THE
DAYS OF HIS FLESH

THE EARTHLY LIFE OF
OUR LORD AND SAVIOUR JESUS CHRIST

BY THE REV.
DAVID SMITH, M.A., D.D.

BAKER BOOK HOUSE
Grand Rapids, Michigan

4862

232
Smi

Reprinted 1976 by
Baker Book House Company

ISBN: 0-8010-8089-4

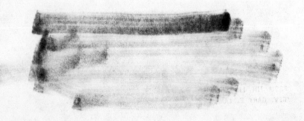

PHOTOLITHOPRINTED BY CUSHING - MALLOY, INC.
ANN ARBOR, MICHIGAN, UNITED STATES OF AMERICA
1976

FOREWORD

A life of Christ first published in 1905 would seem hopelessly out-dated by now in view of the advances in New Testament scholarship since then; but this book proves a happy exception. Shorter than Alfred Edersheim's definitive study but, like it, a classic, *The Days of His Flesh* surmounts its time frame by excellent use of the ancient sources, as well as a rich delving into the church fathers, the rabbinical traditions, and even the secular classics—the full and necessary matrix for a proper understanding of the life and ministry of Jesus.

A Presbyterian minister in Scotland and later professor of theology in Londonderry, Dr. David Smith approached his subject with both heart and mind, reverence and research—a combination needed more than ever in today's theological climate. In an era when theologians were either cordially affirming or despising Renan, Strauss, and the other higher critics, David Smith staked out a different approach to the New Testament. He affirmed the miracles and other supernatural elements in the life of Jesus with the conviction of a Fundamentalist. However, he also carefully, honestly, and constructively criticized his Gospel sources.

Some conservatives, accordingly, may dislike Dr. Smith's technical introduction to this book. Hopefully, they will read it with the same integrity the author devoted to each paragraph of this material, and then go on to the rest of his text, which they will doubtless find more congenial. Those of more liberal persuasion, conversely, may favor the introduction over the book. And yet every theological shading can read these pages with much profit.

The credits in this life of Christ are many, not least Dr. Smith's ingenious explanations of some of the "hard sayings" of Jesus, for whom he never loses an ounce of reverence throughout this study. Indeed, he closes his work with a prayer to his subject!

No attempt has been made to offer a thorough revision of the text in light of contemporary New Testament scholarship, but wherever historical or archaeological evidence since Dr. Smith's time directly contradicts a conclusion of his—a rare enough instance—this has been duly noted in the text or footnotes. Similarly, a few of the many archaic English spellings and phrases from Smith's era have been updated—in cases where they would mislead the reader. Most have been retained, however, since their meaning can be discerned from the context.

Some, of course, will surely fault parts of David Smith's chronology for the life of Christ, or other aspects of his interpretation, but this is standard treatment accorded any study of the person and work of Jesus. Generally, Dr. Smith steers an independent and interesting course through the critical vicissitudes of his era, and, indeed, of ours today.

The Days of His Flesh, then, is well worth this literary resurrection, and should prove a handsome addition to Baker Book House's Twin Brooks Series.

Paul L. Maier
Western Michigan University
September, 1976

PREFACE

THE aim of this work is two-fold. In the Introduction I have endeavoured to vindicate the historicity of the evangelic records and adduce reason for believing, in opposition to an influential school of modern criticism, that they present Jesus as He actually lived among men, and not as He appeared to a later generation through a haze of reverence and superstition. And in the subsequent chapters I have sought, by interpreting what the Evangelists have written, to justify the Church's faith in Him as the Lord from Heaven. It might be well for such as lack taste or aptitude for technical discussion to pass over the Introduction.

My thanks are due to the Rev. W. Robertson Nicoll, LL.D., who invited me to undertake the task and has guided me in its execution; to the Rev. Professor Marcus Dods, D.D., New College, Edinburgh, the Rev. Professor James Stalker, D.D., United Free Church College, Aberdeen, the Rev. George Reith, D.D., College Church, Glasgow, the Rev. H. A. A. Kennedy, D.Sc., Callander, and the Rev. S. G. MacLennan, M.A., Sherbrooke United Free Church, Glasgow, who read my MSS. and gave me profitable criticism; to J. D. C. S. and C. A. S. who have aided me much, especially in preparing the Indexes; and to the Rev. James Angus, Stirling, for his counsel and sympathy.

D. S.

TULLIALLAN U.F. MANSE,
KINCARDINE-ON-FORTH, N.B.

v

PREFACE TO THE EIGHTH EDITION

In the present edition I have corrected several clerical errors and made a few additions to the notes.

My one desire in writing this book was to help others to a deeper knowledge of the Lord Jesus by showing them what I had seen of His grace and glory; and I bless Him for many testimonies that He has owned my poor service.

D. S.

4 THE COLLEGE,
LONDONDERRY.

CONTENTS

CONTENTS

CONTENTS

CONTENTS

CONTENTS

CONTENTS

INTRODUCTION

THE EVANGELIC RECORDS

§ 1. OUR Lord Jesus Christ was a Jew according to the flesh, and the story of His life and teaching was preserved after the Jewish method. That method was oral transmission, and its efficiency is attested by the amazing fact that it was not at the earliest until the third century of our era that the Rabbinical literature was reduced to writing. It was at least a century before the birth of Jesus that the *Halacha* and *Haggada* came into existence, and during all those centuries that voluminous and ever-growing literature was carried in the memories of the Rabbis and their disciples and orally transmitted from generation to generation.[1] " Commit nothing to writing " was the maxim of the Rabbis,[2] prompted originally by their reverence for the Written Law (תּוֹרָה שֶׁבִּכְתָב). They subsequently claimed for the Oral Law (תּוֹרָה שֶׁבְּעַל פֶּה) no less antiquity and even greater worth,[3] alleging that it had been delivered to Moses on Mount Sinai along with the Written Law, had come to Ezra and the Great Synagogue through the Prophets, and had been transmitted orally ever since ;[4] nevertheless they still adhered to the maxim, and the diligence of the Rabbis was directed to the immaculate transmission of the Oral Law. " Raise up many disciples " was their motto,[5] and their disciples were drilled in the multitudinous precepts of that interminable tradition until they had them by heart. The lesson was repeated over and over till it was engraved upon their memories, and hence the term for Rabbinical instruction was *Mishnah*, " repetition." [6] Nor

---

[1] *Cf.* the rhapsodes, who recited the Homeric poems from memory (Jos. *C. Ap.* i. § 2) ; the Druids : " magnum ibi numerum versuum ediscere dicuntur . . . neque fas esse existimant ea litteris mandare " (Cæs. *De Bell. Gall.* vi. 14).

[2] Jost, *Gesch. des Jud.* i. 367.   [3] Lightfoot on Mt. xv. 3.

[4] Lightfoot, i. p. 517 ; W. R. Smith, *O.T. in Jew. Ch.* p. 60.

[5] Taylor, *Say. of Fath.* i. 1.

[6] Greek δευτέρωσις. *Cf.* Jer. *Algas. Quæst.* x.

was it only while they sat at the Rabbis' feet that the disciples learned their lesson. It must never be out of their minds. "Two that sit together without words of the Law," said R. Chananiah ben Teradion, "are a session of scorners; for it is said : 'Nor sitteth in the seat of the scornful' (Ps. i. 1); but two that sit together and are occupied in words of the Law, have the Shekinah among them : for it is said : 'Then they that feared the Lord spake often one to another, etc.' (Mal. iii. 16)." "He who is walking by the way and study-ing," said R. Jacob, "and breaks off his study (*Mishnah*) and says : 'How fine is this tree ! how fine is that tree ! and how fine is this fallow !' they account it to him as if he were guilty of death."[1] Nothing must interrupt a man in his study, not even the sacred office of burying the dead, unless there were no one else to perform it.[2]

It is marvellous how the faculty of remembrance was fostered by this method. Eliezer ben Hyrcanus, one of the five disciples of R. Jochanan ben Zakai, was likened to "a plastered cistern which loseth not a drop."[3] "Should any of us," says Josephus,[4] "be questioned about the laws, he would repeat them all more easily than his own name. Indeed from the very dawn of understanding[5] we learn them off and have them, as it were, engraved on our souls." Such had been the historian's own precocity that at the age of fourteen he was consulted by the High Priests and the rulers about *minutiæ* of the Law.[6]

The study of the Law was thus a purely mechanical exercise, and the least disposition to originality would have been fatal to proficiency. The qualifications were a retentive memory and scrupulous adherence to the letter of the tradi-tion. It must be handed on exactly as it had been received, *ipsissimis verbis* or, as the phrase was, "in the tongue of the Rabbi" (בִּלְשׁוֹן רַבּוֹ) ;[7] and, if a disciple forgot a word of his *Mishnah*, it was accounted to him as if he were guilty of death.[8] "He who teaches anything," said R. Eliezer, "which he has not heard from his master, provokes the divine Majesty

---

[1] Taylor, *Say. of Fath.* iii. 3, 11 ; Lightfoot on Lk. xxiv. 32.
[2] Wetstein on Mt. viii. 21.　　　　[3] Taylor, *Say. of Fath.* ii. 10.
[4] *C. Ap.* ii. § 18.　　[5] *Cf.* 2. Tim. iii. 15.　　[6] *Vit.* § 2.　　[7] *Eduj.* i. 3.
[8] Taylor, *Say. of Fath.* iii. 12.

to depart from Israel."[1]   And no statement was authoritative unless it were prefaced by " R. So-and-so says."[2]

§ 2. Such was the Jewish method, and it was at once natural and inevitable that the Apostles, being Jews, should follow it in recording the life and teaching of Jesus. The prejudice against "committing anything to writing" was carried over into the Christian Church, and even St Chrysostom regarded written records as a *dernier ressort*.[3] The record of the Lord's words and works was the tradition of the Apostles; but they did not so entitle it. They remembered how Jesus had condemned the tradition of the Scribes (Mt. xv. 3, 6); and, moreover, the word παράδοσις sounded ominously in their ears, since it meant "betrayal" as well as "tradition" (*cf.* Mt. xxvi. 45-6 = Mk. xiv. 41-2). They used another term, very beautiful and significant— "the True Deposit."[4] The meaning of the term is well illustrated by Herodotus' story of the Spartan Glaukos to whose custody a certain Milesian committed half his wealth, and who refused to deliver up the "deposit" when it was reclaimed.[5] It furnished a striking metaphor. "God," says St Paul, "hath put in our keeping (θεμένος ἐν ἡμῖν) the Word of Reconciliation" (2 Cor. v. 19). "They that lie," says Hermas,[6] "make themselves defrauders of God, not rendering unto Him the deposit which they received." "Show yourselves proved bankers" is one of the most striking of the ἄγραφα of Jesus;[7] and it is remarkable that it was interpreted in the primitive Church as inculcating the duty of distinguishing between true and false scriptures, as bankers test coins whether they be genuine or counterfeit.[8] The apostolic account of the sayings and doings of Jesus was the True

---

[1] Lightfoot on Mt. xxiii. 7.   [2] Lightfoot on Mt. vii. 29.

[3] *In Matth.* i *ad init.* *Cf.* Iren. *Adv. Hær.* iii. 2.

[4] 2 Tim. i. 14: τὴν καλὴν παραθήκην. καλός (*cf.* p. 349, n. 2) was used of *genuine* as opposed to *counterfeit* coin. *Cf.* Xen. *Mem.* iii. i. § 9: διαγιγνώσκειν τό τε καλὸν ἀργύριον καὶ τὸ κίβδηλον. 1 Thess. v. 21.

[5] Her. vi. 86. *Cf.* Lev. vi. 2, 4 (LXX); Plin. *Ep.* x. 101: the accused Christians pled "se sacramento non in scelus aliquod obstringere, sed ne . . . fidem fallerent, *ne depositum appellati abnegarent.*"

[6] *Past. M.* iii. § 2. *Cf.* Eus. *H. E.* iii. 23.

[7] Orig. *In Joan.* xix. § 2: τὴν ἐντολὴν Ἰησοῦ λέγουσαν· δόκιμοι τραπεζῖται γίνεσθε. *In Matth.* xii. § 2; *In Luc. Hom.* i. *Cf.* Cab. *Tab.* § 15.

[8] Clem. Rom. *Hom.* ii. § 51.

Deposit, and it was the sacred duty of those to whose
custody it had been committed to guard it no less faithfully
than the Rabbis guarded the tradition of the elders.   It was
a two-fold vigilance that they must exercise.   They must see
to it, on the one hand, that nothing was lost, and, on the other,
that it suffered no change.   With a reverent sense of their responsibility they must hand it on unimpaired and uncorrupted.
"The True Deposit guard by the Holy Spirit that dwelleth in us."

   " O Timothy," says St Paul, "guard the Deposit, turning
away from profane babblings and oppositions of the Knowledge
falsely named, which certain professing missed the mark as
regards the Faith" (1 Tim. vi. 20-1).   Heretical teachers
had been busy at Ephesus, certain persons (τινες) well known,
whom the Apostle might have named and whom Timothy
would immediately identify.   The epistle is full of them
(i. 6-7 ; iv. 1-3, 7 ; vi. 3-5).   They were heretics of the
blatant sort, loud-mouthed and shallow-minded, puffed up
with windy vanity (cf. vi. 4).   It would seem that their
teaching was of two kinds.   Some were of a philosophical
turn and unsettled the minds of the believers by their metaphysical disputations—"oppositions of the Knowledge falsely
named" (cf. Col. ii. 8).   Others again tickled the fancies of
their hearers with silly and unhistorical legends which the
Apostle justly brands here as βεβήλους κενοφωνίας and in iv. 7
as βεβήλους καὶ γραώδεις μύθους—the sort of fables wherewith
the apocryphal Gospels crowd the Silent Years.   The circulation of those base counterfeits discredited the True
Deposit.   " O Timothy," pleads St Paul, "guard the Deposit."   Non enim, says Erasmus, vult aliquid addi traditis.
This passage reveals a necessity which emerged at that stage
of the history of the primitive Church and which must have
cost the Apostles much anxious thought—the necessity of
effectively safe-guarding the evangelic tradition and preserving
it alike from mutilation and corruption by committing it to
writing and stereotyping it in a permanent record.   Littera
scripta manet.   It would be in consequence of this anxious
solicitude for the True Deposit that the canonical Gospels
were put into shape and an authoritative version of the
evangelic history given to the Church.[1]

[1] Cf. Chrysost. l.c.

§ 3. Ere the story was written, there was a class of teachers in the primitive Church whose function it was to go about instructing the believers in the oral tradition and drilling it into their minds after the fashion of the Rabbinical schools.[1] They were named the Catechisers (οἱ κατηχοῦντες) and their scholars the catechumens (οἱ κατηχούμενοι) [2]—an expressive name, since κατηχεῖν signifies to *din* a thing into a person's ears by incessant iteration.[3] Their *Mishnah* was called "teaching" (διδασκαλία), and it was hard and disagreeable work with none of the inspiration of preaching about it. St Paul, borrowing the phrase which the Rabbis used of their *Mishnah*, speaks of it as "labour."[4] Nevertheless it was a most necessary service at a time when there was no written record and believers were dependent on oral instruction for their knowledge of the Gospel history; and St Paul was careful to remind the Church of the debt which it owed to its Catechisers.

§ 4. The oral tradition emanated from the Apostles, being their testimony to the things which they had seen and heard.[5] It was preserved and disseminated far and wide by the Catechisers; and, when the Evangelists composed their narratives, they simply reduced the oral tradition to writing, each adopting the version of it which was current in his locality. The First Gospel represents the tradition as it circulated in Judæa, and, though it was not written as it stands by Matthew, it was certainly derived from him and is stamped with his authority.[6] The Second Gospel represents the tradition as it circulated in the Roman Church, and

---

[1] *Cf.* Wright, *Compos. of the Four Gosp.*; *Synops.*

[2] Gal. vi. 6. *Cf.* Lk. i. 3; Acts xxi. 21.

[3] *Cf.* Chrysost. *In Joan.* xviii: In old days, after some crisis in his experience, a man got a new name as a memorial of the goodness of God, that it might be continually dinned into the ears of those who heard the name (ἐνηχῆται τοῖς ἀκούουσιν).

[4] 1 Tim. v. 17. *Cf.* Lightfoot on Lk. v. i.

[5] Lk. i. 2. Clem. Alex. speaks (*Strom.* I. i. § 11; fragm. of *Hypotyp.* in Eus. *H. E.* ii. 1) of a tradition received from the Lord after the Resurrection by Peter and James, John and Paul (*cf.* 1 Cor. xi. 23), and transmitted by them. *Ep. ad Diogn.* xi: ἀποστόλων παράδοσις φυλάσσεται. Justin M. calls the Gospels τὰ ἀπομνημονεύματα τῶν ἀποστόλων.

[6] Mt.'s Gospel, according to ancient and credible testimony, was a Hebrew, *i.e.* Aramaic, book of *Logia*. It is probably the basis of our First Gospel. *Cf.* Papias in Eus. *H. E.* iii. 39; *ibid.* iii. 24; Iren. *Adv. Her.* iii. 1; Orig. *In Matth.* i; Jer. *Script. Eccl.* under *Matthæus*.

it has this connection with Peter, that Mark was his companion and enjoyed the advantage of hearing his discourses.[1]
At the request of the believers at Rome, it is said, he wrote
a short Gospel, and, when Peter heard it, he approved it and
sanctioned the reading of it by the Church.[2] The Third
Gospel, composed by Luke, the physician of Antioch and
the companion of Paul, represents the tradition as it circulated
in Asia Minor and Achaia, and is pervaded by the spirit
of the Apostle of the Gentiles.[3] The Evangelists were not
authors but editors ; they reduced the oral tradition to writing, and therefore it is that their books are entitled, not the
Gospel *of*, but the Gospel *according to* Matthew, Mark, Luke.

§ 5. The evangelic tradition has thus been preserved in
three editions : the Judæan, the Roman, and the Greek ; and
it is a striking evidence of the fidelity wherewith the True
Deposit was guarded that these three editions, though circula-
ting in regions so remote and diverse, have remained so true
to their common source. So little variation have they under-
gone in their independent transmission that it is possible to
arrange the first three Gospels—hence called the Synoptics—
in parallel columns, exhibiting almost verbal agreement. And
such divergences as they display make it clear that their
agreement is not due to inter-dependence : the earliest Gospel
did not set the type, its successors being merely revised
editions of it. Compare, for instance :

Mt. ix. 6.	Mk. ii. 10-1.	Lk. v. 24.
ἵνα δὲ εἰδῆτε ὅτι ἐξουσίαν ἔχει ὁ υἱὸς τοῦ ἀνθρώπου ἐπὶ τῆς γῆς ἀφιέναι ἁμαρτίας—τότε λέγει τῷ παραλυτικῷ Ἔγειρε ἆρόν σου τὴν κλίνην καὶ ὕπαγε εἰς τὸν οἶκόν σου.	ἵνα δὲ εἰδῆτε ὅτι ἐξουσίαν ἔχει ὁ υἱὸς τοῦ ἀνθρώπου ἀφιέναι ἁμαρτίας ἐπὶ τῆς γῆς — λέγει τῷ παραλυτικῷ Σοὶ λέγω, ἔγειρε ἆρον τὸν κράβαττόν σου καὶ ὕπαγε εἰς τὸν οἶκόν σου.	ἵνα δὲ εἰδῆτε ὅτι ὁ υἱὸς τοῦ ἀνθρώπου ἐξουσίαν ἔχει ἐπὶ τῆς γῆς ἀφιέναι ἁμαρτίας—εἶπεν τῷ παραλελυμένῳ Σοὶ λέγω, ἔγειρε καὶ ἆρας τὸ κλινίδιόν σου πορεύου εἰς τὸν οἶκόν σου.

On the supposition that Mt. is a revision of Mk., and Lk. a
revision of both, the retention of that awkward parenthesis
throughout and the introduction of two or three merely verbal
and quite insignificant alterations are inexplicable. The truth
is that each Gospel is an independent reproduction of the
apostolic tradition, and the differences are such variations as
were natural and inevitable in the process of oral transmission.

[1] Papias in Eus. *H. E.* iii. 39.　　　[2] Jer. *Script. Eccl.* under *Marcus*.
[3] *Ibid.* under *Lucas* ; Iren. *l.c.*

§ 6. The Evangelists were not so much authors as editors, and their task was one which required no little discrimination. Since the oral tradition covered the whole of our Lord's ministry, they had before them a huge mass of material, and it was impossible for them to incorporate all of it in their books (*cf.* John xx. 30-1). They had perforce to omit much which possessed exceeding value and interest, much which they no doubt would gladly have included and we would gladly have learned. Some fragments of the omitted material have reached us by other channels to our great enrichment. To St Paul we owe the preservation of one exquisite *logion* (Acts xx. 35), and on the pages of the Fathers we find others which in not a few instances may well be authentic.[1] Moreover, it was the custom of readers in early days to write comments on the margins of their MSS., and it sometimes happened that a copyist, mistaking such an annotation for an accidental omission, would innocently insert it in his text. Often worthless stuff was thus intruded into the sacred narrative, but occasionally the interpolation was an authentic fragment of the tradition which had reached the reader's ears and which he desired to preserve. Such are that precious *logion*, included in T. R. but rejected on documentary evidence by Tisch., W. H., and R.V.: " Ye know not what spirit ye are of. For the Son of Man came not to destroy but to save men's lives " (Lk. ix. 55-6) ; the Pericopè (John vii. 53—viii. 11), which is probably a reader's marginal note over against viii. 15, and which has its true place among the Lord's encounters with the rulers during the Passion-week ;[2] the prayer of Jesus at the Crucifixion (Lk. xxiii. 34). After Lk. vi. 4 one MS. interpolates an incident which also may be an authentic fragment of the oral tradition.[3] Dr Duff, the celebrated missionary, found this inscription in Arabic on the gateway of the mosque of Futtehpore Sikri : " Jesus, on whom be peace, has said : ' The world is merely a bridge ; you are to pass over it and not to build your dwellings upon it.' "[4]

---

[1] *Cf.* Westcott, *Introd. to the Stud. of the Gosp.*, Append. C ; Resch, *Agrapha* in Gebhardt and Harnack's *Text. u. Untersuch.* v. 4.

[2] In a few MSS. the Pericopè stands after Lk. xxi. 38. *Cf.* W. H. n.

[3] D : τῇ αὐτῇ ἡμέρᾳ θεασάμενός τινα ἐργαζόμενον τῷ σαββάτῳ εἶπεν αὐτῷ· Ἀνθρωπε, εἰ μὲν οἶδας τί ποιεῖς, μακάριος εἶ· εἰ δὲ μὴ οἶδας, ἐπικατάρατος καὶ παραβάτης εἶ τοῦ νόμου. *Cf.* p. 135.

[4] Dr Geo. Smith's *Life of Duff*, ii. p. 164.

§ 7. Not only were the Evangelists obliged to omit much of the oral tradition, but they exercised no small measure of editorial freedom. It may easily, be understood that they found their material in a somewhat sporadic condition. Like the rhapsodes who, while they carried the forty-eight books of the Homeric poems in their memories, recited on each occasion only a particular episode, the Catechisers would on each occasion repeat over only so much of the tradition. In this way it got broken up into sections, and the chronological sequence was lost. Consequently, when they took in hand the business of editing it, the Evangelists found themselves face to face with a large assortment of disconnected material, much as though a modern editor had before him a pile of loose leaflets which he must weave into a continuous narrative. To ascertain the historical sequence was, to a large extent, impossible; nor was it indeed any great matter to the Evangelists. Their aim was not to chronicle the events of the Lord's ministry but to pourtray Himself; and therefore they arranged their material rather topically than chronologically, bringing together passages which, though they might belong to different occasions, illustrated some aspect of His work or person.[1]

§ 8. An instructive example of the editorial method of the Evangelists is furnished by that long discourse commonly called " the Sermon on the Mount " (Mt. v.-vii.). It is really not a single discourse but a collection of discourses delivered to different audiences and on different occasions. One special aim of the First Evangelist, following the lines of Matthew's Book of Logia, was to report the teaching of Jesus ; and, just as Luke, in pursuance of his design to exhibit the Grace of Jesus, has transferred the Lord's visit to the Synagogue of Nazareth, when "they all marvelled at the words of grace that proceeded out of His mouth," from its actual position well on in His ministry to the very commencement, setting it there as a sort of frontispiece to show his readers at the outset " the grace of the Lord Jesus Christ " (Lk. iv. 16-30 ; cf. Mt. xiii. 54-8 = Mk. vi. 1-6), so the First Evangelist has woven several discourses into one and placed it at the beginning of his Gospel as a sample of the Lord's

---

[1] Cf. Pliny's arrangement of his epistles : "Collegi, non servato temporis ordine (neque enim historiam componebam), sed ut quæque in manus venerat."

teaching.   Nor is it difficult to resolve it into its component parts and restore each to its historical setting.

1. Mt. v. 1-16, 39b-42, 44-8, vii. 1-6, 12, 15-27 is the Ordination Address to the Twelve.   Cf. Lk. vi. 20-38, 41-9, xi. 33.

2. Mt. vi. 9-15, vii. 7-11 belongs to the Lesson on Prayer Cf. Lk. xi. 1-13.

3. Mt. vii. 13-4, with viii. 11-2, is the Lord's answer to the question : "Are there few that are being saved?"   Cf. Lk. xiii. 23-30.

4. Mt. vi. 19-34, belongs to the Discourse on Worldly-mindedness.   Cf. Lk. xii. 13-34.   Observe how the discourse in Mt. fits on to the parable in Lk. : "So is he that layeth up treasure for himself and is not rich towards God (Lk.).   Lay not up for yourselves treasures, etc." (Mt.).

5. There remains Mt. v. 17-39a, 43, vi. 1-8, 16-8.   All this is peculiar to Mt. except, v. 25-6, which is given by Lk. as an unconnected *logion* (xii. 58-9).   Is it possible to place this section in its historical setting?   It is remarkable that the conclusion of "the Sermon on the Mount" (Mt. vii. 28-9), is identical with the observation which Mk. and Lk. make on the impression produced by our Lord's discourse in the Synagogue of Capernaum (Mk. i. 22 = Lk. iv. 32) ; and it is an attractive and reasonable inference that this homeless section of "the Sermon on the Mount" is nothing else than a report of that discourse.   If it be so, then the Evangelists have divided between them the oral tradition's narrative of what happened at Capernaum ; Mt. reproducing, at least in part, its report of the discourse, and Mk. and Lk. its account of the miracle (Mk. i. 21-8 = Lk. iv. 31-7).[1]

A kindred example is furnished by Mt.'s report of the Lord's commission to the Twelve (x. 5-42).   Much of it was doubtless spoken in that connection, but the Evangelist has introduced *logia* spoken on other occasions, fragments of the abundant teaching which Jesus addressed to the Twelve during His intercourse with them.   Lk. has distributed the material between the commission of the Twelve and that of the Seventy (ix. 3-5 ; x. 2-12) ; and he has betrayed his editorial method by first including x. 4 in the latter and

[1] Mt. v. 38-9a and 43 are editorial additions.   Observe the abbreviation of the recurrent formula: "Ye have heard, etc.," when alien matter is introduced (*vv.* 31, 38, 43).

subsequently reporting the Lord's allusion to it as a command to the Twelve (xxii. 35). Again, Mt. has prematurely included in the commission to the Twelve a prediction of persecution (x. 17-22) which Mk. (xiii. 9-13) and Lk. (xxi. 12-7) have put with more probability in the apocalyptic discourse. It may be added that Mt. x. 34-42 is apparently a series of disconnected *logia*, and Mk. has given *v.* 42 a more appropriate setting in the discourse on humility in Peter's house (ix. 41).

§ 9. It was nothing unusual for the Evangelists to introduce thus, in what they deemed appropriate places, *logia* connected with incidents which they had omitted. Lk. omits the discourse in the Synagogue of Capernaum, but he has preserved, though with little relevance to the context, one memorable fragment of it (Lk. xvi. 17 = Mt. v. 18). Lk. reports the question : " Are there few that are being saved ? " and the Lord's answer (xiii. 23-30) ; Mt. omits the question, but, true to his purpose of reporting the teaching of Jesus, he gives the answer, partly in one connection, partly in another (vii. 13-4 ; viii. 11-2). Lk. alone records our Lord's entertainment by one of the rulers of the Pharisees (xiv. 1-14) ; but Mt. has, suitably enough, inserted a sentence of His discourse on that occasion in his report of the Great Indictment (Mt. xxiii. 12 = Lk. xiv. 11). Lk. omits the Great Indictment, but he gives in another and obviously unhistorical though not unfelicitous connection the exquisite apostrophe wherewith, according to Mt., it closes (Lk. xiii. 34-5 = Mt. xxiii. 37-9) ; and he reports a large part of it as a discourse of Jesus at a Pharisee's table (xi. 37-52)—an impossible connection, since Jesus would never have committed so gross a discourtesy. He omits the ambitious request of the sons of Zebedee (Mt. xx. 20-8 = Mk. x. 35-45) ; but he gives a fragment of the Lord's rebuke on that occasion in connection with the contention in the Upper Room (xxii. 25-6), where the actual answer was the acted parable of the feet-washing (John xiii. 1-17). Mt. omits the contention in the Upper Room, but he inserts in the Great Indictment a passage (xxiii. 8-12) which belongs thereto (*cf.* John xiii. 13-5).[1]

[1] The Evangelists frequently insert in what they deem suitable places *logia* whose original connection is quite lost, their present connection being often

Another example is furnished by the triple account of the
Passover in the Upper Room. Lk. mentions not only the
distribution of the bread and wine at the institution of the
Supper, but the mixing of the cup wherewith, according to
the paschal rubric, the feast began, and tells how, when Jesus
had taken this first cup, He made the announcement : " I
shall not hereafter drink of this fruit of the vine until that
day when I shall drink it with you new in the Kingdom of
My Father " (xxii. 17-8).   Mt. and Mk. make no mention
of the first cup, but they record the solemn announcement,
appending it to the distribution of the sacramental cup at the
close of the feast (Mt. xxvi. 29 = Mk. xiv. 25).

§ 10. Again the Evangelists make no scruple to introduce
an incident in unchronological order because it illustrates the
theme in hand.   Thus, at ix. 51 Lk. makes Jesus bid farewell to Galilee and set out on His last journey to Jerusalem ;
yet he afterwards recounts much that happened in Galilee.
The explanation is that *vv.* 51-6 serve to illustrate *vv.* 49-50,
being a further instance of the disciples' intolerance and the
Lord's disapprobation thereof.   The Evangelist, arranging
his material topically rather than chronologically, has brought
the two passages into connection, and, having started a new
section of the tradition, he continues it, with sundry interpola-
tions (ix. 57—x. 16, 21-4), down to x. 42.   With such
scrupulous fidelity does he reproduce the tradition that he
retains its preface to the forestalled passage (ix. 51), thus
betraying his procedure and enabling us to refer the passage
to its rightful position after xviii. 14.[1]

A cognate instance occurs in the parallel accounts of the
supper at Bethany (Mt. xxvi. 1-13 = Mk. xiv. 1-9 = John
xii. 1-11).   Mt. and Mk. seem to put it two days before the
Passover, whereas John expressly puts it six days before the
Passover.   The truth is that it happened as John relates, and
Mt. and Mk., following perhaps the catechetical practice, bring
the story of what befell at Bethany into juxtaposition with
the Betrayal (Mt. xxvi. 14-6 = Mk. xiv. 10-1).[2]   The idea

artificial and verbal. *Cf.* Mt. xii. 33-7 = Lk. vi. 43-5. *Logia* on divorce, about
which the Champion of the oppressed would say much, are inserted here and there.
Cf. Mt. v. 31-2 ; Lk. xvi. 18.

[1] xvii. 11 resumes ix. 51.   [2] *Cf.* Aug. *De Cons. Ev.* ii. § 153.

evidently is that the traitor's foul deed was provoked by the Lord's rebuke. It was a stroke of revenge.

§ 11. Such free manipulation of their material on the part of the Evangelists was not only warrantable but inevitable. The oral tradition was all in confusion, and, when they undertook the task of editing it, they could do naught else than exercise their discretion in the arrangement of its disconnected sections. And they set to work in no reckless spirit. It is remarkable that hand in hand with their freedom in arranging it went a scrupulous regard for its literal reproduction, a steadfast determination to preserve its language intact. This appears in their welding of the sections. They did not as a rule hold themselves at liberty to forge new links of connection, but retained the prefaces which they found in the tradition even when by so doing they introduced inconsistencies into their narratives. Thus, Mt. begins his third chapter with the formula: "And in those days," though he is resuming his narrative after an interval of thirty years. At the beginning of "the Sermon on the Mount" (v. 1) he makes the auditors *the disciples*, at the end *the multitudes*; the explanation being that v. 1 is the tradition's preface to the Ordination Address and vii. 28-9 its comment on the discourse in the Synagogue (*cf.* Mk. i. 22 = Lk. iv. 32). The triple tradition relates the healing of the withered hand immediately after the plucking of the ears of corn (Mt. xii. 9 = Mk. iii. 1 = Lk. vi. 6); but, whereas, Mt. puts the incidents on the same day, Lk. puts them on different Sabbaths and Mk. says vaguely: "He entered again into a synagogue." Probably the tradition contained some intervening matter, involving a space of time between the incidents. Mt. has simply let the tradition's preface stand; Mk. has modified it just enough to avoid a positive misstatement; while Lk. has more boldly inserted "on another Sabbath." *Cf.* Mt. xiii. 1 = Mk. iv. 1 = Lk. viii. 4; Mk. iv. 35 = Lk. vii. 22 = Mt. viii. 18. According to Mk. v. 43a = Lk. viii. 56b, after the raising of Jaïrus' daughter Jesus enjoined silence regarding the miracle—an injunction which in the circumstances could not be observed. The fact is that in the tradition the miracle in the house of Jaïrus was followed by the healing of two blind men in private, and the injunction was addressed to them (Mt. ix. 27-31). Mk. and Lk. omit the latter miracle, but they retain the injunction and attach it to the former, oblivious of the incongruity. Mt. rightly represents the discourse on cross-bearing at Cæsarea Philippi as addressed to "the disciples" (xvi. 24); according to Mk. it was addressed to "the multitude with His disciples" (viii. 34); according to Lk. "to all" (ix. 23). Perhaps the confusion is due to the isolation of the passage in catechetical teaching. Inculcating an important lesson, it would be often repeated and would easily be misentitled. In Mt. xv. 39 = Mk. viii. 10 it is said that Jesus and His disciples "embarked in *the* boat," though no boat has been mentioned, nor is it to be supposed that they should have a boat at their disposal on the eastern shore of the Lake after a long journey by land. Probably the tradition contained some explanation which the Evangelists do not reproduce, and they would not tamper with the tradition by striking out "the" and writing "*a* boat." Once more, after the Zacchæus-incident Lk. gives the parable of the Pounds. It was probably spoken in the synagogue of Jericho on the following day, the Sabbath; yet it is introduced by "And while they were listening to these things" (xix. 11), as though it followed immediately after the incident of the meeting with Zacchæus. "These things" refers to the previous part of the discourse in the synagogue, recorded by the tradition but omitted by the Evangelist.

Mt. viii. 16 has "evening having come"; Lk. iv. 40 "the sun setting." Such variations were natural in the course of oral transmission. Probably both were current, and Mk., anxious that nothing should be lost, combined them: "Evening having come, when the sun set" (i. 32). Mt. iii. 11 has "carry His sandals"; Mk. i. 7 and Lk. iii. 16, "unloose His sandal-strap" (*cf.* John i. 27). Both were common phrases for *menial service*, and would readily get interchanged in oral transmission. Sometimes, however, a supposed equivalent creates a false impression, as when Lk. (iv. 2) substitutes "He ate nothing" for Mt.'s "He fasted" (iv. 2).

§ 12. With such scrupulous fidelity did the Evangelists "guard the Deposit." Nevertheless it was inevitable that the tradition should suffer somewhat in the process of oral transmission, and there are sundry mishaps which have manifestly befallen it.

1. *Slips of memory*. Mt. and Lk. put the temptations in the wilderness in different orders (Mt. iv. 1-11 = Lk. iv. 1-13) —precisely the sort of confusion incidental to oral transmission. Perhaps they were arranged mnemonically by the Catechisers : as they succeed each other in human life, appetite alluring youths, glory men, wealth the aged (Mt.) ; in the order of severity, hunger being easier to bear than poverty, and poverty than contempt (Lk.).[1] The actual order is probably the reverse of Mt.'s. The temptation to turn the stone into a loaf was certainly the last. It happened at the close of the forty days, and, when Jesus grew faint with hunger, no more was possible.

Whereas Mk. and Lk. give one demoniac at Gerasa and one blind man at Jericho, Mt. gives two in each case (Mt. viii. 28 = Mk. v. 2 = Lk. viii. 27 ; Mt. xx. 30 = Mk. x. 46 = Lk. xviii. 35). Mt. and Mk. put the latter miracle as Jesus was leaving Jericho, Lk. as He was approaching it. These are obviously slips of memory. Mt.'s duplication of the blind-man may be due to confusion with ix. 27-31.

It is another slip of memory when for Mk.'s "except a staff only," Mt. and Lk. substitute "neither a staff" (Mk. vi. 8 = Mt. x. 10 = Lk. ix. 3). It is natural that the clauses should get assimilated in the course of repetition.

2. *Fusion of similar but really distinct passages.* After the first of His encounters with the rulers during the Passion week Jesus completed their discomfiture by a couple of parables. There the controversy ended (Mt. xxi. 45-6 = Mk. xii. 12 = Lk. xx. 19); yet Mt. adds the parable of the King's Marriage-feast (xxii. 1-14). It is hardly doubtful that this parable is a fusion of two others—the Great Supper (Lk. xiv. 15-24) and another about a marriage-feast and an unworthy guest. *Cf.* the parable of the Pounds (Lk. xix. 11-28), which evidently fuses a parable about a nobleman who went into a far country to receive a kingdom, and the parable of the Talents (Mt. xxv. 14-30).

3. *Emendation of what was deemed* (1) *incredible or* (2) *unintelligible.*

---

[1] Wetstein on Lk. iv. ۷.

(1) Mt. xiii. 13 softens down Mk. iv. 11-2 = Lk. viii. 10. It seemed incredible that the parabolic teaching had a judicial purpose. So in Mk. vi. 3 = Mt. xiii. 55 the sentiment of reverence took offence at the idea of the Lord engaging in a menial handicraft and altered "the carpenter" into "the carpenter's son." The process was subsequently carried a step further, some MSS. either omitting Mk.'s "the carpenter" or assimilating it to Mt.'s "the carpenter's son"; so that Origen could reply to a gibe of Celsus that nowhere in the canonical Gospels is Jesus called a carpenter.[1]   It was a like sentiment that glorified Mk. i. 38 : "To this end came I forth," *i.e.* from Capernaum, into Lk. iv. 43 : "For this end was I sent," *i.e.* into the world ; and it is perhaps in consequence of Gentile ignorance of the character of the Jewish rulers that the Baptist's invective, which was actually hurled at them (Mt. iii. 7), is represented by Lk. as addressed to the multitudes (iii. 7). In order to safeguard the divinity of Jesus His question to the Young Ruler : "Why callest thou Me good?" (Mk. x. 18 = Lk. xviii. 19) is changed in Mt. xix. 17 (approved reading) into "Why askest thou Me about what is good?"—a theological gloss which removes the pivot of the argument.

The editor's hand appears in the parallel reports of the Beatitudes (Mt. v. 2-12 = Lk. vi. 20-6). Jesus said simply "the poor," "those that hunger" (Lk.) ; and, in order to guard against an Ebionitic interpretation, Mt. wrote "the poor *in spirit*," "those that hunger *after righteousness*."[2] Probably with a view to symmetry Lk. has reduced the Beatitudes to four, setting over against each a corresponding *Woe*. It is impossible that Jesus should have spoken the *Woes* to the newly ordained Twelve ; and they are precisely the sort of homiletic additions which the Catechisers would be apt to make.

---

[1] *C. Cels.* vi. 36.

[2] Some think, on the contrary, that Mt.'s is the authentic report and Lk. omitted the qualifications, finding here an instance of the latter's alleged Ebionitic tendency. *Cf.* Schmiedel, art. *Gospels* § 110 in *E. B.* ; Strauss, *Leb. Jes.* ii. vi. § 76. Keim speaks of "the morose world-hating Ebionite of Luke's source." It is surely a *reductio ad absurdum* of the theory that Schmiedel discovers opposite tendencies in Lk.—Universalism and Particularism.

(2) A striking instance of the tendency to emend what seemed unintelligible occurs in the narratives of the anointing at Bethany. According to John xii. 3 Mary anointed the *feet* of Jesus; according to Mt. xxvi. 7 = Mk. xiv. 3, His *head*. The former is the true account, and so it would stand in the apostolic tradition; but, since the anointing of the head at feasts was as usual as the anointing of the feet was extraordinary, the Catechisers, not knowing who the woman was or wherefore she did so strange a thing, innocently substituted *head* for *feet* and dropped the unintelligible circumstance of her wiping His feet with her hair.

Misunderstanding of the Lord's announcement of Peter's denial is responsible for much confusion. Mt. has: " In the course of this night, ere a cock crow, thrice shalt thou deny Me " (xxvi. 34); Mk.: " To-day, during this night, ere a cock crow twice, thrice thou shalt deny Me " (xiv. 30); Lk.: " A cock shall not crow to-day until thrice thou deny that thou knowest Me " (xxii. 34); John : " A cock shall not crow until thou deny Me thrice " (xiii. 38). They all agree that Jesus predicted a threefold denial, and so they all represent it as coming to pass (Mt. xxvi. 69-75; Mk. xiv. 66-75; Lk. xxii. 56-62; John xviii. 16-8, 25-7); but they recount different denials. Paulus reckons, between the four, at least eight denials.[1] The truth would seem to be that the announcement ran: " Ere a cock crow, twice and thrice," *i.e.* repeatedly, " thou shalt deny Me." [2] The expression was misunderstood, and what seemed an obvious and very slight correction was made in the process of oral transmission. Then the fulfilment was twisted into artificial agreement with the prediction, at all events in the Synoptics. Though he recounts three denials, John lays no stress on the number as fulfilling the Lord's prediction. *Cf.* John xviii. 27 with Mt. xxvi. 75 = Mk. xiv. 72 = Lk. xxii. 61.

4. *Mutilation of obscure* LOGIA. Under this category falls Mt. vi. 22-3 = Lk. xi. 34-6. While Lk. gives this as an isolated *logion*, Mt. inserts it in the Discourse on Worldly-mindedness; and it is very suitable to the latter connection, since it is certainly a *logion* about covetousness. ἁπλοῦς has in

[1] *Cf.* Strauss, *Leb. Jes.* III. iii. § 129.
[2] E. A. Abbott, art. *Gospels* § 14 in *E. B.*

Biblical 𝔾reek the sense of " liberal " and πονηρός that of " churlish " or " niggardly " [1]; and St Chrysostom in his discourse on the parable of the Ten Virgins says that " dark " was a colloquialism for " uncharitable." [2] This much seems clear, yet it does not suffice to explain the *logion*. The perplexity lies in the apparent confusion of literal and metaphorical, the eye of the body and the eye of the mind. Euthymius Zigabenus, after St Chrysostom, follows quite another line of interpretation, taking " single " as " healthy " and " evil " as " diseased." The truth in all probability is that the *logion* has got hopelessly mangled in the course of oral transmission, nor does Lk.'s embellished version tend to its elucidation.

Another *crux interpretum* is Mk. ix. 49-50. It probably blends a *logion* about the wholesome use of sacrifice with that perspicuous *logion*, Mt. v. 13 = Lk. xiv. 34-5. The addition : " and every sacrifice shall be salted with salt " (*cf.* Lev. ii. 13) is an interpretative gloss valuable only as showing that the passage was a puzzle in the earliest times.

5. *When an Old Testament prophecy found its fulfilment in some incident of the Lord's ministry, the tradition was apt to be modified into more precise agreement with it.* Thus, in the story of the Triumphal Entry, Mt., thinking of Zech. ix. 9 and, like our A.V., misinterpreting the Hebrew as though it meant " an ass and a colt " instead of " an ass, even a colt," introduces two animals and incomprehensibly represents Jesus as riding upon both (Mt. xxi. 1-11 : *cf.* Mk. xi. 1-11 = Lk. xix. 29-44 = John xii. 12-9).

6. *Confusion due to an erroneous presupposition in the minds of the editors.* The Eschatological Discourse exemplifies this. As reported by the three Synoptists, it deals with two great crises : the destruction of Jerusalem, which was accomplished by the army of Titus in A.D. 70, and the Lord's Second Advent, which is still future ; and the difficulty is that, according to the Evangelists' reports, Jesus has brought these two events into immediate connection, declaring that His Second Advent would follow hard after the destruction of Jerusalem and be witnessed by that generation (Mt. xxiv. 29, 34 = Mk.

---

[1] Hatch, *Ess. in Bibl. Gk.* pp. 79-82 ; Rom. xii. 8 ; Ja. i. 5 ; Herm. *Past. M.* ii. § 4. *Cf.* Lightfoot and Wetstein.

[2] *In Matth.* lxxix.

xiii. 24, 30—Lk. xxi. 32). What must be said of this ? It
is remarkable that two passages which Mt. incorporates with
the Eschatological Discourse, are given by Lk. in other connections (Mt. xxiv. 23-8, 37-40 (Mk. xiii. 21-3) = Lk. xvii.
20-37 ; Mt. xxiv. 43-51 = Lk. xii. 39-46) ; and here lies a
clue to the solution of the problem. It is likely that, as the
end drew near, Jesus spoke much about the future ; and, when
the Evangelists took in hand the task of editing the oral tradition, they would find many scattered sayings relative thereto ;
and these they would dispose in what they judged suitable
connections. And where could such fugitive fragments find a
more fitting shelter than in this great prophetic discourse?

It was a perfectly legitimate procedure ; yet it was not
without its perils, and it chanced that in this instance the
Evangelists laboured under a peculiar disqualification. They
shared the prevailing expectation that the Second Advent was
imminent ;[1] and, with this idea in their minds, it is no marvel
that, when they compiled the Lord's sayings about the future,
they should have brought the destruction of Jerusalem and
the final Judgment into immediate connection. This is in no
wise the representation of Jesus. He taught that the progress
of His Kingdom would be a long development, like the
ripening of harvest, the growth of a tiny mustard-seed into a
great tree, the operation of leaven (Mt. xiii. 24-33 ; Mk. iv.
26-9). And even in this discourse there is a striking
evidence of the Evangelists' faithfulness in reproducing the
oral tradition. Though they shared the current expectation
of an immediate Return, they have preserved sayings of Jesus
which correct their error (Mt. xxiv. 6 = Mk. xiii. 7 = Lk. xxi.
9 ; Mt. xxiv. 8 = Mk. xiii. 9 ; Mt. xxiv. 14 = Mk. xiii. 10).
And Mt. has preserved two parables—the Ten Virgins and
the Talents—which belong to the Eschatological Discourse,
and which show beyond all question what really was the
Lord's teaching about His Second Advent. The argument
turns, in the former, on the tarrying of the Bridegroom and,
in the latter, on the prolonged absence of the Master.

7. *Comments inserted in the tradition as* LOGIA *of Jesus.*
Mt. xii. 40 is an instance. It is absent from Lk. xi. 29-

---

[1] *Cf.* 1 Cor. x. 11; xv. 51; Phil. iv. 5; 1 Thess. iv. 15 *sqq.* ; Heb. x. 25;
Ia. v. 8; 1 Pet. iv. 7; 1 John ii. 18 ; Rev. i. 1, 3 ; iii. 11 ; xxii. 7, 10, 12, 20.

30, and not only does it lack the savour of a genuine *logion* of Jesus but it spoils the argument. Jonah's adventure with the whale was no "sign" to the Ninevites, who knew nothing about it. It was his preaching that was a sign to them; and this is what Lk. says. Obviously the verse is no saying of Jesus, but a homiletic gloss which found its way into the Judæan tradition in the course of catechetical instruction and was unsuspectingly received by the Evangelist. Probably Lk. xx. 18 had a similar origin.

Another instance is found in the narrative of the healing of the bloody flux. To the remark of the disciples: "Thou seest the crowd pressing about Thee, and sayest Thou, 'Who touched Me?'" Jesus really, as Mk. represents (v. 32), made no reply. Lk., however, puts a comment of the tradition on His lips, imputing to Him a singularly crude and materialistic idea: "Some one touched Me; for I recognised power having gone forth from Me" (viii. 46; *cf.* Mk. v. 30).

Another instance is Mt. xxiv. 15-21 = Mk. xiii. 14-9 = Lk. xxi. 20-4. The section exhibits several suspicious features: (1) It is the only passage in the Eschatological Discourse where a definite event of history is predicted; and herein it hardly agrees with Mt. xxiv. 36 = Mk. xiii. 32. (2) The express citation from the Book of Daniel is not in the Lord's manner. (3) It is impossible that He should have shared the Judaistic scrupulosity about Sabbath-observance (Mt. xxiv. 20). It is related by Eusebius that on the eve of the catastrophe the Christians, "in accordance with a certain oracle," forsook the doomed city and took refuge in the Peræan town of Pella;[1] and it is very probable that this section is nothing else than that oracle. In the excitement of that awful crisis the prophet who counselled retreat, might well be deemed inspired; and the oracle which came from his lips, would be accepted as a command of the Risen Lord, and would, with no sense of impropriety, be incorporated with the Eschatological Discourse.

Lk. xxii. 43-4, is bracketed by W. H. on documentary evidence as "an early Western interpolation." A passage so dear to religious sentiment cannot be relinquished without

---

[1] *H. E.* iii. 5.

a pang, but it is certainly unhistorical. It combines two
distinct legends which were entered originally as marginal
notes and were introduced by some copyist into the text,
not too skilfully, since *v.* 44 had better precede *v.* 43.
The angelic strengthening availed little, if it was followed
immediately by the agony and bloody sweat.

§ 13. It was inevitable that such mishaps should befall
the tradition, and they are the less serious that they are not
only easily detected but, for the most part, easily rectified.
It has already appeared how effectively the parallel narratives
of the Synoptists check each other, and there is another and
even more effective instrument of rectification. It is not the
least of the services which John has rendered to the Church
that, writing his Gospel with the Synoptics before him, he set
himself, in the fulness of his personal knowledge, not merely
to supplement but, where necessary, to correct them. His
double emendation of the Synoptic report of the Supper at
Bethany has already been remarked, and instances no less
striking occur wherever he traverses ground already covered
by his predecessors. In fact he never tells a story which
they have already told without either emending or supple-
menting their narratives in some particular. The following
instances may be adduced.

The Feeding of the Five Thousand (Mt. xiv. 13-21 =
Mk. vi. 30-44 = Lk. ix. 10-17 = John vi. 1-14). John
mentions that the Passover was near, thus fixing the date.
Again, while Mk. represents the multitude as accomplishing
the long detour round the head of the Lake in less time than
the boat took to sail across and arriving first at the eastern
side (*v.* 33), John makes it plain that the boat arrived first,
and Jesus was already seated with His disciples on the
mountain-slope when He beheld the multitude approaching
(*vv.* 3-5). A comparison of Mt.'s narrative reveals how Mk.
was led astray. Mt. xiv. 14 preserves the language of the
tradition : "And having come forth," *i.e.* from His retreat on
the mountain, "He saw a great multitude." Mk. understood
"having come forth from the boat," and inserted, by way of
explanation, "and outwent them" (*v.* 33). Again, by
mentioning His prompt inquiry of Philip (*vv.* 5-6) John
brings out what the Synoptists overlook, that Jesus designed

the miracle from the first : it was no after-thought suggested by the hunger of the multitude. Further, John's mention of the attempt to acclaim Him king (*v.* 15) explains the Lord's energetic compulsion of the disciples to re-embark (Mt. xiv. 22 = Mk. vi. 45).

The Triumphal Entry (Mt. xxi. 1-11 = Mk. xi. 1-11 = Lk. xix. 29-44 = John xii. 12-9). John's account of the incident itself is somewhat meagre, and he would probably have let the Synoptic narrative suffice but for the necessity of explaining so remarkable an outburst of popular enthusiasm. It was the Lord's first appearance in Jerusalem since the raising of Lazarus ; and it was the fame of that stupendous miracle that earned Him the ovation (John xii. 17-8).

The Announcement of the Betrayal (Mt. xxvi. 21-5 = Mk. xiv. 18-21 = Lk. xxii. 21-3 = John xiii. 21-35). Mt. (*v.* 23) and Mk. (*v.* 20) represent Jesus as answering the universal inquiry " Is it I ? " with an open indication of the traitor ; and it is inexplicable that Judas should forthwith have condemned himself by dipping in the dish and that the rest of the disciples should still have had no suspicion of him, suffering him to go out and accomplish his design. The mystery is cleared by John's explanation that the indication of the traitor was given secretly to himself (*vv.* 25-6).

The Announcement of the Desertion is represented by Mt. (xxvi. 31-5) and Mk. (xiv. 27-31) as made by Jesus when the company had left the Upper Room and were on the way out to Gethsemane. It is incredible that it should have been made then, just when they needed all their fortitude and when the communion-peace was in their souls ; and John gives it its true place early in the evening (xiii. 36-8 ; *cf.* Lk. xxii. 31-4).

The Trial before the High Priests (Mt. xxvi. 57-xxvii. 1 = Mk. xiv. 53-xv. 1 = Lk. xxii. 54-xxiii. 1 = John xviii. 12-27). According to Mt. and Mk. it would appear that there were two trials before the High Priest Caiaphas : an informal examination immediately after the Arrest while it was yet night, and a hasty trial before the Sanhedrin in the morning to pass formal sentence. Lk. seems to have perceived the improbability of this, and represents the prisoner as merely detained at the High Priest's house until it was day and the

Sanhedrin might convene, suffering the while insult and mal-
treatment at the hands of His guards. John makes the situation plain. There were really two trials, but the first was
merely a precognition before Annas, the High Priest
emeritus, to whose house Jesus was conducted immediately on
His arrest. The second was the formal examination before
Caiaphas, the High Priest in office, at the meeting of
Sanhedrin in the morning.

The Trial before Pilate. The Synoptists suppose that the
Jewish rulers were present at the trial (*cf.* Lk. xxiii. 14);
John is at pains to explain that they remained outside the
Praetorium (xviii. 28). The governor examined Jesus within doors, and
had to come forth when he would confer with the rulers (xviii. 29, 33,
38; xix. 4, 9, 13).

§ 14. John does more than correct the Synoptic narratives:
he supplements them. Indeed it was said in early days that
this was his great purpose in writing another Gospel;[1] and
there is no lack of evidence that, as he wrote, he had the
work of his predecessors before him and studiously excluded
from his narrative whatever they had adequately recorded,
assuming indeed that his readers had the Synoptics in their
hands. Thus, he omits the Baptism of Jesus, yet he makes
a reference to it (i. 32-3) which would be unintelligible without the Synoptic account (Mt. iii. 13-7 = Mk. i. 9-11 = Lk.
iii. 21-2). He has greatly enriched the evangelic history.
But for him the very names of Nathanael, Nicodemus, and
Lazarus would have perished, and of Thomas nothing except
his name would have survived. It was, however, one special
and serious defect in the Synoptics that chiefly moved him to
take up his pen. They narrate with much fulness the Lord's
labours in Galilee, but He prosecuted also an important
ministry in Judæa, principally in Jerusalem. This is unrecorded in the Synoptics, and to rescue it from oblivion was,
according to ancient tradition, the special task to which John
addressed himself. And his representation is confirmed by
every consideration of reason and probability. Jesus must
have visited Jerusalem in the course of His ministry, and,
when He was there, He would assuredly do the work of the
Kingdom of Heaven. Since Jerusalem was the sacred capital,

[1] Eus. *H. E.* iii. 24 ; Chrysost. *In Matth.* i.

it was necesssry that the Messiah should manifest Himself there and assert His claims before the supreme tribunal of the nation.   Nor is the silence of the Synoptists inexplicable. They simply reproduced the oral tradition ; and, since it took shape under the Apostles at Jerusalem where the incidents of the Judæan ministry were well known, there was no need that it should include these.   It related only what had befallen in distant Galilee.

§ 15. Yet the Synoptists are not wholly silent regarding the Judæan ministry.   They relate two incidents which beyond question belong to it.   One is the entertainment of Jesus in the house of Martha, recorded by Lk. alone (x. 38-42).   The other is the clearing of the Temple-court ; and it is recorded by all the Synoptists, though they have misplaced it (Mt. xxi. 12-3 = Mk. xi. 15-7 = Lk. xix. 45-6).   It occurred, as John gives it (ii. 13-22), at the outset of the Lord's ministry.   So remarkable an incident could not well be passed over by the Synoptists ; and, since they had omitted the early visit to Jerusalem, they included the incident in their narrative of the Passion-week when He had gone up to die.[1]

There are, moreover, numerous Synoptic passages which, if not absolutely unintelligible without the Johannine narrative, are wonderfully illumined by it.   Thus, the calling of Simon, Andrew, and John at the very outset of the Galilean ministry (Mt. iv. 18-22 = Mk. i. 16-20) is hardly credible without the Johannine account of their meeting with Jesus at Bethany and their subsequent intercourse with Him (i. 35-42).   Jesus would not have chosen men whom He had not tested and approved ; and, even if it be supposed that, with His unerring insight, He had read their hearts and perceived their fitness, it is inconceivable that they should without preparation have responded to His call.   Again, unless it had been already conferred upon him (John i. 42), it is difficult to account for the mention of Simon's surname of Peter or Cephas in the lists of the Apostles (Mt. x. 2 = Mk. iii. 16 = Lk. vi. 14).   It may indeed be urged that it was

[1] So Wetstein, Neander, Ewald.   Others (Strauss, Baur, Keim) follow the Synoptists in putting the incident at the close.   Of course it is possible, though very unlikely, that there were two clearings of the Temple-court (Chrysost., Aug., Euth. Zig., Theophyl., Erasm., Paulus, Olshaus., Heng., Ebrard, Schleierm., Mey., God., West.).

actually bestowed at Cæsarea Philippi (Mt. xvi. 18) and is
here used by anticipation; but in fact the Lord's exclamation at Cæsarea : " I tell thee that thou art Peter," was not
the bestowal of the name but a delighted recognition of
Simon's worthiness of it, as though He had said : "Behold the
justification of the confidence which I placed in thee at our
first meeting ! " Again, does not Mt. x. 5 imply John iv. ?
To have dealings with the Samaritans would never have
occurred to the Twelve, steeped as they were in Jewish
prejudice, but for the Lord's example. And is it not
reasonable to connect the Lord's answer to the question of
the Baptist's disciples (Mt. ix. 15 = Mk. ii. 19-20 = Lk. v.
34-5) with John iii. 29 ? It is as though He had said :
"Recollect your master's words. He called Me the Bridegroom, and said it was meet that the Bridegroom's friends
should rejoice." According to Mt. xxvi. 61 = Mk. xv.
29, Jesus was accused before the Sanhedrin of having
boasted that He could pull down the Temple and rebuild it
in three days; and the saying on which the charge was
based, is found in John ii. 18-21. "How often would I "
in the Lord's apostrophe to unbelieving Jerusalem (Mt. xxiii.
37-9 = Lk. xiii. 34-5) is unintelligible if, according to the
Synoptists, His ministry had been prosecuted exclusively in
Galilee; but it agrees well with the Johannine representation
of extensive labours in Judæa. The charge against Jerusalem
that she stoned them that were sent unto her, is recognised
as no mere flight of rhetoric, no mere allusion to her treatment of the prophets in bygone days, when it is remembered
that, according to John (viii. 59 ; x. 31-9), Jesus had twice
at least escaped being stoned by the rulers in the Temple court.

It is tempting to find at this point in the Johannine
narrative a home not only for this *logion*, but for another which
Mt. and Lk. report in different connections : Mt. xi. 25-7 =
Lk. x. 21-2. How apt it would be on the lips of Jesus as
He left Jerusalem, rejected by her wise men, but accepted by
the multitude ! And it is remarkable how Johannine the
logion is (*cf.* John iii. 35 ; xiii. 3 ; i. 18 ; vi. 46, 65 ; x. 15).[1]

---

[1] *Cf.* Lk. xiii. 32-3 with John xi. 9 ; Mt. xxi. 22 = Mk. xi. 24 with John xvi. 23.
How Johannine is Mt. xxiv. 36 = Mk. xiii. 32, one of Schmiedel's "absolutely
credible passages" (art. *Gospels* § 139 in *E. B.*)

§ 16 It is a misfortune that, comprehending only the ministry of Jesus, the apostolic tradition began, as a glance at Tischendorf's *Synopsis Evangelica* discovers, with the appearance of John the Baptist (Mt. iii. 1-4 = Lk. iii. 1-3 = Mk. i. 1-5), and its testimony is thus lacking to the miracle of the Lord's Birth. Mt. and Lk. have preserved the wondrous story, and the question is : Whence did they derive their information and what is its value as history? They certainly were persuaded of its truth. Lk., at all events, asserts the carefulness of his investigation and the reliability of his information (i. 1-4); and the Hebraistic style of his early narrative (i. 5—ii.), so unlike the pure Greek of his prologue, proves how faithfully he adhered to his sources, whatever these may have been.

It seems certain that the narratives are based on the testimony of Joseph and Mary. The facts were known only to them, and from them ultimately the story, if it be true, must have proceeded. Mt. has preserved the account which was given by Joseph and which circulated in Jerusalem. It is related from his standpoint, describing how he felt and what he did ; and the description of him as " a kindly man " and therefore loath to take harsh measures even when, as it seemed, he had suffered a foul wrong, is the tribute of his intimates to the good Joseph. The Judæan origin of the story furnishes, moreover, a reasonable explanation of the only real disagreement between the Evangelists in those early narratives. According to Mt. it seems as though Bethlehem were the home of Joseph and Mary. There Jesus was born, and it was after the return from Egypt that Joseph, apprehensive lest Archelaus should prosecute his father's murderous design, fixed his household's abode at Nazareth. According to Lk. Joseph and Mary dwelt at Nazareth, and it was the requirement of the census that brought it about that they were at Bethlehem when Jesus was born. Their going to Nazareth when all was over, was not a migration but a return home. It is likely that Lk.'s is the true account and Mt.'s modification of it is due to Judæan contempt for Galilee, especially Nazareth. The Messiah's connection with Galilee was distasteful to the men of Jerusalem, and they suppressed it as far as possible.

As Mt. has preserved Joseph's story, so Lk. has preserved Mary's. Is there not an evidence of this in his repeated remark about her keeping what befell and pondering it in her heart? (ii. 19, 51). She kept it to herself at the time and imparted it long after when occasion arose. Here is an instance of that sympathy with women-folk which characterised the gentle Lk. and made him record certain incidents over-looked by the other Evangelists (vii. 11-5 ; 36-50 ; viii. 2-3 : x. 38-42 ; xi. 27 ; xxiii. 27-9). Not a little of the precious material which he has added to the common store of the evangelic tradition, was probably derived from those devoted women who had attended Jesus during His ministry and with the heroism of love stood beside the Cross ; and his story of the Lord's Birth is distinguished by feminine touches (*cf.* ii. 40, 52). It may be that he heard it from the friends of Mary ; but, if she was indeed, as the *Protevangelium* represents, a mere girl only twelve years of age at her betrothal, it is most likely that she was still alive in the home of the Beloved Apostle (*cf.* John xix. 27) when Lk. was at Jerusalem with Paul (Acts xxi. 15 *sqq.*), and he may have heard it from her own lips. It does not detract from the historicity of his narrative that he has clothed it in poetic garb, quoting apparently from the hymnology of the primitive Church (*cf.* i. 46-55 ; 68-79 ; ii. 14 ; 29-32).

§ 17. There is another and still graver defect in the oral tradition. Comprehending only the ministry of our Lord, it ends with the Crucifixion and omits the supreme event of the Resurrection. Its failure, just where its testimony is most needful, is matter for profound regret ; but it should be distinctly understood that, whatever it may mean, it does not mean that the Apostles knew nothing of the Resurrection or had any doubt regarding it. On the contrary, they believed it with exultant faith, and it was the constant burden of their preaching. For St Paul it was the supreme fact, the very foundation of the Faith (*cf.* 1 Cor. xv. 14-20 ; Rom. x. 9). At the commencement of his ministry he had a confer-ence with the Apostles, the men who had been with Jesus, and laid his Gospel before them ; and in after days he publicly claimed that they had approved it (Gal. i. 18—ii. 19). It is beyond question that they believed with absolute certainty that the Lord had been raised from the dead by the power of God ; and it was that conviction which rescued them from despondency and sent them forth with resolute hearts to preach and die.   They must have been right well assured that their faith was true, or it would never have nerved them to sacrifice and toil and martyrdom.[1]   Why then is the Resurrection omitted from the apostolic tradition ?   In regard to the omission of the Lord's Birth and the Silent Years it is enough to say that the Apostles included in the tradition only what they had themselves seen and heard ; but they had been witnesses of the Resurrection.

§ 18. There are two considerations which go some way toward a solution.   One is that, when the tradition took shape, the wonder of the Resurrection was at its height. The purpose of the tradition was to prevent the facts of the Lord's ministry from being forgotten or distorted ; but the Resurrection was an amazing and overwhelming fact which had happened but yesterday and was fresh in every mind. The very fact that it was deemed needless to record it is an evidence of its notoriety and certainty.   And it was deemed all the more needless forasmuch as the Lord's Return was believed to be imminent.   It was enough, the Apostles thought, to proclaim the fact that He had risen, and keep His words and works fresh and clear in remembrance. Again, it is remarkable, though in no wise inexplicable, that the Apostles always speak with a certain reticence about the Resurrection.   They proclaim the fact, but they refrain from entering into particulars.   As time went on and still the Lord did not return, John, the last surviving eye-witness, yielded to the importunities of the believers and wrote the wondrous story.[2]

> " Imminent was the outcry ' Save our Christ ! '
> Whereon I stated much of the Lord's life
> Forgotten or misdelivered, and let it work."

Yet even John hesitated when he came to speak of the Resurrection.   The twenty-first chapter of his Gospel is an after-thought, a subsequent addition, " a postscript," says Rénan, " from the same pen as the rest."   He stopped when he had told what happened in Jerusalem during the first week.

[1] cf. Isidor. Pelus. Ep. ii. 212.　　　　　　[2] Eus. H. E. iii. 24.

Here he ended his Gospel, and it was probably not only the importunities of the Ephesian elders but a desire to silence the wild story which had got abroad regarding himself (xxi. 24), that moved him to resume his pen and reveal what had happened at the Sea of Galilee. In truth it is no marvel that the Apostles should have maintained such reticence. The story was too sacred to be divulged. The Risen Lord had manifested Himself unto them and not unto the world, and they remembered His word : " My mystery is for Me and the Sons of My House." [1]

§ 19. When the Synoptists undertook the task of composing their Gospels, they laboured under this disadvantage, that the Apostles had dispersed in prosecution of their missions, and were inaccessible for enquiry and consultation. In the oral tradition they had, so far as it went, an amplitude of trustworthy material ; but it stopped short at the Crucifixion, and for the episode of the Resurrection they had to content with such information as they could glean among the believers. This was all that they had to work upon, and from the fact that their narratives comprise hardly anything beyond the visit of the women to the Sepulchre, it is a fair inference that they learned only what the women had divulged. And this meagre material would be distorted at once by the excitement of the moment (*cf.* Mt. xxviii. 8 ; Mk. xvi. 8) and by the subsequent process of transmission from mouth to mouth. The result is that in their account of the Resurrection the Synoptic narratives, elsewhere so remarkably accordant, bristle with discrepancies which refuse to be harmonised even by the most violent expedients. It is hardly too much to affirm that, as they stand, they agree only in their unfaltering and triumphant proclamation of the fact that Jesus rose and appeared to His disciples.

1. The visitants to the Sepulchre : Mary Magdalene and the other Mary (Mt. xxviii. 1) ; Mary Magdalene, Mary the mother of James, and Salome (Mk. xvi. 1) ; "women who had followed Him from Galilee," including Mary Magdalene, Joanna and Mary the mother of James (Lk. xxiii. 55 ; xxiv. 1, 10) ; Mary Magdalene alone (John xx. 1),

---

[1] Clem. Alex. *Strom.* v. 10. § 63: παρήγγειλεν ὁ κύριος ἔν τινι εὐαγγελίῳ· μυστήριον ἐμὸν ἐμοὶ καὶ τοῖς υἱοῖς τοῦ οἴκου μου. *Cf.* Clem. Rom. *Hom.* xix. § 20.

though her "*we* know not" in *v.* 2 may mean that she had companions.

2. The time of the visit: "late on the Sabbath, when the light was dawning unto the first day of the week"[1] (Mt. xxviii. 1), *i.e.* at nightfall; "very early, when the sun had risen" (Mk. xvi. 2); at "deep dawn" (Lk. xxiv. 1); "early, while it was yet dark" (John xx. 1).

3. The object of the visit: to embalm the Lord's body (Mk. xvi. 1; Lk. xxiv. 1); to see the Sepulchre (Mt. xxviii. 1; John xx. 1).

4. They bought the spices after the Sabbath was past (Mk. xvi. 1); they had bought them on the Friday evening between the burial and the commencement of the Sabbath (Lk. xxiii. 56).

5. The stone was rolled away after the women's arrival: there was a great earthquake. and an angel descended, rolled it away, and sat upon it (Mt. xxviii. 2-3); on their arrival they found the stone already removed; no mention of an earthquake nor, thus far, of an angel (Mk. xvi. 3-4; Lk. xxiv. 2; John xx. 1).

6. One angel (Mt. xxviii. 2, 5; Mk. xvi. 5); two (Lk. xxiv. 4; John xx. 12).

7. The angel outside the Sepulchre, seated on the stone which he had rolled away (Mt. xxviii. 2, 5); inside, seated on the right side (Mk. xvi. 5); the Sepulchre empty when the women entered, and, while they were wondering, the two men suddenly appeared beside them in flashing raiment (Lk. xxiv. 3-4); on her return to the Sepulchre after informing Peter and John that it was empty, Mary, as she peered in, saw the two "sitting one at the head and the other at the feet where the body of Jesus had lain" (John xx. 1-12).

8. The angels bade the women go and tell the disciples that the Lord had risen and would meet them in Galilee (Mt. xxviii. 7; Mk. xvi. 7); no command: the angels merely remind them that, while yet in Galilee, Jesus had predicted His Betrayal, Crucifixion, and Resurrection (Lk. xxiv. 6-9).

---

[1] Not the light of morning but the light of the lamps kindled at nightfall, when, according to Jewish reckoning, the day began (*cf.* Lk. xxiii. 54). See Lightfoot and Wetstein. *Cf.* Moulton's *Gram. of N. T. Gk.* i. pp. 72 *sq.*

9. The women, hastening away from the Sepulchre, "said nothing to any one, for they were afraid" (Mk. xvi. 8)[1]; they "told the whole story to the Eleven and all the rest," but gained no credence (Lk. xxiv. 11); as they were hurrying to tell the disciples, Jesus Himself met them and reiterated the angel's behest (Mt. xxviii. 8-10), and their story evidently was believed (*v.* 16); Mary Magdalene of her own accord, ere she saw the angel, ran, not to the Eleven, but to Peter and John and told them that the Sepulchre was empty; and they immediately repaired thither (John xx. 2-10. *Cf.* Lk. xxiv. 24. Lk. xxiv. 12 is spurious.)

10. Jesus did not repulse the women, including Mary Magdalene, when they laid hold on His feet (Mt. xxviii. 9); He repulsed Mary (John xx. 17).

11. The Risen Lord asked for food and ate it in the disciples' presence (Lk. xxiv. 41-3); this is omitted in John xx. 19-25.

12. Lk. xxiv. represents the Ascension as taking place from Mount Olivet late on the Resurrection-day, crowding all the Lord's appearances into that brief space and making Jerusalem and its neighbourhood the scene of them all. Mt. xxviii. 16-20 and John xx. 26-xxi, imply a long interval, spent partly at Jerusalem, partly in Galilee. There was a tradition in early times, that Jesus rose and ascended on the self-same day,[2] and Lk. adopted it in his Gospel Afterwards in the *Book of Acts* he corrected his error (i. 3)

§ 20. Thus discordant are the evangelic accounts of the Resurrection, and it may seem as though there were no escape from the dilemma which Strauss presents: either we must "adhere to one of the four accounts as pre-eminently apostolic, and by this rectify the others," or we must "confess that in all the evangelic accounts of these first tidings of the Resurrection we have before us nothing more than traditional reports." But we are not shut up to these alternatives. An

---

[1] Mk.'s Gospel is broken off abruptly here, *vv.* 9-20 being a later supplement of lesser authority. There is no knowing what the missing conclusion may have contained. The apocryphal *Ev. Petr.* gives an account closely resembling Mk.'s of the women's visit to the Sepulchre. It concludes "Then the women, affrighted, fled," and proceeds to narrate an incident similar to John xxi. 1. *sqq.* The MS., however, breaks off after a few sentences.

[2] *Cf. Ep. Barn.* xv. § 9.

attentive scrutiny of the narratives discovers order amid their chaos and a firm foot-hold for faith. The fact is that there are three distinct strata of evangelic testimony to the Resurrection, each possessing a peculiar value :

(1) The common rumour reported by the Synoptists (Mt. xxvii. 62-6, xxviii. 11-5 ; xxviii. 1-10, 16-20 ; Mk. xvi. 1-8 ; Lk. xxiii. 56-xxiv. 11 [12], 36-53). These traditions are valueless as history, yet they constitute a testimony of no little weight to the fact of the Resurrection, proving that it was universally recognised and was much talked of. And, moreover, loose and inaccurate as they may be, they are never very far from the truth. They are in every case vague reports, distorted versions of actual occurrences.

(2) Lk.'s research (cf. i. 1-4) has rescued from oblivion that story of what befell Cleopas and his unnamed companion on the road to Emmaus (xxiv. 13-35). The story carries its own credentials. It shines amid its surroundings like a gem in a heap of dust. Perhaps the Evangelist got it from Cleopas, whose Greek name suggests that he belonged to the circle of Joanna, the wife of Chuza, Herod's steward. Throughout his narrative there is evidence of close intimacy between Lk. and this circle of believers.

(3) The clear and full narrative of John (xx-xxi). The Lucan passage and the Johannine narrative stand out distinct and strong, and the more closely they are scrutinised, the more convincingly do they attest their title to historicity. There is at least one point where they are linked together and attest each other. Lk. xxiv. 24 is a plain contradiction not only of Mk. xvi. 8 but of Lk. xxiv. 11. It agrees, how-ever, with John xx. 3-10.

§ 21. As soon as the true nature of the Synoptic narratives is recognised, the history of the Resurrection is disencumbered of several bewildering accretions and assumes a distinct and harmonious shape. It is a minor yet not un-important gain that the real errand of the women to the Sepulchre stands revealed. It was not that they might embalm the Lord's body (Mk. and Lk.). That had already been done by Joseph and Nicodemus (John xix. 39-40) in the women's sight (Mt. xxvii. 6 ; Mk. xv. 47 ; Lk. xxiii. 55). And, moreover, the body had lain over thirty hours in the

Sepulchre ere they visited it, and must already have suffered decomposition. Their real errand was to see the Sepulchre (Mt., John), if haply the soul had reanimated its clay.[1] Again, the Synoptics represent Jesus as performing carnal functions with His spiritual body. According to Lk. xxiv. 41-3 He ate in the presence of His disciples. It is incredible that He should have carried to Heaven a body which needed food, and that such a body should have been capable of passing through closed doors (John xx. 19 ; *cf.* Lk. xxiv. 36). Two theories have been advanced in this connection. One is the blunt and obvious notion that when He ate the broiled fish, He acted κατ' οἰκονομίαν. He ate supernaturally, and the miracle was designed to establish the disciples' faith and assure them of the reality of His presence.[2] The other, which is more subtle, is that between the Resurrection and the Ascension, His body underwent a process of sublimation. It was " in a state of transition and change, upon the boundary of both worlds, and possessed the impress or character both of this world and of the next."[3] It is indeed conceivable that there should have been such a process, gradually purifying His body of fleshly qualities and advancing it to a glorified condition ; but it is difficult to conceive the possibility of His body being at the same stage so sublimated that it could pass through closed doors and so gross that it required food. Nor is it necessary to maintain a position so embarrassing and indeed grotesque. Only in Lk. xxiv. 41-3 is it said that the Risen Lord ate, and the statement is absent from John's parallel narrative (xx. 19-25). It belongs to the Synoptic cycle of unhistoric tradition, and is obviously a faint echo of John xxi. 5, 9, 13. It is remarkable that alike in Lk.'s narrative of the supper at Emmaus and in John's narrative of the breakfast on the shore of the Lake it is plainly implied that, while He gave food to His disciples, Jesus Himself took none (Lk. xxiv. 30 ; John xxi. 12-3).

Lk. xxiv. 39 is wanting in John's parallel narrative. Ignatius quotes the curious saying, though in a somewhat less gross form : " Grasp, handle Me and see that I am not

[1] *Cf.* p. 369.
[2] Joan. Damasc. *De Fid. Orthod.* iv. 1 ; Euth. Zig.
[3] Martensen, *Chr. Dogm.* § 172. *Cf.* Orig. *C. Cels.* ii. 62.

a bodiless dæmon; "[1] and Jerome says that Ignatius quoted it from the apocryphal *Gospel of the Hebrews.*[2] This reveals its nature. It is simply one of the unhistorical traditions which floated about the primitive Church, and Lk., ever watchful for fresh material, heard it and incorporated it in his Gospel. It may be that Paul had heard this tradition which represents the Risen Lord as saying: "A spirit hath not flesh and bones as ye behold Me having," and had it in view when he wrote: "This I say, brethren, that flesh and blood cannot inherit the Kingdom of God, neither doth corruption inherit incorruption" (1 Cor. xv. 50).

§ 22. It appears as the result of this investigation that the evangelic history is worthy of all acceptation. Indeed it may be questioned whether any other history carries such credentials or is entitled to equal reliance. It contains indubitably a certain admixture of unreliable elements; but these are easily distinguished, and so far from discrediting the mass serve rather to approve its value. One of our Gospels is the testimony of the best beloved and most spiritually minded of the men who had companied with Jesus to the things which he had seen and heard (*cf.* 1 John i. 1-3);[3] and, though the others were not written by Apostles, yet they embody the tradition which emanated from the Apostles and was transmitted with reverent fidelity. In the Gospels Jesus is set before us as He appeared to the men with whom He companied in the days of His flesh.

But, though it be allowed that the Gospels truly record the doings of Jesus, do they accurately report His sayings? One of the marvels of modern literature is Boswell's report, so minute and accurate withal, of his hero's conversation; and the explanation is that, as he states in his introductory chapter, he "had the honour and happiness of enjoying his friendship for upwards of twenty years; had the scheme

---

[1] *Ep. ad Smyrn.* iii: λάβετε, ψηλαφήσατέ με καὶ ἴδετε ὅτι οὐκ εἰμὶ δαιμόνιον ἀσώματον.

[2] *Script. Eccl.* under *Ignatius.*

[3] It is impossible to enter here into the question of the authenticity of the Fourth Gospel. Suffice it to say that the traditional date is practically conceded. Baur put the date about A.D. 170, but the stress of evidence has pushed it further and further back, until it is now put in the last decade of the first century. *Cf.* Moffatt, *Hist. NT.* p. 495.

of writing his life constantly in view; acquired a faculty
in recollecting, and was very assiduous in recording, his
conversation, of which the extraordinary vigour and vivacity
constituted one of the first features of his character." But
even that vigorous and vivacious conversation must quickly
have faded from the listener's memory had he not hastened
to write it down while it was still ringing in his ears. And
thus it was that Damis of Nineveh, the Boswell of Apollonius
of Tyana, succeeded in preserving his master's conversation.[1]
There is, however, no evidence that the Apostles pursued
this course. They wrote from memory; and, though they
might here and there reproduce the *ipsissima verba* of a
memorable epigram, they could, as a rule, recall only the drift
of what they heard. And thus, it would appear, all that
remains of Jesus' teaching is a far off echo. Seldom, if ever,
is it given us to quote a sentence and say: "The Lord
spoke these words." The utmost that we can say is: "He
spoke after this manner."

One cannot, however, read the words of Jesus as they
are reported by the Evangelists without demurring to this
conclusion. There are no words like them. How they
sparkle and glow on the pages of the Gospels![2] It is neither
exaggeration nor irreverence to say that they are embedded
in the evangelic narrative like jewels in a setting of base
metal. One knows instinctively where Jesus ceases and the
Evangelist begins. It is like passing into another atmosphere.
In a quiet nook of Scotland lies a little town, remote from
the throng of cities and the highways of commerce. It is
an old-world place, and certain of its red-tiled and moss-
grown dwellings bear dates of the seventeenth and sixteenth
centuries over their crumbling lintels. Built here and there
into their rude walls one observes blocks of masonry, broken
and defaced yet skilfully shaped and carved with quaint
devices. How comes it that they are found in so unworthy
a setting? Hard by stand the grey ruins of an ancient
castle which, if tradition be true, sheltered King Robert the
Bruce ere he had won Scotland's liberty; and, when "the
rude forefathers of the hamlet" were minded to build them

[1] Philostr. *Apoll.* i. 19.
[2] *Cf.* Just. M. *Dial. c. Tryph.*, ed. Sylburg., p. 225 C.

dwellings, that venerable pile served them as a convenient quarry.   At a glance one recognises those fragments of nobler handiwork amid their alien setting.   And even thus do the words of Jesus shine on the pages of the Evangelists. It is indeed indubitable that they have suffered some measure of change and are not always written precisely as they came from His lips ; but the change is generally inappreciable. As they stand on the sacred page, they attest their originality. They are no far-off echoes but living voices, as fresh and powerful now as when they were first heard by the Sea of Galilee or in the city of Jerusalem.   They palpitate with life, they throb with emotion, and they make our hearts to burn within us, reminding us how He said : " The words which I have spoken unto you, they are spirit and they are life " (John vi. 63).   No other than He could have spoken them ; and, if it be asked how it came to pass that the Apostles were able to reproduce them, what answer is possible save that they had received the fulfilment of His promise : " The Advocate, the Holy Spirit which the Father will send in My name, He shall teach you all things and remind you of all things which I said unto you " (John xiv. 26)?

THE DAYS OF HIS FLESH

CHAPTER I

THE WONDROUS BIRTH

Lk. i. 26-
38; Mt. i.
18-25; Lk.
ii. 1-39;
Mt. ii. 1-23.

" Altitudo, quid hic jaces
In tam vili stabulo?
Qui creâsti cœli faces,
Alges in præsepio?
O quam mira perpetrâsti,
Jesu, propter hominem !
Tam ardenter quem amâsti
Paradiso exulem."—*Med. Hymn.*

THE life of our Blessed Lord and Saviour Jesus Christ differs in one momentous respect from every other which has ever been lived on earth. It did not begin when He was born. In the prologue of his Gospel St John, borrowing a great conception of Alexandrian speculation, calls Him " the Word, who was in the beginning, was with God, and was God, through whom all things were made, in whom was life, and the life was the light of men."[1] " And the Word was made flesh and tabernacled among us, and we beheld His glory." And St Paul, albeit in simpler language, advances an equally tremendous claim. He affirms the pre-existence of Jesus ; nay, only a generation after Jesus had departed and while many who had been with Him in the days of His flesh still survived, he assumed it as already an article of faith which his readers would never dream of disputing. " Ye perceive the grace of our Lord Jesus Christ, that for your sakes He became poor when He was rich, that ye, by His poverty, might become rich." " Let this mind be in you which was also in Christ Jesus, who, in God's form primally existing, deemed it not a prize to be on an equality with God, but emptied Himself, having taken a slave's form, having been made in men's likeness."

Here is an exceeding wonder. What manner of person must Jesus have been when the men who companied with

Pre-existence of Jesus.

John i. 1-18.

2 Cor. viii. 9.

Phil. ii. 5-7.

Asserted by Himself.

[1] *Cf.* Paul's cosmic Christology : Col. i. 15-7.

1

Him in the days of His flesh, who saw Him eating and drinking, who knew Him in all the intimacies of daily intercourse, could thus think and speak of Him? It is difficult to conceive how they could make so transcendent a claim on His behalf, had He not Himself advanced it. And such is indeed the representation of the Evangelists. Over and over

Mt. v. 17. again He declared that He had *come*. "Think not that I came to pull down the Law or the Prophets. I came not to

Lk. xix. 10. pull down but to complete." "The Son of Man came to

Mt. xx. 28 seek and save what is lost." "The Son of Man came not to
=Mk.x.45.
Cf. John ix. be served but to serve, and to give His life a ransom for
39. many." "What," He enquired of His offended followers at
John vi. 62. a crisis in His ministry, "if ye behold the Son of Man ascending where He was before?" And at its close He

John xvii.5. prayed : "Glorify Thou Me, O Father, by Thine own side with the glory which I used to have, ere the world was, by Thy side." His birth was an Advent. It was the Incarnation of One who had been from all eternity in the Bosom of God.

Born of a   It is in no wise surprising that the Birth of such an one
virgin. should have been unique. He was conceived by the operation of the Holy Spirit in the womb of a virgin, a new creation of God's hand, a divine man, a second and greater Adam.[1] His mother Mary dwelt at Nazareth, and had been betrothed to one Joseph who followed the trade of carpenter and, if tradition be true, was much her senior.[2] He was a kindly man,[3] and on discovering her condition he was disposed to deal leniently with her and put her away privily, sparing her shame as far as he might ; but, ere he could carry out his purpose, he was apprised in a vision of the wondrous truth.

The Cen-   When Mary's time was near, it happened, untowardly, as it
sus. seemed, but in truth according to the purpose of God, that she must needs set out with him on a long journey. The Emperor Augustus, that master of state-craft, had ordained that every fourteen years an estimate should be made of the

---

[1] See Append. I.

[2] So the apocryphal *Protev.* viii-ix. ; *Ev. de Nat. Mar.* viii. ; *Hist. Jos.* xiv.

[3] Such is the meaning of δίκαιος in Mt. i. 19. *Cf.* Chrysost. *In Matth.* iv : δίκαιον ἐνταῦθν τὸν ἐνάρετον ἐν ἄπασι λέγει. ἔστι μὲν γὰρ δικαιοσύνη καὶ τὸ μὴ πλεονεκτεῖν· ἔστι δὲ καὶ ἡ καθόλου ἀρέτη. . . . δίκαιος οὖν ὢν, τουτέστι χρηστὸς καὶ ἐπιεικής. Hatch, *Ess. in Bib. Gk.*, p. 51.

population and resources of the Empire, in the proud Roman phrase "the whole world," all the conquered provinces and tributary kingdoms which lay under the sway of the sovereign city from the Euphrates to the Atlantic, from Britain to the Cataracts of the Nile.[1] Had Judæa been then, as in later days, a mere province, her census would have been taken after the Roman method, which enrolled the people wherever they chanced to reside ; but, since she was still a kingdom, it was taken after the Jewish method, which required each to repair to his ancestral seat and there report himself. Since Joseph was " of the house and ancestry of David," he must needs betake himself to Bethlehem, David's city, a three days' journey from Nazareth. And, notwithstanding her condition, he took Mary with him, not caring in the peculiar circumstances to leave her amid curious and ill-judging people. Near Bethlehem her pangs came upon her. There stood hard by a *caravanserai*, one of those rude structures adjoining the highways of the East for the convenience of travellers, and consisting of an open court-yard for the beasts with a raised platform along the walls, roofed over and divided into compartments where the travellers lodged.[2] So many were afoot that every lodgment was already occupied, and there was nothing for it but that Mary should lie down on the litter in the court-yard among the asses, kine, and camels. And there she brought forth her Child and cradled Him in a manger. It is a singular instance of the irony of history that, when Rome was sacked by Alaric, some of her high-born citizens, men and women both, escaped and found an asylum at Bethlehem.[3] In the holy town where her imperial pride had given the Lord of Glory a manger for a cradle, that remnant of her citizens sheltered, homeless and starving, in the day of her calamity.

As he sat in his gilded palace, master of the world, Augustus little dreamed that far away in despised Judæa a

Margin notes: Journey of Joseph and Mary to Bethlehem.

The Saviour's Birth.

---

[1] On the historicity of Lk. ii. 1-3 see Ramsay, *Was Chr. Born in Bethl. ?* *Cf.* Chrysostom's express assertion in his sermon *In Jes. Chr. Diem. Nat.* that at that time, probably A.D. 386, the records of the Jewish census were lying among the state-papers at Rome and might be inspected by any who desired.

[2] The tradition that Jesus was born in a cave (Just. M. *Dial. cum Tryph.*, ed. Sylburg., p. 296 ; Orig. *C. Cels.* i. 51) may be due to Is. xxxiii. 16, which Justin quotes.

[3] Jer. *Comm. in Ezech. lib. iii. Prœm.*

King had been born whose name would be continued as long
as the sun, and whose dominion would extend from sea to
sea when Rome's empire had perished and her glory become
a memory of the past. God hid these things from the wise
and understanding, but He revealed them unto babes. That
night on the pasture lands around Bethlehem, where in days
long gone by David had tended his father's sheep and Amos
had driven his herds and dressed his sycamores, a company
of shepherds kept watch over their flock.[1] Those shepherds
were a brave and hardy and withal a somewhat lawless race ;
and, honourably as it figures in the Holy Scriptures, their
calling had in later days fallen into disrepute. " Let no man,"
said R. Gorion, " make his son a muleteer, a camel-driver, a
barber, a sailor, a shepherd, an inn-keeper ; forasmuch as their
craft is a craft of robbers." [2] Yet it was to a company of
shepherds that the first announcement of the Lord's birth was
made. They were reclining under the star-lit sky and whiling
away the hours of vigil with flute and song,[3] when suddenly
an angel hovered above them and soothed their alarm with
good tidings of a great joy : " There was born for you to-day
a Saviour, who is Messiah the Lord." It was good tidings
indeed, and wonderful as good, that Israel's long-promised,
long-expected Deliverer had come, and that He had come to
redeem even them. It was a happy augury of the grace
which should afterwards be revealed, that, when the Herald
Angel winged his way from Heaven, he passed by the Holy
City and sought those poor sons of the wilderness, proclaiming
that the Messiah had come to save the lost, to call not the
righteous but sinners.

The shepherds.

" And this," said the angel, " is a sign for you : ye shall
find a babe wrapped in swaddling clothes, and lying in a
manger." Then, as though Heaven had opened, the sky was
filled with a multitude of the heavenly host and rang with the
music of a heavenly song :

The angels' song.

---

[1] Jerome, writing at Bethlehem, thus describes the wilderness of Judæa (*Comm.
in Am. lib. i. Prœm.*): "Quia humi arido atque arenoso nihil omnino frugum gignitur,
cuncta sunt plena pastoribus, ut sterilitatem terræ compensent pecorum multitudine."

[2] Wetstein on Lk. ii. 8.

[3] Two explanations, according to Euth. Zig., were given of ἀγραυλεῖν : (1) *to pipe
in the fields*, (2) *to bivouac in the fields by night*.

" Glory in the highest unto God,
   And on earth peace
   Among the men of His good pleasure."

The vision faded, and the shepherds, hastening over the fields, found it as the angel had said.

Israel's religion had sunk very low in those days. Her priests were Sadducees, her teachers Pharisees. Nevertheless she had still a godly remnant, the Lord's hidden ones, who nourished their souls on the Holy Scriptures and lived quiet lives of faith and prayer, staying their hearts on the promises and hoping, like watchers for the morning, for the appearing of the Messiah. And to two of these His advent was revealed. It happened forty days after His birth. He had already been " circumcised on the eighth day " according to the Jewish Law, receiving then His name JESUS. It was a sacred and heroic name in Israel. It is the same as Joshua, and had been borne by Moses' successor ; by that true priest who aided Zerubbabel in the restoration of the Temple and served in Zechariah's vision as a type of Messiah's salvation ; by that wise and godly Jerusalemite, Joshua ben Sira, Jesus the son of Sirach, who in the first quarter of the second century wrote the Book of Ecclesiasticus, the gem of the extra-canonical Jewish literature, a book which, as appears from more than one echo of it in His teaching,[1] our Lord loved. It meant *Jehovah is Salvation*, and it had served as a battle-cry during the Maccabean struggle." But what gave it its peculiar suitability for the Holy Child was not its historic associations but its prophetic significance. " Thou shalt call His name JESUS," the angel had said, " for He it is that will save His people from their sins."

A month later in obedience to the Law Mary, accompanied by Joseph, took her Child from Bethlehem to Jerusalem, at once to make the offering for her own purification and to pay the five shekels which were the ransom for the life of her first-born son. The offering of purification was properly a lamb, but in case of poverty " a pair of turtledoves or two young pigeons " sufficed ; and this " offering of

The godly remnant.

The circumcision of Jesus. Cf. Acts vii. 45 ; Hebr. iv. 8.

2 Macc. viii. 23 ; xiii. 15.

Cf. Ecclus. xlvi. 1.

His presentation in the Temple.

Lev. xii.

Num. xviii. 15-6.

---

[1] *Cf.* Mt. vi. 7 with Ecclus. vii. 14 ; Mt. vi. 14-5 = Mk. xi. 25-6 with Ecclus. xxviii. 2 ; Lk. v. 39 with Ecclus. ix. 10 ; Mt. xi. 28-30 with Ecclus. li. 23-7 ; Lk. xii. 16-21 with Ecclus. xi. 18-9.

[2] According to *Pseudo-Matth. Ev.* xv. they left the *stabulum* and went into Bethlehem on the sixth day after the Birth.

the poor," as it was called,[1] was all that Mary could afford.
There was in Jerusalem in those days an aged saint named

Symeon. Symeon, one of those who in that dark and calamitous time
were expecting the dayspring from on high and the consolation of Israel. "It had been revealed to him that he should
not see death until he saw the Lord's Messiah"; and, like an
imprisoned exile, he was yearning for his release. He was in
the sacred court, engaged in the offices of devotion, when the
Holy Family entered; and, recognising the Child, he took
Him in his arms and blessed God with a glad heart: "Now
unloosest Thou Thy slave, Lord, according to Thy word in
peace, because mine eyes have seen Thy salvation." Not in
vain had Symeon mused on the Messianic Scriptures. While
his contemporaries were dreaming of a victorious King, he had
laid to heart the prophecies of a suffering Redeemer; and he
forewarned Mary what would be: "Behold, this Child hath
been set for the falling and rising up of many in Israel, and
for a sign gainsaid, and through thine own soul shall a sword
pass, that thoughts out of many hearts may be revealed."

Anna. While Symeon was speaking, another saint appeared on
the scene—an aged prophetess named Anna, who, since she

Lk. ii. 37
R.V. had been a widow for eighty-four years, must have been over
Cf. 1 Tim. a hundred years of age.[2] She haunted the Temple, giving
v. 5. herself night and day to fasting and prayer. Entering the
sacred court while Symeon was still speaking, she took up the
refrain of praise, and afterwards spoke of the Holy Child to
such as, like herself, "expected Jerusalem's redemption,"
quickening their hope and preparing a welcome for Him when
He should be manifested unto Israel.

Universal Nor was it only to a chosen few in the land of Israel that
expectation the Messiah's advent was revealed. It is no wonder that in
of the Re-
deemer's those dark days, when the Jewish people were groaning under
advent. the Roman yoke, the Messianic hope should have revived and
the belief arisen that the Redeemer was at hand. So utter
was the nation's need of Him that, it was felt, His advent could
no longer be delayed. The wonder is that beyond the
borders of the Holy Land a like expectancy prevailed. Yet,

[1] Lightfoot on Lk. ii 24.
[2] Cf. Plin. H. N. vii. 50 for instances of longevity in N. Italy when the census
was taken in the reign of Vespasian.

if it be true that "coming events cast their shadows before," it is in no wise strange that there should have been premonitions of the greatest event in the world's history. One who lived through the crisis, has vividly pourtrayed the unrest and alarm of Europe on the eve of the Reformation, when distress abounded, lawlessness prevailed, unbelief was rampant, and "the whole world was in travail with some great evil." [1] And even so it was when the fulness of the time had come and God was about to send forth His Son. A single instance may suffice. It is related by Plutarch [2] that a ship, bound for Italy and laden with merchandise and passengers, was becalmed one evening "off the isles Echinades." She had drifted nigh to Paxos when suddenly a voice was heard from the island calling aloud "Thamûs!" Thamûs was the Egyptian pilot. Twice was he called and held his peace, but the third time he answered. And then the voice charged him : "When you come over against Palôdes, announce that the Great Pan is dead." The ship's company were amazed and reasoned with themselves whether it were better to obey the behest or pay no heed. Thamûs decided, if there were wind, to sail past in silence, but, should there be a calm at the place, to proclaim what he had heard. When they came over against Palôdes, there was neither wind nor wave, and Thamûs, looking from the stern to the land, cried : "The Great Pan is dead!" Straightway there arose a loud mourning, not of one but of many, mingled with wonderment. Such stories—and they are many [3]—reveal what despair had filled men's hearts when Jesus came. It seemed as though the world's sun had set and its night were hastening on. Humanity was crying out for deliverance ; and it is remarkable that, perhaps because the Hope of Israel had been noised abroad, even the heathen were turning their eyes toward Judæa, thence expecting the Deliverer. [4]

---

[1] Erasm. *Colloq. Puerp.*, written in 1525, two years before the siege of Rome.

[2] *De Defect. Orac.* § 17.

[3] *Cf.* the rumour at Rome in A.D. 34 of the appearance in Egypt of the Phœnix (Herod. ii. 73 ; Plin. *H. N.* x. 2 ; Philostr. *Apoll.* iii. 49), whose advent at intervals of 1461 years, marked the end of one cycle and the beginning of another. Since it had last been seen in the reign of Ptolemy Euergetes (B.C. 247-22) the *Annus Magnus* had still some 1200 years to run. Tac. *Ann.* vi. 28.

[4] *Cf.* Suet. *Vesp.* § 4 ; Tac. *Hist.* v. 13 ; Jos. *De Bell. Jud.* vi. 5. § 4.

The star-
led
Wizards. It is therefore in no wise incredible that, when the Messiah appeared, there came strangers from afar, enquiring after Him. " Behold, Wizards from the East arrived at Jerusalem, saying · ' Where is the new-born King of the Jews? For we saw His star in the East and came to do obeisance unto Him.' " They were astrologers, and their craft, which read men's destinies on the face of the sky, was in great repute in an age when religion was dead and superstition had usurped its place. Its home was the mystic East, but the Chaldæan soothsayer was a familiar figure in the West, especially at Rome, where, like his successor in medieval Europe, he exerted a potent and too often malign influence not only over the multitude but over statesmen and princes.[1] Tradition, probably on the ground of their triple offering, has it that those Wizards were three in number, and makes them kings, by name Caspar, Melchior, and Balthasar. In their distant home[2] they had observed a strange star, and it has been ascertained that there were astronomical phenomena about that time. These could not escape the observation of the Wizards ; and it was natural that, when some strange star swam into their ken, they should hail it as a prognostication of a royal birth.[3] They knew not where it might have
Cf. Gen.
xliii. 11 ; 1
Kings x. 2. occurred, but, furnishing themselves with fit offerings, they set forth on their quest. As they travelled westward, they would learn of the expectation which centred in Judæa ; and they bent their steps toward Jerusalem, arriving two years after their setting out.[4] " Where," they eagerly inquired, " is the new-born King of the Jews? For we saw His star in the East, and came to do obeisance unto Him."

Alarm of
Herod. Since it was believed that His birth would be heralded by a star,[5] who could this King of the Jews be but the Messiah?

[1] *Cf.* Hor. *Od.* i. 11 ; Juv. iii. 43 ; Tac. *Ann.* vi. 20-1 ; *Hist.* i. 22. Severe measures against them : Val. Max. i. 3. § 2 ; Dion. Cass. xlix. 1 ; Suet. *Tib.* § 36 ; Tac. *Hist.* ii. 62 ; *Ann.* ii. 32. See Erasm. *Adag.* under *Qui bene conjiciet, hunc vatem.*

[2] Persia (Chrysost., Theophyl., Euth. Zig.) ; Arabia, (Just. M., Tert.).

[3] *Cf.* Orig. *C. Cels.* i. 59; Wetstein on Mt. ii. 2.

[4] On the assumption that the star appeared at the time of the Birth it has been inferred that Jesus was two years old when the Wizards arrived. But, according to Abarbanel, the star which heralded Moses' birth, appeared three years before.

[5] *Cf.* Num. xxiv. 17. The pseudo-Messiah of A.D. 132 was called Bar-cochba, Son of a Star.

The city was greatly moved and Herod was seized with
alarm. He had won the throne by adroit craft, and knew
with what hatred he was regarded by his indignant subjects.
All along he had been haunted by nervous dread lest he
should be driven from the throne which he had usurped and
retained only by favour of Rome ; and to secure himself and
his heirs in the tenure thereof he had imbrued his hands in
much innocent blood. From two quarters chiefly was danger
to be apprehended. On the one side there were the representatives of the ousted dynasty of the Asmonæans, and he
had set himself to extirpate them, not sparing even his wife
Mariamne, a daughter of that honoured house, and the sons,
Alexander and Aristobulus, whom she had borne him.[1] And
on the other side there were the Rabbis who, indignant that *Cf.* Deut.
an alien should sit upon the throne of Israel, made no secret xvii. 15.
of their disaffection ; and he had signalised the commencement
of his reign by a massacre of the members of the Sanhedrin.[2]

And, now, when he heard of a new-born King of the Jews
who would thrust himself and his successors from the throne,
it seemed as though all his precautions, his scheming and his
sinning, would prove unavailing. At every hazard the danger His san-
must be averted, and he determined to slay the infant guinary
Redeemer. First, however, he must find Him, and he turned resolution.
for guidance to the Sanhedrin. Thirty years before he had
destroyed the august court, but it had been reconstituted soon
after ;[3] and now the tyrant convenes the dishonoured council
and demands of it, as the recognised authority on such questions, where the Messiah should be born. "At Bethlehem,"
was the answer in accordance with the prevailing conviction
derived from the prophetic Scriptures.[4] Straightway Herod had
a private interview with the astrologers, and, directing them
to Bethlehem, bade them seek out the Child and, when they
had found Him, bring him word, that, as he professed, he
might go himself and do obeisance unto Him. It was a
transparent device. Herod was no longer the astute diplomatist
of earlier days. The aged tyrant appears here as on the
pages of the Jewish historian—a decrepit dotard, suspicious

[1] Jos. *Ant.* xv. 7. §§ 4-6, xvi. 11. §§ 2-7 ; *De Bell. Jud.* i. 22. §§ 3-5, 27. §§ 2-6.
[2] Jos. *Ant.* xiv. 9. § 4 ; Lightfoot on Mt. ii. 4.
[3] Jos. *Ant.* xv. 6. § 2. [4] See Wetstein on Mt. ii. 6.

and malignant as ever, but feeble even to imbecility in his very violence. It was a transparent device, nor were the heaven-guided Wizards deceived by it. They repaired to Bethlehem, and, finding the Child, they bowed before Him and presented their offerings—gold, frankincense and myrrh. "The gold," says the good monk of Constantinople after the manner of the ancient interpreters, "is a symbol of kingship, for subjects pay tribute of gold to their kings; and the frankincense of deity, for frankincense was burned unto God; and the myrrh of mortification, for herewith the ancients anointed the dead that they might not rot nor smell."[1] They found the Child, but they did not carry word to Herod. They returned by another way to their own country.

Massacre of the Innocents. The baffled King would not be diverted from his purpose. It was two years since the star had appeared, and, since the Child might have been born at any time during the interval, he ordered a massacre of all the male children of two years old and under in Bethlehem and its neighbourhood. "Then was fulfilled," says the Evangelist, with exquisite felicity applying an ancient Scripture to the tragedy, "that which **xxxi. 15.** was spoken through Jeremiah the prophet:

> 'A voice in Ramah was heard,
>   Weeping and lamentation great:
>   Rachel weeping for her children;
>   And she would not be comforted, because they are not.'"

Ramah was a village on the border of Benjamin on the highway between Bethel and "Ephrath, which is Bethlehem." There Jacob buried Rachel when she died in giving birth **Gen. xxxv. 16-20.** to Benjamin, the Son of her Sorrow. Her tomb was by the way-side, and, as the exiles passed it on their way to Babylon, it seemed to the prophet as though Rachel were weeping for her children's woes. Later legend placed Rachel's tomb at Bethlehem,[2] and in the lamentation over the slaughtered innocents the Evangelist again heard Rachel weeping for her children.

Flight to Egypt. The Infant Redeemer was snatched from the tyrant's fury. Warned of the impending danger Joseph took Him

---

[1] Euth. Zig. *Cf.* Orig. *C. Cels.* i. 60; Chrysost. *In Matth.* viii; Claudian, *Epigr.* 49.   [2] *Hist. Jos.* vii.

and His mother by night and fled with them to Egypt.[1] In
that historic land, where of old their fathers had groaned in
bondage, the Jews had settled in large numbers and prospered
exceedingly.[2] There the exiles would find a secure asylum.
And there they remained, for a year according to tradition,[3]
until the death of the bloody tyrant, when they travelled
back to the land of Israel and reoccupied their long forsaken
home in Nazareth.[4]

It is a striking tribute to our Blessed Lord that His
Birth is recognised as the watershed of history. When He
appeared, the foundation of the city of Rome was the starting-
point of chronology; but His Birth was ere long recognised
as the birth of a new world, and about the middle of the sixth
century of our era Dionysius Exiguus, abbot of a monastery
at Rome, proposed in his *Cyclus Paschalis,* that Christians
should thenceforth reckon from that supreme event ; and
the proposal met with immediate and universal acceptance.
It is certain, however, that in fixing the commencement of
the Christian era Dionysius erred by several years ; and it
is a singular fact that, though our Lord's Birth is the supreme
event of history, it is difficult, perhaps impossible, to determine its precise date.

The Birth of Jesus the beginning of a new era.

It is certain that Jesus was born before the death of King
Herod, which occurred in the spring of B.C. 4 ;[5] but how long
before can be only approximately determined.   He was born
while the census of Quirinius was in progress ; and since the
year B.C. 8 was appointed for this, the first of the imperial enrol-
ments, it seems as though there were here a sure datum.   It
appears, however, that the Judæan census had been considerably
delayed by the troubles wherewith Herod was encompassed.
The miserable quarrel betwixt him and his sons, Alexander and
Aristobulus, which issued in their execution, was at its height ;[6]

The year.

[1] Lk. omits the Flight to Egypt. *Cf.* his silence in *Acts* regarding Paul's retiral
to Arabia (Gal. i. 17).

[2] In Philo's time there were no fewer than a million Jews in Egypt. The city
of Alexandria was divided into five districts, of which two were called " Jewish "
because the inhabitants were mostly Jews (*In Flacc.* §§ 6, 8).

[3] *Hist. Jos.* viii.   [4] *Cf.* Introd. § 16.

[5] Schürer, *H. J. P.* i. 1, p. 464 *sqq.*

[6] Jos. *Ant.* xvi. 11. §§ 2-7 ; *De Bell. Jud.* i. 27. §§ 2-6.

and in B.C. 9 or 8 he went to Rome in order to lay his grievance before the Emperor.   On his return he found Judæa
suffering from the depredations of the brigands of Trachonitis,
who had been emboldened by his absence and encouraged
by the unscrupulous Arabian, Syllæus.   He led an army into
Arabia, and Syllæus, smarting under defeat, addressed a piteous
appeal to Augustus, representing Herod's invasion as an un-
provoked aggression.   The indignant Emperor sent a severe
letter to Herod.   " I have hitherto," he wrote, " treated you
as a friend, but now I shall treat you as a subject."[1]   Only
with extreme difficulty did the luckless King regain the imperial favour, and two full years elapsed ere he was at leisure
to turn his attention to the business of the census, which is
thus brought down probably to B.C. 5.

Again, St. Luke states that the Baptist's ministry began
during the governorship of Pontius Pilate (A.D. 26-36[2]) and
in the fifteenth year of the government of Tiberius, that is, in
A.D. 25, since the government of Tiberius began, not with his
accession in A.D. 14, but with his assumption in the latter part
of A.D. 11 as Augustus' colleague with " equal authority in all
the provinces and armies."[3]   If at His baptism early in A.D.
26 Jesus had turned thirty, He was born in B.C. 5.   It agrees

Lk. iii. 23. herewith that when He was at Jerusalem celebrating the Feast
of the Passover at the commencement of His ministry, the

John ii. 20. Herodian Temple had been forty-six years abuilding.   Herod
ascended the throne in July, B.C. 37, and since the work of restoring the Temple began in the eighteenth year of his reign,[4]
that is in B.C. 20, this would be the year A.D. 26.[5]

The day. Western Christendom celebrates 25th December as the
Birth-day of our Lord, but this also is an error.   When He
was born, the shepherds were keeping watch by night over
their flocks in the wilderness of Judæa ; and, since the flocks
were taken out to pasture about Passover-time and kept there
until the middle of October when winter set in,[6] His birth fell

[1] *Ant.* xvi. 9. § 3.   [2] Eus. *H. E.* i. 9.

[3] Vell. Paterc. ii. 121; *cf.* Tac. *Ann* i. 3. (Recent scholarship challenges this
traditional claim, and the "fifteenth year . . . of Tiberius" is more likely
A.D. 29. —ED.)

[4] Schürer, *H. J. P.* i. 1, p. 410.

[5] *Cf.* Ramsay, *Was Chr. Born at Bethl. ?* pp. 224-5.   The ministry of Jesus
lasted three years, and according to Tert. *Adv. Jud.* § 8 He died during the consul-
ship of Rubellius and Fufius, *i.e.* A.D. 29 (*cf.* Tac. *Ann.* v. 1).

[6] Lightfoot on Lk. ii. 8.

betwixt April and October. Nor is it difficult to understand why the Western Church fixed upon 25th December. Toward the close of that month the Romans kept their festival of the Saturnalia, abandoning themselves to revelry.[1] Albeit marred by debauchery, it was a season of peace and good-will. While it lasted, it were impious to begin a war or execute a criminal, and friends sent gifts to each other.[2] And there is one curious custom which must not be forgotten : for a whole day freedom was granted to the slaves.[3] Many of the primitive Christians belonged to this oppressed class ; and it was natural that, while their heathen fellows were spending the day of freedom in riot, they should keep it as a holy festival, celebrating the Birth of their Lord who had redeemed them with His precious blood and delivered them from the bondage of Rom. vii corruption into the liberty of the glory of the children of [21.] God.

[1] Senec. *Ep.* xviii ; "*Decembris est mensis cum maxime civitas desudat.*"
[2] Suet. *Aug.* § 32 ; Mart. vii. 53 ; xiv. 1.   [3] Hor. *Sat.* ii. 7.

CHAPTER II

THE SILENT YEARS

Lk. ii. 40-
52; Mk. vi.
3=Mt. xiii.
55-6.

" Very dear the Cross of shame
    Where He took the sinner's blame,
    And the tomb wherein the Saviour lay,
    Until the third day came ;
    But He bore the self-same load,
    And He went the same high road
    When the carpenter of Nazareth
    Made common things for God."—WALTER C. SMITH.

Galilee. GALILEE, the ancient heritage of Naphtali, Asher, Zebulon, and Issachar, was the fairest region of the Land of Israel. It was a country of green hills and fertile valleys, abounding in springs and rivulets. There the poet of the *Song of Songs* *Its beauty.* had his home, and, as we read that exquisite idyll, we seem to scent the fragrance of the lovely land and move amid its i. 6, ii. 1-3, varied enchantments. We see the blossoming vineyards, the iv. 13, valleys gay with roses and lilies, the laden apple-trees of the vi. 11. wood, the orchards of pomegranates ; the flocks feeding in the pastures or resting in the shade at noon, and the kids ii. 14, 15, playing beside the shepherds' tents ; the doves nesting in the 17 clefts of the rocks, the foxes making havoc of the vineyards, ii. 17, 11. the gazelles leaping on the hills. We drink the cool air of i. 12-3, iv. morning and breathe the breath of Spring. We smell the 6, 14, vii. perfume of spikenard, myrrh, frankincense, and mandrake, 13, iv. 11. ii. 15, v. 1, and far-wafted odours of Lebanon. We hear the song of the i. 7, iv. 1, vine-dressers, the hum of bees, the bleating of sheep and ii. 12, iv. 15, 12. goats, the cooing of the wood-pigeon, the prattle of brooks and the gurgle of hidden springs.

Nor despite the rude vicissitudes of history had Galilee lost aught of its charm when the Lord dwelt there. It was *Its fertility.* still a fair and pleasant land, and withal exceeding fertile, giving to the Holy Land, according to R. Jonah,[1] its title to be called " a land flowing with milk and honey." Affording

[1] Lightfoot, ii. p. 404.

14

a plenteous sustenance, it had a teeming populace. "It is easier," said R. Eleasar, "for a man to rear a legion of olives in Galilee than a single child in the Land of Israel."[1] "The country," says the Jewish historian,[2] "was fat and rich in pasture and planted with all manner of trees, so that by its geniality it allured even the least zealous in husbandry. Therefore it was all worked by the inhabitants, and no part of it was idle. Yet were there also frequent cities, and the multitude of villages had in every case, by reason of the fertility, a large population, so that the smallest had upwards of fifteen thousand inhabitants." On this reckoning, since the cities and villages of Galilee numbered two hundred and four,[3] the population would be over three millions; and, though it may be deemed incredible that an area of some hundred square miles should have supported so vast a multitude, yet, after all deductions, the population was un-questionably very great. During the Jewish War Josephus levied from Galilee a hundred thousand recruits;[4] nor is it possible to read the Gospels without being impressed by the size of the crowds which, at the shortest notice, gathered about Jesus wherever He went.

> *Its popu-lousness.*

> *Mk. i. 45; ii. 4; iii. 8; vi. 31; Lk. xii. 1.*

Galilee is the Hebrew *Galil*, "Circle"; and the land was called originally *Galil haggoyim*, "Circle of the Gentiles," since, unlike Judæa which was bounded by deserts, she was encompassed by heathen nations—Phœnicia, Decapolis, Samaria. In the time of the Maccabees so hardly was she pressed by "those of Ptolemais and Tyre and Sidon and all Galilee of the Aliens" that her Jewish inhabitants were con-veyed South "with their wives and their children and all that they had" and settled in Judæa; nor was it until the days of John Hyrcanus (B.C. 135-105) that she was repeopled by Jews and restored to the Jewish dominion. In our Lord's time the population was mainly Jewish, insomuch that she was called no longer Galilee of the Gentiles but simply Galilee. Heathen elements still remained: Phœnicians, Syrians, Arabians, and Greeks; and hence Rénan infers that the Galileans were a mongrel race and "it is impossible to ascertain what blood flowed in the veins of him who has con-

> *Gentile elements.*

> *Is. ix. i.*

> *1 Macc. v. 14-23.*

---

[1] *Cf.* Wetstein on Mt. xxvi. 53.
[2] Jos. *De Bell. Jud.* iii. 3. § 2.
[3] Jos. *Vit.* § 45.
[4] *De Bell. Jud.* ii. 20. § 6.

tributed most to efface the distinctions of blood." It would, however, appear that the Gentiles in Galilee dwelt apart in exclusive colonies,[1] and betwixt them and the Jews bitter enmity prevailed, breaking out from time to time into sanguinary conflict.[2]

Galilean Jews patriotic and religious.

The truth is that the presence of the heathen in their midst, so far from corrupting the Jews of Galilee, rather quickened their patriotism and strengthened the tenacity wherewith they clung to the traditions of their race. Albeit a more liberal spirit prevailed there than in the southern stronghold of Rabbinism, nowhere was patriotism so intense or religion so ardent. Josephus had been governor of Galilee and knew its people well, and his testimony is that " they were warriors from infancy, and cowardice never had hold of the men." [3] The names of Hezekiah and Judas the Galilean are eloquent of the heroism of the race and their readiness to risk their lives in desperate enterprises for the glory of God and the liberty of Israel.

Despised by Judæans.

Nevertheless the Galileans were despised by the proud Judæans. Judæa was the home of orthodoxy, the shrine of Israel's sacred institutions. Hers were Jerusalem, the Temple, the Sanhedrin, the great Teachers ; and she boasted of these distinctions and disdained the boorish folk of Galilee. The ignorance of the latter was a by-word, and, when they visited Jerusalem at the festal seasons, their manners, dress, and accent were the jest of the citizens. Since they spoke with a strong burr, the instant they opened their mouths their nationality

Cf. Mt. xxvi. 73= Mk. xiv. 70.

was discovered, and their confusion of the gutturals sometimes occasioned ludicrous blunders. A Galilean woman once said to her neighbour : " Come, and I will give you butter to eat," and it seemed as though she said : " May a lion devour you ! " [4] The Judæans derided the Galileans, but their contempt was probably not unmingled with jealousy. The contrast between their own barren land and fair and fruitful Galilee awoke their envy. " Why," asked the Rabbis, bent on finding even here an evidence of divine favour, " are

---

[1] *E.g.* Carmel was in the hands of the Syrians, and Scythopolis also was a Syrian town (Jos. *De Bell. Jud.* ii. 18. § 1).

[2] Jos. *Vit.* § 6 ; *De Bell. Jud.* ii. 18. §§ 1 *sqq.*

[3] *De Bell. Jud.* iii. 3. § 2.

[4] *Cf.* Lightfoot, ii. 232-3 ; Wetstein on Mt. xxvi. 73.

there none of the fruits of Gennesaret at Jerusalem? Lest they that come up to the feasts should say: 'We had not come save to eat of the fruits of Gennesaret.' Why are not the hot waters of Tiberias at Jerusalem? Lest they that come up to the feasts should say: 'We had not come save to bathe in the baths of Tiberias.'"[1] The contempt of the Judæans was certainly unjust. They had a saying: "Out John vii.52. of Galilee a prophet ariseth not," regardless that not a few of Israel's greatest prophets had been Galileans. Though Tisbeh in Gilead was his birth-place, Galilee was the scene of Elijah's ministry, as it was the scene also of that of his successor, Elisha of Abel-Meholah. Jonah, Hosea, and Nahum were of Galilee. In after days, to say nothing of the prophetess Anna, though St Paul was born at Tarsus in Lk. ii. 36. Cilicia, his parents, according to St Jerome, had belonged to Acts xxii. 3. the Galilean town of Gischala and quitted it on its capture by the Romans.[2] And it is surely the most impressive of history's revenges that Galilee, once the jest and scorn of Judæa, has for nigh two thousand years been esteemed the holiest region on the earth, "blessed and hallowed of the precious body and blood of our Lord Jesu Christ; in the which land it liked him to take flesh and blood of the Virgin Mary, to environ that holy land with his blessed feet." Galilee gave the Messiah a home, Judæa gave Him a cross.

Among the mountains of Galilee, just where they drop Nazareth. down precipitously to the Plain of Esdraelon, lies a hollow amphitheatre; and on its north-western slope nestled the town of Nazareth where the Holy Child was nurtured, "increasing in wisdom and stature and favour with God and men." The people of Nazareth had an evil reputation even among their fellow Galileans, who had a proverb: "Out of Nazareth can John i. 46. there be aught good?" And their behaviour to Jesus, when He visited their town and preached in their Synagogue in the course of His ministry, is evidence that they were of a Lk. iv. 28- passionate and lawless temper. But, whatever the faults of [30]. its people, Nazareth was a lovely spot, worthy of the en-

---

[1] Lightfoot, ii. 227; Wetstein on John v. 4.
[2] *Script. Eccl.* Jerome says Paul was born at Gischala, "quo a Romanis capto cum parentibus suis Tarsum Ciliciæ commigravit."

comium of Antoninus the Martyr who likened it to Paradise.[1]
The houses were built of white lime-stone hewn out of the
calcareous mountains which girt it round; and, when the
Talmud mentions among the districts which produced wine
for the drink-offerings, the White City on the Hill,[2] in all
likelihood it is Nazareth that is meant. The town is closed
in by the encircling ramparts of hills; but climb the over-
hanging brow, and, behold, what a panorama opens to the
view! Northward, the ridge of Lebanon and the snow-capped
peak of Hermon; eastward, the Jordan-valley and the
mountains of Gilead; southward, the Plain of Esdraelon,
Israel's historic battle-field; westward, Mount Carmel and
the sheen of the Mediterranean. Round the foot of the hill
wound the Great West Road, "the Way of the Sea," the
route of the caravans betwixt Damascus and the Mediterranean sea-ports; while southward ran the road to Egypt,
thronging with merchants, and the road to Jerusalem, along
which, as the festal seasons drew near, companies of pilgrims
took their joyous way to the Holy City.

The home of Jesus: His brothers and sisters.
Lk. ii. 7.

Mt. xiii. 55-6=Mk. vi. 3.

John vii. 3-5.

Mk. iii. 21. 31.

ii. 40.

Such were the surroundings amid which our Saviour
passed His holy childhood and grew to man's estate.
There were other children in the home; for Jesus was
Mary's first-born, and she subsequently bore to Joseph
four others, James, Joseph, Judas, and Simon, besides
several daughters. It is pathetic that, though after the
Resurrection they came over to His cause, during His
ministry the Lord's brothers not merely rejected His claims
but sneered at them; and once they went so far as to
pronounce Him mad and attempt to lay hands on Him
and hale Him home to Nazareth; illustrating the proverb
so often on His lips that "a prophet hath no honour among
His own people."[3] Nevertheless, whatever estrangement may
have shadowed His life in after years, it appears from what
little the Evangelists relate that He had a sweet and happy
childhood. "The Child," says St Luke, "grew and waxed

[1] Wetstein on Mt. ii. 23. [2] *Menach.* 9. 7.
[3] In the interests of the doctrine of Mary's Perpetual Virginity (*cf.* Aug. *In Joan. Ev. Tract.* xxviii. § 3) two theories have been held regarding our Lord's brethren. (1) They were sons of Joseph by a former marriage (Orig., Clem. Alex., Epiphan.). *Cf.* J. B. Lightfoot, *Gal.* pp. 252-90. (2) They were His cousins, sons of Mary, the wife of Alphæus, sister to the Virgin (Jer., Aug.). *Cf.* p. 147, n. 2.

strong, being filled with wisdom ; and God's grace was upon Him." Joseph was only a humble carpenter, earning a *His "father."* scanty livelihood by daily toil, and luxury was unknown in the home where the Lord of Glory passed His wondrous childhood ; yet, poor though it was in worldly gear, it was rich in better possessions. It evinces a spirit of earnest piety that, though the attendance of women was optional,[1] Mary accompanied her husband year by year when he went up to the Passover at Jerusalem. Joseph was a kindly *Lk. ii. 41.* man, and he took the Holy Child to his heart, well deserving to be called his " father."[2] The harsh discipline *Lk. ii. 33,* of his childhood's home at Eislεben haunted Martin Luther *41, 43, 48.* all his days ; and, since the word "father" conjured up in his mind the image of one who would beat him, he could never repress an involuntary shudder when he repeated the *Pater noster.* Not such was the Lord's remembrance of the good Joseph, and it is no irreverence to recognise in His master-thought of the Heavenly Fatherhood a tribute to the fatherly love which had cherished Him in His childhood, anticipating His every need and withholding no good thing from Him. Even as the shepherd-psalmist had desired *Mt. vi. 8;* naught better for himself than that God should be his *vii. 11.* Shepherd, dealing with him as he dealt with his sheep, so *Ps. xxiii. 1.* Jesus, looking abroad over the whole domain of human experience for an emblem of the divine Love which He had come to manifest, found none so apt as that human love which had done so much for Him and which He so gratefully remembered. And no less well did Mary discharge *His* her office by the Child whom God had given her. Would *mother.* it not be from her that He had learned that caressing motherword, *Talitha,* "My lamb," which rose to His lips beside *Mk. v. 41.* the couch of Jaïrus' daughter ?

The apocryphal Gospels tell much about the Lord's *Education* school-days and His behaviour toward His teachers and His play-mates ; but of all this nothing is recorded by our

---

[1] *Cf.* Lightfoot on Lk. ii. 43 ; Wetstein on Lk. ii. 41.

[2] *Cf.* Talmudic anecdote in Lightfoot on Lk. iii. 23. Offence was taken at the word as seeming to conflict with the virgin-birth ; and in Lk. ii. 48 some ancient authorities omit "Thy father and I" ; at *v.* 33 for "His father" some read "Joseph" ; at *v.* 41 for "His parents" some Latin cursives have *Joseph et Maria* ; at *v.* 43 "His parents" becomes "Joseph and His mother."

Evangelists. They mention incidentally that He could both
read and write, and it would have been strange indeed had
He grown up uninstructed. "Our ground is good," says
Josephus, [1] "and we work it to the utmost; but our chief
ambition is for the nurture of our children." According to
R. Salomo, a father had as well bury his son as neglect
his instruction.[2] It was recognised that youth is the
golden season of opportunity. "He who learns as a lad,"
said R. Elisha ben Abujah, "to what is he like? To ink
written on fresh paper. And he who learns when old, to
what is he like? To ink written on used paper." [3] And it
was a saying of R. Judah the Holy that "the world exists
by the breath of school-children."

At home.   A Jewish child's education began in his home. His
parents were his first teachers. St Paul testifies that
Timothy's faith was an inheritance from his grandmother
Lois and his mother Eunice, and that from his infancy he
had known sacred literature. Certainly Joseph and Mary
would not be less assiduous than other parents in the task
of instructing their Child. And He was an apt pupil,
"making progress," as it were *pari passu*, "in wisdom and
age." Costly as copies of the Scriptures were, they were
found by the emissaries of Antiochus in B.C. 168 in not
a few homes in the cities of Judah; and it may well be
that, poor though he was, Joseph had acquired a copy at
least of the Law. Nor would he be unmindful of the injunction: "These words which I command thee this day,
shall be upon thine heart: and thou shalt teach them
diligently unto thy children, and shalt talk of them when
thou sittest in thine house, and when thou walkest by the
way, and when thou liest down, and when thou risest up."

The House of the Book.   At the age of six or seven years [4] a Jewish boy was sent
to the elementary school, called, because the material of
instruction was the Book of the Law, the House of the Book.[5]
It was attached to the Synagogue; and, since every village
had its Synagogue, every village had also its school.[6] Thence

Marginal references:
Lk. iv. 16; John viii. 8.
2 Tim. i. 5; iii. 15.
Lk. ii. 52.
1 Macc. i. 56-7.
Deut. vi. 6-7.
Cf. Lk. v. 17.

---

[1] *C. Ap.* i. § 12.   [2] Wetstein on 2 Tim. iii. 15.   [3] Taylor, *Say. of Fath.* iv. 27.
[4] According to the ordinance of Joshua ben Gamla (A.D. 63-5), which was
merely a reinforcement of existing requirements. *Cf.* Schürer, *H. J. P.*, II. ii. p. 49.
[5] בֵּית הַסֵּפֶר.   [6] See Lightfoot on Mt. iv. 23.

such as desired to pursue their studies further passed into The House of the Midrash. the Scribal College, the House of the Midrash,[1] where the great Rabbis taught. There was a House of the Midrash at Jabne, where R. Eleasar and R. Ismael taught in a place called the Vineyard;[2] but the leading college was at Jerusalem. It was within the Temple-precincts, probably in Cf. Lk. ii. 46. the Synagogue of the Temple. Though the main business was the drilling of the disciples in the oral tradition,[3] it was customary also to propound problems, the Teachers putting questions to the disciples and hearing questions from them with a view to the elucidation of difficulties.[4] The Teachers occupied a slightly elevated dais, while the disciples sat round in a circle on the floor, " powdering themselves in the dust of the feet of the wise," [5] whence St Paul's phrase : Acts xxii. 3. " I was educated at the feet of Gamaliel."

Jesus never attended any of these colleges, not being John vii. 15. designed for a Rabbi. It was required of every Jewish father Handicraft. that he should teach his son some honest craft, failing in Ecclus. vii. 14. which he was as if he taught him robbery.[6] " Hate not laborious work " was the precept of one of Israel's wise men ; and even the Rabbis had their handicrafts.[7] Saul of Tarsus, though designed for a Rabbi and studying in the Rabbinical college at Jerusalem, learned the craft of tentmaking, an equipment which stood him in good stead in the days of his Acts xviii. 3. apostleship.[8] Like every Jewish lad Jesus was put to work ; Mk. vi. 2-3. and very naturally he followed Joseph's calling, fashioning for the peasants of Nazareth those ploughs and yokes which in after days furnished Him with heavenly parables.[9]

Jesus never attended a Rabbinical college, yet on one The Child Jesus at the Passover. memorable occasion He was found sitting at the feet of the Rabbis in the House of the Midrash at Jerusalem. At the age of twelve a Jewish boy was reckoned " a son of the

---

[1] בֵּית הַמִּדְרָשׁ.

[2] Sometimes the classes met in an upper room in a private house, like the Christian ἐκκλησία in early days (1 Cor. xvi. 19; Col. iv. 15). Taylor, *Say. of Fath.* i. 4 ; Lightfoot on Acts i. 13.

[3] *Cf.* Introd. § 1.

[4] Lightfoot on Lk. ii. 46.

[5] Taylor, *Say. of Fath.* i. 4, n. 11.

[6] Lightfoot on Mk vi. 3.

[7] Delitzsch, *Jewish Artisan Life*, chap. v.

[8] Taylor, *Say. of Fath.* i. 11, n. 22.

[9] Just. M. *Dial. c. Tryph.*, ed. Sylburg., p. 316 C. *Cf.* Introd. § 12, 3, (1).

Law "[1] and entered upon all the privileges and responsibilities of an Israelite, including attendance at the Feast of the Passover.[2] It was probably in A.D. 8 that Jesus, twelve years old the previous summer, joined with Joseph and Mary the train of pilgrims travelling southward to Jerusalem to keep that sacred feast which year by year in the month Abib or Nisan, our April, was celebrated in commemoration of Israel's deliverance from her bondage in Egypt. The hundred and twenty-second Psalm describes the joy wherewith a young Israelite of old obeyed the summons to join the festal company and the wonder which filled his soul when at last his feet stood within the gates of the ancient capital and his eyes beheld the sacred Temple. Even such would be the emotion of the youthful Jesus on this memorable occasion. Often had he heard from Joseph and Mary of the Holy City and Mount Zion. He had longed for the day when He should go thither and see it all with His own eyes ; and now at length His desire is fulfilled.

Left behind in Jerusalem.   The week of sacred solemnity was like a wondrous dream to the Holy Child. He would feast His eyes on the impressive pageant and drink in all that He heard. When the festival was over, the train of Galileans started on the homeward journey, and Joseph and Mary set out with the rest, unwitting that they were leaving Jesus behind. Amid the confusion of the crowded city[3] the mishap might easily occur ; and, inasmuch as the men and the women travelled in separate bands, the children accompanying either parent, His absence would alarm neither Joseph nor Mary, since each would suppose that He was in the other company.[4] When the caravan halted at the end of the first day's march, they missed him, and hastened back enquiring and looking for Him all along the road in case He should have lagged behind. But not a trace of their lost Child did they discover until they reached Jerusalem ; and there they found

[1] בַּר מִצְוָה.   [2] See Lightfoot and Wetstein on Lk. ii. 42.

[3] At one Passover the High Priests, at the request of the procurator Cestius Gallus (A.D. 63-6), estimated the worshippers in the city. From the number of lambs slain in the Temple (256,500), they reckoned the worshippers at 2,700,200, exclusive of those who took no part—unclean persons and foreigners (Jos. *De Bell. Jud.* vi. 9. § 3). They came from all parts (Acts ii. 8-11).

[4] *Cf.* Bede in *Cat. Aur.*

Him, on the third day after their setting out, seated in the Found at the feet of the Rabbis. House of the Midrash among the disciples at the feet of the Rabbis, listening to them and asking them questions, at once delighting and amazing them by His singular and unearthly intelligence.[1] What would those grave and venerable teachers, as they marvelled at His understanding and answers, have felt, had it been revealed to them Who that wondrous Child really was? "Therefore," says old Euthymius, " let us that are teachers fear, recognising that in our midst is the Christ, attending how we teach."

His parents were amazed, and Mary, forgetting, in her joy Discovery of divine kinship and Messianic vocation. at the recovery of her lost treasure, the august presence in which she stood, broke into gentle chiding: "Child, why didst Thou thus to us? Behold, Thy father and I were seeking Thee in sore distress." Wondrous things had happened to the Holy Child during the Passover-week. God had spoken to His soul and discovered to Him Who He was and wherefore He had come into the world. "Why is it," He replied wistfully as one whose thoughts were far away, " that ye are seeking Me? Did ye not know that it is in My Father's House [2] that I ought to be?" This is the earliest recorded saying of our Blessed Lord, and it is no wonder that it puzzled Joseph and Mary. It strikes the keynote of all His after-life. Henceforth He called no one on the earth His father and owned no carnal kinship; He realised that He had one only business among the children of men, the mighty work of their redemption, and He kept it ever before Him, never resting, never faltering, never turning back.

Nevertheless He quietly returned to Nazareth and resumed His return to Nazareth.

[1] It is an ancient and inveterate misconception that He was confounding them by His superior wisdom. The *Ev. Infant. Arab.* (L-LII) represents Him as expounding hard questions of theology, astronomy, physics, metaphysics, and anatomy, "things which no creature's intellect reaches." So *Ev. Thom.* xix. *Cf.* Origen: "He was questioning the Teachers; and, because they could not answer, He Himself was answering the questions which He asked." "He was questioning the Teachers, not that He might learn aught, but that by questioning He might instruct them" (*In Luc. Hom.* xviii, xix).

[2] ἐν τοῖς τοῦ Πατρός μου either (1), " in My Father's House," which is the patristic rendering; *cf.* εἰς τὰ ἴδια (John xvi. 32; xix. 27); or (2) "about My Father's business"; *cf.* 1 Tim. iv. 15; Plat. *Phaed.* 59 A: ὡς ἐν φιλοσοφίᾳ ἡμῶν ὄντων. Decisive in favour of (1) is a saying of Jesus quoted by Irenæus (*Adv. Hær.* v. 32) from the elders, *i.e.* Papias and his circle: ἐν τοῖς τοῦ Πατρός μου μονὰς εἶναι πολλάς. *Cf.* John xiv. 21: ἐν τῇ οἰκίᾳ τοῦ Πατρός μου μοναὶ πολλαί εἰσιν.

His simple and duteous life. For eighteen years He toiled with hammer and saw, knowing all the while Who He was and wherefore He had come, yet hiding the wondrous secret in His breast and never, until His hour arrived, revealing it by word or sign. Nor were those silent years lost. They served in the providence of God as a preparation for the work which had been given Him to do. All the while He would be brooding over those Sacred Scriptures which spake of Him, foretelling His Advent and prefiguring His Redemption. And He would be looking abroad, with keen eye and sympathetic heart, upon the world which He had come to save. To the unwitting folk of Nazareth He seemed as one of themselves, but to Him they were His Father's lost children ; and, as He mingled with them, He would take earnest notice of them, entering into their thoughts, considering their temptations, and sharing their sorrows, that, when the time should come, He might speak to them as One who knew their hearts and had understanding of their needs.

CHAPTER III

THE MESSIAH'S CALL

Mt. iii. 1-17=Mk. i. 1-11=Lk. iii. 1-18, 21-22.

"Dum baptizat, baptizatur,
Dumque lavat, hic lavatur
Vi lavantis omnia.
Aquæ lavant et lavantur ;
His lavandi vires dantur
Baptizati gratia."—HENR. PIST.

EIGHTEEN years have elapsed when the curtain is again lifted, and it rises on a stirring scene. A great prophet has appeared, and from Jerusalem and all Judæa and all the country about the Jordan an eager multitude is pouring down to the scene of his ministry at Bethany just across the river at the place where the Israelites under Joshua had crossed over into the Promised Land.[1] It was John, son of an old priest named Zacharias who had exercised his obscure ministry somewhere in the hill-country of Judæa.[2] Some thirty years ago, six months before the Birth of Jesus, his wife Elisabeth, after long childlessness, had borne him a son, and the glad parents had consecrated him to the Lord's service. Elisabeth was a kinswoman of Mary, but the families had dwelt far, almost the whole length of the land, apart, and John and Jesus had grown up strangers one to the other.

While Jesus was toiling in the workshop at Nazareth, John, a holy Nazirite, was leading a life no less obscure in the wilderness of Judæa,[3] like his predecessor Amos who

John the Baptist at Bethany beyond Jordan.

Lk. i. 36.

John i. 33.

His early life. Lk. i. 15; cf. Num. vi. 2-3.

---

[1] Cf. Onomast. Called " Bethany beyond Jordan" to distinguish it from the village of Lazarus. On T. R. Bethabara see W. H. Notes.

[2] Lk. i. 39 : εἰς πόλιν Ἰούδα, either "to a city of Judah," possibly the priestly town of Hebron (cf. Josh. xxi. 13), or "to the city called Judah." Adopting the latter Rénan, after Reland, regards Judah as a corruption of Juttah (Josh. xv. 55, xxi. 16); but Caspari with more probability identifies it with the modern Khirbet el-Jehud, i.e. City of Judah, adjoining ʿAin Karim, the traditional site. Cf. Warfield in Expositor, Apr. 1885; P. E. F. Q., Jan. 1905, pp. 61 sqq.

[3] Lk. i. 80 does not mean that he was a hermit, but simply that he led a rural life away from the capital. The antithesis of ἐν ταῖς ἐρήμοις is ἐν τῇ πόλει. Cf. 2 Cor. xi. 26.

Am. i. 1; had been a herdsman and a dresser of sycamores in that very
vii. 14. region eight centuries before.   Like Amos too, while he plied
his labours, he had busied himself with meditation, pondering
how it fared with hapless Israel and what might be God's
purpose concerning her.   Hard by, in the desolate region
bordering on the Dead Sea, the Essenes had their abodes,
those blameless anchorites who had left the world that they
might spend their days in toil, chastity, meditation, prayer,
and fasting ; and it may well be that he had intercourse with
them, even as in his zealous youth Josephus, the future
historian of the Jews, passed three years in the wilderness
under the austere rule of the hermit Banûs.[1]   But he belonged
to no sect.   He was himself a master and had gathered about
him a band of disciples.[2]

His call.   When he reached the age of thirty, "the Word of God
came unto John," as it had come to the ancient prophets, and
he must needs utter the thoughts which glowed within him, as
Am. iii. 8. a burning fire shut up in his bones.   "The lion hath roared :
who will not fear ?   The Lord God hath spoken : who can
but prophesy ? "   The fame of his preaching quickly attracted
curious and ever-increasing crowds ; and ere long Bethany
beyond Jordan was the scene of a mighty revival.   It was
indeed a striking coincidence that just where Israel of old
had entered the Land of Promise, the door of the Kingdom
of Heaven should in those last days be opened.

Secret of   What was the secret of the preacher's power ?   It was
his power :
   1. A manifold.   *He was a prophet, and it was long since a prophet's*
prophet. *voice had been heard in the land.*   The last of that "goodly
fellowship " had been Malachi, and during the four centuries
which had elapsed since his death, the oracles of God had
1 Sam. been mute.   As once of old, "the Word of the Lord was
iii. 1. precious in those days ; there was no open vision " ; and
men were lamenting like the Psalmist of the Maccabean age :
Ps. lxxiv. 9. "We see not our signs : there is no more any prophet ;
neither is there among us any that knoweth how long."
The successors of the prophets were the Rabbis, those servile

----

[1] *Vit.* § 2.

[2] Clem. Rom. *Hom.* ii. § 23: as Jesus had twelve disciples, answering to the
months of the year, John had thirty, answering to the days of the month.   The idea
that Jesus was a disciple of John (Rénan, Brandt) is the wildest of vagaries,
destitute alike of reason and of evidence.

worshippers of a dead past, who busied themselves with exposition of the Law and conservation of the Tradition of the Elders with never a living word from a living God. And now at length a prophet's voice is heard with that ring of assurance and that note of authority which never fail to awaken a response in the souls of men.

The nation was ripe for a revival. Its miseries had revived the Messianic Hope and created an expectation of its immediate fulfilment; and it is no marvel that, when John proclaimed with unfaltering conviction and impassioned earnestness that the Kingdom of Heaven, that is, the Reign of the Messiah,[1] was at hand, he won unhesitating credence. Moreover, it was understood that the Messiah's Advent would, in accordance with an ancient promise, be heralded by a prophet like unto Moses; and in later days, when there was no open-vision and there seemed no prospect of a new prophet appearing, the idea arose that one of the old prophets would return and usher in the Messianic Kingdom. Some thought of Jeremiah, but the general expectation pointed to Elijah.[2] It chimed in with this idea when John appeared in the wilderness of Judæa "in the spirit and power of Elijah," wearing a dress like his and living like him on such simple fare as the wilderness afforded,[3] and announced the approach of One mightier than himself.

And even had it lacked such singular reinforcement, John's preaching must have produced a profound impression. *It dealt with themes which never fail to awaken a response in the human heart—sin and judgment, repentance and forgiveness.* These were the themes which on the lips of George Whitefield

2. Preparedness of the people.

Deut. xviii. 15.

Lk. i. 17.

2 Kings i. 8; 1 Kings xvii. 2-7.

3. Nature of his preaching.

---

[1] See Dalman, *Words of Jesus*, pp. 91 *sqq.*, Lightfoot and Wetstein on Mt. iii. 2. Mt.'s "Kingdom of Heaven" is identical with Mk. and Lk.'s "Kingdom of God," *Heaven* being a reverential substitute of the later Jews for *God*. *Cf.* Taylor, *Say. of Fath.* iv. 7, n. 8.

[2] Mt. xi. 14; *cf.* Mal. iv. 5. John i. 21. Mt. xvi. 14=Mk. viii. 28=Lk. ix. 19. Mt. xvii. 10-3=Mk. ix. 11-3. *Cf.* the belief that John Huss would return to Bohemia a hundred years after his death and complete his work.

[3] *Camel's hair*, either the hairy skin (in Mk. i. 6 D has ἐνδεδυμένος δέῤῥην καμήλου) or cloth woven of the hair. According to Chrysost. and Jer. John's dress was a protest against the luxurious fashion of his day—loose robes of soft wool. *Locusts* were eaten by the poor (Lightfoot, Wetstein), but according to some John's locusts were a sort of bean (Euth. Zig. on Mt. iii. 14). *Wild-honey*, either bee-honey or palm-honey. See Diod. Sic. xix. 731; Plin. *H. N.* xv. 7; Suidas under ἀκρίς.

melted the hearts of the colliers of Kingswood, till the tears poured from their eyes and "made white gutters down their black cheeks." Twenty thousand gathered to hear the message, and "hundreds and hundreds of them were soon brought under deep conviction, which happily ended in sound and thorough conversion."

4. The definiteness of his demand.

And not only had John a distinct message but he *made a definite demand*. His message was "The Kingdom of Heaven is at hand," and his demand "Repent." It was an imperious demand, brooking no delay. The Messiah was at hand and would presently appear, an awful Avenger, a ruthless Reformer. His fan was in His hand and He would thoroughly cleanse His threshing-floor, gathering the wheat into the granary but burning up the chaff with unquenchable fire. Already His axe was laid to the root of the trees, and every tree that did not produce good fruit, would be hewn down and cast into the fire. The expectation prevailed that the Messiah would come as a victorious King, terrible to the heathen but gracious to Israel; John, however, announced judgment not on the heathen only but on the sinners in Israel, and the quickened consciences of his hearers sided with the prophet. "What shall we do?" they cried, and he answered "Repent." It was a saying of the Rabbis: "If Israel repent but for a single day, forthwith the Redeemer will come";[1] and the call to repentance came most fitly from the lips of the Messiah's herald. Nor was it merely a profession of penitence that was exacted by John. He required of the penitents that they should submit to the rite of Baptism, thereby earning for himself the title of "the Baptist." This served to deter the unworthy, since only such as were deeply earnest would undergo the ordeal. And the rite was doubly symbolic, at once typifying the inward cleansing of the penitent and prefiguring the better Baptism of the Messiah. "I indeed baptise you in water unto repentance, but He that cometh after me is mightier than I, whose sandal-strap I am not worthy to unloose:[2] He will baptise you in the Holy Spirit and fire."

Very searching and practical was John in his examination

---

[1] *Hieros. Taan.* 64. 1: "Si resipuerit Israel vel uno die, illico adveniet redemptor." See Lightfoot on Mt. iii. 2.

[2] See Introd. § 11.

of candidates for Baptism.   He laid his finger on every man's
besetting sin and demanded its surrender.   Was the candi-
date rich ?   Then, in terms which recall the Lord's dealing ^{Mt. xix. 21}
with the Young Ruler, he bade him share his possessions with ^{=Mk. x. 21=Lk.}
the poor.   Was he a tax-gatherer ?   Then let him adhere to ^{xviii. 22.}
the prescribed tariff and refrain from over-charging.[1]   Was he
a soldier ?   Then let him have done with bullying, false-accusing,
and mutineering.[2]

It is a remarkable evidence of the Baptist's power that his ^{Approach}
preaching drew to Bethany not only the simple and the rude ^{of Phari-sees and}
but not a few of the men of education and of rank.   " He ^{Sadducees}
saw many of the Pharisees and Sadducees coming unto the
Baptism."   It was no whit more surprising that sanctimonious
Pharisees and courtly Sadducees should mingle with the jostling
rabble than that, belonging as they did to rival and bitterly
antagonistic sects, they should be found thus in company.
In after days, forgetting in a common enmity their mutual
antagonism, they co-operated against Jesus ; but wherefore are
they united now ?   It may be that the religious authorities at
Jerusalem, ever vigilant and astute, learning what was in progress down by the Jordan, had, as in the case of Jesus by and
by, recognised the expediency of taking the movement under
their patronage and employing it to strengthen their hold upon
the multitude ; and those Pharisees and Sadducees came as
deputies from the Sanhedrin to spy upon the work and carry
back a report.   When, however, they found themselves face
to face with the preacher and listened to his impassioned
eloquence, they too were carried away.   Whatever may have
been their motives, they were disposed to show themselves
friendly to the prophet, and actually presented themselves for
baptism.   " He," said Jesus to the rulers, reminding them more ^{John v. 35.}
than a year after of the testimony which John had borne to
Himself, and quoting perhaps their own verdict upon him,
" was 'the lamp that burneth and shineth,' and ye were minded ^{Cf. Ecclus.}
for a season to rejoice in his light." ^{xlviii. 1.}

It was not hidden from John what manner of men they ^{His recep-}
were.   He knew well their inveterate hypocrisy and hollow ^{tion of them.}

[1] Lightfoot on Mt. v. 46 ; Schürer, *H. J. P.* i. 11, pp. 70-1.
[2] On the behaviour of soldiers *cf.* Luc. *Mer. Dial.* 15 ; Wetstein on Lk. iii. 14 ;
Mayor on Juv. xvi. 10.

formalism, and distrusted their professions. They had indeed been impressed by his lurid picture of the coming judgment, but it was fear and not penitence that awed them. As he looked at them, he thought of a scene which he had often witnessed in the wilderness, when the parched brushwood caught fire and the reptiles rushed from their lairs in mad terror.[1] "Ye offspring of vipers!" he cried; "who warned you to flee from the coming wrath?" His Baptism was not for such. Let them demonstrate their sincerity by abjuring their vain hope. It was their boast that they were Abraham's children, and they reasoned that, since God had made a covenant with Abraham and his seed after him, He was their God and they were His people; forgetting that a man is Abraham's son not because he has Abraham's blood in his veins but because he has Abraham's spirit in his heart.

John viii. 33-59; Gal. iii. Like Jesus and St Paul afterwards, John assails this vain confidence, the situation furnishing him with a dramatic argument. On that great day, well-nigh fifteen centuries before, when a path was opened through the flood and Israel passed over on dry land, Joshua had taken twelve stones, one *Josh. iv.* for each tribe, from the river-bed and "laid them down in the place where they lodged that night." There, it was said,[2] they remained unto that day; and, pointing to those grey monuments, the prophet cries: "Think not to say within yourselves: 'We have Abraham as our father.' For I tell you that God is able from these stones to raise up children unto Abraham." And so He did when from the Gentiles, those stony-hearted worshippers of stones, He raised up a seed unto Abraham, heirs according to the promise.[3]

Galileans at Bethany. Tidings of the revival had travelled northward and brought some all the way from Galilee to hear the wondrous prophet and perchance share in the blessing which, like the manna of old, was falling in the wilderness. Among them were five young men who were marked out for a great destiny —John, two brothers, Andrew and Simon, and Philip, all from the shore of the Lake of Galilee, and Nathanael from the upland village of Cana. John and Andrew not merely obeyed the prophet's call to repentance, but joined the company of

---

[1] G. A. Smith, *H. G.* p. 66.   [2] Jer. *Ep.* xxvii, *Ad Eustoch. Virg.*
[3] *Cf.* Iren. *Adv. Hær.* iv. 13; Clem. Alex. *Protrept.* i. 4.

his disciples. By and by another Galilean appeared on the scene. It was Jesus. His coming occasioned no remark, since in outward seeming He differed in no wise from the rest.

Presently He approached John and offered Himself as a candidate for Baptism. Then was the discovery made. It was not the way of the stern prophet to administer the solemn rite ere he was satisfied of the sincerity of each candidate's penitence and his purpose to lead a life of new obedience ; and when Jesus presented Himself, he would subject Him to a searching examination. But, ere it had proceeded far, he was stricken with astonishment. If, when Jesus was only twelve years of age, " His understanding and His answers " had amazed the Rabbis in the House of the Midrash at Jerusalem, it is no marvel that now, after eighteen years of communion with God and meditation on the Scriptures, He should have amazed the Baptist. One thing above all else would excite the latter's wonderment. When candidates for Baptism presented themselves in response to the prophet's warnings and appeals, it was ever with trembling contrition and humble confession ; but Jesus evinced neither guilt nor fear. In another such a mood would have argued insensibility and unfitness for the rite ; but as John surveyed that serene form and that holy face radiant with the peace of God, his soul bowed in reverence and awe, and, like every mortal who ever came under the gaze of Jesus in the days of His flesh, he realised his own unworthiness. As Peter in the Upper Room remonstrated : " Lord, dost *Thou* wash *my* feet ? " so John would have hindered him, saying : " *I* have need to be baptised by *Thee*, and comest Thou to me ? "

[margin note: Jesus a candidate for Baptism.]

It is indeed an exceeding marvel that the Holy One should have taken His place amid that throng of penitents and sought to participate in a rite which symbolised the cleansing away of sin ; and the explanation lies in His answer to the Baptist's protest : " Suffer it just now ; for thus it is becoming for us to fulfil every ordinance." Jesus was " born under the Law," and, " though He was a Son, He learned obedience." In His helpless infancy He endured the rite of Circumcision which signified the putting away of the defilement of the flesh ; and after He reached manhood He paid year by year the Temple-tax, though as the Son of God whose House

[margin note: "Numbered with the transgressors."]

[margin note: Cf. Hebr. ii. 10.]

Mt. xvii. the Temple was, He might have claimed exemption. He
24-27. had not come to pull down the Law but to complete it, and
Mt. v. 19. throughout His holy life He sedulously submitted Himself
to its requirements.   He was born under the Law that He
Gal. iv. 4-5 might redeem them that were under the Law, that we might
receive the adoption.   And therefore it was that He would
be numbered with the transgressors at the Jordan, making
Himself sin for us.   It was, in the language of St Chrysostom,
as though He had said : " As I was circumcised that I might
fulfil the Law, I am baptised that I may ratify grace.   If
I fulfil a part and omit a part, I leave the Incarnation
maimed.   I must fulfil all things that hereafter Paul may
write : ' Christ is the fulfilment of the Law unto righteousness for every one that believeth.' " [1]

His dis-   Thus far John knew not who Jesus was, but it was presently
covery to discovered to him that He was none other than the Messiah.
John.
Cf. Is. xi. He had learned from the Scriptures by what mark he should
2 ; lxi. 1. recognise the Messiah when He appeared.   He would see the
John i. 33. Spirit descending and remaining upon Him.   And now the
sign is given.   When God makes His revelations, He ever
makes them in such ways as men are able to understand, with
gracious condescension employing their ideas, albeit erroneous,
as the vehicles of His communications.   He made known
the Saviour's Birth to the Wizards by a star ; and, since John
was a Jew, He dealt with him as a Jew.   The Jewish
imagination, fastening on that passage in the first chapter
Gen. i. 2. of the Book of Genesis which speaks of " the Spirit of God
brooding upon the face of the waters," according to the
Rabbinical comment, " like a dove hovering over its young,"
loved to figure the Spirit as a dove.[2]   And there was
another idea which had lodged itself in the minds of the
later Jews.   The voice of prophecy was mute, and men,
longing to hear the silence broken and remembering perhaps
how their poets in old days had styled the thunder the Voice
Ps. xxix. of Jehovah, persuaded themselves that ever and anon God
spoke from Heaven, sending forth at perplexing crises what
they called *Bath Kol*, the Daughter of a Voice.[3]

[1] *In Sanct. Theoph. Serm.*
[2] Wetstein on Mt. iii. 16.   See Conybeare in *Expositor*, June 1894, pp. 451-8.
[3] See Lightfoot on Mt. iii. 17 ; xii. 39.

Being a child of his age and people, the Baptist shared The Dove and the Voice. those ideas, and God employed them to reveal the Messiah to him. As Jesus after His baptism stood praying on the river bank, "behold, the heavens were opened and the Spirit Lk. iii. 21. of God as a dove descended upon Him ; and, behold, a Voice out of the heavens : ' This is My beloved Son, in whom I am well pleased.' "   It was a distinct attestation of His Messiah- ship, since *the Son of God* was a Jewish title for the Cf. John xi. 27 ; xx. 31. Messiah.   The vision was seen and the voice was heard by Jesus and by John, and by no others.   Even so it Mt.iii. 16= Mk. i. 10; John i. 32- 34. was when the Lord manifested Himself after the Resurrection : His glorified body was invisible to the eye of sense, and only those perceived Him who were endowed with the gift of spiritual vision.   Jesus and John were thus enlightened, and they beheld the vision and heard the voice, while the multitude saw nothing and heard nothing.   It was fitting that it should happen thus.   For them alone was the revelation designed—for Jesus, that He might know that His hour had come, and for John, that he might recognise the Messiah.

[1] There was a Jewish tradition that " the Messiah would not know Himself nor have any power until Elijah (*cf.* Mt. xi. 14) came and anointed Him and made Him manifest to all."   See Just. M. *Dial. cum Tryph.*, ed. Sylburg., p. 226 B.

CHAPTER IV

THE MESSIAH'S TEMPTATION

Mt iv. 1-11
=Lk. iv. 1-
13=Mk. i.
12-3

"Saviour, breathe forgiveness o'er us;
All our weakness Thou dost know;
Thou didst tread this earth before us,
Thou didst feel its keenest woe;
Lone and dreary,
Faint and weary,
Through the desert Thou didst go."—JAMES EDMESTON.

Retiral to the wilderness. THE hour had come, and Jesus must abandon His peaceful life and address Himself to His Mission. He had long been brooding over it in the seclusion of Nazareth; but, when the hour arrived, He realised the magnitude of the ordeal, and, Gal. i. 15-7 like St Paul when after his conversion he "conferred not with flesh and blood, but went away into Arabia," He hastened from the faces of men that He might collect His thoughts and in communion with God gain light and strength. West of the Jordan lay a wild tract, rugged and barren,[1] the haunt Mk. i. 13; of fierce beasts and still fiercer bandits who by their deeds of Lk. x. 30. violence had earned for the steep road from Jericho to Jerusalem the ghastly name of the Ascent of Blood.[2] Thither, impelled by the Holy Spirit, who had taken possession of John iii. 34. Him at His Baptism and thenceforth dwelt in Him "without measure," Jesus retired. And there for forty days[3] He pondered the work which had been given Him to do, wrestling with perplexities which crowded upon Him and hardly attaining to clear certainty of the way which He must take.

The Temptations: It was a mighty task which lay before Him, and He questioned within Himself by what path He should pursue it, resolute to obey the Father's will yet distracted by alluring

---

[1] Jos. *De Bell. Jud.* iv. 8. § 3.

[2] Josh. xv. 7. Jer. *Ep.* xxvii, *Ad Eustoch. Virg.*: "Locum Adomim, quod interpretatur sanguinum, quia multus in eo sanguis crebris latronum fundebatur incursibus." *Cf.* p. 328. See Lightfoot on Lk. x. 30; G. A. Smith, *H. G.* p. 265.

[3] Perhaps a round number. *Cf.* Gen. vii. 12; Num. xiii. 25; Ezek. iv. 6; Deut. ix. 9; 1 Kings xix. 8.

34

voices.[1] As he wandered meditative over that dreary desert, 1. A worldly Messiah-ship. He found Himself on the summit of a lofty mountain, perhaps that mountain overlooking Jericho whereof Josephus speaks : " The city stands on a plain, but over it hangs a mountain bare and barren, of very great length, all irregular, and uninhabited by reason of its sterility." [2] Very striking would be the prospect from that height, and the imagination would travel further than the eye. At His feet lay Jericho, that fair City of the Palms, reposing on its lovely champaign ; and Deut. xxxiv. 3. westward through the clear atmosphere might be descried the white walls and gleaming minarets of the Sacred Capital. The land of Israel spread before Him, and, as His eye followed its lines of busy highway, conducting to Egypt, Arabia, Persia, Damascus, and the ports of the Mediterranean, those outlets to the Isles of Greece and imperial Rome, there rose before Him a vision of " all the kingdoms of the world and the glory of them."

And this world He had come to redeem. It was natural The Jewish ideal. that the question should occur how best He might accomplish this mission and win the teeming myriads of mankind. And it was inevitable that the Messianic ideal which prevailed among His contemporaries should present itself before Him. It was expected that the Messiah would be a victorious King who should emancipate Israel from the tyranny of the Gentiles and set up the fallen throne of David in more than its ancient glory. If He were indeed the Messiah, must He not appeal to the ardent patriotism of His people and, announcing Himself as the long expected Deliverer, rally them about Him and disown the dominion of Rome ? Mad as they may appear, such projects were cherished by thousands of indignant Jews in those days of national humiliation. Only the other year Judas the Galilean had raised the standard of rebellion and set the land aflame. The insurrec- tion had indeed come to naught, but the fire was still smouldering and needed only a breath to fan it into a fierce conflagration. A new party had arisen in Israel, bearing the significant name of the Zealots ; and they were eagerly watching their opportunity to resume the baffled enterprise.

---

[1] On the order of the Temptations see Introd. § 12. 1.
[2] De Bell. Jud. iv. 8. § 2.

Jesus had merely to proclaim Himself the Messiah come to restore the Kingdom unto Israel, and thousands upon thousands would have mustered to His side. Such was the rôle which it was expected the Messiah would play, and truly it would have been no ignoble enterprise to unfurl the banner of liberty, a second and greater Judas Maccabæus. Judas of Gamala had failed, but Jesus of Nazareth had the hosts of Heaven at His command.

Mt. xxvi. 52-3.

The true ideal. As He looked abroad upon the world which He had come to win, this course must have opened before Him ; but He resolutely turned from it, knowing that He had come to achieve a better salvation than deliverance from the Roman yoke. The current Messianic ideal was in truth a worldly dream. Had Jesus embraced it, He might indeed have won "all the kingdoms of the world and the glory of them." Did not the anti-Christ in after days sit upon the throne of the Cæsars? But far other was the Kingdom of the true Messiah. "The Spirit of the Lord God is upon Me, because the Lord hath anointed Me to preach good tidings unto the meek; He hath sent Me to bind up the broken-hearted, to proclaim liberty to the captives and the opening of the prison to them that are bound, to proclaim the acceptable year of the Lord." That was His Mission. The path whereunto He was called, was a lowly path of service and sacrifice ; and, though at its end there stood not a Throne but a Cross, He set His face like a flint to walk therein.

Is. lxi. 1-2; Cf. Lk. iv. 17-9.

Alliance with the rulers. But was there not another way? Might He not ally Himself with the Jewish rulers? Indeed it appears that the Sanhedrin from motives of policy would gladly have taken Him under its patronage. After His first public appearance at Jerusalem that high court deputed one of its members, the good Nicodemus, to wait upon Him privately, evidently with the design of coming to an understanding with Him.[1] And, had He welcomed their overtures, He might have gone forth upon His Mission in peace and prosecuted it unmolested.

[1] There is thus a measure of reason in the fantastic idea of Bengel and Lange that the Tempter in the wilderness was a deputy from the Sanhedrin who, after the Baptist's testimony tracked Jesus to His retreat and urged Him to adopt the Messianic ideals of the age and secure the patronage of the rulers. Bengel indeed allows that the Tempter was Satan, supposing merely, on the ground of the thrice repeated " It is written," that he had assumed the guise of a Scribe.

It was an alluring prospect, yet Jesus turned away from it. A like temptation had been presented to the Baptist when the Sanhedrin sent its delegates to Bethany; and he had flung it from him with indignant scorn. And Jesus no less than John knew what manner of men the rulers were, and perceived the motives which prompted their overtures. Corrupt and worldly-minded, they desired to have to do with the new movement only that they might control it. They durst not crush the prophet whom the multitude revered, and therefore they would adopt the safer course of patronising him and making him their creature. If the alliance was impossible for John, it was still more impossible for Jesus. He had His commission from God and needed not the sanction of men, least of all men like these. He was the foe of priestcraft and ceremonialism, and He could not ally Himself with the very system which He fought even unto the death.

Perhaps another thought occurred to Jesus as that vision of "all the kingdoms of the world and the glory of them" floated before Him. There is this apparent contradiction in His ministry, that He was at once the Messiah of Israel and the Saviour of the World; and this makes the supreme pathos of His earthly life, that, with an " ocean and abyss of philanthropy "[1] in His heart, He should have been shut up to a single family of mankind and restrained from pouring forth His universal compassion. It is very plain, if it may be said with fitting reverence, that He fretted all the days of His ministry against the limitation of His Mission, and was grieved by the thought of that great outer world hungering for salvation and perishing in its sore need. It was a hard necessity that was laid upon Him throughout the days of His humiliation to confine His grace and restrain the outgoings of His heart. The veiling of His love cost Him more than the veiling of His glory. As He beheld that far-reaching vision, would He not be tempted to overleap His barriers and betake Himself to the broad field of the world outside the land of Israel? And He would conquer the temptation by recalling how God's purpose of redemption had been wrought out all down the ages. Its arena had

Limitation of His Mission.

---

[1] Chrysost. *In Matth.* v: τὸ πέλαγος καὶ τὴν ἄβυσσον τῆς φιλανθρωπίας τοῦ Θεοῦ.

been the little land of Israel, and there, as in soil providentially prepared, must the Messiah sow the good seed of His Kingdom. Had He, as the Tempter suggested and His enemies once surmised that He intended, forsaken Israel and gone to the Gentiles, it would have fared ill with Christianity. It is significant that the Greek Fathers were wont to speak of the Faith as a " philosophy "; and, had Jesus preached among the Greeks, they would have accounted Him a philosopher and not a Saviour, and His teaching a philosophy and not a Gospel.

John vii. 35.

It is likely that among the heathen He would have been better entreated,[1] but this was no allurement to Him. He knew that He had not come to be welcomed and honoured but to be rejected and slain, a sacrifice for the sin of the world. " It was necessary that the Messiah should suffer these things and enter into His glory." And He knew this from the beginning. It was no late discovery, no unexpected *dénouement*, no unwelcome necessity which He would fain have evaded.[2] He contemplated it from the first. At the very outset of His ministry He puzzled the sign-seeking rulers with a mystic prophecy of His Passion and Resurrection. In His conversation with Nicodemus He spoke of the necessity of the Son of Man being " lifted up," a phrase which signified at once His elevation on the Cross and His subsequent glorification. And shortly after the commencement of His Galilean ministry He predicted the coming of days when the Bridegroom should be taken away and the sons of the bride-chamber mourn. There is profound truth in the tradition that Jesus never was seen to laugh but oftentimes to weep.[3] He had come into the world to die. All the days of His flesh He was bearing the load of its guilt. The Cross was His goal, and its shadow lay dark and dread upon His path. " It was necessary that the Messiah should suffer these things "; and therefore He abode in the land of Israel.

Jesus came to die.

Lk. xxiv. 26.

John ii. 18-22.

John iii. 14.

Mt. ix. 15= Mk. ii. 19-20=Lk. v. 34-5.

When He had thus refused to ally Himself with the world, Jesus was assailed by an opposite and subtler temptation. Might He not ally Himself with God? That was an age

2. A spectacular Messiahship.

[1] *Cf.* p. 418.
[2] Keim: "It was the death of the Baptist which, weighing on the mind of Jesus, first matured in him the presentiment of his own near departure."
[3] *Ep. of Lent.*; "Aug." *Serm.* ccviii. § 9.

which loved marvels and, except it saw signs and portents, would not believe. It expected that the Messiah would show signs in attestation of His claims, and every impostor that arose in Israel sought to win credence by a pretence of miraculous power.[1] The multitude and the rulers both continually demanded signs of Jesus in the course of His ministry ; and the idea presented itself to Him in the wilderness that He might establish His claims by gratifying this universal desire. His thoughts turned to the Holy City gleaming afar on her mountain throne ;[2] and He pictured Himself ascending to the Wing of the Temple, that lofty parapet whence James, the Lord's brother, was hurled some thirty-eight years later,[3] and, in sight of the multitude which would throng the sacred court at the approaching Passover, casting Himself headlong from that dizzy height. God would intervene ; for was it not written of the Messiah : "His angels will He command concerning Thee, and on their hands they shall bear Thee up, lest Thou ever dash Thy foot against a stone"? Unseen hands would support Him and bear Him in safety to the ground, and the wondering multitude would shout "Hosanna" and hail Him as the Messiah.

Jesus rejected this course as, in the language of Scripture, a "tempting of God." It is indeed the privilege of the sons of God to encounter with quiet and steadfast hearts whatsoever befalls them in His providence ; but should any rashly incur danger, should he court it vain-gloriously, "acting presumptuously in carnal confidence," he has no warrant to expect God's intervention.[4] And the idea of winning applause by a spectacular display was abhorrent to Jesus. Wonder is not faith ; and He desired, not the acclamation of a gaping

Margin refs: John iv. 48. John vii. 31. Cf. John vi. 30; John ii. 18; Mt. xii. 38=Lk. xi. 16; Mt. xvi. 1=Mk. viii. 11. Ps. xci. 11, 2. Tempting God. Deut. vi. 16.

[1] Mt. xxiv. 24=Mk. xiii. 22. *Cf.* Theudas (Jos. *Ant.* xx. 5. § 1 ; Eus. *H. E.* ii. 11); the Egyptian impostor (Jos. *Ant.* xx. 8. § 6 ; *De Bell. Jud.* ii. 13. § 5).

[2] The Temptation was from first to last a spiritual conflict waged within the Lord's breast. It were a misuse of Jewish imagery to conceive that the Devil appeared in bodily shape or actually transported Him to Jerusalem. At the same time the mention of the Devil or Satan should not be explained away as a mere accommodation to contemporary theology. Jesus repeatedly spoke of a personal power of evil, and Keim insists that the question must be regarded as "scientifically quite open." *Cf.* Gore, *Dissert.*, pp. 23-7.

[3] Eus. *H. E.* ii. 23.

[4] *Cf.* Aug. *De Civit. Dei.* xvi. 19: "Si periculum, quantum caveri poterat, [Abraham] non caveret, magis tentaret Deum quam speraret in Deum."

multitude, but the homage of believing souls, born of a reason-able recognition of His claims. Throughout His ministry He shrank from being accounted a mere wonder-worker, and, whenever He wrought a miracle, He would fain have done it, as it were, by stealth. His grace was the evidence of His Messiahship, and such as had experience of it, required no other evidence. The craving for signs bespoke a carnal mind.

3. A selfish Messiah-ship. Towards the close of His sojourn in the wilderness, exhausted by the protracted conflict and faint with long abstinence, Jesus was assailed by the last and subtlest of His temptations. Around Him lay fragments of limestone, and, as His eye rested on a lump, the idea occurred to Him that He might relieve His hunger by miraculously converting it into a loaf. And He could have done it. Ere many days elapsed, He changed water into wine, and twice in the course of His ministry He multiplied a handful of bread into a meal for thousands. Yet He would not do it; and the explana-tion lies in the fact that of all the miracles which He wrought in the course of His ministry, not one was wrought on His own behalf. His power, ever alert to the cry of others' need, slumbered when His own was great. His Mission demanded this self-abnegation. He had come to bear our load and drink our cup, and it was necessary that He should experience the uttermost of our woe, in order that He might be touched Hebr. iv. with the feeling of our infirmities. Had He exerted His 15. miraculous power to save Himself from suffering, He would have cancelled that great act of self-renunciation whereby He assumed our nature that He might dwell here, a man of sorrows and acquainted with grief. At every step of His progress through the world He denied Himself, resolutely sharing the woes which He had come to heal.

"Such was the life He livèd; self abjuring,
His own pains never easing,
Our burdens bearing, our just doom enduring,
A life without self-pleasing!"

The sinless-ness of Jesus. His temptation in the wilderness most strikingly evinces the sinlessness of our blessed Lord. When Saul of Tarsus retired to the solitude of Arabia, he was haunted by the remembrance of his "exceeding madness" against Jesus

and His saints.   It clung to him all his life, and during that
season of retirement he would mourn over it and vow with
sore contrition to make the future, so far as he could, a
reparation of the past.   But far otherwise was Jesus employed
during His sojourn in the wilderness.   He could look back
without regret or shame.   It was not the past that concerned
Him, but the future ; and His only thought was how He
should do the Father's will, and accomplish the work which
had been given Him to do.   The past had left no regret, and
He faced the future, not with tears of penitence and vows of
reparation, but with a prayer for guidance and a steadfast
resolution to recognise no law save the Father's will and seek
no end save His glory.   It was a spotless life that the
Messiah consecrated to the work of the world's redemption.

CHAPTER V

THE MESSIAH'S MANIFESTATION UNTO ISRAEL

"Salve sancta facies
Nostri Redemptoris,
In quâ nitet species
Divini splendoris."—*Med. Hymn.*

Deputation
from the
Sanhedrin
to the
Baptist.
IN the meantime what had been transpiring at Bethany? The Pharisees and Sadducees who had presented themselves as candidates for baptism and been so scornfully rejected, had quitted the scene of their humiliation and carried a report to the Sanhedrin. It is an evidence of the impression which he had made upon them, that the rulers did not straightway take vengeance on the audacious prophet. They feared him ; they thought it possible that he might be the Messiah or the Messiah's herald.[1] And therefore they resolved to despatch a deputation to interview him and ascertain what he claimed to be.

The composition of the deputation is remarkable. There were two great parties in the Jewish state in those days—the Sadducees and the Pharisees. The former were the aristocratic order ; and, albeit sceptics, acknowledging, it is said, only the books of Moses as authoritative and rejecting the doctrines of the Resurrection and Immortality,[2] they enjoyed a monopoly of the lucrative offices of the priesthood. Being more subservient to the Roman government than the patriotic Pharisees, they had this for their reward. Strong, however, in the favour of the populace, the Pharisees constantly overbore their rivals in the councils of the Sanhedrin.[3] It was they that conceived the idea of a deputation to Bethany : it was " sent on the motion of the Pharisees,"[4] but they stood aloof from the negotiation,

---

[1] *Cf.* p. 27.   [2] *Cf.* p. 404.   [3] Jos. *Ant.* xiii. 10. § 6 ; xviii. 1. § 4.
[4] In John i. 24 omit ol. ἐκ of *the ultimate agent. Cf.* iii. 1 ; ix. 40 ; xi. 19 ; xviii. 3.

42

entrusting it to a party of Priests and Levites. It was an astute device. Since John was a priest's son, a priestly deputation would presumably be acceptable to him.

And, when they approached him, they were received not merely with courtesy but with the utmost frankness. "Who art thou?" was their first question; and, divining their thought, he hastened to assure them that he was not the Messiah. "What then?" they asked. "Art thou Elijah?" "I am not," he replied. "Art thou the Prophet?" "No." He might indeed have answered the latter two questions in the affirmative, since he actually performed the part of the prophet of Jewish expectation; and in this sense Jesus by and by declared him "Elijah that should come." But John knew that, whatever might be the truth about that current expectation, he was no ancient prophet returned to life; and it evinces his absolute sincerity and his utter freedom from the fanatic temper that he would not encourage a delusion in order to enhance his prestige and influence. *John's disavowal of Messiahship.* *Mt. xi. 14; Mt. xvii. 10-3=Mk. ix. 11-3.*

It would lift a load from the deputies' minds when they heard those explicit disavowals. John was not, as they had feared, the Messiah, nor was he even the Prophet; and they had been disquieting themselves in vain when they trembled for the impending judgment and stayed their hands from taking vengeance on the bold preacher. His confession had divested him of his terrors, and they might now with impunity deal with him as they listed. Forthwith they altered their tone. "Who art thou?" they persisted, "that we may give an answer to them that sent us. What sayest thou about thyself?" "I am," John answered, quoting the ancient prophet's description of the return of the exiles from Babylon, "a voice of one crying in the wilderness: 'Prepare the way of the Lord.'" "Then why," they demanded with Sadducean brusquerie,[1] "art thou baptising, if thou art not the Messiah nor Elijah nor the Prophet?" Here they spoke on the Pharisees' behalf. John's Baptism would be no offence to the Sadducees. They would account it simply another of those endless ablutions which, to their no small amusement, the Pharisees practised with indefatigable assiduity. "Lo!" they sneered, "the Pharisees will presently be cleansing the *Relief of the deputies.* *Is. xl. 3.*

---

[1] Jos. *De. Bell. Jud.* ii. 8. § 14.

sun for us."[1] But it was an offence to the Pharisees.
Since ceremonial ablution was their affair, they regarded it as
an invasion of their peculiar province ; and the deputies were
apparently echoing the complaint of their colleagues when
they demanded of John what right he had to baptise.
Formerly the fiery prophet would have blazed with indignation,
but since he had seen the Lord's blessed Face, he had been
clothed with meekness, and he felt only a great compassion
for the blindness of those arrogant men. "I baptise in water,"
he answered, "but in the midst of you standeth One whom
ye know not, even He that cometh after me, whose sandal-
strap I am not worthy to unloose."

Manifestation of Jesus as the Messiah.

Next day Jesus reappeared at Bethany. He had fought
His battle and attained to clear certainty regarding the
path which He should take in the prosecution of His Mission.
There was something unearthly in His look, and John gazed
at Him ; then, turning to the bystanders, he cried : "Behold,
the Lamb of God that taketh away the sin of the world."
He had learned much from the Scriptures. Unlike most of
his Jewish contemporaries, who formed their expectation of
the Coming Deliverer after those magnificent yet secular
pictures of a King that should break in pieces the oppressor
and reign gloriously in Zion, he conceived of the Messiah,
in accordance with a profounder ideal born of the nation's
Is. liii. woe, as a sin-bearer, led like a lamb to the slaughter. That
was a great hour when John pointed to Jesus and declared
Him the Messiah. His mission was accomplished. He had
ushered in the Greater than himself.

Andrew and John join Him.

No more is recorded of that day's doings, but the story
of what befell in the course of the next two days is among
the most memorable on the pages of the New Testament.
It is the story of the Lord's meeting with five of His future
disciples, and every sentence is crowded with significance and
throbs with emotion. It chanced on the morrow that John
the Baptist was standing with two of his disciples. One of
them was Andrew, and the other, though unnamed, was
certainly St John. It was the manner of the Evangelist to
conceal himself thus. *Amavit nesciri et pro nihilo reputari.*
The Baptist espied Jesus walking to and fro, and, looking

[1] *Cf.* Edersheim, *Life and Times of Jesus the Messiah*, i. p. 312.

upon Him, repeated his declaration: "Behold, the Lamb of
God!" The two disciples heard, and they understood. It was
their master's farewell. He was pointing Jesus out to them
that they might betake themselves to Him and be thenceforward His disciples. They timidly approached the newly
discovered Messiah; and, as they followed Him wonderingly,
He suddenly wheeled round and, says the Evangelist, "beheld
them." It is the same word that the Baptist employed when
he said: "I have *beheld* the Spirit descending as a dove from John i. 32
Heaven"; and its meaning is that it was a solemn and glad
spectacle that met the eyes of Jesus. In these two, following
Him with reverent and wondering faces, He recognised the
forerunners of the great multitude which should yet believe on
His name and call Him Lord. "What are ye seeking?"
He enquired. They were abashed and confounded, thinking
that He resented their intrusion; and they stammered out:
"Rabbi, where lodgest[1] Thou?" "Come," He answered
kindly, "and ye shall see."

It would be a poor lodging, perhaps some fastness in Interview
the wilderness where Jesus slept with no covering but His with Jesus
cloak and no roof but the canopy of heaven. He conducted
them thither that they might see the poverty of His condition and realise how they must fare if they cast in their
lot with Him. And they stood the test. It was ten o'clock
in the forenoon[2] when they joined Him, and they stayed
with Him the livelong day, returning to their abodes at
night-fall with wonder and gladness in their souls and never
a doubt that He was indeed the Messiah. It is noteworthy
that this great day when Jesus, resting from His conflict,
rejoiced in the birth of those two souls, seems to have been
the Sabbath.[3] It was the supreme crisis in the lives of
the two. They never forgot it. When he wrote his
Gospel some seventy years later, the scene was still clear
and vivid in St John's memory. He recalled the very
hour.

[1] *Cf.* p. 449. [2] Append. II.
[3] Since the marriage of a virgin was, according to Rabbinical law, celebrated
on the fourth day of the week, *i.e.* Wednesday (*cf.* Lightfoot on John ii. 1), the
order of events was this: Sabbath, John and Andrew with Jesus; Sunday, Simon
brought to Him; Monday, the start; Tuesday, on the road; Wednesday, arrival
at Cana and marriage in the evening.

Simon.   As soon as morning broke,[1] impelled by that sacred instinct which ever prompts one who has found Jesus, to bring others to His blessed feet, Andrew sought his brother Simon and acquainted him with his discovery. "We have found the Messiah!" he cried—"the speech," says St Chrysostom, "of a soul travailing for His advent, expecting His arrival from above, overjoyed on the appearance of its expectation, and eager to impart the good tidings unto others." He conducted Simon to Jesus and forthwith Simon's heart was won.

John i. 42. The Evangelist tells how it came to pass: "Jesus looked upon him." What was there in the Face of Jesus that the mere sight of it should have sufficed to win men, yea, and rebuke the erring and overwhelm them with remorse? A look from that Face conquered Simon at Bethany; and, in the hour of his shame in the courtyard of the High Priest,

Lk. xxii. 61-2 a look from it recalled him to his allegiance. "The Lord turned and *looked* upon Peter. And Peter went outside and wept bitterly." It was a wondrous Face.[2] It haunted St John to his dying day. It stood in his remembrance for all that is most blessed and all that is most awful. Would he realise the joy of Heaven? He thinks of that Face:

Rev. xxii. 3-4. "His servants shall minister unto Him, and they shall see His Face." Would he realise the terror of the Day of

Rev. xx. 11. Judgment? Again he thinks of that Face: "I saw a great white Throne and Him that sat thereon, from whose Face fled the earth and the heaven, and no place was found for them."

Surnamed "Cephas." John ii. 25.   The Face of Jesus searched men and discovered the secrets of their hearts. "He read every one, and had no need that any should testify concerning the man; for He Himself ever read what was in the man." And, looking upon Simon with "those eyes of far perception," He saw what manner of man he was and what grace would yet make him. It was the fashion in Israel that, when a man passed through some experience which made him a new creature, he should

---

[1] In John i. 41 b(Ital.) has *mane*, pointing to a reading πρωΐος which is probably original and certainly preferable to either πρῶτος (T. R., Tisch.) or πρῶτον (W. H.). The latter would mean that the first thing Andrew did was to find his brother; the former, that he was beforehand with John.

[2] *Cf.* Jer. on Mt. ix. 9: "Certe fulgor ipse et majestas divinitatis occultæ quæ etiam in humana facie relucebat, ex primo ad se videntes trahere poterat aspectu."

get a new name, commemorative of the occasion and expressive of the transformation. And Jesus gave a new name to Simon : "Thou art Simon : thou shalt be called Cephas." Cephas meant Rock, being the Aramaic of Peter. The name was prophetic. For many a long day Simon retained his character of vacillation and impetuosity ; but grace wrought upon him its divine transformation, making him at the last a rock of strength to his brethren and the *Cf.* Lk. Church's steadfast foundation-stone. It was of the Lord's xxii. 32, Mt. xvi. 18, kindness that he got his new name ere he had earned it. It would be a constant incentive to him, reminding him of his Master's generous confidence and prompting him to prove worthy thereof.

The day following Jesus won two others to faith in His Departure Messiahship. He must needs set out for Galilee that for Cana. morning, since He had engaged to attend a wedding at Cana on the evening of the next day but one ; John, Andrew, and Simon, as it happened, being also bidden to it. Another of the Galileans who had come south to share in the blessing Philip. of the revival, was a man named Philip ; and he had witnessed all that had transpired and would fain have imitated the example of his three countrymen and attached himself to Jesus. It seems, however, that, being somewhat retiring in his disposition, he held back. Jesus had observed him and read his thoughts. It chanced that Philip too had been bidden to the wedding, and, as Jesus was setting out with the three, He noticed him taking the northward road and invited him to join the company.[1]

Philip gladly obeyed and fared onward, listening to Jesus Nathanael, with kindling heart. Soon the barren wilderness was left behind, and he espied an acquaintance some distance ahead reclining under a fig-tree by the wayside. It was Nathanael of Cana, who was betaking himself to his townsman's wedding. He was a devout Israelite, and he had been at Bethany and heard the Baptist's testimony to Jesus ; and he was travelling home much tumbled up and down in his mind. He was deeply impressed, and would fain have welcomed Jesus as the Messiah ; but his judgment held him back.

---

[1] "Follow Me," literally (*cf.* John xxi. 19-20), not figuratively as in Mt. viii. 22 ; ix. 9.

He was an earnest student of the prophetic scriptures,[1] and
Cf. Mt. ii. 4-6. these plainly declared that the Messiah would be born at
Bethlehem. Jesus, however, was from Nazareth, His birth-
place, as Nathanael supposed; and, apart from the testimony
of the Scriptures, it seemed incredible that the Holy One
should come from a place of so evil a reputation. He would
fain have accepted the Baptist's testimony and rejoiced in the
Redeemer's advent, but he could not sophisticate his reason
or make his judgment blind. And he had lain down under
the fig-tree less to rest than to think.

As he lay lost in meditation, Jesus and His company
approached. Philip spied his acquaintance and, hurrying to
him all out of breath, greeted him with the exultant announcement, jerking it out disjointedly : "Whom Moses in the Law
wrote of—and the Prophets—we have found—Jesus, Joseph's
son—the Man from Nazareth!" Provoked by a glib
credulity which saw no difficulty where to himself all was
dark, Nathanael eyed him cynically and retorted with the
proverb : "Out of Nazareth can there be aught good?"
"Come and see," answered Philip, wisely eschewing disputation. Nathanael obeyed. As he approached, Jesus said to
His companions : "Behold, an Israelite truly, in whom is no
guile!" It was a precise description of Nathanael's intellectual
attitude, and he exclaimed in wonderment : "Whence dost
Thou read my thoughts?" "Ere Philip hailed thee," Jesus
replied, "while thou wast under the fig-tree, I saw thee."
"Rabbi," cried Nathanael, saluting Him with the titles of the
Messiah, "Thou art the Son of God! Thou art King of
Israel!" What had so suddenly inspired him with such
complete conviction? It was not alone the Lord's keen
observation and swift comprehension, though that was a
prophetic attribute of the Messiah.[2] Nathanael was won even
as Simon had been won before him. He "beheld that face
that doth minister life to beholders," and his soul bowed in
wonder and adoration.

A disciple like Nathanael was worth winning. He was
not the man to be lightly tossed to and fro. His very

[1] Cf. Aug. In Joan. Ev. Tract. vii. § 17: "Intelligere enim debemus ipsum
Nathanaelem eruditum et peritum Legis fuisse." Chrysost. In Joan. xix ; In
Servat. Nost. Jes. Chr. Diem Nat. Serm. xxxi.
[2] Is. xi. 3 marg. Cf. Lightfoot on Mt. xii. 25.

slowness to believe save on sure evidence was a pledge of his steadfastness once he had attained to conviction. Never would he repent of the decision which he had that day made after so much travail of soul and wrestling of spirit. He had seen enough to persuade him of the Lord's Messiahship, and fresh evidence would continually crowd upon him. " Because," said Jesus, " I said unto thee ' I saw thee beneath the fig-tree,' dost thou believe? Greater things than these shalt thou see." There was a wondrous experience in store for these men who had believed on His Name and who, as they companied with Him, would behold ever more and more of His glory. " Verily, verily I tell you," He says with evident Gen. xxviii. allusion to the story of Jacob's vision at Bethel, " ye shall see 12. the Heaven opened and the angels of God ascending and descending upon the Son of Man."

Here for the first time Jesus employs that name, the Son The nick- of Man, wherewith throughout His ministry He loved to name "Son designate Himself. Since it is nowhere explained in the of Man." New Testament, its meaning is a matter of surmise; and it appears reasonable to connect it with the scene enacted by the bank of the Jordan when Jesus was manifested unto Israel. The Baptist had pointed to Him and proclaimed Him the Messiah. " Behold, the Lamb of God, that taketh away the sin of the world! This is He of whom I said : ' After me cometh a man who hath been put in advance of me.' " It seems strange that the announcement should have produced apparently so little result. Why did not the multitude flock to the Lord's side and greet Him with glad hearts? Only two approached Him and only five believed on His name. It looks a sorry outcome of the Messiah's manifestation unto Israel ; yet it is hardly surprising. The announcement must have fallen on incredulous ears and aroused a sense of disappointment and indeed resentment. The Jews were looking for a glorious Messiah. They called Him " the Son of God," the title which had of old been borne by the King of Israel as God's representative and vice-gerent. And, cf. Ps. ii. when the Baptist pointed to Jesus, a peasant from despised 6-7. Nazareth, and said : Behold, the Messiah ! " they would exclaim in derisive incredulity : " This the Messiah ? A Galilean ! a Nazarene ! a carpenter ! " The phrase for " the common folk" in those days was "the sons of man";[1] and the multitude would cry : "This is no Son of God ; he is one of the sons of man." Jesus would overhear their murmurings, and would catch up their contemptuous epithet. *A son of* John vii. *man !* one of the common folk, "the people of the earth," 49. whom the rulers despised. Yes, that was His designation, and He would wear it all the days of His ministry and be known as "The Son of Man."

He acted thus not in a spirit of bravado by way of exhibiting His disdain. On the contrary, it was a happy device, and had a deep and gracious purpose. The title "Son of Man" served as a continual protest against that secular ideal of the Messiahship which more than anything else hindered His recognition and acceptance ; and in assuming it Jesus designed to make men think and perchance discover that the true Messianic glory was not what they conceived—not the glory of earthly majesty but the glory of sacrifice. And He had the further design of identifying Himself with the weak and despised, and thus revealing His grace. And the Jews should have recognised the suitability of the title ; they would have recognised it, had they not been blinded by their worldly ideal. *The Son of the Fallen* was a Rabbinical title of the Messiah,[2] and it was closely analogous to the title "Son of Man." It should have been no stumbling-block to them when the Messiah came bearing this name of lowliness and of sympathy with the weak and despised. Rather should they have hailed Him gladly and recognised in the name He bore the fulfilment of their expectation. "Behold, the Son of the Fallen!"

If this be indeed its origin, the title was in the first instance an opprobrious epithet, in fact a nickname ; and Jesus transfigured it by bearing it. Nor was it the only nickname which was thrown at Him while He dwelt among men. The Pharisees in Galilee, offended by His kindness

---

[1] בְּנֵי אָדָם.   *E.g.* "א ב דֶּרֶךְ, "the common custom"; לְשׁוֹן ב "א, "the common parlance." *Cf.* "son of man" in O.T. In Pss. viii. 4, cxliv. 3, cxlvi. 3, it is equivalent to "man" with the implication of *mortal weakness.* In Ezek., where the prophet is over sixty times addressed as "son of man," it has a like signification, "expressing the contrast between the prophet, as one of mankind, and the majesty of God" (Davidson).

[2] Derived from Am. ix. 11.   *Cf.* Lightfoot on Acts xv. 16.

towards the outcasts, styled Him "the Friend of Tax-gatherers Mt. xi. 19 and Sinners"; and the rulers at Jerusalem in their Judæan =Lk. vii. 34. pride called Him "a Samaritan," one of the contemptuous John viii. epithets wherewith the Rabbis branded such as did not sit at 48 their feet.[1] It is indeed only a conjecture that the name originated thus, but it is not without attestation. Wherever it occurs in the Gospels, it is Jesus Himself that uses it. The Evangelists never call Him "the Son of Man"; and what is the explanation if it be not that it was a name of scorn, and they would not bestow it on the Lord whom they loved and revered? As soon would they have termed Him "the Friend of Tax-gatherers and Sinners" or "the Samaritan." And, moreover, Jesus never used it save in two connections: in connection with His present humiliation and suffering, and Mt. viii. 20 in connection with His future glory. Nor is there any in- =Lk. ix. 58; Mt. consistency between these two usages seemingly so wide xvii. 22= apart. When He used the title in the latter connection, it Mk. ix. 31 =Lk. ix. was always with the design of startling His hearers. Thus, 44; etc. John i. 51; at the outset of His ministry it was nothing but a term of Mt. xiii. 41; xxv. 31; contempt; and, when He said to Nathanael: "Ye shall see Mt. xxvi. 64 the Heaven opened and the angels of God ascending and =Mk. xiv. 62=Lk. descending upon the Son of Man," it was a prophecy of the xxii. 69. glory which they would yet discover in one so lowly. And so, when at the close He replied to the High Priest's question whether He were the Messiah: "I am, and ye shall see the Son of Man seated at the right hand of power and coming with the clouds of Heaven." It would have been no marvel had He said "the Son of God"; but, when He said "the Son of Man," it seemed a preposterous claim. It was credible Cf. Ps. only to such as had discovered the glory which was hidden lxxx. 17. beneath His humiliation. It was the very opprobriousness of the epithet that gave point and force to His declaration.[2]

---

[1] *Cf.* p. 342. [2] *Cf.* Append. III.

CHAPTER VI

John ii. 1-
11.

THE FIRST MIRACLE

> " To Thee our full humanity,
> Its joys and pains belong ;
> The wrong of man to man on Thee
> Inflicts a deeper wrong.

> " Thy litanies, sweet offices
> Of love and gratitude ;
> Thy sacramental liturgies,
> The joy of doing good."—WHITTIER.

Cana of Galilee. THE village of Cana, called Cana of Galilee to distinguish it from the Phœnician Cana near Tyre, lay, if it be rightly identified with the modern Kefr Kenna, some four or five miles north-east of Nazareth.[1] It was three days' journey from Judæa to Galilee,[2] and Jesus and His companions, setting out in the morning, would arrive on the third day in good time for the marriage-feast.

The marriage-feast. The occasion is for ever memorable forasmuch as it witnessed the Lord's first miracle. The feast was celebrated *Cf. vv.* 9-10. after night-fall in the house of the bride's father, the bridegroom furnishing the entertainment ;[3] and they were evidently humble folk, since there were no slaves in waiting. Those who discharged that office are designated by the Evangelist "attendants,"[4] being probably members or friends of the family. Since she not only lent a helping hand but gave directions, it is not unlikely that Mary was a relative, and Jesus may thus have been a kinsman after the flesh of the *Lack of wine.* bridegroom or the bride.[5] It was a poor home, and in the course of the entertainment the supply of wine became exhausted. The mishap was known only to the attendants, and Mary betook herself to Jesus and privately informed Him of the embarrassing situation.

---

[1] Henderson, *Palestine*, § 108.　　[2] Jos. *Vit.* § 52.　　[3] *Cf.* p. 425, n. 2.
[4] διάκονοι, not δοῦλοι.　　[5] Calvin.

Wherefore did she appeal to Him? It is evident that she expected some singular intervention on His part, nor is it strange that she should have done so. She knew what had happened recently. If it be true that, as the apocryphal *Gospel of the Hebrews* averred,[1] she and His brethren had accompanied Him thither to share the blessings of the great revival, she had witnessed what transpired at Bethany beyond Jordan and had heard the Baptist's testimony. And, even though she had not been present, she must have heard the story from the lips of others. The five disciples had come with Jesus to Cana, and they would tell her what they had seen and heard. It is no wonder that she appealed to Jesus. He had been declared the Messiah, and in that untoward accident she recognised an opportunity for Him to manifest His glory. It may be that St Chrysostom does her an injustice when he conceives her as actuated by a vain-glorious ambition to gain *éclat* in the eyes of the company as the mother of the Messiah;[2] but she shared her contemporaries' secular ideal of the Messiahship, and her fond heart yearned for the exaltation of the Son of her love. And therefore, thinking that it afforded a welcome opportunity, she approached Him and informed Him of the emergency.[3]

She addressed Him with affectionate familiarity and unfaltering confidence, and for the first time in all her experience she received a harsh answer from those gentle lips. "What," He said, "have I to do with thee, woman? Mine hour hath not yet come." It is true that the speech was less harsh than it sounds to modern ears. There was no rudeness in the appellation, "woman." It was frequently employed in situations which demanded not merely courtesy but reverence, corresponding nearly to "lady."[4] Nor was it incompatible even with tender affection. Jesus' last word to Mary, as He hung on the Cross and commended her to the care of the Beloved Disciple, was: "Woman, behold thy son." And as

Mary's appeal to Jesus.

His response.

John xix. 26.

---

[1] Jer. *Adv. Pelag.* iii. [2] *In Joan.* xx.

[3] Calvin: she expected no miracle, but wished Him to "remove the disgust of the guests by some pious exhortation, and at the same time relieve the shame of the bridegroom." Equally quaint is Bengel's idea: she wished Him to take His departure, that the others might follow His example, ere the failure of the wine was known.

[4] *E.g.* Soph. *O.T.* 934 : a messenger to Queen Jocasta.

for the question : " What have I to do with thee ? " it was a
common phrase of dissent and remonstrance.[1] The speech
was really less harsh than it sounds to modern ears ; nevertheless it was strange language for a son to use to his mother
and very unlike what Mary had been wont to hear from the
lips of Jesus ; and it must have surprised and pained her.
What did it mean ? It was the Messiah's assertion of the new
relation wherein He stood toward the world. In that hour
when He accepted His vocation, old things had passed away
and all things had become new. Thenceforth He owned no
human kinship. He was no longer the son of Mary. He
was the world's Redeemer, and none but spiritual ties bound
Him to the children of men, according to that word of His

Mt. xii. 46-
50=Mk.
iii. 31-5=
Lk. viii. 19-
21.

in after days : " Whosoever doeth the will of My Father in
Heaven, he is My brother and sister and mother." It was a
hard word for Mary to hear. It would seem to her as
though a great gulf had suddenly yawned betwixt her and
the Son of her love, and she would taste the bitter fulfilment

Lk. ii. 35.

of old Symeon's prediction that a sword would pass through
her soul. Yet she concealed her pain and, confident that He
would interpose, bade the attendants do whatever He might
direct.

"Mine
hour."

The words, " Mine hour hath not yet come," disclose
what was passing in the Lord's breast. " Mine hour " or " My
time " is a phrase which was frequently on His lips during the
course of His earthly ministry, always in reference to some
momentous crisis. When His brethren urged Him to betake
Himself to Jerusalem, and manifest Himself to the world, He

John vii. 3-
6.

answered : " My time hath not yet arrived." He knew that,
when He went to Jerusalem, the Cross was His goal ; and,
when His hour arrived, He would go thither ; yet the prospect
was awful to Him. " Father," He prayed, " save Me from this

John xii.
27; xvii. 1.
Mt. xxvi.
45.

hour " ; and again : " Father, the hour hath come. Glorify
the Son, that the Son may glorify Thee." " Behold," He cried
in Gethsemane, " the hour hath drawn nigh, and the Son of
Man hath been betrayed into sinners' hands." In these
instances the phrase refers to the supreme crisis of His Passion,
and, when He used it at the marriage-feast, it referred to

---

[1] Cf. 2 Sam. xvi. 10. κοινόν is understood ; cf. Luc Merc. Cond. §25: τί κοινὸν
λύρᾳ καὶ ὄνῳ ; Euth. Zig. interprets : " What concern is it of Mine and thine ? "

another and very solemn crisis. He was standing on the
threshold of His ministry, conscious of His miraculous power,
and He was questioning whether that were the hour to put it
forth. The great crises are wont to come in simple guise.
Had Jesus found Himself confronted by some mighty task
like cleaving the sea or turning the river into blood, He would
never have hesitated ; but the supplying of wine to a company
of peasants seemed so trivial, so unworthy of the Messiah, so
insufficient for the inauguration of the Kingdom of Heaven.
"Can this be the call of God?" was the question which He
was debating with Himself, still unresolved, when Mary's
appeal broke in disturbingly upon Him. It was a momentous
crisis ; and in that hour of perplexity, searching of soul, and
enquiring after the Father's will, it was revealed to Him what
"the works of the Messiah" must be—not dazzling marvels, Mt. xi. 2.
as the Jews expected, but lowly deeds of service and compassion.[1]

And His way was at length made plain before His face. The
Ranged along the wall for the washing of the guests' feet on miracle.
their arrival and the ceremonial ablution of their hands before Mk. vii.
meat, stood six large water-pots containing each some twenty 2-5; Lk.
to thirty gallons. They had been drained at the beginning of xi. 38.
the entertainment, and Jesus ordered that they should be re-
filled. The attendants, mindful of Mary's injunction and
doubtless aware of the wonder which invested Him, obeyed
with a will, filling them up to the brim. "Draw some now,"
He commanded, "and carry it to the Master of the Feast."[2]
It was water in the jars, but, behold, it was wine in the flagons !

It was an amazing miracle, and St Chrysostom observes [3] Its reality.

[1] Of the many which have been offered, the following explanations of this profound passage may be noted: (1) Aug. *In Joan. Ev. Tract.* viii : Jesus had to do
with Mary only as man. As man He died, but His hour for that had not yet come.
(2) Chrysost. *In Joan.* xxi : The company did not know that the wine had failed.
"Let them first perceive this, and come to Me in their need and ask help." Man's
extremity is the Lord's opportunity, and His grace is never vouchsafed until the need
of it is realised. (3) Calvin : It was an assertion of His dignity which would brook
no interference and accept no dictation. "Hoc autem loco temporis ad agendum
sumendi et eligendi arbitrium sibi vindicat."

[2] ἀρχιτρίκλινος, the classical συμποσίαρχος, ἄρχων or βασιλεὺς τῆς πόσεως, Lat.
rex or *magister convivii, arbiter bibendi* ; chosen by cast of dice "to conduct the
banquet." *Cf.* Becker, *Charicles*, p. 341. The Jews in later times had a similar
usage (Ecclus. xxxii. 1-2).

[3] *In Joan.* xxi.

how careful the Evangelist is to attest its reality. Lest it should be supposed that the jars were wine-jars and the water, mingling with the dregs, made a sort of thin wine, he explains that they were water-pots and stood there for purposes of ablution. Nor did Jesus simply by a creative act fill the empty jars with wine. This had been perhaps a greater miracle, but it had been less credible, since the suspicion might have been entertained that the wine had not been created but surreptitiously introduced. Moreover, Jesus did not Himself fetch the water but employed the attendants, that, should any question arise, they might testify : " We drew the water."   And, finally, the Master of the Feast is brought in as a witness. He was the first to taste the wine, and he remarked upon its excellence. He hailed the bridegroom and bantered him merrily. " Every man," he cried, quoting apparently an apt proverb, " serveth the good wine first, and, when they have drunk deep, the worse ; but thou hast kept the good wine until now." [1]

Analogy to nature.

It was a wondrous miracle, but, as St Augustine justly observes,[2] it is not incredible to one who recognises the divinity of Jesus. " He made the wine that day at the marriage in the six water-pots who every year makes it in the vines. For, even as what the attendants put into the water-pots was turned into wine by the Lord's operation, so too what the clouds pour forth is turned into wine by the same Lord's operation." [3]   And most fitly did it serve to in-

---

[1] There were ribald scoffers like Woolston and Venturini in Chrysostom's day There was no miracle, they alleged. The guests were intoxicated and could not tell water from wine.   Chrysostom allows the intoxication of the guests, but, judging rather by the fashion of his dissolute city of Antioch than by the evidence of the narrative, insists on the sobriety of the ἀρχιτρίκλινος, whose business it was to keep order.   But (1) the speech of the ἀρχιτρίκλινος was playful : he quoted a proverb. (2) Had the company been intoxicated Jesus would not have furnished material for further excess.   (3) In those days at any rate the Jews were a temperate people. Cf. Jos. C. Ap. ii. § 25.   Drunkenness was a distinctively Gentile vice (1 Pet. iv. 3), and the N.T.'s sternest prohibitions of it are found in epistles to Gentile churches. Cf. Rom. xiii. 13 ; 1 Cor. v. 11 ; Gal. v. 21 ; Eph. v. 18 ; 1 Thess. v. 7.

[2] In Joan. Ev. Tract. viii. § 1.

[3] This was a favourite argument in early days. Cf. Iren. Adv. Hær. iii. 11. § 9 ; 17. § 7 ; Chrysost. In Joan. xxi. Of course, as Strauss points out, our Lord's action was more than an acceleration of natural processes, which produce only the grape and must be followed by the artificial processes of pressing, straining, and fermenting ; nevertheless the argument is not without validity.

THE FIRST MIRACLE

Evangelist, "His glory." It was no dazzling display of
regal splendour but a gracious work of kindly sympathy, and
it revealed, in contrast to the prevailing expectation, what the
glory of the Messiah really was. And it served, on the other
hand, to mark Him out from His Forerunner. John was an
ascetic, unsocial and austere; but Jesus was a lover of men,
and He dwelt in their midst all the days of His flesh, their
Brother and Friend, sharing their joy and their sorrow. The
world was in His eyes no unhallowed domain; it was the
outer court of the Father's House. He did not frown on
mirth. He had come that men might have joy and that
their joy might be full. And, though He was Himself
unbound by earthly ties, He deemed them holy, and it grieved
Him when they were profaned.[1] He had not come to
condemn the world but to redeem it; and He dwelt lovingly
among the children of men, ennobling their common life by
His gracious fellowship. And therefore He went to that
marriage-feast, a sympathetic guest, rejoicing in the bridegroom's joy.

And, like every other that He wrought, this miracle has a
symbolic significance. The Master of the Feast spoke more
truly than he knew when he said jestingly: "Thou has kept
the good wine until now." "Not simply wine," says St
Chrysostom, "but the best of wine. Such are Christ's
wondrous works, far fairer somehow and better than those
that are perfected by Nature. When He straightened a
halting limb, He rendered it better than those that were
whole." Yea, even sin when repented of and forgiven, is
used by Him for the soul's discipline and enrichment. Was
it not the remembrance of his sin that inspired St Paul's
passion of gratitude and devotion? Had he never been Saul
the persecutor, he had never been Paul the Apostle. Thus
does Jesus turn our dross to gold, our loss to gain, our misery
to bliss. "O blessed sin which hath won such a Redeemer!"

[1] *Cf.* His frequent protests against divorce.

CHAPTER VII

AT THE PASSOVER

John ii. 12;
ii. 13-22=
Mt. xxi. 12-
3=Mk. xi.
15-7=Lk.
xix. 45-6;
John ii. 23
—iii. 21.

" Jesu spes pœnitentibus,
    Quam pius es petentibus,
    Quam bonus te quærentibus,
    Sed quid invenientibus ? "—S. BERNARD.

Visit to
Caper-
naum.
AFTER the marriage Jesus did not return to Nazareth. He had heard the Heavenly Call and had bidden farewell to His earthly home and His kindred after the flesh ; and, when He left Cana, He betook Himself to Capernaum with His disciples who all except Nathanael dwelt in that town by the shore of the Lake of Galilee. Mary and His brethren went with Him, whether merely to bear Him company or to visit kinsfolk there. Whatever their errand may have been, Jesus had other thoughts. He designed Capernaum as the seat of His ministry, and He went thither to view the field of His labours and perhaps make preparation for His settlement.

The
Passover :
April A.D.
26.
He stayed there "not many days." The Passover was approaching, and He must repair to Jerusalem and participate in the celebration. Ever since His twelfth year He had gone up annually with the train of pilgrims from Galilee, but on this occasion it was not the mere custom of the Feast that took Him thither. He would go up as the Messiah. It was fitting that His public ministry should open in the sacred capital and His first appeal be addressed to the rulers of the nation.

Traders in
the
Temple-
court.
On His arrival He betook Himself to the Temple, and in the forecourt, the Court of the Gentiles, a strange scene greeted His eyes. In those degenerate days an unseemly practice prevailed in connection with the celebration of the Passover. Victims were required—lambs for the paschal sacrifice as well as the offering of purification, bullocks for the thankoffering, and doves for the poor folk's offering of purification ; and the greedy priests had found here an opportunity for swelling

their revenues. Ostensibly for the convenience of the worshippers but really for their own enrichment they had instituted a cattle-market in the sacred court. It was an astute but disgraceful trick, securing them both price and purchase, since the victims which they sold in the court were presently returned to them at the altar. They had instituted also a money-market on a double pretext. Since many of the worshippers, Jews of the Dispersion, came from distant lands and had only heathen money, which was reckoned unclean, they must needs, ere they could purchase their offerings, exchange it into Jewish currency. And so the money-changers with their cash-boxes were there, exacting their *agio*.[1] They were employed also in another and more offensive transaction. Every adult Israelite, rich or poor, had to pay an annual tax of half a shekel to the Temple-revenue. On the first day of the month Adar or March intimation was made that all should have the money in readiness ; on the fifteenth the collectors sat in every town receiving payment ; on the twenty-fifth they sat in the Temple-court, and all outstanding payments must then be made on pain of distraint. It sometimes happened that a poor man's garment was arrested.[2] It was a heartless exaction, and it would grieve the Lord that God's poor should thus be plundered for the enrichment of a luxurious and irreligious priesthood.

Such was the scene which confronted Him when He entered the sacred precincts. The court was reeking with the stench of cattle and resounding at once with their lowing and bleating and with the vociferations of buyers and sellers wrangling and screaming after the Oriental fashion. And there sat the money-changers in their booths, their tables loaded with piles of small coin, quarrelling loudly and bitterly with their clients over the rate of discount or threatening needy creatures with the legal penalty unless their half-shekels were forthcoming. And all this in the court of the Lord's House, which should have been a peaceful harbour, a quiet retreat, whither the weary and heavy laden might betake

Their expulsion by Jesus.

---

[1] St John employs two words for *money-changers*, which set the scene vividly before us: (1) κερματισταί from κέρμα (κείρω), "small change." (2) κολλυβισταί from κόλλυβος (said to be a Phœnician word), *i.e.* καταλλαγή, *agio*. Cf. Becker, *Charicles*, p. 291 ; *P. E. F. Q.*, Jan. 1904, pp. 49-51.

[2] Lightfoot on Mt. xxi. 12

themselves, sure of finding there, in communion with God, rest unto their souls! Centuries earlier a prophet had raised his protest against a like desecration and sighed for the day when there should be no more a trader in the House of the Lord of Hosts;[1] and it is no marvel that the spectacle should have raised a storm of indignation in the breast of Jesus. He had witnessed it before, but hitherto He had gone up to the Passover as an ordinary worshipper: now He is the Messiah and assumes the Messiah's authority. Among the litter that strewed the court were pieces of rope, cast off tethers and baggage-cords; and, snatching up a handful of these and plaiting them into a scourge, He herded the sheep and oxen out of the sacred precincts. Then He assailed the money-changers, overturning their tables and scattering their ringing coins over the pavement. The doves in their coops could not be driven, and perhaps He had a feeling of tenderness for those "offerings of the poor." He used no violence upon them, but bade their owners carry them thence. "Make not," He cried, "My Father's House a market-house!"[2]

Why they offered no resistance. It may seem surprising that the traders should have given way before Jesus when He assailed them single-handed and armed only with a scourge, and that the rulers, with the Temple-guard at their beck, should have suffered His audacity to go unchallenged and unpunished.[3] Yet it is really no marvel. For one thing, Jesus was assailing an abuse which, while it enriched the Sadducean priesthood, must have been felt by the people as a grievous wrong. The multitude would applaud the bold reformer, recognising Him as their champion against aristocratic tyranny and priestly exaction; and, though the rulers despised the multitude, they also feared them, knowing the excitability and fierceness of their passions. Moreover, in the conscious guilt of the offenders Jesus had a still stronger reinforcement. They knew that they were in the wrong. They might indeed have pled speciously that it was no profane traffic. If the victims might be sacrificed at the Temple-altar, might they not be sold in the Temple-court? And was it not right that the worshippers, especially those from afar,

---

[1] Zech. xiv. 21 (Hebr.): "Canaanite," *i.e.* Phœnician merchant; Vulg. *mercator.*

[2] On the position of this incident in the Synoptics see Introd. § 15.

[3] Origen (*In Ev. Matth.* xvi. § 20) regards it as a miracle.

should find fit offerings ready to hand? Yet, gloze it as they might, they knew that it was sacrilege and that their aim was neither the glory of God nor the convenience of the worshippers but their own enrichment. Conscience made cowards of them all. The traffickers retired tumultuously, and their masters stood by, resentful yet making no interference. Their sin had found them out. And they had another and more commanding reason for submission. They knew what had passed at the Jordan several months earlier, and they would have an uneasy misgiving that possibly John had spoken the truth and Jesus was indeed the Messiah. Galilean peasant as He was, He had a strange majesty about Him, and had He not called the Temple "His Father's House"? When He broke into their midst and swept the desecrators before Him, they would remember that oracle of the last of the Prophets of Israel: "The Mal. iii. 1. Lord, whom ye seek, shall suddenly come to His Temple; and the Messenger of the Covenant, whom ye delight in, behold, He cometh, saith the Lord of Hosts."

The real surprise is that Jesus should have performed Assertion this audacious act of reformation at all. It was an open of Messiah ship at assertion of His Messiahship, and it is remarkable that, know- Jerusalem, ing how false was the Messianic ideal of His time, He was Galilee. accustomed to recoil from the Messianic honours which the multitude would have thrust upon Him. His manner was to walk among the people meek and lowly in heart, revealing His grace by deed and word, and letting it steal into their hearts and persuade them that He was of a truth the Redeemer of Israel. This was indeed the course which He pursued in Galilee, where He laboured month after month throughout His three years' ministry; but it is important to observe that He adopted another method in Jerusalem. He paid only a few brief visits to the sacred capital in the course of His ministry; and, since it was necessary that He should employ each opportunity to the utmost and present His claims to the rulers and citizens with all emphasis and clearness, He never visited Jerusalem without in one way or another asserting His Messiahship.

And He never made a more startling assertion thereof Perplexity than this at the outset of His ministry, when He entered the of the rulers. Temple and, claiming it as His Father's House, vindicated its sanctity.   Nor was its meaning misunderstood.   "Can this be the Messiah?" asked the rulers, and they made two approaches to Jesus in order to ascertain the truth.   Since it

John vii. 31. was expected that, when the Messiah came, He would work miracles, there seemed to the rulers[1] a short and conclusive method of settling the question whether Jesus were the Messiah, and no sooner was order restored than they approached Him and with all courtesy presented Him with a

(1) They request a sign. challenge: "What sign showest thou unto us, forasmuch as thou doest these things?"   It was the very temptation which had presented itself to Him in the wilderness when the Devil suggested that He should cast Himself headlong from the Wing of the Temple in sight of the wondering throng.   So soon did the Tempter, who had departed from Him "till

Lk. iv. 13. further opportunity," return and renew the conflict.   The rulers were sincerely perplexed, and they made the proposal in all good faith; and Jesus met them graciously.   He granted them a sign, though not such a sign as they desired.   "Break up this sanctuary," He said, "and in three days I will raise it again."   He referred to His Death and Resurrection, and of course His meaning was hidden from them.   It was His wont all through His ministry to utter such dark sayings, not to mystify His hearers, but to provoke them to reflection.   They were all puzzled, the disciples and the rulers alike.   Not till the prophecy had been fulfilled did the former understand it; and as for the latter they were shocked, deeming it mad arrogance and rank blasphemy.   "During forty and six years," they exclaimed, "hath this Sanctuary been abuilding, and thou—in three days wilt thou raise it again?"   The saying was much discussed and long remembered, and three

Mt. xxvi. 60-1=Mk. xiv. 57-8; cf. Acts vi. 14. years later, when He was arraigned before the Sanhedrin, it was raked up in a distorted form and made the basis of a false accusation.[2]   Yet they might have guessed somewhat of His

---

[1] John ii. 18: "The Jews," according to Johannine usage, the unbelieving section of the nation, especially the rulers, in contrast to the friendly multitude.

[2] Criticism for the most part allows the genuineness of this singularly attested *logion* and seeks to invalidate its testimony to our Lord's foresight of His end by making it a prediction not of the Resurrection but of the abolition of the Jewish system and the introduction of a spiritual religion. *Cf.* Strauss, *Leb. Jes.* iii. i. § 114.   But (1) this is opposed to the Evangelist's interpretation (ii. 21-2); (2) Jesus always insisted that He had not come to abolish but to fulfil the ancient

meaning. He said, not "this temple," but "this sanctuary." The Temple was the entire edifice, all that lay within the sacred precincts ; the Sanctuary was the central shrine with its two chambers, the Holy Place and the Holy of Holies ;[1] and, while the former was always used literally, the latter often bore a figurative meaning. "Know ye not," says St Paul to the Corinthians, "that your body is a sanctuary of the Holy Spirit that is in you?" And it is this figurative sense that the word bore on the lips of Jesus. "He was speaking of the sanctuary of His body." 1 Cor.
vi. 19.

The perplexity of the rulers was only increased by the Lord's reply to their appeal, and, as the days went by, it was increased still more. Though He would not show a sign in attestation of His Messiahship, He wrought miracles which produced a profound impression, convincing not a few that He was indeed the Messiah. "Many," says the Evangelist, "confided in His title,[2] when they beheld the signs which He did ; yet Jesus on His part would not confide Himself unto them." He knew the thought that was in their hearts when they gave Him the name of Messiah. They were dreaming of a victorious King who should deliver Israel from her bondage to the heathen and set up the fallen throne of David, and it grieved Him that His gracious works should foster within them that carnal delusion which dominated the minds of the Jews in those days and more than aught else blinded them to the Messiah's true glory.

So extreme did the perplexity of the rulers become that they took counsel together and resolved to approach Him once more in the hope of arriving at an understanding. Whether He were the Messiah or not, it were well to attach Him to themselves, and they proceeded as they had done in the case of the Baptist. To the latter they had sent a deputation of Priests and Levites ; to Jesus they sent a single delegate, choosing him, with characteristic astuteness, from the ranks of the Pharisees. Since Jesus was a man of the people, they deemed it expedient to entrust the errand (2) They
send a dele-
gate to
Him.

---

religion (Mt. v. 17-9). (3) He said λύσατε, not λύσω, and the rulers would never have dreamed of destroying the ancient order.

[1] ναός (ναίω, *inhabit*), the Habitation of God, His presence-chamber ; τοῦ ναοῦ in Mt. xxiii. 35=τοῦ οἴκου in Lk. xi. 51. *Cf.* Trench, *N.T. Synon.* pp. 10 sqq.

[2] ἐπίστευσαν εἰς τὸ ὄνομα αὐτοῦ. *Cf.* Mt. xxiv. 5=Mk. xiii. 6=Lk. xxi. 8 : ἐπὶ τῷ ὀνόματί μου, *i.e.* claiming the title Messiah.

[3] John iii. 1 : ἐκτῶν Φαρ. proves him a delegate. *Cf.* p. 42, n. 4.

to a representative of the popular party. And, moreover, there was a prominent Pharisee who seemed well suited for the delicate negotiation—one Nicodemus, a venerable Rabbi and a member of the high court of the Sanhedrin.[1] Albeit somewhat timid, he was a man of judicial temper and kindly nature, and his rectitude, which offended his colleagues when they were bent on injustice, commanded their respect.

Nico-demus.

John vii. 50-2.

Since it was desirable that the negotiation should be conducted secretly, Nicodemus waited till nightfall and under covert of the darkness betook himself to Jesus. Where was the scene of the memorable interview? It was not in the city. When Jesus visited Jerusalem, He never passed the night within its gates. During the festal seasons the capital was crowded. There was no accommodation within its circumscribed area for the multitude that came up to worship in the Temple, and many lodged in the open country. Such was the custom of Jesus. Every evening, weary of disputing the livelong day with His adversaries and teaching the people in the Temple-court, He would bid the city farewell and, crossing the Kedron, climb the slope of Olivet, and there bivouac till morning beneath the star-lit canopy of Heaven.

Scene of the inter-view.

Lk. xxi. 37 =Mk. xi. 19; Lk. xxii. 39.

Appreciating at its proper value the popular enthusiasm which His miracles had evoked, Jesus had received coldly those who hailed Him as Messiah; but to Nicodemus He accorded a gracious welcome, hearing his errand and, late though it was, seeking, in a long conversation whereof the Evangelist has recorded only such fragments as clung to his memory, to show him some glimmering of heavenly truth.[2] His unerring intuition read the thoughts of the old Rabbi's heart and perceived beneath the crust of years of formalism the stirring of unrest and desire. Nicodemus was not merely the Sanhedrin's delegate. The Holy Spirit had been at work in his soul, and he came to Jesus with a hungry heart, an earnest and anxious enquirer.

Gracious reception.

---

[1] Nicodemus is the Jewish name Nakdimon. Hellenic or Hellenised names were very common at that period not only among the time-serving Sadducees but among the patriotic Pharisees and the common people; *e.g.* Philip, Andrew. *Cf.* Schürer, *H. J. P.* II. i. 47; Wetstein on Mt. iv. 18.

[2] John iii. 1; "*But* there was a man," contrasting His reception of Nicodemus with His distrust of the others. *Cf.* Acts v. 1. Both our versions miss this, A.V. omitting δέ and R.V. rendering it "now."

With studious courtesy he stated his errand. The rulers The
knew not what to make of the Lord's miracles, and Nicodemus question.
had been deputed by his colleagues to wait upon Him and ask
what they meant. Of this much they had no doubt, that Jesus
was a God-sent teacher, and they thought it probable that He
was indeed the Messiah. " Rabbi," said their delegate, " we
know that Thou art a teacher come from God ; for no one can
do these signs which Thou doest, unless God be with him."
Thus he opened the question, thinking to learn not only on
his colleagues' behalf but on his own whether the miracles were
" the works of the Messiah " ; but Jesus brushed the question Mt. xi. 2.
aside and brought Nicodemus face to face with a more urgent The reply.
and wholly personal concern : " Verily, verily I tell thee, unless one be born anew,[1] he cannot see the Kingdom of God."
The Kingdom of God was the Messianic era. The Jews
were looking for it, and they thought that it would be signalised by manifestations of power and pomp. Jesus here
declares it a spiritual order invisible to the eye of sense.
The Kingdom of God was in the midst of the unbelieving
Jews, yet they never saw it, because they were spiritually
blind. The light shone in the darkness, and the darkness
comprehended it not. When Nicodemus and his colleagues
wondered at His miracles and disputed whether they were
evidences of His Messiahship, they were on a wrong track.
They must be born anew that they might see the Kingdom
of God.

The declaration amazed Nicodemus. It is true that Bewilder-
regeneration was a familiar idea to him. The Rabbis said of ment of Nico-
a proselyte from heathenism that he was " as a child newly demus.
born." But regeneration was only for converts from heathenism. " All Israel," they said, " has a portion in the world to
come." [2] It was incredible to Nicodemus that the Jews should
be required to enter into the Kingdom of Heaven by that
door of humiliation, on the self-same terms as the despised

---

[1] It is a question whether ἄνωθεν here means "from above" or "anew."
Chrysost. *In Joan. Hom.* xxiii : τὸ ἄνωθεν ἐνταῦθα οἱ μὲν ἐκ τοῦ οὐρανοῦ φασὶν, οἱ δὲ
ἐξ ἀρχῆς.   Not only is the latter sense stereotyped in theological language (ἀναγέννη-
ησις, *regeneratio*), but our Lord's saying is thus quoted by Just. M. (*Apol.* ii. p. 94
A) : καὶ γὰρ ὁ Χριστὸς εἶπεν· ἂν μὴ ἀναγεννηθῆτε, οὐ μὴ εἰσέλθητε εἰς τὴν βασιλείαν
τῶν οὐρανῶν.   Nonnus in v. 3 has τὸ δεύτερον, and in v. 7, ἑτέρην βαλβῖδα
γενέθλης.

[2] Lightfoot on John iii. 3.

Gentiles. It never occurred to him that Jesus could mean that. The very idea was revolting to his Pharisaic instincts, and he refused to entertain it. Half resentful, half puzzled he replied : "How can a man be born when he is old? Can he enter a second time into his mother's womb and be born?"

Attempt of Jesus to explain. So unspiritual and slow of heart was Nicodemus, though versed in all the lore of the Rabbinical schools. Jesus dealt very patiently with him and sought to open a way whereby the truth might enter his mind through the barrier of life-long prejudices. "Verily, verily I tell thee," He said, explaining the idea of regeneration, "unless one be born of water and the Spirit, he cannot enter into the Kingdom of God." It was an allusion to the Baptist's great word : "I baptise you in water unto repentance, but He that cometh after me shall baptise you in the Holy Spirit."[1] The Lord's attitude toward the work of John was identical with His *Mt. v. 17.* attitude toward the Mosaic Law : He came not to pull it down but to complete it. Repentance remained, and the renewal of the Holy Spirit was added thereto, making a full salvation. This is regeneration—repentance unto remission of sins and renewal by the Holy Spirit ; and this two-fold experience is the indispensable condition of entrance into the Kingdom of Heaven. The unspirituality of his ideas, common to him and his contemporaries, was the secret of all Nicodemus' misunderstanding. When he heard of regeneration, he thought of a carnal birth. And Jesus sought, after His own exquisite manner, to bring the spiritual truth home to his heart. As they sat there on the mountain, the cool breeze, fragrant with far-wafted odours, whispered among the foliage and kissed their brows, and Jesus made it a parable of the operation of the Holy Spirit. "Marvel not that I said to thee : 'Ye must be born anew.' The wind bloweth[2] where it will, and the voice thereof thou hearest, but knowest not whence it cometh and where it goeth. So is everyone that is born of the Spirit."

---

[1] There is thus no reference, as the Fathers and many moderns suppose, to Christian Baptism.

[2] τὸ πνεῦμα πνεῖ, "the breath breatheth." πνεῦμα, like רוּחַ and *spiritus*, means both "breath" and "wind." The Holy Spirit is the breath of God. *Cf.* Ezek. xxxvii. 9 ; John xx. 22. Vulg. : "Spiritus ubi vult spirat."

Nicodemus was only the more puzzled. "How can these things come to pass?" he faltered. His bewilderment was inexcusable. Had he never felt the stirring of God's Spirit in his soul, or heard the whisper of the heavenly voice, "soft as the breath of even," pleading, upbraiding, consoling? Such slowness of heart was amazing, and all the more that Nicodemus was a Rabbi. "Art thou the teacher of Israel," Jesus exclaimed, "and recognisest not these things?" Truly, if Nicodemus were a fair representative of his order, it was not from the wise and understanding that the Messiah must expect recognition, but rather from "the people of the land," who, ignorant as they might be, had open minds void of pre-possession and receptive of the truth. Such were the five men who had already attached themselves to Him. Simple Galileans though they were, they had understood what was hidden from Nicodemus and the rest of his order. And Jesus adduces them as witnesses to the truth of all that He has said: "Verily, verily I tell thee, what we know we are talking of, and what we have seen we are testifying; and our testimony ye do not receive." He had spoken of the common and familiar operations of the Holy Spirit, and was it likely that minds which had misunderstood such "earthly things," would understand "heavenly things"—the high truths of His Kingdom? *(margin: Increased bewilderment of Nicodemus.)*

Jesus held much further discourse ere the interview terminated, addressing Himself, it would seem, from this point onward rather to the disciples than to Nicodemus. When St John wrote his Gospel many years later, he retained an imperfect recollection of the wondrous things which had fallen upon his ears that great night, and he made no attempt to reproduce the discourse, merely indicating its trend. It would seem that Jesus spoke of His Passion and Resurrection. Following up, perhaps, what He had said in their hearing a few days before in answer to the rulers' request for a sign, He told His hearers that, "as Moses had lifted up the serpent in the wilderness, even so must the Son of Man be lifted up." He spoke of God's great love, how He had "so loved the world that He had given His only-begotten Son, that every one that believed in Him might not perish but have Eternal Life." And He spoke of the solemn responsibility which *(margin: Further discourse of Jesus, primarily to the disciples,)* must rest on all who heard the message of salvation. Such themes they could at that stage comprehend only very imperfectly, but, while they listened, their hearts would be stirred to wonder and enquiry ; and, as time passed and they penetrated ever deeper into the mystery of their Lord, they would recall His discourse and recognise the meaning of much which at the moment was hidden from them. That night in the Mount of Olives Jesus began a task which employed Him all through His ministry—the instruction of the men whom He had chosen to be with Him, and their preparation for the trust which should devolve upon them when He had returned to His Glory and left them to carry His salvation to the ends of the earth.

Nicodemus would go away in utter bewilderment. Yet the good seed had been sown in his heart, and after many days it sprang up and bore rich and abiding fruit.

CHAPTER VIII

AMONG THE SAMARITANS

"Quærens me sedisti lassus,
Redemisti crucem passus :
Tantus labor non sit cassus."—THOMAS DE CELANO.

John iii. 22-
36 ; Mt.
xiv. 3-5=
Mk. vi. 17-
20=Lk, iii.
19-20 ; Mt.
iv. 12=Mk.
i. 14=Lk.
iv. 14=
John iv. 1-
3 ; John iv.
4-42.
Sojourn in
Judæa.

WHEN the Feast was over, Jesus let the train of Galilean worshippers depart and tarried with His disciples in Judæa. It would seem that He betook Himself to the scene of His Baptism down by the Jordan, on purpose, no doubt, to recall the great experiences which had been vouchsafed to Him there, to consecrate Himself afresh to the work which had been given Him to do, and to enjoy a quiet season of meditation and communion ere entering upon His Galilean ministry. John was there no longer. The rulers had declared war against him and had driven him away. Safe nowhere within their jurisdiction, he had settled in Samaria near the frontier of Galilee, and was continuing his ministry at a place called Ænon, that is *Springs*, situated, according to ancient tradition, eight Roman miles south of Scythopolis and near to Salim and the Jordan.[1]   Bethany beyond Jordan was no longer thronged by an eager multitude hanging on the prophet's lips and crying "What must we do?" and thither Jesus repaired with His disciples.   His miracles at Jerusalem had excited no small wonderment, and a great crowd thronged after Him exceeding, alike in number and in enthusiasm, that which had gathered about John.   It would seem that Jesus, busied with His own high thoughts, left His disciples to deal much as they would with the multitude ; and, since two of them at least had been disciples of John, it is in no wise surprising that they adopted his methods and administered to penitents

---

[1] Jer. *De Loc. Hebr.*   Cf. Sanday, *Sacred Sites*, pp. 33-5.

the rite of Baptism. Jesus, the Evangelist is careful to mention, took no part in the administration.[1]

The Baptist at Ænon. Tidings of what was passing in Judæa reached John at Ænon. His disciples had fallen into controversy with a Jew[2] about ceremonial purification, the question at issue being probably the validity and authority of their Master's Baptism, a much vexed question at that crisis and for many a long day after; and in the course thereof their opponent had twitted them with the decline of their Master's popularity, telling them of the stir which the new prophet was making in Judæa. In sore discomfiture they betook themselves to John and told him what they had heard. He did not share their chagrin. He had all along declared that his ministry was merely a preparation for the Messianic Kingdom, and he rejoiced that the Greater than he had come and was winning His rightful recognition. " Ye yourselves bear me witness that I said, ' I am not the Messiah,' but ' I have been commissioned in advance of Him.' He that hath the bride is the bride-groom ; but the friend of the bridegroom that standeth and heareth him, greatly rejoiceth by reason of the bridegroom's voice. This then is my joy which hath been fulfilled. He must increase but I grow less." It was a noble declaration, revealing the greatness and generosity of the man. His own honour was nothing to him ; the cause was all, and, if only it prevailed he was content to be cast aside and forgotten.

Sudden departure of Jesus by reason of (1) apprehension of annoyance from the rulers ; Suddenly Jesus left Judæa and hastened northward, impelled by two motives. One was that tidings of the new movement down by the Jordan had reached the rulers at Jerusalem to their no small perturbation. They had been congratulating themselves that they were rid of John, and, behold, another and more powerful prophet had arisen and was carrying on his work. Jesus foresaw that a deputation from the Sanhedrin would presently appear on the scene ; and, weary of bootless disputation and reluctant to precipitate the inevitable crisis, He abruptly withdrew. And there was (2) tidings of the Baptist's arrest. another and more weighty reason for His sudden departure. Evil tidings had reached His ears. The Baptist had been

John i. 25;
Mt. xxi. 24-
7=Mk. xi.
29-33=Lk.
xx. 3-8.

---

[1] The Christian Sacrament of Baptism was not instituted until after the Resurrection (Mt. xxviii. 19). Jesus never baptised.

[2] John iii. 25 : μετὰ 'Ιουδαίου Tisch., W. H. ; μετὰ 'Ιουδαίων T. R.

arrested by Herod Antipas, one of the three sons of Herod
the Great among whom on the death of the latter his kingdom
had been portioned. Under the title of Tetrarch he ruled
over Galilee and Peræa. He had none of his father's
dexterity and none of his strenuous and indomitable energy;[1]
but he had all his father's vices—craft, cruelty, and licentious-
ness. Josephus ascribes the arrest to political considerations.
Observing the excited crowds that gathered round the
Baptist, the suspicious tetrarch dreaded a popular insurrection
and deemed it prudent to avert the danger by removing the
leader of the movement.[2] It is indeed likely that this is the
reason which Antipas alleged, yet he would hardly on the
strength of a mere suspicion have adopted so extreme a
measure, nor, had the Baptist been regarded as a plotter of
sedition, would his disciples have been allowed access to [Mt. xi. 2, 3]
him in his prison, lest they should act as his agents. The [=Lk. vii. 18-9, 22.]
Gospel-story records the shameful truth, passing over the
flimsy pretext in contemptuous silence. The tetrarch had
married the daughter of Aretas, King of Arabia.[3] This
ill-fated union was probably nothing more than a stroke of
policy. Arabia bordered upon Peræa, and Antipas thought
by allying himself with Aretas to secure peace upon his
southern frontier. After a while he visited Rome, and, while
lodging with his half-brother Herod Philip,[4] who lived as a
private citizen in the imperial capital, became enamoured of
the latter's wife, Herodias, a daughter of their half-brother
Aristobulus. The ambitious woman encouraged the tetrarch's
advances and agreed to forsake her husband and marry
Antipas on condition that he would divorce the daughter of
Aretas. The stipulation was prompted by jealousy. There
was no occasion for divorce, forasmuch as the Jewish law
allowed the king eighteen wives.[5]

It was a monstrous transgression, combining heartlessness,

---

[1] Josephus (*Ant.* xviii. 7. § 2) describes him as ἀγαπῶν τὴν ἡσυχίαν.

[2] *Ant.* xviii. 5. § 2.   [3] *Ibid.* § 1.

[4] Mt. xiv. 3 = Mk. vi. 17 = Lk. iii. 19 T. R. Josephus calls him simply Herod,
the family name. Since they were only half-brothers, it is the less strange that two
of Herod's sons should have been named Philip, the other being the tetrarch of
Ituræa and Trachonitis (Lk. iii. 1) who married Salome, Herodias' daughter. *Cf.*
Schürer, *H. J. P.* I. ii. 22.

[5] Schürer, *H. J. P.* I. i. p. 455.

treachery, adultery, and incest ; and John, after the manner of the ancient prophets and prophetic men in all ages, had sought out the guilty tetrarch and upbraided him to his face. At the moment Antipas quailed before the withering denunciation, and, had he been left to himself, he would have endured the affront. But the incident was noised abroad. It came to the ears of the Jewish rulers, and in pursuance of their quarrel with the Baptist they fanned the flame of the tetrarch's resentment.[1] Above all, Herodias was concerned. She had, in full measure, a bad woman's vindictiveness, and it was doubtless at her instigation chiefly that the bold prophet was arrested.

Through Samaria.

When He heard the heavy tidings, Jesus hurried north- ward. " It was necessary," says the Evangelist, " that He should pass through Samaria." There was indeed an alternative route, and, had He been bound direct for Galilee, He might have followed it, setting out from Bethany beyond Jordan, travelling up the eastern bank, and entering Galilee by the ford of Bethshean.[2] And, had He followed this route, it is likely that He would have fallen in with the Baptist by the way. Antipas had despatched the prisoner to his strong- hold of Machærus to the east of the Dead Sea,[3] and it is probable that, while Jesus was hastening northward, John was being dragged in chains down the other side of the Jordan. But it was not the Lord's purpose to meet with John and snatch him from his doom. Not thus had the Messiah come " to proclaim liberty to the captives and the opening of the prison to them that were bound." He hastened northward not to deliver John but because in the fall of that brave leader He recognised a call to step into the breach and unfurl the banner of His Kingdom in Galilee. And it was necessary that He should pass through Samaria, since Ænon was in Samaria, and He must visit the scene of the Baptist's labours if perchance He might win his dispirited followers. And there was yet another reason in the secret counsel of God. As the event proved, great work awaited Him in Samaria. The harvest was ripe for His sickle at the town of Sychar.

[1] From Mt. xvii. 12 = Mk. ix. 13 it appears that the rulers had a hand in John's arrest. παρεδόθη in Mt. iv. 12 = Mk. i. 14, perhaps implies *betrayal*. *Cf.* Mt. xxvi. 45 = Mk. xiv. 41.

[2] G. A. Smith, *H. G.* p. 256.   [3] Jos. *Ant.* xviii. 5. § 2.

The Galileans were accustomed to pass through Samaria Feud
when they went up to Jerusalem in companies at the festal Jews and
seasons,[1] but for solitary or defenceless travellers the eastern Samaritans.
route was safer. The Samaritans were hated by the Jews
and hated them in return with a bitter hatred. They were a
mongrel race. Their history began with the fall of the
northern Kingdom of Israel. In B.C. 721, when Shalmaneser
took Samaria, he carried Israel away into Assyria and brought
men from Babylon and Cuthah and Avva and Hamath and
Sepharvaim, and placed them in the cities of Samaria.[2]
Those heathen allied themselves with the remnant of the
children of Israel that had been overlooked in the deportation,
and blended their heathen religion with the worship of
Jehovah. Thus the Samaritans originated, and in B.C.
536 they would fain have aided the returned exiles in
rebuilding the Temple. Their offer was contemptuously Ezr iv. 1-3.
rejected, and ever after there was bitter animosity betwixt
them and the Jews. They set up a rival temple on Mount
Gerizim[3] and subjected the Jews to ceaseless annoyance.
They maltreated and sometimes slew Jewish travellers through
their territory.[4] One Passover-season during the governorship
of Coponius (A.D. 6-9), when according to custom the priests
had thrown open the gates at midnight, some Samaritans
stole in and polluted the Temple by scattering human bones
in the porches ; and ever after the perpetration of this wanton
outrage Samaritans were excluded from the sacred precincts.[5]

Of course the Jews retaliated. " With two nations," says the Ecclus. l.
Son of Sirach, " is my soul vexed, and the third is no nation : 25-6.
they that sit upon the mountain of Samaria, and the
Philistines, and that foolish people that dwelleth in Sichem."
On Jewish lips " Samaritan " was a term of abuse. The John viii.
Samaritans were cursed in the Temple ; their food was 48.
reckoned unclean, even as swine's flesh.[6] Indeed the Jews
had a worse hatred of the Samaritans than of the heathen,
herein exemplifying that singular fact whereto the history of
religion bears abundant and deplorable witness, that quarrels
are ever bitterest where differences are least and grounds of

---

[1] Jos. *Ant.* xx. 6. § 1.
[2] 2 Kings xvii ; Jos. *Ant.* ix. 14. § 1 ; x. 9. § 7.
[3] Lightfoot on John iv. 20.   [4] Lk. ix. 51-6 ; Jos. *Ant.* xx. 6. § 1.
[5] Jos. *Ant.* xviii. 2. § 2.   [6] Lightfoot on John iv. 8.

toleration most ample.   The Samaritans had much in
common with the Jews.   They accepted the Pentateuch, and,
if they rejected the rest of the Scriptures, so also, it seems, did
the Sadducees.[1]   They observed the Sabbath, practised the
rite of circumcision and all the other Mosaic ceremonies, and
celebrated the yearly festivals.   And, however it might be
tainted, they had Jewish blood in their veins.   And they
were proud thereof, though Josephus accuses them of claiming
kinship with the Jews in prosperity and disowning it in
adversity : they reckoned their descent from Joseph[2] and

John iv. 12. called Jacob their father.

Sychar.   After a two days' journey Jesus and His disciples found
themselves about six o'clock in the evening[3] approaching
the town of Sychar which, if it be rightly identified with the
modern El 'Askar, lay under the southern slope of Mount
Ebal.[4]   Less robust than His companions He was exhausted
with the long day's travel.   Within a mile of Sychar there
was a celebrated draw-well which, according to local tradition,
had been dug by the patriarch Jacob and was called then, as

Jacob's it is to this day, Jacob's Well.   The low parapet which
Well. enclosed it, offered an inviting seat to weary wayfarers.
Jesus sank down upon it, and the disciples left Him to rest
and pushed on toward the town to purchase provisions.[5]

Jacob's Well was had in great repute not only for its sanctity
but for the quality of its water.   There were other springs
in the neighbourhood, like that at El 'Askar which gushes
from Mount Ebal ; but, tainted by the calcareous soil, their
waters were unpalatable and injurious.   Being over a hundred
feet deep, Jacob's Well was fed from the bowels of the
earth ; its water was cool and sweet and healthful, and it is
no wonder that the people of Sychar, like their descendants

---

[1] *Cf.* p. 404.   [2] *Ant.* ix. 14. § 3 ; xi. 8. § 6 ; xii. 5. § 5.
[3] *Cf.* Append. II.
[4] See Hasting's *D. B.* under *Sychar* and *Jacob's Well* ; Taylor, *Say. of Fath.*,
Additional Note 48.
[5] In consequence of their proximity to them and the necessity of passing
through their territory the Jews were compelled in practice to compromise their
theoretic estimate of the Samaritans as unclean.   Their food, theoretically like
swine's flesh, was allowed unless mingled with their wine or vinegar ; their land
was clean, *i.e.* its fruits might be eaten ; their water was clean, *i.e.* it might be
used for drinking and washing ; their houses were clean, *i.e.* Jews might lodge in
them.   Lightfoot on John iv. 4, 8.

at the present day, should have been wont to fetch their drinking water thence.[1] As Jesus sat on the parapet, a woman approached with her empty pitcher, and He asked her for a drink. He was thirsty and needed refreshment, but He had a deeper reason for His request. The woman was one of the outcasts of society, and it needed not the eye of Jesus to read her character. It was written upon her face and advertised by her bearing. She was a sinner, and the heart of the Sinner's Friend went out toward her. Therefore He accosted her, if haply she would talk with Him and unbosom her guilt. *The Samaritan Woman.*

She answered, after the manner of her sort, impudently, and not without surprise. "How," she sneered, "dost thou, though thou be a Jew, ask drink of me, though I be a woman, a Samaritan woman?" "If," replied Jesus, "thou hadst known ' the gift of God ' and Who it is that saith to thee ' Give Me to drink,' thou wouldst have asked Him, and He would have given thee living water." Orientals called water, that precious boon, " the gift of God " ; and " living water " meant water from a running spring.[2] The Lord's speech puzzled the woman ; yet there was that in His voice and look which arrested her, and she answered with sudden courtesy : " Sir, thou hast nothing to draw with, and the pit is deep : whence hast thou ' the living water ' ? " Then, resuming her tone of insolence, she added : " Art *thou* greater than our father Jacob, who gave us the pit and himself drank from it and his sons and his cattle ? " " Everyone," said Jesus, " that drinketh of this water will thirst again ; but whosoever drinketh of the water which I shall give him, shall never thirst ; but the water which I shall give him will become within him a well of water springing up into life eternal." This seemed to her sheer absurdity, stark insanity, and she cried with feigned reverence, making a mock of Him : " Sir, give me this water, that I thirst not neither come all the way here to draw." *The colloquy.* *Cf. Ecclus xxiv. 21.*

---

[1] *P. E. F. Q.*, Jan. 1897, pp. 67-8; Apr. 1897, pp. 149-51 ; Jul. 1897, pp. 196-8. G. A. Smith, *H. G.* pp. 367-75.

[2] *Cf. Didache,* vii. Jacob's Well is at the present day " not an '*ain,* a well of living water, but a *ber,* a cistern to hold rain water " (*P. E. F. Q.* Jul. 1897, p. 197); it was certainly an '*ain* originally. *Cf.* Smith, H. G. p. 374.

Finding her impervious to gentleness, Jesus tried another way. He laid His hand upon her sin. " Go," said He, " call thy husband, and come here." That was a home-thrust. She winced, and faltered : " I have not a husband." " Well saidst thou : ' I have not a husband,' " He replied, casting her sin in her face ; [1] " for five husbands hast thou had, and now he whom thou hast is not thy husband. This is true that thou hast said." She was amazed. How could this stranger be acquainted with her shameful story ? " Sir," she stammered, essaying to divert the conversation into another channel by raking up that old controversy betwixt Jew and Samaritan, " I perceive that thou art a prophet. Our fathers in yonder mountain [2] worshipped ; and ye say that in Jerusalem is the place where it is necessary to worship———." " Believe me, woman," Jesus interrupted, sweeping the quibble aside and bringing the reluctant sinner face to face with God's real demand, " that there is coming an hour when neither in yonder mountain nor in Jerusalem will ye worship the Father. Ye worship what ye know not, we worship what we know, because salvation is of the Jews. But there is coming an hour, and it now is, when the true worshippers will worship the Father in spirit and truth ; for the Father seeketh such for His worshippers. God is a Spirit, and they that worship must worship in spirit and truth." Still she sought a loophole for escape, an excuse for delay. When that hour arrived all would be put right, and for the present what need to trouble ? " I know that Messiah is coming. When He hath come, He will declare unto us everything." " I," said Jesus with solemn and startling emphasis, " am He—I that am talking to thee."

Meanwhile the disciples had done their errand in Sychar, and just as Jesus made that great announcement, they

Amaze-
ment of the
disciples.
appeared on the scene in utter amazement. " They were marvelling," says the Evangelist, " that He was talking with a woman." And they might well marvel. It was wonder enough to find their Master in close and earnest converse with a Samaritan, but it was a still greater wonder that He should

---

[1] How did Jesus know the woman's past ? Was it revealed to Him by God ? Cf. John viii. 28. Or did He merely make a general allusion to her past, which the Evangelist has particularised from fuller knowledge ?

[2] I.e. Gerizim, towering behind them to the south-westward.

talk with a woman. Among the Jews women were very lightly esteemed. A Jew might not greet a woman;[1] he might not talk with a woman on the street, even if she were his own wife or daughter or sister.[2] In the Morning Prayer the men blessed God "who hath not made me a Gentile, a slave, a woman."[3] There was a strict sort of Pharisee nicknamed the Bleeding Pharisee, because he went about with closed eyes lest he should see a woman, and knocked his head against walls until it bled.[4] It was impiety to impart the words of the Law to a woman : sooner should they be burned.[5] The disciples might well marvel when they found their Master in converse with a woman, and such a woman.[6]

They stood aghast, neither attacking her nor remonstrating with Jesus. And she never heeded them. She had heard great tidings, and she hurried away to tell them, forgetting her water-pot. The disciples produced the provisions which they had procured, and invited Jesus to partake thereof. They had left Him weary and hungry, but His weariness and hunger were both forgotten in the rapture of that great hour. "I have food to eat," He said, " whereof ye know not " ; and, as they questioned each other whether some one could have brought Him food during their absence, He continued : "My food is to do the will of Him that sent Me, and finish His work."

Emotion o. Jesus.

Cf. Pss. xlii. 3; cf. 4.

The woman had meantime hastened with winged feet to the town. "Come," she cried to the townsfolk,[7] "see a man who told me all that I have done ! Can it be that this is the Messiah ? " Her words made a great stir. That whole region had of late been ringing with the Baptist's preaching, and it may even be that some of the people of Sychar had been at Ænon and heard his announcement that the Messiah

---

[1] Lightfoot on Lk. i. 29,

[2] Lightfoot and Wetstein on John iv. 27..

[3] Taylor, *Say. of Fath.* pp. 15, 26, 137-40. *Cf. P. E. F. Q.*, Oct. 1905, p. 349.

[4] Lightfoot on Mt. iii. 7.

[5] Lightfoot on John iv. 27. *Sot.* 21. 2 : " Whoso instructs his daughter in the Law, teaches her evil ways."

[6] R. Chanina and R. Oschaja were shoemakers in a town noted for its immorality, and, when harlots came to them for shoes, they would not raise their eyes, lest they should behold them (*Pesach.* 113. 2).

[7] τοῖς ἀνθρώποις = " the folk," not τοῖς ἀνδράσιν.

had come. They caught at the woman's suggestion that this wondrous Man who had come into their neighbourhood, was none other than the Messiah, and they poured out to see Him.

Reason thereof. Jesus espied them hastening toward Him, and the spectacle excited within Him strong emotion. " Have ye not a saying," He cried to the disciples, "'It is yet four months and the harvest cometh'?[1] Lo, I say unto you, lift up your eyes and behold the fields that they are white for harvest!" It was the very outset of His ministry. He had hardly begun to sow the good seed of His Kingdom, and, lo, a rich harvest was before Him! In that great hour when He sat on Jacob's Well and beheld the throng of Samaritans hurrying forth to hear the Word of His Salvation, the temptation which had assailed Him in the wilderness, again rushed upon Him. Already had He tasted the bitterness of Jewish unbelief; and, when He saw that multitude and read in their eager faces the hunger of their human hearts and their souls' yearning after God, He chafed at the limitations of His mission and questioned if it were indeed the Father's will that He should confine His grace to Israel, while the great world without was perishing for lack of knowledge. The harvest was ripe before His eyes, and it grieved Him that He must stay His hand and refrain from thrusting in the sickle. He longed for the day when the river of His grace would burst its bounds and stream abroad over the thirsty earth; and, if it may be said with befitting reverence, there is a tone of envy in His congratulation of the disciples that for them had been reserved this high ministry, this supreme consummation of which the prophets had dreamed and for which the saints had toiled: " Already he that reapeth receiveth wages and gathereth fruit unto life eternal, that both he that soweth and he that reapeth may rejoice together. For herein is the saying true: 'He that soweth is one and he that reapeth another.' I have sent you forth to reap that whereon ye have not laboured. Others have laboured, and ye into their labour have entered."

Ministry at Sychar. Very rich were the first-fruits which the Lord reaped at Sychar. So eager were its people, prepared as they

[1] Simply a husbandman's proverb. There is here no chronological datum.

were by the preaching of John, to hear His word that, at
their entreaty, He tarried with them two days; and, when
He took His departure, He left many of them, not marvelling
at His miracles—for it is not written that He wrought a
single miracle among them,—but rejoicing in His Salvation.
"It is no longer," they said to the woman, "because of thy
talk that we are believing. For we have heard for ourselves,
and know that this is in truth the Saviour of the World."

CHAPTER IX

John iv. 43-
54; Mt. iv.
13-6=Lk.
iv 31; Mk.
i. 14-5=
Mt. iv. 17

SETTLEMENT AT CAPERNAUM

" Clear silver water in a cup of gold,
   Under the sunlit steeps of Gadara,
   It shines—His Lake—the Sea of Chinnereth—
   The waves He loved, the waves that kissed His feet
   So many blessed days. Oh, happy waves !
   Oh, little, silver, happy Sea, far-famed,
   Under the sunlit steeps of Gadara ! "—SIR EDWIN ARNOLD.

Departure **IT** was not without regret that Jesus bade farewell to those
from
Sychar. kindly Samaritans and turned His face northward. He knew
well what difficulties awaited Him in Galilee. It was His own
country, and was it not proverbial that " in his native place
a prophet hath no honour " ? [1] Already during His sojourn
in Jerusalem had He got a taste of Israel's unbelief and
unspirituality. The rulers had required a sign, and the faith
of the multitude had been mere wonder. What marvel
though He were loath to quit Sychar where, though He had
wrought no miracle, He had been recognised as the Saviour of
the World, and begin the weary conflict with Israel's
unbelief ?

Arrival in   No sooner had He crossed the frontier than He found His
Galilee. forebodings realised. Those Galileans who had been at the
Feast, had witnessed His miracles and on their return had
spread the fame thereof. As He travelled through the
country, He was the object of gaping wonderment. He
Mt. iv. 13. repaired first of all to His old home at Nazareth, proceeding
thence toward Capernaum, the headquarters of His future
ministry. On the way betwixt Nazareth and Capernaum lay
Cana, and it was natural that He should stop there, at once to

---

[1] *Cf.* p. 214. John iv. 44 seems a *non sequitur*. Should not "for" be
"although"? (1) Orig. *In Joan.* xiii. § 54 : His own country was Judæa ; dishonoured there He went into Galilee. (2) Chrysost. *In Joan.* xxxiv : His own country
was Capernaum in lower Galilee ; He went to Cana in upper Galilee. (3) Euth.
Zig.: Nazareth was His own country (*cf.* Mt. xiii. 54) ; He "left" it (Mt. iv. 13),
i.e. hurried past it. Perhaps the idea is : just because Galilee was unbelieving, He
went thither.

visit the friend whose wedding He had recently blessed with At Cana,
His presence and perchance to discover what impression had
been produced by the miracle which He had wrought.   At
seven o'clock in the evening a stranger arrived at the village
in hot haste, seeking Jesus.   He was a distinguished personage, The
"a courtier" the Evangelist calls him, meaning probably an courtier.
official under Herod Antipas, the tetrarch of Galilee.   He was
in sore trouble.   His only son,[1] a mere child, was lying sick
of a deadly fever at Capernaum.   Galilee was ringing with
the fame of the Lord's miracles at Jerusalem, and the news of
His arrival in Galilee inspired the anxious father with a great
hope.   He left the couch of his dying child and, seeking out
Jesus, implored Him to go down to Capernaum and heal his
darling.

The request grated upon the Lord's ears.   It seemed to Hesitation
chime in with the prevailing sentiment.   Everyone was of Jesus.
wondering at His miracles and no one was giving a thought
to His message of salvation.   Was it thus with the courtier?
He had travelled all the way from Capernaum to seek healing
for his child ; but had he any sense of a still deeper need ?
If the shadow of death had not fallen upon his home, would
he ever have sought Jesus at all?   And, if the boon which he
craved were denied him, would he have any care for the
Kingdom of Heaven ?   Thus Jesus questioned within Himself
when the eager suppliant approached Him.   It seemed as
though unspiritual Israel were speaking through that man's
lips, and He exclaimed, addressing not the courtier but his
generation : "Unless ye see signs and wonders, ye will in no
wise believe."   "Lord," cried the troubled father, "come
down ere my child die !"   That agonised entreaty broke open
the flood-gates of the Lord's compassion.   It showed Him
that the courtier was no mere sign-seeker.   Defective as his
faith might be, he had a great sorrow in his heart, and to
such an appeal Jesus never turned a deaf ear.   He hastened
to grant the suppliant's prayer, exceeding what he had asked The
or imagined.   He did not go down to Capernaum and lay miracle.
His hand upon the child and recover him of his sickness.   He
sent His word and healed him on the instant across the inter- Cf. Ps. cvii.
vening distance.   "Go thy way," He said.   "Thy son liveth." 20.

---

[1] Such is the force of οὐ ὁ υἱός.

Since Capernaum was nigh twenty miles away and the night was at hand, the courtier would rest till morning ere setting out on his return-journey, and when he was still on the way, he met his slaves hastening to meet him with the joyful tidings that his boy had recovered.   On enquiry he ascertained that the fever had ceased in the very hour when Jesus said, " Thy son liveth " ; and it is no marvel that he and his whole household were won to faith.   It has been suggested, not without probability, that the courtier may have been Chuza, Herod's steward.[1]   It is not recorded that Chuza ever rendered any great service to the Kingdom of Heaven, but his wife Joanna was one of that noble band of women who ministered of their substance to the Lord and His Apostles, and lingered, with love stronger than death, about His Sepulchre.[2]

Lk. viii. 3; xxiv. 10.

Caper-
naum.

From Cana on the uplands Jesus descended to the Lake of Galilee and took up His abode at Capernaum.   It is some- what disappointing that the precise situation of this town, so dear and sacred to the Christian heart, is debated.

> " The waters glass no sail ; the ways have shrunk
>   Into a camel-path ; the centuries
> With flood and blast have torn the terrace bare
> Where the fox littered in the grapes. Ask not
> Which was ' His City ' 'mid this ruined life !
> None surely knoweth of Capernaum
> Whether 'twas here, or there."

For some thirteen centuries there have been two claimants to recognition—Tell-Hum near the head of the Lake, and Khan-Minyeh some three miles lower down ; nor has the diligence of modern exploration succeeded in adjudicating betwixt them.   The balance of evidence would seem to incline toward the latter, but the question still remains, and probably must always remain, undecided.[3]   Whatever its

---

[1] Godet on Lk. viii. 3.

[2] It is very generally assumed by modern critics and even by Wetstein, that this story is the Johannine version of the miracle of the healing of the Centurion's servant (Mt. viii. 5-13 = Lk. vii. 1-10).   Ewald regards the Johannine narrative as the more accurate, whereas Keim finds it replete with exaggerations designed to heighten the wondrousness of the miracle and glorify Jesus.   The theory is perhaps as old as the 2nd c. (cf. Iren. Adv. Hær. ii. 33. §1), and Chrysost. argues powerfully against it (In Joan. xxxiv).

[3] G. A. Smith, H. G. p. 456 ; Henderson, Palestine, § 113 ; art. Capernaum in D. B. and E. B. ; Sanday, Sacred Sites, pp. 36-48 ; P. E. F. Q., July 1907, pp. 220 ff. (Since D. Smith's time, the site of Capernaum has been established. —ED.)

precise position may have been, Capernaum was exquisitely situated. It stood on the north-west shore of the lovely Lake of Galilee, called of old the Sea of Chinnereth. "Seven seas," said the Lord, according to the Rabbis, "have I created, but of them all have I chosen none save the Sea of Chinnereth."[1] It was an inland lake some thirteen miles in length by eight at its broadest ; and it lay 682 feet below the level of the Mediterranean, sheltered from the upland breezes and basking in tropical heat. Its water was sweet to the taste[2] and swarmed with fish. Its blue expanse, girdled by crags of yellow limestone, "clear silver water in a cup of gold," was in our Lord's day dotted over with boats speeding to the breeze or hanging by their nets. The banks were studded with populous and busy towns : on the West Chorazin, Capernaum, Magdala, Tiberias, Sinnabris, Taricheæ ; on the East Bethsaida, Gerasa, Gamala, Hippos.·.

Num. xxxiv. 11; Josh. xiii. 27.

Since it is never mentioned in the Old Testament, it is likely that Capernaum came into existence after the Exile. The name means *Village of Nahum*, and tradition makes it the burial-place of the ancient prophet.[3] It was a most prosperous place, and three circumstances conduced thereto. First, it was the principal harbour of the fishermen who plied their business on the Lake. And a very thriving business it was. A little to the south lay the town of Taricheæ, that is *Pickleries*, where the fish were salted, and whence they were exported in kegs far and near.[4] It would seem that the fisher-quarter of Capernaum down by the water-side was called Bethsaida or *Fisher-home*, in full Bethsaida of Galilee, to distinguish it from the Peræan town of Bethsaida Julias on the other side of the Lake. It was the home of the fisherfolk, and there dwelt Simon Peter, Andrew his brother, and Philip.[5]

Reasons of its prosperity :

1. Fishing industry.

John i. 44; xii. 21.

---

[1] Wetstein on Mt. xiv. 34. [2] Jos. *De Bell. Jud.* iii. 10. § 7.

[3] Καφαρναούμ= כְּפַר נַחוּם. *Nahum* means " consolation," and Origen (*In Joan.* x. § 6) interprets "Field of Consolation."

[4] G. A. Smith in *E. B.*, art. *Trade and Commerce* § 78.

[5] Caspari, *Chronolog. and Geograph. Introd.* § 95. It is certain, despite G. A. Smith's argument to the contrary (*H. G.* p. 457 *sq.* ; art. *Bethsaida* in *E. B.*), that there were two Bethsaidas, B. Julias on the E. and another B. on the W. (1) After the feeding of the 5000 near Bethsaida Julias (Lk. ix. 10) Jesus sent the disciples " to the other side unto Bethsaida " (Mk. vi. 45). John vi. 17 proves that Bethsaida

2. Fertility of Land of Gennesaret. Moreover, Capernaum was enclosed behind and on either side by the Land of Gennesaret. The Rabbis were boundless in their praises of this fair and fertile tract which extended along the north-west shore of the Lake, thirty furlongs in length by twenty in breadth. Its name, they said, meant "Gardens of Princes." They identified Gennesaret with Chinnereth, and it got this name, they said, because "its fruits were sweet as a harp's sweet music."[1] And no less glowing is the description which the sober historian Josephus gives of this goodly land.[2] "It refuses not any plant by reason of its fatness, and the well-tempered air suits the different kinds. The hardy walnut flourishes in vast plenty, also the palm which is nourished by heat, and hard by the fig-tree and olive for which a softer air has been appointed. One would call it an ambition of Nature, which has done violence to itself to bring together plants that are at enmity, and a generous strife of the seasons, each, as it were, laying claim to the country. The royallest sorts, grape-cluster and fig, it supplies during ten months without intermission. For in addition to the good temperature of the climate it is watered by a most fertilising spring which the people of the country call Capernaum." This rich fruitfulness augmented the town's prosperity, and the scenes and employments of the fair garden furnished Jesus with many an apt and telling image: the ploughman, the vinedresser, the birds, the rain and the sunshine.

3. The Way of the Sea. Mt. iv. 15: cf. Is. ix. 1. Once more, the *Via Maris*, the great high-way which bore a heavy stream of traffic betwixt Damascus and the Levant, now a caravan of laden camels, then a Roman legion or a troop of Herod's soldiers on the march with gleaming armour and measured tread, skirted the north of the Lake. Capernaum was the first station on the route on **Mt. ix. 9-** the hither side of the Galilean frontier, and it had a custom-**10.** house with a staff of taxgatherers. There was also a Roman

---

was not distinct from Capernaum. (2) John (xii. 21) speaks of "Bethsaida of Galilee," plainly by way of distinguishing it from another Bethsaida. *Cf.* art. *Bethsaida* in *D. B.*; Henderson, *Palestine*, §§ 112-3.

[1] Wetstein on Mt. xiv. 34. Gennesaret, גַּנֵּי שָׂרִים. Chinnereth, כִּנּוֹר = *harp*.

[2] *De Bell. Jud.* iii. 10. § 8.

garrison in the town, and one of the officers had built a *Mt. viii. 5, 9; Lk. vii. 3-5.*
synagogue and presented it to the people.

Capernaum was thus no obscure village but a busy hive *Suitability as head-quarters of the Lord's ministry:*
of cosmopolitan life and multifarious activities. And it was
excellently situated for the purposes of the Lord's ministry.
Nowhere else could He have exercised so varied an influence *1. Central.*
or secured so extensive a hearing. Speaking in Capernaum
He spoke to the world. Southward lay the land of Palestine,
eastward populous Peræa, northward heathen Phœnicia ; and
St Mark affirms that, ere His ministry was far advanced, He *Mk. iii. 7-10.*
attracted hearers from all these quarters.

In reading the story of the Galilean ministry one marvels *2. Near Emmaus.*
at the number of sick folk that were continually being
brought to Jesus for healing ; and it may be a partial
explanation that some ten miles along the shore from
Capernaum, hard by Tiberias, the splendid capital which
Herod Antipas had recently built for himself and with
servile adulation had named after the Roman Emperor,[1] was
the sanatorium of Emmaus,[2] whither to this day, especially
in June and July, the very season when Jesus began His
ministry at Capernaum, invalids resort in order to bathe in
the medicinal waters which there well up warm from the earth.[3]
The proximity of those springs was one reason for Herod's
choice of the site of his new capital. The fame of Jesus would
reach Emmaus, and the sufferers, fired with a new hope, would
have themselves conveyed to Capernaum, if haply the wondrous Physician would lay His hand upon them and heal them.

When Jesus came to Capernaum, He found an expectant *Arrival of Jesus.*
audience. All Galilee was talking of His doings at the
Passover, and the people of Capernaum had special reason for
wonderment. John, Simon Peter, Andrew, and Philip were
their townsmen, and they had arrived before Jesus. It is
likely that they had parted from Him on the frontier of
Galilee and sought their homes while He repaired to Nazareth.
At all events they were already at Capernaum and had
resumed their occupations ere He appeared. And they
would talk of all that they had witnessed at Bethany and
Sychar. Moreover, the town had just been astonished by

---

[1] Jos. *Ant.* xviii. 2. § 1.   [2] G. A. Smith, *H. G.* p. 450.
[3] Plin. *H. N.* v. 15 ; Jos *Ant.* xviii. 2. § 3 ; *De Bell. Jud.* ii. 21. § 6 ; iv. 1. § 3.

the healing of the courtier's child and by that distinguished family's profession of faith in Jesus. It is no wonder that His appearance created a mighty stir and that He was observed with eager curiosity.

His initial message was at once old and new. The time hath been fulfilled," He said, "and the Kingdom of Heaven hath drawn nigh. Repent and believe in the Gospel." When John the Baptist appeared in the wilderness of Judæa, this had been the burden of his preaching : " Repent, for the Kingdom of Heaven hath drawn nigh"; and Jesus deliberately took up his cry. His purpose was to associate Himself with His forerunner and make it clear that He had not come to overthrow his work but to carry it on. It was no politic concealment of His claims in order to bring Himself into line with John when He announced merely that the Kingdom of Heaven had *drawn nigh*. It was ever thus that He spoke. When He sent forth the Twelve, He charged them to proclaim: "The Kingdom of Heaven hath drawn nigh," and He taught His disciples to pray : "Thy Kingdom come." He was indeed the Messiah, and His advent was the advent of the Messianic Kingdom ; yet the Kingdom of Heaven never comes until it is recognised and welcomed. The Pharisees once asked Him when the Kingdom should come, and He told them that it was " in their midst." It was in their midst, but not in their hearts ; it had drawn nigh, but had not come to them.

He took up John's message, but He added thereto something wholly new when He bade His hearers not only " repent " but " believe in the Gospel." The Gospel—the Good Tidings, "the Good Tidings of God," "the Good Tidings of the Kingdom "— is a word which was never heard from John's lips, nor was the thought of it in all his preaching ; but it was the keynote of the Lord's preaching from first to last. And no word could more truly express what He wrought for the children of men. "Removal of punishment," says St Chrysostom,[1] "absolution of sins, righteousness, sanctification, redemption, adoption, inheritance of Heaven, and kinship with the Son of God He came announcing to all, to His enemies, to the unfeeling, to them that sat in darkness and shadow. What could match these Good Tidings ? "

Marginal notes:
His initial message. Mk. i. 15.

Mt. iii. 2.

Mt. x. 7.
Mt. vi. 10=
Lk. xi. 2.

Lk. xvii. 20-21.

Mk. i. 14;
Mt. iv. 23.

[1] *In Matth.* i.

CHAPTER X

THE LORD'S CHOICE OF THE MEN WHO SHOULD BE WITH HIM

Mt. iv. 18-22 = Mk. i. 16-20 ; Lk, v. 1-11 ; Mt. viii. 19-22 = Lk. ix. 57-62.

" In simple trust like theirs who heard,
   Beside the Syrian sea,
The gracious calling of the Lord,
Let us, like them, without a word,
   Rise up and follow Thee."—WHITTIER.

NOT the least important task which engaged Jesus in the course of His ministry, was the formation and instruction of an inner circle of disciples. All who believed on Him were called disciples ; and, though they did not follow Him whithersoever He went, they rendered good service to His cause by remaining in the places where His grace had found them and testifying what He had done for their souls. But this was not enough. It was a great work that Jesus had undertaken, and He needed helpers. He needed also faithful comrades who would continue with Him in His temptations and afford Him support and sympathy in His hours of weakness and disappointment. Above all, a day was coming when He must depart, and, unless there were loyal hands to take it up and carry it forward, His work would fall to the ground. Formation of a disciple-band. Lk. vi. 13; John iv. 1; vi. 60, 66-7.

All this Jesus foresaw from the outset ; and no sooner had He entered upon His active ministry than He set about choosing the men who should be with Him continually. Since the time was short and they would have much to learn, much also to unlearn, it was needful that they should be chosen as early as might be. Yet haste were perilous. Ere they were called to a trust so high and solemn they must be tried and evince their fitness.

There were four of the men of Capernaum whom, ere He settled there, Jesus had sufficiently approved—the two brothers Simon and Andrew, John, and Philip. Down at Bethany beyond Jordan they as well as Nathanael of Cana, Disciples already won.

had given their hearts to Him, and it had been so ordered by the providence of God that they had been in His company almost ever since. They were engaged once more in their old employments, but the time had come when they must leave all and cast in their lot with Jesus. It chanced one morning that He was down by the water-side where the fishermen beached their boats, and the people were pressing upon Him to hear the Word of God from His lips and
Discourse by the Lake. almost, in their eagerness, thrusting Him into the Lake. He espied hard by two skiffs which had come ashore after an unsuccessful night's fishing. One of them belonged to Simon and Andrew, who were washing their nets on the beach, and the other to John and his brother James, who were in the skiff with their father Zebedee, mending their nets. Jesus got into the former and bade Simon push her out a little way from the shore. And there He sat and discoursed to the multitude ranged along the sloping beach down to the very brink.

The haul of fish. His discourse ended, He addressed Himself to a greater task. " Put out into the deep," He said to Simon, " and let down your nets for a haul." It seemed a useless attempt. Night was the time for fishing, when all was still and there was no glare upon the water.[1] Yet such was the ascendancy which Jesus had won over those men, that they immediately complied. " Master," said Simon in fisher phrase,[2] " all through the night we toiled and took nothing, but on the strength of Thy word I will let down the nets." To their amazement they made a huge haul. So many fish were in the net that it was like to break.[3] They beckoned to their mates, James and John, to put off to their assistance, and the fish loaded both the boats well-nigh to sinking.

Simon's amazement. Simon was a big-hearted, impulsive man who always blurted out the thought of the moment, often speaking unadvisedly and immediately regretting it. He was amazed at the miracle. He had indeed seen Jesus work greater miracles, but never one which touched him so closely. " Depart from

---

[1] *Cf.* Plin. *H. N.* ix. 23.

[2] ἐπιστάτης, properly a sailor's word, " captain." *Cf.* Lk. viii. 24 ; Xen. *Œc* xxi. 3.

[3] διερρήσσετο (Imperf.). *Cf.* ὥστε βυθίζεσθαι αὐτά, Vulg.: " ita ut *pene* mergerentur."

me ; for I am a sinful man, Lord," he cried, no longer calling Him " Master " but exchanging his fisher phrase for one more reverential. Here, as on another and greater occasion, he " knew not what he was saying." That the Lord should Lk. ix. 33. depart from him was really the last thing that he desired. " Fear not," said Jesus. " Henceforward thou shalt be a catcher of living men."

The laden skiffs made their slow way to shore, and, when Call of Jesus had disembarked, He said to Simon and Andrew : Simon and Andrew, " Follow Me, and I will make you to become fishers of men." James and Then, going along the beach to the other boat, he addressed John. a like call to James and John. They all obeyed. They abandoned everything, and cast in their lot with the homeless Son of Man. Their earthly employment was a parable of their divine vocation.[1] As David was taken from the sheep- 2 Sam. vii cote to be a shepherd to Israel, and Paul from his tent- 8 ; Ps. lxxviii. making to be a maker of heavenly tabernacles, so they were 70-71 ; taken from their boats to be fishers of men.[2] 2 Cor. v. 1-4.

Jesus was very careful in the choice of the men who A Scribe should be with Him. In every recorded instance He made rejected. the choice, and there are three incidents which exemplify His procedure. Once He was accosted on the road by a Scribe, one of the order of learned Pharisees, otherwise styled Lawyers or Doctors of the Law. They were the Teachers of Cf. John Israel, and bore the honourable title of Rabbi.[3] " There iii. 10. approached Him *a single Scribe*," says St Matthew, meaning perhaps that the incident was unique or else depicting by a graphic touch the manner of the great man's approach, not amid a jostling multitude but in solitary state.[4] " Teacher," he said, " I will follow Thee wherever Thou goest."

It was a request for enrolment in the Lord's company, and the motive which prompted it is very apparent. The Scribe was persuaded that Jesus was the Messiah ; and, entertaining the current ideal of the Messianic Kingdom, he was confident that, when the Master came to His throne and dispensed

---

[1] *Cf.* Orig. *In Num.* xvii. § 4.

[2] Mt. and Mk. recount simply the call, but they imply Lk.'s miracle. Jesus might have hailed Simon and Andrew out on the deep (*cf.* John xxi. 5), but it is incredible that He should have shouted His solemn call across the water. The casting of the net (Mt. Mk.) implies the previous putting out into the deep (Lk.).

[3] Schürer, *H. J. P.* ii. 1, pp. 313 *sqq.*

[4] See, however, Moulton's *Gram. of N. T. Gk.* i. pp. 96 *sq.*

honours and offices among His faithful followers, He would
award the chief dignity to one so distinguished in rank and
learning.[1] It is no marvel that he should have reasoned thus.

Mt. xx. 20-
28 = Mk. x.
35-45. Not many days before the Crucifixion James and John were
dreaming the selfsame dream. Jesus promptly dissipated
the illusion which was floating before the aspirant's imagination, showing in a single brief sentence what must be the
lot of such as followed Him wherever He went. "The
foxes," He said, "have holes, and the birds of the heaven
nests ; but the Son of Man hath not where to lay down His
head." The Scribe was dreaming of a golden future, but
behold the reality—a life of sacrifice, privation, contumely !
Was he prepared for this?

A reluctant
disciple
compelled. Jesus received no one into His company until He was
satisfied of his fitness ; but, on the other hand, when He was
satisfied thereof, He would admit no excuse. Once He
addressed the great call to a disciple who, tradition says,[2]
was none other than Philip and who certainly resembled
Philip in his timorousness and diffidence. The man demurred
and pled a prior claim: "Lord, permit me first to go away
and bury my father." "Leave the dead," Jesus sternly
replied, "to bury their own dead, but thou—follow thou
Me."[3]

At the first blush the Lord's behaviour here seems very
cruel. Is it possible that the gentle Jesus detained a son
from the sacred duty of paying the last tribute of reverence
to his dead father? It was indeed the manner of the Rabbis
to trample on natural affection, arrogating to themselves the
first place in their disciples' regard and service. "If," they
said, "a disciple's father and his master have lost aught, his
master's loss has the precedence ; for his father indeed brought
him into this world, but his master, who has taught him
wisdom, has introduced him into the world to come. If his
father and his master be carrying a burden, let him remove
his master's burden first and then his father's. If his father
and his master be in captivity and he have not wherewith
to redeem both, first let him redeem his master and

[1] *Cf.* Chrysost., Jer., Hil.
[2] Clem. Alex. *Strom.* III. iv. § 25.
[3] Chrysost. and Clem. quote the *logion* in this spirited and probably authentic
form : ἄφες τοὺς νεκροὺς θάψαι τοὺς ἑαυτῶν νεκρούς, σὺ δὲ ἀκολούθει μοι.

then his father." [1]   And they insisted that, unless there were no other to discharge it, even the sacred office of burying the dead should not interrupt the study of the Law.[2]

It seems as though the behaviour of Jesus in this instance fully matched the arrogance and inhumanity of the Rabbis; but a little consideration places it in another light and reveals the disciple's plea as a palpable evasion. There is force in St Chrysostom's observation that the work of burial was not all. " It had been further necessary to busy himself about the will, the division of the inheritance, and all the rest that follows thereupon; and thus wave after wave would have caught him and borne him very far from the haven of truth. Therefore He draws him and nails him to Himself." [3]   A great issue was at stake, and even though the disciple's father had been dead, it were no marvel that Jesus, apprehensive lest he should be lost to the Kingdom of Heaven, should have detained him.   But in fact his father cannot have been dead; he cannot even have been dying.   Immediate inter- *Cf.* Acts v. ment is necessary in the sultry East; and, had his father 6. been either dead or dying, the disciple should have been at home performing the funeral rites or closing the dying eyes; and it would have been utter shamelessness had he excused himself from following Jesus on the score of a duty which he was all the while palpably neglecting.   And the truth is that his excuse was a mere pretext for delay.   He craved a truce from following Jesus that he might tend his father in his declining years, employing a phrase which is common to this day in the unchanging East.   It is told [4] that, when a youth was counselled by a Syrian missionary to complete his education by travelling in Europe, he answered : " I must first bury my father."   His father was in excellent health, and the youth meant merely that domestic duties had a prior claim.   Jesus did not make light of those sacred duties, but he declared that the claims of the Kingdom of Heaven are paramount, and those to whom the heavenly call is addressed

---

[1] *Cf.* Taylor, *Say. of Fath.* iv. 17, n. 21.

[2] Introd. § 1.

[3] Contact with a dead body made a Jew unclean for seven days (Num. xix. 11 *sqq.*), and there were seven days of mourning (Ecclus. xxii. 12).

[4] Wendt, *Lehr. Jes.* ii. 70, n. 1, E. T.

must obey it at every hazard, considering that, "if they venture all for God, they engage God to take care of their concernments."

A half-hearted volunteer rejected. Another time there came a man to Jesus and said : " I will follow Thee, Lord ; but first permit me to bid farewell to my household."[1] Like the Scribe he volunteered, and like Philip he craved respite. And his request seems most reasonable. It resembles Elisha's when Elijah cast his mantle 1 Kings xix. 19-21. upon him : "Let me, I pray thee, kiss my father and my mother, and then I will follow thee." Elisha was busy ploughing, and it seems as though the ancient story leaped into the mind of Jesus and suggested His reply. "No one," He said, adapting a familiar proverb,[2] "having put his hand upon a plough and looking backward,[3] is well set for the Kingdom of God." A disciple who hankers after the past is like a ploughman who, instead of fixing his eye steadily ahead, looks backward or aside, letting the share swerve and drawing a crooked furrow.

It may seem strange that, while Elijah let Elisha go and kiss his father and mother, Jesus should have dealt so sternly with this man ; but in truth the cases were very different. Elisha did not volunteer, and, when he was called, he instantly left his oxen and ran after Elijah with eager alacrity ; but this man took the first word and betrayed his half-heartedness by accompanying his offer with a reservation. He was persuaded that he ought to cast in his lot with Jesus, and he proposed a compromise. Nor was Jesus for a moment deceived. He read the man's thoughts. He perceived that he was divided betwixt his home and the Kingdom of Heaven, and clearly foresaw what the issue would be if he had his way. Should he go home and announce his intention of following Jesus, his friends would cry out against it, and, overborne by their arguments and entreaties, he would abjure the resolution which he had taken in an hour of enthusiasm. Once let him taste the delight of

---

[1] ἀποτάξασθαι τοῖς εἰς τὸν οἶκόν μου, either "take leave of those in my house" (cf. 2 Cor. ii. 13 ; Acts xviii. 18) ; or "renounce the things in my house," renunciare negociis domesticis (cf. Lk. xiv. 33).

[2] Cf. Plin. H. N. xviii. 49 : " Arator nisi incurvus prævaricatur."

[3] βλέπων εἰς τὰ ὀπίσω. Some MSS., Orig., Cyrill., Chrysost., Athanas. have στραφεὶς εἰς τὰ ὀπίσω, "facing right round."

home, and it would happen with him as with the lotus-eaters :

> "Surely, surely, slumber is more sweet than toil, the shore
> Than labour in the deep mid-ocean, wind and wave and oar ;
> Oh rest ye, brother mariners, we will not wander more."

Jesus knew the peril of dallying with conviction and the imperious necessity of instant obedience to the heavenly vision which comes to a man but once and quickly fades.

CHAPTER XI

Mk. i. 21=
Lk. iv. 31;
Mt. v. 17-
30 (Lk. xii.
58-9),
33-7; vi. 1-
8, 16-8; vii.
28-9; Mk.
i. 22-8=Lk.
iv. 32-7.

IN THE SYNAGOGUE OF CAPERNAUM

" 'Was it,' the Lord then said, ' with scorn ye saw
The old law observed by Scribes and Pharisees?
I say unto you, see *ye* keep that law
More faithfully than these.' "—MATTHEW ARNOLD.

The Jewish Synagogue. ONE Sabbath Day soon after His settlement at Capernaum, probably the first Sabbath thereafter, Jesus repaired to the Synagogue. The synagogal system was an institution of later Judaism, and it was admirably adapted to foster the religious life of the nation.[1] Every town, nay, every village had its synagogue, which exercised a powerful and beneficent influence upon the community. It was controlled by ten Officials. officials, who must be men of leisure and learning that they might devote themselves to the administration of their offices and the study of the Law. Eight of them had clearly defined functions. Three composed a court for the settlement of cases within their province, including debt, theft, loss, restitution, seduction, the admission of proselytes, elections ; and they were called the Rulers of the Synagogue. Another Lk. iv. 20. was the Officer of the Synagogue, and his business was to lead the prayers, see to the reading of the Law, and on occasion preach. He was styled also the Angel or Messenger of the Church and the Overseer of the Congregation. There were also three Deacons who cared for the poor, collecting alms from house to house and at the meetings of the congregation. These seven were known as " the Seven Good Men of the Town." Then there was the Targumist or Interpreter who, as the Scripture passages were read low in his hearing, rendered them aloud in the vernacular. The congregation assembled twice on the Sabbath—in the forenoon and again in the evening ; and there were also two week-day meetings, on Monday and Thursday, the second and

[1] *Cf.* Lightfoot on Mt. iv. 23 ; Schürer, *H. J. P.* II. ii. pp. 52 *sqq.*

fifth days of the week. It was a peculiarity of the synagogal system that any qualified worshipper might deliver the sermon;[1] and, when the Ruler of the Synagogue observed such an one in the congregation, he would ask him if he had " any word of exhortation unto the people." This custom afforded Jesus a golden opportunity, whereof He gladly availed Himself from the very outset of His ministry. Acts xiii. 15. Lk. iv. 15; Mt. iv. 23; ix. 35.

On that Sabbath after His settlement at Capernaum He repaired to the Synagogue and at the Ruler's call discoursed to the congregation. It was the first formal sermon that He ever preached, and happily a report of it has been preserved by St Matthew, embedded in that precious collection of our Lord's sayings commonly called " The Sermon on the Mount."[2] It was a great discourse, and it is in no wise surprising that it made a profound impression upon an audience accustomed to the dreary ineptitudes of Rabbinical teaching. "They were astonished at His teaching; for He was teaching them as one that had authority, and not as their Scribes." Jesus in the Synagogue of Capernaum.

It was in truth the Manifesto of the Messiah. Jesus knew what suspicion His teaching must arouse in minds jealous for traditional orthodoxy. His association with the Baptist was in itself sufficient to create a prejudice against Him. John had broken with the religion of his day. He had kept aloof from Jerusalem and was never found in the Temple; and he had pictured the Messiah as a ruthless reformer, axe and winnowing-fan in hand. It was therefore needful that Jesus should at the outset of His ministry declare His loyalty to the ancient faith. "Think not," He began, "that I came to pull down [3] the Law or the Prophets. I came not to pull down but to complete. For verily I tell you, until the heaven and the earth pass away, a single iota or a single tip [4] shall in no wise pass away from the Law until everything come to pass." And thus indeed it was that Jesus ever regarded the Scriptures and their sacred institutions. He reverenced the Temple, calling it His Father's House. His sermon. Assertion of His loyalty to the Law. Lk. ii. 49; John ii. 16; Mt. xvii. 25-6.

[1] Cf. Lk. iv. 16; Phil. De Septen. vi.   [2] Cf. Introd. § 8.

[3] καταλῦσαι: cf. Mt. xxiv. 2=Mk. xiii. 2=Lk. xxi. 6; Mt. xxvi. 61=Mk. xiv. 58; 2 Cor. v. 1.

[4] Proverbial, like "the dot of an i or the stroke of a t." Cf. Lightfoot and Wetstein. In the early Church a momentous controversy turned on the iota of difference betwixt ὁμοούσιος and ὁμοιούσιος.

He kept the Feasts. He loved the Old Testament. It was His armoury in His controversies and a never-failing fountain of refreshment to His weary spirit. The Scriptures spake of Him ; their every ordinance was a prophecy of His salvation ; and He had come to complete them as the day completes the dawn, as the substance completes the shadow. He gave what they promised.

Enlargement of its scope.
Cf. Mt. xi. 11=Lk. vii. 28.
"Therefore," He continues, alluding evidently to John the Baptist, " whosoever shall unloose one of these commandments, even the least, and teach men so, least shall he be called in the Kingdom of Heaven ; but whosoever shall do and teach, he shall be called great in the Kingdom of Heaven. For I tell you that, unless your righteousness exceed that of the Scribes and Pharisees, ye shall in no wise enter into the Kingdom of Heaven." In this bold sentence He, as it were, flings down the gauntlet ; He strikes the first blow in the conflict which He waged even unto death against that spirit of externality and formalism which was the curse of contemporary Judaism. And in the remainder of His discourse He makes good His claim that so far from relaxing the obligation of the Law He required a fuller and deeper obedience, citing three of its precepts and showing in regard to each how the Rabbis narrowed it and how He widened it and increased its content.

Thoughts even as acts :
(1) Hatred even as murder.
" Ye have heard that it was said to them of old : ' *Thou shalt not kill.*' " According to the Rabbinical interpretation this precept of the Decalogue took cognisance merely of *acts*, but Jesus extends its scope and comprehends within the sweep of its prohibition *thoughts* as well, not only the deed of violence but the disposition which prompts it. " It was said to them of old time : ' *Thou shalt not kill ; and whosoever killeth shall be liable to the Judgment.*' But I tell you that everyone that is angry with his brother shall be liable to the Judgment ; and whosoever shall say to his brother : ' Raka ! ' shall be liable to the Sanhedrin ; and whosoever shall say : ' Thou fool ! ' shall be liable to the Gehenna of Fire."

Our Lord's meaning here is obscure only because He employs certain terms which are no longer familiar. The Judgment was the court of the Rulers of the Synagogue. And what of " Raka "? The word has long been a puzzle to

interpreters.[1]   It would seem that it was a mere interjection.
St Augustine learned this from " a certain Hebrew " whom
he questioned on the subject.   " He said it was a word
which had no signification but expressed the emotion of a
disdainful mind."   And St Chrysostom further explains that
it was used in Syriac much like "you" in addressing a
servant or a beggar : " Begone, you ! "   " Tell so-and-so,
you ! "[2]   The Sanhedrin was the supreme court of the
Jewish nation, which took cognisance of cases of blasphemy
and which alone could pronounce sentence of stoning.   Then
what was the Gehenna of Fire ?   Gehenna is the Græcised
form of Ge-Hinnom, the Valley of Hinnom, which lay outside the southern wall of Jerusalem.[3]   Once a pleasant spot,
it was profaned by the worship of Moloch, and at the Jer. vii. 31-
Reformation under Josiah it was defiled.   Thither the re- 3; 2 Kings xxiii. 10.
fuse of the city was conveyed and the bodies of the worst
criminals were cast out a prey to pariah dogs and carrion
birds.   It was choked with putrefaction and stench, and fires
were kept burning to purify the poisoned atmosphere.[4]   In
later days that horrid den, where the worm died not and the Mk. ix. 48;
fire was not quenched, became a symbol of the place of cf. Is. lxvi. 24.
doom.   Here, however, it bears its literal and not its eschatological significance.

And now the Lord's meaning is very plain.   In terse and
graphic language which would arrest His hearers and strike
home to their consciences, He depicts a double *crescendo* of
sin and punishment.   On the one side He set an ascending
scale of offences, each rising out of and including the last :
Anger, Contempt, Abuse.[5]   Over against these grades of sin
stand their appropriate punishments : for Anger the Judgment,
for Contempt the Sanhedrin, for Abuse the Gehenna of Fire.
He that is angry with his brother is even as the culprit who

---

[1] Generally connected with Hebr. רֵק, *empty*.   Jer. : "inanis aut vacuus, quem
nos possumus vulgata injuria absque cerebro nuncupare."   A.V. marg. : " Vain
fellow " ; *cf.* Ja. ii. 20 ; ὦ ἄνθρωπε κενέ.   Otherwise derived from Gk. ῥάκος, *rag;*
f. Aug. *De Serm. Dom. in Mon.* i. § 23.

[2] *In Matth.* xvi.   This use of σύ is a familiar classical idiom.   *Cf.* Soph. *O.T.*
532.   Lat. *Heus tu !*

[3] גֵּי הִנֹּם, γέεννα   *Cf.* Orig. *C. Cels.* vi. 25-6.

[4] *Cf.* Lightfoot, ii. *Præfat. ad Lect.*

[5] *Cf.* Aug. *De Serm. Dom. in Mon.* i. § 24.

is arraigned before the Rulers of the Synagogue. He whose
anger passes into contempt is as guilty as the blasphemer
who is haled before the Sanhedrin. And he who adds abuse
to contempt is on a level with those vile criminals whose
bodies are cast forth into the loathsome pit of Gehenna.

By such picturesque instances Jesus illustrates and
enforces His doctrine, so novel and amazing to Jewish ears,
that the thought of hatred is in God's judgment no less
heinous than the deed. The Jews were very scrupulous
about external purity, and it was laid down in their Law that,
if on his way to the Temple to offer his Paschal Lamb a man
should recollect that he had leaven in his house, he should
hasten back and remove it, and then, when he had purged his
house, carry his offering to the altar.[1] But far more needful
is it, Jesus declares, that the worshipper should purge his
heart ere making his approach to God. " If therefore thou
art offering thy gift at the altar and there rememberest that
thy brother hath aught against thee, leave there thy gift
before the altar, and go thy way : first be reconciled to thy
brother, and then come and offer thy gift."

(2) Lust   " Ye have heard," Jesus continued, adducing a second
even as
adultery. instance of His doctrine, " that it was said : ' *Thou shalt not
commit adultery.*' But I tell you that every one that eyeth
a woman with the intent to lust after her hath already
committed adultery with her in his heart." This sentence
is well weighed and scrupulously just.[2] It is not said that
desire is sin. Desire visits every breast ; and only when it is
harboured and cherished, does it pass into sin and make the
man an offender. And truly the thought of lust is even as
the act. It is restrained only by the lack of opportunity.
And it is ever within a man's breast that the issue is
determined. The sin which puts him to an open shame, is no
sudden catastrophe but the climax of a long course of secret
sinning. He has already been defeated on the hidden battle-
field of his soul.

The consciences of His hearers would confess the truth of
this doctrine of Jesus. It needed no proof, and He followed
it up with a counsel which at first sounds very strangely on

[1] *Cf.* Wetstein, Lightfoot.
[2] *Cf.* Aug. *De Serm. Dom. in Mon.* i. §§ 33-4.

His lips. "If thy right eye ensnare thee,[1] tear it out and fling it from thee; for it is expedient for thee that one of thy members be destroyed and not thy whole body flung into Gehenna. And if thy right hand ensnare thee, hack it off and fling it from thee , for it is expedient for thee that one of thy members be destroyed and not thy whole body go away into Gehenna." It is told of the ancient philosopher Democritus that, lest he should behold vanity, he put out his eyes;[2] nor was Origen the only saint of early days who, in faithful though erring obedience to the Lord's behest, mutilated his flesh for the Kingdom of Heaven's sake.[3] It is difficult to believe that this was indeed the Lord's requirement. It is alien from the spirit of Him who came not to destroy the body but to redeem it and to bestow upon the children of men "more life and fuller"; and is it not also inconsistent with His doctrine that the supreme necessity is inward purity, purity not alone of act but of thought? A man might be a thief at heart though he cut off his hands lest he should steal; and might still retain his passions, though he plucked out his eyes lest he should behold vanity. The pure in heart alone are guiltless in God's judgment; and they walk unscathed amid the world's allurements, and have no need to seclude themselves either by closing the avenues of sense or by repairing to a hermitage. "He that can apprehend and consider vice with all her baits and seeming pleasures, and yet abstain, and yet distinguish, and yet prefer that which is truly better, he is the true wayfaring Christian. I cannot praise a fugitive and cloister'd vertue, unexercis'd and un-breath'd, that never sallies out and sees her adversary, but slinks out of the race, where that immortall garland is to be run for not without dust and heat."[4]

Self-multilation is in truth no heroic act. Rather is it the resource of one who, half cowardly, shrinks from the moral conflict and, half unbelieving, will not yield himself unreservedly to the grace which bringeth salvation. And assuredly it was never in the thoughts of Jesus. "If," says St Chrysostom,[5] "He had been speaking of members, He

[1] Such is the proper meaning of σκανδαλίζειν. σκανδάληθρον = the *spring* of a trap. Suidas: σκανδάληθρα· τὰ ἐν ταῖς παγίσιν ἐπικαμπῆ ξύλα. See Wetstein.

[2] Tert. *Apol.* § 46.   [3] Eus. *H. E.* vi. 8.

[4] Milton, *Areopag.*   [5] *In Matth.* xvii,

Gal. iv. 15

would not have spoken of one eye nor of the right alone, but of both. For the man who is ensnared by the right eye, will obviously be likewise affected by the left also." St Augustine aptly quotes the phrase "I love you more than my eyes."[1] 1 Sam. xi 2; Exod. xxix. 20. The right member was accounted superior; and, when Jesus spoke of the right eye and the right hand, He meant the dearest and most precious possessions. His counsel is: "Seek after purity of heart, and count no sacrifice too costly or too painful that you may win it."

(3) Truth in the inward parts. "Ye have heard that it was said to them of old: ' *Thou shalt not break an oath, but thou shalt render unto the Lord thine oaths.*' But I tell you not to swear at all." It is surprising that Jesus should speak thus. All over the ancient world the oath was held in high veneration, and not least in Gen. xxii 16-8; Hebr. vi. 16-8. the land of Israel.[2] It is written in the Old Testament that, when the Lord made His promise to Abraham, "purposing to show more abundantly unto the heirs of the promise the immutability of His purpose," He confirmed it by an oath. Rom. i. 9-10; 1 Cor. xv. 31; 2 Cor. xi. 31; Gal. i. 20. Mt. xxvi. 63-4. And not only was St Paul accustomed to support his asseverations by oaths, but Jesus Himself let the High Priest put Him on oath when He stood before the Sanhedrin. The truth is that, when He bade His hearers in the Synagogue of Capernaum abstain from the swearing of oaths, He was speaking, if it may be said with befitting reverence, in a spirit of playful raillery and, moreover, was condemning rather the abuse of the practice than the practice itself.

It is an evidence of prevalent abuse that the pious Essenes, like the Quakers, eschewed swearing, deeming it worse than perjury.[3] And indeed the abuse was manifold. It was a serious aspect of the case that custom had divested the practice of its solemnity. Light use of oaths is ever characteristic of a godless time. So it was in England in Chaucer's day.

> "Vengeance shal not parten from his hous,
> That of his othes is outrageous.

---

[1] *De Serm. Dom. in Mon.* i. § 37. *Cf.* Deut. xxxii. 10; Ps. xvii. 8; Prov. vii. 2; Zech. ii. 6. ὀφθαλμός and *oculus* frequently in classics in sense of "darling." *Cf.* Catull. iii. 5.

[2] *Cf.* Josh. ix. 19; Jud. xi. 35; Herod. vi. 86; Plaut. *M. G.* **v.** 21-4; Hor *Sat.* ii. 3. 179-81.

[3] Jos. *De Bell. Jud.* ii. 8. § 6.

> By Goddes precious herte, and by his nailes,
> And by the blood of Crist, that is in Hailes,
> Seven is my chance, and thin is cink and treye:
> By Goddes armes, if thou falsely pleye,
> This dagger shal thurghout thin herte go."[1]

And even so it was among the Jews in our Lord's Day. In
their common intercourse they would invoke the most august
and sacred institutions with thoughtless and irreverent hearts.
They would swear by the heaven, forgetting that it was God's
Throne: by the earth, forgetting that it was His footstool . Is. lxvi. 1.
toward Jerusalem, forgetting that it was the City of the Great Ps. xlviii. 2
King; by their heads, never considering, says Jesus with a
stroke of humorous sarcasm, that they could not make a
single hair white or black.

It is a still more serious aspect of the case that the
Rabbis, like the Jesuits whom Pascal satirises in the *Provincial
Letters*, had developed a monstrous system of casuistry,
distinguishing betwixt oaths which were binding and oaths
which it was no sin to break. If a man swore by the
Sanctuary, it was naught; but if he swore by the gold of
the Sanctuary, he was bound. If he swore by the altar, it
was naught; but if he swore by the gift upon the altar, he
was bound. If he swore by Jerusalem, he was not bound
unless he looked intently toward Jerusalem as he swore.[2]
Such casuistry is ruinous to the moral sense; and even where
there is no evasion, the practice of oath-taking is subtly
mischievous, being "apt to introduce into the laxer sort of
minds the notion of two kinds of truth—the one applicable
to the solemn affairs of justice, and the other to the common
proceedings of daily intercourse."[3] Jesus required "truth in
the inward parts." When the heart is simple and sincere,
then *Yea* and *Nay* are all-sufficient. The man's word is as
good as his bond. It may be said of him as of the Essenes
of old that "everything that is spoken by him is stronger
than an oath."

From the exposition of His doctrine that God regards Protest
thoughts as well as acts, Jesus proceeds by natural transition to against
inculcate the necessity of heart-religion. And assuredly, if ever acting"

---

[1] *The Pardoneres Tale.*
[2] Mt. xxiii. 16, 18. Lightfoot and Wetstein on Mt. v. 33-7
[3] Lamb's Essay on *Imperfect Sympathies.*

the exhortation was needed, it was in that age.   The religious
teachers were the Pharisees, and they had made religion a
hollow and heartless form.   By a single stinging epithet
Jesus pourtrays them.   He terms them "hypocrites," and
hypocrite meant properly an actor on the stage of the theatre.
And truly the Pharisees were mere play-actors.   Their
sanctity was a mask, their whole life an elaborate posturing
before admiring spectators.[1]

"Take heed," says Jesus, "not to do your religion[2] before
men with the intent of being a spectacle unto them ; [3] else
have ye no recompense in the judgment of your Father in

Cf. Tob Heaven."   Almsgiving, Prayer, and Fasting were the chief
xii. 8. exercises of religion in those days, and Jesus in graphic and
vigorous language depicts the manner of the Pharisees in each
(1) in alms- of these.   "When thou doest alms, sound not a trumpet
giving ; before thee, as the playactors do in the synagogues and in
the streets, that they may be glorified by men.   Verily I tell
you, they have their full recompense."   The ancient Law,
ever humane and merciful, had a tender regard for the poor,[4]
and there are not a few truly noble sayings of the Rabbis
inculcating the sacred duty of ministering to their necessities.
"Let thy house," said R. Joses ben Jochanan of Jerusalem,
"be opened wide ; and let the needy be thy household." [5]
And almsgiving had a prominent place in the worship of the
Synagogue.   It was a beautiful and truly pious usage, yet it
was grievously abused by the Pharisees.   They made it an
occasion of self-glorification.   See them as they deposit their
gift in the offertory-box in the Synagogue or drop it into the
beggar's hand in the street.   See how they court observation,
"sounding," says Jesus, "a trumpet before them." [6]   R. Eliezer

---

[1] Aug. *De Serm. Dom. in Mon.* ii. § 5.

[2] Reading δικαιοσύνην. δικαιοσύνη the generic term ; ἐλεημοσύνη, προσευχή,
νηστεία specific instances. δικαιοσύνη = צְדָקָה often in the sense of *alms* (Hatch,

Ess. in Bib. Gk. pp. 49 *sqq.*) ; *cf.* Tob. ii. 14 ; 2 Cor. ix. 9 ; Acts x. 4.   Hence
T. R. ἐλεημοσύνην.

[3] πρὸς τὸ θεαθῆναι, "with the intent of being a θέατρον." *Cf.* 1 Cor. iv. 9.

[4] Deut. xv. 7-11 ; Lev. xix. 9-10 ; *cf.* Ps. xli. 1 ; Prov. xxi. 13.

[5] Taylor, *Say. of Fath.* i. 5.

[6] *Cf.* Achill. Tat. viii : αὕτη δὲ οὐχ ὑπὸ σάλπιγγι μόνον ἀλλὰ καὶ κήρυκι
μοιχεύεται.   Greek proverb αὐτὸς ἑαυτὸν αὐλεῖ (Erasm. *Adag.* under *Adulatio*).
Calvin thinks they actually blew a trumpet to summon the beggars, but the phrase is
merely a vigorous metaphor. *Cf.* Chrysost. *In Matth.* xix ; Lightfoot and Wetstein.

commended the charity which was done in secret, the giver knowing not to whom he gave nor the recipient from whom he received ;[1] but not such is the manner of these playactors. They do not give their alms by stealth, as though they would hide from the left hand what the right is doing. They resemble the worshippers whom old Thomas Fuller describes : " I have observed some at the church-door cast in sixpence with such ostentation, that it rebounded from the bottom, and rang against both sides of the bason (so that the same piece of silver was the alms and the giver's trumpet) ; whilst others have dropped down silent five shillings without any noise."

The sacred exercise of Prayer furnished those playactors (2) in with a great opportunity.   Standing was the prescribed prayer; attitude,[2] and the face must be turned toward the Sanctuary. Eighteen prayers must be offered daily ;[3] and, if the hour of prayer found the man riding on an ass, he must dismount and assume the due posture ; if it found him in the street, he must stand and pray on the spot.[4]   Here lay the opportunity of the Pharisees.   They would deliberately so arrange it that the hour of prayer might find them at the corners of the *Cf.* Prov. streets, the chief places of concourse ; and there they would vii. 12. strike their ostentatious attitude of devotion.[5]   " When ye pray," says Jesus, " ye shall not be as the playactors ; forasmuch as they love to take their stand in the synagogues and at the corners of the streets and pray, in order that they may be a sight to men.   Verily I tell you, they have their full recompense.   But thou, when thou prayest, enter into thy chamber and after shutting thy door pray to thy Father that is in secret ; and thy Father that seeth in secret shall grant thee thy desire."

Moreover, the Pharisees delighted in long prayers.   " Every one," they said, " that multiplies prayer is heard."[6]   This notion also Jesus assailed with the sharp arrows of His scorn.   It was, He declared, a heathenish notion, and those sanctimonious Pharisees with their endless iterations were

---

[1] Wetstein on Mt. vi. 1.
[2] *Ber.* 26. 2 : " Stare nihil aliud fuit quam orare.''
[3] Lightfoot on Mt. i. 17 ; vi. 9.   [4] *Ber.* 16. 1.
[5] Lightfoot on Mt. vi. 5.
[6] Lightfoot on Mt. vi. 7.   *Cf. Didache,* viii.

1 Kings xviii. 26. no better than the priests of Baal who cried from morning even until noon, " O Baal, hear us ! " God is no reluctant deity to be wearied with importunate entreaties, but a gracious Father. " In praying do not babble [1] like the heathen ; for they think that in their much speaking they will win a hearing. Be not then like unto them ; for your Father knoweth what things ye have need of ere ye ask Him."

(3) in fasting. The practice of Fasting also was very congenial to the Pharisees. They fasted every Monday and Thursday [2] ; and since it happened opportunely that these were the days when the Synagogue met, it was given them to display themselves to the assembled worshippers in their guise of woe. Their fasting was not merely abstinence from meat and drink. They did not wash or anoint themselves, they went barefoot, and they sprinkled ashes on their heads,[3] " making their faces unsightly that they might be a sight to men in their fasting."

Cf. Is. lviii. 5. And thus, to win the praise of sanctity, they displayed themselves in a mask of fictitious woe to the gaze of an admiring world. " Fools," cries Thomas Fuller, " who, to persuade men that angels lodged in their hearts, hung out a devil for a sign in their faces ! " " But thou," said Jesus, humorously prescribing a method of fasting which really meant the abandonment of the usage, " when thou fastest, anoint thy head and wash thy face." What manner of fast were this for which men array themselves as for a joyous festival ?

Astonishment of the congregation. The sermon made a profound impression upon the hearers. What they chiefly remarked was the " authority " wherewith the Preacher spoke. This note rang out in every sentence : in His criticism of the religion of the day and still more in His definition of His attitude toward the Law. The very assertion that He had not come to pull down the Law or the Prophets was amazing to minds habituated to well-nigh idolatrous veneration of the Scriptures ; and their wonderment would increase when He proceeded to quote precept after precept and

---

[1] Jer., Aug. : "Nolite multum loqui." *Cf.* Ecclus. vii. 14. βαττολογεῖν = "say the same thing over and over"; variously derived : (1) from Battus, a foolish poet who delighted in pompous iterations (Suidas). Ovid. *Met.* ii. 688 *sqq.* (2) From the Libyan King Battus, (Herod. iv. 155), so named from his stammering (βατταρίζειν). (3) Onomatopoetic (Hesychius). *Cf.* Lightfoot, Wetstein, Erasm. *Annotat.* and *Adag.* under *Battologia, Laconismus.*

[2] Lightfoot on Mt. ix. 14. *Cf.* p. 324. [3] Lightfoot on Mt. vi. 16, 17.

oppose to each His "*but I tell you.*" And with what masterful confidence He spoke of the Kingdom of Heaven and prescribed the conditions of entrance into it, calmly arrogating to Himself the Messiah's prerogative! It is no marvel that "they were astonished at His teaching."

In the congregation there was one of those unhappy creat- A de-ures who, in the language of that time, were called *demoniacs*. moniac. Every age has its peculiar ideas which to after generations seem often no better than grotesque superstitions ; and in our Lord's day it was universally believed, not only by the Jews, but by the Greeks and the Romans, that all sorts of ailments were due to the operation of malignant spirits. According to the Demoni-Egyptians the human body was composed of thirty-six parts, acal pos-and each part was under the dominion of a dæmon, its health session. depending on the dæmon's good-will [1] The idea of demoniacal possession originated in Persia,[2] and by the time of our Lord it had rooted itself not only in popular belief but in science and philosophy, despite the protests of certain physicians who assigned diseases to natural causes.[3] It was a general opinion that the dæmons were the spirits of the wicked dead.[4] Body and soul alike were believed to be open to their invasion, moral excesses as well as physical distempers being ascribed to their malign influence.[5] There were lying spirits, unclean spirits, deceiving spirits.[6] Nowhere, however, was possession so plainly and appallingly recognised as in raving madness and in epilepsy with its paroxysms of foaming and choking.[7]

The idea is of course simply a fantastic notion of a dark Did Jesus age unskilled in natural science, and it was nothing strange believe in that the people of the New Testament should have entertained it? it. But it is disconcerting that it seems to have been enter-tained by Jesus also. When He healed a demoniac, He would

[1] Orig. *C. Cels.* viii. 58.

[2] Plin. *H. N.* xxx. 2 ; Plut. *De Defect. Orac.* § 10.

[3] Orig. *In Matth.* xiii. § 6 ; *cf.* Wetstein on Mt. iv. 24, pp. 282-3.

[4] Philostr. *Apoll.* iii. 38 ; Jos. *De Bell. Jud.* vii. 6. § 3. According to *Enoch* xv. 8 (*cf.* Just. M. *Apol.* i., ed. Sylburg., p. 44 B) the progeny of the sons of God and the daughters of men (Gen. vi. 1-4).

[5] Lightfoot on Mt. xvii. 15 and Lk. viii. 2. *Cf.* Jer. *Vit. Hil. Erem.* : a *virgo Dei* possessed by *amoris dæmon.*

[6] 1 Kings xxii. 20-3 ; Philostr. *Apoll.* iii. 38. Mt. i. 27 ; Mk. x. 1 ; etc. ; Acts viii. 7 ; Rev. xvi. 13 ; Philostr. *Apoll.* iv. 20. 1 Tim. iv. 1 ; 1 John iv. 6 ; Philostr. *Apoll.* iv. 25.

[7] Mt. viii. 28-34 = Mk. v. 1-20 = Lk. viii. 26-39. Mt. xvii. 14-21 = Mk. ix. 14-29 = Lk. ix. 37-43. Jos. *Ant.* vi. 8. § 2.

address the supposed dæmon, rebuking it and commanding it to come out of the man. That He should thus share the limitation of His age is at the first blush somewhat of a shock to faith ; yet, even if it be allowed, there is perhaps no real occasion for disquietude. When the Lord of Glory came down to earth, He assumed the nature of the children of men, being "made at every point like unto His brethren" ; and it might be accepted as a welcome evidence of the reality of the Incarnation if He were found to have shared the scientific and metaphysical conceptions of His contemporaries.

Iebr. ii. 17.

Evidence to the contrary: (1) Detachment of Jesus from current theories.

Nevertheless there are counter facts which demand consideration. Not the least weighty is our Lord's singular detachment from current theories. He never entangled His teaching with contemporary ideas ; He never made a statement which has been discredited by the progress of human knowledge.[1] When the Inquisition condemned Galileo, it appealed not to the Gospels but to the Book of Joshua in support of the Ptolemaic astronomy ; when the evolutionary theory was propounded, it was not with the teaching of our Lord but with the cosmogony of Genesis that it seemed to conflict ; and criticism may assign what date or authorship it will to the Old Testament writings unchecked by His authority. If it so be that Jesus gave His sanction to the idea of demoniacal possession, it is the solitary instance where He involved Himself with the passing opinions of His day.

(2) Difference betwixt His methods and the exorcists'.

Cf. Acts xix. 13-6.

Moreover, there was a wide difference betwixt His treatment of the demoniacs and the methods of His contemporaries, the exorcists. Exorcism was an elaborate art ; and indeed, grotesque and superstitious as it was, it is very credible that it exercised a beneficent influence, at all events in cases of mental derangement. Its practitioners and their patients alike sincerely believed in the reality of demoniacal possession and in the efficacy of the prescribed ceremonies ; and it is in no wise incredible that frenzied minds were calmed and their hallucinations dispelled by the potent influences of a masterful personality and a strong faith.[2] Even a man of letters and affairs like Josephus believed in the craft. Its principles, he tells us, were ascribed to King Solomon ; and he relates in

[1] *Cf.* Romanes, *Thoughts on Religion*, p. 157.
[2] Jesus expressly attests the success of the exorcists (Mt. xii. 27).

all good faith a wonder wrought by a Jewish exorcist, Eleazar, in presence of Vespasian, his sons, his officers, and a large number of his soldiers. Eleazar applied to the nostrils of a demoniac a ring which had under its seal one of the roots prescribed by Solomon, and drew out the dæmon through the sufferer's nose. By way of attestation a basin full of water was placed hard by, and in obedience to the exorcist's command the departing dæmon overturned it.[1] The most potent of the magical roots was named Baaras after the lonely valley near Machærus where it grew. In colour it resembled fire, and toward evening it emitted a bright glow. When approached, it shrank into the ground unless means were taken to prevent it.[2] To grasp it was certain death, and it was secured by a gruesome device. They dug away the earth all round it, then tied a dog to it, and the animal's struggles wrenched up the stubborn root. The dog instantly died, as it were, a substitute for the man. Thereafter the root might be handled safely; and, if applied to the possessed, it drove out the dæmons which had entered into them.[3]

Such were the methods of His day, but Jesus eschewed them all. He employed neither root nor incantation. He simply spoke His word of power, and straightway the sufferer was healed, his frenzy calmed, his reason restored. Surely He knew right well what the ailment was. He approved as little of the theory of the exorcists as of their methods; and it is an example of His gracious wisdom that He condemned neither. The idea of possession was rooted in the minds of the men of that generation. The sufferers were firmly persuaded that dæmons lodged within them, so much so that, when they spoke, they fancied it was not them- Mk. i. 24 ▪ selves that spoke but the dæmons, even as a madman will Lk. iv. 34 imagine himself some great person and deport himself accordingly. When a physician has to deal with such a case, he does not reason with the patient, but rather humours him.[4]

---

[1] *Ant.* viii. 2. § 5.

[2] πρὶν ἄν τις οὖρον γυναικὸς ἢ τὸ ἔμμηνον αἷμα χέῃ κατ' αὐτῆς.

[3] *De Bell. Jud.* vii. 6. § 3. *Cf.* Tob. vi.-viii; Philostr. *Apoll.* iv. 10.

[4] *Cf.* Samuel Warren, *Diary of a Physician*, chap. xiv; Shak. *Com. of Err.* IV. iv:

> "*Adr.* Is't good to soothe him in these contraries?
> *Pinch.* It is no shame; the fellow finds his vein,
> And, yielding to him, humours well his frenzy."

And Jesus dealt with the demoniacs after the manner of a wise physician. He did not seek to dispel their hallucination. He fell in with it and won their confidence. And, once He had achieved this, He had gained the mastery over them and could do with them what He listed. The yielding up of the will was ever the indispensable condition of the Lord's miracles. Where faith was lacking, He could do no mighty work.

(3) His avoidance of the term "demoniac." There is another and conclusive evidence that, though He graciously accommodated Himself to the popular idea, He did not Himself share it. Demoniacal possession was not a phrase of Jesus.[1] Very significant is His message to John the Baptist, when the latter sent from his prison asking if He were indeed the Messiah. "In that hour," says the Evangelist, "He healed many of sicknesses and plagues and evil spirits, and on many blind He bestowed sight." Then He made His answer. "Go and report to John the things which ye saw and heard : that blind men recover sight, lame walk, lepers are cleansed, deaf hear, dead are raised, poor have the Gospel preached to them." It seems as though, in this enumeration, He omitted the demoniacs. In truth He includes them, but He employs another phraseology than the Evangelist. All the sufferers perhaps whom Jesus mentions, certainly the blind and the deaf,[2] were, in common parlance, demoniacs, but Jesus deliberately eschewed the name. He knew the truth. With gracious condescension He accommodated Himself to the ignorance of men, but He did not share it. It is remarkable that St John never records an instance of the healing of a demoniac. Yet he alludes to the idea of possession, telling how Jesus was thrice accused of "having a dæmon"—once by the multitude and twice by the rulers. And he relates how Jesus healed at least one who, in popular phraseology, was a demoniac and would probably have been so designated by the other Evangelists—the paralytic at Bethesda. It is a striking coincidence, revealing the Beloved Disciple's comprehension of his Master's mind.

Healing of the demoniac in the Synagogue. The demoniac in the Synagogue of Capernaum on that memorable Sabbath was evidently an epileptic. His behaviour

Margin references:
Mt. xiii. 58 =Mk. vi. 5-6. *Cf.* Acts xiv. 9.

Lk. vii. 21-2.

vii. 20; viii. 48 : x. 20.

v. 1-14; *cf.* Lk. xiii. 11.

[1] On Mt. x. 8 see p. 216, n. 2.
[2] *Cf.* Mt. xii. 22 ; Mt. ix. 32 = Lk. xi. 14 (κωφός either *deaf* or *dumb*).

and the description of him as " in the power of an unclean Cf. Mk. ix. 18, 25-6. spirit" point to that distressing malady and its disgusting concomitants. Like the rest he was powerfully affected by the sermon. The excitement proved too much for him, and he was taken with a violent fit. " Ha !" he cried ; " what have we to do with Thee, Nazarene Jesus? Didst Thou come to destroy us ? I know who Thou art—the Holy One of God." It was a characteristic piece of demoniacal raving. It was the dæmon, not the man, that spoke ; and, recognising Jesus as the Messiah, the foe of the powers of Hell, it trembled for itself and its confederates. Jesus after His wont fell in with the delusion. " Be muzzled ! " He said sternly, addressing the dæmon in colloquial phrase,[1] as though it were a wild beast, " and come out of him." A violent paroxysm ensued. The man wallowed on the floor and uttered a wild scream. Then he lay still. The fit was past. He was healed.

The wonder of the congregation was boundless. The sermon had astonished them ; the miracle amazed them. By a simple command with neither ceremony nor incantation Jesus had cast out the dæmon. " What is this ? " they said one to another. " A new teaching with authority ! And He chargeth the unclean spirits, and they hearken unto Him ! "

[1] φιμώθητι. *Cf.* Mk. iv. 39 ; Mt. xxii. 34.

CHAPTER XII

A MISSION THROUGH GALILEE

Mt. viii. 14
7=Mk. i.
29-34=Lk.
iv. 38-41 ;
Mk. i. 35-9.
=Lk. iv.
42-4; Mt.
iv. 23-5 ;
Mt. viii. 2-
4=Mk. i.
40-5=Lk.
v. 12-6.

"To Thee they went—the blind, the dumb,
  The palsied, and the lame,
  The leper with his tainted life,
  The sick with fevered frame."—E. H. PLUMPTRE.

Healing
of Peter's
mother-in-
law,

LEAVING the Synagogue, Jesus went home with Simon Peter, accompanied by James and John. Peter and Andrew kept house together, and not only the wife of the former but her mother also was an inmate of the dwelling. On their arrival they found that the elder woman had been stricken by the deadly malaria so prevalent on the marshy shores of the Sea of Galilee.[1] The anxious friends appealed to Jesus, and He approached the couch and rebuked the fever, even as He afterwards rebuked the winds and the waves on the storm-tossed Lake, and, grasping the sufferer's hand, raised her up. The cure was instantaneous and complete. As the storm sank to rest at His word and a great calm ensued without the long, rolling swell which is wont to follow the subsidence of a tempest, so the abatement of the fever was followed by no lingering convalescence. She arose in full strength and resumed her domestic offices. Jesus abode for the remainder of that day under Peter's roof. Indeed it would seem that He lodged there ever afterwards while He sojourned at Capernaum. The grateful inmates constrained Him, and the benediction of His presence was their ample recompense.

Mt. viii. 26
=Mk. iv.
39=Lk.
viii. 24.

Cf. Mt.
xvii. 24-5.

of many of
the towns-
folk.

With the setting of the sun the Jewish Sabbath ended,[2] and no sooner were they relieved of the obligation of the Sabbath-law than the townsfolk congregated at the door of Peter's house. The miracle in the Synagogue had been noised abroad, and they brought their sick to Jesus. All sorts of sufferers were there, but none so pitiable as the

[1] Cf. John iv. 52 ; Jos. Vit. § 72.   [2] Cf. Lightfoot on Mt. viii. 16.

demoniacs with their wild cries.   Jesus welcomed them all, laying His hands on every one of them and healing them.

It would be late ere the gracious work was done, and Jesus would be weary when He went to rest.   Nevertheless He was early astir.   While it was still night, He quitted the house and, stealing through the silent streets, betook Himself to a lonely spot, perhaps on the uplands behind the town ; and there gave Himself to prayer.   When the rest of the household awoke, they missed Him.   The tidings of His disappearance got abroad, and a great search ensued.   The disciples, it would seem, were at no loss where to seek Him, perchance because it was His habit to repair to that retreat. It was His accustomed oratory, and they pursued Him thither. "They are all in quest of Thee," they said when they found Him.   They expected that He would hasten back and resume His ministry in the town, but He had determined otherwise. He had resolved to withdraw for a season from Capernaum and make a tour through Galilee, carrying the glad tidings of the Kingdom of Heaven.   "Let us go elsewhere," He said, "into the adjoining towns, that there also I may preach. For it was in order to this that I came out here." [1]

Retiral of Jesus ere daybreak to a lonely spot.

What moved Him to leave Capernaum so soon ?   He had just begun His ministry there, and, to all outward appearance, the tide of success was flowing strong.   Certainly it was needful that the adjoining towns also should hear the Evangel, but might they not have waited a while until He had satisfied the eager desire of Capernaum ?   Why did He turn His back upon so great an opportunity ?   It was because He had a just appreciation of the situation, and rated the multitude's enthusiasm at its proper value.   They were seeking Him not that they might hear His message of salvation but that they might see His miracles, eager for the healing of their bodies, unconcerned about the sickness of their souls.   They were hailing Him as the Messiah, but He knew what that sacred title meant on their lips. Astonished by His miracles, they thought that their dream of a worldly king and an earthly kingdom was about to be realised.   Therefore the enthusiasm of the multitude displeased Him, and He would leave Capernaum until it should

Resolution to withdraw from Capernaum for a season.

Lk. iv. 41 = Mk. i. 34.

[1] See Introd. § 12, 3, (1).

Lk. iv. 42. subside. They would fain have hindered His departure. They gathered round Him and hemmed Him in, but He broke from them and went His way with His disciples.

Mission in Galilee. In the course of that mission through Galilee He prosecuted an active ministry, and His fame travelled far. " He

Mt. iv 23- went about in the whole of Galilee, teaching in their
5. synagogues, and preaching the good tidings of the Kingdom, and healing every kind of sickness and every kind of infirmity among the folk. And His fame went abroad into the whole of Syria ; and they brought unto Him all that were ill with various diseases and holden with torments, possessed, and lunatic, and paralytic ; and He healed them. And there followed Him large multitudes from Galilee, and Decapolis, and Jerusalem, and Judæa, and the other side of the Jordan." It was a wondrous time, yet the Evangelists, perhaps since their interest centred in Capernaum, have preserved only a single incident, one drop of the plenteous rain which fell on Galilee during that season of her merciful visitation. It happened in one of the cities of Galilee. Jesus was apparently within doors [1] when He was visited by a miserable creature,

A leper. " a man full of leprosy." This awful disease, fostered by insanitary conditions and poor diet, is to the present a sore scourge in the squalid East. It was regarded by the Jews with singular awe as a divine stroke. It was accounted incurable, and the sufferer's only hope lay in the special help

Num. xii. of God.[2] He dragged on his wretched existence, a living
12. corpse. In the early Latin Church, when a man was stricken with leprosy, they celebrated the last rites and read the burial service over him ; and this ghastly usage was in entire accordance with the Jewish sentiment. "These four," says the Talmud, "are reckoned as dead—the blind, the leper, the poor, and the childless."[3] The leper was an outcast.

2 Chr. xxvi. He had to live apart. Even as of old he had been banished
20-1=1
Kings xv.5. from the camp of Israel, so in later days he was not suffered
Num. v. 1- to enter a walled town. He had to rend his garments, go
4.

---

[1] (1) Mk. says that Jesus "thrust him out" (ἐξέβαλεν) and he "went out" (ἐξελθών), i.e. from the house. (2) The command of Jesus : "Tell no man," implies that the miracle was wrought within doors and not in public.

[2] 2 Kings v. 7 ; Jos. Ant. iii. 11. § 3 : ἂν δέ τις ἐξικετεύσας τὸν Θεὸν ἀπολυθῇ τῆς νόσου.

[3] Lightfoot on Lk. ix. 60.

bareheaded, wear a covering over his mouth, and cry : Lev. xiii
"Unclean! unclean!" If the wind blew from his direction, 45.
he must come no nearer, said R. Jochanan, than four cubits ; no
nearer, said R. Simeon, than a hundred cubits. He was admitted
to the Synagogue, but he must be the first to enter and the
last to leave, and must occupy a special enclosure ten hand-
lengths high and four cubits broad. The penalty, should he
transgress his limits, was forty stripes.[1]

It was one of these hapless creatures that visited Jesus in His cleans-
that city of Galilee. Regardless of legal restrictions, he ing.
entered the city and made his way along the streets. He
left pollution on his trail, yet his progress was unimpeded :
all stood aside, none would lay hands on him. Reaching the
house where Jesus was, he burst in, knelt before Him, flung
himself on his face, and cried : "Lord, if Thou wilt, Thou
canst cleanse me." He had no hope in man, but he had hope
in the Divine Physician. Had Jesus been a Rabbi, He would
have recoiled in disgust and indignation. R. Meir would not eat
eggs from a street where there was a leper. When R. Eleazar
saw a leper, he hid himself. When R. Lakisch saw one, he
pelted him with stones, crying : "Away to thine own place,
lest thou pollute others!"[2] But Jesus treated this poor
supplicant after another fashion. A great compassion filled
His heart at the sight of the

"maimèd form, swollen and scarred and bent
Out of all human semblance" ;

and He stretched out His hand and laid it on the wretch.
"I will," He said ; "be cleansed." And instantly the rotting
flesh became sound and sweet.

It was a perilous thing that He had done. Not only had The Lord's
He contracted ceremonial pollution, but He had trespassed behest.
upon the province of the priest, with whom it lay to pronounce
a leper clean. Should it be noised abroad, it would confirm
the suspicion that He made light of the Law and its ordinances, and give the rulers a specious pretext for accusing Him
and impeding Him in the prosecution of His ministry. Since,
however, the incident had happened within doors, it might be
kept secret, and Jesus addressed Himself to the man with the

[1] Lightfoot and Wetstein on Lk. xvii. 12.   [2] Wetstein on Lk. xvii. 12.

profuse and energetic gesticulation which Orientals use. He
eyed him sternly, knitting His brows and shaking His head
after the manner of one who would enjoin secrecy.[1] "See!
say nothing to any one," He commanded ; "but go thy way,
Lev. xiv. 1- show thyself to the priest and offer for thy cleansing what
32. Moses prescribed, for a testimony unto them." By repairing
to Jerusalem and submitting himself to the priest for examination the man would display all due respect for constituted
authority and would relieve his Benefactor of the suspicion
of encouraging violation of the Law. And it was necessary
that he should forthwith hasten on his errand and, meanwhile
at least, tell no one of his cure. Perhaps, if he lingered to
recount the wondrous story, the news might reach Jerusalem
before him, and then the priest might refuse to pronounce
him clean.[2] Yet this was not the Lord's main apprehension.
He foresaw that, were it noised abroad, so remarkable a
miracle would excite wonderment and draw a curious throng.
He had quitted Capernaum to escape the applause of the
carnal multitude, and now He dreads a like outbreak of
enthusiasm. The man must forthwith begone, nor must any
in the city learn what had happened. Great issues were at
stake, and Jesus accompanied His energetic behest with
action equally energetic, laying hold upon him and thrusting
Mk. i. 43. him out of the house.

The man's dis-obedience. Unhappily His importunities were disregarded. No sooner
was the man out of doors than he published broadcast the
story of his healing. It may be that he was actuated by
gratitude and deemed it unmeet to hold his peace, reasoning
within himself that he owed it to Jesus to make His goodness
known, and forgetting that he could render to his Benefactor
no better tribute than obedience. His self-willed course was
a grievous error. It issued in the very consequence which
Jesus had foreseen. The tidings spread, and great was the
excitement. Large crowds assembled to gaze at the wonder-
worker, nor did He escape when He quitted that city. The

---

[1] Mk. i. 43 : ἐμβριμησάμενος. See Euth. Zig. on Mt. ix. 30. The verb mean:
properly to *snort* (*cf.* Æsch. *Sept. c. Theb.* 461), the metaphor being a horse
champing its bit in rebellion against its load. Cyrill. Lex. Voss.: δεῖ δε γινώσκειν ὅτι
ἀπὸ μεταφορᾶς τῶν μασσωμένων χαλινῶν τοῦ ἵππου δι' ἀγανάκτησιν τοῦ βάρους κεῖται
ἡ λέξις. *Cf.* Germ. *anschnautzen.*

[2] Wetstein, Bengel.

tidings had travelled far and wide, and, wherever He went, He was beset. " He could no longer openly enter into a city." He kept to the open country, busying Himself with prayer ; but even thus He could not escape. The cúrious folk discovered His whereabouts, and from every direction they thronged out all agape. Further prosecution of His ministry was impossible. The disobedience of the healed leper, albeit perhaps well meant, had this immediate consequence, that it brought the mission in Galilee to an abrupt and premature conclusion.

CHAPTER XIII

THE GATHERING STORM

Mt. viii. 5-
13=Lk.
vii. 2-10;
Mt. ix. 1-8
=Mk. ii. 1-
12=Lk. v.
17-26.

" From thence read on the story of His life.
His humble carriage, His unfaulty ways,
His canker'd foes, His fights, His toil, His strife,
His pains, His poverty, His sharp assays,
Through which He past His miserable days,
Offending none, and doing good to all,
Yet being maliced both of great and small."

EDMUND SPENSER.

Return to
Caper-
naum.

IT seems probable in view of the extent of His circuit and
the abundance of His labours that our Lord's mission through
Galilee occupied a considerable period. Most likely the
summer was past ere He returned to Capernaum. During
His absence the aspect of the situation had changed. It was
indeed impossible that He should have been forgotten, since
the fame of His doings in the uplands would reach the
dwellers by the Lake; but their excitement had subsided and
their life had resumed its accustomed routine. On the other
hand, the rulers had taken alarm. They had marked the
amazing popularity of Jesus and, recognising Him as a
dangerous rival, had resolved, without meanwhile proclaiming
open war against Him, to keep jealous watch over His every
act and word and movement.

The cen-
turion and
his slave.
Mk. ii. 1.

Their new attitude speedily became apparent. The
return of Jesus made no small stir. The word passed from
mouth to mouth, " He is home ! " It was glad tidings to at
least one man in the town. He was a centurion in the army
of Herod Antipas, and, though a Gentile, he was well disposed
to the Jewish people. He belonged in all probability to
that class of Gentiles who, without actually becoming proselytes and submitting to the rite of circumcision, reverenced
the Jewish faith and observed certain of the Jewish usages;[1]

[1] Schürer, *H. J. P.* II. ii. pp. 311 *sqq.*

and he had won the esteem of his fellow-citizens by building a synagogue and presenting it to them—a not uncommon act of generosity.[1] And he was a kind-hearted as well as a public-spirited man. In those days slaves were commonly treated with monstrous barbarity. It is told of the freedman Pallas, the wicked favourite of the Emperor Claudius and brother to Felix, Governor of Judæa, that he was wont to sig- nify his pleasure to the slaves of his household by a nod or a gesture ; and, if more were needed, he used writing, lest his voice should be degraded by addressing creatures so abject.[2] Yet were there exceptions. "Live with your slave kindly," said Seneca, enjoining what he practised ; "courteously admit him to conversation, to counsel, and to your board. Let some dine with you because they are worthy, others that they may be so."[3] And it sometimes happened that by extreme fidelity and devotion slaves laid their masters under obligation and won their confidence and friendship.[4] This centurion had a slave whom he held in high esteem, and to his grief the trusty retainer had been stricken with paralysis. Like every one else in Capernaum, he had heard the fame of Jesus ; and it may be that, since they were both in the service of Herod Antipas, he had learned more of His grace from the courtier whose son had been so wonderfully restored a few months previously. The cry "He is home !" reached his ears, and he resolved to seek the aid of the mighty Healer.

Acts xxiii. 24 sqq.

John iv. 46- 54.

Learning his purpose, the elders of the Synagogue volunteered to intercede with Jesus on his behalf. It is no mere fancy on St Chrysostom's part when he charges them with sycophancy and pictures them compassing their patron with observances and, pompous ecclesiastics as they were, running his errand with obsequious alacrity.[5] Probably, however, they had a further motive for intruding their offices. It chagrined them that the centurion should call in the aid of one whom they viewed with jealousy and suspicion ; and,

Embassy of Jewish elders.

---

[1] Lightfoot on Lk. vii. 5.   [2] Tac. *Ann.* xiii. 23.   [3] *Ep.* xlvii.

[4] For instances see Senec. *De Benef.* iii. 22-7.   *Cf.* Lightfoot on Lk. vii. 2.

[5] *In Matth.* xxvii. Erasmus comments, satirising his *bête noire*, the monkish fraternity : "Ad eundem modum et hodie quidam quæstui prætexentes pietatem adulantur divitibus. Benigne largitur fratribus, extruxit nobis monasterii partem, favet ordini nostro, tantum legavit, fraudatis etiam liberis."

not daring to protest, they sought to secure their prestige as far as they might. They knew the modesty of the centurion and his reverence for Jesus ; and, feigning approval of his purpose, they professed to have influence with the wondrous prophet and proffered their mediation. It was a cunning stroke of policy. Should Jesus heal the slave at their desire, to them would accrue no small measure of the glory. The centurion consented, and they approached Jesus and required His services, addressing Him with a brusquerie in striking contrast to the reverential tone wherewith they referred to their patron. " He is worthy," they explained, " that thou shouldst do him this favour. For he loveth our nation and himself built us the Synagogue."

Embassy of friends of the centurion. It would have horrified the centurion had he heard how they urged his suit. And indeed it would seem that he had misgivings. Scarcely had they departed on their errand when he despatched a second embassy, some friends like-minded with himself. They met Jesus and the elders a little way from the house, and delivered the centurion's message. *His request.* " Lord," he had bade them say, " trouble not to come ;[1] for I am not fit that Thou shouldst come in under my roof. Wherefore neither did I deem myself worthy to come unto Thee. But command by a word, and let my servant be healed." Surely it was in his mind how Jesus had spoken His mighty word at Cana and the courtier's child had on the instant been healed at Capernaum. That miracle had revealed to him somewhat of the power of Jesus. He was a soldier and his thought was cast in a military mould. " I," he argued, " am a man ranked under authority with soldiers under myself ; and I say to this one ' Go,' and he goeth ; and to another ' Come,' and he cometh ; and to my slave ' Do this,' and he doeth it." He pictured a spiritual hierarchy after the model of the military organisation which he knew so well. Though only a subordinate officer subject to his superiors, he had authority over his soldiers ; and, if he had only to issue his commands and they were executed, might not Jesus, whom he recognised as the Lord of all principalities and powers, do

---

[1] μὴ σκύλλου. σκύλλεσθαι = ἔρχεσθαι with the added idea of *fatigue.* Eus. *H. E.* i. 13 (Abgarus to Jesus): ἐδεήθην σου σκυλῆναι πρός με. " σκύλλεσθαι πρός τινα dicitur qui longius et molestius iter facit ad aliquem " (Heinichen's Eus. *H. E.,* Index iv). Cf. *Expositor,* Apr. 1901, pp. 273-4.

the like and much more? There was no need for Him to approach the sufferer: let Him but speak the word, and ministering angels would hasten to fulfil it. It may have been a grotesque and somewhat heathenish conception, yet it bespoke profound reverence and boundless faith, and it gladdened the heart of Jesus. It was the fullest recognition that He had yet received, and it was the more remarkable coming, as it did, from a Gentile, a representative of that great outer world which Jesus regarded with such exceeding tenderness and earnest desire. He marvelled, it is written, and, turning to the attendant multitude, exclaimed : " Verily I tell you, not even in Israel have I found faith like this ! " [1]

Such praise of a Gentile was offensive to Jewish ears, and would the more embitter the rulers. They maintained their attitude of jealous surveillance, nor was it long ere they found an opportunity for joining issue with Jesus. He was engaged teaching, apparently in the Synagogue of Capernaum, though not on the Sabbath but at one of the week-day services.[2] During His mission in Galilee His fame was noised all over the land, and some of the attendant multitude were from distant Jerusalem. The Sanhedrin, it would seem, had taken alarm, and deputies had been sent to Capernaum to co-operate with the local authorities in controlling and, if possible, suppressing the movement, just as Saul of Tarsus in

Jealousy of the rulers.

Mt. iv. 25.

Acts xxii. 5.

---

[1] Mt.'s narrative of this incident is simpler than Lk.'s, omitting the double embassy and representing the centurion as coming in person to Jesus. In early times the theory was held that the Evangelists relate distinct incidents. "This solution," Chrysostom drily observes, "is easy, but the question is whether it be true." The truth is that Mt.'s interest centres in the centurion's faith and the Lord's commendation thereof, and he has omitted unessential details. *Cf.* his simplification of the narrative of the healing of the paralytic (ix. 1-8 = Mk. ii. 1-12 = Lk. v. 17-26). It is no discrepancy that Mt. has παῖς and Lk. δοῦλος (παῖς in v. 7). παῖς was used for " slave," like נַעַר, *puer. Cf.* Wetstein. On Mt. viii. 11-2 *cf.* Introd. § 9.

[2] The scene cannot have been Simon's house, as is mostly assumed. No private dwelling could have accommodated so many, and their intrusion would have been a gross incivility. There is nothing in the narrative to countenance Ewald's supposition that the people were outside and Jesus addressed them from the window. The synagogue seems to be indicated by (1) the presence of the Rabbis. It is incredible that they should have pressed into the lodging of Jesus at the head of a jostling crowd. (2) Mk.'s συνήχθησαν. *Cf.* συναγωγή and patristic σύναξις = *conventus.* Had it been the Sabbath, Jesus would have been charged with Sabbath-breaking as well as blasphemy; *cf.* Mt. xii. 9-14 = Mk. iii. 1-6 = Lk. vi. 6-11; Lk. xiii. 10-7.

after days was sent to Damascus, with credentials from the
High Priest and all the Presbytery, to bring the believers
there to Jerusalem in bonds.   Hence it came to pass that the
Cf. Mt. foremost seats in the Synagogue were occupied by an impos-
xxiii. 6. ing array of official personages, and, as He taught, Jesus was
under the jealous scrutiny of their cold, stern eyes.   There
was a huge congregation.   The Synagogue was crowded, and
many who had failed to gain admittance were thronging
about the entrance and straining their ears to catch the
preacher's voice.

A paralytic   In the course of the service a company of four men
carried by
four. approached the Synagogue, carrying a light couch whereon
lay a helpless paralytic.   They were bringing him to Jesus.
On their arrival they encountered an unforeseen obstacle.
The Synagogue was packed, nor could they even get near the
door.   It was a keen disappointment alike to the bearers and
to the invalid.   But they were resourceful men and would not be
baulked.   A bold device suggested itself to them.   A flight
of steps gave access to the flat roof, and the stalwart bearers
ascended with their inert burden.   They knew precisely where
the preacher sat and, prising up several of the flag-stones
and digging through the substructure heedless what discomfort
or even danger they might inflict on the assemblage below,
they made a sufficient aperture and lowered the couch till it
rested on the floor in front of Jesus.[1]

"Thy sins   It was a daring, indeed a lawless proceeding, yet it was
are
forgiven." very grateful to Jesus.   It revealed what utter confidence the
bearers and the sufferer alike had in His power and pity.[2]   As
He looked down on the wistful face, He read the man's story.
He was a sinner as well as a sufferer, his infirmity, it would
seem, being the penalty of unbridled excess.[3]   But, though

---

[1] Lk.'s account is somewhat different.   He has in view a Roman building with
a tiled roof and an opening (*impluvium*) in the centre.   *Cf.* Becker, *Gallus*, pp. 64,
257.   Through this and not through a rough breach he represents the couch as
being lowered.   *Cf.* Ramsay, *Was Christ Born in Bethlehem?* pp. 57 *sqq.*

[2] It has been maintained both in ancient and modern times that it is the faith
of the bearers exclusively that is alluded to (Mt. ix. 2 = Mk. ii. 5 = Lk. v. 20), the
sufferer, paralysed alike in mind and in body, being incapable of faith—an instance
of "the vicarious virtue of faith."   So Jerome ; Bernard. *Super Cant. Serm.*
lxvi ; Bruce, *Galilean Gospel*, pp. 163 *sqq.*   According to Chrysost. *Serm.*
lxii it was the faith of the bearers and the paralytic both.

[3] Wetstein on Mt. ix. 2.

his body was crippled, his mind was active enough, and, as he lay in helplessness, he was enduring the sharp stings of remorse. He had secured the good offices of those four friends to bring him to Jesus, not only for healing, but for pardon. This was at once his chief need and his chief desire. Jesus perceived his case and greeted him with the gracious assurance : " Courage, child ! Thy sins are forgiven."

Thereat a murmur ran round the circle of Pharisees and Rabbis. Jesus, they thought, had delivered Himself into their hands. He had committed a grievous sin, nothing less than blasphemy, thereby rendering Himself liable to the extreme penalty of the Jewish law. " Why," they muttered one to another, " doth this fellow talk thus ? He is blaspheming. Who can forgive sins except God alone ? " Their whisperea thought was not hidden from Him. He turned upon them, and, with that quick resourcefulness which ever characterised Him, demanded : " Which is easier—to say ' Thy sins are forgiven,' or to say ' Arise and walk ' ? " They made no reply, yet they could be in no uncertainty. It was an article of Jewish theology that, until a man was absolved of his sin, he could not be healed of his sickness.[1] Forgiveness was the necessary preliminary of healing, and, if Jesus did the latter, He would prove abundantly that He had done the former also. Therefore, that they might know that the lowly Son of Man had authority to forgive sins, He bade the paralytic arise, lift his couch, and go away home. The man obeyed. He had been carried helpless into the Synagogue, and he quitted it carrying his couch and sturdily jostling his way through the throng. The rulers were silenced, and the awe-stricken people glorified God, confessing that they had never seen the like.

His argument in this encounter constitutes not the least significant of our Lord's testimonies regarding Himself. It is widely alleged that in no authentic utterance did Jesus ever claim to be divine. It is only the Fourth Gospel that represents Him as asserting His oneness with the Father " The sentence ' I am the Son of God,' " writes one,[2] " was

Charge of blasphemy against Jesus.

His reply.

The Lord's assertion of His oneness with God.

John x. 30

---

[1] *Nedar*, 41. 1 : " Nullus ægrotus a morbo suo sanatur donec ipsi omnia peccata remissa sunt." See Wetstein.

[2] Harnack, *What is Christianity?* p. 145.

not inserted in the Gospel by Jesus Himself, and to put that sentence there side by side with the others is to make an addition to the Gospel." Surely, however, in this narrative, if nowhere else, the allegation encounters a direct and emphatic contradiction. His adversaries charged Jesus with blasphemy forasmuch as He had usurped a peculiar prerogative of God ; and how did He answer the charge? Did He hasten to repudiate the imputation and disclaim all thought of putting Himself on an equality with God? On the contrary, He confronted them with a demonstration of His right to forgive sins. He allowed that absolution was God's peculiar prerogative and He vindicated His title to exercise it, herein not merely asserting but proving His oneness with the Father.

[1] *Cf.* Chrysost. *In Matth.* xxx.

CHAPTER XIV

THE OFFENCE OF BEFRIENDING SINNERS

Mt. ix. 9-
17=Mk. ii.
13-22=Lk.
v. 27-39.

"A great sinner, when converted, seems a booty to Jesus Christ; he gets by saving such an one; why then should both Jesus lose his glory, and the sinner lose his soul at once, and that for want of an invitation?"—JOHN BUNYAN.

THENCEFORTH it was open war betwixt Jesus and the rulers. They set themselves to find occasion against Him, searching diligently for something in His conduct or speech which might either bring Him within the grasp of their Law or discredit Him with the multitude. One thing they observed in Him which offended them much and afforded them a fair pretext for assailing Him : He took to do with the outcasts of society. There was no class in those days so obnoxious to Jewish sentiment as the Tax-gatherers or, to call them by their Latin name, the Publicans. The imperial government farmed out the business of gathering in the revenues of tributary provinces, the lessee undertaking to render so much annually to the exchequer. Should his province yield less, he must make good the deficiency, and whatever more it might yield was his legal emolument. Since only wealthy men durst run the risk, the business was in the hands of powerful capitalists of the equestrian order. It was their interest to extort the utmost from their provinces. They did not conduct the business directly but employed agents to collect the revenue from the various districts ; and these underlings are the tax-gatherers who figure in the Gospel-story. They carried on the rapacious work, bearing the brunt of the popular odium, while their superiors waxed fat securely in the distant capital and were belauded as " an ornament of the State, a bulwark of the Republic." [1]

All over the Empire there was a bitter cry against the local tax-gatherers. Plutarch complains thus of their vexa-

The Lord's kindness to the outcasts.

The Tax-gatherers.

Resentment against them.

[1] Cic. *Pro Planc.* § 9.

tious impudence : " It is not when they tax obvious imports that we are aggrieved and angry at the tax-gatherers, but when they examine private articles and meddle with bags and baggage which they have nothing to do with. Yet the law permits them to do this, and they suffer if they do not." [1] They were regarded by their indignant victims as simply " licensed robbers," " wild beasts in human shape." [2] " The tax-gatherers gave the necklace to the merchant! After this will not wolves drop lambs from their mouths and lions let fawns go free from their teeth to their dams, when even a tax-gatherer has let go such a prize ? " [3]

Especially in Palestine. Nowhere was the indignation so hot as in Palestine, where the payment of tribute to Rome was resented not merely on the patriotic ground that she was a foreign tyrant but on the religious ground that she was a heathen power. Acknowledgment of her dominion was disloyalty to the theocracy. The tax-gatherers were regarded by the Jews with bitter hatred and utter abhorrence.[4] Their cash-boxes were objects of especial loathing. Their money was unclean, and no Jew might accept it, whether as payment or as alms, on pain of defilement. " Assassins, robbers, and tax-gatherers " was the Rabbinical category ; and the Gospels couple " tax-gatherers and sinners," " heathen and tax-gatherers." They were the pariahs of Israel. If a man swore an oath to a tax-gatherer, he was under no obligation to keep it. A tax-gatherer was disqualified from serving as a witness. He was excluded from religious fellowship.[5] He was a sinner well-nigh beyond redemption.[6] And indeed there was little injustice in this estimate. No man with a shred of self-respect would have engaged in an occupation which was held in such ill repute ; and, since they were treated as outcasts, it was inevitable that the tax-gatherers should set public opinion at defiance and run recklessly to excess of riot. The

Mt. ix. 10, xi. 19, Lk. xv. 1 ; Mt. xviii. 17.

---

[1] *De Curiosit.* § 7.

[2] Chrysost. *In Matth.* xxxi ; *Serm. in Publ. et Phar.*

[3] Iamblichus in Suidas under τελώνης.

[4] *Cf.* Lightfoot on Mt. v. 46, Mk. ii. 16, Lk. xix. 2 ; Wetstein on Mt. v. 46 ; Schürer, *H. J. P.* I. ii. pp. 68-71.

[5] *Hieros. Dem.* 23. 1 : " Religiosus, qui evadit publicanus, pellendus est e societate religiosa."

[6] *Ba. Kam.* 94. 2 : " Difficilis est admodum pœnitentia publicanorum."

Greek satirist did them no injustice when he classed tax-gatherers in one vile category with whoremongers, brothel-keepers, parasites, and informers and arraigned the villainous gang in fetters before the judgment-seat of Minos in the nether world.[1]

Such were the tax-gatherers. Being a frontier town on that great artery of commerce, the Way of the Sea, Capernaum had a large staff of tax-gatherers; and it chanced that, as He passed by the custom-house, Jesus spied one, Levi the son of Alphæus, seated at his table. "Follow Me," He said, and Levi instantly obeyed and joined the little band of the Lord's comrades. A great future lay before the man. Like Simon he got a new name, and he lives in the world's gratitude and reverence as Matthew the Apostle and Evangelist.[2] *Jesus calls a tax-gatherer named Levi.*

It seems all too sudden, and long ago the Neoplatonist philosopher Porphyry and the apostate Emperor Julian scoffed at the story, arguing that it implied either mendacity on the part of the Evangelists, or folly on the part of the man who followed a stranger at his beck.[3] But in truth it was not so sudden as it seems. Levi must have heard the fame of Jesus; and, though he was an outcast from the Synagogue, it may be that, when Jesus preached on shore or field, he had stood and listened on the outskirts of the crowd. And his heart was accessible to the good tidings of the Kingdom of Heaven. He was a tax-gatherer of the most obnoxious type. He was, as his name indicates, a Jew, yet he had hired himself to the Roman government to do the heathen's work for the heathen's gold, profiting by the shame and oppression of his countrymen. Such a man stood continually on a pillory of scorn and execration, and he must have felt the misery of his situation. Nor is it possible that the memory of earlier and better days should have quite died out of his heart; and, when he heard the message and beheld the works of the Messiah, he would realise what he had lost by making himself an outcast from the hope of Israel. His heart had thus been prepared, and it is no marvel that, when *Levi's preparation for his call.* *Cf.* Lk. xix. 2-3.

---

[1] Luc. *Menipp.* § 11. *Cf.* Theophr. *Char.* xiii (vi).

[2] Mt. ix. 9 = Mk. ii. 14 = Lk. v. 27. According to Clem. Alex. (*Strom.* iv. 9. § 71), Orig. (*C. Cels.* i. 62), Neander, Ewald, Keim, Matthew and Levi were different persons.

[3] Ierome on Mt. ix. 9.

he heard the Lord's gracious call, he gladly and gratefully obeyed it.

He gives an entertainment to his friends. And he forthwith did a grandly heroic thing. He gave an entertainment in his house,[1] assembling a great company of tax-gatherers and others of a like stamp and inviting also Jesus and His disciples. His design is evident. He had said farewell to his evil life, and he brought together his old associates, his boon-companions at many a merry carousal in that very hall, that he might confess Jesus before them and tell what He had done for his poor soul. Thus quickly had the tax-gatherer been transformed into a herald of salvation. The guests would gather eagerly, curious to know what it all meant. And Jesus would very gladly attend.

Jesus attends with His disciples.
ii. 15. It would seem that the hearts of the outcasts had been stirred. "They were many," says St Mark, "and they were for following Him."[2] Yet they were shut off from Him by an insurmountable barrier, excluded as they were from the Synagogue and debarred from mingling with the multitude which thronged about Him out of doors. The heart of Jesus yearned for them, and Levi's entertainment afforded Him an opportunity of getting into close quarters with them.

The Pharisees scandalised.
Cf. Lk. vii. 36-7. The lynx-eyed Pharisees observed whither He went. The banqueting-hall, after the fashion of the day, stood open, and they stole in, forgetful of their dignity and heedless of the pollution which they incurred by entering that unhallowed house. With horror largely feigned they accosted the disciples : "With the tax-gatherers and sinners he is eating and drinking !" Wherefore did they thus surreptitiously address the disciples instead of taking Jesus to task ? Were they afraid to face Him after their recent discomfiture ? Or was it, as St Chrysostom suggests,[3] that they thought basely to discredit Him with His followers and detach them from Him ?

---

[1] Lk. v. 29. Mt. ix. 10 has simply "in the house." Mk. ii. 15 : "He," i.e. Jesus, "was reclining at table in his," i.e. Levi's, "house." Keim insists that ἐν τῇ οἰκίᾳ αὐτοῦ must mean "in the house of Jesus." But it is inconceivable that Peter's house should have accommodated so large a company, and αὐτοῦ may quite well refer to Levi and αὐτὸν to Jesus in the same sentence. Cf. Lk. v. 29.

[2] Another reading (אBL) is καὶ ἠκολούθουν αὐτῷ καὶ γραμματεῖς τῶν Φαρισαίων. καὶ ἰδόντες, κ.τ.λ., i.e. the Pharisees dogged His steps and observed whither He went.

[3] In Matth. xxxi.

Jesus caught their hissing whisper, and, ere the embarrassed disciples could utter a word, He flung His answer in His accusers' faces: "They that are strong have no need of a physician, but they that are ill." The terse epigram was an unanswerable vindication of His attitude toward those outcasts, and it involved at the same time a high claim on His own behalf. He was the Physician of souls, and His mission was the healing of their manifold distempers.[1] It was therefore right that, wherever the plague was rife, there He should be in the exercise of His ministry of mercy. " I came not," He explained with manifest irony, "to call righteous men but sinners."[2] He took His critics at their own valuation. They were righteous? Granted : then they were naught to Him. They had no need of His gracious offices. His irony pierced like a rapier through their mask of sanctity. Despite their pretensions they were in a worse case than the sinners whom they scorned. They too were sick, but they did not know it. And herein lay the desperateness of their condition. The insidious disease was doing its fatal work unperceived and unarrested.

The Lord's defence.

Such was His defence, and He added a stern and humiliating rebuke : "Go ye, and learn what this meaneth : 'It is mercy that I desire and not sacrifice.'" Jesus loved this quotation from the ancient prophet, so apposite as it was to the Pharisaic spirit of His day. He spoke in keen satire. The Scribes were the official exponents of the Scriptures ; and there, in presence of that despised company, He accused them of ignorance of their own proper lore, and contemptuously bade them begone and acquaint themselves with its very rudiments.

His rebuke.

Hos. vi. 6.

Cf. Mt. xii. 7.

Again the Lord's adversaries had been worsted, and again they cast about for some way to be avenged. It chanced that there was a company of the Baptist's disciples at Capernaum ; and they had this in common with the Pharisees, that they were assiduous in their observance of the practice of fasting. Jesus never fasted, and here His unscrupulous adversaries saw their opportunity. They conferred with

A fresh plot.

The disciples of John and fasting.

[1] Cf. Diog. Laert. *Antisth.* vi. 6 : ὀνειδιζόμενος ποτὲ ἐπὶ τῷ πονηροῖς συγγενέσθαι, Καὶ οἱ ἰατροί, φησί, μετὰ τῶν νοσούντων εἰσὶν ἀλλ' οὐ πυρέττουσιν.

[2] Lk. v. 32 : "to repentance," a theological gloss, introduced into T. R. of Mt. ix. 13 and Mk. ii. 17.

John's disciples, and induced them to approach Jesus and
question Him about His neglect of a usage which had
scriptural sanction and was highly esteemed by the religious
world.[1]   It was an astute device.   Evidently they not only
thought to embroil Jesus with the disciples of John and
prevent their accession to His cause, but hoped that He would
condemn fasting and furnish them with a pretext for denouncing
Him as a sacrilegious innovator.   It argues great simplicity
on the part of those earnest men that they should have
been so easily entrapped.   Fasting was the one thing which
they had in common with the Pharisees.   And had they not

Mt. iii. 7-   heard their master's denunciation of that "brood of vipers"?
10.   Did they not remember how those smooth-tongued ecclesiastics
had persecuted him and never rested till they had him
incarcerated in the dungeon of Machærus?

The Lord's   Unconscious that they were the tools of the wily and male-
answer.   volent rulers, they approached Jesus and propounded their
question.   They came in all honesty, and Jesus, according to
His wont with earnest enquirers, received them graciously.
He began with a gentle reproach.   It should have seemed
nothing strange to them that He and His disciples never
fasted.   Did they not remember their Master's declaration

John iii. 29.   on the eve of his arrest?   "He that hath the bride is
the bridegroom, but the friend of the bridegroom that
standeth and heareth him, greatly rejoiceth by reason of the
bridegroom's voice.   This then is my joy which hath been
fulfilled."   So John had told them, and reminding them of
their master's words,[2] Jesus asks them : "Can the friends of
the bridegroom [3] mourn so long as the bridegroom is with
them?"   With the glad tidings of the Kingdom of Heaven in
their ears sadness was no fitting mood for His disciples.
They were no band of mourners but rather resembled a
wedding company.   "Yet," He adds with sudden solemnity,
"there will come days when the bridegroom shall be taken
away from them ; and then they shall fast."   He knew the end

---

[1] According to Mt. it was the disciples of John that approached Jesus ; according
to Lk., the Pharisees ; according to Mk., both.   Probably the disciples of John
interviewed Jesus at the instigation of the Pharisees.

[2] Chrysost. *In Math.* xxxi : ἀναμιμνήσκων αὐτοὺς τῶν Ἰωάννου ῥημάτων.

[3] The Synoptic οἱ υἱοὶ τοῦ νυμφῶνος is Hebraic for οἱ φίλοι τοῦ νυμφίου, οἱ
παράνυμφοι.

from the beginning, and saw the Cross before Him dark and grim.[1]   The thought of it went to His heart like a sudden stab.

Then by a couple of homely metaphors He justified His neglect of fasting.   His Gospel was a new thing and must not be encumbered with remnants of the old economy.   To accept the new and withal cling to the old would be disastrous.   It would be like "stitching a patch of unfulled rag on an old cloak": when the patch got wet, it would shrink and tear the rotten stuff, making a worse rent.   It would be like "putting new wine into old skins": when the wine fermented, it would crack the unsupple leather and burst it, and wine and skins would both be lost.   Thus disastrous would it be to carry the old usages of Judaism into the new life of the Kingdom of Heaven.   It would not save Judaism, and would perpetuate the ancient bondage, annulling the glorious liberty of the children of God.[2]

Jesus had nevertheless a generous sympathy with those who clung to their ancient traditions and had difficulty in accommodating themselves to the new order; and He spoke a deep and gracious word, intended, probably, rather for His own disciples than for the disciples of John: "No one after drinking old wine desireth new; for he saith, 'The old is excellent.'"[3]   It was no fresh metaphor.   The Rabbis had used it,[4] and in his exquisite book which our Jesus loved, another Jesus, the son of Sirach, had written: "Forsake not an old friend; for the new is not comparable to him.   As new wine, so is a new friend: if it become old, thou shalt drink it with gladness."   The Lord's language was not original, but, as He used it, it taught a new lesson, and it were well had the disciples laid it to heart.   Had the advocates of Christian liberty remembered this large-minded word of

His generous sympathy with lovers of the old order.

Ecclus. ix. 10.

---

[1] On the ground of the *a priori* impossibility of an intimation of the Passion thus early Keim puts this incident "between the Baptist's embassy and his death or after his death," which, it is alleged, first revealed to Jesus His fate.   "The Gospels," he remarks with delicious naïveté, "though they quite agree among themselves as to the early date of the controversy, do not agree with us."

[2] Chrysostom (*In Matth.* xxxi), in order to make room for fasting, ingeniously supposes our Lord to mean that His disciples were still weak and had need of forbearance.   They could not endure the burden of ordinances.   The time would come when they would fast, but that time was not yet.

[3] Reading χρηστός.   T. R. χρηστότερος.

[4] *Cf.* Wetstein on Lk. v. 39; Taylor, *Say. of Fath.* iv. 28-9.

Jesus, it would have done much to soften the asperity of
that bitter controversy betwixt Judaism and Paulinism which
well-nigh rent the Apostolic Church asunder.   It would have
taught them to sympathise with brethren who clung tenaciously
to usages endeared by life-long association, and to bear more
gently with their prejudice and slowness of heart.

CHAPTER XV

THE 'OFFENCE OF SABBATH-BREAKING

Mt. xii. 1-14=Mk. ii, 23—iii. 6=Lk. vi. 1-11

"It is better to plough upon holy days than to do nothing, or to do viciously."
                                                        JEREMY TAYLOR.

OF all their sacred institutions there was none which the Jews regarded with such veneration as the Sabbath; and indeed, according to its original institution, there was none which was more worthy of veneration. The Mosaic Law, always humane, had ordained that every seventh day should be given to holy rest for the refreshment alike of body and of spirit. To devout Israelites it seemed as though even inanimate nature shared in the Sabbath's repose, and they told of a river which flowed for six days and ceased on the seventh, hence called the Sabbatic River.[1] Nay, even to Gehenna the benediction extended, and, while the Sabbath lasted, the doomed had rest from torture. It was a beneficent ordinance, but the Rabbis had turned it into an oppressive bondage. The Mosaic enactment was sufficiently stringent; yet they deemed it too lax, and amplified and defined it with vexatious ingenuity.[2] "In it," said the commandment, "thou shalt not do any work"; and they drew up a catalogue of forty works save one which were forbidden and which, if done wittingly, rendered the offender liable to the doom of stoning, and, if done inadvertently, must be expiated by a sin-offering. Nor did they stop here. Those thirty-nine works were primitive or, in Rabbinical phrase, "fathers," and each had its subsection of derivative works or "descendants." Thus, ploughing was one of the thirty-nine, and under it was classed digging. And digging included much. For example, it was forbidden to draw a chair along the ground lest it should make a rut; and,

The beneficent institution of the Sabbath.

Exod. xx. 8-11; xxiii. 12.

The grievousness of Rabbinical legislation.

---

[1] Lightfoot, ii. p. 416; Plin. *H. N.* xxxi. 18. Josephus (*De Bell. Jud.* vii. 5. § 1), differing from both Pliny and the Talmud, says it flowed only on the seventh day.

[2] See Lightfoot and Wetstein on Mt. xii. 2; Edersheim, *Life and Times*, Append. XVII; Schürer, *H. J. P.* II. ii. pp. 96-105.

though it was permissible to spit on a pavement and rub the expectoration with the foot, it was debated whether it were permissible to perform the operation on the earth, forasmuch as the foot would scratch the surface. Another of the " fathers " was carrying a burden, and it had a large brood of " descendants." To walk with a crutch or a wooden leg was permissible ; but to go on stilts was forbidden, since it was not the stilts that carried the man but the man that carried the stilts. Neither was it permissible to wear false teeth or a superfluous garment. A tailor must not go abroad with his needle nor a scribe with his pen toward sunset on Friday, lest the Sabbath should begin ere his return and find him abroad with his burden. Another " father " of work was reaping, and this included the plucking of an ear or a blade. A woman must not look into her mirror on the Sabbath Day, lest she should discover a grey hair and be tempted to pluck it out. This would be a sort of reaping.

Rabbinical casuistry. These are but a few instances of the Rabbinical amplifications and definitions of the Sabbath-law, but they suffice to show how grievous a burden the holy Day of Rest had become in our Lord's time. The worst of it all was that, since the Rabbinical legislation was in practice impossible, it was found necessary to have recourse to casuistry. A useful device was the fiction of *Erubhin* or Connections. Thus, the limit of the Sabbath Day's journey was two thousand cubits beyond the city[1] ; but, if a man desired to travel further, he had only to deposit food for two meals at the boundary on the Friday. This made the boundary, by a technical fiction, his home, and he might journey thence on the Sabbath two thousand cubits further. Again, it was unlawful to convey anything from one house to another on the Sabbath Day ; but, when several houses surrounded a courtyard, the inhabitants had only to deposit food in the courtyard on the Friday, and then the whole area was reckoned as one dwelling. Like the Jesuits, the Rabbis had recourse to the fiction of " intention " ; and they found here an effectual method of evading the precepts of Sabbath-observance. For example, it was unlawful to eat an egg which had been laid on the Sabbath Day ; but let it be understood that the hen was intended for the table, and then

---

[1] Lightfoot on Lk. xxiv. 50 and Acts i. 12.

the egg, being simply a part which had fallen from the hen, might lawfully be eaten.

One Sabbath [1] toward the close of the first year of His ministry [2] Jesus was passing with His disciples along the path which, after the Jewish fashion, [3] led through the midst of a corn-field. The grain was fast ripening for the harvest, and the yellow stalks were nodding on either hand. The disciples were hungry, and they plucked the full ears and, rubbing out the grain betwixt the palms of their hands, ate it as they went. Their action was observed by certain watchful Pharisees, who recognised in it their opportunity. It was not indeed a theft, since it had the sanction of the Law. "When," it is written, "thou comest into the standing corn of thy neighbour, then thou mayest pluck the ears with thine hand ; but thou shalt not move a sickle unto thy neighbour's standing corn." The offence lay in this, that it was done on the Sabbath. And it constituted a double violation of the Sabbath law : when the disciples plucked the ears, they were reaping ; when they rubbed out the grain, they were threshing. [4]

The disciples pluck ears of corn on the Sabbath.

Deut. xxiii. 25.

All eagerness and gesticulation the Pharisees approached Jesus. "See," they cried, "what they are doing on the Sabbath—a thing which is not allowed!" Not an instant did He hesitate. He faced them contemptuously and once more charged them with ignorance of the Scriptures : "Did ye never read what David did when he had need and hungered, himself and his company? how he entered into the House of God and ate the shew-bread." [5] There is no evidence that this incident occurred on a Sabbath, and our Lord does not cite it as an instance of Sabbath-breaking but as an illustration of a broad and far-reaching principle. What David did at Nob was a double violation of the Law. He was a layman ; yet he intruded into the sacred shrine, and he ate the consecrated bread which only the priests

Jesus vindicates them.

1 Sam. xxi. 1-6.

---

[1] See Append. IV.

[2] It fixes the time of the year that the ears were ripe in the field. The harvest began in April, early enough sometimes for the unleavened bread of the Passover to be baked of new flour. *Cf.* Orig. *In Joan.* xiii. § 39.

[3] *Cf.* Lightfoot on Mt. xiii. 4.   [4] *Cf.* Wetstein.

[5] Mk.'s "in the days of Abiathar the High Priest" is a gloss. The priest in question was Ahimelech.

might eat. This constituted a precedent, establishing the
principle that there are occasions when the Law may with
impunity be set aside. And, if a more directly pertinent
instance were desiderated, it was furnished by the constant
practice of the priests in the Temple. On the Sabbath Day
they slew and dressed the sacrificial victims and did much
other work. " There is," it was said, " no Sabbath-observance
in the Temple at all." [1] All this was reckoned no impiety,
since it was done in the service of the Temple. " And I tell
Cf. Mt. xii. you," says Jesus, "that something greater than the Temple
41-2. is here." He meant Himself, the Lord of the Temple ; and
His hearers would remember how at the previous Passover
He had called the Temple His Father's House and swept the
desecrators from its precincts.

Man more   Since there were occasions which justified the setting
than the aside of the Law, it did not forthwith follow that, because
Sabbath.
they broke the Sabbath, the disciples were guilty. It must
first be considered whether occasion had arisen. Jesus
maintained that occasion had arisen, and it was nothing
else than their hunger. " If ye had recognised," He says,
quoting once more that prophetic sentence which He loved,
" what this meaneth : ' It is mercy that I desire and not
sacrifice,' ye would not have condemned the faultless." This
was no new doctrine of the Sabbath, but rather a reversion
to the original design of that humane and beneficent institution. " The Sabbath was made for man's sake, and not man
for the Sabbath's." And, forasmuch as He was the Friend
of man, Jesus claimed authority over it : " The Son of Man
is Lord even of the Sabbath."

Story of a   Jesus was no rude iconoclast. He revered the Law ;
man work- and His desire was not to destroy it but to clear away the
ing on the
Sabbath. rubbish of human invention wherewith it had been overlaid,
and disclose its divine simplicity and majesty, adding to it
withal fresh sanction and significance. Yet it was part of
His humiliation that He had to endure not only the contradiction of sinners but their approbation. Even as in after
Rom. vi. 1. days His free mercy was made a pretext for " continuance in
sin, that grace might abound," so in the days of His flesh
such as were disposed to laxity would justify themselves by

[1] *Cf.* Lightfoot and Wetstein on Mt. xii. 5.

His teaching and screen themselves behind His example.   It
is said [1] that on that very Sabbath Day He observed a man
working, perhaps reaping his field.   So flagrant a violation
of the Sabbath law, so audacious a defiance of religious
sentiment, must have excited general wonderment and
indignation ; and it is likely that the spectators would charge
Jesus with the responsibility.   What but the example of the
disciples and the Lord's vindication thereof had emboldened
the man to that shameless profanation ?   He sternly accosted
the offender.   " Man," [2] He said, enunciating a great principle,
" if thou knowest what thou art doing, blessed art thou ; but,
if thou knowest not, cursed art thou and a transgressor of the
Law."   It was no light thing that the man was doing, and
the question was: Had he seriously considered the matter
and come to the deliberate conclusion that, in view of some
higher obligation, he ought to disregard the Law ?   Or was
he simply a godless worldling who had given the matter no
serious thought and cared for nothing but his temporal
interest ?

On another Sabbath Day Jesus was teaching in the *Jesus heals
a withered
hand on the
Sabbath.*
Synagogue, and it chanced that among His hearers there was
a man whose right hand was atrophied.   It is said that he
had been a mason, and he made his appeal to Jesus : " I was
a mason, winning a livelihood with my hands.   I pray Thee,
Jesus, that Thou restore me to soundness, lest I have the
shame of begging my meat." [3]   The Pharisees were sitting
round intent.   Only when life was in danger, did the Law
permit healing on the Sabbath ; [4] and, since his life was in
no danger, it would be a breach of the Law should Jesus
grant the man's prayer and heal his hand.   They watched
what He would do.   He bade the man advance and take his
stand in the midst of the circle.   Then He looked round on
His enemies and demanded : " Is it allowed on the Sabbath
to do good or to do evil, to save life or to kill ? "   The
question was skilfully put.   Had they been asked whether it

[1] *Cf*. Introd. § 6.

[2] ἄνθρωπε, half contemptuous, half indignant.   *Cf*. Lk. xii. 14 ; xxii. 58, 60.

[3] *The Gospel of the Hebrews*, quoted by Jerome on Mt. xii. 13 : " Cæmentarius
eram manibus victum quæritans ; precor te, Jesu, ut mihi restituas sanitatem, ne
turpiter mendicem cibos."

[4] *Cf*. Lightfoot and Wetstein on Mt. xii. 10.

was lawful to heal on the Sabbath, they would unhesitatingly
have answered : " Not unless the man's life be in danger " ;
but to allow that it was lawful to do good would have been
to give their consent to the miracle. Yet to deny it were
monstrous. They discreetly held their peace. Jesus, grieved
by their inhumanity, swept an indignant glance round the
reverend circle. " What man of you will there be," He cried,
" who shall have one sheep, and, if it fall on the Sabbath into a
pit, will not lay hold on it and lift it ? How much then is a
man better than a sheep ? Therefore it is allowed on the
Sabbath to do well."

It was an effective illustration. The Rabbis had decreed
that, if a beast fell into a pit on the Sabbath Day, its owner
should ascertain whether it had sustained injury. If it had
not, then he must supply it with bedding and food, and let it
remain till the Sabbath was past ; but, if it had, he must take
it out and kill it. Since, however, this rule was found too
hard, they had recourse to casuistry and enacted that in any
case the owner should take out his beast *with the intention of
killing it*, though he should not actually do so.[1] It is no
wonder that Jesus was indignant. They would strain the law
where their property was at stake ; but, where a poor fellow-
creature was concerned, they would not abate a jot of its
rigour. " Stretch forth thy hand," He said. The man obeyed,
and his hand was restored to soundness.

Alliance of
Pharisees
and
Herodians.

The Pharisees had not a word to say ; yet they were
enraged. It would cut them to the quick that they had been
openly put to shame, and they left the Synagogue and held a
council with the Herodians. It was a monstrous confederacy.
The Herodians were apparently a northern sect of the
Sadducees, so called from their obsequious observance of the
Tetrarch Herod Antipas.[2] Herod was a vassal of Rome, and
Cf. Mt. xxii.
16 = Mk.
xii. 13.
it is characteristic of the Herodians that they acquiesced in
the Roman domination and advocated the payment of tribute
to the heathen tyrant. They were traitors alike to Israel

---

[1] See Lightfoot and Wetstein on Mt. xii. 11.

[2] Orig. *In Matth.* § 26. Jerome on Mt. xxii. 16 makes them Herod's soldiers.
Cf. Chrysost. *In Matth.* lxxi. Tertullian (*De Præscript. Hær.* § 45) says they were
so called because they regarded Herod as the Messiah. Certainly their adulation of
Herod amounted to hero-worship ; according to a scholium on Pers. v. 180 they kept
his birthday like a Sabbath. They were Sadducees (*cf.* Mt. xvi. 6 = Mk. viii. 15).

and to Israel's God.   Betwixt them and the Pharisees, those champions of patriotism and orthodoxy, there was a natural and implacable feud, yet they both forgot their animosity for the nonce and made common cause against Jesus.   They took counsel together and resolved that He must die.   Had He not been fenced about by the favour of the multitude, they would have wreaked instant vengeance upon Him.   It was necessary that they should proceed cautiously, but from that day they pursued their bloody purpose with unslacking persistence, and never rested until they saw it, as they vainly supposed, accomplished on Calvary.

CHAPTER XVI

John v.

THE POOL OF BETHESDA

"The Father worketh hitherto,
And Christ, whom I would serve in love and fear,
Went not away to rest Him, but to do
What could be better done in heaven than here,
And bring to all good cheer."—WALTER C. SMITH.

Visit to
Jerusalem. JESUS had completed the first year of His ministry. The Passover had come round once more, and He went up to Jerusalem to keep the Feast.[1] During His sojourn in the Holy City He was narrowly watched. The Sanhedrin's emissaries had brought a report of His doings in Galilee, and it was a heavy indictment. He had been found guilty of blasphemy in usurping the divine prerogative of forgiving sin ; of unseemly association with the outcasts ; of neglect of fasting ; above all, of laxity in the matter of Sabbath-observance. The first and the last were capital offences. It mattered not that He had triumphantly vindicated Himself on each count : their defeat only exasperated His adversaries and whetted their resentment.

The Pool
of
Bethesda.
Neh. iii. 1 ;
xii. 39. They soon found occasion against Him. There was by the Sheep Gate a pool which, since it had medicinal properties, was known by the beautiful name of Bethesda, "House of Mercy."[2] Its water had a reddish tinge, due probably to chalybeate admixture, though tradition ascribes it to the blood of the slaughtered victims which the priests washed in it. At the Passover-season the spring, full-fed by the Winter rain, bubbled up periodically—a perfectly natural phenomenon, occasioned doubtless by the action of volcanic forces in the

---

[1] Cf. Append. V.
[2] T. R., Bethesda. Tisch., W. H., Bethzatha, "House of the Olive." The variant Bethsaida, "House of Fish," is due to the tendency to substitute a familiar name for an unfamiliar. There cannot have been fish in a mineral well.

bowels of the earth.[1]   Of all the medicinal wells in Jerusalem [2] there was none so remarkable as Bethesda.   It was accredited with a powerful efficacy during its periodic ebullition, and it had been surrounded with five porches, that the waiting sufferers might not be crowded together and infect each other with the ceremonial pollution of their various diseases.[3]

It was a wonderful pool, and the popular imagination wove legends in its honour.   One of these is very familiar, since it has intruded into the text of our English Bible and is commonly regarded as a portion of St John's narrative.[4] It ascribes the periodic ebullition to the visitation of an angel who came down and stirred the pool.   And there is another which gives a yet more marvellous explanation.[5]   When Adam, it is said, was a-dying, he sent his son Seth to the angel that guarded Paradise, to crave a portion of the Tree of Life, that he might have health ; and the angel gave him a bough.   Ere Seth could return, his father was dead ; and he buried him and planted the bough upon his grave.   There it flourished and became a tree.   In course of time, when Solomon's Temple was a-building, the tree was hewn down ; but it would not be fitted to any part, and therefore it was laid over a stream to form a bridge.   By and by the Queen of Sheba came with her offerings, and she would not walk over that bridge because she saw the tree and recognised that the Redeemer of the world would suffer thereon.   Long after the Jews took it and cast it into a stagnant pool, and it imparted a wondrous virtue to the putrid water.   And there it remained until the day of our Lord's Passion, when it was taken out and fashioned into a cross.   And hence it is that the Cross is called the Tree. *Acts v. 30; Gal. iii. 13; 1 Pet. ii. 24.*

During His sojourn at Jerusalem Jesus visited Bethesda on the Sabbath Day and found there a throng of sufferers, blind, lame, and palsied, waiting for the ebullition.   One *Healing of a paralytic at Bethesda.*

---

[1] Jerome, *De Loc. Hebr.* Cf. Conder's art. in Hasting's D.B.; Sanday, *Sacr. Sit.* pp. 55-8.

[2] *Cf.* Wetstein on John v. 4.

[3] *Cf.* Lightfoot on John v. 2 and Lk. xvii. 12.

[4] Vers. 4 om. אBC*D, Nonn., Tisch., W. H., modern critics generally. ἐκδεχόμενον τὴν τοῦ ὕδατος κίνησιν is better attested ; om. Tisch., W. H.

[5] Daniel, *Thes. Hymnol.* II. c., n. 3.   *Cf. Travels of Sir John Mandeville,* chap. ii.

particularly engaged His attention and elicited His compassion—an old man who, apparently as the result of early
Cf. v. 14. excess, had been paralysed for eight and thirty years.[1]   All
that weary time he had persistently dragged himsel to
Bethesda, but never had he succeeded in getting into the
pool at the efficacious moment.   He had none to help him,
and others less infirm had always forestalled him.   Yet he
had never relinquished hope ; and on that great Sabbath he
was still at his station, crouching on a poor mat and eagerly
watching for the bubbling of the water.   Jesus not only saw
his misery but read his shame.   " Wilt thou be made whole ? "
He asked by way of arresting the paralytic's attention.
" Sir," was the answer, " I have no man to put me into the
pool when the water is troubled ; and, whilst I am going,
another steppeth down before me."   He hoped that the
pitiful stranger would help him into the pool when the time
came, but Jesus purposed a better thing.   " Rise," He said,
" lift thy mat, and walk."   So entirely had the man's confidence been won that he obeyed without demur, attempting
in faith an impossibility.   In the act vigour pulsed through
his palsied frame ; and he left the porch hale and erect, and
walked homeward through the city, carrying his mat.

Indigna-   The rulers noticed him as he went, light of foot and
tion of the
Rulers. glad of heart.   They do not seem to have recognised him
as the erstwhile paralytic, so little care did those hireling
Cf. Ezek. shepherds of Israel bestow upon the sick and broken of their
xxxiv. 4. flock.   But they observed that he was carrying his mat, and
they angrily challenged him for so flagrant a violation of the
Sabbath law.[2]   He replied that the man who had made him
whole, had bidden him lift his mat and walk.   It was news
to them that he had been healed, but for that they cared
nothing.   They did not ask wonderingly : " And who is he

---

[1] In view of certain points of similarity, actual or alleged,—"the illness, the
culpability, the helplessness, the call of Jesus, the controversy with the Pharisees
on the subject of blasphemy, as well as the period—in the early part of Jesus'
ministry"—Keim makes this miracle a mere embellishment, *Johannino more*, of
the Synoptic story of the paralytic at Capernaum (Mt. ix. 1-8=Mk. ii. 1-12=Lk.
v. 17-26).   It seems to have escaped the ingenious critic that he had been forestalled.   Chrysostom (*Serm.* lxii) refers to "inconsiderate readers" in his day,
" Greeks, Jews, and many of the heretics," who identified the incidents.

[2] Jer. xvii. 21-2 ; Num. xv. 32-6 ; *Shabb. Per.* 10: " Qui autem quidpiam
Sabbato dextrâ gerit aut sinistrâ aut in sinn suo aut super humeros, reus est."

that made thee whole?" The breach of their law was their sole concern. "And who is the fellow," they cried with swelling indignation, "that bade thee, 'Take it up and walk'?" He could not tell. Anxious to escape the applause of the throng at Bethesda, Jesus had stolen away and disappeared.

By and by the man repaired to the Temple. Jesus was on the outlook for him [1] and quietly accosted him. "See," He said, "thou hast been made whole. Sin no more, lest something worse happen to thee." How mercifully the Lord dealt with that poor sinner! He did not open up his shameful past at Bethesda. In the hearing of the throng He spoke never a word which would have put him to shame ; but, more solicitous for the salvation of his soul than for the healing of his body, He sought him out and, taking him apart, brought his sin to his remembrance and charged him to have done with it.

Jesus finds the man in the Temple.

When Jesus let him go, the man repaired to the rulers and told them that it was Jesus that had made him whole. What prompted him to take this step? Was he a monster of ingratitude who, in order to clear himself of the guilt of Sabbath-breaking, did not scruple to betray his Benefactor? It would seem that this opinion, which has still its advocates,[2] was held in early days, and St Chrysostom argues strenuously against it.[3] The man, he points out, told the rulers, not that it was Jesus who had bidden him carry his mat, but that it was Jesus who had made him whole ; testifying to the miracle of mercy which had been wrought upon him, and thinking that it must needs evoke their wonder and adoration. Had he deliberately betrayed his Benefactor, he would indeed have been a veritable "wild beast," yet even so fear must have restrained him. He had experienced the power of Jesus, and the warning : "lest something worse happen to thee," was ringing in his ears. And, it may be added, his presence in the Temple reveals what spirit he was of. He had gone thither with a grateful and penitent heart to give thanks for the mercy which had been vouchsafed to him, and vow to lead thenceforth a new life.

The man informs the rulers.

---

[1] Vers. 14 εὑρίσκει. *Cf.* John i. 41, 43, 45.
[2] *E.g.* Farrar.   [3] *In Joan.* xxxvii.

Their attack on Jesus. Probably he knew nothing of the rulers' hatred of Jesus; and it was in all simplicity and good faith that he went and told them the name of the gracious stranger, never dreaming what would ensue. The rulers swooped down upon Jesus and accused Him of violating the Sabbath law. His defence. Knowing their fondness for doctrinal refinements, He met them with an argument which, profound though it was, closely resembled in form the theologising of the Rabbinical schools. " My Father," He said, " even until now is working, and I am working." God never ceases from His beneficent operations. On the Sabbath even as on other days He makes His sun to rise and His rain to fall. The Sabbath River of Jewish fable might stay its flood every seventh day, but the river of His loving kindness is ever full and ever flowing. And therefore, when Jesus wrought that work of mercy on the Sabbath, He only emulated His Father.

His claim to equality with God. The argument involved a startling claim. The Son of God was a Messianic title, and, since the Jews never expected a divine Messiah,[1] Jesus might have called God His Father without claiming deity. It would have been merely a claim to Messiahship; and, though it might have seemed audacity or imposture, it could not have been reckoned blasphemy. But Jesus claimed more than Messiahship : He claimed deity ; and He made this plain to the rulers. " He called God His peculiar Father, making Himself equal to God." And thus in the eye of the Jewish law He stood guilty of two capital offences—Sabbath-breaking and blasphemy ; and His adversaries were the more exasperated and the more resolute to put Him to death.

Vindication thereof. As was His wont whenever He visited Jerusalem, Jesus boldly advanced His claims. He asserted His unique relationship to God ; and, when the rulers cried out against what they deemed His blasphemy, He reiterated and amplified His assertion. As the Son of God He stood in a unique relation to the Father, a relation involving complete accord of will and action ; and by the Father's appointment life and judgment were at His disposal. " Verily, verily I tell you

---

[1] Cf. Just. M. Dial. c. Tryph., p. 268 A, ed. Sylburg. : καὶ γὰρ πάντες ἡμεῖς τὸν Χριστὸν ἄνθωρπον ἐξ ἀνθρώπου προσδοῶκμεν γενήσεσθαι. Lightfoot on John v. 17 and Acts xiii. 33.

that he that heareth My word and believeth Him that sent Me hath Eternal Life and into judgment cometh not, but hath passed out of death into life. Verily, verily I tell you that an hour is coming and now is when the dead shall hear the voice of the Son of God, and they that have heard shall live." Did it seem incredible that one so lowly should be Lord of Eternal Life, the Resurrection, and the Last Judgment? Nay, rather was it a revelation of the Father's mercy. " He gave Him authority to do judgment because He is the Son of Man"— because He is our Divine Brother, not one who cannot be touched with the feeling of our infirmities, but one who was in all respects tempted like as we are.

> " Thou knowest, not alone as God, all knowing ;
> As Man our mortal weakness Thou hast proved ;
> On earth, with purest sympathies o'erflowing,
> O Saviour, Thou hast wept, and Thou hast loved."

"The Father judgeth none, but all the judgment hath He given to the Son. And He gave Him authority to do judgment because He is the Son of Man."

These were tremendous claims ; and, lest His adversaries should, as on a subsequent occasion, quote their legal maxim that testimony on one's own behalf counts for nothing, Jesus pointed out that His claims had received very powerful attestations. They had been attested, first of all, by John the Baptist. It was little more than a year since the rulers, profoundly impressed by the stern prophet's preaching, had sent a deputation to him, and he had testified to the Messiah-ship of Jesus. And His claims were attested also by His miracles. He had wrought miracles in Jerusalem at the previous Passover, and Nicodemus, the Sanhedrin's delegate, had confessed them an evidence that God was with Him. The fame of His miracles in Galilee had reached the ears of the rulers, and that very day He had wrought another in their midst. His miracles attested His claims. " The works which I do testify concerning Me, that the Father hath com-missioned Me." And, finally, there was the testimony of the Holy Scriptures. Had the rulers had the Word of God abiding in them, they would have believed Jesus. Yet they professed boundless reverence for the Scriptures. Among those who have no part in the world to come, the Rabbis

[Marginal notes: Its three-fold attestation : John viii. 13-4. (1) By John the Baptist. John i. 19-27. (2) By His miracles. John ii. 23. John iii 2. (3) By the Holy Scriptures.]

reckoned those who said that the Law had not been given from Heaven.[1] They maintained that every word of it had been written by God's own finger. It had been given out of Heaven to Moses, and the only question was whether he had received it book by book or all at once.[2] They pored over the Law with incessant and laborious diligence, counting the words, nay, the very letters, and discovering in each a mystic significance.[3] If ever men searched the Scriptures, it was the Rabbis ; nevertheless, when the Redeemer came of whom the Scriptures spoke, whose features were delineated on their every page, and whose salvation was foreshadowed by their every ordinance, they did not recognise Him. And the reason is that they searched the Scriptures with prejudiced minds, not to discover the truth but to buttress their own opinions. They had a great controversy with the Sadducees over the question of the hereafter, and they searched the Scriptures for evidence of their doctrines of the immortality of the soul and the resurrection of the body. They found what they sought, but they missed the testimony which the Scriptures bore to the Saviour who should come. "Ye search [4] the Scriptures," said Jesus, " because ye think that in them ye have 'Eternal Life' ; and it is those Scriptures that testify concerning Me, and ye will not come unto Me that ye may have Life." And truly it is no marvel that they missed the supreme significance of the Scriptures. They did not approach them as humble and reverent learners. Their sole desire was to display their exegetical acumen and win the applause of men. And those Scriptures which, while professing to revere them, they so abused, would rise up and condemn them at the last. Yes, Moses would be their accuser. "For," says Jesus, "if ye had believed Moses, ye would have believed Me. For it was concerning Me that he wrote."

---

[1] Lightfoot on Acts iv. 2.　　　　　　　　　　　[2] *Gitt.* 66. 1.

[3] *Cf.* Lightfoot on Lk. x. 25. סוֹפְרִים, *scribes*, meant literally "counters."

[4] ἐραυνᾶτε, best taken as Indic. not Imper. On the contrary see Wetstein ; Field, *Notes.*

CHAPTER XVII

THE TWELVE APOSTLES

"Gloriosus Apostolorum chorus."

Mk. iii. 7-12; Mt. x. 2-4=Mk. iii. 16-9a= Lk. vi. 13b 16 (Acts i. 13).

WHEN the Feast was over, Jesus returned to Capernaum and resumed His ministry. His popularity was greater than ever. A vast multitude had gathered from the whole of Syria—not only from Galilee and Judæa but from Peræa in the East, Phœnicia in the North, and Idumæa in the South. And the enthusiasm was boundless. "They were falling upon Him," says St Mark, "that they might touch Him, as many as had plagues." It was impossible for Him to preach amid such wild confusion, and He had recourse to an expedient which had already served Him. He bade His fisher disciples keep a little boat in constant readiness that, when the crowd jostled Him, He might get into it and, pushing out from the shore, employ it as His pulpit. If the enthusiasm of the multitude had swelled thus high, the hostility of the rulers had risen to an equal pitch. They had declared open war against Jesus. They had resolved upon His death, and it was only His popularity that stayed their hands. He knew their purpose, and His thoughts went forward to the time when they would have wrought their murderous will upon Him.

He had foreseen that event from the first and had been making preparation for it, that, when He should fall, His cause might not perish. From the ranks of His disciples He had chosen a band of men to be constantly with Him, to aid Him in the work of the Kingdom of Heaven, and to continue it after His departure. Since it was the purpose of God that the Gospel should be preached to Israel first, He had chosen twelve, corresponding to the ancient tribes;[1] and He gave them a title expressive of their function, styling them "Apostles," which means not merely messengers but delegates

Back in Capernaum.

Enthusiasm of the multitude.

Lk. v. 3.

Hostility of the rulers.

Choice of the Twelve.

Cf. Mt. x. 6.

[1] *Cf.* Mt. xix. 28; Barn. *Ep.* § 8.

bearing a commission and, so far as their commission extends, wielding their Master's authority.[1]

Simon
Peter and
Andrew.
John xxi.
15-7.
John i. 44.
Mt. iv. 18
Mk. i. 16.

Who were those twelve men? First come the two brothers, Simon, surnamed Peter, and Andrew. Their father's name was John, and they belonged to Bethsaida, the harbour town of Capernaum. They had both been fishermen on the Lake, and they had met with Jesus down at Bethany beyond Jordan in the morning of His ministry. Of Andrew nothing very remarkable is recorded by the Evangelists, but there is a steadfast and credible tradition that he was crucified at Patræ in Achaia; and it is said that he hung alive on the cross for two days, teaching the people all the while.[2] It would seem that, like Peter, James, and John, he

Mk. xiii. 3.
John i. 35-
42.

enjoyed a special intimacy with the Master; and, since he brought Simon to the newly-found Messiah, he has the distinction of being the first missionary of the Kingdom of Heaven. It was truly a priceless service that he rendered when he brought his brother to Jesus. Simon Peter was the chief of "the glorious company of the Apostles." "The mouth of the Apostles" St Chrysostom styles him,[3] "the ever ardent, the coryphæus of the Apostle choir." In point of intellect indeed he was in no wise comparable to John; yet he had a greatness of his own. If John was "the disciple whom Jesus loved," Peter was the disciple who loved Jesus.[4] That impulsive disciple, so prone to err, so quick to repent, deserves to be held in admiration and reverence. He was continually blundering, and in the panic of the last dread crisis he was guilty of a dire infidelity; nevertheless his very blunders were born of the ardour of his love for Jesus, and in

Lk. xxii.
61-2.
John xxi.
17.

the hour of his unfaithfulness a look from that dear Face broke his heart. When all was over, he could lift his eyes and say: "Lord, Thou knowest all things; Thou perceivest that I love Thee." And right nobly did he vindicate his protestation. For some forty years he did the work of an apostle, and then, if tradition be true, he died a martyr's death at Rome in the last year of Nero's bloody reign. He was sentenced to

---

[1] Lightfoot on Mt. x. 1. *Cf.* J. B. Lightfoot, *Gal.* pp. 92-101.
[2] Abdiæ, *Hist. Apost.* iii. § 41.
[3] *In Matth.* liv. *Cf.* Clem. Alex. *De Div. Serv.* § 21.
[4] *Cf. Aug. In Joan Ev. Tract.* cxxiv. § 4.

crucifixion and at his own request, since he deemed himself unworthy to die like his Lord, he was fastened head-downward to the cross.[1]

Next come other two brothers—James, presumably the elder, and John who had this double bond of fellowship with Andrew, that they had both been disciples of the Baptist and were the earliest to attach themselves to the Messiah. Like Simon and Andrew they had been fishermen on the Lake in company with their father Zebedee and were called from their boats and nets at the commencement of the Lord's Galilean ministry. Since he employed several paid hands, Zebedee had evidently a prosperous business. It nowhere appears that he was in any wise a remarkable man, but his wife was distinguished equally by the strength of her character and by the earnestness of her piety. Her name was Salome ; and, since, it would seem, she was a sister of the Virgin, her sons were cousins of Jesus after the flesh.[2] She was an ambitious woman, but her ambition was all for her sons ; and this fault, if fault it were, was amply atoned by her devotion to Jesus. She was one of the brave women who surrounded the Cross and visited the Sepulchre on the first day of the week. Her sons inherited her ardent spirit, and Jesus playfully designated them Boanerges, that is, Sons of Thunder,[3] in allusion probably to their fiery temper during the earlier days of their discipleship.[4] It was they who would fain have called down fire from Heaven, after the manner of Elijah, upon the unfriendly village of Samaria ; and was it not something of the old fire that blazed up in John long after-

[Marginal references:]
James and John.
Mk. i. 19.
20=Mt. iv. 21-22.
Mt. xx. 20. 1.
Mt. xxvii. 56=Mk. xv. 40.
Mk. xvi. 1.
Lk. ix. 54. 5.

---

[1] Jer. *Script. Eccl.* under *Simon Petrus* ; Eus. *H. E.* iii. 1.

[2] *Cf.* Mt. xxvii. 56 = Mk. xv. 40 with John xix. 25. John enumerates four women at the Cross : (1) the mother of Jesus, (2) her sister, (3) Mary the wife of Clopas, (4) Mary Magdalene. Perhaps modesty kept him from saying that (2) was his own mother Salome (*cf.* Mt. = Mk.). Jerome in a doctrinal interest (see p. 18, n. 3) held that only three women are enumerated by John, the second being " the sister of Jesus' mother, viz. M. the wife of Clopas (Alphæus)," and that it is her children (Mk. xv. 40 = Mt. xxvii. 56), really His cousins, that are called " the Lord's brethren." But (1) it is unlikely that two sisters were called Mary ; (2) James the Little (Mk. xv. 40) was an apostle, and none of " the Lord's brethren " were apostles (*cf.* Acts i. 13-4).

[3] בְּנֵי רְגֶשׁ. *Sheva* was popularly pronounced *oa. Cf. Moasada* for *Masada* (מצָדה). See Lightfoot on Mk. iii. 17.

[4] Jerome regards the epithet as descriptive of their eloquence.

wards when, learning that Cerinthus was in the public baths at Ephesus, he hurried from the building lest the roof should fall and he should share the heretic's doom?[1]

The sons of Zebedee and Peter won the special confidence of Jesus and enjoyed a peculiar intimacy with Him. They were "the inner circle of the elect."[2] It was the privilege of Peter and John to glorify their Lord by long years of honourable and fruitful ministry, but for James it was ordered otherwise. Herod Agrippa put him to a martyr's death. The tragedy is recorded by St Luke in a single sentence: **Acts xii. 2.** "He slew James, the brother of John, by the sword"; but tradition is more generous of details, whatever be their value.[3] James, so runs the story, was accused by a scribe named Josias. He was sentenced to death, and, as they were dragging him along by a halter, his accuser, moved to penitence by the apostle's testimony,[4] fell at his feet, crying: "Pardon me, thou man of God; for I have repented of the things which I have spoken against thee." James kissed him and answered: "Peace to thee, child, peace to thee, and pardon for thy transgression." Josias avowed himself a Christian on the spot, and they were beheaded together, the apostle and his accuser.[5]

Philip and Nathanael Bar Talmai. Next come Philip and Bartholomew. The former, like Andrew and Peter, belonged to Bethsaida, and he first met **John i. 44.** with Jesus down at Bethany beyond Jordan. On that memorable occasion he evinced a retiringness which lends **Lk. ix. 59-60=Mt. viii. 21-2.** credibility to the tradition that he was the disciple who would fain have excused himself from obeying the Lord's call on the score of domestic obligations.[6] It would seem from his **John xiv. 8-9.** remark in the Upper Room and the Lord's reply that he was somewhat slow of heart and dull in spiritual understanding; yet he had his peculiar aptitudes which justified his election to the apostleship. There is room in the Lord's service for

[1] Iren. *Adv. Hær.* iii. 3. § 4; Eus. *H. E.* iii. 28.
[2] Clem. Alex. *De Div. Serv.* § 36: τῶν ἐκλεκτῶν ἐκλεκτότεροι.
[3] Eus. *H. E.* ii. 9; Suid. under Ἡρώδης: Abd. *Hist. Apost.* iv. §§ 8-9.
[4] According to later legend, by his healing a paralytic on the road "in the name of Jesus Christ for whose faith I am being led to death."
[5] A legend, irreconcilable with the facts of history, has it that James preached in Spain and was buried at Compostella. Daniel, *ibid.*; Lightfoot on Acts xii. 2. The shrine of St James of Compostella was a favourite resort of medieval pilgrims.
[6] *Cf.* p. 90.

the exercise of all sorts of gifts, and it would seem that Philip, being of a practical turn, was charged with the duty of catering for the disciple-band.[1] It appears that he was on terms of special intimacy with Andrew.[2]

John vi. 8; xii. 21-2.

And what of Bartholomew? It is said that he wrote a Gospel and that he preached to the Indians,[3] but outside the catalogues of the Apostles his name is never mentioned in the New Testament. It were strange indeed had one of the Twelve been thus buried in oblivion ; and it is provocative of speculation that Bartholomew is really not a name but a patronymic, Bar Talmai, the son of Talmai.[4] There is much reasonableness in the suggestion that the Son of Talmai was none other than Nathanael of Cana, that earnest Israelite so well versed in the Scriptures whom Jesus found on the road northward from Bethany beyond Jordan deliberating the question of His Messiahship.[5] The identification has no little probability. Even as the other Evangelists never mention Nathanael, so St John never mentions Bar Talmai. He intro- duces Nathanael on two occasions : the first at the beginning, when he met with Jesus on the way to Cana ; and the other at the close, when with six others he witnessed the manifesta- tion of the Risen Lord by the Lake of Galilee. Since the four others who in the latter instance are mentioned by name, were all apostles, it is a reasonable inference that Nathanael also was an apostle. And it is a further confirmation that Philip and Bar Talmai are coupled in the catalogues of the Apostles. Since Philip was a friend of Nathanael and brought him to Jesus, it was fitting that they should be sent forth in company on their missionary labours.

John i. 45- 51.
John xxi. 1-14.

Next come Thomas and Matthew. Thomas is not a name but an epithet, meaning, like its Greek equivalent Didymus, the Twin ;[6] and it is credibly reported that the name of this

Judas the Twin, and Matthew.
John xi. 16; xxiv. 29; xxi. 2.

---

[1] *Cf.* Beng. on John vi. 5.   [2] Philip was buried at Hierapolis (Eus. *H. E.* iii. 31).

[3] Jer. *In Comm. super Matth. Prooem.*; *Script. Eccl.*

[4] *Cf.* Bar Jonas, Bar Timæus. Talmai (2 Sam. xiii. 37) Græcised Θολομαῖος. Jos. *Ant.* xiv. 8. § 1 ; xx. 1. § 1.

[5] Lightfoot, Wetstein. The identification was unknown to Augustine who sug- gested (*In Joan. Ev. Tract.* vii. § 17) that Nathanael was excluded from the apostle- ship because he was a learned man and Jesus chose unlearned men to confound the world. *Cf. In Psalm.* lxv. § 4.

[6] תְּאוֹם, Aram. with art. תְּאוֹמָא, ὁ δίδυμος.

apostle was Judas.[1] He was styled the Twin for distinction's sake, since there were two others among the Twelve who bore that unhappy name. The earlier Evangelists merely mention

xi. 16; xiv. 5; xx. 24-9; xxi. 2.

him as one of the Apostles, but St John has rescued him from oblivion and revealed what manner of man he was. He shared to the full the slowness of heart which characterised all the Twelve while the Lord was with them ; but his predominant characteristic was a disposition to look always at the dark side and hug despair. He was gloomy and querulous, yet withal he had a great devotion to Jesus. It was he who, when the Master insisted on venturing again into hostile Judæa and the rest were minded to let Him go alone, cried : " Let us also go, that we may die with Him ! " There was something of the hero about that despondent apostle.

Tradition credits the Twin with the authorship of a Gospel,[2] and this adds interest to his association with the Evangelist whose *Sayings of Jesus* is the basis of the first of the canonical Gospels. Was it because the memory of his shameful past had wrought in Matthew, the erstwhile tax-gatherer, a spirit of meekness that Jesus assigned him a comrade whose querulousness must have made him at times difficult to endure ? In former days he had been called Levi, but, when he met with Jesus and became by His grace a new man, he got, in accordance with ancient custom, a new name—Matthew, the Gift of the Lord. And it is very remarkable that, whereas St

Mt. ix. 9= Mk. ii. 14 =Lk. v. 27.

Mark and St Luke, when they tell the story of his call, give him his old name of Levi, never hinting, in their tender charity, who that tax-gatherer was, St Matthew himself, when he tells the story, calls the tax-gatherer Matthew, publishing his identity. And in their catalogues of the Apostles St

Mt. x. 3= Mk. iii. 18 =Lk. vi. 15.

Mark and St Luke call him simply Matthew ; but, when St Matthew comes to his own name, he says, " Matthew the Tax-gatherer," deliberately blazoning his shame abroad in order to magnify the grace of Jesus ; like John Bunyan when he put on the title-page of his autobiography that poignant sentence : " I have been vile myself, but have obtained mercy, and I would have my companions in sin partake of mercy too."

---

[1] Eus. *H. E.* i. 13 : Ἰούδας ὁ καὶ Θωμᾶς. *Act. Thom.*
[2] The apocryphal *Ev. Thom. Cf.* Jer. *In Comm. sup. Matth. Proœm.*

Next come James, the Son of Alphæus, and one who is
named by St Matthew Lebbæus, by St Mark Thaddæus, and by
St Luke Judas, the Son of James.[1]   In allusion doubtless to
his stature James was entitled the Little [2] to distinguish him
from James the Son of Zebedee.   If Alphæus be indeed
identical with Clopas,[3] then his mother was Mary, one of the
women who stood beside the Cross and visited the Sepulchre
on the Resurrection morning.   It is possible that Alphæus
the father of James was the same as Alphæus the father of
Levi the tax-gatherer.[4]   Tradition says that James also had
been a tax-gatherer,[5] and it is likely that he was one of the
company at that memorable feast which Levi made in his
house when he bade farewell to his old life and entered on his
new life of discipleship under his new name Matthew.   If
these identifications be allowed, then great indeed was
the glory of that home which furnished to the Kingdom of
Heaven a father, a mother, and three sons, two of them
apostles.

Cf. Mk. xv. 40.

And what of James the Little's comrade?   His name was
Judas and his father's James.   Since there were two others of
the Apostle-band named Judas, he bore two distinctive epithets.
To mark him out, on the one hand, from the despondent Judas
the Twin he was styled Thaddæus, the Aramaic Taddai, which
means " the Courageous "; and to mark him out, on the other
hand, from the cold and worldly-minded Judas Iskarioth he
was styled Lebbæus, the Aramaic Libbai, which means " the
Hearty." [6]   Once only does he figure in the Gospel-story.
When Jesus in His farewell address in the Upper Room
promised to manifest Himself to such as loved Him, he ex-

Marginal notes: James the Son of Alphæus (Clopas) and Judas Libbai or Taddai. Mk. xv. 40. John xix. 25; Mk. xv. 40; Mk. xvi. 1. Mk. ii. 14.

---

[1] Ἰούδας Ἰακώβου, not "the *brother* of James" (Bez., A.V.)—an arbitrary
identification of the Apostle with the author of the Epistle. *Cf.* Jer. *Ep. ad
Paulin.*: "Jacobus, Petrus, Joannes, Judas Apostoli septem epistolas ediderunt tam
mysticas quam succinctas." Nonnus, *Paraphr. S. Ev. Joan.* xiv. 84-5 : Ἰούδας υἱὸς
Ἰακώβοιο.

[2] μικρός cannot mean *natu minor*. *Cf.* Lk. xix. 3 : τῇ ἡλικίᾳ μικρός.

[3] Ἀλφαῖος and Κλωπᾶς both represent חֲלְפִּי. In John xix. 25 read *Clopas* and
distinguish Cleopas (Lk. xxiv. 18). Κλεόπας = Κλεόπατρος, as Ἀντίπας = Ἀντίπατρος.

[4] It is curious that for *Levi* some ancient authorities give *James* in Mk. ii. 14.

[5] Chrysost. *In Matth.* xxxiii : δύο τελῶναι, Ματθαῖος καὶ Ἰάκωβος.

[6] Thaddæus = תַּדַּי ; Lebbæus = לִבַּי, *corculus* (Jerome) Dalman, *Words of
Jesus*, p. 50. Lightfoot derives Lebbæus from the town of Lebba (Plin. *H. N.*
v. 17).

John xiv. 22. claimed : " Lord, what hath come to pass that to us Thou art about to manifest Thyself, and not to the world ? " The question merely shows that Judas cherished the same secular ideal of the Messianic Kingdom as his fellow-apostles and the rest of the Jews. He was dreaming of an earthly throne and

Cf. John vii. 5. expecting that Jesus would presently " manifest Himself to the world," casting aside His disguise and flashing forth in regal splendour ; and he marvelled what could have happened to prevent this consummation.

Simon the Zealot and Judas the man of Kerioth. Last come another Simon and another Judas. To distinguish him from Simon Peter the former is designated the Cananæan or Zealot. He was a member of that fraternity of desperate patriots who, amid the commotion attendant on the

Acts v. 37. census of A.D. 7, had pledged themselves to undying hostility against the Roman government ;[1] and it was a bold thing that Jesus did when He enrolled him among His followers. It exposed Him to the suspicion of the Roman authorities. When the Jewish rulers arraigned Him at the last before the procurator Pontius Pilate, it was on a political charge. They

Lk. xxiii. 2. represented Him as a dangerous revolutionary. And it would lend plausibility to their allegation that one of His intimates was a member of that seditious sect. The Zealots were the extreme opposites of those Jews who, setting patriotism and religion alike at naught, took service as tax-gatherers under the Roman government ; and it is a striking evidence of the wideness of the Lord's sympathy that Simon the Zealot should have been enrolled with the tax-gatherers Matthew and James in the apostolic brotherhood, and that men so diverse should have found in His discipleship a common meeting-place.

Simon's comrade was Judas, styled, to distinguish him from Judas the Twin and Judas the son of James, Judas Iskarioth, that is, the Man of Kerioth, a town in the south of Judæa.[2]

---

[1] *Cf.* p. 35. Καναναῖος = קַנְאָנִיָּא. Despite Lk.'s τὸν καλούμενον Ζηλωτὴν the epithet has been greatly misunderstood. (1) Jerome, Bede, Tyndale, Coverdale, Great Bible : " Man of Cana." (2) Bishops' Bible, A.V. : " Canaanite," confounding Καν. with Χαναναῖος (*cf.* Mt. xv. 22).

[2] אִישׁ קְרִיוֹת, Ἰσκαριώθ, Ἰσκαριώτης. Jerome (on Mt. x. 4 ; Ps. cviii (cix). 10 ; *De Nom. Hebr.*) doubted whether the name was derived from the town of Judas or from his tribe, Issachar, explaining it in either case as connected with

His father was named Simon, and he also belonged to Kerioth.[1]
Judas was distinguished from his fellow-apostles in that he
was apparently the only one who was not a Galilean.   Jesus
marked the various aptitudes of His followers, and assigned to
each the office for which he was fitted.   He entrusted Philip
with the business of the commissariat, and, since Judas had
an aptitude for finance, He made him treasurer.

Judas turned traitor and sold Jesus to the priests, and his *The Lord's
choice of*
admission into the apostle-company presents one of the most *Judas a*
perplexing problems of the Gospel-history.   Long ago the *problem.*
philosopher Celsus made the treachery of Judas the ground of
an envenomed attack.   Jesus, he sneered, inspired in His
deluded followers less loyalty than a general inspires in his
troops, aye, less than a brigand-chief inspires in his gang
of desperadoes.[2]   And truly, though the infamy rests
with the traitor, it seems to imply a lack of discernment on
the part of Jesus that He should have trusted Judas and
received him into the circle of His intimates.   The emphatic
declaration of St John that "He knew from the first who *vi. 64; cf.*
should betray Him," is indeed a vindication of the Lord's *71.*
foresight, but it seems only an aggravation of the difficulty.
If He foresaw the issue, wherefore did He deliberately choose
Judas?   And wherefore did He appoint him to an office
which would excite his cupidity?   "Who," it has been argued,
"places the weak in a situation which so constantly appeals to
his weak point as to render it certain that he will sooner or later
give way to the temptation?   No truly: Jesus assuredly
did not so play with the souls immediately entrusted to him,
did not exhibit to them so completely the opposite of what
he taught them to pray for, 'Lead us not into temptation,' as *Mt. vi. 13*
to have made Judas, of whom he foreknew that he would
become his betrayer out of covetousness, the purse-bearer of his
society; or, if he gave him this office, he cannot have had
such a foreknowledge."[3]

From the earliest days the problem has pressed for a *Theories.*

שָׂקַר, *price, wages*—a prophecy of the thirty pieces of silver.   Keim thinks of Koreæ
on the northern border of Judæa.   Ewald, deeming it unlikely that Judas was a
Judæan, suggests Kartah (Josh. xxi. 34).
[1] According to the true reading of John vi. 71, xiii. 26 : Σίμωνος Ἰσκαριώτου.
[2] Orig. *C. Cels.* ii. 12.   [3] Strauss, *Leb. Jes.* III. ii. § 118.

solution and has provoked much ingenious speculation.   The Cainites, that fantastic sect of the Gnostics, held that Judas had advanced beyond the Jewish ideas of his fellow-apostles and attained to the heavenly *gnosis*. He betrayed Jesus because he knew that His death would break the power of the evil spirits, the rulers of this world.[1] Another theory of early days is that Judas was indeed a covetous man and sold his Master for greed of the thirty pieces of silver, but he never thought that Jesus would be slain.   He trusted that He would escape from the grasp of His enemies as He had done before ; and, when he saw Him actually condemned, he was over- whelmed with remorse.[2]   Akin to this is the more modern theory that he calculated upon the multitude rising and rescuing Jesus from the rulers.[3]   Like the rest of the disciples, it is urged, Judas was discontented with the Lord's inexplicable procrastination in proclaiming Himself King of Israel and rallying the nation to His side, and he thought to force His hand and precipitate the *dénouement*.   " His hope was that, when at length actually arrested by the Jewish authorities, Christ would no longer vacillate ; he would be forced into giving the signal to the populace of Jerusalem, who would then rise unanimously." [4]   Again it has been supposed that Judas' faith in his Master's Messiahship was wavering.   If, he reasoned, Jesus were indeed the Messiah, no worldly power could harm Him : on the contrary, opposition would only serve to bring out His glory ; while, if He succumbed, it would be an evidence that He was not the Messiah ; God would have pro- nounced againt Him, and His death would be merely His desert.[5]

According to the Evangelists the be- trayal a crime.

vi. 70.

xxii. 3-4.

Those theories aim at justifying Judas and vindicating the Lord's election of him to the apostleship, but they are all mere fancies not only absolutely unsupported but directly discountenanced by the evangelic narratives.   " Did I not," said Jesus according to St John, " choose you the Twelve ? and of you one is a devil."   " And Satan," says St Luke, " entered into Judas, that is called the Man of Kerioth, being of the number of the Twelve ; and he went away and

---

[1] Iren. *Adv. Hær*. i. 28. § 9 ; Epiphan. *Hær*. xxxviii. § 3.
[2] See Theophyl. on Mt. xxvii. 4.   [3] Paulus.
[4] De Quincey, Rosegger.   [5] Neander, *Leb. Jes. Chr.* § 264.

conferred with the High Priests and the Captains how he might betray Him unto them." The Evangelists represent the betrayal as a horrible, nay, diabolical crime.[1]

And their representation should be simply accepted. The Lord's choice of Judas with clear prescience of the issue is indeed a dark mystery, but it is in line with the providential conduct of human affairs and runs back to the ancient and abiding problem of the relation betwixt divine foreknowledge and human freedom. Even as God knew the issue when He raised Saul to the throne of Israel, so Jesus from the beginning perceived what was in Judas and knew the part which he would play. And may it not be affirmed without presumption that He recognised him as God's instrument for the accomplishment of His eternal purpose of salvation? It was by the determinate will and foreknowledge of God that Jesus was betrayed into the hands of sinners, and it was by the determinate will and foreknowledge of God that the traitor was numbered with the Twelve. Nevertheless Judas was not chosen because he would turn traitor, but because he had in him at the outset the possibility of higher things. And this is the tragedy of his career, that he yielded to the baser impulses of his nature and suffered them to usurp dominion over him. Cupidity was his damning quality. In common with the rest of the Apostles he entertained the prevailing conception of the Messianic Kingdom; and, recognising Jesus as the Messiah, he joined His cause in the expectation of attaining to worldly greatness and reward when his Master was seated upon the throne of Israel. As time went on, his hope grew dim; and, when during the Passion-week he perceived the inevitable issue, he resolved to abandon what he deemed a falling cause and, in a spirit at once of revenge and of despair, carry with him what poor spoil he might, securing some small recompense for the sacrifices which he had made. If he could not have a place beside

The old problem of divine foreknowledge and human freedom.

[1] Volkmar regards the story of the betrayal as a tendency-fiction. "The motive for inventing a traitor," says Strauss (*New Life*, i. p. 376), "is considered by the acute author of this theory to lie in the wish of the Pauline party to make room for the Apostle of the heathen in the college of Twelve, which could not be done except by ejecting one of them, the treason of the Jewish people to Jesus being transferred to him." The theory was rejected by Strauss and Keim, but it has been revived in a modified form by Cheyne, *E. B.* art. *Judas* § 10.

the Messiah's throne, at least he would have the thirty pieces of silver.

General estimate of the Twelve.

It would seem that the Apostles were all young men, Simon Peter being apparently the only one who was married. Certainly they were all younger than Jesus, who was as a father among them in love and admonition.[1] Some of them came to Him from the houses of their fathers; and He required them to love Himself more than father or mother, brothers or sisters. It was natural that He should choose as His Apostles young men still unenslaved by custom, still unpossessed by prejudice, still receptive of new truths, still sensitive to wonder and hope.[2] And most of them, indeed all except, perhaps, Nathanael the son of Talmai,

Mt. xi. 25; cf. Acts iv. 13.

were destitute of worldly learning, unlike their future compeer St Paul. Yet they had better gifts. At least two of them had been disciples of John the Baptist, and probably all, except the two tax-gatherers, had led blameless if not pious lives.[3] And all, except the traitor, nobly requited the confidence which Jesus had reposed in them. They gave themselves, in the power of the Holy Spirit, to their mission, and some, perhaps most, of them sealed their testimony with their blood.[4]

[1] He styled them "children" (Mk. x. 24 ; John xiii. 33) and promised that He would not leave them "orphans" (John xiv. 18).

[2] Darwin to J. D. Hooker (*Life of Darwin*, p. 230): "Nearly all men past a moderate age, either in actual years or in mind, are, I am fully convinced, incapable of looking at facts under a new point of view."

[3] Utterly erroneous is the inference from Mt. ix. 13=Mk. ii. 17=Lk. v. 32 that the Apostles had all been great sinners. Barn. *Ep.* v. § 9.

[4] On the subsequent careers of the Twelve *cf.* Chrysost. *Serm. in xii. Apost.*; Eus. *H. E.* iii. 1 ; Abd. *Hist. Apost.*; Daniel, *Thes. Hymnol.* II. ccxxiii. Papias (Fragm. xi. in *Patr. Apost. Op.* from Georg. Hamart.) says that John as well as James ὑπὸ Ἰουδαίων ἀνῃρέθη in fulfilment of Mk. x. 38-9.

CHAPTER XVIII

THE ORDINATION OF THE TWELVE

Mt. v. 1 =
Mk. iii. 13.
5 = Lk. vi.
12-3a ;
Lk. vi. 20-
38, 41-9 ;
xi. 33 = Mt.
v. 2-16, 39b-
42, 44-8 ;
vii. 1-6, 12,
15-27.

" Qui generosus miles est,
Sibi ducat honori
Cum duce Jesu millies
In campo crucis mori."—*Med. Hymn.*

THE ordination of the twelve Apostles, His comrades and *The ordin-* successors, was a momentous departure, and Jesus, according *ation* *address.* to His wont at every great crisis, betook Himself to His upland oratory and spent the livelong night in prayer.[1] In the morning He called them about Him, and solemnly ordained them ; and then He discoursed to them of their high vocation, showing them how great was the trust which had been committed to them and what manner of men they must be. He began with congratulation. " Blessed are ye " *The Beati-* was His opening sentence, and it would seem most natural to *tudes.* the Twelve with their Jewish dream of an earthly Kingdom. Extreme would their astonishment be when they heard Him further. He pronounced them " blessed," not because they would have places by His throne in Jerusalem, but because they would be poor, lowly, sorrowful, despised, and persecuted. Every sentence of His benediction was in Jewish ears an astounding paradox.[2]

It is always the tendency of worldly prosperity to draw the heart away from God, but it was especially so amid the

---

[1] The site of the *Mons Beatitudinum* has been much debated. Tabor, says Jerome in opposition to "nonnulli simplicium fratrum " who thought of Olivet. An early western tradition identifies it with the Horns of Hattin (*Kurûn Hattin*), at whose bases lies a level expanse, corresponding to the τόπος πεδινός of Lk. vi. 17. *Cf.* Caspari, § 108. Probably, however, Lk. vi. 17-9 is an editorial conflation of Mt. viii. 1 and Mk. iii. 7-12. It interrupts and confuses the narrative. The likelihood is that τὸ ὄρος (Mt. v. 1) denotes no particular hill but the high land bounding Gennesaret on the west. *Cf.* Josh. xvii. 16 ; xix. 50, where הָהָר, LXX τὸ ὄρος, is not " the hill," but " the hill-country."

[2] On the differences between the parallel versions of the Beatitudes see Introd. § 12, 3, (1).

disasters which pressed upon Israel almost without intermission after the Babylonian Captivity. When the nation was under heathen domination, disloyalty to Jehovah was the condition of worldly advancement, and such as stood faithful sank into obscurity and suffered contempt and persecution. And thus it came to pass that " poor " was practically synonymous

Cf. Is. liii. with "godly," and "rich" with "ungodly." The *poor*, the
9. *needy*, the *meek*, the *humble* were thus almost technical terms.[1] They signified the godly remnant in Israel.[2] When Jesus pronounced the Twelve "blessed," because they belonged to that order, it was probably His purpose to dispel their dream of worldly felicity in the Messianic Kingdom. He told them what must be their lot as His Apostles, as though challenging their courage to accept it. He would have them at the outset clearly understand the conditions of their ministry lest they should embark upon it in ignorance and abandon it in disappointment. Yet withal He added high encouragements. One was that, when they suffered, it would be *for His sake*. Another was that, though persecution must be their earthly portion, their recompense would be great in Heaven. And, moreover, it was a heroic calling. They would be in the ranks with the prophets of old time who had suffered persecution and often martyrdom. When He thus spoke, Jesus advanced a high claim on His own behalf. " He hints here," says St Chrysostom, " at His own dignity and His equal honour with the Father. As the Prophets, He says, suffered for the Father's sake, so you shall suffer all this for Mine."[3]

The calling   It was not, however, of themselves and their fortunes but
of the   of their mission that Jesus would have the Twelve think ;
Twelve.   and, alluding perhaps to the Essenes who forsook the world and lived hermit lives, holy but unserviceable, in the seclusion of the wilderness, He shows them, by two vivid metaphors, whereunto they were called—not to pious repose but to

"The salt active and beneficent service.[4] " Ye," He says, " are the salt
of the of the earth." This is a figure which our Lord loved and
earth." which He frequently employed. And it would go home to
Cf. Mk. ix.
50 ; Lk.
xiv. 34-5.   [1] πτωχός, πένης, πραΰς, ταπεινός. See Hatch, *Ess. in Bib. Gk.* pp. 74-7 ; Harnack, *What is Christianity ?* pp. 91-2.
[2] *Cf.* p. 5.   [3] *In Matth.* xv.
[4] *Cf. Ep. ad Diogn.* vi : ὅπερ ἐστὶν ἐν σώματι ψυχή, τοῦτ' εἰσὶν ἐν κόσμῳ Χριστιανοί.

His fisher disciples. They knew how quickly in that sultry climate their fish would spoil unless salted without delay. And they knew also that nothing was more worthless than salt which had lost its saltness and become insipid, as the salt of Palestine readily does "when in contact with the ground or exposed to rain and sun." "Such salt soon effloresces and turns to dust—not to fruitful soil, however. It is not only good for nothing itself, but it actually destroys all fertility wherever it is thrown. . . . So troublesome is this corrupted salt, that it is carefully swept up, carried forth, and thrown into the street. There is no place about the house, yard, or garden where it can be tolerated."[1] Even such are savourless disciples. "Ye are the salt of the earth ; but. if the salt become insipid, wherewith shall it be salted? For nothing doth it avail any longer save to be flung out and trodden down by the people."

"Ye are the light of the world," said Jesus again. That a light may serve its purpose it must be conspicuous, and the mistake of the Essenes was that they hid their light. They were indeed holy men, but they led secluded lives and exerted no influence upon their fellows. Jesus required that it should be otherwise with His disciples. The Lake of Galilee was girt round by high-perched towns—Gerasa. Gamala, Aphek, and Hippos—that stood like beacons and caught the eye from afar. "A city," says Jesus, turning the landscape into a parable, "cannot be hid when set upon a hill.[2] Neither do they light a lamp and put it under the bushel-measure, but on the lamp-stand, and it shineth for all that are in the house. Even so let your light shine before men, that they may see your fair works and glorify your Father in Heaven."

"The light of the world."

Such was the calling of the Twelve—not to dream of honour and reward in an earthly kingdom, but to seek, with utter self-forgetfulness, the glory of God and the salvation of their fellow men. Thus early Jesus hints at the universality of their mission and the world-wide destina-

---

[1] Thomson, *Land and Book*, chap. xxvi.

[2] *Cf.* 1897 Oxyrhynchus *Logia* 7 : λέγει Ἰησοῦς· πόλις ᾠκοδομημένη ἐπ᾽ ἄκρον [ὄ]ρους ὑψηλοῦ καὶ ἐστηριγμένη οὔτε πε[σ]εῖν δύναται οὔτε κρυ[β]ῆναι. Evidently amplified from Mt. vii. 24-5.

tion of His Gospel. He says, "Ye are the light," not of Israel, but "of the world." Theirs was the privilege where-unto Israel had been called of old, but whereof she had proved herself unworthy, declining into narrowness and isolation.

Jesus had warned the Apostles that they must lay their account for persecution, and He proceeded to instruct them how they should comport themselves therein, adducing, after the picturesque manner which He loved, several examples of the sort of treatment which they would encounter. Smiting on the face was a common form of insult in the East.[1] A fine of two hundred *zuzim* or *denarii* was imposed for the offence, and, if the aggressor inflicted a second blow with his other hand, the fine was doubled.[2] The injury was insignificant, but the indignity was extreme. Even a slave, says Seneca, would prefer scourging to a buffet.[3] Such contumely the Twelve would encounter in the prosecution of their mission. "Whoever," says Jesus, "smiteth thee on the right cheek,[4] turn to him the other also." Again, it was legal for a creditor to take his debtor's raiment in pledge; but the ancient Law, with its accustomed humanity, provided that the poor man's cloak, which served also as his blanket, should be restored to him at sunset, lest he should have no covering while he slept. "Him," says Jesus, "that would go to law with thee · and take thy coat, let him have thy cloak also."[5] Though their coats might be legally retained, they were entitled to claim their cloaks at nightfall; but He bids them forego this right, cheerfully submitting to illegal spoliation. Once more, there prevailed throughout the Roman Empire a system of forced service which empowered soldiers to employ both men and beasts as their baggage-bearers.[6] The outrage was bitterly resented, and by none

Marginal notes:
Cf. Is. lx. 1-3.

Injunctions to meek endurance:

of insult;

of extortion; Prov. xx. 16.

Exod. xxii. 26-7; *cf.* Am. ii. 8.

of tyranny.

---

[1] *Cf.* 1 Kings xxii. 24; Mt. xxvi. 67; Acts xxiii. 2; 1 Cor. iv. 11; 2 Cor. xi. 20.

[2] *Cf.* Lightfoot on Mt. v. 39, and Mk. vi. 37.　　[3] *De Constant. Sap.* § 4.

[4] The *left* cheek would naturally be first struck, and some MSS. omit *right* (*cf.* Lk. vi. 29). Its addition heightens the idea of contumely, the right being *pars potior* (*cf.* Mt. v. 29, 30).

[5] Lk. vi. 29, perhaps from unacquaintance with the Jewish law, puts the *cloak* first—the order of stripping.

[6] ἀγγαρεία, a Persian word; originally a system of communication by relays of mounted couriers. *Cf.* Herod viii. 98; Xen. *Cyrop.* viii. 6. § 17; Esth. vii. 10; Æsch. *Agam.* 273; Hatch, *Ess. in Bib. Gk.* pp. 37-8; Deissmann, *Bib. Stud.* pp. 86-7; Taylor, *Say. of Fath.* iii. 18, n. 30.

more than by the proud Jews. "Do not resent it," says Jesus to the Twelve. "Submit cheerfully. Whosoever shall impress thee for one mile, go with him two." And then He crowns those strange injunctions with another, the strangest of all : "To him that asketh of thee give ; and from him that would borrow of thee turn not away."

These are amazing counsels, and they have occasioned no **Difficult to interpret.** little bewilderment. It was roundly asserted in St Augustine's day that they were contrary to the ethics of the State. "Who," it was asked, "would suffer aught to be taken away from himself by an enemy, or would not wish to requite their mischief to the spoilers of a Roman province by the right of war?" St Augustine replied that "those precepts pertained more to the preparation of the heart which is within than to the work which is in the open"; pointing out that, when Jesus was smitten on the face by the High Priest's officer, He **John xviii. 22-3.** did not actually turn the other cheek, but meekly remonstrated.[1] And it is thus that interpreters mostly reason, smoothing away the sharpness of the Lord's requirements and accommodating them to what is deemed practical necessity. Some, however, like the Quakers and Count Tolstoï, accepting them literally and fully, read here a condemnation of the existing order of society. Non-resistance, Tolstoï maintains, is the very essence of Christianity, and it is contrary to the Gospel for an individual to seek legal redress or a nation to have recourse to war even in self-defence.

It is, indeed, beyond doubt that the literal and universal **Not general rules of conduct.** application of those precepts would involve the abolition of the magistrate's office and the soldier's profession ; yet it is impossible to acquiesce in the conclusion that this was our Lord's intention. He did not require the Centurion of Capernaum to abandon the military profession. He granted his prayer and eulogised his faith, nor was it any obstacle to his entrance into the Kingdom of Heaven that he was a soldier. And the Apostles were loyal to the existing order of society. St Peter bade his readers "submit themselves **1 Pet. ii. 13-4.** to every ordinance of man' for the Lord's sake." St Paul required that prayer should· be offered "for kings and all **1 Tim. ii. 1-2.** that are in authority," and on 'one memorable occasion made

[1] *Ep. ad Marcell.* cxxxviii. §§ 9-13.

Acts xxv.
11. his appeal as a Roman citizen to the judgment of the Emperor. The early Christians, moreover, as the apologists frequently point out in refutation of heathen accusations, led peaceable and law-abiding lives. They prayed for the Emperor; they engaged in the multifarious pursuits of their communities; nay, they even enlisted in the Roman army and gave a good account of themselves as soldiers.[1] In truth the adoption of those precepts as general rules of life would end in disaster. What, for instance, of the command, "Give to every one that asketh of thee"? The saintly William Law demoralised his whole neighbourhood by giving away £2500 every year. Indiscriminate giving would be ruinous alike to the giver and to the recipient. St Augustine shrewdly observes: "'Give to every one that asketh,' He says, not 'Give everything to him that asketh'; that you may give what you can honourably and justly give. To every one that asketh of thee thou wilt give, although thou wilt not always give what he asks; and sometimes thou wilt give something better when thou hast corrected one that asks things unjust."[2]

Addressed to Apostles. What then must be said of those precepts of our Lord? All difficulty vanishes the moment it is recognised that they were addressed, not to a promiscuous audience, but to the Apostles. Jesus was not enunciating a general code of Christian ethics but instructing the Twelve how they should comport themselves as the heralds of His Kingdom.[3] Not indeed that He required a loftier goodness of them than of the rank and file of His disciples, but their vocation imposed upon them a peculiar necessity for self-abnegation and self-effacement. St Paul acted on this principle when he

1 Cor. vi. recognised that there were certain things which, though
12; x. 23. lawful for him as a Christian, were not expedient for him as an Apostle, and when, to silence malicious slanders, he
1 Cor. ix. waived his title to claim maintenance of the Church of Corinth according to the Lord's ordinance that "they that preach the Gospel should live by the Gospel." And this

---

[1] Tert. *Apol.* §§ 30, 37, 42. *Cf. Ep. ad Diogn.* v; Eus. *H. E.* v. 5: the Thundering Legion.

[2] *De Serm. Dom. in Mont.* i. § 67.

[3] Jerome on Mt. v. 39: "Ecclesiasticus vir describitur, imitator ejus qui dicit: 'Discite a me, quia mitis sum et humilis corde.'"

necessity, which was laid upon the first Apostles, is laid equally upon their successors in each generation. "The Lord's bond-servant must not strive, but be gentle toward all." He is no true minister of the Gospel who is not ready to endure meekly "the contradiction of sinners" after the example of the Master "who, when He was reviled, reviled not again ; when He suffered, threatened not." 2 Tim. ii. 24.

1 Pet. ii. 23

It is likely that, when Jesus gave those counsels, He had the Zealots in His eye. One of the Twelve was a Zealot, and the rest would all, except perhaps Judas, be in sympathy with the wild schemes of those desperate patriots. The military impressment would be especially galling to them, and Jesus here seeks to win them to a calmer mood. Is it irreverence to think that there is a tone of playful humour in His counsels? When He says : "Whoever will impress thee for one mile, go with him two," He speaks after the manner of the Rabbi who said : " If thy neighbour call thee an ass, put a saddle on thy back." [1] He would have them recognise their impotence and the futility of resistance, which would only aggravate their misery by provoking the oppressor to greater severity. "If," says the Stoic Epictetus,[2] "there be an impressment, and a soldier arrest your ass, do not resist, do not even grumble ; or else you will get beaten and lose your ass all the same." Jesus spoke playfully, calming the indignant hearts of His disciples ; yet beneath His smile lay a serious purpose. Resistance was unavailing, and He indicates a better way. " Fire," says St Chrysostom,[3] " is not quenched by fire, but by water," and meek endurance puts the oppressor to shame. " He will not inflict a second blow, though he be more savage than any wild beast, but will condemn himself for the first." It is not craven submission that Jesus counsels here, but, on the contrary, that noble dignity which meets insult and outrage with proud disdain.

Reference to the Zealots.

There is, however, a still higher pitch of heroism. It is no great achievement that a man should submit because he is too weak to resist, his heart all the while afire with indignation and athirst for revenge. It is a nobler attitude when he disdains the injury, but noblest of all when he regards the wrongdoer with a great compassion. And this

Command to love enemies.

---

[1] Wetstein on Mt. v. 41.   [2] *Dissert.* iv. § 1.   [3] *In Matth.* xviii.

is the spirit which Jesus bade His Apostles cherish. "Love your enemies," He said, "do good to them that hate you, bless them that curse you, pray for them that despitefully use you. All things whatsoever ye would that men should do to you, so do ye also to them." [1]

Incentives thereto :

(1) the example of God ;

This is a great requirement, and, lest it should seem to them impracticable, Jesus sets before the Twelve strong arguments and lofty motives. He reminds them of their heavenly kinship and the obligation which it imposed. It was no great thing that they should love those that loved them, and be affable to their brethren. The tax-gatherers, the heathen did as much ; and a loftier virtue was demanded of them, the sons of God. Their Heavenly Father should be their example ; and He was kind towards the unthankful and evil, He made His sun rise upon evil and good, and sent rain upon righteous and unrighteous. *Noblesse oblige.* "Show yourselves compassionate, even as your Father is compassionate."

(2) the duty of seeking even an enemy's salvation ;

And it would slay resentment in their hearts and fill them with a great compassion, if they remembered their mission and recognised even their persecutors as objects of apostolic solicitude, immortal souls to be won for God, "Heaven's possible novitiates." And the worst might be gained if only he were sought in patience, faith, and hope. "Love your enemies, and do good, and lend, despairing of no man." [2]

(3) consideration of one's own faults.

Then, adopting a lighter, almost playful tone, Jesus passes to another argument. Remember, He says, your own faults, and you will look with kinder eyes on those of others, and find it easier to make allowance for them. There was a Jewish

[1] The Golden Rule is introduced in different connections in Mt. vii. 12 and Lk. vi. 31. So memorable a *logion*, being often quoted, would readily wander from its place. Others had said something similar before Jesus. *Cf.* Tob. iv. 15 : "What thou hatest, do to none." To a Gentile who mockingly asked to be taught the whole Law while he stood on one foot, Hillel replied : "What is hateful to thyself, do not to thy neighbour. This is the whole Law ; the rest is commentary." See Wetstein and Lightfoot on Mt. vii. 12 ; Taylor, *Say. of Fath.* pp. 142-3. Gibbon (*Decl. and Fall*, chap. liv, n.) denies the originality of the Golden Rule : "a rule which I read in a moral treatise of Isocrates, four hundred years before the publication of the gospel. ἃ πάσχοντες ὑφ' ἑτέρων ὀργίζεσθε, ταῦτα τοῖς ἄλλοις μὴ ποιεῖτε" : not observing that the rule on the lips of other teachers was *negative*, on His *positive*.

[2] Lk. vi. 35 : μηδένα ἀπελπίζοντες. The reading μηδὲν ἀπελπίζοντες ("despairing of nothing," "never despairing") is due to the elision of the first a. A.V. "hoping for nothing again," an unwarrantable rendering.

proverb which frequently occurs in the Talmud : "With what measure a man measures, others will measure to him."[1] Jesus quotes it. "Judge not," He says, "and ye shall not be judged ; condemn not, and ye shall not be condemned ; release, and ye shall be released ; give, and it shall be given unto you ; good measure, pressed down, shaken together, running over, shall they give into your bosom. For with *Cf.* Pss. what measure ye measure it shall be measured unto you again. lxxxix. 12 cxxix. 7. Why," He continues, quoting another proverb, characteristically Oriental in its grotesque exaggeration, "seest thou the chip that is in thy brother's eye, but the log that is in thine own eye considerest not ?[2] Or how wilt thou say to thy brother : 'Let me cast out the chip out of thine eye'? and, behold, the beam is in thine own eye. Thou play-actor! cast out first from thine own eye the beam, and then shalt thou see clearly to cast out the chip from thy brother's eye."

While Jesus would have His disciples look thus kindly Necessity even upon their persecutors, He would have them also, in for discrimination. the interests of their ministry, cultivate a spirit of discernment. And He bade them be on their guard against two sorts of men whom they would encounter in the prosecution of their mission. They would meet with some whom it were vain to think of winning—obdurate men, wise in their own conceits or wedded to their sins. These they must let alone. "Give not," *Cf.* 2 Pet. He says apparently in proverbial language, "what is holy to ii. 22 ; Prov. xxvi. the dogs, neither cast your pearls before the swine, lest they 11. trample them under their feet, and turn and rend you."[3] Even so had the wise man said of old : "He that correcteth a Prov. ix. 7. scorner getteth to himself shame : and he that reproveth a wicked man getteth himself a blot." And · He bade them also beware of false prophets—impostors who would call themselves by His name and claim His authority only to gain profit or honour, "ravening wolves in sheeps' clothing,"

"Such as for their bellies' sake
Creep, and intrude, and climb into the fold."

---

[1] *Cf.* Lightfoot and Wetstein on Mt. vii. 2 ; Dalman, *Words of Jesus*, p. 225.
[2] Another Jewish proverb. *Cf.* Lightfoot. It has been suggested that ὀφθαλμός here represents עין, *a well* : "a chip in your neighbour's well, a log in your own." See Bruce in *Exp. Gk. Test.*   [3] *Cf.* Wetstein.

The Apostolic Church knew well the plague of the false prophet, and branded him with the stinging epithet " Christ-trafficker." [1]   " Not everyone," it was said, " that speaketh in the Spirit is a prophet, but only if he have the Lord's manners."   And even while Jesus lived, there were un-authorised claimants to apostolic prerogatives.   Such an one was that unknown man who awoke the indignation of the disciples by casting out dæmons in their Master's name, albeit he followed not with them.[2]   They were for interdicting him. " Hinder him not," said Jesus ; " for there is none who will do a mighty work in My name and will be able lightly to speak evil of Me."   Even such is the test which He proposes here. " From their fruits ye shall recognise them.   Do they gather grape-clusters from thorns or figs from thistles " ?

Mk. ix. 38-41=Lk. ix. 49-50.

The worthlessness of lip-homage.

Is. xxix. 13; cf. Mt. xv. 7-9=Mk. vii. 6-7.

All down their history lip-homage had been a besetting sin of the Jews.   " This people," the ancient prophet had said, " draw nigh unto Me, and with their mouth and with their lips do honour Me, but have removed their heart far from Me "; and, if the accusation was just in Isaiah's day, it was ten-fold more just in our Lord's.   The holy men of that generation were the Pharisees, and they were naught else than solemn play-actors.   Jesus foresaw that this baleful spirit would invade His Church, and He warned His Apostles against its insidious operation.   He required not mere homage of the lips, be it ever so effusive, but loyal obedience to the Heavenly Father's will.   And, says Euthymius, the good monk of Constantinople, " the Son's commandments are the Father's will." Since the Holy Spirit works in strange ways and pours His grace through what seem unlikely channels, a bad man may not merely profess the Lord's name but do the Lord's work.   The Twelve were commissioned to " heal the sick, raise the dead, cleanse lepers, cast out dæmons " ; and one of the Twelve was Judas, the Man of Kerioth.   But on the great Day of Judgment their masks will be stripped off and the play-actors will stand revealed.   " Lord, Lord," they will cry, " did we not in Thy name prophesy, and in Thy name cast out dæmons, and in

Mt. xxiv. 24=Mk. xiii. 22.

Mt. x. 4, 8.

---

[1] *Didach.* §§ 11-2.

[2] This indubitably authentic incident is of itself sufficient to discredit the theory that the warning against false prophets is an interpolation of the apostolic age (Hilgenfeld, Keim, etc.).

Thy name do many mighty works?" "And then," says Jesus, "I will declare plainly to them : 'I never knew you. Depart from Me, ye that work iniquity!'"

There was an ancient proverb which likened vain and unenduring work to building on sand;[1] and, perhaps with it in His thoughts, Jesus closes with a solemn and impressive parable. He depicts two builders. One was a prudent man ; and, sparing no pains, he dug down to the bed-rock and laid his foundation sure and strong. Winter came with its rain and flood and tempest, and they spent their fury on the house ; but it stood fast ; "for it had been founded upon the rock." The other builder was a foolish man, and, taking the easy way, he planted his house without a foundation upon the sand. It looked as well as the other, perhaps better, being tricked out for display ; and no harm befell while the fair weather lasted. But winter came and the floods swept away the loose sand ; and the house collapsed. "It fell, and the fall of it was great." The prudent builder, said Jesus, represents the man that heareth these words of Mine and doeth them ; the foolish builder the man that heareth them and doeth them not. Jesus and His teaching are inseparable, and it is impossible for a man to be loyal to Him and neglect it.

Parable of two builders.

[1] εἰs ψάμμον οἰκοδομεῖs. Erasm. *Adag.* under *Inanis Opera.*

CHAPTER XIX

Lk. xi. 1-13
=Mt. vi. 9-
15, vii. 7-11
=Mk. xi.
25.

A LESSON IN PRAYER

> " O man, forgive thy mortal foe,
> Nor ever strike him blow for blow;
> For all the souls on earth that live
> To be forgiven must forgive.
> Forgive him seventy times and seven :
> For all the blessèd souls in Heaven
> Are both forgivers and forgiven."—TENNYSON.

Thus far nothing about Prayer in the teaching of Jesus. IT was of the utmost moment that the Twelve should be prepared for the ministry whereto they had been chosen, and Jesus was unremitting in the task of their instruction. It was in truth His supreme business ; and, whenever He had them alone, walking with them by the way, reclining at table, sitting on the hill-side, or sailing on the Lake, He would discourse to them of the things that belonged to His Kingdom and to their vocation. There was, however, one omission which they observed and wondered at. Amid all His teaching He had never taught them how to pray. And this was the more surprising forasmuch as He was Himself unwearied in prayer. He would rise a great while before day and betake Himself to His upland oratory. That was His constant retreat ; and, whenever they missed Him, they sought Him there, sure to find Him busy in communion with God. And, moreover, other teachers instructed their disciples in the art of prayer. The Rabbis prescribed eighteen forms of prayer for daily repetition,[1] and John the Baptist had furnished *Lk. v. 33.* prayers to His disciples and enjoined diligent and frequent use thereof.[2]

" Lord, teach us to pray." The Twelve wondered at their Master's seeming neglect ;

[1] *Cf.* p. 103.

[2] One of the prayers which John taught his disciples was :

> " God make me worthy of Thy Kingdom and to rejoice in it ;
> God show me the baptism of Thy Son," *i.e.* the Messiah.

See Nestle, *E. B.*, art. *Lord's Prayer* § 1, n. 6.

168

and once, finding Him at prayer, probably at daybreak in
His wonted retreat, one of them appealed to Him : " Lord,
teach us to pray, even as John also taught his disciples."
Jesus granted the request and furnished His Apostles with
that form commonly called " the Lord's Prayer." In the
primitive Church it was called simply " The Prayer," and was
held in high esteem, being repeated thrice daily.[1]

> "Our Father that art in Heaven,   The
>   Hallowed be Thy Name ;   Praye..
>   Thy Kingdom come ;
>   Thy Will be done,
>   as in Heaven, also upon the earth.
> Our bread for the approaching day
>   give us to-day.
> And forgive us our debts
>   as we also have forgiven our debtors ;
> And lead us not into temptation,
>   but rescue us from the Evil One. [2] "

Jesus gave this prayer to the Twelve, not to be their Its charac-
only prayer, but to serve them as a model and show them teristics.
what manner of petitions they should offer before the Throne
of Grace : " Thus pray ye." And the prayer has several Mt. vi. 9.
striking characteristics. It is *brief*, recalling the Lord's warnings Mt. vi. 7 ;
against the babbling prayers of the heathen and the long Mk. xii. 40
prayers of the Pharisees. It is *simple*, suiting the lips of a 47. =Lk. xx.
little child. It is *catholic*, addressing not the Lord God of
Israel but the Heavenly Father. It is *spiritual*, concerning
itself primarily with God's Glory, His Kingdom, and His
Will, and only secondarily with the worshipper's needs.
And what are the boons which it craves? Bread, pardon,
and deliverance from temptation. It concerns itself almost
exclusively with the things of God and the needs of the
soul, asking only the simplest provision for the body. Such
was the Lord's constant requirement. " Seek first," He said
on another occasion, "your Heavenly Father's Kingdom Mt vi. 33=
Lk. xii. 31.

[1] *Didach.* § 8. Lk.'s version (xi. 2-4) is briefer than Mt.'s (vi. 9-13), omitting,
according to the approved reading, the third petition and the latter clause of the
sixth, besides minor variations. Mt.'s is the version which was current in the
Apostolic Church, agreeing almost exactly with the version in the *Didache*. The
doxology of Mt. vi. 13 T. R. is a liturgical addition. *Cf. Didach.* : " For Thine is
the power and the glory for ever."

[2] τοῦ πονηροῦ may be neut. but it is most probably masc. *Cf.* Mt. xiii. 19 ; Eph.
vi. 16 ; 1 John ii. 13-4. See Taylor, *Say. of Fath.* pp. 186-90.

and His righteousness, and all these things—food, drink, and clothing—shall be added unto you." And like this is another saying which is ascribed to Him : " Ask the great things, and the little things shall be added unto you; ask the heavenly things, and the earthly things shall be added unto you." [1]

"Our bread for the approaching day." The only difficulty which the Prayer presents is found in the fourth petition, the solitary petition for temporal good ; and it lies in the phrase which our English versions render " our daily bread" with the marginal alternative " our bread for the coming day." [2] It is certain that the latter is the true rendering, and the difficulty is that it seems inconsistent with our Lord's teaching elsewhere. " Be not anxious for the morrow," He says in His discourse of worldly-mindedness ; Mt. vi. 34. " for the morrow shall be anxious for itself. Sufficient for the day is the evil thereof " ; yet here He puts on His disciples' lips a prayer as it seems, for the morrow's bread, nay, a prayer that they may be furnished to-day with provision against the morrow.

The Prayer a morning prayer. It seems a stark contradiction ; but, when the situation is apprehended, the difficulty vanishes. Jesus was accustomed to rise "a great while before day " and betake Himself to prayer, seeking in communion with the Father invigoration for the work which lay before Him. At that early hour the day which was just breaking, was in common parlance designated indifferently " to-day " or " the approaching day." [3]

[1] Orig. *Select in Pss.*, Lommatzsch, xi. p. 432 : αἰτεῖτε τὰ μεγάλα, καὶ τὰ μικρά ὑμῖν προστεθήσεται· αἰτεῖτε τὰ ἐπουράνια, καὶ τὰ ἐπίγεια προστεθήσεται ὑμῖν. Cf. *Berac.* 31. 1 : "Forsan homo precatur pro necessariis sibi, et postea orat.' Lightfoot on Lk. xi. 1.

[2] ἐπιούσιος is ἅπαξ λεγόμενον. According to Origen (*De Orat.* § 27) a coinage of the Evangelists. The Prayer was doubtless given in Aramaic. In the *Gospel of the Hebrews*, Jerome found מָחָר "quod dicitur crastinum," which attests the derivation of ἐπιούσιος from ἡ ἐπιοῦσα (ἡμέρα), "the on-coming day." The alternative derivation from ἐπί and οὐσία (εἶναι)—"bread for our essential being," *i.e.* spiritual bread,—which seems to have been first advocated by Origen (*l.c.*), is etymologically impossible, since the ι of ἐπί was always elided in composition before a vowel. Cf. J. B. Lightfoot's *Fresh Revision*, Append.

[3] Cf. Plat. *Crit.* 43A-44B : Crito comes to the prison "very early, at deep dawn " (cf. Mk. xvi. 2 = John xx. 1 = Lk. xxiv. 1), and tells Socrates that the ship from Sunium will arrive "to-day " (τήμερον). Socrates replies that it will not come "to-day " (οὐ μέντοι οἶμαι ἥξειν αὐτὸ τήμερον), and presently repeats his assertion, substituting "the approaching day " for "to-day " (οὐ τοίνυν τῆς ἐπιούσης ἡμέρας οἶμαι αὐτὸ ἥξειν ἀλλὰ τῆς ἑτέρας).

It was probably early in the morning when Jesus was found at prayer by His disciples and gave them this lesson in prayer; and He conceived of them as following His example and beginning each day before the Throne of Grace.   The prayer which He taught them, is a morning prayer, and it craves not " the morrow's bread " but simply provision for the incoming day : " Our bread for the approaching day give us to-day," or, as St Luke has it, " day by day."   So far from lending sanction to anxiety about the morrow the petition implies a spirit of utter unworldliness.   It conceives of the disciples as not knowing when the day broke where they should find the day's food and seeking it with filial confidence from their Heavenly Father.   It may be that there is an allusion to the Manna, the bread which God rained from Heaven for the Israelites in the wilderness.   It came down morning by *Exod. xvi;* morning, a gift from His hand, and they had no need to be *Ps. lxxviii.* *23-5. Cf.* anxious for the morrow.   Each morning they gathered of it *John vi. 31-* every man according to his eating ; and, if they gathered more *5.* and left it until the next morning, it bred worms and stank. " Bread for the approaching day " was all they needed.   The morrow's provision was in God's hands.

It were, however, of no avail that the disciples had a model *Conditions* after which to fashion their prayers, unless they had the spirit *of true prayer:* of prayer in their hearts ; and Jesus proceeded to inculcate two great lessons.   First, in explanation of the petition, " Forgive us our debts as we also have forgiven our debtors," *(1) a for-* He told them that, unless they forgave, they could not be *giving spirit;* forgiven.   The son of Sirach had written : " Forgive thy *Ecclus.* neighbour the hurt that he hath done thee ; and then thy sins *xxviii. 2.* shall be pardoned when thou prayest " ; and the Lord adds His sanction to this doctrine.   " If," He says, " ye forgive men their trespasses, your Heavenly Father will forgive you also ; but, if ye forgive not men, neither will your Father forgive your trespasses."   Even so had He spoken in His discourse in tho Synagogue of Capernaum : " If thou art offering thy gift *Mt. v. 23-4* at the altar and there rememberest that thy brother hath aught against thee, leave there thy gift before the altar, and go thy way ; first be reconciled to thy brother, and then come and offer thy gift."   And in after days St Paul reiterated the lesson, reinforcing it with the gracious compulsions of the

32. Lord's finished redemption: "Show yourselves kind one toward another, compassionate, forgiving each other, even as God also in Christ forgave you."

(a) earnestness.   Then He inculcated the necessity of earnestness in prayer, setting forth the lesson by a bold and striking parable. "Which of you," He asked, "shall have a friend, and shall go to him at midnight and say: 'Friend, lend me three loaves; since a friend of mine hath arrived at my house from a journey, and I have nothing to set before him'? And the other shall answer from within and say: 'The door is now shut, and my children and I are in bed. I cannot rise and give unto thee.' I tell you," said Jesus, "though he will not rise and give unto him because he is his friend, yet because of his persistence he will rise and give unto him as many as he needeth. And I tell you, ask, and it shall be given unto you; seek, and ye shall find; knock, and it shall be opened unto you. For everyone that asketh receiveth, and he that seeketh findeth, and to him that knocketh it shall be opened."[1]

Of course Jesus did not mean that God is like a selfish neighbour who must be plagued into complaisance; nor would He have His disciples ·besiege God with importunities and insist on getting their desires, forgetful that their Heavenly

Mt. vi. 8. Father was wiser than they and "knew whereof they had need ere they asked Him." His purpose was not to set forth God's character, but to show after what manner men should

Cf. Ecclus. vii. 10. pray. The parable is a warning against listlessness and half-heartedness. It teaches that prayer is not the mumbling over of stereotyped formulæ, but a serious and strenuous business demanding the undivided energy of mind and heart, after the manner of Onias, styled the Circle-maker, who, when the people in time of drought asked him to pray for rain, drew a circle and, standing in the midst of it, prayed thus: "Lord of the world, Thy sons have turned their eyes on me, because I am as a son of Thy house. Before Thee I swear by Thy great name that from this circle I will not depart unless Thou first have mercy on Thy sons."[2]

---

[1] Cf. Cromwell to his daughter, Bridget Ireton, 25th October 1646: "To be a seeker is to be of the best sect next to a finder; and such an one shall every faithful humble seeker be at the end. Happy seeker, happy finder!" Erasm. Adag. under Qui instat extundit.

[2] Ortho, Hist. Doct. Misn. pp. 66-7.

How far it was from the Lord's purpose to liken God to a selfish neighbour appears in the sequel, where He deduces from the parable an *a fortiori* argument : If even a selfish man yields to entreaty, much more will God. "What man is there of you who, if his son shall ask of him a loaf, will give him a stone, or, if he shall ask a fish, will give him a serpent, or, if he shall ask an egg, will give him a scorpion?[1] If ye then, being evil,[2] know how to give good gifts unto your children, how much more shall your Father that is in Heaven give good things[3] to them that ask Him?" Here is a repetition of the ancient prophet's moving argument: "Can a woman forget her sucking child, that she should not have compassion on the son of her womb? Yea, these may forget, yet will not I forget thee." Is. xlix. 15.

It is indeed surprising that Jesus should have so long withheld from His disciples instruction in prayer, but it is still more surprising that the lesson which He at length gave them at their request, should have been what it is. He taught them nothing new. He simply reiterated certain truths which other teachers had already enunciated ; and as for the Prayer which He gave them for a model, beautiful as it is, it is nothing else than a mosaic of snatches from the Jewish liturgy, especially the Morning Service. There is not a sentence, a phrase, or an idea in it which has not its Jewish parallel.[4] *Nothing new in this lesson in prayer.*

"Our Father that art in Heaven," says the Prayer : "Be bold as a leopard, and swift as an eagle, and fleet as a hart, and strong as a lion, to do the Will of thy Father that is in Heaven," said R. Judah ben Thema, "*Our* Father," says the Prayer ; and the Rabbis required that, when man prayed, he should "associate himself with the Congregation," praying not in the singular but in the plural number.[5]

"Hallowed be Thy Name ; Thy Kingdom come," says

---

[1] Proverbial phrases. *Cf.* Sen. *De Benef.* ii. § 7 : "Fabius Verrucosus beneficium ab homine duro aspere datum panem lapidosum vocabat." Erasm. *Adag.*: ἀντὶ πέρκης σκορπίον. Wetstein on Mt. vii. 10 : "For a fish a fisherman sometimes catches a water-snake."

[2] *Cf.* Introd. § 12, 4.

[3] For Mt.'s ἀγαθά Lk. has Πνεῦμα ῞Αγιον, which is probably a theological gloss, though Jesus might have so spoken : *cf.* Mk. iii. 29 ; xii. 36.

[4] See Wetstein on Mt. v. 16 ; vi. 9-13 ; Taylor, *Say. of the Fath.*, Exc v.

[5] Lightfoot on Mt. vi. 9.

the Prayer; and in their prayers the Jews were wont to couple the hallowing of God's Name and the coming of His *Cf.* Zech. xiv. 9. Kingdom. "Any benediction," said R. Judah the Holy, "wherein no mention is made of the Name, is no benediction." "Any benediction," said R. Jochanan, "wherein no mention is made of the Kingdom, is no benediction."

"Thy Will be done, as in Heaven, also upon the earth," says the Prayer; and it is written in the Talmud: "What is a brief prayer? R. Eliezer says: 'Do Thy Will in Heaven above, and give rest of spirit to them that fear Thee below.'"

"Our bread for the approaching day give us to-day," says the Prayer; and the Jews prayed: "We thank Thee for the food wherewith Thou dost feed and sustain us continually every day."

"Forgive us our debts as we also have forgiven our debtors," says the Prayer, and Jesus the son of Sirach had said the like. It is also written in the Talmud: "Let each bethink himself how we every day pile up our sins before God. It is our duty to forgive our neighbour also his trespasses after the pattern of the mercy which God shows unto us."

"Lead us not into temptation," says the Prayer: "Never," said R. Judah, "let a man lead himself into the hands of temptation; for, behold, David, King of Israel, led himself into the hands of temptation, and he fell." And it is a petition of the Jews' Morning Prayer: "Lead me not into the hands of sin, nor into the hands of transgression and iniquity, nor into the hands of temptation." "Rescue us from the Evil One," says the Prayer: "Be it Thy good pleasure," R. Judah was wont to pray, "to rescue us from shameless ones and shamelessness, from the evil man and from the evil assault, from evil affection, from an evil companion, from an evil neighbour, from Satan the Destroyer."

The nature of true Christian prayer. It is indeed very remarkable that Jesus should not only have so long withheld instruction in prayer from His disciples but, when they craved it, should, as it seems, have put them off with a handful of excerpts from the Jewish liturgy and a couple of precepts which other teachers had already enforced. And the explanation is that the time for teaching them how to pray had not yet arrived. In His discourse to the Eleven on the night of His betrayal He vouchsafed to them an intimation which is full of significance. He told them that after His departure the Advocate, the Spirit of *John xvi. 7, 13; 23-4.* Truth, would come unto them and guide them in all the Truth; and then He added: "In that day ye shall not ask Me for anything. Verily, verily I tell you, if ye shall ask the Father for aught, He will give you it in My Name. Hitherto ye have not asked for anything in My Name: ask, and ye shall receive, that your joy may be fulfilled."

This is the distinction of Christian prayer, that it is *"In My Name."* offered in the Name of Jesus, pleading His merit and claiming acceptance on the ground of His infinite sacrifice. It is written in the *Epistle to the Hebrews*: "Having therefore, *x. 19-22.* brethren, boldness to enter into the Holy Place by the Blood of Jesus by the way which He dedicated for us, a new and living way, through the Veil, that is, His flesh; and having a great High Priest over the House of God, let us approach with a true heart in fulness of faith." By His Death and Resurrection Jesus established a new relation betwixt God and men; He "finished transgression, and made an end of sins, and made reconciliation for iniquity, and *Dan. ix. 24.* brought in everlasting righteousness"; He gave to every believing soul a sure pledge of acceptance with God. But all this was hidden from the disciples while their Lord companied with them in the flesh; and not till He had finished the work which had been given Him to do, and sent the Holy Spirit unto them, did they perceive the difference which He had made, and realise the wonder and blessedness of their standing before God.

Mt. viii. 1
=Lk. vi.
17a=Mk.
iii. 20; Mk.
iii. 22-30=
Mt. xii. 22-
37 (ix. 32-
4)=Lk. xi.
14-5, 17-26;
Mt. xii. 38-
45=Lk. xi.
16, 29-36,
24-6; Lk.
xi. 27-8;
Mt. xii. 46-
50=Mk.
iii. 21, 31-5
=Lk. viii.
19-21.

CHAPTER XX

RENEWED CONFLICT

"Men spurned His grace; their lips blasphemed
The Love who made Himself their slave;
They grieved that blessed Comforter,
And turned against Him what He gave."—FABER.

Jesus re-
sumes His
ministry in
Caper-
naum.
AFTER ordaining the Twelve Jesus descended from the uplands and entered into Capernaum to resume His ministry.
No sooner had He got home to Peter's house than a crowd
gathered. The fame of His doings during the festal season,
His miracle at Bethesda and His encounter with the rulers,
had reached Galilee, and the excitement was greater than
ever. So insistent was the throng about the door, so eager
to see and hear Him, that, in the language of St Mark, Jesus
and His disciples "could not even eat bread." The acclamation, however, was broken by a discordant and ominous note.
His doings at Jerusalem had exasperated the rulers, and
the Sanhedrin had sent emissaries to co-operate with the
local authorities; and they watched Him with jealous and
malignant eyes, angry at the enthusiasm of the multitude
and eager to find occasion against Him.

Hostility of
the rulers.

Charge of
alliance
with Satan.

Mt. xii. 23.
An occasion soon presented itself. A blind and dumb
lunatic was brought to Jesus, and He healed him.[1] It was a
striking miracle, in truth three miracles in one; and the
spectators were amazed. "Is it possible," they said one to
another, "that this is the Son of David."[2] The Pharisees
were bitterly chagrined. The reality of the miracle was
beyond dispute, but some objection they must raise in order
to stay the tide of popular enthusiasm and discredit Jesus;
and they devised an accusation whose palpable absurdity

[1] Only the dumbness is mentioned by Lk. xi. 14. It is probable that Mt. ix.
32-4, is an abbreviated duplicate of this incident assimilated to Lk.'s version and
inserted where it stands in view of Mt. x. 25.
[2] *I.e.* the Messiah. Some MSS. add ὁ Χριστός.

176

betrays the desperateness of their case. They asserted that He was in league with the Devil : " This fellow does not excel the dæmons but by Beelzebul,[1] prince of the dæmons."

The insinuation reached the ears of Jesus, and He took up the charge and, with indignant contempt, tore it to tatters. First, He demonstrated its absurdity.   It was a common-place, almost a proverb, that disunion was ruinous alike to kingdoms, to cities, and to houses ;[2] and if Satan expelled Satan, he was divided against himself, and how could his kingdom stand ?   Then He retorted their accusation upon themselves.   What of the Jewish exorcists ?   " If it be by Beelzebul that I expel the dæmons, by whom is it that your sons expel them ?   Therefore *they* shall be your judges." Finally, since the hypothesis of alliance with Satan was absurd, it could only be by the Spirit of God that He expelled the dæmons, and it followed that the Kingdom of God had made its appearance among them, that is to say, He was the Messiah.   He had proved Himself the triumphant adversary of Satan.   " How can one enter into the strong man's house and plunder his goods, unless he first bind the strong man ?   And then he will plunder all his house."[3]

His reply.

After thus refuting the foolish and malignant accusation of the Pharisees, Jesus brought against them a counter charge, the most awful that can be imagined.   He told them that there was a sin which could never be forgiven, and they had committed it.   They had blasphemed against the Holy Spirit. They had witnessed that gracious miracle, and they had known that it was a work of God ; yet they had hardened their hearts and pronounced it a work of the Devil.   It was pardonable that they should speak against Jesus, since He presented Himself in lowly guise as the Son of Man, and they might despise and reject Him, not knowing what they did.   But it was another matter when they did despite to the

His counter charge : blasphemy against the Spirit.

---

[1] Beelzebub, " Lord of flies," the god of Ekron who had in early days threatened to rival Jehovah in the affection of Israel.   He was subsequently regarded as the chief of the evil spirits and designated contemptuously Beelzebul, " Lord of dung."   Lightfoot on Mt. xii. 24 and Lk. xi. 15.   Less probable is the explanation " Lord of the mansion " (זבול) *i.e.* the nether world.

[2] Wetstein on Mt. xii. 25.

[3] Mt. xii. 30 = Lk. xi. 23 ; Mt. xii. 33-7 = Lk. vi. 43-5 ; homeless *logia.   Cf.* Introd. § 9, n. 1.

Spirit of Grace, refusing His testimony, stifling the voice of conscience, and calling good evil. That was a sin which could never be forgiven. It betokened that their hearts were hopelessly hardened, fenced about with an impenetrable barrier of malicious prejudice, and utterly impervious to repentance ; and where there is no possibility of repentance,

John iii. 18. there is no possibility of forgiveness. The man "hath already been judged." He is like Friar Alberigo in the *Divina Commedia* whose soul was in the Inferno while his body still tenanted the upper world. " I tell you," says Jesus, " that all their sins shall be forgiven unto the sons of men, and their blasphemies, however much they shall blaspheme. And whosoever shall speak a word against the Son of Man, it shall be forgiven unto him. But whosoever shall blaspheme against the Holy Spirit, hath never forgiveness, but is in the grip of an eternal sin."[1] The sin is eternal because it can never be forgiven, and it never can be forgiven because the man can never repent.

Request for a sign. It was the emissaries from Jerusalem who had accused Jesus of being in league with the Devil. He had put them to silence and to shame, and they durst not renew the attack. But they had allies in the local Pharisees, and some of the latter presently approached Him, feigning perplexity and asking Him to resolve their doubts regarding His Messiahship by working a miracle in their presence. A like request had been made by the rulers in the Temple-

John ii. 18. court at the commencement of His ministry ; and, while refusing it, He had dealt with it graciously, since it had been made in all sincerity. It was, however, a very different spirit that prompted these Pharisees. What need had they of another sign after all that they had already witnessed ? The truth is that they had no desire to be convinced. They probably hoped that, should He accede to their proposal, He would fail in the attempt ; and, if He succeeded, they would have treated the sign as they had treated all His previous miracles. It is no wonder that Jesus refused. Even when the request was made in all good faith, He would not work a miracle in attestation of His claims, forasmuch as they rested on a deeper and more spiritual sort

[1] אBL ἁμαρτήματος. T. R. κρίσεως. Other variants : ἁμαρτίας, κολάσεως.

of evidence. And, when it was made in the spirit of those Pharisees, it was naught else than rank impiety. It was like the challenge of the English man of science whc some while ago proposed a short and simple test of the efficacy of prayer : that there should be two hospitals or two wards in the same hospital, and the patients in both should receive the self-same treatment ; but the one set should be made the objects of special prayer by believers and the others left to the operation of natural law ; the issue determining whether there be any efficacy in prayer.[1] What else than blasphemy were such a proceeding ? God will not be experimented upon. "Without faith it is impossible to be Hebr. xi. 6. well-pleasing unto Him ; for he that approacheth God must have faith that He is and unto them that diligently seek Him proveth a rewarder."

Jesus contemptuously refused the request of the Pharisees. His reply. "It is an evil and adulterous generation," He said, "that seeketh after a sign ; and no sign shall be given unto it except the sign of Jonah the prophet."[2] The sign of Jonah was his preaching, which, without any miracle, won the men of Nineveh to repentance. They "believed God, Jon. iii. 5. and proclaimed a fast, and put on sackcloth, from the greatest of them even to the least of them." And no other sign would Jesus grant to those obdurate Pharisees. Their unbelief was without excuse. It proved them harder of heart than the very heathen. The Ninevites had repented at the preaching of Jonah : "and, behold," says Jesus, "something greater than Jonah is here !" The Queen of Sheba had come from the ends of the earth to hear the wisdom of Solomon : "and, behold, something greater than Solomon is here !"

And truly that generation was in a very evil case. Its bane was Pharisaism, which made religion a matter of mere external conformity to the multitudinous observances of the ceremonial law ; and what availed the show of sanctity when the heart remained untouched and the soul unsatisfied ?

---

[1] *Cf.* Rénan's "commission, composed of physiologists, physicists, chemists, persons accustomed to historical criticism," who should sit in judgment on a case of resurrection. Introd. to *Vie de Jes.*

[2] *Cf.* Introd. § 12, 7.

It sometimes happens that a sufferer finds temporary relief; but, since the root of his distemper remains, it presently recovers its vigour and breaks out more powerfully than ever. The Jews had their explanation of this familiar phenomenon. They believed that the sufferer was possessed by a dæmon. It had been driven out and banished to the wilderness which was its proper haunt.[1] But it was ill content there, desiring embodiment that it might work its unholy desires;[2] and, watching its opportunity, it re-entered the man, resuming its interrupted sway with intensified ferocity. Such was the Jewish belief, and Jesus makes use of it here. "When the unclean spirit is gone forth from the man, it passed through waterless places seeking rest, and findeth it not. Then it saith: 'Into my house will I return whence I came forth'; and, when it hath come, it findeth it unoccupied and swept and garnished. Then it goeth and taketh with itself seven other spirits more evil than itself, and they enter and dwell there. And the last state of that man proveth worse than the first. Thus shall it be also unto this evil generation." It is an awful yet familiar moral tragedy that Jesus here depicts. During the Reign of the Saints ungodliness was repressed with a strong hand, and it seemed for a season as though England had been exorcised. But men's hearts remained unchanged, and they fretted at the restraint. The Restoration came, and the nation, flinging off its bonds, plunged into a very riot of excess. The unclean spirit returned in sevenfold strength, and the last state of the nation proved worse than the first. Mere reformation is insufficient. Unless the dispossessed soul be filled by the grace of the Holy Spirit, there is no true and abiding salvation.

Acclamation of the bystanders. The encounter attracted an ever-increasing throng of spectators. It seemed a very unequal contest. Jesus stood alone against the power and pride of the rulers; yet He stood undaunted, like St Ambrose confronting the sinful Emperor in the porch of the Church of Milan, like Luther proclaiming his resolution at the Diet of Worms, like Knox declaring the truth to Queen Mary. It was a heroic scene,

[1] Is. xiii. 19-22; xxxiv. 13-4; Tob. viii. 3; Bar. iv. 35; Rev. xviii. 2.
[2] Clem. Rom. *Hom.* ix. § 10.

and the spectators would watch its progress with breathless
interest and would greet His triumph with a murmur of
applause. A voice was lifted in admiration—the voice of
a woman in the crowd. "Blessed," she cried, "is the womb
that carried Thee, and the breasts which Thou didst suck!"
It was a womanly exclamation. "O that I had a son like
that!" was the thought of her heart. The tribute, so
spontaneous, so eloquent of sympathy and goodwill, would
be very precious to Jesus; and it was in no spirit of reproof
that He replied, telling her of a still higher blessedness:
"Nay rather, blessed are they that hear the Word of God
and keep it."

Hard after this interruption came another. Word was
passed to Jesus that His mother and brethren were standing
on the outskirts of the crowd and craved speech with Him.
They had arrived while His controversy with the Pharisees
was in progress, and had been unable to push their way
through the dense throng. What had brought them thither?
Tidings, no doubt exaggerated and perverted, of His doings,
especially His recent encounter with the rulers at Jerusalem,
had reached Nazareth and had seriously perturbed His kinsfolk, especially His brethren who all through His ministry
treated Him disdainfully and rejected His claims. His
doings seemed to them sheer madness, and they concluded
that their brother, always a dreamer in their eyes, had lost
His reason. Apprehensive perhaps lest the consequences of
His quarrel with the rulers might extend to themselves,
they determined to avert the danger by getting hold of
Him and keeping Him under control. With this design
they had come down to Capernaum, and they waited on
the outskirts of the crowd until they should have an opportunity of seizing Him and carrying Him off. The controversy, however, continued long, and, waxing impatient, they
sent a message that they were there and desired to talk
with Him.

Mary was with them, but it is hardly possible that, knowing
the wonder of His birth, she should have shared their coarse
opinion. Her feeling was probably solicitude for His safety.
She had heard of His quarrel with the rulers and, dreading the
issue, would gladly have had Him conveyed away from the

Attempt of His kins-folk to arrest Him as mad.

Mk. iii. 21.

Mary's participation there in.

scene of strife to peaceful Nazareth.   Nevertheless her interference must have pained Jesus.   A few moments previously
an unknown woman had envied the mother who bore Him,
and there was that mother in alliance, if not in sympathy, with
those who deemed Him mad!   Whatever her motive, Mary's
conduct betrayed an utter misapprehension of His Messianic
vocation and a culpable distrust of Him who, while her son
after the flesh, was yet, as she knew, her Lord.   The Spartan
mother of old gave her son his shield as he went forth to
battle, and bade him either bear it home triumphant or fall
upon it on the stricken field ; and Mary should have cheered
the Son of her love in the prosecution of His holy warfare.

His re-
pudiation
of earthly
kinship.

Jesus divined the purpose of His mother and brethren.
On the threshold of His ministry, when Mary would have
prescribed what He should do at the wedding at Cana, He
repressed her with the question : " What have I to do with thee,
woman ? " and now He meets the interference of His kinsfolk
with a fresh and more explicit repudiation of earthly kinship.
" Who," He asks, " is My mother ? and who are My brethren ? "
Then He stretched out His hand toward His disciples and
cried : " Behold, My mother and My brethren !   For whosoever shall do the will of My Father in Heaven, *he* is My
brother and sister and mother."   The Kingdom of Heaven is
not carnal but spiritual, and only such as know the Father's
love and seek His glory are of the kindred of Jesus.

CHAPTER XXI

TEACHING BY PARABLES

Mt. xiii. 1-23, 34-5, 51-2=Mk. iv. 1-20, 33-4=Lk. viii. 4-15, 18.

" The simplest sights we met—
The Sower flinging seed on loam and rock ;
The darnel in the wheat ; the mustard-tree
That hath its seed so little, and its boughs
Wide-spreading ; and the wandering sheep ; and nets
Shot in the wimpled waters,—drawing forth
Great fish and small :—these, and a hundred such,
Seen by us daily, never seen aright,
Were pictures for Him from the page of life,
Teaching by parable."—SIR EDWIN ARNOLD.

IT is remarkable that at the commencement of the second year of His Galilean ministry, when the rulers' hostility had thrown off all disguise and the people's enthusiasm had grown greater than ever, Jesus adopted a new method of teaching. He "spoke in parables to the multitudes, and without a parable would He speak nothing to them." It was indeed no novel method. It had been employed by the ancient prophets, and was much in vogue with the Rabbis.[1] And this commended it to Jesus. He was always careful to accommodate Himself to the usages of His contemporaries, and the originality of His teaching lay less in the revelation of new truths than in the disclosure of an undreamed of significance in truths already familiar. "Every scribe," He said, "that hath been made a disciple unto the Kingdom of Heaven is like a householder who flingeth forth out of his store things new and old."[2] The Rabbis, those slavish repeaters of tradition, who prefaced their every statement with " R. So-and-so saith," had in their store only " things old " ; but the Christian teacher must, after the manner of his Lord, combine the new with the old,

Teaching by parables.

Cf. 2 Sam. xii. 1-6 ; Is. v. 1-6 ; Ezek. xvii. 3-10 ; xxiv. 3-5.

Mt. xiii. 52.

---

[1] R. Meir was specially distinguished in parabolic teaching. Cf. Lightfoot on Mt. xiii. 3. Some of the Rabbis' parables closely resembled parables of Jesus, but in the instances adduced they were the imitators, since He lived first.

[2] The Kingdom of Heaven is here personified. Cf. Mt. xxvii. 57. The Fathers generally understand καινά καὶ παλαιά as the N.T. and the O.T. Cf. Chrysost. In Matth. xlviii : The Jews brought forth παλαιά but not καινά, and the heretics who rejected the O.T. (Marcionites), καινά but not παλαιά.

recognising each fresh revelation as a development and enrichment of the ancient heritage of truth.

A method of training the Twelve.
It was primarily for the sake of the Twelve that Jesus adopted the parabolic method. He had chosen the men who should continue His work after His departure, and it was of paramount importance that they should be prepared for their high vocation. His interest thenceforth centred in the Twelve, and He devoted Himself more and more exclusively to the task of their instruction. His parabolic teaching was a device for the achievement of this great end. He would speak to the multitude in parables, and by and by, when He was alone with the Twelve, He would explain the parables to them. It was not an abandonment of the multitude. It was a partial and temporary slackening of His efforts to win the world that He might be at leisure to furnish the instruments whereby that great work should be accomplished.

Mk. iv. 33-4; cf. Mt. xiii. 36, 51; Mt. xv. 15 =Mk. vii. 17.

Its judicial aspect.
At the same time His adoption of the parabolic method of teaching had a judicial aspect. For the most part, while transported with wonder at His miracles, the multitude had no heart for His teaching. Like their fathers in Isaiah's day, they "heard, but did not understand; they saw, but did not perceive." For a whole year Jesus had been seeking vainly to win an entrance for His Evangel into their dull hearts, and He would no longer essay the unprofitable task. When He spoke in their hearing, it would thenceforth be by parables, "that," He says, quoting the language of the ancient prophet, "seeing they might see and not perceive, and hearing might hear and not understand, lest haply they should turn and be forgiven." [1] Jesus was weary of the unprofitable multitude, so enthusiastic about His miracles, so impervious to His teaching, and He adopted the parabolic method in order to chill their unspiritual ardour. If they had missed the significance of His plain teaching, much more would they miss that of His parables, which even the Twelve needed to have interpreted to them, and which would simply bewilder and offend the unthinking multitude. His parabolic teaching was thus a dispensation of

Is. vi. 9.

[1] This has always seemed a hard saying. Cf. Introd. § 12, 3, (1). It is rejected by some modern critics as unhistorical: Keim (quoting Strauss approvingly) speaks of "the paradoxical and astonishingly morbid meaning which the pessimist Gospels, despairing of the Jewish people, have more or less introduced into his words." Schmiedel, E. B. art. Gospels § 128 (g); Jülicher, E. B. art. Parables.

judgment. It was as a fan wherewith he purged His floor, separating the chaff from the grain.

His first parable was spoken by the shore of the Lake. The A crowd had gathered about Him, so large and so eager that parable of the Sower. He resorted to His old expedient of getting into a boat, pushing out from the land a little way, and thence discoursing to the multitude on the beach.[1] He taught them much, and it was all in parables, whereof one was especially memorable. " Hearken ! " He said. " Behold, the sower went forth to sow." As he scattered his seed, some of it fell on the path which ran through the midst of the field,[2] and lay on the hard surface till it was trampled by the passers by or devoured by the birds. Some fell on places where the soil was shallow, a mere sprinkling of earth upon the rock-bed ; and it took root and sprang up quickly, but, since it had no deep loam to strike its roots into and draw nourishment from, it as quickly withered away. Some fell on ground which had not been cleared of weeds. The soil was good enough, and, had it been clean, it would have grown a plenteous crop; but side by side with the corn-blades thistles sprang up. It was a struggle betwixt the two, and the rank weeds got the best of it, and choked the tender blades. The rest of the seed fell on good ground, soft and deep and clean ; and it sprang up and produced ears of various fulness, one grain multiplying itself thirty-fold, another sixty-fold, another an hundred-fold.

" He that hath ears," said Jesus, challenging His audience Questions to reflection, " let him hear." And indeed reflection was Twelve. needed. Even the Twelve were puzzled, and, when they were alone with Jesus, they asked Him two questions. " Wherefore," said they, wondering at the novel method of teaching, " speakest Thou unto them in parables?" and Jesus told them of His resolution to give Himself thenceforth to the task of revealing to them the mysteries of the Kingdom of Heaven and leave the unreceptive multitude alone. Then they enquired what the parable meant. They should have seen some glimmering of its spiritual signifi-

[1] Chrysost, *In Matth.* xlvi : κάθηται παρὰ τὴν θάλασσαν ἁλιεύων καὶ σαγηνεύαν τοὺς ἐν τῇ γῇ.

[2] *Cf.* p. 133.

cance, and their dulness disappointed Jesus. " Ye know not this parable ! And how will you read all the parables ? " It seemed an unpromising beginning. Nevertheless He patiently expounded the parable to them. The seed repre-sented the Word, and the different kinds of soil different kinds of hearers. First, there was the pathway where the seed could not strike root and was presently trampled down by passing feet or devoured by birds ; and this represented such as " hear the Word and do not take it in.[1] " Their fault may be stupidity, or it may be levity of mind, a fatal lack of seriousness. No sooner has the voice of the preacher ceased than they forget his message. They do not lay hold of it and ponder it. It gains no lodgment in their souls. " When any one heareth the Word of the Kingdom and doth not take it in, the Evil One cometh and snatcheth away what hath been sown in his heart. This is the seed that has been sown by the wayside."

*Interpreta-tion of the parable:
(1) the path-way;*

The shallow soil represented a class only too common in times of religious revival—hearers who, carried away by their emotions, manifest great zeal and make extravagant pro-fessions. Presently, however, they encounter difficulties, or are called to suffer for their religion ; and they lose heart and fall off. " When they hear the Word, immediately with joy they receive it ; and they have no root in themselves, but are temporary ;[2] then, when tribulation or persecution hath arisen for the Word's sake, immediately they are made to stumble." A time of persecution is ever a time of sifting. When Pliny assumed the governorship of Bithynia during the reign of Trajan, he found the ancient religion well-nigh extinct and Christianity professed all over the province ; and he took prompt and vigorous measures to repress " the wicked and extravagant superstition." Some stood faithful, but most bowed before the storm and reverted to their old allegiance. The heathen temples, long forsaken, were once more thronged with worshippers, the disused rites were celebrated anew, and the traffic in sacrificial victims recovered its former

(2) the shallow soil;

---

[1] συνίημι like our colloquial " take it in," expressing both the reception of the seed into the ground and the reception of the Word into the mind. Mt. xiii. 23 : ὁ τὸν λόγον ἀκούων καὶ συνιείς=Mk. iv. 20 : οἵτινες ἀκούουσιν τὸν λόγον καὶ παραδέ-χονται.

[2] πρόσκαιροι : cf. 2 Cor. iv. 18 ; Hebr. xi. 25.

activity.[1] Jesus had no quarrel with enthusiasm, but He would
have men understand that discipleship was a high and heroic
enterprise, and would have no one enter upon it unless he had.
counted the cost and was prepared to carry it out at all hazards.

Peculiarly tragic is the case of that third class of hearers (3) the un-
whom Jesus likens to uncleaned soil. They are men with cleaned
excellent possibilities. They hear the Word and receive it, soil;
and it takes root in their hearts ; but side by side with it
there springs up a noxious growth—"the anxieties of the
world, and the deceitfulness of riches, and the lusts of other
things."[2]   Sometimes it is the urgency of worldly affairs
that drives the thought of higher things out of the man's
heart. He is too busy to care for the things that belong
to his eternal peace ; and soon his Godward aspirations,
unnourished by prayer and meditation, wither and die.
Or luxury enfolds him and eats like a canker into his
soul. Or there emerges a choice betwixt the Lord's
requirement and worldly interest, and the latter wins the
day. Or perhaps it is that some fleshly lust has taken
root in his soul, and he suffers it to retain its hold instead
of resolutely tearing it up and flinging it out of his life. And
it strikes its roots ever deeper and stronger, until it chokes the
tender shoots of heavenly grace and holds undisputed dominion.

There remains the fourth class of hearers, who are likened (4) the good
by our Lord to good soil. " These are such as in a true and soil.
good heart,[3] having heard the Word, hold it fast and bear
fruit."   It is very noteworthy that they exhibit various
degrees of excellence. They all bear fruit, but some thirty-
fold, some sixty-fold, some an hundred-fold. " If," says St
Chrysostom,[4] " the ground was good and the sower and the
seeds all alike, why did it bear here an hundred-fold, here

---

[1] Plin. *Ep.* x. 101.

[2] Chrysost. *In Matth.* xlv: " It is possible, if you will, to prevent this evil growth
and use riches aright. Therefore it is that He did not say ' the world' but ' the
anxiety of the world,' not ' riches' but ' the deceitfulness of riches.'" αἱ περὶ τὰ
λοιπὰ ἐπιθυμίαι, a delicate allusion to things unnamable.

[3] Lk. viii. 15: ἐν καρδίᾳ καλῇ καὶ ἀγαθῇ, wanting in Mt. xiii. 23=Mk. iv. 20 ;
an editorial addition to differentiate the fourth class of hearers more precisely. The
second and the third class no less than the fourth "hear the Word and take it
in." The phrase betrays Lk.'s Greek culture. In the classics καλὸς κἀγαθός=
"a perfect gentleman." *Cf.* Arist. *M. Mor.* ii. 9. § 2.

[4] *In Matth.* xlvi.

sixty-fold, and here thirty-fold ?   The difference was due to
the nature of the ground ; for even where the ground was
good, the difference in it was great.   You see, it is not the
husbandman that is to blame, nor the seeds, but the land that
receives them.   And here, too, the philanthropy is great,
because God does not require one measure of excellence,
but receives the first, and does not reject the second, and
gives the third a place."   Believers have not all equal
capacities or endowments, but it is enough that each should
do what lies within him and prove faithful to the trust
committed to him, employing his faculties, whatever they
may be, with diligent hand and devoted heart.   There is
room in the Kingdom of Heaven not only for a St John and
a St Paul but for the nameless multitude that love the Lord
and serve Him loyally in their obscure places.[1]

The parable the Lord's judgment of His ministry.   Those types of hearers were sketched from life.   They had
all come under the Lord's observation.   In truth the parable
of the sower is nothing else than His estimate of His year's
ministry in Galilee.   To a superficial observer it might seem
that the success had been very great.   The whole land had
been stirred, and not only Galilee but Judæa, nay, the heathen
territories of Syrophœnicia and Perœa had contributed to the
throng that had poured into Capernaum to see His wondrous
works and hear His gracious words.   But Jesus knew how
little all that enthusiasm was worth.   Many were wayside
hearers, forgetting as soon as they heard.   And many had
attached themselves to Him and called themselves His
disciples because they deemed Him the Messiah and expected
Him presently to take unto Him His great power and reign ;
and He knew that, when they discovered their mistake and
saw a cross where they had looked for a throne, they would
fall off.   He appraised the popular enthusiasm at its proper
value.   He knew that a day was coming when the multitude's
acclamation would turn to execration, and the faith even of
His Apostles would fail.   He estimated the result of His
year's labour, and His verdict was : *abundant sowing, scanty
fruit*.   Yet He did not speak in bitterness.   His labour had
not been in vain.   He had won His own, and they sufficed.

---

[1] Mt. editorially appends to the parable of the Sower a group of eight parables
about the Kingdom of Heaven.

CHAPTER XXII

RETREAT ACROSS THE LAKE

Mt. viii. 18,
23—ix. 1 =
Mk. iv. 35—
v. 20 = Lk.
viii. 22-39.

"The winds were howling o'er the deep,
 Each wave a watery hill ;
The Saviour waken'd from His sleep ;
 He spake, and all was still.

"The madman in a tomb had made
 His mansion of despair :
Woe to the traveller who stray'd
 With heedless footsteps there !

"He met that glance, so thrilling sweet ;
 He heard those accents mild ;
And, melting at Messiah's feet,
 Wept like a weanèd child."—HEBER.

JESUS did not remain long in Capernaum. Beset by the multitude and harassed by the rulers, it was impossible for Him to give Himself to the task of instructing the Twelve. He resolved to create opportunity, and one evening He said : "Let us cross over to the other side." In haste to set out, He dismissed the multitude and, "just as He was," without rest or refreshment after the day's labour, got into the boat. The people were loath to let Him go, and some procured boats and put off along with Him.

The em-
barkation.

Cf. Mk. iii. 9.

  Jesus sat in the stern-sheets while His fisher-disciples managed the boat. It was a long sail of some seven miles ; and, weary with the labour of the day and lulled by the gentle motion of the boat and the plash of prow and sides, He sank into a profound sleep, His head pillowed on the steersman's seat.[1] The Lake of Galilee is liable to sudden storms. It lies deep in its hill-girt basin, and after a sultry day the cool air from the uplands will often rush down the ravines with terrific violence.[2] That evening, as the little fleet crept along in the fading twilight, a storm of unusual severity burst upon it, a hurricane of wind with black, driving clouds and

Jesus
sleeps.

A sudden
storm.

---

[1] Mk. iv. 38 : τὸ προσκεφάλαιον, properly *a pillow for the head*, then *a cushion for sitting on*. See Wetstein. It would be no luxurious pillow. Euth. Zig. : ξύλινον δὲ τοῦτο ἦν ἐπὶ τῆς πρύμνης κατεσκευασμένον.

[2] Thomson, *Land and Book*, chap. xxv.

189

pelting rain.[1] Instantly the Lake was in wild commotion.
The waves smote the frail vessels, breaking over them and
filling them fast. A little more and they must founder. All
the while Jesus was sleeping peacefully, undisturbed by the
howling wind, dashing waves, and beating rain. The terrified
Jesus stills it. disciples woke Him. " Master, Master ! " they cried, " we are
perishing." He awoke and surveyed the scene undismayed.
" Why," He asked, reassuring them with gentle rebuke, " are
ye cowardly, O ye of little faith ? "[2] And then He addressed
the tumultuous elements as though they had been raging
beasts. " He rebuked the wind, and said to the sea : ' Silence !
Be muzzled ' ! "[3] And they obeyed. When a storm subsides
naturally, the wind gradually abates, and long after it has died
away, the sea still heaves and swells. But at the word of
Jesus " the wind sank to rest, and there ensued a great calm."
The other boats shared the deliverance, and their crews were
stricken at once with wonder and with dread.[4] " What
manner of man is this," they asked one of another, " that even
the wind and the sea obey Him ? "

Gerasa.   They came to land on the eastern shore near the town of
Gerasa, which survives in ruins to this day with its ancient
name modified to *Khersa.* " It was a small place, but the
walls can be traced all round, and there seems to have been
considerable suburbs. . . . It is within a few rods of the shore,
and an immense mountain rises directly above it." Save here
the whole eastern shore of the Lake slopes gently to the
water's edge, but here the mountain comes down abruptly
with a steep declivity. Hard by the ruins of the town are
the remains of ancient tombs hewn out of the face of the
mountain.[5]

---

[1] λαῖλαψ. Suid. : ὁ μετ'ἀνέμων ὄμβρος καὶ σκότος.

[2] Mt. : ὀλιγόπιστοι. Mk. : πῶς οὐκ ἔχετε πίστιν ; Lk. : ποῦ ἡ πίστις ὑμῶν ;
ὀλιγόπιστος was a favourite word of Jesus. *Cf.* Mt. vi. 30=Lk. xii. 28 ; Mt. xiv. 31 ;
xvi. 8.

[3] *Cf.* p. 109. Verg. *Æn.* i. 66 : " et *mulcere* dedit *fluctus* et tollere vento."
Chrysost. *In Matth.* xxix : ὥσπερ εἰκὸς δεσπότην ἐπιτάττοντα θεραπαινίδι καὶ
δημιουργὸν κτίσματι.

[4] Mt. viii. 27 : οἱ ἄνθρωποι, explained by Mk. iv. 36 : καὶ ἄλλα πλοῖα.

[5] T. R. gives Γαδαρηνῶν in all the three Evangelists ; but W. H. with the best
authorities read Γερασηνῶν in Mk. and Lk., Γαδαρηνῶν in Mt. Tisch. reads in Lk.
Γεργεσηνῶν, which is probably an alternative or mistaken form of Γερασηνῶν. See
E. B. art. *Gerasenes.* Since Gadara lay several miles inland S.E. of the Lake,

RETREAT ACROSS THE LAKE 191

Jesus disembarked and took His way up the mountain. His errand is hardly doubtful. It would be very early in the morning when the storm-tossed voyagers came to land, and it was His wont to betake Himself for prayer to some solitary place "a great while before day." A favourite oratory of His was the mountain-top. Such was His errand now; and, as He went His way up the hill-side, an appalling adventure befell Him. He was passing the burial-place when there rushed forth a man,[1] liker a wild beast than a human being. He was, in the parlance of that age, a demoniac; that is to say, he was a lunatic, but his lunacy was of a dreadful sort. He was a raging madman. In those days, ere Christianity had imbued society with its humane and beneficent spirit, there were no asylums, and such miserable wretches were suffered to roam at large. They were wont to haunt burial-places, tearing their garments and crouching during the night in the open tombs.[2] The Gerasene madman was the terror of the neighbourhood. Attempts had been made to fetter him, but with the strength of frenzy he had always burst his bonds, and he roamed over the mountain, howling and bruising his naked body against the sharp rocks.

When he espied Jesus, he uttered a cry not of fury but of fear, then ran to Him and prostrated himself before Him. Forthwith there ensued an extraordinary scene. Jesus addressed Himself resolutely to the task of healing the madman. It was necessary first of all that He should gain the mastery over him; and, falling in, according to His wont,

A madman among the tombs.

Cf. Mt. xiv. 23 = Mk. vi. 46 = John. vi. 15.

Jesus encounters him.

Γαδαρηνῶν is impossible. It is due to the tendency to substitute a familiar name for an unfamiliar. Besides Peræan Gerasa there was, according to Origen (*In Joan.* vi. § 24) a Gerasa (Gergesa) on the eastern side of the Lake, "an ancient city on the lake now called Tiberias, and in its neighbourhood there is a precipice flanking the lake, from which, it is pointed out, the swine were thrown down by the dæmons." To Thomson (*Land and Book*, chap. xxv) is due the identification of Gerasa (Gergesa) with the modern Khersa. *Cf.* Smith, *H. G.* p. 459; Sanday, *Sacred Sites*, pp. 25-9.

[1] *Cf.* Introd. § 12, 1.

[2] Lightfoot and Wetstein on Mt. viii. 28. *Cf.* Jerome's description of the spectacle which met the eyes of Paula when she visited the tombs of Elisha, Obadiah, and John the Baptist at Sebaste (*Ep.* xxvii, *Ad Eustoch. Virg.*): "Namque cernebat variis dæmones rugire cruciatibus, et ante sepulchra sanctorum ululare homines more luporum, vocibus latrare canum, fremere leonum, sibilare serpentum, mugire taurorum; alios rotare caput et post tergum terram vertice tangere, suspensisque pede fœminis vestes defluere in faciem."

Ineffectual attempts to cure him. with the hallucination of the disordered brain, He sternly addressed the supposed dæmon and commanded it to come forth from the man. It was an attempt to master the lunatic by an assertion of authority. But it proved unavailing. It only excited a paroxysm of frenzy. " What have we to do Cf. Lk. i. 32, 35, 76. with Thee, Jesus, Son of the Most High God?[1] Hast Thou come here ere the time to torment us?"

Foiled thus, Jesus made a second attempt. " What is thy name?" He asked quietly, thinking to recall the madman to himself. But this device also proved unsuccessful. The idea that he was possessed had taken hold of the man. He believed that not one dæmon but thousands had entered into him. Wherever Rome's invincible legions came, they seemed the very embodiment of resistless tyranny. Their name had Cf. Mt. xxvi. 53. passed into a proverb among the Jews, and this poor creature conceived himself possessed by a legion of dæmons. " My name," he answered, speaking as their mouthpiece, " is a legion."

Incident of the swine. And then, still speaking for the dæmons, he prayed : " Send us not away into the wilderness."[2] The authority of the Lord's calm personality was beginning to gain ascendancy over him. He recognised that he must yield ; and, still identifying himself with the dæmons, he dreaded banishment to the wilderness, the abhorred haunt of disembodied dæmons. It chanced that a huge herd of swine, numbering some two thousand, was feeding at a distance, and an idea occurred to the madman. " Send us," he cried, proposing a compromise, " into the swine." It was an insane notion, yet Jesus welcomed it. It furnished Him with an opportunity of getting the man under His control. " Away ! " He cried, and forthwith an amazing thing happened. The swine rushed wildly down the mountain-side, over the precipice, into the Lake, and were drowned.

Beneficent strategy. What was it that happened? Intent on gaining ascendancy over him, Jesus had all along, like a wise physician, humoured the madman's fancy ; and in this wild suggestion He recognised an opportunity for achieving His beneficent

---

[1] *I.e.* the Messiah. This stamps the man as a Jew. The population on the eastern side of the Lake was mixed, partly Jewish, partly Gentile.

[2] Mk. ἔξω τῆς χώρας, outside of the cultivated land where men dwell, *i.e.* into the wilderness, the haunt of disembodied dæmons ; *cf.* Mt. xii. 43=Lk. xi. 24. See p. 180. Lk. has εἰς τὴν ἄβυσσον, *i.e.* into Hell.

purpose.   He feigned acquiescence.   "Away!" He said to
the supposed dæmons, and therewith pressed the swine into the
service of His humane endeavour.   He was Lord of man and
of beast, and, even as He directed a shoal of fish into the net ^{Lk. v. 4-6;} of His disciples, so He compelled the herd of swine to work ^{John xxi. 6.}
His will.   He smote the creatures with a sudden panic, and
they rushed down the incline to their destruction.   The
stratagem was entirely successful.   The man believed in his
possession by six thousand dæmons and in the feasibility of
their transference to the swine ; and, when he heard the Lord's
command and straightway saw the headlong rush of the
maddened beasts, he was assured of his deliverance.   The
dæmons had left him ; they had entered into the swine and had
been plunged into the Lake.   And they could trouble him no
more ; for, since, according to Jewish ideas, the sea was one of
the three doors into Gehenna,[1] they had been swept into the
Abyss, incurring the very doom which they had deprecated. Lk. viii. 31.
He was dispossessed.   There was no doubt about it : had he
not seen it with his own eyes ?   His frenzy was calmed, and
he yielded himself to the will of Jesus.

It would seem that the man had previously had to do The mad-
with Jesus.   No sooner did he espy Him than he recognised man's re-
Him : he greeted Him by name, and hailed Him as the of Jesus.
Messiah.[2]   Nor is this inexplicable.   It is impossible that
such a frenzy of madness should have been of long continuance,[3] and ere his seizure the man must have heard the fame
of the wondrous Prophet ; nay, it is most likely that he had
crossed over to Capernaum and heard Him preach and witnessed His miracles.   He had been impressed, but he had
stifled conviction ; and now, when he espies Jesus, the idea
presents itself to his disordered mind that He has come in
haste to begin that terrible work of vengeance which, accord- Cf. Mt.
ing to Jewish expectation, the Messiah would execute upon viii. 29.
the Devil and his minions at the Last Judgment.[4]

---

[1] One door in the desert (Num. xvi. 33), the second in the sea (Jon. ii. 2), the
third at Jerusalem (Is. xxxi. 9).   See Lightfoot on Mt. v. 22.   Cf. Rev. xiii. 1.

[2] In other cases where they recognised Jesus, the demoniacs obviously had previous knowledge of Him.   Cf. Mk. i. 24 = Lk. iv. 34.

[3] Lk.'s χρόνῳ ἱκανῷ is a vague phrase and may denote no more than several
weeks or even days.   Cf. Acts xiv. 3 ; xxvii. 9.

[4] See Wetstein on Hebr. ii. 14 ; Charles on Enoch xvi. 1.

When their beasts had perished, the swine-herds fled away
and spread the news in the town and neighbourhood ; and
presently a crowd assembled at the scene of the disaster.
There they found Jesus and the maniac—a maniac no longer
but sitting at his Benefactor's feet, clothed and sane.　They
learned what had occurred ; and what did they do ?　They
should have rejoiced in their neighbour's deliverance ; they
should have bowed before the Deliverer and blessed Him with
reverent and grateful hearts ; and they should have hasted
and brought all the sufferers within their borders and besought
Him to heal them likewise.　But they did none of these
things.　They were seized with superstitious dread, and they
took alarm lest some further disaster should befall their
possessions.　It was dangerous to have Jesus in their
midst, and they would fain be relieved of His presence.
"They began to beseech Him to depart from their
borders." [1]

And He gave them their desire.　He had sought the
eastern shore that He might be alone with His Apostles and
instruct them in the mysteries of the Kingdom of Heaven ;
and His design had been frustrated.　He found Himself in
the midst of an excited and unfriendly multitude.　To return
to Capernaum was His only course, and He repaired to His
boat.　The erstwhile madman followed Him and, as He was
embarking, craved permission to accompany Him ; but Jesus
refused.　He had other work for the man to do.　"Away
home," He said, "to thy friends, and announce to them what
great things the Lord hath done for thee, and how He had
mercy on thee."

When Jesus wrought a miracle, He was wont to enjoin
secrecy and command that "no man should know it" ;
and He departed from His custom in this instance because He was quitting the country and had no need to
dread the assembling of a gaping multitude, greedy of wonders
but regardless of His message.　He desired that His miracle
should be published abroad, if haply it might speak for Him
when He was gone.　With a heart full of gratitude the man
"went away and began to proclaim in Decapolis what great

[1] Jerome thinks they were moved by reverence like Peter when, after the
draught of fish, he cried : "Depart from me ! "

things Jesus had done for him ; and they all marvelled." It was not given him to bear Jesus company and be numbered with His Apostles, yet he was appointed to another and no less sacred ministry. He remained in his own land and among his own people, a living monument of the grace which had blessed him and would fain have blessed them all.

CHAPTER XXIII

BACK IN CAPERNAUM

Mt. ix. 18-
26=Mk. v.
21-43—Lk.
viii. 40-56;
Mt. ix. 27-
31.

"Veniet quidem mors: sed somnus erit dilectis Domini, et ecce hæreditas ejus.
Erit janna vitæ, erit initium refrigerii, erit sancti illius montis scala, et ingressus in
locum tabernaculi admirabilis quod fixit Deus et non homo."—S. BERNARD.

The return. WHEN He came ashore again at Capernaum, Jesus was
enthusiastically received. The people had been loath to let
Him go the previous evening, and, when His boat was sighted
steering homeward, they crowded down to the landing-place
and bade Him welcome. Among the rest came one who was
not wont to mingle with the jostling throng. It was Jaïrus,[1]
The request one of the rulers of the Synagogue,[2] and he was in sore
of Jaïrus. trouble. His only child, a daughter twelve years of age, was
dying,[3] and he implored Jesus to come and save her. Some
Lk. vii. 2-5. time previously a deputation of the elders of the Synagogue
had waited on Him and interceded with Him on behalf of
the Centurion's loved slave, and it may be that Jaïrus had
been one of them. In any case he must have been
cognisant of their mission. And now, remembering what the
Lord had done, he turns to Him for succour in his own day
of need. Jesus at once complied and set forth for the ruler's
house, escorted by a large crowd. Their interest, excited by
the prospect of witnessing another miracle, was intensified by
the rank of the suppliant.[4]

A woman   It was certain that Jesus could heal the sick, but never
with an
issue of yet had He been known to raise the dead, and it seemed of
blood.

[1] The Hebr. *Jair* (Num. xxxii. 41; Deut. iii. 14; Jud. x. 3).

[2] *Cf.* p. 94. Mt.'s ἄρχων is synonymous with Mk.'s εἷς τῶν ἀρχισυναγώγων
and Lk.'s ἄρχων τῆς συναγωγῆς. *Cf.* Schürer, *H. J. P.* II. ii. p. 64.

[3] Mt., abbreviating the story (*cf.* Mt. viii. 5-13=Lk. viii. 1-10 for a similar
abbreviation) makes Jaïrus say at the outset that she was dead. Chrysostom (*In
Matth.* xxxii) supposes him to have inferred that she had died since he left home,
making his trouble as serious as possible in order to arouse the Lord's compassion.

[4] Chrysost. *In Matth.* xxxii : ἠκολούθουν πολλοὶ ὡς ἐπὶ θαύματι μεγάλῳ καὶ διὰ
τὸ πρόσωπον τὸ παραγεγονός.

the utmost importance that He should arrive in time. There
was not a moment to lose. The anxious father would fret at
the obstruction of the multitude, and what would be his consternation when an incident occurred which brought Jesus to a
halt? Amid the throng there was a woman who for twelve
years had been afflicted with a distressing malady, an issue of
blood which had baffled the skill of her physicians. "She had
suffered many things," says St Mark with a stroke of satire,[1]
"of many physicians, and had spent all that she had, and had
got no benefit, but rather had grown worse." Nor is this
at all surprising when one considers the methods of the
physicians of that period. Pliny mentions their prescriptions
for the ailment in question, specifying among the rest a
poultice of fresh ass's dung and a draught of goat's urine.[2] It
is little wonder that unflattering things were said about
physicians in those days. "To live under doctor's orders,"
said one Latin proverb, "is sorry living." "A doctor," said
another, "is worse than a robber. The robber takes your
money or your life; the doctor takes both." And it is
written in the Talmud that "the best of doctors is ripe for
Gehenna."[3]

The woman had mingled with the crowd, and she crept The tassel
up behind Jesus and stealthily laid hold of the tassel of His of His cloak.
cloak.[4] "If," she said to herself, "I touch only His clothes, I
shall be saved." Like the citizens of Ephesus who carried Acts xix.
home to their sick folk handkerchiefs and aprons which 12.
had been in contact with St Paul's body, she thought
that there was a magical efficacy in the mere touch of
Jesus. It was indeed a superstitious idea; yet there was
faith in it, and the faith was richly rewarded. "Straightway the fountain of her blood was dried up, and she perceived
in her body that she had been healed of the plague." She

[1] Lk., himself a physician, puts it more gently (viii. 43).
[2] *H. N.* xxviii. 77. For the Jewish prescriptions see Lightfoot on Mk. v. 26.
[3] Erasm. *Adag.* under *Insalubritas* and *Solis medicis licet impune occidere.*
Kiddusch. 4. 24. *Cf.* Erasmus' serio-comic description of what he endured at the
hands of doctors and his happy deliverance: "Iratus medicis Christo medico me
commendo. Stomachus intra triduum restitutus est hausto pullo gallinaceo contuso
et cyatho vini Belnensis" (*Ep.* v. 25 : *Rhenano suo*).
[4] Every Jew wore a tassel, κράσπεδον, צִיצִית, on each of the four corners of his
ἱμάτιον in accordance with Num. xv. 38-40; Deut. xxii. 12. *Cf.* Schürer, *H. J. P.*
II. ii. pp. 111-12.

purposed to steal away unobserved, rejoicing in her cure, but a greater blessing was in store for her.   Amid the pressure of the jostling crowd Jesus had distinguished the nervous grasp of that feeble hand clutching the tassel of His cloak.[1]   He had recognised it as a claim upon His sympathy and succour, and had promptly responded to the mute appeal.   He knew neither who the suppliant was nor what might be the trouble ; but He felt the touch of trembling faith, and that sufficed.   It unlocked the flood-gates of His pity and His power, and, ere He knew what the need was, He supplied it.   " It seems absurd," says Calvin, " that Christ should have poured forth His grace, not knowing whom He was benefiting " ; but surely it is rather an evidence of His compassion and His willingness to bless all that come unto Him.   In the days of His flesh, when He shared the limitations of humanity, He did not wait until He knew His suppliants ere He granted their hearts' desires.   It was enough for Him that they needed His aid and were willing to receive it.

"Who touched My clothes?"   The woman thought to steal away unobserved, but Jesus insisted on discovering her.   He turned round amid the throng and demanded : " Who touched My clothes ? "[2]   The disciples were astonished, and Peter, ever the spokesman, exclaimed : ' Thou seest the multitude pressing about Thee, and Thou sayest, ' Who touched Me ? ' ! "   Jesus vouchsafed no answer, but looked round with searching scrutiny to discover who it was.[3]   The woman, " trembling like a guilty thing surprised," came forward and avowed herself, telling the whole story. " Daughter," He said, " thy faith hath saved thee.   Go in peace."

Discovery of the woman.   It was natural modesty that had made her court conceal-ment, and it seems cruel that Jesus should have dragged her forward and compelled her to divulge her secret in presence of the crowd.   And, moreover, it seems contrary to His wont. He was accustomed to enjoin secrecy on the recipients of

---

[1] Aug. *Serm.* lxxvii. §6 : "Nam isti premunt, illa tetigit.   Corpus ergo Christi multi moleste premunt, pauci salubriter tangunt."

[2] Chrysost. (*In Matth.* xxxii) thinks that Jesus knew and desired that the woman should confess of herself.   *Cf.* Theophyl., Euth. Zig., Calv., Trench.   But He really did not know.   "Anything like feigning ignorance ill comports with the candour of His character " (Godet).

[3] *Cf.* Introd. § 12, 7.

His miraculous grace ; and it would, one might think, have accorded better with His practice to let the woman steal away, content that a miracle had been wrought and pleased that it should remain undiscovered. Assuredly His insistence on knowing who had touched Him was not prompted by a desire to be glorified in the sight of the people.[1] For His own sake He would gladly have let the miracle go unobserved by the wonder-loving multitude, but for the woman's sake He would not have it so. Had she been suffered to steal away, she would have lost the chief blessing of her life. She would have gained the healing of her body, but she would have missed the healing of her soul; she would have proved the power of Jesus, but she would have remained a stranger to His love. It was worth her while to be put to shame before the multitude that she might hear that gracious word : " Daughter, thy faith hath saved thee. Go in peace."

Tradition says that the woman's name was Veronica,[2] and that she came from the Phœnician city of Cæsarea Philippi. Early in the fourth century a house in the city was pointed out as hers, and at the gates of the house stood a monument —a lofty pedestal of stone and thereon the brazen image of a woman kneeling with outstretched hands before the brazen image of a man wearing a mantle and extending his hand toward her. At his feet, reaching up to the tassel of his mantle, grew a strange kind of herb which cured all sorts of disease. It was said that the images represented Jesus and the woman, and that she had erected the monument in commemoration of her Saviour's kindness.[3] And indeed it seems in no wise unlikely that the woman was a Gentile. Had she been a Jewess, she durst not have gone abroad in her uncleanness, infecting everyone whom she touched with ceremonial pollution. It may well be that she was a Gentile, and, hearing the far-borne fame of Jesus, had sought Him in her extremity.

The monument at Cæsarea Philippi.

Lev. xv. 19-30.

Mk. iii. 7-8.

Jesus was still speaking to the woman when a message was brought to Jaïrus which extinguished the last ray of hope in his breast. " Thy daughter is dead. Make the Teacher

The house of mourning.

---

[1] *Cf.* Chrysost. *In Matth.* xxxii : καίτοιγε τινὲς τῶν ἀναισθήτων φασὶ δόξης αὐτὸν ἐρῶντα τοῦτο ποιεῖν.
[2] *Ev. Nicod.* vii.
[3] Eus. *H. E.* vii. 18.

travel no further." [1] Jesus overheard [2] and said calmly : " Fear not ; only believe." They reached the house, and Jesus entered, taking with him only Peter, James, and John, the favoured three. There confronted Him a scene of wild commotion. In accordance with ancient custom hired mourners had been fetched in to lead the dirge with flute and voice ; [3] and a crowd of acquaintances also had gathered, some for friendship's sake with sorrow in their hearts, others with an eye to the funeral feast.[4] It was all very painful to Jesus. It was not thus that He viewed death. In truth he wholly disallowed it, forasmuch as "all live unto God," and " over the ocean of darkness and death flows an infinite ocean of light and love." He never spoke of "death": His word was "sleep." [5] He was pained by the scene. "Why," He exclaimed, "are ye making a tumult and weeping? The child is not dead but sleepeth." [6] His words were greeted with derision. He expelled the scoffers and entered the chamber, admitting only the parents and the three disciples. Then He took the little hand and spoke as a mother would to her darling. " *Talitha, kûm*, My lamb, rise!" And, lo, the sleeper heard and woke. It was no lingering convalescence, no protracted recovery. She arose in full health, retaining no trace of the sickness which had brought her down to death. "Immediately she arose and walked about." Jesus bade the parents give her some food. The command recalled

Margin notes: Lk. xx. 38 · "Talitha, Kûm."

---

[1] For the meaning of σκύλλειν cf. p. 118.

[2] Mk. v. 36 אBLΔ παρακούσας. παρακούειν may mean (1) *neglect to hear ; cf.* Mt. xviii. 17 ; (2) *make as though one did not hear*, see Field, *Notes ;* (3) *overhear.* Only (3) is possible here. Had Jesus either neglected to hear or pretended not to hear, He would have said nothing.

[3] The custom prevailed among both Jews and Gentiles ; *cf.* 2 Chron. xxxv. 25 ; Jer. ix. 17-8 ; Am. v. 16 ; Lightfoot and Wetstein on Mt. ix. 23 ; Becker, *Charicles*, pp. 387 *sqq.*, *Gallus*, pp. 506 *sqq. Cf.* the modern custom (*P. E. F. Q.*, Oct. 1905, p. 349).   [4] Lightfoot on Mt. ix. 23.

[5] The primitive Christians learned both the phrase and the thought ; *cf.* Mt. xxvii. 52 ; Acts vii. 60, xiii. 36 ; 1 Thess. iv. 13-5. *Cemetery* is κοιμητήριον, "sleeping-place." Chrysost. *Serm. in Cæmet. Appellat.*: " Before the Advent of Christ death was called death. . . . But, since Christ came and died for the life of the world, death is no longer called death but slumber and falling asleep (ὕπνος καὶ κοίμησις)."

[6] Interpreted as a declaration that the child had merely swooned by Paulus, Keim, Schleiermacher, and even Olshausen and Neander. Lk. is careful to explain that she was really dead : *vv.* 53, 55.

them from their amazement ; and, when they saw her eat, they would be assured of the reality of her resuscitation.[1]

It was an astounding miracle, the greatest that Jesus had ever yet wrought. It was the first time He had raised the dead, and, knowing what excitement it would occasion when it was noised abroad, He quitted the house and hastened homeward. As He passed along the street, two blind men besought His aid. Eager to reach home, He hurried on, and they followed Him clamorously. " Have pity on us," they cried, " Thou Son of David ! " Still He paid no heed. They pursued Him to the door, and, when He entered, they pressed in after Him. Then He addressed them. " Have ye faith," He asked, " that I can do this ? " " Yea," they replied. His heart was overflowing with pity. They could not see His kind face, but they could feel His gentle hand ; and, anxious to make amends for His apparent harshness and assure them of His sympathy, He touched their sightless eyes. "According to your faith," He said, " be it done to you," and their eyes were opened. He foresaw the result should the miracle get abroad. It would add fresh fuel to the popular excitement and increase His embarrassment. And therefore He laid a prohibition on the two men, enforcing it with all the emphasis of look and gesture.[2] "See ! " He said. " Let no one get to know about it." His prohibition, however, was unavailing. They went out and told the story far and near.[3]

Two blind men.

---

[1] On the injunction to silence about the miracle *cf.* Introd. § 11.

[2] ἐνεβριμήθη : *cf.* p. 114.

[3] Chrysostom (*In Matth.* xxxiii), thinking that the prohibition was not seriously meant but designed merely as an example of humility, praises them for disregarding it and styles them " heralds and evangelists."

CHAPTER XXIV

IN THE HOUSE OF SIMON THE PHARISEE

" Jesum quærens convivarum turbas non erubuit,
Pedes unxit, lacrimarum fluvio quos abluit,
Crine tersit et culparum veniam promeruit.

" Suum lavit mundatorem, rivo fons immaduit,
Pium fudit flos liquorem, in ipsum refloruit ;
Cœlum terræ dedit rorem, terra cœlum compluit."

Med. Hymn. *De B. Maria Magdalena.*

Departure from Capernaum. AFTER those three miracles, especially the raising of Jaïrus' daughter, it was impossible for Jesus to remain in Capernaum. The excitement would be intense ; and, that He might prosecute His ministry, He must betake Himself elsewhither. He had already sought to escape from the multitude by crossing over to the eastern side of the Lake ; but He had found no repose there, and He resolved, as He had done the previous **Mk. vi. 1,** year, to strike inland and go on a missionary tour through **6b=Mt. ix.** Galilee. It appears that He quitted Capernaum immediately **35=Lk.** **viii. 1.** and betook Himself in the first instance to the town of Magdala which lay a few miles southward on the shore of the Lake.[1]

Invitation to a Pharisee's house. The raising of Jaïrus' daughter had this peculiarity, that, whereas most of His miracles hitherto had been wrought among the multitude, it was wrought on behalf of a leading ecclesiastic, one of the principal men of Capernaum; and it procured Jesus consideration where hitherto He had been disdained as a mere demagogue. The change speedily became apparent. On His arrival at Magdala He received an invitation to the house of a Pharisee named Simon. Simon had doubtless heard of the wondrous thing which had happened to his colleague at Capernaum ; and, desiring to know more about Jesus, who, he recognised, was certainly a great prophet

---

[1] The modern *Mejdel.* Smith, *H. G.* p. 455 and *E. B.* art. *Magdala.*

and might perchance be more,[1] he made a feast in his house and invited Him to it. Jesus accepted the invitation. Such gatherings were agreeable to Him, not because He relished feasting, but because, unlike His ascetic forerunner, He loved to mingle with men, and an entertainment afforded Him an opportunity for converse about the things of the Kingdom of Heaven. Hitherto His entertainers had belonged mainly to the disreputable order of the Tax-gatherers, and His intimacy with them had earned Him the nick-name "the Friend of Tax-gatherers and Sinners"; but now it is a Pharisee that bids Him to his house. It is St Luke that relates the incident, and he has recorded two other occasions on which Jesus went to a Pharisee's house and accepted a Pharisee's hospitality, thus rescuing from oblivion a striking feature of the Lord's earthly ministry. It is a revelation of the wideness of His sympathy that He should have been the friend at once of Tax-gatherers and of Pharisees; and it is a pleasant discovery that the Pharisees were not all His enemies.[2]

Lk. xi. 37 sqq.; xiv. 1 sqq.

Simon was a truly pious man, but he was not exempt from the prejudices of his order. He felt it an act of condescension on his part to admit Jesus to his house and his table; and he stood upon his dignity, receiving Him with supercilious hauteur and making a difference between Him and the other guests. When the Lord entered, He got no kiss of welcome from His host; no slave unloosed His sandals and bathed His dusty feet; and, when He had taken His place at table, no cool, fragrant ointment was poured upon His head.[3] All these observances of common courtesy were omitted in His case, but He took no notice, comporting Himself with characteristic dignity.

Discourtesy to Jesus.

Cf. 1 Sam. x. 1; Acts xx. 37; Mt. xxvi. 48; John i. 27; 1 Tim. v. 10; Ps. xxii. 5.

When the company had taken their places, reclining after the Oriental fashion on couches ranged slantwise about the table, a singular incident occurred. While the guests were arriving, a woman had stolen in amongst them[4]; and it was evident what manner of woman she was, since she wore her

A sinful woman at Jesus' feet.

---

[1] According to the reading ὁ προφήτης in *v.* 39 he thought He might be the Messiah's forerunner. *Cf.* p. 27.

[2] *Cf.* p. 305.

[3] See Wetstein on Mt. xxvi. 7.

[4] *Cf. v.* 45: ἀφ' ἧς εἰσῆλθον. The reading εἰσῆλθεν would imply that she had entered in the course of the meal.

hair unbound, and this among the Jews was the harlot's token.[1]   Had it been a tax-gatherer's house, her presence would have been in no wise incongruous ; but a harlot in the house of a Pharisee !   What did she there ?   She had come in quest of Jesus.   The fame of His doings at Capernaum had reached her ears, and perhaps she had heard Him preach since His coming to Magdala.   She had discovered the misery of her condition, and, when she heard the Evangel, her heart kindled with hope.   Might not Jesus do for her what He had done for others as vile as she ?   She learned that He was to be the guest of Simon, and she resolved to go unbidden to the Pharisee's house and cast herself at the Saviour's feet.   And she would not go empty-handed.   The Friend of Sinners had won her heart, and she must bring Him some tribute of love and reverence.   She procured an alabaster vase of fragrant ointment,[2] and brought it with her to the Pharisee's house. Stealing in among the guests, she observed how Jesus was slighted ; and, when He had taken His place on His couch, she approached and took her station by His feet.   The big tears dropped upon them as she stooped, and she wiped them away with her loose tresses, and fondly kissed those blessed feet and poured the ointment over them, not daring to approach His head.[3]

Horror of the Pharisee.   The host was horrified.   The touch, nay, the very sight of the woman was, to his mind, a pollution.[4]   " Had such a woman," says St Augustine,[5] " approached that Pharisee's feet, he would have said, in the language of Isaiah : ' Depart from me, touch me not; for I am clean.' "   He was speechless with horror and vexation.   To think that he had been so deceived !   He had taken Jesus for a prophet and in that capacity had invited Him to his house ; but certainly He was no prophet, or He would have discerned the woman's character and spurned her from Him.   He said nothing, bearing himself with perfect decorum ; for despite his Pharisaic pride he was

Is. lxv. 5.

---

[1] Jer. *Ep.* xxii, *Ad Eustoch.* : " laxius, ut crines decidant, ligatum caput." *Chetub.* 72. 1 : A mark of evil character in a woman, " si prodeat in publicum capite aperto."   *Cf.* Lightfoot on John xii. 3.

[2] Plin. *H. N.* xiii. 3 : " Unguenta optime servantur in alabastris."

[3] Orig. *In Matth. Comm. Ser.* § 77 : " Non fuit ausa ad caput Christi venire sed lacrymis pedes ejus lavit, quasi vix etiam ipsis pedibus ejus digna."

[4] *Cf.* p. 77.   [5] *Serm.* xcix. § 2.

a man of good breeding and not ungenerous nature ; and it
evinces an unusual delicacy that, when he saw the woman
lavishing caresses on the feet of Jesus, he merely concluded
that He lacked discernment. There were others of his order *Cf.* Mt. xi.
who would have put a worse construction on the incident. 19=Lk. vii. 34.
He said nothing, but his thoughts were written on his face, and
Jesus read them there, thus proving Himself indeed a prophet
and more than a prophet. " Simon," He said, accosting him The Lord's
courteously, " I have something to say to thee," [1] and Simon *defence :
little for-*
answered with equal courtesy : " Teacher, say on." "A certain *giveness,
little love.*
creditor," said Jesus, " had two debtors. The one owed him
five hundred *denarii* and the other fifty ; and, as they had
nothing to pay, he freely forgave both. Now which of them
will love him more ? " " I suppose," answered Simon with an
air of indifference, as though resenting the irrelevance of the
question, " the one whom he forgave the more." " A correct
judgment ! " said Jesus, and forthwith applied the parable,
showing Simon the bearing of his innocent admission. He
turned to the woman crouching at His feet, and said to the
host in speech rhythmic with emotion : " Thou seest this
woman ? I entered into thine house : water to Me upon My feet
thou gavest not, but *she* with her tears rained upon My feet and
with her tresses wiped them. A kiss to Me thou gavest not,
but *she*, ever since I entered, did not cease fondly kissing [2]
My feet. With oil [3] My head thou didst not anoint, but *she*
with perfume anointed My feet. Wherefore I tell thee, forgiven are her sins, her many sins, because she loved much.
But one to whom little is forgiven, little loveth."

For the argument's sake Jesus accepted Simon's estimate Shall we do
of the difference betwixt himself and the woman in point of *evil that
good may*
sinfulness, likening him to a debtor who owed fifty *denarii* and *come?*
her to a debtor who owed five hundred. Granting the justice
of this estimate, He pointed to the devotion of the poor outcast and the coldness of the proud Pharisee, and asked if it
was any wonder that He bestowed His regard where it met .
so generous a response. It was a just argument and excel-

---

[1] Beng. : "Comis præfatio."

[2] φίλημα, καταφιλοῦσα. *Cf.* φιλήσω, κατεφίλησεν (Mt. xxvi. 48-9=Mk. xiv. 44-5).

[3] The rich used ointment, the poor oil (Wetstein on Mt. xxvi. 7). Even the latter was withheld from Jesus.

lently adapted to beat down His host's pride; but it seems to lead to a very startling conclusion. If they that are little forgiven love little, then were it not well that men should sin greatly in order that, being greatly forgiven, they may greatly love, "doing evil that good may come"? It is incredible that Jesus should have intended this; and the fact is that He accepted Simon's estimate of the difference betwixt himself and the woman in respect of sinfulness simply for the sake of the argument, even as elsewhere, in order to justify His care for the sinful, He allowed the claim of the Pharisees that they were "whole and had no need of a physician," that they were "righteous and had no need of repentance." Simon was superior to most of his colleagues in that he recognised that he had some little need of forgiveness; but he had much of the Pharisaic blindness and very imperfectly perceived his actual condition. It is ever characteristic of a true saint that, with the vision of God's transcendent holiness before his eyes, he realises his sinfulness and abases himself to the dust. It is told of St Francis of Assisi that one day an angry brother pelted him with contumelious epithets—thief, murderer, drunkard, and the like. The saint meekly confessed that it was all true; and, when his assailant asked in astonishment what he meant, he replied: "All these and still worse crimes had I committed, had not the favour of Heaven preserved me."[1] Had Simon known the plague of his own heart, he would have taken the sinner's place side by side with that poor outcast. When Jesus said: "One to whom little is forgiven, loveth little," He was allowing the Pharisee's assumption in order that He might meet him on his own ground. Stated absolutely, the law would stand: "One who thinks that he needs little forgiveness, loves little."[2] A man's love for Jesus is ever commensurate with his sense of the debt he owes Him.

Rom. iii. 8.

Mt. ix. 12
=Mk. ii.
17=Lk. v.
31.
Lk. xv. 7.

Who was
the sinful
woman? St Luke is the only evangelist who tells this exquisite story,[3] and it is remarkable that he has withheld the woman's

---

[1] Erasm. *Coll. Exeq. Seraph.*

[2] Aug. *Serm.* xcix. § 6: "O Pharisæe, ideo parum diligis, quia parum tibi dimitti suspicaris: non quia parum dimittitur, sed quia parum putas esse quod dimittitur."

[3] By many modern critics it is regarded as a Pauline adaptation of the story of the anointing in the house of Simon the Leper. The opinion is as old as Origen's

name. She must have been well known in the primitive
Church, and it is impossible that her name should have been
hidden from the evangelist who made research his especial Lk. i. 1-4.
care. He must have known it, and he doubtless concealed it
deliberately, reluctant to blazon abroad the shame of one who
had so greatly repented and been so greatly forgiven. Is it
possible to penetrate the secret and discover who she was?
It is curious that, whereas the Greek Fathers seem to have
been content that she should remain unknown, the Latin
would not have it so and insisted upon a twofold identification.

First, they recognised that sinful woman, who by the Identifica-
greatness of her love proved how greatly she had been Mary Mag-
forgiven, as no other than Mary Magdalene; and the idea dalene.
won universal acceptance in Western Christendom and
has rooted itself ineradicably in religious art and literature.
Nor is it without justification. It seems indubitable that
Mary had been a sinful woman, and loved Jesus so well
because He had rescued her from shame. When first she
appears on the pages of the Gospel-story, she is styled " Mary, Lk. viii. 2.
the Magdalene as she is called, from whom seven dæmons had
gone out." Immorality was reckoned a form of demoniac
possession,[1] and, the number *seven* being the symbol of completeness, sevenfold possession meant utter abandonment
thereto. And so, when it is said that Jesus cast seven
dæmons out of Mary, the meaning is that she had been the
slave of her passions and He rescued her from their unhallowed
dominion.[2] Magdala was a wealthy city, being, says the
Talmud, one of three cities whose tribute was conveyed in wag-
gons to Jerusalem. It had, however, a shameful reputation : it
was destroyed, according to the same authority, for its harlotry.[3]
When she met with Jesus, Mary had her abode at Magdala ; and
from the sinful town where she had plied her sinful trade, she got

---

day ; and the great scholar of Alexandria, while holding that the incidents were
distinct, regarded the identification as not unreasonable on the principles of spirit-
ualising exegesis. *In Matth. Comm. Ser.* § 77.

[1] *Cf.* p. 105.

[2] *Cf.* Mt. xii. 45=Lk. xi. 26. The grace of the Holy Spirit is called "seven-
fold"; *e.g.*, S. Odo Clun. *De S. Mar. Mag.* :

" Qui septem purgat vitia,
Per septiformem gratiam."

[3] Lightfoot on John xii. 3.

the epithet which distinguished her ever after.[1]   Nor is it
without significance that St Luke first introduces Mary the
Magdalene immediately after the incident in the Pharisee's
house, albeit, loath to reveal her shame, he does not expressly
identify her with the sinful woman.   This at least is certain,
that it must have been some wondrous experience of the
Lord's grace that inspired Mary with that love, stronger than
death, which she bore Him.

Identification with Mary of Bethany.

John xi. 2.

St Augustine carries the identification still further.   He
appeals to St John's parenthetical comment at the beginning
of his narrative of the raising of Lazarus: " Now it was the
Mary that anointed the Lord with perfume and wiped His
feet with her tresses, whose brother Lazarus was sick "; taking
this as a reference to the anointiug in the Pharisee's house
already recorded by St Luke.[2]   And, if this be indeed the
reference, the two-fold identification is certain.   It must,
however, be acknowledged that the argument is somewhat
precarious.   It is indeed possible that St John was alluding
to the earlier anointing, unrecorded by himself but recorded
by St Luke ; yet it is also possible and perhaps more probable
that he referred to the subsequent anointing at Bethany which
he narrates in the next chapter, and to which, since it was
well known, he could refer by anticipation.

The anointing at Bethany a re-enactment of the scene in the Pharisee's house.

John xii. 3.

If this were all the evidence, it would furnish a very precarious argument for the identification of the sinful woman with
Mary of Bethany.   But in St John's narrative of the anointing
at Bethany there is a delicate and pathetic touch which seems
to attest it beyond controversy.[3]   As Jesus reclined at table
Mary brought her precious nard and anointed His feet and
wiped them with her hair.   There is here a double surprise :
that she should have anointed His feet and not His head, and
that she should have wiped them with her hair.   And what
is the explanation ?   Is it not that Mary's act was no mere
tribute of affection and reverence to her Lord but a grateful

[1] Lightfoot (on Mt. xxvii. 56) suggests that Magdalene may be the Talmudic
מנדלא, " hair-braider," *i.e.* harlot (*cf.* I Pet. iii. 3 : ἐμπλοκῆς τριχῶν), the epithet
which Jewish virulence applied to Mary, the mother of Jesus.

[2] Aug. *De. Cons. Ev.* ii. § 154.   On the contrary, Chrysostom (*In Joan.* lxi),
expressing the Eastern opinion, says : οὐχ αὕτη ἐστὶν ἡ πόρνη ἡ ἐν τῷ Ματθαίῳ οὐδὲ
ἡ ἐν τῷ Λουκᾷ ἀλλ' ἑτέρα τις σεμνή.

[3] *Cf.* Introd § 12, 3, (2).

reminiscence of that day when, a weeping penitent, she had
bent over His feet in the Pharisee's house and with her loose
hair wiped off the tears which dropped on them like rain?
That scene she could never forget; and, to assure Jesus that
she cherished it in lively and grateful remembrance, she acted
it all over again. It was indeed, as He designated it, "a
beautiful work." Its significance was hidden from the rest of
the company, but He comprehended and appreciated it.

Mt. xxvi. 10
=Mk. xiv.
6.

Is not this a powerful, nay, an irresistible reinforcement of
the identification of Mary of Bethany with the sinful woman
in the Pharisee's house? And there is a reinforcement hardly
less strong of her identification with Mary Magdalene. If
Mary of Bethany be other than Mary Magdalene, then she
was not present at the Cross and the Sepulchre. Mary
Magdalene is mentioned among the brave women who, heedless of insult and violence, followed Jesus to Calvary and
stood, with breaking hearts, as near as they might until the
tragedy was ended, and then escorted His mangled body to
Joseph's garden and saw it laid to rest. And on the Resurrection-morning she returned "early, while it was yet dark,"
to the Sepulchre and was rewarded with the first vision of
the Risen Lord. But no mention is made of Mary of
Bethany. Is it possible that, dwelling hard by just over the
brow of Olivet, she should have sat at home securely,
heedless what befell the Master whom she loved so well and
to whom she owed so much?

If other
than Mary
Mag-
dalene,
Mary of
Bethany
absent from
the Cross
and the
Sepulchre.

Mt. xxvii.
56=Mk.
xv. 40.

Mt. xxvii
61=Mk.
xv. 47.
John xx. 1,
11-8.

There is a further confirmation of the twofold identification in the curious silence of the earlier evangelists regarding
the family at Bethany. Once only are they mentioned, and
by St Luke alone; and he takes evident pains to prevent
their recognition. He indeed makes mention of Martha and
Mary, but none of Lazarus; nor does he tell where the sisters
dwelt. And St Matthew and St Mark exhibit a similar
reserve. When they tell the story of the anointing at
Bethany, they say merely that it occurred in the house of
Simon the Leper and that the "beautiful work" was wrought
by "a woman." It is St John who explains that Lazarus was
one of the guests, that Martha served, and that the woman
was Mary. This reserve is remarkable, and the manifest
studiousness of it is a refutation of the modern contention

The
Synoptists'
silence re-
garding the
family at
Bethany.
Lk. x. 38-
42.

Mt. xxvi. 6-
7=Mk. xiv.
3.
John xii. 1.
3.

that the story of Lazarus is a Johannine fiction unknown to the earlier evangelists.[1]   It is evident that they knew it and took pains to conceal it, drawing a veil over that sweet home. Perhaps their principal motive was apprehension for the safety of Lazarus.   When the rulers observed the effect of

John xii. 9-11. his resurrection in disposing the populace to believe in Jesus, they were minded to put him to death ; and, when the Apostles fashioned the Evangelic Tradition, they made no mention of him, lest they should exasperate his enemies further.   But this was not their sole motive. Mary had sinned, and, with tender solicitude for that dear family, they would not bruit her story—how Jesus had found her in her shame at far northern Magdala and restored her forgiven and cleansed to her home at Bethany.   Notoriety would have been at once perilous and painful to Lazarus and his sisters. Many years elapsed ere St John wrote his Gospel ; and by that time they had passed " to where beyond these voices there is peace," and the aged Evangelist could speak freely with no other concern than the exhibition of the grace of Jesus.   Yet even he was silent about Mary's sin forasmuch as her memory was sacred in his eyes.

Modern distaste for the identification.   It must be confessed that this identification of the sinful woman with Mary Magdalene and then with Mary of Bethany finds little favour in these days.[2]   In some quarters it is pronounced baseless, and in others it is deemed an intolerable outrage on Christian sentiment that one who had been an harlot should be supposed to have stood so near the Lord and been so beloved by Him.[3]   The latter contention assuredly deserves no sympathy but, on the contrary, emphatic reprobation.   It is nothing else than a revival of the ancient spirit of Pharisaism.   It was even so that Simon spoke : " This man, had he been a prophet, would have recognised who and of what sort the woman is who is touching him, that she is a sinner."   A truly Christian heart would rather rejoice to

[1] E. A. Abbott, *E. B.* art. *Lazarus* § 3.
[2] Schmiedel, *E. B.* art. *Mary* § 26 : "The identification of Mary Magdalene with the sinner of Lk. 7 36-50 cannot be called felicitous. . . . Even less happy, however, is the identification of Mary Magdalene with the sister of Martha."   The identification is powerfully advocated by Hengstenberg on John xi. 1-46.
[3] J. B. Mayor in Hastings' *D. B.* art. *Mary* ; Godet on Lk. vii. 36-50 ; Andrews, *Life of our Lord*, p. 284. *Cf.* Orig. *In Matth. Comm. Ser.* § 77.

believe that one who had fallen so low was lifted so high, seeing therein a radiant illustration of the grace of Him who came to call not the righteous but sinners. So it seemed to the holy men of medieval days who out of the fulness of their faith and desire poured those sweet hymns which were as springs of living water in a desert land. None ever loved Jesus more passionately or worshipped Him more reverently than St Bernard of Clairvaux; and he deemed it no offence but a soul-gladdening marvel that the harlot who rained hot tears on His feet in the Pharisee's house, was none other than Lazarus' sister Mary who anointed Him at Bethany, none other also than Mary the Magdalene who brought sweet spices to the Sepulchre.[1]

[1] *Serm. In Fest. B. Mar. Mag.* See Daniel, *Thes. Hymnol.* I. cxc; ccccxxxix; II. xl; Append. LIII. *Cf.* Herbert's *Marie Magdalene*.

Lk. viii. 1-3
= Mt. ix.
35 = Mk.
vi. 6b ; Mt.
xiii. 54-8 =
Mk. vi. 1-
6a = Lk. iv.
16-30 ; Mt.
ix. 36-x. 16,
24-42 = Mk.
vi. 7-13 =
Lk. ix. 1-5,
x. 1-12, vi.
40, xii. 2-9,
51-3, xvii.
33 ; Lk.
ix. 6.

CHAPTER XXV

ANOTHER MISSION THROUGH GALILEE

" Measure thy life by loss instead of gain ;
Not by the wine drunk, but the wine poured forth ;
For love's strength standeth in love's sacrifice ;
And whoso suffers most hath most to give."—H. E. H. KING.

Ministering women.

FROM Magdala Jesus proceeded on His projected tour through Galilee, accompanied not only by the Twelve but by a band of women who had experienced His loving-kindness and followed Him with grateful hearts. Mary Magdalene was one of them. She quitted the scene of her shame and went with her Saviour, a witness to His redeeming grace. Another was Joanna, wife of Chuza, the steward of Herod ; and, if it be a true conjecture that Chuza was the courtier whose child John iv. 46- Jesus had healed at the commencement of His ministry,[1] 54 it is no marvel that she should have attended Him in loving ministration. Another was Susanna ; and, though nothing is now known of her beyond her name and her devotion, she must, since her name is mentioned without designation, have been well known in the primitive Church. Only these three are named, but there were many others. It is likely that Joanna was not the only lady of means among them, and they undertook the gracious office of ministering of their substance to Jesus and the Twelve.[2]

At Nazareth

Thus attended Jesus struck inland and travelled to Nazareth. It was apparently His first visit since the beginning of His ministry to that town where He had spent the Silent Years, and where His mother and the rest of her family still resided ; and His appearance excited much interest. His fame had reached Nazareth, and its people were curious about their distinguished townsman. He experienced afresh, however, the truth of the proverb that

[1] Cf. p. 82.
[2] Lk. viii. 3 : αὐτοῖς BD Tisch., W. H., R.V. αὐτῷ אALM, T. R.

"a prophet has no honour in his own country."[1]   They all knew Him, and they knew His kinsfolk; and their knowledge of Him after the flesh was like a veil that hid from them His glory.   He would fain have blessed them, but they lacked faith ; and, where faith was lacking, His grace could find no entrance.   "He could there do no mighty work, save that on a few infirm folk He laid His hands and healed them. And He wondered by reason of their faithlessness."[2]

On the Sabbath Day He repaired to the Synagogue ; and when, according to custom, the Ruler invited Him to address the congregation,[3] He gladly availed Himself of the opportunity.   According to the synagogal order of service the sermon followed the *Aphtarah* or lesson from the Prophets; and this was read by the preacher, who stood while he read it as a mark of reverence for the Holy Scriptures, and then sat down and delivered his discourse.[4]   There was a prescribed lectionary, and it chanced that the lesson for that Sabbath was from the Book of Isaiah.   The Officer handed Jesus the proper volume, and He unrolled it and found the passage, which, as it chanced, included the sixty-first chapter where the prophet announces to the exiles in Babylon their approaching deliverance : "The Spirit of the Lord is upon me, because He anointed me ; to preach good tidings to the poor hath He sent me forth, to proclaim to the captives deliverance and to the blind recovery of sight, to let the bruised go free,[5] to proclaim the acceptable year of the Lord."   Jesus read those gracious words; then, rolling up the volume and handing it back to the Officer, sat down.   Every eye was riveted upon Him, and He began His discourse.   "To-day," He said, "hath this Scripture been fulfilled in your ears."   Nothing more of the discourse is recorded, but it is plain that it was an assertion of His Messiahship and a proclamation of the graciousness of His mission.   And it was a wondrous discourse.   The fame of His preaching had reached the people of Nazareth, but,

Sermon in the Synagogue.

---

[1] *Cf.* p. 80.

[2] On the relation between Lk. iv. 16-30 and Mt. xiii. 54-8 = Mk. vi. 1-6 *cf.* Introd. § 8.

[3] *Cf.* p. 95.   [4] See Lightfoot on Lk. iv. 16.

[5] This clause : ἀποστεῖλαι τεθραυσμένους ἐν ἀφέσει is interpolated from Is. lviii. 6.   Was the Evangelist quoting from memory, or did Jesus quote the words and dwell upon them in His discourse ?

when they heard it, they confessed that it far surpassed what had been told them. "They all testified to Him and wondered at the words of grace that proceeded out of His mouth." Grace was the keynote of the sermon from the first sentence to the last.

The hearers aggrieved. Their souls were stirred, yet they would not yield to the prompting of the Holy Spirit. Prejudice asserted itself, and their hearts rose up in rebellion. It was customary after a sermon for the hearers, if they desired, to address questions to the preacher;[1] and presently the Synagogue was a-buzz with excited conversation. The congregation had a double grievance against Jesus. First, who was He that He should advance such claims? "Is not this man the carpenter,[2] the son of Mary and brother of James and Joses and Judas and Simon? And His sisters—are they not all with us? Whence then hath this man all this?" That He was singularly gifted they durst not dispute; but jealousy is strong in the human breast, and they were angry at His manifest superiority to themselves. And, further, had He not put a slight upon Nazareth? He had gone to Capernaum and there exercised His marvellous gifts? Why had He not settled among His own people and made His own town famous?

Jesus reasons with them. Jesus listened to their questionings and upbraidings, and answered them gently and winsomely. Aggrieved at His neglect of Nazareth and His preference for Capernaum, they had quoted the proverb: "Physician, heal thyself";[3] and, capping proverb with proverb, He answers: "Verily I tell you, 'No prophet is acceptable in his native place.'"[4] Had they not, by their attitude toward Him since His coming amongst them, proved the truth of the proverb and justified His action? And there was precedent for what He had done. Had not Elijah in the time of the great famine been sent to a widow in Zarephath, a heathen city, though there was many a widow in Israel? And in the days of Elisha there was no

1 Kings xvii. 8 sqq.

---

[1] Cf. Lightfoot on Mt. iv. 23; Wetstein on Mt. iv. 23.

[2] Cf. Introd. § 12, 3, (1).

[3] Frequent in ancient literature. The Talmud has: "Medice, sana claudicationem tuam." See Wetstein. The two proverbs here quoted by Jesus are combined in 1897 Oxyrhynchus Logia, 6: λέγει Ἰησοῦς· οὐκ ἔστιν δεκτὸς προφήτης ἐν τῇ πατρίδι αὐτοῦ, οὐδὲ ἰατρὸς ποιεῖ θεραπείας εἰς τοὺς γινώσκοντας αὐτόν.

[4] πατρίς, "native town." See Field, Notes, on Mt. xiii. 54.

MISSION THROUGH GALILEE 215

lack of lepers in Israel, yet the prophet had cleansed only 2 Kings v.
Naaman the Syrian. Those ancient prophets had far outdone
Jesus. He had merely preferred one Jewish town to another,
they had passed Israel by and blessed Gentiles.

It was an almost playful argument, and it should have Uproar in the Syna-gogue.
soothed His hearers; but it had precisely the opposite effect.
Aware of His singular tenderness for outcasts, they took fire at
His allusion to the grace which had of old been shown to the
heathen. Instantly the Synagogue was in an uproar. The
evil behaviour of the Nazarenes was proverbial, and they arose Cf. John i. 46.
and thrust Jesus outside their town, and dragged Him up the
hillside to a precipice, meaning to hurl Him over. It was The Cliff of Precipita-tion.
a shameful scene. Jesus had been at school with some of
those men, and many a time, when they were playmates, had
He clambered in their company to the Cliff of Precipitation.
And now they are howling about Him and dragging Him to
a cruel death. Their murderous project, however, was un-
accomplished. Something arrested their fury. Was it the
memory of old days that stayed their hands and awoke
ruth in their hearts? Or were they overawed by His calm
and dauntless bearing?

> "Veluti magno in populo cum sæpe coorta est
> Seditio, sævitque animis ignobile vulgus,
> Jamque faces et saxa volant, furor arma ministrat;
> Tum, pietate gravem ac meritis si forte virum quem
> Conspexere, silent, arrectisque auribus adstant;
> Ille regit dictis animos et pectora mulcet." [1]

By the time they had reached the summit, their fury had
abated, and "He passed through their midst and went His
way."

Jesus must have been deeply pained by His experience Grief of the True Shepherd.
at Nazareth. He had come to His own home and His own
had not received Him. It would have been no marvel had John i. 11.
He turned away in anger and abandoned that stiff-necked
and rebellious race. But no such thought visited His gracious
heart. Resentment was swallowed up by a great compassion.
He laid the blame not upon the people but upon their
teachers. These were the shepherds of Israel, and they had
neglected their charge, letting their sheep wander untended Cf. Ezek. xxxiv.

[1] Verg. *Æn.* i. 148-54. *Cf.* Luc. *Dem.* § 64.

216 THE DAYS OF HIS FLESH

and unsought. The heart of the True Shepherd was grieved within Him. " He saw the multitudes and He had compas-

Num.xxvii. sion for them, because they were weary [1] and scattered, 'as
17. sheep that have no shepherd.'"

Commis-   It was a piteous spectacle, and it moved the Lord not
sion of the merely to compassion but to more strenuous endeavour. It
Apostles. was impossible for Him to cope with the work single-handed,
so short was the time and so wide the field; and He resolved
upon a departure which He had all along contemplated. He
had ordained the Twelve to be not merely His successors
but His fellow-labourers, and they had already profited sufficiently by His instruction to set their hands to the work.
Grieved by the sore need which He beheld on every side, He
turned to them. "The harvest," He said, "is great, but the
labourers few. Pray therefore of the Lord of the harvest that
He thrust forth labourers ₂into His harvest." It was more
than an exhortation; it was a challenge like that which had
Is. vi. 8. been addressed to the prophet of old: "Whom shall I send?
and who will go for us?" and, as He spoke, Jesus would scan
the faces of the Twelve, hoping that the prophet's response
would leap from their lips: "Here am I! Send me." What
availed it to pray for labourers, if they would not themselves
press forward into the service? And who so fit as they, the
men who had been with Jesus, who had seen His heart and
heard His instruction? Yet they stood irresponsive, knowing
well what the Master desired, yet each waiting for his comrade
to step forward. Jesus would not be baffled. Since they did
not volunteer, He pressed them into the service; since they
did not hasten to the harvest, He thrust them forth. He
called them to Him and laid His command upon them. He
sent them forth in couples to travel through Galilee, preaching
and healing in His name.[2]

The Lord's   Ere they went their various ways, He addressed to them
Address : words of direction and encouragement.[3] First, He defined
Limitation their mission. Their business in the meantime was with
of their Israel. To the north and to the east lay heathen territory
mission.

---

[1] ἐσκυλμένοι, "fatigued by travel." *Cf.* p. 118.

[2] Mt. x. 8 is probably an editorial version of Mk. vi. 7 = Lk. ix. 1-2, modelled on Mt. xi. 5 = Lk. vii. 22. It does not appear that the Twelve raised the dead.

[3] *Cf.* Introd. § 8.

and to the south Samaria, but they must confine themselves within the bounds of Galilee. "Into a road to Gentiles depart not, and into a city of Samaritans enter not; but go rather unto the lost sheep of Israel's house." It is very significant that such a prohibition should have been necessary. No Jew would have dreamed of preaching to Gentiles or Samaritans, and the idea would never have entered into the Apostles' minds had not Jesus, by His sympathy with aliens, set them the example. The time, however, had not yet arrived for the world-wide proclamation of the Gospel, and they must meanwhile preach to none but Jews.

Then He told them how they should equip themselves. *Their equipment.* They must take nothing for their journey save a staff;[1] and this they would need, since they must travel far and would oftentimes be weary and foot-sore. But nothing else must they take: no bread, no wallet, no money. They must go hardily shod with sandals[2]; nor must they take a pair of under-coats, as travellers were wont to do, whether for change of raiment or for double clothing in cold weather.[3] Thus unprovided must they go, and the reason was twofold. They were going on an urgent errand, and they must not stay to equip themselves nor encumber themselves with baggage; nay, they must not pause even to salute anyone by the way after the elaborate fashion of Oriental courtesy.[4] And *Cf. 2 Kings iv. 29.* they were entitled to maintenance in requital of their service. "Worthy," said Jesus, "is the labourer of his food." Perhaps *Cf. 1 Cor. ix. 14.* too there is a deeper significance in the command. It was required that no one should set foot upon the Temple-mount with staff or shoes or purse or with dust upon his feet;[5] and it may be that Jesus meant to impress upon His Apostles the sacredness of their mission. They were entering, as it were, upon holy ground.

They must go poor, but in no wise as mendicants. On *Their entertainment.* the contrary, they were the bearers of a priceless boon which

---

[1] *Cf.* Introd. § 12, I.

[2] It is unnecessary to suppose a discrepancy between Mt.'s μηδὲ ὑποδήματα and Mk.'s ὑποδεδεμένους σανδάλια. Shoes were worn by well-to-do travellers, sandals by the humbler sort. *Cf.* Lightfoot and Wetstein.

[3] See Wetstein on Mt. x. 2. *Cf.* the Baptist's injunction (Lk. iii. 11).

[4] *Cf.* Hastings' *D. B.*, art. *Salutation.*

[5] See Wetstein and Lightfoot.

the recipients could never repay, and whoever entertained

Mt. x. 40-1. them would win a rich reward. When therefore they arrived at a town, they must not crave alms, but must discover who was worthy to have them under his roof; and when they had made their choice, they must remain under that roof all the

Cf. Ecclus. xxix. 24. time of their sojourn in the town. "Pass not," says Jesus, "from house to house." Did He mean that they must not waste in a round of social functions the precious time which should be devoted to the prosecution of their mission? or that they must not vex their host by quitting his house for another more luxurious? And, while they were under his roof, they must bear themselves graciously and considerately, " eating what was set before them," finding no fault and accommodating themselves in all respects to the customs of the household. Sometimes, however, they would be ill received; and, when they and their message were rejected, they must take their departure, but not without a solemn protestation. " Into whatsoever city ye enter and they do not receive you, go forth into its streets and say : ' Even the dust that hath stuck from your city to our feet, we wipe off against you.[1] Nevertheless recognise this, that the Kingdom of God hath come nigh.' Verily I tell you, it shall be more tolerable for the land of Sodom and Gomorrha at the Day of Judgment than for that city."

Persecution in store. What had happened at Nazareth was a forewarning of what awaited the Apostles in the prosecution of their ministry. " Behold," says Jesus, " I am sending you forth as sheep in the midst of wolves. Prove therefore ' prudent as the serpents and simple[2] as the doves.'" It was a proverbial maxim,[3] warning against recklessness on the one hand and time-serving on the other. They must lay their account for persecution, and they must encounter it fearlessly, never playing the coward and holding their peace, but confessing their Lord openly and proclaiming at all hazards the message wherewith He had charged them. " What I tell you in the darkness,

---

[1] *Cf.* Acts xiii. 51. A graphic rejection of the unbelievers : they were as heathen. A heathen land was unclean, and a Jew wiped its dust from his feet when he passed into the Holy Land. *Cf.* Lightfoot and Wetstein on Mt. x. 14.

[2] ἀκέραιοι, literally *unmixed, unadulterated*, from κεράννυμι. The rendering *harmless* is based on a false derivation from κεραΐζω, κέρας.

[3] See Wetstein on Mt. x. 16.

speak in the light ; and what ye hear in the ear proclaim upon the housetops." What though they suffered? They had strong consolations. Their Master had gone that way before them. "A disciple is not above the Teacher, nor a slave above his lord. If they have styled the master of the house Beelzebul, how much more them of his household?" =Mt. xii. And, though their enemies might slay their bodies, they could not slay their souls. It mattered little what they might suffer, so long as they did not, by cowardice and unfaithfulness, yield themselves to the Devil. "Fear them not," says Jesus; "but I will warn you whom to fear: Fear him that after killing hath authority to cast into Gehenna. Yea, I tell you, fear him." And had they not in every strait the assurance of God's wise and loving providence? They were in His hands, and He would watch over them. He cared for the meanest of His creatures, even for the sparrows, so insignificant that a penny [1] would purchase a pair, while if the purchaser took twopence' worth, he got one extra.[2] "Are not five sparrows sold for twopence? and one of them"—even the odd one which is thrown into the bargain—"shall not fall on the ground [3] without your Father.[4] But as for you, even the hairs of your head have all been numbered. Fear not; ye are worth more than many sparrows."

It is noticeable what pains Jesus took to disabuse His Apostles of any illusions which they might be cherishing. He was calling them to strife, suffering, and sacrifice; and He would have them recognise the fact and consider whether they had courage to face the ordeal and go through with it. "Think not that I came to cast [5] peace upon the earth. I came not to cast peace but a sword. For I came to set a man at variance against his father, and a daughter against her mother, and a daughter-in-law against her mother-in-law; and the man's foes shall be those of his household." And He went further. He pointed to the dearest and holiest of human affections, and claimed, not for God nor for the

The Lord's Challenge.

---

[1] ἀσσάριον, a *penny*; κοδράντης, a *farthing*. *Cf.* Mk. xii. 42.
[2] *Cf.* Mt. x. 29 with Lk. xii. 6. Two sparrows were the offering at the cleansing of a leper: Lev. xiv. 4. See Lightfoot on Lk. xii. 6.
[3] For ἐπὶ τὴν γῆν Chrysostom has εἰς παγίδα, "into a snare."
[4] *Cf.* Spanish proverb : "A leaf stirs not on the tree without the will of God."
[5] The metaphor is from sowing seed. *Cf.* Wetstein.

Kingdom of Heaven, but for Himself, a prior devotion: "He that loveth father or mother above Me is not worthy of Me; and he that loveth son or daughter above Me is not worthy of Me." Nay, He went further still, and claimed that for His sake they should be ready to endure the worst suffering and the uttermost ignominy. In those days "cross-bearing" was not, as in modern religious phraseology, a mere metaphor, lightly applied to ordinary and often sentimental afflictions, but a stern and terrible reality. Crucifixion was the doom of the vilest criminals; and the Apostles had often seen poor wretches carrying their crosses to the place of execution, to hang there in shame and agony, moaning out their lives. Jesus knew that the world's enmity must be His portion, and He claimed that His Apostles should be ready to share it: "He who doth not take his cross and follow after Me, is not worthy of Me." On the lips of a Socrates or an Alexander such claims would have seemed the language of insanity and would have been greeted with derision; yet Jesus made them, not once but constantly, and the men who stood nearest to Him and knew Him best, acknowledged that they were just.

The Apostles' response.

It is no wonder that the Lord's address, appealing as it did to their noblest instincts, fired the hearts of His Apostles. It was a challenge to chivalrous heroism. "He that hath found his life," said Jesus in the language of a general exhorting his troops on the eve of battle,[1] "shall lose it; and he that hath lost his life for My sake shall find it." What though they should fall on the field? They would win immortality. Better die a glorious death than purchase life at the cost of honour. When Francis of Assisi heard the Apostolic Commission read by the priest in the chapel of the Portiuncula, it thrilled through his soul, and he threw aside his staff, wallet, purse, and shoes and devoted himself from that hour to his high mission. And it is no wonder that the Apostles responded to the appeal when they heard it warm and impassioned from the Lord's own lips. They bade Jesus and the women farewell and went their several ways two by two, "preaching the Gospel and healing everywhere."

[1] Wetstein on Mt. x. 39: "Proverbium est militare." Cf. Xen. Anab. iii. 1. § 43.

CHAPTER XXVI

THE CLOSING SCENE OF THE BAPTIST'S LIFE

Mt. xi. 1;
Lk. vii. 11-
7; Mt. xi.
2-19=Lk.
vii. 18-35 ;
Mt. xiv. 6-
11=Mk.
vi. 21-8.

"John, than which man a sadder or a greater
Not till this day has been of woman born,
John like some lonely peak by the Creator
Fired with the red glow of the rushing morn."—MYERS.

THE Apostles went their several ways, and Jesus, accompanied Scanty re-
by the faithful women, went His. Of the doings of the cord of the mission.
Twelve nothing is recorded, not because they did nothing
worthy of record, but because the task of the Evangelists was
to tell not of the Apostles but of the Lord. Had they known
the story, they would have recounted what He did and said
as He travelled through Galilee, teaching and preaching in its
cities ; but it was hidden from them. The Apostles were
absent on their own errands ; and, since they included in their
tradition only what they had seen and heard, they have left
at this point a blank page.

St Luke's research, however, has rescued one precious The mir-
fragment from oblivion ;[1] and, if she was indeed the mother acle at Nain.
of the child whom more than a year before Jesus had
snatched from death, it is likely that his informant may have
been Joanna. An experience so like her own would appeal
to her. In the course of His mission Jesus came into the
south of Galilee and approached the town of Nain, which lay
seven miles south-east of Nazareth between ancient Endor
and Shunem.[2] He was attended not only by the women but
by a band of disciples, converts whom He had lately won, and
a crowd which followed out of curiosity. A mile eastward
from the town still lies the ancient burial-ground ; [3] and, as

[1] It is hardly doubtful that the Nain incident belongs to the mission in Galilee.
(1) How else would He have been so far from Capernaum ?   (2) Lk. puts it before the
message from John the Baptist, which in Mt. follows the departure of the Twelve.
Nothing can be inferred from Lk. vii. 11, where the reading is ἐν τῷ ἑξῆς (χρόνῳ),
"subsequently," not ἐν τῇ ἑξῆς (ἡμέρᾳ), "next day."

[2] Jer. De Loc. Hebr.

[3] Sanday, Sacr. Sit. pp. 24-5.   It was required that a Jewish burial-place should

R   221

Jesus approached, He met a *cortege* wending its mournful way thither.   It was the funeral of a young lad, a widow's only son ; and the broken-hearted mother was conspicuous among the women folk who, in accordance with Jewish custom, headed the procession.[1]   There was a large company of sympathetic mourners ; and it is no wonder that the heart of Jesus, that fountain of compassion, overflowed at the sight. " Weep not," He said to the sorrowful mother, and laid an arresting hand on the open bier.[2]   " Lad," He said, " arise ! " and the boy sat up and began to talk.[3]   The spectators were stricken with awe.   " A great prophet," said some, thinking

2 Kings iv. of Elijah and his miracle in the village of Shunem hard by, " hath arisen among us."   " God," said others, " hath visited His people."

Envoys from John the Baptist.

Jesus was still prosecuting His mission when two strangers approached Him and sought an interview.   They were disciples of John the Baptist, who had been arrested by Herod Antipas at the commencement of the Lord's ministry and had lain a prisoner ever since in the fortress of Machærus.   It was a weary time, and its protraction was due to the play of opposing influences on the mind of the vacillating tyrant.   In the first flush of his resentment Antipas would have had him executed had he dared ; but, knowing how greatly the multitude revered the prophet, he dreaded an insurrection should he destroy their idol.[4]   He therefore kept John under arrest, and presently a still more powerful dread took possession of him.   He had repeated interviews with the prisoner, and his guilty soul quailed before that fearless man, so helpless yet so majestic.   " He was much perplexed [5] and gladly listened

be 8 *stadia*, *i.e.* a Roman mile, outside the town.   *Cf.* Lightfoot on Lk. viii. 12 and vol. ii, p. 582.

[1] Because woman had brought death into the world.   *Cf.* Wetstein on Lk. vii. 13.

[2] *Cf.* Jos. *Ant.* xviii. 8. § 3.

[3] Philostratus (*Apoll.* iv. 45) tells a story which is evidently designed (1) to rival this miracle of Jesus, and (2) to suggest that it was not really a case of resurrection from the dead but merely of resuscitation from a swoon.

[4] The popular sentiment is evinced by the fact that, when some eight years later, in A.D. 36, Antipas was defeated by Aretas of Arabia, the Jews interpreted the disaster as God's vengeance for the murder of the Baptist. See Jos. *Ant.* xviii. 5. § 2.

[5] Mk. vi. 20: אBL, Tisch., W. H., R.V. πολλὰ ἠπόρει. ACD, T. R. πολλὰ ἐποίει.

to him." It was the supreme crisis in the tetrarch's life. His conscience was stirred, and he was disposed to obey its dictates and yield to the importunities of the Holy Spirit; but, alas, he was hampered by his evil past. Herodias held him back. For her sake he had sinned, and now that he was minded to repent, he was fast bound by the fetters which he had himself forged. She was bitter with all a bad woman's bitterness against the Baptist for his denunciation of her infamous marriage, and clamoured for his' death. Torn this way and that, the tetrarch had neither executed his prisoner nor set him at liberty, but had held him in durance all that weary time. It seems that he showed him not a little indulgence and made his captivity as easy as possible, allowing his disciples free access to their master.   Mt. xi. 2 = Lk. vii. 18.

And they had kept John acquainted with the progress of events in the outer world and, more particularly, with the doings of Jesus, whom he had hailed as the Messiah and announced as such to the multitude at Bethany beyond Jordan. He listened with eager interest to every report of "the works of the Messiah"; and, as time went on, misgivings arose within him. He began to doubt if Jesus were really the Messiah after all, and he sent that deputation of two of his disciples to request a plain declaration.   John's doubt as to the Messiahship of Jesus.

Mt. xi. 2.

And wherefore did he doubt? What had happened to shake his assured conviction? It has been supposed that he had lost heart. His long imprisonment had broken his spirit, and he was aggrieved at the neglect which he had suffered.[1] Jesus had busied Himself in Galilee, and had let him lie in prison, never lifting a hand to deliver him or even sending him a message of sympathy and encouragement. This, however, is a baseless opinion and one that does less than justice to the brave prophet. If he had lost heart, he would hardly have appealed to Jesus. On the contrary, he would have humbled himself before Antipas and endeavoured to make peace with him. Nor was John the man to lose heart. He was of heroic stuff, the sort of man that holds his own interest cheap so long as the cause which is dearer to   Reason thereof.

[1] Lightfoot, Wetstein. According to Tertullian (*Adv. Marc.* iv. § 18) John's doubt was due to the passing of the prophetic spirit from him to Jesus, *ut in massalem suam summam.*

him than life, is advancing.[1]   With noble self-abnegation he
John iii.
27-30. had stepped aside and left the field open for Jesus ; and he
would have been well content to rot in the deepest dungeon
of Machærus, had he only been assured that the Kingdom of
Heaven was winning its way.

His Mes-
sianic ideal   And it was precisely this that troubled him : it seemed to
him that the Kingdom of Heaven was not advancing.   He
heard of the doings of Jesus, and, wonderful as they were,
they were not, in his judgment, "the works of the Messiah."
Like the rest of the Jews, John had an imperfect ideal of the
Messiah, and he doubted the Messiahship of Jesus because it
did not square with his ideal.   It is indeed true that he did
not share the Messianic ideal which commonly prevailed.   The
Jews of that generation looked for a king of the lineage of
David, a conqueror who should crush the heathen and make
Israel once more a free nation ; and they could not believe
in the Messiahship of Jesus because He had not a crown on
His head and an army at His back.   John had another and
nobler ideal.   In fact, he had two ideals, more or less inconsistent, which lay side by side in his mind.   On the one hand
he looked for a Messiah who should play the part of a
Mt. iii. 12
=Lk. iii.
17. reformer : "Whose fan is in His hand, and He will thoroughly
cleanse His threshing-floor, and He will gather His wheat
into the barn, but the chaff He will burn up with fire un-
Mt. iii. 10
=Lk. iii. 9. quenchable."   "Already the axe hath been set to the root of
the trees.   Every tree therefore that bringeth not forth good
fruit, is being hewn down and flung into the fire."   On the
other hand, building on the fifty-third chapter of Isaiah, he
looked for a suffering Messiah, not merely a martyr but a
John i. 29. Redeemer, a sacrificial Victim :   "Behold, the Lamb of God
that taketh away the sin of the world."   He heard of the

---

[1] *Cf.* Chrysost. *In Matth.* xxxvii. (1) Chrysostom's view is that John had
himself no doubt and asked the question for the sake of his disciples in order to
persuade them to cast in their lot with Jesus. So Jer., Hil., Isid. Pel., Theophyl.,
Euth. Zig., Calv., Beng. (2) John had really no doubt about the Messiahship of
Jesus but marvelled at His delay in assuming His rightful majesty and thought to
precipitate His self-manifestation (Fritzsche, Hase, Neander). (3) Strauss cuts the
knot by denying the historicity of the earlier narratives, especially the Fourth
Gospel's, which represent John as recognising and announcing the Messiahship of
Jesus. He does not now begin to doubt whether after all Jesus is really the
Messiah, but rather begins to wonder if He may not be the Messiah. "We have
here not a decaying, but a growing certainty."

doings of Jesus, and he recognised the greatness and wonder of them ; but they were not, as he conceived, "the works of the Messiah." Jesus realised neither of his Messianic ideals. He was not a Reformer. "He did not strive nor cry, neither Mt. xii. 19. did any one hear His voice in the streets." Where were the winnowing-fan and the axe? Neither was He a Sufferer ; for these were the days of the Lord's popularity. He was the idol of the populace, the hero of the hour.

Therefore was John perplexed. Had he heard of Jesus inaugurating a crusade against the abuses of the day, he would have been satisfied : "Behold, the Messiah with winnowing-fan and axe !" Or had he been told that He was undergoing persecution, that He had, like himself, been arrested and thrown into prison, then also he would have been satisfied : "Behold, the Messiah ! He is led as a lamb to the slaughter." But he heard none of these things. Jesus was neither a Reformer nor a Victim : could He be the Messiah ?

What ailed John was not so much a mistaken ideal as His im-impatience. His ideal was in a sense true. Jesus *was* a patience. Reformer : He had come to make all things new. And He would be a Sufferer : the Cross was His goal. But the time for these things had not yet arrived, and John was impatient for the consummation. He did not, he could not, deny the Messiahship of Jesus. There was much that seemed to attest it, yet much was lacking which he deemed essential. He wavered betwixt *Yea* and *Nay* ; and such was his confidence in Jesus, such his inclination to believe, that he resolved to refer the question to Him and accept His decision.

His messengers sought Jesus and presented to Him their The Lord's master's enquiry. "Art *Thou* the Coming One, or are we to reply. look for another?" The Lord was engaged with a throng which included many sick folk desirous of healing. Vouchsafing at the moment no reply, He continued His beneficent work in the envoys' presence. Then He addressed them. "Go," He said, "and announce to John the things which ye hear and behold : blind are recovering sight, and lame are walking, lepers are being cleansed, and deaf are hearing, and dead are being raised, and poor are having the Gospel preached to them.[1]   And blessed is he who stumbleth not at Me."   It seems a stern, almost unfeeling reply.   He spoke no word of sympathy, He sent no message of cheer to that brave soul languishing in prison and questioning whether the crowning act of his heroic ministry had not been a fatal blunder.   It seems almost a cruel reply, but in truth Jesus spoke both kindly and wisely.   Had He answered categorically : " Yes, I am the Messiah," the Baptist would have accepted His verdict ; but he would have accepted it blindly, and his doubts would have remained unresolved.   He would have been haunted still by harassing uncertainty.   Jesus took a better way.   He bade the envoys tell their master what they had heard and witnessed, and let him judge.   The evidence was overwhelming.   It was not indeed the sort of evidence that John was looking for ; but it was his expectation that was at fault, and Jesus had faith in his sincerity, his candour, his open-mindedness, his willingness to reconsider his opinions and abandon them if he found them untenable.

His eulogy on John. As soon as the messengers had taken their departure, Jesus pronounced a glowing eulogy on John.   He knew what the bystanders were thinking.   They were charging the Baptist with vacillation and cowardice.   His faith, once so assured, had been shaken ; adversity had broken his spirit. Such was their judgment, and Jesus assailed it and exposed the absurdity of it, recalling those great days when they had crowded down to the Jordan and listened spell-bound to the inspired prophet's eloquence.   It was impossible to remember the scene and think John irresolute or cowardly.   " What went ye forth into the wilderness to behold ?   A reed shaken by wind ? "   Nay, there had been no irresolution, no vacillation about that stern preacher of doom.   " But what went ye forth to see ?   A man clothed in soft raiment ?   Behold, they that wear soft raiment are in kings' palaces."   Had John been a cowardly weakling whom adversity could daunt, he would not have followed that stern, ascetic life ; he would have been a supple courtier.   " But what went ye forth to see ?   A

[1] Passive use of εὐαγγελίζομαι. Cf. Hebr. iv. 2, 6. Euth. Zig. takes it as a Middle : The marvel was that poor men like the Apostles should preach. τί γὰρ πενέστερον ἀλιευτικῆς ; " Preaching the Gospel to the poor " (cf. p. 158) is coupled with His miracles, because this also was a special work of the Messiah. Cf. Is. lxi. 1 : Lk. iv. 18.

prophet? Yea, I tell you, and something more than a prophet. This is he of whom it hath been written : ' Behold, I send My messenger before Thy face, who shall prepare Thy way before Thee.' " John was indeed what he had claimed to be—the Forerunner of the Messiah, the Elijah of Jewish expectation who should come and restore all things.[1] A greater man had never lived.

Yet John had a serious limitation. He utterly mis- John's conceived the Messianic Kingdom. " Verily I tell you, there limitation. hath not arisen among them that are born of women a greater [2] than John the Baptist ; yet one that is but little in the Kingdom of Heaven is greater than he."[3] John conceived the Messiah as a stern Reformer, and he was eager for the inauguration of the new and better era. He had broken with the old order ; he had forsaken Temple and Synagogue, and assailed the rulers with fierce denunciation. He had inflamed the Zealot-temper and set the land afire.[4] Men were thinking to establish the Kingdom of Heaven by violent and revolutionary methods. They were like an army storming a city and seizing the booty with wild and eager hands. " The Law and the Prophets," says Jesus, " were until John the Baptist ; but from his days until now the Kingdom of Heaven is being stormed, and stormers are plundering it."[5] This spirit and these methods Jesus viewed with profound disapprobation,[6] recognising as He did the value of the ancient faith, as a preparation for His perfect revelation, and the

[1] Mal. iv. 5-6. See Lightfoot on Mt. xvii. 10. *Cf.* p. 27.

[2] προφήτης in Lk. vii. 28 is an interpretative addition, inconsistent with περισσότερον προφήτου.

[3] μικρότερος, not equivalent to Superlat. but a regular Comparat. : " one that is comparatively little in the K. of H." *Cf.* Mt. xxiii. 11. " The expression is used because all members of the Kingdom of God as such are great, and because some can only be spoken of as *comparatively* little " (Wendt). Chrysost., attaching ἐν τῇ βασ. τῶν οὐρ. to μείζων, takes the words as an assertion of the Lord's own superiority to John : " I that am less in age and in the opinion of the people, am greater than he in the Kingdom of Heaven." Jerome says this was a common interpretation in his day. Erasmus approves it.

[4] This was the reason which Antipas alleged for arresting John. *Cf.* p. 71.

[5] Mt. xi. 12-3 = Lk. xvi. 16. In Lk. this remarkable logion is an isolated fragment, but more intelligible than in Mt. who reverses the clauses. Commonly interpreted as a description of the influx of all sorts of disreputable people into the Kingdom of Heaven—a welcome spectacle to Jesus but shocking to the Pharisees. Wetstein, Bruce.

[6] *Cf. Ep. ad Diogn.* vii : βία γὰρ οὐ πρόσεστι τῷ Θεῷ.

Mal. iii. 1.

spirituality of the Kingdom of Heaven.   He had the Baptist
in His eye when He said at the outset of His ministry:

Mt. v. 19. "Whosoever looseth one of these least commandments and
teacheth men so, least shall he be called in the Kingdom of
Heaven."   And now He reiterates the declaration with still
greater emphasis: "One that is but little in the Kingdom of
Heaven is greater than he."

Unreason- The Lord's purpose in thus speaking was not to censure
ableness of John, but to bring home to His hearers their unreasonable-
that gener-
ation. ness.   God had tried first one way to win them, and then,
when they remained obdurate, He had tried another way, like
the huntsmen, says St Chrysostom, who, determined that
their quarry shall not escape, press upon it from all sides at
once.   First John had arisen, and his austerity had displeased
them.   Then Jesus came, and He was no wilderness-recluse.
He dwelt among them, a gracious friend, going, when they
bade Him, to weddings and feasts.   But they were no better
pleased.   John had been too austere, Jesus was too genial.
"Whereunto," says Jesus, "shall I liken this generation?"
And He compares them to children playing in the sunny
market-place their game of charades in which one company
would act a part, and another company would sit by and, if
they guessed what it was, would join in with the actors.[1]   It
was bad enough that the men of that generation were like
children playing at religion, but it was worse that they were
like petulant children.   First they were for acting a marriage,
and they were aggrieved because John would not dance to
their piping; then they were for acting a funeral, and were
aggrieved because Jesus did not join in their wailing.
"Whereunto shall I liken the men of this generation?   They
are like children that sit in a market-place and call to one
another, saying: 'We piped to you, and ye did not dance;
we chanted the dirge to you, and ye did not beat your
breasts.'[2]   For John the Baptist hath come neither eating or
drinking, and ye say: 'He hath a dæmon!'   The Son of
Man hath come eating and drinking, and ye say: 'Behold,

---

[1] Cf. Calvin.

[2] Proverbial; cf. Æsop, *Fab.* 27: "The Piping Fisherman."   The παιδία represent the Jews, οἱ ἕτεροι John and Jesus (Mt. xi. 16: ἑτέροις Tisch., W. H.; ἑταίροις
T. R., Erasm.).   Chrysost. understands οἱ ἕτεροι as the Jews, John and Jesus being
the complainers; but ἐθρηνήσαμεν, κ.τ.λ. must then precede ηὐλήσαμεν, κ.τ.λ.

a glutton and wine-bibber, a friend of tax-gatherers and sinners ! ' " [1]

His appeal to Jesus was the Baptist's latest act.   Herodias Execution
of John. at length got her desire, winning by craft what had been denied to her importunities and blandishments ; and the blow so long impending fell on the heroic captive.   The birth-day of Antipas [2] had come round, and, to celebrate the occasion, he summoned his leading nobles and officers to a banquet in the princely castle of Machærus.[3]   In the midst of the revel an unexpected diversion was introduced by Herodias.   She had, by the husband whom she had so shamelessly abandoned, a daughter named Salome, who by and by became the wife of Philip the tetrarch of Trachonitis.[4] The young princess, a mere girl some seventeen years of age, was sent by her wicked mother into the banquet-chamber to entertain the wine-inflamed company by executing a lewd dance before their lascivious eyes.   It was a shameless performance, unbefitting alike a princess and a maiden.[5] Nevertheless it evoked rapturous applause, and the gratified host assumed an air of maudlin magnificence.   He was only a humble vassal of Rome, but in popular parlance he was styled " the King," a reminiscence of the days of Herod the

Mk. vi. 14,
25, 26, 27 ;
Cf. Mt. xiv.
1 = Lk ix.
7 (iii. 19).

[1] The sententious aphorism, Mt. xi. 19b = Lk. vii. 35, is probably an interpolation.

[2] It is doubtful whether the occasion was his birth-day or the anniversary of his accession. γενέθλια was the proper term for the former, but γενέσια also was so used (Suid.), and it is so understood here by Orig. and Chrysost. Birth-day celebrations were associated by the Jews with idolatry (Lightfoot) ; only Pharaoh (Gen. xl. 20) and Herod Antipas are recorded in Scripture to have celebrated their birth-days (Orig., Jer.).

[3] Josephus (*Ant.* xviii. 5. § 2) fixes the scene of the execution at Machærus, nor does Mk. vi. 21 imply that the banquet took place at Tiberias, Antipas' northern capital. οἱ πρῶτοι τῆς Γαλιλαίας would repair to Machærus. The castle there had been built by Herod the Great in magnificent style. It commanded a fine prospect and had salubrious springs hard by (Jos. *De Bell. Jud.* vii. 6. §§ 2-3).

[4] Jos. *Ant.* xviii. 5. § 4.   In Mk. vi. 22 Tisch. reads τῆς θυγ. αὐτῆς τῆς Ἡρωδ. W. H. read τῆς θυγ. αὐτοῦ Ἡρωδ., which makes her the daughter of Antipas and her name Herodias. Keim finds this incident unhistorical. He puts the death of John " very shortly before the year 36." Philip the tetrarch died in the year 33-4 after living several years with Salome in barren wedlock. Therefore at John's execution she was not a κοράσιον but a widow. In truth, however, it is Keim's chronology and not the Gospel narrative that is in error. John was executed probably in A.D. 28. Cf. Schürer, *H. J. P.* I. iii. 28, n. 29.

[5] Hor. *Od.* iii. 6. 21-4. Chrysost. *In Matth.* xlix : ἔνθα γὰρ ὄρχησις, ἐκεῖ ὁ διάβολος.

Great; and his vain soul loved the title.   He summoned the
girl before him, and, sublimely oblivious of the fact that he
durst not dispose of a single acre of his territory without the
Emperor's sanction, vowed, in a strain of Oriental munifi-
Cf. Esth. cence, to grant whatever boon she might crave, were it half of
v. 6. his kingdom.   She went out and consulted with her mother,
and that wicked woman, exulting in the success of her
stratagem, bade her request the head of John the Baptist
served up, like some dainty viand,[1] on a trencher.   The
tetrarch was deeply distressed and would gladly have withdrawn from his engagement; but, according to that age's
code of honour,[2] he durst not, and sorely against his will he
sent an executioner to behead the prophet in his cell.   The
deed was done, and the dripping head was brought on a
trencher into the banquet-hall and presented to Salome.
She bore the ghastly trophy to Herodias; and it is said [3]
that, not content with feasting her eyes upon it, that she-
devil emulated the barbarity of Fulvia and pierced with a
bodkin the once eloquent tongue which had denounced
her sin.

[1] Chrysost. : ὡς περὶ τινος ἐδέσματος διαλεγομένη.
[2] *Cf.* Jud. xi. 30-5 ; Herod. ix. 109 ; Ovid. *Met.* ii. 44-52.
[3] Jer. *Adv. Ruff.* iii.

CHAPTER XXVII

ANOTHER RETREAT ACROSS THE LAKE

> " Bone pastor, panis vere,
> Jesu, nostri miserere.
> Tu nos pasce, nos tuere,
> Tu nos bona fac videre
>   In terra viventium."—S. Thomas Aquinas.

Mt. xiv. 12 =Mk. vi. 29; Mt. xiv. 1-2= Mk. vi. 14-6=Lk. ix. 7-9; Mt. xiv. 13-21= Mk. vi. 30-44=Lk. ix. 10-7=John vi. 1-14; Mt. xiv. 22-33=Mk. vi. 45-52= John vi. 15-21.

JOHN'S disciples conveyed their master's mutilated corpse, it is said, to Sebaste, the capital of Samaria, not far from Ænon, the scene of his later ministry, and buried it there beside the tombs of Elisha and Obadiah.[1]   And then in their desolation they sought Jesus and told Him what had befallen. He was deeply moved. He brought His mission to an end, and, betaking himself to Capernaum, awaited the return of the Twelve. Presently they arrived, brimming over with talk about what they had seen and done; but Jesus had no heart to listen. No sooner had they all reassembled than He bade them withdraw from Capernaum and accompany Him to the other side of the Lake. *Sorrow of Jesus.*

Wherefore did He depart so soon?   He and His company needed a breathing-space after the labour of their mission, and the people of Capernaum were overjoyed to have Him back in their midst. Wherefore did He not stay awhile? For one thing, shocked by the tragedy, He had no heart to engage in His wonted employments. He craved a season of retirement that He might give Himself to communion with God. And there was no chance of repose at Capernaum. The town was all excitement and enthusiasm. "Come ye yourselves apart," He said to the Twelve, "into a lonely place and rest a little." There was more than met the eye in the prevailing excitement. A plot was on foot among the people, and the disciples were privy to it. It was nothing less than a design to precipitate the Messianic consummation by compelling Jesus *He resolves to seek the eastern shore by reason of (1) His need of repose; (2) a Messianic plot;*

---

[1] Jer. *De Loc. Hebr.*   See p. 191, n. 2.

to assume forthwith what they deemed His rightful dignity and come forward as the King of Israel. The multitude and the disciples both had long been fretting at His inexplicable procrastination, and they had resolved to seize Him and acclaim Him King. The ringleaders were intent on the business, and Jesus observed them going to and fro, so eager that " they had no leisure even to eat." The mad scheme must be frustrated, and Jesus determined to escape to the eastern shore.

Cf. John vi. 15.

(3) curiosity of Herod Antipas regarding Him.

He had yet another reason for His sudden departure. Herod Antipas had heard the fame of His extensive activity. It can hardly indeed have been the first rumour that had reached his ears, but, arriving just after the execution of John when the tetrarch's conscience was ill at ease, it greatly disturbed him. He wondered who Jesus could be, and, when he consulted his attendants, they informed him of the various opinions which were in circulation : how some thought that He was Elijah come back, according to Jewish expectation, to prepare Israel for the Messiah's advent, and others that He was simply a prophet like the great ones of old.[1] Neither theory satisfied Antipas. His crime haunted him. His guilty soul was shaken by superstitious dread ; and, Sadducee though he was, denying the doctrine of the Resurrection,[2] the idea took possession of him that the murdered Baptist had risen from the dead, endowed, as befitted a visitant from the unseen world, with mysterious and miraculous powers. It came to pass with Antipas as with many an unbeliever.

> " Just when we are safest, there's a sun-set touch,
> A fancy from a flower-bell, someone's death,
> A chorus-ending from Euripides,—
> And that's enough for fifty hopes and fears

---

[1] According to Lk. popular surmise was three-fold : *John raised from the dead, Elijah, one of the ancient prophets redivivus* ; Herod was simply perplexed. Keim pronounces this version " the more probable one," but it is likely that Lk. deemed it impossible that the Sadducean tetrarch should have entertained the idea that John had risen from the dead, and attributed it to the populace. Chrysost. suggests harmonistically that Herod first (in accordance with Lk.) contemptuously rejected the various theories, and then (in accordance with Mk. and Mt.), as the fame of Jesus increased, adopted the popular opinion. If the reading ἔλεγον were adopted in Mk. vi. 14, the discrepancy would disappear, φανερὸν γάρ . . . εἷς τῶν προφητῶν being a parenthetical account of the popular opinion.

[2] *Cf.* Mt. xvi. 6 with Mk. viii. 15. See Lightfoot and Wetstein.

As old and new at once as nature's self,
To rap and knock and enter in our soul,
Take hands and dance there, a fantastic ring,
Round the ancient idol, on his base again,—
The grand Perhaps ! We look on helplessly.
There the old misgivings, crooked questions are."

It is a pathetic evidence of the human heart's profound need of God, that, when it abjures faith, it becomes a prey to abject superstition.

Antipas was anxious to see Jesus that he might ascertain the truth ; and, since his capital of Tiberias stood on the shore of the Lake within ten miles of Capernaum, it was expedient that Jesus should withdraw. Though it is hardly likely that the tetrarch would have done violence to Him, thereby increasing his already intolerable load of guilt, it would have been an unpleasant experience to be haled into his presence ; and Jesus resolved to avoid the embarrassment by crossing the Lake. On the other side He would be in the territory of Philip beyond the jurisdiction of Antipas.

He embarked with the Twelve ; and, steering north-east- Near Beth-ward, they came to land near Bethsaida Julias on a level saida strip of well-watered and fertile land, covered, since it was Julias. spring-time, with a fresh carpet of green grass. Jesus hoped John vi. 4. to find there a quiet retreat ; but His departure had been observed, and a vast crowd set out from Capernaum and travelled round the head of the Lake to join Him on the other side.[1] It was a considerable detour, and, ere they arrived, Jesus and His disciples had landed and retired to the upland behind the plain. Presently He espied them approaching, travel-worn and some in piteous plight; for there were sick folk among them who had dragged themselves all that weary way in the hope of being healed. The heart of the True Shepherd was smitten with compassion for the shepherdless throng. He quitted His retreat and, bidding them kindly welcome,[2] discoursed to them and healed their sicknesses.

And He did more. When He beheld the long train defiling Feeding round the Lake and crowding the green champain, He the multi-tude.

---

[1] *Cf.* Introd. § 13.

[2] Lk. ix. 11 : ἀποδεξάμενος. *Cf.* viii. 40. 1 Tim. i. 15 : πάσης ἀποδοχῆς ἄξιος. Acts xv. 4 : παρεδέχθησαν, al. ἀπεδέχ.

addressed Philip the purveyor.[1] "Wherewith are we to buy bread, that these may eat?" Philip was astounded. He cast his eye over the multitude and, guessing their number, estimated the cost of providing them with a meal. Perhaps he calculated thus: A *denarius*, approximately a shilling, was a fair day's wage in those days;[2] and, taking five as an average household and putting its expenditure for a day's food, three meals, at a half *denarius*, he made a swift reckoning. If a half *denarius* would provide three meals for five, two hundred *denarii* would be required to provide a single meal for six thousand. There was a crowd of five thousand men besides women and children, all hungry with travel and fasting. "Two hundred shillings' worth of bread," said the master of the commissariat in despair, "is not sufficient that each may take a little."[3]

Five loaves and two fishes. There meantime the matter rested. While Jesus was busy teaching and healing, the disciples investigated their resources; and, as it drew toward evening, they urged Him to dismiss the multitude that they might procure themselves food in the neighbouring villages. "Give *ye* them to eat," He answered. They protested that it was impossible, and Philip's friend Andrew [4] explained that all the available provision was five poor barley-loaves [5] and two little fishes which a fisher-lad, attracted by the crowd, was offering for sale.[6] "But these," he added, "what are they among so many?" Jesus vouchsafed no explanation, but bade the disciples prepare for a repast; and such was their confidence in Him that they obeyed His behest without demur. They disposed the people in hundreds and fifties over the grassy sward, an arrangement which prevented confusion and ensured that none should be overlooked, besides making it easy to calculate the number of the company. When all were in

[1] *Cf.* p. 149.

[2] For a vinedresser (Mt. xx. 1-16); for a Roman soldier (Tac. *Ann.* i. 17). *Cf.* Wetstein on Mt. xx. 2.

[3] Carr in *Expositor*, Jan. 1890. Since, however, 200 *denarii* was a standing sum among the Jews, being the fine frequently imposed for serious offences (*cf.* Lightfoot on Mk. vi. 37), it may be that Philip merely quoted it off-hand as an impossible sum.

[4] *Cf.* p. 149.

[5] A realistic touch preserved by John. Barley was food for cattle and slaves. *Cf.* Wetstein on John vi. 9.

[6] *Cf.* Euth. Zig. on Mt. xiv. 17

place, Jesus blessed the food and doled it out to the disciples for distribution among the people ; and, behold, the scanty store became an exhaustless fountain.[1]   He gave and gave, and still the provision grew in the Creator's hands.   " Two hundred shillings' worth of loaves is not sufficient," Philip had declared, " that each may take a little " ; but the five barley-loaves and the two little fishes which Jesus blessed, afforded an abundant meal.   " They did all eat and were filled."   Nay, there was not merely enough but enough and to spare.   When a Jew went on a journey, he carried a basket with provision lest he should incur defilement by eating strangers' meat. His basket was the Jew's badge, and it was the butt of heathen ridicule.[2]   The wandering Apostles had their baskets, and, at the bidding of their Master, who would have nothing wasted and perhaps designed that they should retain evidences of the miracle,[3] they collected the fragments of the feast and found enough to fill their twelve baskets.

There is a peculiarity about this great miracle which Signifi-
furnishes a clue to its real significance.   It was not the cance of
Lord's wont to exert His miraculous power unless it was miracle.
needed and there was no other way ; and it seems as though
in this instance He departed from His custom.   There was
apparently no necessity for the miracle.   The multitude could
easily have procured food in the neighbourhood.   Such was Mk. vi. 36
the suggestion of the disciples, but Jesus disregarded it : He =Mt. xiv.
was bent on working the miracle.   And the truth is that He 15=Lk. ix
had a purpose far beyond the relief of the multitude's hunger. 12.
His soul had been stirred within Him by recent events,
especially the Baptist's death, and His emotion was more
than natural grief at the tragic end of one whom He had
loved and who had held a unique and intimate relation
toward Him.   In that dark tragedy He recognised a premonition of His own impending doom.   They had wrought
on John all their will, and even so would the Son of Man Mt. xvii.
suffer at their hands.   He had indeed foreseen it all along and 12.
shuddered at the dread prospect ; but now it had assumed, as
it were, a palpable shape, and the horror of it swept over Him

---

[1] Chrysost. *In Matth.* 1: οἱ πέντε ἐν ταῖς χερσὶ τῶν μαθητῶν ἐπήγαξον. Jer. :
" Frangente Domino seminarium fit ciborum."

[2] Juv. iii. 14 ; vi. 542.   [3] Chrysost. *In Matth.* 1.

like a great flood. Already He was tasting the bitter cup which He must presently drink to the dregs. The Psalmist's

Ps. lv. 5-8. plaint was the language of His stricken soul : " Fearfulness and trembling are come upon Me, and horror hath overwhelmed Me. And I said : O that I had wings like a dove ! Then would I fly away, and be at rest. Lo, then would I wander far off, I would lodge in the wilderness. I would haste Me to a shelter from the windy storm and tempest."

A prophecy of the Last Supper. It was no slight aggravation of His anguish that, while the Cross was in His view, His disciples were dreaming of a throne and conspiring with the multitude to acclaim Him King. He had retreated to Bethsaida that He might be alone with the Twelve and perchance convey to their dull minds some higher and truer conception ; and it vexed Him when the inevitable multitude appeared on the scene. Yet He would not relinquish His purpose, and, as soon as He

John vi. 5. espied them, He formed a design and resolved upon the miracle ere the occasion for it had arisen. The Passover, as St John significantly observes, was near, that sacred feast which all down the ages had pointed Israel backward to the redemption from Egypt and forward to a still grande·· redemption. A year later the great consummation was accomplished, and the Redeemer instituted the new Passover-feast which has ever since commemorated His infinite sacrifice. It was no unpremeditated impulse that moved Him when, on His betrayal-night, He took the bread and blessed it and brake it and gave it to His disciples, saying : " Take, eat ; this do in remembrance of Me." Long before He assembled His followers in the Upper Room, He had planned what He

Lk. xxii. 15. would do, and " with desire had desired to eat that Passover with them ere He suffered." For a whole year at least He had purposed it ; and, when He fed the multitude at Bethsaida, the sacrament was before His mind. The miracle was a prophecy thereof; and, though its significance was hidden at the moment, it was revealed ever more clearly as the issue unfolded.

Sacramental language of the Evangelists. Mt. xiv. 19-20= Can it be accidental that in narrating the miracle each of the Evangelists employs sacramental language ? Recounting the miracle St Matthew says : " He took the five loaves and the two fishes, and blessed and brake and gave the loaves to the disciples and the disciples to the multitudes ; and they did all eat." Describing the scene in the Upper Room, he says : " Jesus took a loaf, and blessed and brake and gave to the disciples, and said : ' Take, eat.' " " Jesus," says St John in his narrative of the miracle, " took the loaves, and blessed them, and gave to them that sat at meat." " The Lord Jesus," says St Paul, delivering the tradition of the Supper, " took a loaf and, having blessed it, brake." Next day, when they had all returned to Capernaum, Jesus discoursed in the Synagogue on the Bread of Life, disclosing the thoughts which had been in His heart when He wrought the miracle. " I am the Bread of Life, the Living Bread that came down out of Heaven. If any eat of My [1] Bread, he shall live for ever ; and the Bread which I shall give for the world's life, is My flesh."

Mk. vi. 41. 2=Lk. ix. 16-7.

xxvi. 26= Mk. xiv. 22=Lk. xxii. 19. vi. 11.

1 Cor. xi. 23-4.

John vi. 22-65.

The miracle added fuel to the enthusiasm of the multitude. Jesus was certainly the Messiah, and they were more bent than ever on carrying out their wild project. The moment seemed auspicious. The Passover was at hand. Jerusalem would be thronged with worshippers ; and they had only to escort Him thither in triumphal procession and acclaim Him King, and He would be hailed by a myriad of voices and installed amid the nation's applause on His ancestral throne. Perceiving their intention, He peremptorily bade the Twelve re-embark and set sail for Bethsaida, the harbour of Capernaum [2] ; and then, eluding the multitude, He stole away to His retreat on the hill-side, and gave Himself to prayer.

Attempt to acclaim Him King of Israel.

The evening deepened into night and a storm arose, but Jesus, engrossed in communion with the Father, was all unconscious of the elemental strife. The dawn was breaking [3] when He rose from His knees ; and, looking down upon the Lake, He descried the boat more than half-way across,[4] battling with wind and wave. In sore jeopardy the disciples

Jesus walks on the Lake.

---

[1] John vi. 51 : τοῦ ἐμοῦ ℵ, Tisch. τούτου τοῦ T. R., R.V., W. H.

[2] *Cf.* p. 83.

[3] *The fourth watch,* between 3 and 6 a.m. The Jews divided the night into three watches, but after the time of Pompeius they adopted the Roman division. See Lightfoot and Wetstein on Mt. xiv. 25.

[4] John vi. 19. The Lake was 40 furlongs (*stadia*) broad. Jos. *De Bell. Jud.* iii. 10. § 7.

were wishing that their Master was with them, when to their amazement they beheld Him hard by. He was walking on the water. He made as though He would have passed them by, and they did not hail Him. When a Jew met a friend by night, he would not greet him lest it should be a dæmon in his friend's shape.[1] Thinking that it was a ghost that they saw, the disciples would not hail Him ; but they were unable to repress a cry of alarm, and it reached Jesus. " Courage ! " He said. " It is I. Fear not." Peter, " ever ardent, ever leaping before his fellows," [2] made reply : " Lord, if it be Thou, bid me come unto Thee upon the waters." " Come," said Jesus. No sooner had he set foot on the waves than fear got the better of the impetuous disciple, and he began to sink. " Lord, save me ! " he cried, and Jesus reached forth a helping hand and grasped him.[3] The alarm of the disciples had by this time been allayed, and they welcomed their Master on board.[4] The wind sank to rest and they sped lightly on their way, and in their wonder and gladness it seemed but a moment till they got to shore. " When Christ is absent from his people, they go on but slowly, and with great difficulty ; but when he joins himself unto them, oh ! how fast they steer their course ! how soon are they at their journey's end ! "

Significance of the miracle.   This is a very amazing story, and all down the centuries it has been a trial to faith and a jest to unbelief. It seems so palpably impossible. " The peculiar difficulty of the narrative," says Strauss, " lies in this, that the body of Jesus appears so entirely exempt from a law which governs all other human bodies without exception, namely, the law of gravitation, that he not only does not sink under the water, but does not even dip into it ; on the contrary, he walks erect on the waves as on firm land." And it seems also so grotesque. It has been the jest of unbelievers ever since the latter half of the second century, when Lucian pelted it with the pitiless artillery of

[1] Wetstein on Mt. xiv. 26.
[2] Chrysost. *In Matth.* li.
[3] Peter's adventure is recorded by Mt. alone. This at least may be said, that it is just the sort of thing that Peter would do.
[4] John vi. 21 : ἤθελον λαβεῖν, they had been afraid, now they were willing. Strauss, bent on making out a discrepancy between John and the Synoptists : "they wished to take him on board, but their actually doing so was rendered superfluous by their immediate arrival at the land." This, however, would require ἀλλὰ εὐθέως.

his keen and biting satire.[1]   What must be said about it?
The eighteenth century naturalism thought to explain it away.
Under stress of the storm, it was alleged, the boat had kept
close to the land, and, when the disciples saw Jesus, He was
not really walking on the water but merely walking along the
shore.   And ever since the time of Strauss it has been the
fashion with unbelievers to regard the miracle as a myth and
discover prototypes of it not only in the Old Testament stories
of the passage through the Red Sea and the parting of the
Jordan before Elisha when he smote its waters with Elijah's
mantle, but in the bold imagery of Hebrew poetry.   "Thy
way," the Psalmist had said, "is in the sea, and Thy path in
the great waters, and Thy footsteps are not known." [2]

2 Kings ii. 13-4.

Ps. lxxvii. 19.

It is impossible, however, to dismiss the story in this easy
fashion; and the truth is that, like the Feeding of the Multitude, the miracle had a great prophetic purpose.   The Lord's
mind was occupied with anticipations of the future—" the
sufferings that should befall Him and the glories that should
follow these"; and He desired to lead the thoughts of the
Twelve thereto and prepare them for what would soon come
to pass.   From the day when He heard of the Baptist's death,
His steadfast aim was to apprise them of the final issue—of
His Death and His Resurrection.   The miracle of the Feeding
of the Multitude had been a picture of the Last Supper, a
prophecy of His Death; and this miracle is a prophecy of
His Resurrection.   It is indeed impossible for a mortal body
to walk upon the water, but an ethereal body is subject to
other laws; and, if it was possible for the Risen Lord to pass
through the closed door and appear in the chamber where His
disciples were assembled, it was possible for Him, assuming
by the power of God the ethereal condition, to walk upon the
water.   The disciples could not at the time comprehend the
ineffable mystery.   Enough if they realised the wonder of
their Lord and were assured that, even when it seemed
victorious, the world's hostility could have no power over
Him.

A prophecy of the Re-surrection.

1 Pet. i. 11.

John xx. 19, 26.

---

[1] *Ver. Hist.* ii. § 4: the Corkfeet (Φελλόποδες) whom he saw in his wonderful
voyage ἐπὶ τοῦ πελάγους διαθέοντας.   *Cf. Philops.* § 13.   "Walking on the water"
was a proverb, denoting *an impossibility*.   *Cf.* Wetstein.

[2] *Cf.* Job ix. 8 LXX : περιπατῶν ὡς ἐπ' ἐδάφους ἐπὶ θαλάσσης.

CHAPTER XXVIII

CONTROVERSIES IN CAPERNAUM

Mt. xiv.
34-6=
Mk. vi. 53-
6; John vi.
22—vii. 1;
Mt. xv. 1-
20=Mk.
vii. 1-23
(Lk. vi. 39).

"Habet Jesus multos amatores regni sui cœlestis, sed paucos bajulatores suæ crucis. Plures invenit socios mensæ, sed paucos abstinentiæ. . . . Multi sequuntur Jesum usque ad fractionem panis, sed pauci usque ad bibendum calicem passionis. Multi miracula ejus venerantur, pauci ignominias crucis sequuntur."—*De Imitat. Chr.* II. xi. § 1.

Perplexity of the people. WHEN the disciples embarked, the multitude did not all disperse. Observing that Jesus did not put off in the boat, some of them lingered in the hope that He would reappear; and not till the morning broke did they think of returning home. During the night a fleet of boats belonging to Tiberias had come to land hard by, driven doubtless by stress of weather; and in these they took passage for Capernaum. On arriving there they found to their astonishment that Jesus had returned before them.

What they should think about Him they knew not. They had been convinced of His Messiahship, and the miracle of yester-eve had strengthened their conviction. It was a current expectation among the Jews that, as Moses, the first Redeemer, had fed the Israelites with bread from Heaven, so would the Messiah, the second Redeemer; nay more, that He would lead them forth into the wilderness of Bashan, and *Cf.* John vi. 30-1. there make the manna descend for them; and was not the wilderness of Bethsaida in Batanea, the ancient Bashan?[1] Surely Jesus was the Messiah, yet wherefore had He refused the Messianic dignity, eluding their grasp and fleeing to the mountain when they would have acclaimed Him King? They were honestly perplexed, and it so happened that an opportunity presented itself that very day for arriving at an understanding. It was one of the two week-days, whether Monday or Thursday, on which there was service in the John vi. 59. Synagogue.[2] Jesus attended and preached, and, in accord-

[1] Lightfoot on John vi. 31.

[2] It cannot have been the Sabbath, or they would not have journeyed across the Lake, the distance being greater than a Sabbath Day's journey.

ance with the custom of the Synagogue, they plied Him with questions.

To a superficial observer it might have seemed at that crisis that Jesus had achieved signal success. He was surrounded by an admiring multitude, persuaded of His Messiahship and eager to witness His recognition by the nation. In His eyes, however, it was an hour of bitter disappointment, of well-nigh utter failure. The multitude's enthusiasm was inspired by a false ideal of His mission. They regarded Him as the Messiah, but they conceived of the Messiah as an earthly king who would free them from bondage and give them abundance of bread. It was this false ideal which had all along made the multitude's applause so distasteful to Him; and now that the crisis had been reached, it was necessary that He should at all hazards disabuse their minds and repudiate the rôle which they would fain thrust upon Him. This He set Himself to accomplish. First of all, He upbraided them with their unspirituality : "Verily, verily I tell you, ye are seeking Me, not because ye saw signs, but because ye ate of the loaves and were filled." And then, interpreting His miracles of yester-eve and yester-night, He spoke in mystic language of His Death and His Resurrection. They were dreaming of a Messiah who would feed them with bread from Heaven. "The Bread of God," He says, "is He that cometh down from Heaven and giveth life to the world. I am the Bread of Life. He that cometh unto Me shall never hunger and he that believeth in Me shall never thirst. Verily, verily I tell you, unless ye eat the flesh of the Son of Man and drink His blood, ye have not life in yourselves. He that feedeth on My flesh and drinketh My blood hath Eternal Life, and I will raise Him up on the last day."

Discourse in the Synagogue.

Such language would sound less strange in Jewish than in modern ears, since, alike in the Scriptures and in the Rabbinical literature, sacred instruction is called *bread* and those who eagerly absorb it are said to *eat* it. "Thy words," says the prophet Jeremiah, "were found, and I did eat them." And it is written in the Talmud : "'Feed him with bread,' that is, Make him labour in the warfare of the Law, as it is said : 'Come, eat of my bread.'" Yet stronger and closely

A test of attachment to Jesus.

xv. 16.

Prov. ix. 5.

similar to the language of our Lord is the Talmudic figure of
"eating the Messiah," which meant receiving Him joyfully
and, as it were, devouring His instruction.[1]   Nevertheless it
was impossible that any of His hearers, even the Twelve at
that stage, should understand the Lord's mystic discourse.
Nor indeed did He mean that they should understand it.
He designed it as a test of their faith.   Would their loyalty
stand the shock of disillusionment?

Wide- | He deliberately made the experiment.   And what was the
spread | result?   It is in no wise surprising that the rulers and their
alienation. | party among the people were horrified and indignant.   "Is
not this man," they cried, "Jesus the son of Joseph, whose
father and mother we know?   How is this man now saying:
'I have come down from Heaven'?"   "How can this man
give us his flesh to eat?"   It was natural that *they* should
assume this attitude, and Jesus would be in no wise disappointed.   But there were others of whom He expected
better—the great mass of people who had espoused His
cause and went by the name of His disciples.   How would
they stand the test?   He had hope of them, but to a large
extent, alas, they belied His confidence.   "This is a hard
word," they said; "who can hear it?" and many of them
"drew back and would no longer walk with Him."   He was
left alone with the Twelve; and He turned to them and,
wistfully scanning their troubled faces, addressed to them the

The | pathetic question: "Are ye also wishing to be gone?"   It
Twelve | appears that they were wavering in their allegiance; and
remain | perchance they might have forsaken Him, had they seen any
faithful. | door of escape.   But they had committed themselves too
deeply.   They had left all and followed Jesus, dreaming of a
royal recompense when He should win His kingdom and His
throne; and, had they abandoned Him, they would have been
a public jest and scorn.   For very shame they durst not.
And they had a nobler reason for standing faithful.   For all
their misconception they loved their Master and had made
great discoveries of His grace.   "Are ye also," He asked,
"wishing to be gone?"   Peter, always the spokesman of the
Twelve and the lover of Jesus, made reply; and his answer
was strangely blended, beginning with a sob of despair and

[1] Lightfoot and Wetstein on John vi. 51.

swelling out into passionate and triumphant faith. "Lord," he cried, "unto whom shall we go away? Thou hast words of Eternal Life. And we have believed and recognised that Thou art the Holy One of God."[1]

It was a poor, faltering confession, and it showed Jesus how feeble was the faith even of His Apostles, and how great their need of instruction in the things of the Kingdom of Heaven and of preparation for the approaching ordeal. Peter was the bravest and most devoted of them all; and, if this were the utmost reach of his faith, what could be expected of the rest? He knew what the issue would be. "Did not I choose you the Twelve?" He said; "and of you one is a devil." Yes, there was one of them who even then was meditating a worse crime than defection. "He was speaking," the Evangelist explains, "of Judas the son of Simon Iskarioth. For this man was about to betray Him, being one of the Twelve." *A traitor in their midst.*

The people had taken offence at Jesus, but they soon found how greatly they needed Him. He continued His ministry of mercy in their midst. What though their dream of a throne in Jerusalem had been dispelled? Their burden of suffering and misery remained, and they found the Lord still merciful and mighty. They brought their sick as heretofore to His blessed feet, that, like the woman with the bloody issue, they might merely touch the tassel of His cloak.[2] The Passover came, but Jesus, aware of the murderous designs of the rulers, remained in Galilee. He was ready to die in due season, but He still had work to do. His hour had not yet come. The rulers were disappointed when He did not appear, and, bent on His overthrow, they sent a deputation of Pharisees and Scribes to co-operate with the authorities at Capernaum. Encompassed as He was by the goodwill of the multitude, those malignants durst not lay hands upon Him, but they kept a jealous watch over Him, hoping to discover some pretext for calling Him to account. *Jesus continues His ministry. Cf. Mt. ix. 20=Lk. viii. 44. John vii. 1. Emissaries of the Sanhedrin.*

Nor was it long ere they discovered one which promised *Offence of eating with unwashed hands.*

---

[1] T. R. : ὁ Χριστὸς ὁ υἱὸς τοῦ Θεοῦ τοῦ ζῶντος is an assimilation to Mt. xvi. 16. It is a singularly unfortunate theory (Keim and others) that this is the Johannine version of Peter's Confession at Cæsarea Philippi.

[2] Chrysost. *In Matth.* li : ἡ γὰρ αἱμορροοῦσα ἅπαντας ἐδίδαξε φιλοσοφεῖν.

success.   No requirement of the Rabbinical law was more
stringent than that of ceremonial ablution, especially the wash-
Cf. Lk. xi. ing of the hands before and after meat.   To eat with un-
27-8. washed hands was accounted a foul pollution,[1] and the penalty
was excommunication.[2]   Moreover, the terrors of superstition
were brought in to reinforce the requirement.   There was
a dæmon named Shibta ; and, should a man touch his food
with unwashed hands, he was exposed to its nocturnal assaults.
It was a truly ridiculous requirement, and it shows how low
Jewish religion had fallen that so puerile a ceremony should
have been deemed essential.   Yet even so abject a superstition may be raised almost to sublimity by the enthusiasm
of its votaries ; and it is told that R. Akiba was once imprisoned by the Romans, and was provided daily with a
supply of water, sufficient for the purposes of ablution and
drinking.   One day, by order of his gaoler, a less supply was
provided.   "Give me water for my hands," said the Rabbi.
"My master," said the disciple who waited upon him, "there
is scarce enough water to drink."   "What shall I do?" Akiba
answered.   "It is better for me to die than to transgress the
ordinances of my ancestors."[3]

The Lord's   Prosecuting a course of espionage, the Lord's enemies
defence. observed that His disciples neglected this momentous rite.
It was a grievous offence, not indeed against the Law of
Moses, but, which was far more heinous in their eyes, against
the Tradition of the Elders.[4]   They approached Jesus and
demanded an explanation, and He answered with a bold and
contemptuous defiance.   He flung in their faces a counter
accusation of monstrous and incredible impiety.   "Why,"
they asked, "do thy disciples transgress the Tradition of the
Elders?"   "Why," He retorted, "do ye on your part transgress
the commandment of God for the sake of your Tradition?"
It was a heavy charge, and Jesus made it good by citing an
amazing instance of Jewish casuistry.   Whatever was vowed to
God was sacred to the uses of religion.   It was *corban*, an offering, and must pass into the hands of the priests.   With perverse

---

[1] *Sot.* 4. 2 : "Quicunque panem edit illotis manibus est instar concumbentis
cum scorto."
[2] Lightfoot on Mt. xv. 2.
[3] Wetstein on Mt. xv. 2 ; Ottho, *Hist. Doct. Misn.* p. 134.
[4] *Cf.* Introd. § 1.

ingenuity this pious ordinance was pressed into the service of irreligious and often wicked ends. Suppose a debtor refused payment: the creditor would say, "What you owe me is *corban*." He dedicated some portion of it, much or little, to the Temple-treasury, and should the debtor still persist in withholding it, he would incur the guilt of robbing God.[1] This was innocent enough, but it was a monstrous iniquity when a son played the trick upon his needy parents, answering their appeal by the very formula which our Lord quotes: "Whatever of mine thou mightest be profited by is *corban*."[2] It was frequently done, and the rulers encouraged it for the sake of the profit which it brought them. The peculiar odiousness of it lay less in the inhumanity itself than in the circumstance that it was perpetrated in the name of God. "Ye playactors!" exclaims Jesus, "admirably did Isaiah prophesy of you, saying: 'This people with the lips honoureth Me; but their heart is far away from Me. But in vain they worship Me, teaching as doctrines men's commandments.'" xxix. 13.

It was a crushing reply, and Jesus turned from His discomfited assailants and addressed the bystanders who had witnessed the rencontre. "Hearken," He said, "and take it in: It is not what goeth into his mouth that defileth the man; but what cometh out of his mouth, this it is that defileth the man." Meanwhile the Pharisees took themselves off in high dudgeon, and the Twelve, dreading their vengeance, remonstrated with Jesus on His temerity. He set their fears at naught. "Every plant," He said, prophesying the doom of the Pharisaic system, "which My Heavenly Father did not plant, shall be rooted out. Let them go!" He cried, surveying His retreating assailants. "They are blind guides; and, 'if a blind man guide a blind, both shall fall into a ditch.'" It was a common proverb,[3] and it served at once as a just characterisation of those proud ecclesiastics and a warning to the bystanders lest they should be misled. What really defiles.

It was the custom of the Twelve to question Jesus by and by about the parables which He had spoken to the multitude in their hearing; and when they got home after the encounter with the Pharisees, they appealed to Him. "Explain to us Dulness of the Twelve. Mk. iv. 33- 4; Mt. xiii. 36.

So Origen (*In Matth.* xi. § 9), his authority being τῶν Ἑβραίων τις.
See Lightfoot on Mt. xv. 5.   [3] See Wetstein.

the parable," said Peter, referring to His sentence about what really defiled a man. It was in truth no parable at all, but, wedded to their Jewish prejudices, they supposed that there must be some hidden meaning in it. The distinction between clean meat and unclean still seemed to them vitally important, and it never occurred to them that Jesus would contemn it. And indeed it is no marvel that they failed to receive His doctrine that nothing defiles a man save impure thoughts.

Acts. x. 9-15. Years after Peter still clung to his Jewish prejudice. Jesus was grieved by their slowness of heart. "Even yet," He exclaimed, "are ye also without understanding?"

Their instruction henceforth the Master's exclusive concern.   The incident confirmed Him in a momentous resolution which He had formed. The time was short, and the Twelve were ill prepared for the task which would devolve upon them when He was gone. They were still very ignorant and unspiritual, and He had resolved to devote Himself thenceforward to the business of their instruction in the things of the Kingdom of Heaven. His ministry at Capernaum was ended. He would quit that town which had so long been blessed with His presence, and seek some retreat where He might be alone with His Apostles and, in close and unbroken converse, reveal to them what they had so much need to know.

CHAPTER XXIX

RETREAT INTO PHŒNICIA

Mt. xv. 21-
9=Mk. viL
24-31.

"O quam mire, Jesu, ludis his quibus diligeris!
Sed cum ludis non illudis, nec fallis nec falleris,
Sed excludis quos includis, notus non agnosceris."

Med. Hymn.

JESUS desired to be alone with the Twelve. Whither should Retreat to the region of Tyre and Sidon.
He betake Himself? He might have crossed to the eastern
side of the Lake, or He might have retired to the interior of
Galilee; but experience had proved that in neither direction
would He find the seclusion which He desired. He must
seek a new retreat. To the north-west of Galilee lay the land
of Phœnicia, once the chief maritime country of the world, but
now a portion of the Roman province of Syria. Its people
were the survivors of the Canaanites, the sinful and idolatrous
race which the Israelites had dispossessed on their entrance
into the Land of Promise. It was an unclean land, abhorred
in Jewish eyes, but for that very reason it seemed to promise
retirement. Thither Jesus turned, and found a lodging in the
district adjacent the once famous sea-ports of Tyre and Sidon,
thinking to sojourn there unrecognised and undisturbed.

Herein, however, He was disappointed. His fame had A suppliant woman.
travelled thither. Visitors from Tyre and Sidon had witnessed
His works in Galilee, and on their return they would tell what Mk. iii. 7-8.
they had seen and heard. His arrival was soon noised through
the country, and presently, as He walked abroad with the
Twelve, He was approached by a suppliant—a widow[1] who
had a lunatic daughter. "Have pity on me, Lord, Thou Son Cf. Mt. ix. 27; Mt. xx. 30, 31 =Mk. x. 47, 48=Lk. xviii. 38, 39; Mt. xxi. 9.
of David!" she cried, giving Him the title wherewith the Jewish
populace loved to hail Him. It was a pathetic appeal, and
might have softened a harder heart than the gracious Son of
Man's. "It was a piteous spectacle," says St Chrysostom,

[1] Mk. vii. 26 in Sinaitic Palimpsest: "That woman was a widow from the
borders of Tyre of Phœnicia." According to Clem. Rom. (*Hom.* iii. § 73; ii. § 19;
xiii. § 7) her name was Justa and her daughter's Bernice, and she was a Jewish
proselyte.

"to see a woman crying with so much feeling, and that woman a mother, and praying for a daughter, and that daughter so ill bested." But Jesus heeded not. He walked on and let her cry. The disciples were moved, and they assumed the office of intercession. They called their Master's attention to the suppliant and besought Him to grant her petition, urging, lest they should seem to accuse Him of heartlessness, the embarrassment of the situation. "Send her away," they said, "for she is crying after us."[1] Silent to her, He answered them: "I was not sent but unto the lost sheep of Israel's house."

Her persistence. It seemed as though the answer closed every door of hope The disciples said nothing further, but the woman would not be repulsed. She followed on, and, when they reached their lodging, she entered[2] with them. They took their places at table and she knelt at His feet and prayed: "Lord, help me!" Then at length He took notice of her and answered her in language suggested by the surroundings: "It is not seemly to take the children's bread and throw it to the whelps." She caught up the word and retorted: "Yea, Lord; for even the whelps eat of the crumbs that fall from the table of their masters." Her insistence prevailed. "O woman!" He cried, "great is thy faith. Be it done unto thee as thou wilt." She went home, and found her daughter healed.

Difficulties of the story: There is no incident in our Lord's earthly ministry more puzzling than this. His behaviour here appears strangely and painfully out of character. Were it related of a Rabbi, it would excite no surprise, and might be quoted as an example of Jewish exclusiveness, strikingly contrasting with the large comprehensiveness of our Lord's attitude toward the heathen. But it is disconcerting to hear such language from the lips of Jesus and see Him behaving to this poor heathen after the very manner of a Pharisee. Some explanation there must be of behaviour so alien to His manner and so contrary to the spirit of His Gospel, which recognises no distinction between Jew and Gentile, embracing every child of Adam with impartial love.

1. The Lord's refusal. The main difficulty lies not in His reluctance to grant the

---

[1] The Lord's reply shows that they desired, not that she should be peremptorily dismissed, but that she should be granted her request.

[2] Mk. vii. 25: εἰσελθοῦσα אLD, Tisch.

suppliant's petition. This is easily enough accounted for, though the common explanation is but partially satisfactory. Jesus, it is argued, was not here obeying the promptings of His heart but accommodating Himself to the requirements of His mission. He had a definite method in the prosecution thereof, and He faithfully adhered to it, developing it in due course and taking each step in order. It was the method which He explained in His parable of the Leaven. His design was to place the Gospel in Israel as in the midst of humanity and let it permeate the whole mass. The insufficiency of this explanation lies here, that, while throughout His earthly ministry Jesus adhered to the principle that He had been sent only to the lost sheep of Israel's house and never sought the aliens, still, whenever aliens crossed His path, like the Samaritan woman and the people of Sychar, or came in quest of Him, like the Centurion of Capernaum, He had no scruple in lavishing His grace upon them as freely as if they had been Jews. And, had He acted in this instance after His wont, He would have received the suppliant graciously and forthwith granted her the desire of her heart. *Mt. xiii. 33 =Lk. xiii. 20-1.*

The truth is that His reluctance was not due at all to the fact that the woman was a Gentile but wholly to the circumstance that He had gone to those parts in search of seclusion. He desired to be alone with the Twelve and impart to them the instruction which they so much needed; and it was with a feeling of dismay that He observed the approach of a suppliant. He foresaw the consequence of granting her petition. The fame of the miracle would go abroad, and He would presently be surrounded by a crowd—sufferers craving relief and others who came only to gaze and admire. Therefore He would fain work no miracle, and He would have been no whit less reluctant had the suppliant been an Israelite. *Due to His desire for privacy.*

The main difficulty lies not here, but in the harshness wherewith He sought to repel the woman. Various considerations have been put forward which doubtless go a certain way toward alleviating it. One is that His harshness was only assumed, and He had two ends in view when He put on that mask of churlishness. He desired, on the one hand, to try the woman's faith and make its triumph more *2. His seeming harshness.*

signal ; [1] and, on the other hand, to show the disciples what
even a heathen was capable of, and thus conquer their Jewish
prejudice and prepare them for His world-wide purpose of
salvation.[2]   Though it surrounds the incident with a theatrical
air, yet surely this interpretation is preferable to that which
regards our Lord as here awaking for the first time to
consciousness of the universality of His mission.   It is at
once offensive to the religious instinct and inconsistent with
fact to suppose that He had until that crisis shared the
narrow prejudices of His time and race, and then had it borne
in upon Him, to His surprise and delight, that the heathen
also were worthy of His grace.[3]

Again, it has been pointed out that, while Jesus speaks
here after the manner of Jewish insolence, styling the heathen
"dogs," [4] He nevertheless employs a diminutive form of the
word—a diminutive of endearment, it is alleged, denoting,
not the unclean pariah dogs which prowled about the streets
after nightfall and devoured the garbage of the gutters, but
the little house-dogs which played about the table at meal-
times and got occasional scraps from their masters.[5]   Perhaps
one was in the room where Jesus and the Twelve were
supping.   It may be so, yet it is equally possible that the
word is a diminutive of contempt, meaning *wretched curs*.[6]

His
language
proverbial. Whatever force these considerations may possess, they
merely soften the harshness and do not obliterate it.   Therefore one gladly welcomes another which seems to have
hitherto escaped notice, and which divests our Lord's words
of every semblance of harshness and transforms the seeming
insult into a good-humoured pleasantry.   He had quitted
Jewish soil and come where the language of Jewish bigotry
was unknown and could not have been understood.   It was
not the brutal epithet of Pharisaic insolence that He employed,
but a familiar proverb.   The Greeks had a saying: "You
starve yourself to feed dogs." [7]   "It was said," explains
Erasmus, "of one who, while too poor to procure the neces-
saries of life, endeavoured to maintain an establishment of

---

[1] Chrysost. *In Matth.* liii ; Aug. *Serm.* lxxvii. § 1.
[2] Neander.   [3] Keim.   [4] *Cf.* Lightfoot and Wetstein.
[5] Wetstein, Laidlaw.   [6] It is contemptuous in Plat. *Euthyd.* 298 D.
[7] Erasm. *Adag.* under *Absurda* : αὐτὸν οὐ τρέφων κύνας τρέφεις.

horses or servants. It will be appropriately employed against
those who, by reason of the narrowness of their means, have
scarce enough to maintain life, yet ambitiously endeavour to
emulate the powerful and wealthy in fineness of dress and
general ostentation. In short, it will be suitable to all who
regard the things which belong to pleasure or magnificence,
neglecting the things which are more necessary." And they
had another proverb : " Never be kind to a neighbour's dog,"
or otherwise : " One who feeds a strange dog gets nothing but
the rope to keep." [1] " The proverb," says Erasmus, " warns
you against uselessly wasting kindness in a quarter whence
no profit will accrue to you in return. A neighbour's dog,
after being well fed, goes back to his former master." And
it was some such familiar adage that Jesus quoted when He
said : " It is not seemly to take the children's bread and
throw it to the whelps." It was a playful reply. It was as
though He had said : " You are a stranger to Me, and why
should I give away to a stranger the blessings which belong
to those of My own household ? "

And now observe the woman's retort. It also is a proverb, as appears from a passage in Philostratus' *Life of Apollonius of Tyana.*[2] Apollonius was attended wherever he went by an admiring disciple, Damis of Nineveh, who served as his Boswell, recording his movements, his doings, and his discourses, and taking note even of little things and *obiter dicta.*[3] Once some one sneered at him for this. " When you collect such trifles, you are acting just like the dogs which eat the scraps that fall from the feast." " If there be feasts of gods," answered Damis, " and gods eat, certainly they have also attendants who see to it that even the scraps of ambrosia are not lost." Here is the very figure, almost the very language, of the woman's retort : " Yea, Lord ; for even the whelps eat of the crumbs that fall from the table of their masters." The resemblance is too close to be accidental, and it is most reasonable to recognise the words as a familiar proverb.[4] Have they not indeed a proverbial

Her retort also proverbial.

[1] Erasm. *Adag.* under *Ingratitudo* : μήποτ' εὖ ἔρδειν γείτονος κύνα. ὅς κύνα τρέφει ξένον, τούτῳ μόνον λῖνος μένει.
[2] I. 19. [3] εἴ τι καὶ παρεφθέγξατο.
[4] The Arabs have a proverb : " It is better to feed a dog than to feed a man," meaning that the dog is more grateful.

ring? The woman caps proverb with proverb, pleasantry with pleasantry.[1]

The Lord's discernment of character. It may seem, however, that this interpretation merely substitutes a new difficulty for the old one. It relieves us indeed from the necessity of imputing to the gentle Jesus the insulting language of Jewish bigotry, but in the unhappy circumstances was not banter well-nigh as cruel as insult? He met the prayer of the grief-stricken mother with playful raillery; and what was this but mockery of her sorrow? What was such "patching of grief with proverbs" but to "charm ache with air, and agony with words"? And how should she have replied to such untimely jesting? Surely after the fashion of the courtier when Jesus met his request that He should come to

John iv. 48-9. Capernaum and heal his dying son, with the rebuke: "Except ye see signs and wonders, ye will in nowise believe." "Sir," he cried, vexed and impatient, "come down ere my child die!" The woman, however, answers raillery with raillery. Was not her behaviour as unnatural as His was cruel?

If, however, the circumstances be considered, the difficulty will disappear. There was indeed raillery in our Lord's reply, but there was no flippancy. There would be a twinkle in His eyes as He spoke, but neither in look nor in tone the faintest suggestion of mockery; and the poor mother would read the kindness of His heart in His gentle face. Nor, though the situation was distressing, was it at all desperate. The courtier's son was dying; but this poor girl was a lunatic, and it was no question of life or death. And there was a world of difference in temperament between the courtier of Capernaum and the Syrophœnician woman. He was an unsmiling Jew, a stranger to "the saving grace of humour"; she was a Greek, nimble of fancy and keen of wit, delighting in quips and cranks, and responding, even in the midst of sorrow, to a playful assault. Our Lord's treatment of her is an instance of His wondrous insight into human character. He perceived at a glance what was in everyone with whom He had to do, and knew exactly how to handle him.

Ministry among the heathen. The incident had the untoward issue which Jesus had foreseen and dreaded. It spread His fame abroad and made

---

[1] "Wisdom's scholars," says Rutherford, "are not fools: Grace is a witty and understanding spirit, ripe and sharp."

seclusion impossible; and thus He was compelled to seek some other retreat where He might hold uninterrupted converse with the Twelve. Eager as He was to address Himself to the urgent task of their instruction, He tarried awhile in Phœnicia. In the providence of God a door had been opened for the Gospel in that heathen land, and Jesus obeyed the call. Instead of retracing His steps southward, He visited Tyre, then travelled northward along the shore of the Mediterranean to Sidon, and, thence fetching a compass, He skirted the southern slopes of Lebanon and Hermon and travelled down the eastern bank of upper Jordan until He reached the Lake of Galilee. It was a memorable episode in the ministry of our Lord. In no other instance did He pass the borders ot Israel, and one would fain know what befell in the course of this His solitary mission to the Gentiles. What did the Saviour of the World, what said He, how fared He, in sea-girt Tyre, that far-famed city, "the mart of nations," "the merchant of the peoples unto many isles," "whose antiquity was of ancient days," and in her mother, Sidon? Unhappily the story is unwritten. Was it distasteful to the Jewish Evangelists that the Lord showed such grace to the Gentiles?[1] Or were they so distraught by the unfamiliar scenes that they retained no distinct remembrance of aught that they saw or heard? Whatever be the explanation, they have told nothing. The sole record of that wondrous mission is St Mark's brief note of the Lord's itinerary: "And again He went forth from the region of Tyre and went through Sidon unto the Sea of Galilee through the midst of the region of Decapolis."[2] It nevertheless appears that His labours were crowned with abundant success. His kindness to the Syrophœnician woman had opened the hearts of her countrymen; and in after days Jesus quoted the reception which Tyre and Sidon had accorded to His Word, as a melancholy and damning contrast to the unbelief of the cities of Galilee.

Is. xxiii. 3; Ezek. xxvii. 3; Is. xxiii. 7, 12.

Mk. vii. 31

Mt. xi. 21 = Lk. x. 13-4.

---

[1] Lk. fails us here. There is a lacuna in his narrative between the Feeding of the 5000 and the Great Confession at Cæsarea Philippi.

[2] Assimilated in T. R. to Mt. xv. 29, which obliterates the Phœnician ministry.

CHAPTER XXX

WANDERINGS

"When he showed himself to Israel, they drove him sometimes into the wilderness, sometimes into the desart, sometimes into the sea, and sometimes into the mountains, and still in every of these places he was either haunted or hunted by new enemies."—JOHN BUNYAN.

Quest for a retreat.
AMID His missionary activities in Phœnicia Jesus never lost sight of His main purpose; and from the moment when He quitted Sidon and turned His face southward, His hope was to find some sequestered nook where, free from intrusion, He might resume His converse with the Twelve. His design, however, was frustrated. A crowd escorted Him on His way, increasing as He went until eventually it numbered upwards of four thousand.

Miracles on the eastern side of the Lake.
It was an urgent necessity that He should rid Himself of the embarrassment; and, when He reached the Lake of Galilee, He made an effort to escape. Somewhere on the eastern side He ascended to the uplands and there sat Him down, thinking that the multitude would respect His desire for privacy and withdraw. But herein He was disappointed. The people of the district welcomed His arrival and brought their sufferers to Him for healing—lame, deaf, maimed, and many other sorts. He had gone up the mountain, but, nothing daunted, they climbed after Him bearing their piteous burdens, and dropped them at His feet.[1] It was not in the Lord's heart to withhold His succour, and He healed them all. One case there was which attracted special notice—that of a deaf stammerer. Since he did not come to Jesus but was carried to Him,[1] it would seem that he was stricken also in mind. To give him hearing and speech without repairing his shattered intellect would have been a small boon, and Jesus made the lesser blessing the means to the greater. He took

---

[1] Mk. vii. 32. *Cf.* p. 493, n. 4.

the man aside, thrust His fingers into the choked ears as though boring them, and moistened the stammering tongue with saliva, which in those days was believed to possess medicinal efficacy.[1] It was a device to stir the torpid mind to expectancy, and it was furthered by an involuntary but effective reinforcement. The piteous spectacle smote the heart of Jesus, and " He looked up to Heaven and groaned." The operation of those kind hands arrested the poor creature's attention, and the look of that pitiful face won his confidence. He yielded himself to the gracious stranger and let Him do with him what He would. " Be opened," said Jesus ; and the miracle was wrought. The deaf ears were unstopped and the stammering tongue unloosed, and he talked aright.

Cf. Mk. viii. 23 ; John ix. 6.

The miracles on the mountain increased at once the enthusiasm of the multitude and the embarrassment of Jesus, and He resolved what He would do in order to escape. He would fain be rid of them ; yet a multitude was always a pathetic spectacle in His eyes, and, as He surveyed that vast assemblage, a great compassion filled His heart. Some of them had followed Him a long distance, all the way from Phœnicia ; and they were now weary ; their provisions were spent, and, since they were in a lonely region, they could procure none. If He left them so, they must perish of hunger. " I have compassion on the multitude," He said to the disciples, " because they have now been with Me three days ; and I will not let them go away fasting, lest they faint on the road." Remembering how He had already fed a still greater multitude, the disciples referred the matter to Him. " Whence have *we* in a wilderness so many loaves as to satisfy so great a crowd ? " It is as though they had said : " It is impossible for us ; we leave it to Thee." Jesus bade them produce what provision they had. It amounted only to seven loaves and a few small fishes, the customary fare of the Galilean peasantry. He took the scanty store and blessed it and served it out to the company, which numbered above four thousand. And it sufficed ; nay, the fragments which remained, filled seven maunds.[2]

Second miraculous feeding.

---

[1] *Cf.* p. 344.
[2] It is widely alleged that the two miracles of feeding are only varying versions of the same incident (Schleier, Strauss, Ewald, Keim, Wright) ; but it is remarkable

Escape by boat to the vicinity of Magadan and Dalmanutha. The multitude would fain have held by Jesus still, but He had devised a way of escape. He had procured a boat,[1] and as soon as the miracle had been wrought, He went down to the Lake and, putting off, left the wistful multitude on the shore. Whither He betook Himself is uncertain, but it would seem that He steered southward and, landing at the lower end of the Lake, took His way inland until He reached a spot which promised seclusion. "He went," says St Matthew, "into the region of Magadan";[2] "He went," says St Mark, "into the parts of Dalmanutha." Both these names are unknown save for their mention here, but there is a place called Ed Delhemîyeh situated on the Jordan a mile north of the point where it is joined by the tributary Yarmûk, the ancient Hieromax; and it may be that this is Dalmanutha, Magadan being an adjacent village.[3] Their very obscurity justified the Lord's expectation that in their neighbourhood He would find an undisturbed retreat.

Arrival of Pharisees and Sadducees. Again, however, He was doomed to disappointment. His presence with that huge following on the eastern shore could not be hid, and His enemies hastened to dog His steps. Scarce had He reached His retreat when a band of Pharisees and Sadducees, probably from Capernaum, appeared on the scene. They had tracked Him thither in order to ply Him with captious questions and perchance betray Him into some fatal declaration. They opened the attack with a renewal of their now hackneyed demand for a sign. In truth they had witnessed signs enough, nor did they dispute the reality thereof, but they pretended that they needed one more convincing. They asked *a sign from Heaven*, "that He should stop the sun," suggests St Chrysostom, "or rein in the moon or hurl down thunder, or the like." The demand stirred more sorrow than indignation in the breast of Jesus. It was a

Demand for "a sign from Heaven."

---

that the narratives have different words for basket (*cf.* Mt. xvi. 9-10 = Mk. viii. 19-20) —κόφινος and σφυρίς (σπυρίς). κόφ. was the Jew's bread-basket and σφ. a Gentile term (*cf.* Epict. iv. 10). The verbal difference corresponds to a difference of nationality, the first multitude being Jewish, the second at least mainly Gentile.

[1] *Cf.* Introd. § 11.

[2] Μαγαδάν ‫א‬BD, Tisch., W. H., R.V.; *Magedan* Vulg. Μαγδαλά .. R. is merely a familiar name substituted for an unfamiliar.

[3] Henderson, *Palestine*, § 114; arts. *Dalmanutha* and *Magadan* in Hastings' *D. B.* Rendal Harris and Nestle suggest that Dalmanutha is simply the Aramaic of εἰς τὰ μέρη mistaken for a proper name. *Cf.* Dalman, *Words of Jesus*, pp. 66-7.

veritable tragedy that was being enacted in His presence. The Pharisees and the Sadducees were natural and hereditary rivals, wide as the poles asunder in creed and policy ; yet, blinded by a common enmity, they had laid aside their mutual antagonism and conspired in this monstrous and unholy alliance.[1] It was surely the very extremity of obduracy, the furthest reach of that sin against the Holy Spirit which hath never forgiveness. " He groaned in His spirit."

It was the third time that our Lord's adversaries had asked for a sign, and it is noteworthy how He received each successive demand. The first was made in Jerusalem during the Passover at the outset of His ministry ; and He acceded to it, albeit the sign which He granted was unintelligible to the rulers and even, at the time, to His disciples. It was the sign of the Resurrection. The second demand He met with indignant contempt, yet to it also He acceded after a fashion, reminding His adversaries how the Ninevites had repented at the preaching of Jonah and bidding them beware lest, with a greater sign than the preaching of Jonah before them, they should remain impenitent. Now, when the demand is a third time made, He meets it with an absolute and contemptuous refusal : " Why doth this generation seek a sign? Verily I tell you, there shall no sign be given to this generation." [2]

The Lord's refusal.

John ii. 18-9.

Mt. xii. 38-42 = Lk. xi. 16, 29-32.

It was impossible for Jesus to hold converse with the Twelve in the presence of those malignant adversaries. He must quit the scene and seek elsewhere a retreat. Whither should He turn? Galilee was closed against Him, and so was the eastern side of the Lake. He had no choice but to betake Himself northward once more and look for a hermitage on heathen soil. He travelled back to the shore and, re-embarking, steered for the upper end of the Lake.[3] It was a sail of some thirteen miles ; and, as the craft slipped gently on

Flight northward.

---

[1] *Cf.* Orig. *In Matth.* xii. § 1.

[2] Mk.'s report of this incident is much superior to Mt.'s. The latter is obviously assimilated to the narrative of the second demand for a sign (Mt. xii. 38-42 = Lk. xi. 16, 29-32). It is further vitiated by the intrusion of the taunt about their skill in reading the signs of the weather and their blindness to the signs of the times (*vv.* 2b-3)—no doubt an authentic *logion* but belonging elsewhere. *Cf.* Lk. xii. 54-6. See W. H.'s note.

[3] Much confusion has resulted from the idea that εἰς τὸ πέραν, " to the other side, " must mean across the Lake from W. to E. or from E. to W. It may, however, equally well mean across the Lake from S. to N.

her way, He embraced the opportunity of instructing the
"The Twelve in the things of the Kingdom of Heaven. "See!" He
leaven of said. "Beware of the leaven of the Pharisees and Sadducees."
the Phari-
sees and He was thinking of the scene which had been enacted a little
Saddu-
cees." before, and He meant to warn them against the blind tradi-
tionalism of the Pharisees and the worldliness of the Sadducees,
Cf. Mk. those aristocratic sycophants of the Herodian court.   The sen-
viii. 15. tence was a prelude to a discourse on the true nature of His
Messiahship ; and, had He been suffered to continue, He would
1 Pet. i. 11. have unfolded to them what they must anticipate—"the sufferings that should befall Messiah and the glories that should follow
these."   His discourse, however, was interrupted.   It chanced
that in the haste of their departure the disciples had neglected
to procure a store of provisions and had only a single loaf on
board.   When He spoke of "leaven," they took Him literally
and supposed that He was giving them directions about getting
bread, forbidding them to purchase it of people with Pharisaic
or Sadducean sympathies.[1]

Dulness of   It was a revelation of the dulness and unspirituality of the
the Twelve. Twelve.   The metaphorical use of the word "leaven" was
common among the Jews,[2] and their misunderstanding of it
was the more inexcusable after all that they had recently
Mt. xv. heard and seen.   Had they profited by the Master's lesson
16-20=Mk.
vii. 18-23. about what really defiled a man, they would never have im-
puted to Him that absurd objection to bread which had
passed through Pharisaic or Sadducean hands.   And how
could they fear want when He was in their midst who had
twice fed thousands with a handful of bread?   "Why," He
cried, "are ye debating within you, O ye of little faith, because
ye did not take loaves?   Do ye not yet understand, neither
remember ye the five loaves of the five thousand, and how
many baskets ye took?   Neither the seven loaves of the
four thousand, and how many maunds ye took?   How
do ye not understand that it was not with reference to loaves
that I said : 'Beware of the leaven of the Pharisees and
Sadducees'?"

---

[1] Euth. Zig. : κωλυθέντες ἀπὸ τῶν Ἰουδαικῶν ἄρτων, ὡς προσεδόκησαν.   Mt. xvi. 5
confusedly represents the incident as occurring after their arrival at the other side.
Mk. viii. 13 states the situation accurately.

[2] *Cf.* Lightfoot on Mt. xvi. 6.

The incident brought home to Jesus afresh how sorely Healing of a blind man at Bethsaida Julias. the Twelve needed instruction. Meanwhile He desisted. The boat sped on her way, and by and by they reached the northern end of the Lake and put in at the embouchure of the upper Jordan. On the left bank of the river a little way inland stood the fine town of Bethsaida. Once a poor village, it had been enlarged and embellished by the tetrarch Philip and styled Bethsaida Julias in honour of Julia, daughter of the Emperor Augustus.[1] Jesus was bound northward and would fain have escaped observation; but, as He passed through the town, His progress was arrested. A blind man was brought to Him for healing.[2] Apprehensive lest a crowd should gather and follow Him on His way, He laid hold of the man's hand and led him outside the town ere addressing Himself to the miracle. Since the avenue of sight was closed, He approached his soul by that of touch. After the manner of the physicians of that age He spat on his eyes, handled them, and inquired if he made out anything. The man looked up. The touch and the voice of Jesus had enkindled his faith, and it leapt forth to meet Him. That instant the miracle was wrought. "I make out the men," he said, "for as trees I see them walking about." An English philosopher tells how a blind man, being asked what was his idea of the colour scarlet, answered that he conceived it to resemble a loud blare of a trumpet. And this blind man, descrying the bystanders, said that he saw men, and he knew that they were men because they walked about, but they were like the fancy which in his darkened mind he had formed of trees. The Lord laid His hands on the bewildered eyes, and they made out everything distinctly.

It seems that the man lived in the country, and Jesus, Escape from. Bethsaida. anxious to avoid publicity, sent him straight home, forbidding him to enter the town. Thus He succeeded in getting clear away and pursuing His journey without a following.

---

[1] Jos. *Ant.* xviii. 2. § 1. Though Philip had raised it to the rank of a city, πόλεως παρασχὼν ἀξίωμα, Mk. still calls it a village (viii. 23, 26). So enduring is custom. *Cf.* the retention of the title of "king" by Herod Antipas (p. 229). It may be that the old village had been left side by side with the new city.

[2] Mk. has assimilated his narrative of this incident to vii. 31-7.

CHAPTER XXXI

THE GREAT CONFESSION

> " Tu beatus es, Bariona,
> Cui aspirat sua dona
> Quasi nato Spiritus.
> Quod caro sanguisque nescit
> Per Patrem tibi patescit
> Revelatum cœlitus."—*Med. Hymn.*

At Cæsarea Philippi. JUST beyond the frontier of Galilee at the base of the majestic Hermon lay the town of Cæsarea Philippi. It was a lovely district. There the Jordan takes its rise. Two springs, says St Jerome[1] propagating an etymological fancy which long maintained its ground and survives to this day among the native Christians, the Jor and the Dan, blend together, and the confluence of their waters makes the stream of that sacred and historic river as the combination of their names forms its name. When the Greeks came thither, they built a shrine in honour of their god Pan and called the town Paneas; and the tetrarch Philip in his turn adorned it and named it Cæsarea after Cæsar Augustus and Cæsarea Philippi after himself to distinguish it from the other Cæsarea, Cæsarea Stratonis, on the Palestinian sea-board.[2]

" Who say the people that the Son of Man is?" There Jesus found the retreat which He had sought so long, and addressed Himself to the task of instructing the Twelve in the things of the Kingdom of Heaven and preparing them for the impending *dénouement*. He began with a matter of supreme moment, a question which demanded immediate settlement. Ever since He had entered on His public ministry men had been debating about Him, and He would fain ascertain what opinion the Twelve had formed and what judgment they had arrived at regarding Him. He lost no time in eliciting an avowal. He walked abroad with them

---

[1] On Mt. xvi. 13.

[2] Jos. *Ant.* xviii. 2. § 1 ; *De Bell. Jud.* ii. 9. §. 1. *Cf.* Schürer, *H. J. P.* II. i. pp. 132-5.

in the neighbourhood of Cæsarea,[1] and it was evident from
His prayerful abstraction that some great concern was on His
mind. At length He spoke. "Who," He asked, "say the
people that the Son of Man is?"[2] He had a purpose in
employing that sobriquet, "the Son of Man." It was His
title of humiliation, and He desired to learn whether they had
discovered His hidden glory and recognised in any measure
what He really was. He did not enquire what the rulers
thought about Him. All too plainly had they avowed their
opinion that He was an impostor and their determination to
compass His destruction. But what was the judgment of
the people? They were indeed full of admiration for His
heavenly teaching and of wonderment at His miracles, but
was that all? Had they attained to any just conception of
His person and mission? "Who," He asked, "say the people
that the Son of Man is?" and the Twelve told Him the
various opinions which they had heard. Some thought, like *Cf.* Mk. vi.
Herod Antipas, that He was John the Baptist; some that 14-6=Lk.
ix. 7-9.
He was Elijah; some that He was another of the old prophets,
perhaps Jeremiah.

Jesus doubtless knew better than the Twelve what the "Who say
people were saying about Him; and it was not for informa- ye that I
am?"
tion that He asked, but in order to open the way for a
question of greater import. Such were the popular opinions.
"But ye," He continues, "who say ye that I am?" It was
a searching and momentous question. Their answer would
define the disciples' attitude toward Him and reveal what
profit they had derived from His teaching and whether they
were fit for the trust which would by and by be committed to
them. Prompt and unwavering came the response: "Thou Peter's
art the Messiah."[3] It was Peter that spoke—Peter, "the great confession.
mouth of the Apostles, the ever ardent, the coryphæus of the
Apostle choir." And it was a great confession. To call
Jesus the Messiah is in any circumstances a great confession,
since it implies the recognition of Him as the Saviour whom

---

[1] Mk.'s εἰς τὰς κώμας K. is a Hebraism meaning much the same as Mt.'s εἰς τὰ
μέρη K. *Cf.* Num. xxi. 32; Josh. xv. 32, 36, 41, etc.

[2] Mt. xvi. 13. με om. אB, Tisch., W. H., R.V. For τὸν υἱὸν τοῦ ἀνθρ. Mk.
and Lk. give με, obliterating a significant and essential touch.

[3] Mt.'s ὁ υἱὸς τοῦ Θεοῦ ζῶντος is a mere expansion, inserted probably as an
antithesis to τὸν υἱὸν τοῦ ἀνθρώπου.

prophets foretold and righteous men desired to see, the Fulfiller of Israel's long hope and humanity's eager desire. But circumstances invested Peter's confession with a peculiar significance and made it very precious in the eyes of Jesus. At the dawn of His ministry the first disciples had attached themselves to Him believing Him to be the Messiah on the strength of the Baptist's testimony and their initial acquaintance with Him. But they were Jews and cherished the Jewish conception of the Messiah and His mission, and their subsequent intercourse with Jesus had proved naught else than a continuous disillusionment. He had deliberately set Himself to combat the prevailing ideal of Messiahship. He had steadfastly trodden the path of humiliation, and they had known Him day by day as the lowly Son of Man, shunning applause and rejecting the regal dignity which misguided enthusiasm would have thrust upon Him. Even John the Baptist, to whom had been vouchsafed such singular attestations of the Lord's Messiahship, had been shaken in his mind ; and it is no marvel that the Twelve also doubted. It was a great confession when the response came prompt and unfaltering : "Thou art the Messiah." It meant that, though indeed they still clung to their Jewish ideal, the Twelve had drunk so deep of their Master's grace and perceived so much of His glory that they could not doubt. In face of all that seemed to contradict their faith, they were persuaded that He was the Messiah, the Saviour of Israel.

Exultation of Jesus.   Jesus hailed the confession with exultant rapture. It furnished Him with welcome evidence that His labour was not fruitless nor His confidence vain. "Blessed art thou, Simon son of John!" He cried ; "for flesh and blood did not reveal it unto thee, but My Father in Heaven." The names which He uses are significant. Simon was the name which the apostle had borne in the old days ere he had met with Jesus, and John means "the grace of the Lord." His confession proved him a new man, a true son of God's grace. That great faith had been taught him by no human wisdom

Mt. xi. 27 =Lk. x. 22.   but by revelation from the Father. "No one," says Jesus elsewhere, "recogniseth the Son but the Father, neither doth any one recognise the Father but the Son, and he to whom the Son may will to reveal Him."

It evinces what worth that great confession had in the His
Lord's eyes that, not content with pronouncing this bene-
promise to
diction on the disciple who made it, He promised him a Peter.
wondrous reward. "I tell thee," He said, making symbolic
use in turn of the surname which He had bestowed upon him
on that memorable day when first they met, "that thou art John i. 42.
Peter, the Rock, and on this rock will I build My Church and
the gates of Hades [1] shall not prevail against it. I will give
unto thee the keys of the Kingdom of Heaven ; and whatsoever thou shalt bind on earth shall stand bound in Heaven,
and whatsoever thou shalt loose on earth shall stand loosed in
Heaven." Of all the sayings of Jesus this is the most sorely
vexed and the most grievously abused. It is the Papacy's
grand proof-text ; and it is surely no less than a tragedy, a
pathetic evidence of human perversity, that on a saying of
Him who combated the priestcraft of His day even unto
death, a new priestcraft should have been built, more enduring than the old, more wide-spread in its dominion, and
more malign in its influence. Suffice it to observe that the
Romanist interpretation is sanctioned by none of the great
Fathers. Origen insists that the promise was made not to
Peter alone but to every disciple who joins in Peter's confession.[2] St Chrysostom holds that the rock was not Peter
but Peter's faith, "the faith of his confession."[3] According
to St Jerome [4] the rock was Jesus Himself. "Even as He
granted light to the Apostles that they might be called 'the
light of the world,' so also upon Simon who believed in the
Rock Christ, He bestowed the name of Peter, the Rock."
And he goes on to speak reprovingly of Presbyters and
Bishops who, "not understanding this passage, assume somewhat of the arrogance of the Pharisees." St Augustine,
influenced by a hymn of St Ambrose, once thought that the
rock was Peter ; but subsequently, while not condemning his
earlier opinion outright, he preferred the view that the rock
was Christ Himself.[5]

It hardly, however, admits of reasonable doubt that, Interpreted
when Jesus said : "Thou art the Rock, and on this rock will
by two
apostolic
concep-
tions.

[1] A proverbial phrase. *Cf.* Is. xxxviii. 10 ; Hom. *Il.* ix. 312-3.
[2] *In Matth.* xii. §§ 10-1.   [3] *In Matth.* lv. *Cf.* Isidor. Pelus. *Ep.* i. 235.
[4] On Mt. xvi. 18-9.   [5] *Retract* i. 21.

I build My Church," He meant Peter.[1]   His words, so highly
figurative, so strongly emotional, are a glowing eulogy of
the Apostle who had gladdened His heart by that great
confession ; and their meaning, hidden from flesh and blood,
has been revealed by the inspiration of the Holy Spirit.
There are two apostolic conceptions which, though they may
not comprehend its entire significance, are yet its best
interpretation.

1. The Church a living temple.

ii. 19-22.

The first is that sublime ideal of the Church as a living
temple built of living stones.   "Ye are no more strangers
and sojourners," wrote St Paul to the Ephesians, "but ye are
the saints' fellow-citizens and members of God's household,
Christ Jesus Himself being chief corner-stone ; in whom all
that is built, being fitly framed together, groweth into a holy
sanctuary in the Lord ; in whom ye also are being built into
an habitation of God in the Spirit."   This is one of the
master-thoughts of apostolic days ; and it is very noteworthy
that it laid hold on St Peter and kindled his imagination.
Had he the Lord's promise at Cæsarea Philippi before his

Is. xxviii. 16.

ii. 4-5.

mind when, echoing the ancient prophet's language, he wrote
in his first epistle : "Coming unto the Lord, a living stone,
by men rejected but with God chosen, precious, yourselves
also, as living stones, are being built a spiritual house."
Here is the very conception of Jesus.   His Church was a
living Temple and her stones living men.   And it was the
peculiar and inalienable honour of Peter that he was the
first stone ever built into that spiritual house.   Others would
follow him in his confession and share in his reward ; yea,
and others might prove worthier than he and shine with
brighter lustre ; yet this was his unique and abiding honour,
that his had been the earliest confession of the glory of
Jesus ; and none could ever wrest from him that proud
distinction.   In that great hour at Cæsarea Philippi the
Church of the Lord Jesus Christ was born ; the first stone of
the Living Temple was laid.

2. The union of Christ and believers.

There is further the magnificent Pauline conception of
the corporate union between Christ and His believing people.

[1] Aug. : " Non dictum est illi, Tu es Petra ; sed *Tu es Petrus.*   "But our Lord,
speaking in Aramaic, would use the same word, כֵּיפָא, in both cases.   πέτρα is due to
the idea that כֵּיפָא is fem.

How marvellous, how audacious is the Apostle's language when he sets forth this ineffable mystery! "We are members of His body." "Your bodies are members of Christ." "We that are many are one body in Christ, and severally members one of another." "As the body is one and hath many members, and all the members of the body, being many, are one body, so also is Christ. . . . And whether one member suffer, all the members suffer with it; or a member be glorified, all the members rejoice with it." "Now I rejoice in my sufferings for your sake and fill up on my part the deficiencies of Christ's afflictions in my flesh for the sake of His body, which is the Church." Here, though clothed with different imagery, is the very thought which Jesus expressed when He said: "I will give unto thee the keys of the Kingdom of Heaven; and whatsoever thou shalt bind on earth, shall stand bound in Heaven, and whatsoever thou shalt loose on earth shall stand loosed in Heaven."[1] The promise was made to Peter, since at that moment he was the sole realisation of the Church, the first and as yet the only stone of that Living Temple. By and by, however, when others had been added, the promise was repeated, and it was then addressed not to Peter alone but to the whole brotherhood. It is an amazing promise, and what is the principle which underlies it, the basis on which it rests? Is it not that profound truth of the corporate unity of the whole Church in Heaven and on earth? One spirit, one life pervades it all. His saints on earth are Christ's witnesses to the world; they are His representatives, and whatsoever they do in His name has His sanction. When they speak, it is not they that speak but His spirit that speaketh in them. Their decisions are ratified in Heaven. "Verily I tell you, whatsoever things ye shall bind on earth shall stand bound in Heaven, and whatsoever things ye shall loose on earth shall stand loosed in Heaven."

Such is the Church's prerogative, but it is hers only as she abides in the unity of the mystic Body. And that unity is twofold. On the one hand there is the unity betwixt the members. "God," says St Paul, "hath tempered the

Marginal references:
Eph. v. 30.
1 Cor. vi. 15.
Rom. xii. 5.
1 Cor. xii. 12, 26.
Col. i. 24.
Cf. Is. xxii. 22.
Mt. xviii. 18.
Mt. x. 20 =Mk. xiii. 11=Lk. xii. 12.
A two-fold union.
1 Cor. xii. 24-5.

---

[1] "Bind and loose," a Rabbinical phrase for *prohibiting and permitting*. See Lightfoot and Wetstein on Mt. xvi. 19.

body together, that there may be no schism in the body, but that the members may have the same care one for another." And Jesus expresses this very truth when He says : "If two of you shall agree on earth concerning anything which they may ask, it shall be done unto them of My Father in Heaven. For where two or three are assembled in My name, there am I in the midst of them." On the other hand there is the unity of the members with their Living Head, and her high prerogative belongs to the Church only as she belongs to Christ, drawing her life from Him and breathing His spirit. "Holding fast the Head," says St Paul, "from whom all the body, being supplied and knit together through the joints and bands, groweth the growth of God." "Abide in Me," says Jesus, "and I in you. As the branch cannot bear fruit from itself, unless it abide in the vine, so neither can ye unless ye abide in Me. I am the vine, ye are the branches. Apart from Me ye can do nothing." The instant the Church is severed from Christ, she ceases to be His representative ; her life is no longer His life, nor her acts His acts. Very strikingly was this truth declared to the disciples on that ever memorable first day of the week when the Risen Lord appeared in their midst. "Whosoever sins ye forgive," He said, "they have been forgiven unto them ; and whosoever ye retain, they have been retained " ; but first " He breathed upon them and said : ' Receive ye the Holy Spirit.' "

Mt. xviii. 19-20.

Col. ii. 19.

John xiv. 4-5.

John xx. 22-3.

CHAPTER XXXII

SUFFERINGS AND GLORY

Mt. xvi.
20–xvii. 13
= Mk. viii.
30–ix. 13 =
Lk. ix. 21-
36.

" Recordare sanctæ crucis
  Qui perfectam viam ducis,
    Delectare jugiter.
  Sanctæ crucis recordare
  Et in ipsa meditare
    Insatiabiliter."—S. BONAVENTURA.

IT was a glad moment for Jesus when He heard from the lips of Peter the confession of His disciples' faith. But no sooner had the flood of exultation subsided in His breast than, fearing lest their testimony should reanimate the popular enthusiasm, He charged them to tell no man that He was the Messiah. Thereafter He made a momentous announcement. Already had He thrown out vague hints of the doom which awaited Him,[1] but the disciples, dreaming their Jewish dream of a worldly kingdom, had missed them all. It was time that they should know the truth, and their confession emboldened Jesus to declare it. He told them that " He must go away to Jerusalem and suffer many things of the Elders and Chief-priests and Scribes, and be killed, and on the third day [2] be raised up."

First distinct intimation of Passion and Resurrection.

    The announcement fell like a thunder-bolt on the ears of the Twelve. They were aghast, and Peter, the lover of Jesus, could not endure it.[3] Horrified and distressed, he clutched his dear Master and broke out into remonstrance. " Mercy on Thee,[4] Lord ! " he cried. " This shall in no wise

Peter's remonstrance.

---

[1] John ii. 19; iii. 14; Mt. ix. 14-5 = Mk. ii. 18-20 = Lk. v. 33-5; John vi. 51, 55. It is remarkable that those intimations of His Death, though made in their hearing, were not addressed to the disciples.

[2] Mk.'s "after three days" is, according to the inclusive reckoning of the ancients, identical with Mt.-Lk.'s "on the third day." *Cf.* Mt. xxvii. 63-4.

[3] In Mk. viii. 32 the Sinaitic Palimpsest reads : "Then Simon Cepha, as though he pitied Him, said to Him, ' Be it far from Thee.'"

[4] Ἴλεώς σοι, sc. εἴη ὁ Θεός, probably a colloquialism. *Cf.* 2 Sam. xxiii. 17 (LXX). See Wetstein.

befall Thee." It may have been an ill-advised speech, very characteristic of Peter, yet it was prompted by tender love, **Agitation of Jesus.** and for that very reason it distressed Jesus. All the days of His ministry the Cross had been before Him, and the prospect had been very awful to Him ; and, though He had set His face like a flint and pressed forward on His way, His heart had oftentimes failed within Him. It was the Father's will that He should die, a sacrifice for the world's redemption ; yet His flesh had shuddered at the grim ordeal, and the temptation had been ever present with Him to turn aside and choose an easier path. At the outset of His ministry it had assailed Him in the wilderness when the Devil displayed before Him the Kingdoms of the world and the glory of them with the promise : " All these things will I give Thee, if Thou wilt fall down and do obeisance unto me." And it had pursued Him all along, conjuring up the horror of the Cross before His eyes and suggesting some smoother way. But He had always turned from the Tempter's allure- ments and, hearkening to the voice which called Him to self-abnegation and self-sacrifice, had set Himself to do the Father's will and accomplish the Father's work. And now the temptation assails Him afresh with powerful reinforce- ment. It was the Devil that spoke, but he spoke through the lips of that loved disciple who a little ago had made the great confession. It was as though the Tempter had assumed Peter's form and were urging his suit with all the moving importunity of tender affection. It is no wonder that Jesus **His reply** was shaken, but not for a moment did He hesitate. He recognised the temptation under its specious disguise. First He glanced round at the other disciples, questioning what *their* thoughts might be, and then from those gracious lips whence blessing was wont to flow, there flashed the sentence : " Get behind Me, Satan ! Thou art a stumbling- block to Me ; forasmuch as thou dost not side with God but with men." [1]

Oblivious- ness of the Twelve. This is the Lord's first distinct intimation of His Death and Resurrection, and it was followed by two others, each **Mt. xxii.** more circumstantial than its predecessor. It seems at

[1] οὐ φρονεῖς τὰ τοῦ Θεοῦ, *non sectaris partes Dei.* *Cf.* Plut. *Brut.* xxvi. § 2 : κα᾽ τοὺς᾽ Ἀπολλωνιάτας ᾔσθετο τὰ Βρούτου φρονοῦντας. See Wetstein.

the first blush a great marvel that, after such plain and _{22-3=Mk.} reiterated forewarnings, the catastrophe should have taken _{ix. 30-1=} _{Lk. ix.} the disciples by surprise. The Crucifixion appeared to _{43-4; Mt.} them a crushing disaster; and, when they heard from the _{xx. 17-9=} _{Mk. x. 32-} women what had befallen on the Resurrection-morning, they _{4=Lk.} _{xviii. 31-3.} were incredulous and deemed it an idle tale; nay, when Peter and John saw with their own eyes the empty Sepulchre, _{John xx.} they were amazed. The event astonished them. They had _{8-10.} never, apparently, anticipated it.

Their obliviousness of such forewarnings is indeed surpris- _{Blinded by} ing, yet is it in no wise incomprehensible. There is nothing _{Jewish pre-} _{judice.} more difficult than to change men's ideals, and the disciples clung with blind and dogged pertinacity to their Jewish _{Lk. xxiv.} expectation of an earthly kingdom. Even after Jesus had _{17-21.} twice announced His Passion, they disputed which of them _{Mt. xviii. 1} should occupy the chief places about His throne. When He _{=Mk. ix.} _{34=Lk. ix.} started on His last journey to Jerusalem, they believed that _{46.} He was going up at last to claim His Kingdom; and after His third and most solemn intimation the sons of Zebedee _{Mt. xx. 20-} conspired with their mother to extort from Him a pledge _{8=Mk. x.} _{35-48.} that they would sit on His right and left. They simply could not comprehend what He meant when He spoke of His Passion. It was, they conceived, beyond the bounds of possibility that the Messiah should die, and they listened amazedly and went on hugging their Jewish ideal. So the Evangelists testify: "They were grieved exceedingly." _{Mt. xvii.} "They were ignorant of this saying, and it was veiled from _{23.} them that they should not perceive it; and they were afraid _{Lk. ix. 45.} to question Him about this saying." "And they took in none of these things, and this saying was hidden from them, _{Lk. xviii.} and they did not recognise the things that were spoken." _{34.} The very fact that it was necessary for Jesus to reiterate the announcement with ever-increasing emphasis, as though striving to force it home, is an evidence of their invincible dulness.

It is strange, but it is not unparalleled. It is matched _{Parallel} by the obstinacy wherewith, despite the Lord's plain _{instances:} _{Mt. xv. 10-} declaration, they clung to their Jewish prejudice against _{20=Mk.} _{viii. 14-23.} unclean meat; by their confident anticipation of His im- _{Acts x. 9-} mediate return despite those parables wherein He had taught _{16.}

that the progress of His Kingdom would be slow and gradual, like the operation of leaven or the growth of seed ;[1] and by their hostility to the admission of the Gentiles into the Church on equal terms with the Jews notwithstanding the Lord's kindness to the outcasts, His preaching at Sychar, and, above all, His ministry in Phœnicia. And herein is revealed not only the disciples' slowness of heart but the depth of their trust in Jesus. They retained their Jewish notion of the Messiah ; yet, though His every word and act conflicted therewith, they clung, with a splendid inconsistency, to their faith in His Messiahship. He was the very opposite of all that, as they believed, the Messiah should be; yet they had seen His glory, they had tasted of His grace, and, in defiance of reason, they rendered unto Him the trust and homage of their souls.

Call to fellowship in His sufferings.   The announcement that their Master must die was a heavy blow to the Twelve ; and what did He do as they stood amazed ?[2] He dealt them, as it seems, another blow. He told them that not only must He suffer but they must share His suffering. There are two claimants to the throne in every man's heart—Self and Jesus; and, if the man would be a disciple, he must yield the throne to Jesus ; and he must say No to Self's blandishments, must take up the cross and lay it on Self's back and send Self away to death. "If anyone is minded to come after Me, let him say No to Self, and take up Self's cross, and escort Me on My way." Already, when He sent them forth on their apostolic mission, He had spoken of "cross-bearing"; but now, with the announcement of His Passion in their ears, they would recognise it as no mere metaphor but a dread reality. It meant for them what it meant for Him.

Mt. x. 38.

An inspiring appeal.   It may seem strange that Jesus should thus add blow to blow. Surely it was enough in the meantime that they should learn what awaited Him. Surely they needed reassurance rather than fresh alarm. In truth, however, He dealt with them very wisely. He invoked their manhood, their chivalry, and their faith. It was a heroic ordeal whereunto they were called, and He challenged their courage

_____

[1] Cf. Introd. § 12, 6.   [2] Cf. Introd. § 11.

to encounter it. He appealed to the love which they bore Him, to the confidence which He reposed in them, and to the sacred cause wherein they were enlisted. Could they not endure the utmost " for His sake and the Gospel's " ? He bade them, moreover, beware lest, in seeking to save their life, they should lose it, " preferring," in the language of the Roman satirist, " life to honour and for life's sake losing the ends of living." " What," He asked, " shall a man be profited, if he gain the whole world but forfeit his life ? or what shall a man give as the price of his life's redemption ? " A man has only one life to live ; and, if he forfeit it, wherewith shall he buy it back ? His final argument was the most moving of all. According to Jewish theology the Messiah would appear in glory at the end of the world and execute judgment ;[1] and Jesus availed Himself of this familiar doctrine. If His disciples failed in the hour of trial and played a craven part, how would they meet Him on that great Day ? how bear the scrutiny of His blessed face ? " Whosoever is ashamed of Me and My words in this adulterous and sinful generation, the Son of Man also shall be ashamed of him when He cometh in the glory of His Father with the holy angels." It was an awful sentence. The thought of that face which they knew so well, turning away at the sight of them for very shame and leaving them there, a scorn to men and angels, must have haunted them and incited them to labour that they might be found worthy on that great Day.

Such was the prospect which lay before the Apostles, and Jesus did not conceal it from them. Yet He closed with a great word of promise and reassurance. Sharp though the conflict would be, victory was certain, and some of them would live to see it. " Verily I tell you, there are some of those that stand here who shall not taste of death until they see the Kingdom of God come in power." And the promise was fulfilled. One of the marvels of history is the rapidity wherewith the Gospel won its way. Scarce three centuries had elapsed ere it conquered the Roman Empire and a Christian was seated on the throne of the Cæsars. None of the Twelve witnessed this consummation, yet they

A promise of victory.

---

[1] Schürer, *H. J. P.* II. ii. pp. 165-8, 181-3 ; Hastings' *D. B.* art. *Eschatology.*

witnessed much. In the course of a single generation the message which they preached in the power of God, had sounded over the known world. Far beyond the borders of Palestine, in Asia Minor. in Greece, in imperial Rome, the Gospel had free course and was glorified. In the year A.D. 58 St Paul could make this claim: "I will not dare to write of any things save those which Christ wrought through me, for the obedience of the Gentiles, by word and deed, in power of signs and wonders, in power of the Holy Spirit; so that from Jerusalem and round about even unto Illyricum I have fulfilled the Gospel of Christ." [1]

Rom. xv. 18-9.

A week elapsed,[2] and, though nothing is recorded of the employments of those days, they would in no wise slip idly away. Weary with His task Jesus took Peter, James, and John and, retiring with them to a mountain, "was transfigured [3] in their presence." According to ancient tradition the mountain was Tabor; [4] and the Greek Church still abides thereby, celebrating the Feast of the Transfiguration under the name of the Thaborion on the sixth of August. It is, however, an impossible fancy. Tabor was situated far away in the south of Galilee well-nigh fifty miles from Cæsarea Philippi; and, moreover, since its summit was occupied by a fort called Itabyrium,[5] it was no fit scene for the enactment of a heavenly mystery. The mountain was plainly in the neighbourhood of Cæsarea Philippi; and probably it was one of the lower heights of Hermon, whose snowy summit[6] towered aloft a little distance northward.

On the Mount.

He went thither to refresh His soul by communion with

The Transfiguration.

---

[1] More specific references have been assigned to this saying: (1) The Transfiguration (Aug., Chrysost., Euth. Zig., Theophyl.). (2) The Resurrection and its effects (Calvin). (3) The Destruction of Jerusalem (Lightfoot, Wetstein). (4) The Second Advent, regarded in the primitive Church as imminent (Meyer and others). Its interpretation as referring to the Second Advent probably accounts for the form which the saying has assumed in Mt.

[2] Mt. and Mk. "after six days"; Lk. vaguely "after these sayings about eight days." Jer. : "Hic medii ponuntur dies, ibi primus additur et extremus."

[3] μετεμορφώθη. Lk., writing for Gentiles and knowing what the word would suggest to minds familiar with classical fables of the metamorphoses of deities, paraphrased it into ἐγένετο τὸ εἶδος τοῦ προσώπου αὐτοῦ ἕτερον.

[4] Jer. *Ep.* xxvii, *Epitaph. Paul.*: "montem Thabor in quo transfiguratus est Dominus."

[5] Polyb. v. 70; Jos. *De Bell. Jud.* iv. 1. § 8.   [6] *Cf.* Mk. ix. 3 T. R.: ὡς χιών.

the Father, and it was while He prayed that the ineffable
wonder was wrought. "His face," says St Matthew, "shone
as the sun, and His garments became white as the light."
"His garments," says St Mark, "became glistering, exceeding
white, as no fuller on the earth can whiten." "His raiment,"
says St Luke, "became flashing white." And two men
appeared in His company. They were Moses and Elijah, and
they talked with Him of "the decease which He was about
to accomplish at Jerusalem." The weary disciples had fallen
asleep, but their slumber was disturbed and, wide awake, they
beheld the wondrous scene. Presently the vision began to
fade, and Peter, ever impetuous, thought to stay the heavenly
visitants. "Master," he cried, "it is well that we should be
here; and let us make three tents, one for Thee and one for
Moses and one for Elijah." It was indeed a foolish speech.
"He knew not," says St Luke, "what he was saying"; and,
had he paused to consider, he would have held his peace.
Nevertheless he had a purpose in his mind; and, wild as it
may have been, it was one which only a generous and loyal
heart could have conceived. He was haunted by the Master's
announcement of His Passion, and the scene on the mountain-
top suggested to him a way of escape. "Wherefore," he
asked himself, "depart from this holy place? Wherefore
descend to the plain and resume the weary conflict? Wherefore go away to Jerusalem and endure that awful doom? Let
us abide here on this hallowed mount and prolong this
heavenly fellowship." While he spoke, a cloud overshadowed
them, and, even as at the Lord's Baptism when the heavens
opened and the Holy Spirit descended upon Him, they heard
a voice. "This is My beloved Son," it said, "in whom I am
well pleased. Hearken unto Him." They fell on their faces
for fear, and lay prostrate until Jesus laid His hand upon them
and bade them arise. When they looked about them, Moses
and Elijah were gone, and they were alone with Jesus.

Mt. iii. 16-7
=Mk. i.
10-11=Lk.
iii. 21-2.

The real import of this wondrous incident emerges only
when it is recognised that, like the Lord's miracle of walking
upon the Lake, it was an anticipation of the Resurrection.
By the power of God the body of Jesus assumed for a season
the conditions of the resurrection-life. It became, in the
language of St Paul, "a spiritual body," and He appeared to

An antici-
pation of
the Resur-
rection.

the three even as when He manifested Himself after He had risen from the dead on the road to Emmaus, in the room at Jerusalem, on the shore of the Lake.   And the miracle had a

Its pur-
pose :
(1) to
strengthen
Jesus ;

twofold purpose.   It was designed, in the first instance, to strengthen Jesus and nerve Him for the dread ordeal which awaited Him.   It was as though the veil had been drawn aside and the eternal world for a little space disclosed to His view.   It was like a vision of home to the exile, like a fore-taste of rest to the weary traveller.   He was granted a glimpse of the glory which He had resigned that He might tabernacle among the children of men, winning redemption for them, and an earnest likewise of the joy that was set before Him.   From the vantage-ground of the Mount of Transfiguration He descried the consummation which awaited Him beyond the Hill of Calvary.   Nor was that the only consolation which was vouchsafed to Him.   His heart had been grieved by the dulness of the Twelve, the folly of the multitude, and the hostility of the rulers, and in that transcendent hour it was revealed to Him how His work was viewed by God and the glorified saints.   Though He stood alone on earth, misunder-stood, forsaken, and persecuted, He had Heaven's sympathy and approval.

(2) to re-
veal to the
disciples
the glory
of the
Passion.

And the Transfiguration had a purpose also in relation to the disciples.   It was designed to reconcile them to the incredible and repulsive idea of Messiah's sufferings by reveal-ing to them the glories that should follow.   What did they hear as they listened to the converse betwixt those two glorified saints who bore the greatest names on Israel's roll of honour ?   They heard them talking of "the decease," or, as

Cf. 2 Pet.
i. 15.

it is in Greek, "the Exodus, which He was about to accomplish at Jerusalem."   In the judgment of Moses and Elijah that issue, which seemed to the disciples an intolerable ignominy and a crushing disaster, was a splendid triumph, like the mighty deliverance which God had wrought for Israel when He brought her by the hand of Moses out of the land of bondage and made her a free nation.   It is very significant that in the copies of St Luke's Gospel which were in use in St Chrysostom's day, this sentence ran : "They spake of the *glory* which He was about to accomplish at Jerusalem." [1]   And

---

[1] Chrysost: *In Matth.* lvii : τὴν δόξαν ἣν ἔμελλε πληροῦν ἐν Ἱερουσαλήμ· τουτέστιν,

such was the conception of her Lord's sufferings which was by and by revealed to the Church. "We behold Jesus," it is written in the *Epistle to the Hebrews*, "by reason of the ii. 9. suffering of death crowned with glory and honour."

Refreshed by communion with the Father and nerved to *The descent from the Mount.* the ordeal by that glimpse of the glory which awaited Him on the other side of Calvary, Jesus on the following day set His face toward the plain. Knowing that, if the story got abroad, it would be misconstrued, He charged His companions that they should not divulge what they had seen until He had risen from the dead. Thereat they fell a-wondering. Though He had already spoken of His Resurrection, linking a prophecy *Mt. xvi. 21 = Mk. viii. 31 = Lk. ix. 22.* thereof to the announcement of His Passion, they had in their amazement missed the promise of hope; but now it is forced upon their attention. It was a dark saying, and they pondered it, questioning one with another what His rising from the dead might signify. Did they, amid their musing and debating, at all connect it with the scene which they had witnessed on the holy mount?

They talked much as they made the long descent, and *The coming of Elijah.* there was one problem especially which engaged their Jewish minds. It was commonly expected that, ere the Messiah's advent, Elijah would reappear on the earth and work a mighty reformation, preparing Israel to welcome her Redeemer; and, in view of what they had witnessed, the disciples knew not what to make of this doctrine. Elijah had indeed come, but wherefore had he come so late and so soon departed? He should have preceded Jesus the Messiah and ere His advent accomplished the promised reformation. They referred the problem to the Master. Elijah's reappearance was of course only a Rabbinical fancy; but Jesus always dealt kindly with the ideas of His contemporaries, and already, on that memorable day when the Baptist's delegates had visited Him, He had given a felicitous interpretation to this Jewish notion. "If ye are willing to receive it," He had said in the *Mt. xi. 14* course of His eulogy of John, " *he* is Elijah that should

τὸ πάθος καὶ τὸν σταυρόν. οὕτω γὰρ αὐτὸ καλοῦσιν ἀεί. Euth. Zig. on Mt. xvii. 3: τινὰ δὲ τῶν βιβλίων οὐκ ἔξοδον ἀλλὰ δόξαν γράφουσι. δόξα γὰρ καλεῖται καὶ ὁ σταυρός. Vossius connects ἐν δόξῃ, not with ὀφθέντες, but with ἔλεγον. ἐν δόξῃ ἔλεγον, i.e. ἐδόξαζον, τὴν ἔξοδον αὐτοῦ, "they glorified His decease."

come." John had actually done what was expected of Elijah. He had come and prepared the Messiah's way before His face.[1] It was an apt and novel application, but the disciples, absent on their apostolic mission, had not heard it. And now He repeats it, taking occasion to make a fresh intimation of the doom which awaited Him. " Elijah," He said, " cometh and will restore all things ; but I tell you that Elijah hath already come, and they did not recognise him, but wrought on him all their will. Thus also the Son of Man is about to suffer by them."

[1] Chrysost. *In Matth.* lviii: οὐκ ἐπειδὴ 'Ηλίας ἦν ἀλλ ἐπειδὴ τὴν διακονίαν ἐπλήρου ἐκείνου.

CHAPTER XXXIII

THE RETURN TO CAPERNAUM

"An vero utilius aut efficacius auxilium aliquod est quam ut ores devote pro tuo fratre, non dissimules redarguere culpas ejus ; ut non modo nullum ei offendiculum ponas, sed et sollicitus sis, quantum praevales, tanquam angelus pacis de regno Dei scandala tollere et occasiones scandalorum penitus dimovere." — S. BERNARD. *De Advent. Dom. Serm.* iii.

MUCH had happened on the plain while Jesus and the three were absent on the Mount. Even as the Pharisees and Sadducees had pursued Him to His retreat in the neighbourhood of Magadan and Dalmanutha, so, when He escaped northward, a band of Scribes followed in His track with an attendant multitude and presently discovered His retreat at Cæsarea Philippi. He was absent when they arrived, but they found the nine and, it would seem, harassed them with petty malignity. An incident occurred which afforded them a welcome opportunity. A man appeared on the scene in quest of Jesus. He had a son who was a lunatic, deaf and dumb, and subject withal to violent fits of epilepsy ; and he brought the unhappy lad for healing. In the absence of Jesus he appealed to the disciples ; and, since they had been empowered by their Master to work such miracles, they readily undertook the task. They failed, however, in the attempt. Great was the glee of the Scribes. They exulted over the crestfallen disciples, and doubtless employed their failure to discredit Jesus with the multitude, alleging that, had He been present, He would have proved equally impotent.

In the thick of the dispute Jesus appeared ; and there was something about Him which amazed the multitude. Was it that His face, like that of Moses when he came down from Mount Sinai, still shone with the glory of His transfiguration ? They ran to greet Him, He enquired the cause of the commotion, and the unhappy father told Him the story. "O

faithless and perverse generation!" He cried when He heard
of the failure of His disciples. "How long shall I be with
you? how long shall I suffer you? Bring him unto Me."
They brought the lad, and, overcome with agitation, he fell
into a violent fit and lay struggling and foaming on the ground.
The poor father's distress was even more piteous than his
child's suffering. "How long time is it," Jesus asked him,
bent on succouring both, "that he hath been thus affected?"
"Since childhood," was the reply. "And often it hath flung
him into fire and into waters to destroy him. But, if Thou
canst do aught, have compassion on us and help us." He was
almost hopeless. The disciples' impotence had shaken his
faith. Where they had failed, he scarce expected Jesus to
succeed. "'If Thou canst!'" returned Jesus, echoing the
despairing appeal. "All things are possible to one that
believeth." The reproach and yet more the tone of that
gracious voice and the look of that blessed face dispelled his
despondency. "I believe," he cried; "help my unbelief!"
Having thus won the father's faith, Jesus addressed Himself
to the healing of the child. "Thou dumb and deaf spirit,"
He said, "I charge thee, come out of him and no more enter
into him." A wild cry and a fierce convulsion, and the child
lay, to all appearance, dead, till Jesus took him by the hand
and raised him and gave him to his father healed.

Reason of the disciples' impotence. It was a striking manifestation of the Lord's power, and
it made a profound impression. There were, however, two
groups that participated neither in the gratitude of the father
nor in the adoration of the multitude. One was the Scribes,
who would stand confounded; and the other the nine disciples.
It was a rebuke to them that the Master had succeeded where
they had failed, and on the way home they debated what it
might mean. Their dread, thinks St Chrysostom, was that
they had lost the grace wherewith He had entrusted them when
He "gave them power and authority over all dæmons and sent
them forth to preach and heal." Perhaps such was their
secret fear; but they were loath to allow it, and, it would
seem, they devised an excuse, flattering themselves that they
were in no wise to blame. It was, they alleged, an exceptionally
difficult and obstinate case, demanding for the mastery of it a
higher power than they possessed. When they reached the

secrecy of their lodging, they appealed to Jesus, and He ruth-lessly swept their excuse aside. " This kind of spirit," they had been saying, " goeth out by naught but by some special power." " This kind," He retorted, " goeth out by naught but by prayer."[1] It was a sharp home-thrust. During His absence on the Mount they had employed themselves amiss, dreaming perhaps of the honours of the Messianic Kingdom and debating about pre-eminence in it. They had refrained from prayer and had suffered the heavenly flame to burn low in their souls. And therefore they had failed. The spirit of the Lord had departed from them.

It was now time for Jesus to quit His retirement ; nor indeed, even had He been minded to protract His sojourn at Cæsarea Philippi, was it any longer possible for Him to be alone there with the Twelve. His retreat had been discovered, and He was beset once more by an importunate multitude and malignant adversaries. He set out for Capernaum, seeking, as He travelled through Galilee, to escape recognition, since His disciples still needed instruction and much might be imparted to them by the way. As they travelled through that pleasant land, He reiterated the dread announcement of His Passion, seeking by dint of emphasis to drive it home and pierce their impervious incredulity. " Set into your ears," He said, " these words : The Son of Man is about to be betrayed into men's hands, and they will kill Him, and on the third day He will be raised." There is here added to His former announcement the grim detail of betrayal. It is no wonder that they " were grieved exceedingly " and " feared to interrogate Him." Did they recall the bitter word which He had spoken in Capernaum on that dark day of desertion : " Did I not choose you the Twelve ? And of you one is a devil " ? Did it dawn upon them that there was a traitor in their midst ?

At length they arrived at Capernaum and went their several ways to their abodes. Jesus lodged in Peter's house ; and, ere they reached it, the disciple was summoned from his Master's side. It was a matter of business that craved his

Journey to Capernaum.

Another announcement of the Passion.

John vi. 70.

The unpaid tax.

---

[1] Mk. ix 29 : καὶ νηστείᾳ is an interpolation· Mt., omitting this striking *logion*, makes Jesus assign ὀλιγοπιστία as the reason of the disciples' failure, introducing here that saying about the power of faith which was spoken in connection with the withering of the barren fig-tree (Mt. xxi. 21 = Mk. xi. 23).

attention.   Of every Israelite twenty years old and upwards an annual tax was exacted for the maintenance of the Temple.[1] It fell due on the fifteenth of Adar or March, and defaulters were required to make payment in the Temple on the twenty-fifth or suffer distraint.[2]   Jesus was liable to the tax and had paid it year by year hitherto ; but, ever since the tidings of John the Baptist's execution had reached His ears, He had been wandering far and wide and had made only a single visit to Capernaum.   It was now toward the end of August,[3] and His tax was still unpaid.   The collectors observed His return and immediately set about recovering the debt.   It is an evidence of the reverence wherewith Jesus was regarded, that they did not accost Himself, but drew Peter aside and broached the matter with studious courtesy [4] : " Doth your Teacher not pay the half-shekels ? "   " Yes," faltered Peter, and hurried home to tell Jesus.

Peter's dis-   An inimitable scene ensued, and it is surely pathetic that comfiture. an incident which is unique in the Gospel-story and reveals a hidden trait of our Blessed Lord, should be little else than a jest for unbelievers and a stumbling-block to faith.   It was one of the rare moments in the Master's ministry when no censorious eye was upon Him and He might freely unbend. He was alone with one who loved Him, and, secure from misunderstanding, He indulged His kindly humour and laughed away the discomfiture of that impulsive and warm-hearted disciple.   It is no wonder that He was amused. Picture the situation.   The demand of the collectors had taken Peter aback.   And it was certainly embarrassing. Jesus and the Twelve had just returned from a long journey. Their resources, never abundant, must have been at a very low ebb, and here was a claim requiring immediate settlement. Peter hurried home and burst in to communicate the dis-

---

[1] A half *shekel* = two (Syrian) drachmæ, τὸ δίδραχμον.   *Cf.* Exod. xxx. 13 (LXX) : τὸ ἥμισυ τοῦ διδράχμου ὅ ἐστι κατὰ τὸ δίδραχμον τὸ ἅγιον.   A *shekel*, corresponding to a Syrian *stater* (Mt. xvii. 27), was worth about 2s. 6d.   See Schürer, *H. J. P.* II. i. pp. 249 *sqq.*   It is noteworthy that the story of the tax is recorded by Mt. alone. It would appeal to the *quondam* tax-gatherer.

[2] *Cf.* p. 59.

[3] The Greek Church celebrates the Feast of the Transfiguration on 6th Aug., and that this date is at least approximately correct is proved by the fact that the Feast of Tabernacles, to which He repaired after no very long stay at Capernaum, fell at the beginning of October.   [4] *Cf.* Chrysost. *In Matth.* lix.

concerting intelligence. It is no wonder that Jesus was amused. He knew all. He had seen the approach of the collectors, and, even had He not guessed their errand, His disciple's face would have told the tale. It might well have vexed Him that, after the solemn things which he had recently seen and heard, Peter should have been so lightly discomposed; yet the situation had an aspect of absurdity, and Jesus was rather amused than vexed.

He took the first word and accosted Peter in a tone of gentle raillery. "What thinkest thou, Simon? The kings of the earth—from whom take they custom or tribute? From their own sons or from other men's?" "From other men's," was the reply. "Then," said Jesus, "their sons are free." The words were playfully spoken, yet they carried a serious significance. In truth they constitute one of the most striking assertions which Jesus ever made of His divinity. He was the Son of God, and the Temple was His Father's House. For His glory it existed, and not on Him rested the obligation of supporting it by pious offerings. He might have claimed exemption from that sacred impost; yet He would not, lest His action should be misconstrued. To such as did not recognise His lordship, it would have seemed a mere violation of the Law, and He dreaded that imputation. At the outset of His ministry He had asserted the sanctity and permanence of the Law; and to the last He manifested a high reverence for its doctrines and institutions, participating in the worship of Synagogue and Temple and appealing to its testimony in vindication of His Messianic claims. Year by year hitherto he had paid the Temple-tax, and He would pay it now, "lest we make them stumble." *The Lord's title to exemption.* *Mt. v. 17-20.*

But wherewithal? That was the problem which was distressing Peter. It never occurred to him that he might resort to his long disused craft. Were there not fish in the Lake and a market to sell them in? Such was the plan which Jesus recommended, but, looking at His disciple's rueful visage, He smiled and plied him with pleasant banter.[1] Stories were rife in those days about lucky fishermen who had found treasures inside fishes. It was in this remarkable fashion, according to Jewish fable, that Solomon recovered his *The shekel in the fish's mouth.*

[1] *Cf.* His reply to Martha (Lk. x. 41).

lost signet.[1]   And there is a Rabbinical story about one
Joseph, a devout Jew remarkable for his strict observance of
the Sabbath.   He had a wealthy neighbour who was warned
by fortune-tellers that his riches would pass into Joseph's
possession.   Alarmed by the prophecy and determined to
prevent its fulfilment, he sold all his property and, purchas-
ing a pearl with the proceeds, took ship and put to sea.   The
pearl was lost overboard, and was swallowed by a fish.   The
fish was caught, and it chanced that Joseph bought it and
found the pearl in its inside.[2]   " Away and cast a hook into
the sea," said Jesus with some such story in His thoughts ;
" and the first fish that riseth, up with it, and open its mouth,
and thou shalt find a shekel.   That take, and give it to them
for Me and thee."   Of course it was a piece of raillery, nor
was Peter so dull as to miss the Master's meaning.[3]

Teaching   That day, perhaps toward evening,[4] the disciples assembled
in Peter's
house. in Peter's house, and Jesus talked with them, continuing His
instruction.   They had need not only to be apprised of high
mysteries like His Passion and Resurrection, but to be purged
of the old leaven of worldliness and imbued with the spirit of
the Kingdom of Heaven ; and in that season of quiet fellowship and lofty discourse He discovered and reproved the
A lesson in thoughts of their hearts.   First He taught them a lesson in
humility.
humility.   He convicted them of worldly ambition, not
flinging the charge in their faces but making them, as it were,
their own accusers.   On the way from Cæsarea Philippi the
disciples had fallen a little behind and, leaving the Master
Cf. Mk. x. to His own high thoughts, had conversed among them-
32. selves.   It is a pathetic evidence of their slowness of heart
that, with the emphatic announcement of His Betrayal and
Passion still echoing in their ears, they persisted in their

---

[1] Sale's *Koran*, xxxviii, n. *e*.

[2] Wetstein on Lk. xiv. I.   *Cf.* story of Polycrates' ring in Herod iii. 42 and
Augustine's anecdote in *De Civit. Dei*, xxii. 8. § 9.

[3] Against the supposition of an actual miracle observe : (1) Mt. does not tell
what happened at the Lake, and, when the Evangelists record a miracle, they relate
not only the Lord's command but its fulfilment.   *Cf.* Mt. xii. 13=Mk. iii. 5=Lk.
vi. 10.   (2) If this were a miracle, it would be the only one which Jesus wrought
on His own behalf.   (3) It would be a grotesque miracle, meriting the gibes of
Paulus and Strauss.   Even Neander is disconcerted and talks vaguely about "an
unusual blessing of Providence."

[4] ὥρᾳ in Mt. xviii. I, not *hour*, but *season*.   Orig. : ἡμέρᾳ.

carnal expectation, and pictured the splendid future which awaited them when their Master should take unto Him His great power and reign a King in Jerusalem. Such was the prospect which floated before their imagination; and, as they journeyed, they beguiled the way with talk thereof, whispered talk not meant for His ears. Ambition and jealousy are ever nigh to one another, and a dispute had arisen "which of them should be greatest[1] in the Kingdom of Heaven."

Nor had it escaped the Master's notice. He said nothing at the time, but, when they were all seated in the house, He enquired what had been the matter of their dispute. They held their peace for shame, and He proceeded to read them a very effective lesson. " If any one desireth to be first," He said, laying down a spiritual law, " he must be[2] last of all and servant of all "; and then He gave them an illustration. There was a child, doubtless Peter's, in the room,[3] and He brought the little fellow into the midst of the circle, and, taking him in His arms after His fond manner with children, *Cf.* Mk. x made him a living parable. It was an apt illustration. A [16.] child is a stranger to ambition and the selfishness which it breeds. " If," says St Chrysostom,[4] " you show him a queen with a crown, he does not prefer her to his mother albeit clothed in rags, but would choose rather his mother in such attire than the queen in her bravery." And such must all be who would be citizens of the Kingdom of Heaven. " Verily I tell you, unless ye turn about and become as the children, ye shall in no wise enter into the Kingdom of Heaven." The error of the Twelve lay not in their desire to be great in the Kingdom of Heaven but in their ideal of greatness. What makes a man great in the world's sight is superiority to his fellows; but in the Kingdom of Heaven he is the greatest who is the readiest to serve and who has ever a large tenderness for such as need service most—the weak and helpless whom the world despises and tramples under foot.

[1] μείζων a regular Comparat. They were all to be great but one greater than the rest. *Cf.* p. 227. See, however, Moulton's *Gram. of N.T. Gk.* i. p. 78.

[2] ἔσται, Fut. almost equivalent to Imperat. *Cf.* Mt. v. 48; vi. 5.

[3] A medieval tradition (Anast. Bibliothec., Sym. Metaphr.) makes the child St Ignatius. The fancy is founded on the saint's title Θεόφορος, *carried by God*; otherwise Θεοφόρος, *carrying God, i.e.* having Christ within him.

[4] *In Matth.* lxiii.

Such was the spirit of Jesus, and only as they shared it were His disciples true to Him.   " Whosoever," He said, " receiveth a child like this in My name, receiveth Me."

A lesson in
charity.   It was a heavy rebuke.   John plucked up courage to reply.   That phrase of the Master " in My name " reminded him of an incident which had happened recently, perhaps while he and James were prosecuting their apostolic mission in Galilee.   " Teacher," he said, " we saw a man in Thy name casting out dæmons, and we tried to stop him, because he was not following us."   What prompted the reminiscence ? Apparently John desired to change the subject and divert the conversation into another channel ;   and probably he would fain prove to Jesus that, much as they merited His censure, they were active in His service and very jealous for His honour.   Nevertheless it was an ill-advised speech, and earned a fresh rebuke.   Whoever that unknown man may have been,[1] he was doing the Lord's work, and his efforts were owned of God.   Of this, however, the disciples took no account.   It was enough for them that he did not belong to their company, and they regarded him as an unauthorised usurper of their prerogatives.   In fact their grievance was a personal one, as John confesses with naïve simplicity.   They interdicted the man, not because he was dishonouring Jesus, but because, though doing the work of Jesus, he did not belong to their company.   It was really not for the Master's honour but for their own that they were jealous.

" Try not to stop him," said Jesus ; " for there is no one who shall do a mighty work in My name and be able soon to speak evil of Me."   Then He enunciated a far-reaching principle : " One who is not against us, is for us."[2]   What though that man were outside the Apostle-company ?   The

[1] Lightfoot conjectures that he was a disciple of the Baptist and wrought miracles in the name not of *Jesus* but of *the Messiah*.   It was not from contempt but from ignorance that he did not follow Jesus.

[2] There is no real contradiction between this and that other *logion* which Mt. includes in the Lord's refutation of the Pharisaic insinuation that He was in league with Beelzebul : "He that is not with Me is against Me" (Mt. xii. 30)—a condemnation of those who, though recognising His claims, yet, for prudential considerations, adopt an attitude of neutrality.   *Cf.* Solon's enactment in the days when Athens was distracted by civil strife, that such as, when a tumult arose, cautiously held aloof until they saw which faction prevailed, should on the restoration of peace be punished as rebels.   Mk. ix. 41 an interpolated *logion*.   *Cf.* Mt. x. 42.

Kingdom of Heaven had need of more ministers than the
Twelve; and it may be that this was one who had himself
been healed by Jesus and, being forbidden like the Gerasene
demoniac to follow in His train, had returned to his home
and his people and was there glorifying his Saviour. And,
even if he should have joined their fellowship and was holding
aloof for unworthy reasons, he still was the Lord's and was
doing the Lord's work in the Lord's name. This is the sole
and all-sufficient test of discipleship, and John should have
recognised it, even as St Paul did in after days when he
rejoiced that, though some did it " for envy and strife, thinking
to add affliction to his bonds," nevertheless "in every way,
whether in pretence or in truth, Christ was being preached."

(margin: Mk. v. 18-20=Lk. viii. 38-9)

(margin: Phil. i. 15-8.)

Jesus was deeply pained by John's story. In that unknown man He recognised a representative of a class which
always engaged His peculiar sympathy and which He called
" the little ones," meaning not children merely but all that
were weak and needed kindness, help, and patience.[1] It
grieved Him that instead of " receiving that little one in His
name " the disciples had driven him away, and instead of
lending him a helping hand had put a stumbling-block in his
path. The ancient law reckoned it a crime to put a stumbling-
block before the blind or make him wander out of the way;
but in the Lord's sight it was infinitely more heinous to put
obstacles on the way to the Kingdom of Heaven. " Whoever
maketh one of these little ones that believe in Me to stumble,
it is better for him if a heavy mill-stone were put round his
neck and he were flung into the sea."[2] The gravity of the
offence lay in contemning what God accounted infinitely
precious. " See," says Jesus, making felicitous use of the
lovely Jewish fancy that the heirs of salvation were attended
by ministering angels,[3] " see that ye despise not one of these
little ones. For I tell you that their angels in Heaven always

(margin: A lesson in consideration for the weak.)

(margin: Lev. xix. 14; Deut xxvii. 18.)

(margin: Cf. Heb i. 14.)

---

[1] Chrysost. *In Matth.* lix: παιδίον γὰρ ἐνταῦθα τοὺς ἀνθρώπους τοὺς οὕτως
ἀφελεῖς φησὶ καὶ ταπεινοὺς καὶ ἀπερριμμένους παρὰ τοῖς πολλοῖς καὶ εὐκαταφρονήτους.
Cf. Mt. x. 42=Mk. ix. 41 ; Ps. cxix. 141.

[2] *Cf.* Jos. *Ant.* xiv. 15. § 10. The phrase had become proverbial : *cf.* Lightfoot
on Lk. xvii. 2. Mt. xviii. 8-9=Mk. ix. 43-8 an interpolation : *cf.* Mt. v. 29-30.

[3] A development of the post-exilic idea that every nation had its guardian angel.
Cf. Dan. x. 13, 20, 21 ; Deut. xxxii. 8 (LXX) : ὅτε διεμέριζεν ὁ ὕψιστος ἔθνη, ὡς
διέσπειρεν υἱοὺς Ἀδὰμ, ἔστησεν ὅρια ἐθνῶν κατὰ ἀριθμὸν ἀγγέλων Θεοῦ.

behold the face of My Father in Heaven. It is not a thing desired in the presence of your Father in Heaven that one of these little ones should perish." [1]   Since it is thus precious in the sight of God and an object of such jealous solicitude to the denizens of Heaven, what else than a crime is light esteem of a human soul?

A lesson in dealing with offenders.   John's story led to the inculcation of another lesson.   The interdict had been a piece of high-handed tyranny.   It was not thus that Jesus would have His disciples deal with offenders, and He laid down a rule of Church-discipline.   Although our Blessed Lord never ordained a precise system of ecclesiastical government, He contemplated the rise of a sacred community which should abide from generation to generation, His witness in the world, the guardian of His truth, and the repository of His grace.   It was unnecessary that He should legislate for it, since it would have the guidance of His Spirit in the ordering of its affairs, and in the Jewish economy there existed ready to hand an ecclesiastical order of divine appointment.   The Rabbis taught that, "when the Messiah came, He would neither abolish nor change aught of the Mosaic rites, but would advance and raise them all to more splendid form and dignity"; [2] and in a sense the expectation was fulfilled. Jesus accepted the Jewish order.   He styled His new community the *Church,* which is the Septuagint rendering of the Old Testament *Congregation*; [3] and such rules as He laid down were, for the most part, reinforcements, with more august sanctions, of the synagogal order. [4]

Here is an instance.   Jesus desired to preclude the recurrence of such rash and irresponsible tyranny; and what did He do?   There was a Rabbinical precept : " If thy neighbour have done thee an injury, convict him betwixt thyself and him alone. For, if he hearken to thee, thou hast gained him.   But, if he do not hearken to thee, speak to him in the presence of one or two, that they may hear it.   If even so he do not hearken, let

---

[1] Mt. xviii. 12-3 an abrupt interpolation of the parable of the Lost Sheep (Lk. xv. 3-7), *v.* 11 being inserted by some copyist in T. R. to relieve the abruptness.

[2] Lightfoot on 1 Cor. xi. 21.   [3] ἐκκλησία, קָהָל, Ps. xxii. 23, 26.

[4] This refutes the theory that the reported sayings of Jesus about the Church are later rules of ecclesiastical order put unhistorically in His mouth. Schmiedel, *E. B.* art. *Gospels* § 136.

him be worthless in thine eyes." [1] This rule of Jewish Church-discipline Jesus reiterated and reinforced : " If thy brother sin, go, convict him betwixt thee and him alone. If he hearken to thee, thou hast gained thy brother.[2] But, if he do not hearken, take with thyself one or two besides, that ' at the mouth of two witnesses or three every word may be established.' And, if he refuse to hearken to them, speak to the Church. And, if he refuse to hearken even to the Church, let him be to thee as the Gentile and the Tax-gatherer." Nothing is lacking in the Jewish precept to make it word for word identical with our Lord's injunction except "Speak to the Church"; but neither was this lacking in the Jewish practice. When, after due admonition, an offender continued obstinate, he was proclaimed publicly in the Synagogue and branded with infamy.[3] It is therefore no new law which Jesus here lays down. Such was the accustomed order of Jewish discipline. And it was a wise and gracious method in complete accord with the Master's spirit. Even so would He have offenders treated — with patience, with brotherly kindness, with an earnest desire to win them, with a resolute determination to exhaust all means to that end and a great reluctance to own defeat and give them over to impenitence.[4]

Deut. xix. 15.

The lesson elicited a question from Peter. " Lord," he asked, " how often shall my brother sin against me, and I forgive him ? Until seven times?" The Rabbinical rule was that after three offences the duty of forgiving ceased ;[5] but Peter thought to be generous and suggested "seven times," seven being the number of completeness and withal a good round number. "Nay," answered Jesus, "the duty of forgiving is inexhaustible. I tell thee not until seven times but until seventy-seven times. If thy brother repent, forgive him. And, if seven times a day he sin against thee and seven times turn unto thee, saying, ' I repent,' thou shalt forgive him." And then He enforced the requirement by one of the most striking parables that He ever spoke. He told how a king had a slave who had run up a huge debt of over £2,000,000.

The inexhaustible duty of forgiving.

Cf. Gen. iv. 24.

---

[1] Wetstein on Mt. xviii. 17.

[2] Chrysost. *In Matth.* lxi : "He did not say, ' Thou hast sufficient revenge,' but, ' Thou hast gained thy brother '; showing that the loss from the quarrel is common."

[3] Lightfoot on Mt. xviii. 17.

[4] Mt. xviii. 18-20 interpolated *logia.*

[5] *Cf.* Wetstein.

It was an impossible sum, such a debt as man never owed to man ; but for this very reason it is the more fitting to represent our debt to God. When the day of reckoning arrived, he could not discharge it, and the king ordered his goods to be seized and his wife and children sold ; but, moved by the wretch's entreaties and promises, he revoked the sentence. The man went out and, meeting a fellow-slave who owed him a paltry £3, 10s., took him by the throat and demanded payment. The luckless debtor fell at his feet and, in the very language which had just come from his own despairing lips, prayed : " Have patience with me, and I will pay thee." But not a moment's respite would he grant. He hardened his heart and flung the poor creature into prison. The king heard the story, and, summoning the ruffian before him, addressed him with indignant severity : " Thou wicked slave ! All that debt I forgave thee when thou didst entreat me : shouldest not thou also have had mercy on thy fellow-slave as I had mercy on thee ? " And he handed him over to the torturers.[1]

"So," adds Jesus with solemn emphasis, pointing the moral, " My Heavenly Father also will do to you, unless ye forgive every one his brother from your hearts." " *My* Heavenly Father " He says significantly. An unforgiving man is no son of God.

[1] *Cf.* Ecclus. xxxiii. 26 ; Jos. *De Bell. Jud.* i. 30. §§ 2 *sqq.* ; *Ant.* xvi. 8. § 1.

CHAPTER XXXIV

LINGERING IN GALILEE

Lk. x. 1;
Lk. x. 13-5
=Mt. xi.
20-4; Lk.
xii. 13-21;
Lk. xii. 22-
34=Mt. vi.
19-34; Lk.
xiii. 1-17.

"Non potestis, O miseri servi Mammonæ, simul gloriari in cruce Domini nostri Jesu Christi et sperare in pecuniæ thesauris, post aurum abire et probare quam suavis est Dominus."—S. BERNARD. *De Dilig. Deo.*

Mournful
retrospect.

JESUS had returned to Capernaum, but not to remain. "The Lk. ix. 51. days for His being received up were being fulfilled, and He steadfastly set His face to go to Jerusalem." His Galilean ministry was ended, and His heart was stirred within Him as He looked back and reckoned what had been accomplished. It was truly a saddening retrospect. How generous had been His love, how cold the response! How abundant His sowing, how meagre the harvest! He was indeed the hero of the populace; but it was His miracles rather than His message that evoked their enthusiasm and won their applause, and His true-hearted disciples were as a drop of a bucket amid Galilee's teeming thousands. Judged by the world's standard His ministry had ended in utter failure. It is no marvel that, as He surveyed that land where He had loved so well and been so ill requited, a cry of mournful upbraiding broke from His lips: "Woe unto thee, Chorazin![1] woe unto thee, Bethsaida! For, if in Tyre and Sidon had the mighty works been done that were done in you, long ago in sackcloth and ashes they had repented. But I tell you, for Tyre and Sidon it will be more tolerable at the Day of Judgment than for you. And thou Capernaum—shalt thou be 'exalted unto Is. xiv. 13-
5. Heaven? Unto Hades thou shalt be brought down.' For, if in Sodom had the mighty works been done that were done in thee, it had been standing even until to-day. But I tell you that for the land of Sodom it will be more tolerable at the Day of Judgment than for thee."

The Lord's design was to travel slowly to Jerusalem, The
Seventy

---

[1] According to Jer. *De Loc. Hebr.* two miles from Capernaum.

289

passing through Samaria and preaching as He went. In every instance it would be His final appeal, and He desired that it should prove effective. And what did He do, thinking to ensure success? Out of the throng of His converts He chose seventy [1] and, ordaining them as apostles in addition to the Twelve, sent them two by two in advance along the route, "unto every city and place where He Himself was about to come." His primary object was to prepare the people for His advent and incline their hearts to welcome His message; but He desired withal to apprise His disciples of a great fact which their Jewish minds were slow to receive. When He elected the first Apostles, He fixed their number at twelve, signifying, since there were of old twelve tribes in Israel, that their mission was to the Jews. He began with the Jews, but He had a larger purpose. He was the Saviour of the world. The time had come for declaring the world-wide destination of His Gospel, the universality of His salvation. According to Jewish reckoning mankind was composed of seventy nations, and Jesus appointed those seventy apostles to signify that His message was for all the nations of the earth.[2]

The division of the inheritance.

Lk. xii. 1.

That the Seventy might get fairly on their way He lingered awhile, travelling about Galilee, it would seem, and revisiting the scenes of His ministry. He was attended everywhere by an eager multitude, and once after a

---

[1] ἑβδομήκοντα אC, Tisch., W. H. ἑβδομ. δύο BDMR, Chrysost. (*In Joan.* xvii), Jer.

[2] Clem. Rom. *Hom.* xviii. § 4. The calculation was based on Gen. x. Sometimes the nations were reckoned at seventy-two. On the grounds mainly of its slender attestation and its universalistic implication it is alleged that the appointment of the Seventy is a Pauline fiction. But (1) this is not the sole omission of Mt. and Mk. at this point. Their narratives leap from Galilee to Judæa (Mt. xix. 1 = Mk. x. 1), and but for Lk.'s research all that happened in the interval would have been lost. He has rescued from oblivion a series of incidents which, though mostly isolated traditions difficult to arrange in chronological sequence, are exceedingly precious. (2) It is no evidence of invention, but merely an example of the freedom wherewith the evangelic editors handled their material, that Lk. has transferred hither part of the address to the Twelve. *Cf.* Introd. § 8. (3) There were other apostles besides the Twelve in the primitive Church (1 Cor. xv. 7). Who were they if not the Seventy? (4) Though Jesus concealed the universal destination of His Gospel at the outset, He knew it all along and revealed it as His disciples were able to receive it. *Cf.* Mt. xxiv. 14 = Mk. xiii. 10. It is a sheer incredibility that He who has broken down every wall of division betwixt the families of the earth and revealed the universal brotherhood of mankind, should never have guessed whither His labour was tending and whereunto it would grow.

discourse a voice from the throng addressed Him. What ailed the man? Was it concern about the great matter of salvation? Nay, that was not in all his thoughts. "Teacher," he said, "tell my brother to divide the inheritance with me." Jesus was deeply pained. It was not that the man meant any dishonour to Him. On the contrary, he had addressed Him with studious courtesy and after his own fashion had paid Him a compliment. It was the function of the Rulers of the Synagogue to settle such disputes;[1] yet so high was his esteem of Jesus that he desired Him to arbitrate, styling Him withal Teacher or Rabbi. Nevertheless Jesus was pained. Worldly matters lay outside His province, and the request revealed how utterly the man misunderstood Him. It jarred upon Him the more cruelly that His mind was at that crisis occupied with solemn anticipations and His heart was yearning for a response to His last appeal. "Man," He answered half in contempt, half in pity, "who appointed Me a judge or a divider over you?"

Then, turning from him disdainfully, He addressed Himself to the multitude and taught them a lesson from the incident. First, He stated a truth: "Take heed and beware of every sort of grasping greed; because it is not so that, when a man hath abundance, his life is derived from his possessions." Then, by way of illustration, He spoke a parable. He described a husbandman who waxed richer year by year until one plenteous harvest-tide he found himself confronted by a difficulty. So abundant was his harvest that his granaries could not contain it. "What shall I do?" he cried. He thought it over and made up his mind. "This will I do: I will pull down my barns and build greater, and will gather there all my fruits and my goods. And I will say to my soul: 'Soul, thou hast many good things laid up for many years. Take thine ease, eat, drink, make merry.'"

Parable of the Rich Fool.

Cf. Lk. xvi. 3-4.

Jesus does not represent this husbandman as in any respect a wicked man. He was rich, but in that there was no wrong. Nay, it was rather to his credit that he had made so much of his farm. There is no suggestion that he had amassed his wealth unrighteously, by keeping back the hire of his labourers or withholding his corn from the market and

Ja. v. 4; Lev. xix. 13; Deut xxiv. 14-5

Cf. p. 94.

292 THE DAYS OF HIS FLESH

Prov. xi. 26. selling it at famine-price. All that is charged against him is that he had been so taken up with worldly affairs that he had neglected the great concerns; he had left out of his reckoning the supreme facts—God, death, judgment, eternity. He seemed to the world and to himself a shrewd, clever man, yet in God's sight he was a fool, and he discovered at the last that he had made a fool's bargain. He said to his soul: "Soul, thou hast many good things laid up for many years. Take thine ease, eat, drink, make merry." But God said to him: "Thou fool! this night thy soul is required [1] from thee."

Consider the pathos and irony of the situation. He had been a hard-working man all his days, toiling late and early, denying himself ease and pleasure, and hoarding every shekel. He had prospered exceedingly, and, when that difficulty about his granaries arose, he discovered how rich he was. He called a halt and reviewed the situation. It was time, he concluded, that he should forbear his drudgery and enjoy a little hard-earned repose; and he could well afford it. He said to his soul: "Soul, thou hast many good things laid up for many years. Take thine ease, eat, drink, make merry." Observe the significance of his speech. He addressed *his soul*, and what did he say to it? Did he say: "Soul, thou hast long enough given thyself to the world, and it is now time that thou shouldst bethink thee of the things that belong unto thine eternal peace"? It may be that at the outset he had purposed that one day he would rally himself thus and apply his heart unto wisdom; but the years had brought their inevitable change. The canker of worldliness had eaten into his soul; his very faculty for religion had suffered atrophy; and he now conceives naught better for *his soul* than taking ease, eating, drinking, making merry. He seemed a successful man, one who had achieved his ambition; but presently he had a rude awakening. All those years he had been filling the cup of his pleasure till it was full to the brim, and he was just putting it to his lips when an unseen hand dashed it from his grasp. All those years he had been building a palace for his soul, and

---

[1] Literally "they require thy soul." This indefinite use of *they* is common in the Rabbinical writings. *Cf.* Taylor, *Say. of Fath.* ii. § 2, n. 7. It is unnecessary and contrary to the purpose of the parable to understand with Wright (*Synops.*): "The peasants, whom you have irritated beyond endurance by your selfishness, are rising in mass against you."

he was surveying it with pride when a breath out of eternity blew upon it, and it collapsed like a house of cards. He said to his soul : " Soul, thou hast many good things laid up for many years.   Take thine ease, eat, drink, make merry." But God said to him : " Thou fool! this night thy soul is required from thee ; and the things which thou hast prepared—— Ps. xxxix. 6. who shall have them ? "   Ay, who should have them ?   His heirs mayhap would quarrel over them like those two brothers whose dispute about their inheritance had occasioned the parable. A disputed will and a lost soul!   Surely a sorry end.   " So," Jesus concludes, " is he that layeth up treasure for himself and is not rich toward God."

This parable Jesus spoke to the multitude, and by and by, Lesson to the Twelve. according to His wont, when He was alone with the Twelve, He expounded it to them in ampler discourse.   " Be not Cf. Mk. v. 33-4. anxious," He said, " for your life what ye shall eat, nor for your body what ye shall put on."   It was an admonition which was very needful.   The Twelve were exposed to such alarms.   They had left all for Jesus' sake.   They were comrades of One who had nowhere to lay down His head, and oftentimes, when they woke in the morning, they knew not what they should eat or where they should shelter at the close of the day. These were questions which must frequently have pressed upon them : " What shall we eat?   What shall we drink ?   Wherewithal shall we array us ? "   Such was their condition while their Master was with them, and it continued after He was gone.   " Even unto the present hour," says St 1 Cor. iv. 11. Paul, " we both hunger and thirst, and are naked, and are buffeted, and have no certain dwelling-place."

In this immortal discourse Jesus says three things regard- Anxiety about worldly concerns: (1) unreasonable; ing anxiety about worldly matters.   First, it is *unreasonable.* " Look at the fowls of the heaven : they do not sow nor reap nor gather into barns, and your Heavenly Father feedeth them.   Are not ye worth more than they?   Mark the lilies of the field how they grow : they labour not nor spin.   Yet I tell you that not even Solomon in all his glory was arrayed like one of these.[1] And if the grass of the field, which to-day is and to-morrow is flung into an oven, God doth thus dress,

---

[1] Jos. *Ant.* vii. 7. § 3 : Solomon was wont to ride forth in his chariot λευκὴν ἠμφιεσμένος ἐσθῆτα.

how much more you, O ye of little faith?"   Jesus here throws
His disciples back on the providence of God, His wise and
almighty government of the world.   He made everything and
He cares for everything.   Everything, great or small, has a
place and a portion in the Creator's beneficent care.   It is an
Cf. Mt. vii. argument *a fortiori*, such as Jesus loved.   If God cares for
11=Lk. xi. lesser things, the birds, the flowers, nay, the very grass, will
13; Mt. xii. He not much more care for you, His children?   It was indeed
12. a mighty and convincing argument on the lips of Jesus, yet it
lacked its highest sanction while the Cross was still future
and its revelation of the love of God and man's infinite value
in His sight yet undiscovered; and it is stated in the fulness
of its triumphant and unanswerable cogency in St Paul's great
Rom. viii. question: "He that spared not His own Son but for us all
32. delivered Him up, how shall He not also with Him freely
give us all things?"

(2) useless,   Again, anxiety about worldly matters is *useless*.   "Which
of you, though ever so anxious, can add to the length of his
life a single cubit?"[1]   It is unavailing to fret about the
future.   If there be trouble in store for us, it will come, and
our part is to do the present duty and leave the future in
God's hands.   Worry about the future simply embitters the
present and does not avert trouble.   The trouble which one
anticipates, seldom comes.   The morrow may have trouble in
store, but it will not be the trouble which one anticipates.
"Therefore," says Jesus, "be not anxious against the morrow;
for the morrow will be anxious for itself.   Sufficient for the
day is the evil thereof."

(3) irre-   Finally, anxiety about worldly matters is *irreligious*.
ligious. "After all these things the heathen seek."   And it is
nothing strange that they, not knowing the Heavenly Father,
should be anxious about food and raiment; but His children
should be otherwise minded.   "Your Heavenly Father knoweth
that ye have need of all these things."   Anxiety about worldly
matters is in truth practical heathenism, and Jesus bids His
disciples decide which God they will worship.[2]   "No man can

---

[1] ἡλικία is here not "stature" but "age."   A cubit would be an enormous
addition to one's stature, and not ἐλάχιστον (Lk. xii. 26).   With the use of *cubit* as
a measure of time *cf.* a similar use of *handbreadth* in Ps. xxxix. 5; also Herbert, 115:
"My inch of life"; *Reliq. Baxt.* I. i. 16: "This hasty Inch of Time."   *Cf.* Wetstein.
[2] Law, *Ser. Call*, chap. i. : "It is as possible for a man to worship a crocodile,

serve two lords; for either he will hate the one and love the other, or he will hold to one and despise the other. Ye cannot serve God *and* Mammon.[1] Therefore I tell you, be not anxious." This is the sovereign remedy: to believe utterly in the Heavenly Father's love and wisdom and make His Kingdom and His righteousness the supreme concerns, leaving all lesser interests in His hands. "Seek ye first His Kingdom and His righteousness, and all these things shall be added unto you." Here is the secret of a quiet heart. "Nothing," says St Chrysostom,[2] "makes men light-hearted like deliverance from care and anxiety, especially when they may be delivered therefrom without suffering any disadvantage, forasmuch as God is with them and stands them in lieu of all."

Jesus was still lingering in Galilee when tidings of a terrible tragedy reached His ears. A company of Galileans had gone up to Jerusalem and had betaken themselves with their offerings to the Temple. They were evidently a devout and peaceable company, but the Galileans were a brave race, always ready for resistance to the Roman tyranny,[3] and those northern strangers had somehow incurred the suspicion of the procurator Pontius Pilate. He set upon them while they were presenting their sacrifices at the altar, and cut them in pieces, mingling their blood with that of their victims. The tragedy seemed the more appalling inasmuch as another had recently happened. A tower at the Pool of Siloam had fallen and killed eighteen persons, probably sick folk who were seeking health from the medicinal waters.[4]

A massacre of Galileans in the Temple.

Some of that ill-fated band had escaped the swords of Pilate's ruffians and fled northward. They came in hot haste,[5] and told Jesus. It is no wonder that they were horrified. What they had witnessed was in itself sufficiently dreadful, but they

According to the Jews a providential judgment.

---

and yet be a pious man, as to have his affections set upon this world, and yet be a good Christian."

[1] μαμωνᾶς = מָמוֹנָא, Aram. for *riches*. Jer.: "Mammona sermone Syriaco divitiæ nuncupantur." It is a mistaken fancy that there was a Syrian deity called Mammon.

[2] *In Matth.* xxxiii.

[3] Jos. *Ant.* xvii. 9. § 3, 10. § 2; xx. 5. § 3, 6. § 1.

[4] *Cf.* Jerome on Is. viii. 6.

[5] παρῆσαν, not "were present," but "had come," "arrived." *Cf.* Mt. xxvi. 50; John xi. 28.

were Jews and entertained a Jewish notion which greatly increased their dismay. It was a rooted conviction in the Jewish mind that prosperity was a token of God's favour and misfortune, on the contrary, an evidence of His displeasure.

Job iv. 7. If a man suffered, he must needs have sinned. "Who," asked Eliphaz the Temanite, "ever perished, being innocent? or **Cf. Pss.** where were the righteous cut off?" The idea appears **xxxvii. lxxiii.** frequently in the Old Testament and in the Talmud, and in the latter it sometimes takes an amusing form. It is told in one place how four hundred casks of wine belonging to a rich scholar went sour, and his friends, like the friends of Job, saw in his misfortune the hand of Providence and bade him inquire into his conduct and discover wherefore the judgment had overtaken him. "Do you then," he asked, "suspect that I have done something wrong because this evil has befallen me?" They replied: "Can we accuse God of having punished thee without a cause?" "Well, then," he returned, "if any one has heard evil of me, let him say so." "We have heard," they alleged, "that his honour keeps back the share of the vineyard that belongs to his gardener." "Has the gardener," he cried, "left me anything? He steals all I have." They disallowed the plea, and insisted that he had defrauded the gardener, quoting the proverb: "Who steals from a thief is no better than the thief."[1]

According to Jesus a providential warning. Such was the Jewish theory of the providential government of the world, and it was a cruel aggravation of the distress of those Galileans. The sting of the disaster lay in their conviction that it was an evidence of divine displeasure. Their brethren were sinners, and the hand of God had smitten them. Jesus did not hold the theory of His contemporaries, **Cf. Mt. v. 15; John x. 1-3.** and He gave it an emphatic repudiation. He did not indeed deny that the disaster had a providential aspect. It was not, however, a judgment. It was a warning, and the nation would do well to give heed thereto. "Think ye," He said, "that these Galileans were found sinners beyond all the Galileans because they have suffered these things? No, I tell you; but, unless ye repent, ye all shall likewise perish. Or those eighteen upon whom fell the tower at Siloam—think ye that *they* were found debtors beyond all the people that dwelt at

[1] Delitzsch, *Jew. Art. Life*, p. 38.

Jerusalem?   No, I tell you ; but, unless ye repent, ye all shall likewise perish."

This prophecy was fulfilled at the destruction of Jerusalem some forty years later, when the towers of Jerusalem were overthrown by the Roman battering-rams and multitudes of her citizens slaughtered in the Temple, their last refuge.   Is it really so that, had they repented, they would have averted that disaster?   Yes, it is literally true that they perished because they disbelieved Jesus and disregarded His call to repentance. They persisted in their wild dream of a Messiah who should "restore the Kingdom unto Israel."   They were continually hailing some impostor as the national Deliverer.   The land was throbbing with unrest and seething with rebellion ; and at length Rome was provoked beyond endurance, and crushed the turbulent nation as a man might crush a troublesome wasp. It was her false ideal of the Messiahship that destroyed Israel. She rejected the true Messiah when He came " meek and lowly in heart," " not striving nor crying nor causing His voice to be heard in the street."   Had she received Him and obeyed His gracious teaching, she would never have incurred Rome's vengeance.   She would have remained unmolested, and might have continued a nation unto this day.[1]

Israel perished because she rejected Jesus.

In order to drive home to the hearts of His hearers this solemn premonition of imminent doom, Jesus spoke a parable. He told how a proprietor had a fig-tree planted in his vineyard.   It was contrary to the rules of husbandry that trees should grow among vines, but an exception was made in favour of the fig-tree.[2]   It was a reasonable expectation that a tree so advantageously situated should yield a plenteous crop, yet this fig-tree proved barren.   For three years in succession the owner sought in vain for fruit upon it.   It took three years for a fig-tree to attain maturity,[3] and there was cause for complaint when as long again elapsed and still no fruit appeared.   The owner lost patience.   " Behold," he said to the vine-dresser, " for three years I have come seeking fruit on this fig-tree and found none.   Hew it down.   Why should it keep the ground idle ? "   " Sir," interceded the vine-dresser, " let it alone for this year also, until I dig about it

The parable of the barren fig-tree.

---

[1] *Cf.* Jos. *De Bell. Jud.* vi. 5. § 4.   [2] Plin. *H. N.* xvii. 18.
[3] Wetstein.

and scatter dung. And, if it produce fruit next year,— ; but, if not, thou shalt hew it down."

Cf. Is. v. 1-7; Ps. lxxx. 8-16. The fig-tree was Israel, which had been favoured above every other nation. The proprietor was God, and the vine-dresser His mercy which refrained His wrath. The three years were Israel's long day of grace culminating in the Redeemer's advent;[1] and the year of respite was the term which would elapse ere the blow fell. It was a solemn declaration. Israel was on probation. Her doom was hanging in the balance. The axe was uplifted, and God was staying His hand until He should see the issue of the final appeal. It proved unavailing, and the blow fell. Jerusalem was overthrown and Israel scattered over the face of the earth.

Healing of a woman on the Sabbath. Another incident occurred while Jesus lingered in Galilee. The scene seems to have been some obscure place, probably some village where He had preached in the course of His ministry. On the Sabbath Day He attended the synagogue, and saw among the worshippers a woman bent almost double, no doubt with rheumatism. For eighteen years she had been thus afflicted, and Jesus took pity on her. He called her to Him and laid His hands upon her, and immediately her crooked form was straightened. The Ruler of that rural synagogue was a different sort of personage from the astute ecclesiastics of Capernaum and Jerusalem. He was a dull and narrow-minded man, a blind stickler for traditional orthodoxy; and he was vexed[2] at what he quite sincerely deemed a heinous sin. Not liking to upbraid Jesus, He remonstrated with the people. "There are six days," he said, "whereon it is right to work. On them therefore come and be healed, and not on the Sabbath Day."

Complaint of the Ruler of the Synagogue.

The Lord's defence. Jesus hastened to interpose, but, sparing the bigot for his sincerity, assailed not him but his order. "Ye play-actors!"[3] He cried. "Doth not each of you on the Sabbath loose his ox or his ass and lead it away to watering? And this

---

[1] More specific references have been assigned to the three years. (1) God came seeking fruit by Moses, by the Prophets, by Jesus (Theophyl.). (2) The three πολιτεῖαι under the Judges, the Kings, and the High Priests (Euth. Zig.). (3) The three years of Jesus' ministry. These are needless subtleties.

[2] ἀγανακτῶν, "vexed," "irritated"; less strong than "angry," "indignant."

[3] ὑποκριταί אBL, Tisch., W. H., R.V. ὑποκριτά T. R.

woman, being a daughter of Abraham, whom Satan hath
bound,[1] behold, for eighteen years—ought she not to have
been loosed from this bond on the Sabbath Day?" It was a
just and damning charge which He brought against those
Jewish bigots. They were scrupulous where they should
have been lax, and lax where they should have been scrupulous.
They were very punctilious about Sabbath-observance when
it cost them nothing ; but, whenever their worldly interest
was involved, they found a pretext for contravening the Law.
"Thou shalt do no work on the Sabbath," said the Law, and
of course the watering of cattle was work. But the
Rabbis found a way out of the difficulty and salved their
consciences by ridiculous refinements. It was permissible,
they said, not only to lead away a beast to watering on the
Sabbath, but to draw water for it, if only the water were not
brought to the beast and placed before it. The beast must
be led to the water and must drink of its own accord.[2]
When their property was involved, they had no scruple in
setting aside the Law ; yet, when it was a question of
succouring a poor, afflicted fellow-creature, they insisted on its
rigid and literal observance.

[1] The Jewish theory of disease. *Cf.* Lightfoot on Mt. xvii. 15. Jesus here
speaks the language of His time : He does not accept the theory.

[2] *Cf.* Lightfoot and Wetstein.

CHAPTER XXXV

THE JOURNEY THROUGH GALILEE

John vii. 2-
10 ; Lk.
xiii. 22-30
=Mt. vii.
13-4, viii.
11-2 ; Lk.
xiii. 31-3;
xiv.-xv.
(Lk. xvii.
5-6; Mt.
xviii. 12-3);
xvi. 1-12,
14-5, 19-31.

" O Shepherd with the bleeding Feet,
    Good Shepherd with the pleading Voice,
        What seekest Thou from hill to hill ?
Sweet were the valley pastures, sweet
    The sound of flocks that bleat their joys,
        And eat and drink at will.
Is one worth seeking, when Thou hast of Thine
        Ninety and nine ? "—CHRISTINA G. ROSSETTI.

Advice of the Lord's brothers. IT was time for Jesus to bid Galilee farewell and turn His steps toward Jerusalem. The Feast of Tabernacles, which began on the fifteenth of Tisri or October, was at hand, and the train of Galilean pilgrims would presently be setting out for the Holy City. Among the rest the brothers of Jesus were getting ready for the journey, and they came to Him and urged Him to accompany them. They were unbelievers, nay, they had derided His claims ; yet His fame was pleasant to them. It was no small distinction to have the great prophet for their brother. They were apparently somewhat coarse-minded men ; and, sharing the Messianic ideal of their day, they were impatient that He had not come forward as King of Israel, and would fain bring His procrastination to an end. Let Him go up to the approaching feast, and there amid the multitude of worshippers declare Himself and rally all who believed in Him and called themselves His disciples. " Remove hence," said they, " and begone to Judæa, that thy disciples also may behold the works which thou doest. For no one doeth aught in secret and seeketh to be himself known openly. If thou doest these things, manifest thyself unto the world."

His reply. It was an insulting speech. They assumed that Jesus was as eager as themselves for notoriety and had been restrained by cowardice.[1] He answered with indignant contempt.

---

[1] Chrysost. *In Joan.* xlvii : πολλῆς δὲ πονηρίας ἦν τὰ λεγόμενα, ἐνταῦθα γὰρ αὐτῷ

"My time hath not yet come, but your time is always ready. The world cannot hate you, but Me it hateth, because I testify concerning it that its works are evil. Go ye up to the feast. I am not going up to *this* feast, because My time hath not yet been fulfilled." Jesus was indeed going up to the feast, but the feast to which He was going up was not the Feast of Tabernacles : it was the Passover six months later. That was the Lord's goal, the one fixed point in His outlook. He knew that it was the Father's will that He should go up to that great feast and offer Himself, the true Paschal Lamb, a sacrifice for the sin of the world ; but the time had not yet come, and He would not forestall it. Unlike His brothers after the flesh, whose time was always ready, He ever abode God's time, observing the indications of His will and following where it beckoned. It was a light thing for them, who had naught to fear, to go up to Jerusalem ; but for Him, who had incurred the hostility of the rulers, it was very perilous, and He durst not fling away His life until His time had come.

There were still six months ere the Feast of the Passover, His departure. yet He must forthwith set His face toward Jerusalem. His purpose was to make a gradual progress southward, preaching as He went, and to reach the sacred Capital in time for the great *dénouement*. When His brothers had left Him and set out upon their journey, He also took His departure, " not openly but in secret," not with a pilgrim throng but with the escort of His twelve disciples. Betwixt Capernaum and the frontier of Samaria lay a long expanse of Galilean territory, thick-set with towns and villages ; and, as He passed from place to place, He preached to the folk. Surely there would be a great tenderness in His heart and an exceeding urgency in His tones. It was the last appeal that they would hear from His lips, and never more would they see His face until that awful Day when He shall come in His glory and sit upon His great white throne to judge the quick and the dead.

Somewhere in the course of His journey through Galilee A theological quibble. an incident occurred. He had preached; His theme had been salvation, and He had pressed His claims upon His hearers and

καὶ δειλίαν καὶ φιλοδοξίαν ὀνειδίζουσι. He thinks that they were in league with the rulers and designed out of jealousy to betray Him to them.

challenged them to decision. There was one in His audience who was deeply impressed yet would fain evade the issue. And what did he do? He acted precisely in the manner of the woman of Samaria. When Jesus probed her conscience, she essayed to raise a side-issue. She dragged in a theological question, the old controversy betwixt the Jews and the Samaritans. "Sir," she said, "I perceive that thou art a prophet. Our fathers in yonder mountain worshipped; and ye say that in Jerusalem is the place where it is necessary to worship." This man resorted to the self-same device. "Lord," he asked, " are they few that are being saved?" It was one of the vexed questions among the theologians of that day. Some held that every Israelite would have " a portion in the world to come," while others held a less hopeful opinion. One Rabbi argued that, as only two of all that came out of Egypt entered the Promised Land, so would it be in the days of the Messiah.[1] The question was an attempt to shirk the real issue. The man had been impressed, but he shrank from the great surrender, and, thinking to create a diversion, he essayed to raise that unprofitable controversy.

John iv. 19-20

The Lord's reply. / It was a palpable evasion, and Jesus brushed it aside and set the real issue before His hearers. " The question is not whether the saved be few or many, but whether you be of the number. Strive to enter through the narrow door. Enter through the narrow gate; because broad and spacious is the way that leadeth to destruction, and many are they that enter through it; because narrow is the gate and straightened the way that leadeth to life, and few are they that find it." The significance of the reply lies in this, that Jesus here quotes an idea whereof the ancient moralists had made great use and which had passed into a common-place, almost a proverb. It is as ancient as the poet Hesiod;[2] and it appears in Kebes' quaint allegory *The Tablet*, a sort of Greek *Pilgrim's Progress*, purporting to be an account of a pictorial tablet which hung in the temple of Kronos and emblematically depicted the course of human life. Kebes saw it and had it explained to him by an old man who kept the temple.

The Narrow gate and the Two Ways.

---

[1] Lightfoot on Lk. xiii. 23.

[2] *O. et D*. 287-92. Pythagoras (B.C. 570-504) elaborated it. *Cf.* Conington on Pers. iii. 56-7.

"'What is the way that leads to the true Instruction?' said I.

"'You see above,' said he, 'yonder place where no one dwells, but it seems to be desert?'

"'I do.'

"'And a little door, and a way before the door, which is not much thronged, but very few go there; so impassable does the way seem, so rough and rocky?'

"'Yes, indeed,' said I.

"'And there seems to be a lofty mound and a very steep ascent with deep precipices on this side and on that?'

"'I see it.'

"'This, then, is the way,' said he, 'that leads to the true Instruction.'"[1]

The allegory of the Two Ways had passed into a sort of proverb, and Jesus here applies it to the great business of salvation, throwing His hearers back on the broad principles of life. It was recognised that, if a man would attain to Virtue or Wisdom, he must face a steep and toilsome way, and climb it with resolute heart. "All noble things," said the proverb, "are difficult"; and salvation, being the noblest of all, is the most difficult. It can be attained only by resolute endeavour, and every man must face the ordeal for himself. It is folly to stand gazing at the height and wondering whether few or many will win it. "There is the narrow gate!" cries Jesus; "yonder is the rugged path! Enter and climb." *The Lord use of the allegory.*

He was speaking to Jews and He gave a Jewish turn to His exhortation, passing abruptly from the image of the Two Ways to another which the Rabbis loved and which Jesus frequently employed in those later days—the image of the great Feast in the Messianic Kingdom. "When once the Master of the House hath arisen and shut the door, and ye have begun to stand outsde and to knock at the door, saying: 'Lord, open to us!' and He shall answer and say to you: 'I know you not whence ye are'; then[2] shall ye begin to say: *The Feast in the Messianic Kingdom. Cf. Lk. xiv. 15; Lk. xiv. 16-24; xvi. 23; Mt. xxii. 1-14; xxv. 1-13; Mt. xxvi. 29=Mk xiv. 25.*

---

[1] Ceb. *Tab.* § 15.

[2] Tisch. makes καὶ ἀποκριθεὶς ἐρεῖ the apodosis. W. H. connect ἀφ'οὗ κ.τ.λ., with the preceding verse and begin a new sentence with τότε ἄρξεσθε. This involves a very abrupt change of metaphor. Perhaps *vv.* 25-30 are an interpolation. *Cf.* Mt. vii. 22-3; viii. 11-2.

'We ate in Thy presence and drank, and in our streets Thou didst teach.' And He shall say : ' I tell you, I know you not whence ye are. Withdraw from Me, all ye workers of unrighteousness ! ' There shall be the weeping and the gnashing of teeth, when ye shall see Abraham and Isaac and Jacob and all the Prophets in the Kingdom of God, while ye are flung outside. And they shall come from east and west and north and south and take their places at the feast in the Kingdom of God. And, behold, there are last who shall be first, and there are first who shall be last." These were terrible words for Jewish ears to hear. Jesus had already announced the doom of impenitent Israel, but here He prophesies a further dispensation wherein, when it was executed, even St Paul Rom. xi. could scarce acquiesce—the ingathering of the Gentiles and their investiture with Israel's forfeited privileges.

A warning. As He travelled southward, Jesus would find Himself in the vicinity of Tiberias, the capital of the tetrarch Herod Antipas, and He was approached by a company of Pharisees. They brought Him a warning. The tetrarch had taken alarm at the popularity of Jesus, and, apprehending a tumult, had re-
Mt. xvii. 12 solved, probably at the instigation of the Jewish rulers who
= Mk. ix.
13. had hounded him on to the arrest of John the Baptist, to dissipate the enthusiasm of the populace by removing their hero. Those Pharisees had discovered his sanguinary purpose. They were not indeed believers, yet they were friendly to Jesus and did not wish to see Him fall a victim to the tetrarch's cruelty. They came to Him and bade Him hasten on His way till He was across the Galilean frontier and beyond the tyrant's jurisdiction. " Begone," they cried, " and take thy way hence ; for Herod is wishing to kill thee." [1]

The Lord's Jesus met their alarm with calm contempt. He bade
defiance. them carry a message of defiance to the wily tyrant. " Go

---

[1] So Hausrath. The prevailing interpretation, ancient and modern, is that their friendship was feigned. They were in league with Antipas, who wished by "this masterpiece of artful, bloodless, pacific stratagem to get Jesus out of the way" (Keim). They thought to " frighten Him from Galilee into Judæa, where He would be more in the power of the Sanhedrin " (Eaton in Hastings' *D. B.*, art. *Pharisees*). Wetstein aptly compares Am. vii. 10 ; Neh. vi. 10 ; Ecclus. xxxvii. 7-8. Had they been traitors, however, Jesus would have hurled His scorn at them and not at Antipas.

your way, and say to this fox : [1] 'Behold, I cast out dæmons and accomplish healings to-day and to-morrow, and on the third day I am perfected.'"   "To-day and to-morrow" was a *Cf.* 1 Sam. Hebrew phrase for "a little longer." [2] A little longer must Jesus xx. 12. ply His ministry in Galilee, and He would continue until the appointed end, fearless of threats. "Nevertheless," He adds with mournful irony, "it is necessary that to-day and to-morrow and the next day I should go My way, because it is not possible that a prophet should perish outside of Jerusalem." His visitors had counselled Him to depart ; and depart He would, but not for fear of Herod. In Jerusalem had all the prophets been slain, and there it was fitting that the greatest of the prophets and their Lord should die.[3]

The intervention of those friendly Pharisees is a pleasant Friendly incident. They belonged to an order which bears a very Pharisees evil reputation. Their name is a by-word for hypocrisy, and they were our Lord's bitter and unscrupulous adversaries. Nevertheless there were good men among the Pharisees. They were Israel's religious teachers, and, though the majority were narrow-minded and hypocritical, there were noble exceptions. Though it does not appear that a single Pharisee attached himself to Jesus during His ministry, there were representatives of the party in the Apostolic Church. Nicodemus Acts xv. 5. and Joseph of Arimathæa were both Pharisees, and it may be that they were not the only members of their order who, *Cf.* John though afraid to confess Him, were disciples at heart. The vii. 48. Jewish Evangelists St Matthew and St Mark saw naught else in the hated order than black malignity, but the kindly eye of the Gentile St Luke discovered even there some soul of goodness, and he has rescued from oblivion other instances besides this which prove that there were Pharisees who were well disposed to Jesus. Thrice he tells of Jesus being bidden vii. 36-50; to the houses and tables of Pharisees ; and, though in each xi. 37-8; xiv. 1-24. instance the host was a proud personage and showed scant courtesy to the man of the people whom he had deigned to distinguish by an invitation to his board, yet the mere invitation evinced a measure of goodwill.

[1] τῇ ἀλώπεκι ταύτῃ, fem: (*cf.* Mt. viii. 20=Lk. ix. 58), as in English "the cow:" So ἡ κύων. *Cf.* the proverb : καθάπερ τὴν ἐν τῇ φάτνῃ κύνα (Luc. *Tim.* § 14).
[2] *Cf.* Wetstein:
[3] On the position of Lk. xiii. 34-5=Mt. xxiii. 37-9 *cf.* Introd. § 15.

A Sabbath-
feast in a
Pharisee's
house.

One of these instances of friendship on the part of Pharisees occurred in the course of that last journey through Galilee. He got an invitation to a Sabbath entertainment in the house of a leading Pharisee. Curiously enough the Sabbath was the great day for social gatherings ; and, though the viands were cooked on the previous day and served cold, it was deemed fitting that they should be specially sumptuous.[1] Indeed St Augustine alleges that, down to his own time, the Jews made the Sabbath a day of unseemly revelry.[2] The host had invited a company of Lawyers and Pharisees to meet Jesus, and they came all agog with curiosity. Nor were they disappointed in their anticipation of witnessing some-

Healing of
a man with
dropsy.
Lk. vii. 37-
8.

thing unusual. There was a man in the neighbourhood who suffered from dropsy, and, like Mary of Magdala, he betook himself to the Pharisee's house and, entering the dining-hall, planted himself with mute appeal before Jesus, hoping that He would observe him and take pity on him. And so it proved. " Is it right," asked Jesus, addressing the company, " to heal on the Sabbath or not ? " The Rabbinical law ordained that only if the patient's life were in danger, was it allowable to apply remedies on the Sabbath ;[3] and they would naturally have replied that, since there was no immediate likelihood of a fatal issue, the man should wait until the morrow for healing. But they knew how Jesus had already handled the question, and they kept silence. He took hold of the sufferer, healed him, and sent him away ; and then He justified His action after His wonted manner by an appeal to the instinct of humanity. " Which of you," He asked, " if his son [4] or his ox fall into a well, will not immediately draw him up on the Sabbath Day ? " The argument was apt and cogent. There was an obvious analogy between dropsy and submergence in a well,[5] and the law permitted the rescue of a beast, much more a human being, from the latter predicament.

The Lord's
table-talk.

It proves the friendliness of those Pharisees that they raised no protest, unlike their colleagues at Capernaum who, when Jesus met them with a precisely similar argument,

---

[1] Cf. Wetstein and Lightfoot.   [2] De Cons. Ev. ii. § 151.   [3] Cf. p. 135.

[4] υἱός is the best attested reading. ὄνος אKL, Vulg., T. R. ; πρόβατον D.

[5] So Jesus compares the loosing of the rheumatic woman from her bond to the loosing of a beast from a stall. Lk. xiii. 15-6.

"went out and took counsel against Him, how they might Mt. xii. 14.
destroy Him." The entertainment went on, and Jesus plied
the company with kindly yet incisive raillery. The place of The chief
honour at a feast was next the host, and there had been some Cf. Mt.
contending for the coveted distinction. The scene had xxiii. 6.
amused Jesus, and He now alludes to it good-humouredly,
ridiculing the self-aggrandisement which courts humiliation.
"If thou covetest honour," He says, quoting a cynical maxim Prov. xxv.
of the wise man of old, "feign humility. Take the lowest 6-7.
place at the feast, and thine host will say to thee: 'Friend,
come up higher.' Then shalt thou have glory in the presence
of thy fellow-guests." For the host also He had a counsel.
"When thou makest a feast, call not thy friends nor thy Whom to
brethren nor thy kinsfolk nor thy rich neighbours, lest haply invite.
they on their part invite thee in return, and a requital be
made thee. But invite poor folk, maimed, lame, blind; and
blessed shalt thou be, because they have nothing to requite
thee with; and it shall be requited thee at the resurrection of
the righteous." It was a playful satire on the ways of
fashionable society with its round of complimentary enter-
tainments which have no friendship in them, and which
squander on pride and luxury what, were it bestowed on the
poor, would profit the recipient and win for the giver the
blessing of God.

With such trenchant table-talk did Jesus enliven the Our Lord's
banquet. His satire pierced home, and one of the company, dislike of
thinking to pass it off, caught at the phrase "the resurrection talk."
of the righteous" and ejaculated sententiously: "Blessed is
he who shall eat bread in the Kingdom of God!" It was
a mere religious common-place, and hardly anything was
more distasteful to Jesus than pious talk which was mere
breath. On one occasion the Apostles, conscious perhaps of
some remissness, said to Him: "Increase our faith"; and He
answered, quoting an Oriental proverb: "If ye have faith as Cf. Mt.
a grain of mustard seed, ye would say to this sycamine tree: xiii. 31-2=
'Be uprooted and be planted in the sea,' and it would obey 2=Lk. xiii.
you."[1] It was a stern and contemptuous rebuke. Their 19.
lack was not faith but devotion. Let them gird themselves
to their task, and God would not fail them. Jesus could not

[1] Lk. xvii. 5-6: an isolated fragment of the Evangelic Tradition.

endure such talk, and He answered that sententious ejacula-
tion at the Pharisee's table with a scathing parable. He told
how a man made a great supper and invited a large company.
When all was ready, he sent them word, according to Oriental
custom,[1] but "they all with one consent began to make
excuse." One had bought a field, and must go and see it;
another had bought five pairs of oxen, and must go and try
Cf. Deut. them; a third had married a wife, and therefore he could not
xxiv. 5. come.[2] The excuses, at all events the first and second, were
palpable pretexts. The men simply did not wish to come,
and each pled the first excuse that occurred to him. Their
language was exceedingly polite, but that was no extenuation,
it was rather an aggravation, of the insolence of their behaviour. What worth is there in lip-homage? "Why,"
Lk. vi. 46. asked Jesus on another occasion, "do ye call Me 'Lord!
Lord!' and do not the things which I say?"

The master of the house was indignant when he learned
how his hospitality had been scorned. He resolved that the
entertainment should go forward, but he would have guests of
another sort. He sent abroad to the streets and alleys of the
city, and brought in the poor and maimed and blind and lame
to the banquet. Still there was room, and He commanded:
"Go forth to the roads and hedges, and constrain them to
come in, that my house may be filled." Is there not a stroke
of humour here? The host was resolved that his preparations
should not be wasted, and he took a mischievous pleasure in
crowding his festal-chamber with that motley assemblage; as
it were, saying to the men who had insulted him: "I need
you not, and I count these outcasts worthier than you." The
significance of this latter part of the parable is very plain.
It is another premonition of the impending judgment. The
denizens of street and alley were Israel's outcasts, the tax-
gathers and sinners who made so ready a response to Jesus;
and those outside the city, who wandered on the highways and
sheltered beneath the hedges—who were they but the Gentiles?

---

[1] *Cf.* Thomson, *Land and Book*, chap. ix: "If a sheikh beg, or emeer invites,
he always sends a servant to call you at a proper time.' This servant often repeats
the very formula mentioned in Luke xiv. 17: 'Come, for the supper is ready.'"

[2] A humorous touch. *Cf. Kidd.* 29. 2: "Dicit Samuel, 'Traditio est ut ducat
quis uxorem et postea applicet se ad discendam Legem.' At R. Jochanan dicit,
'Non molâ collo ejus appensâ addicet se ad studium Legis.'" 1 Cor. vii. 32-3.

Jesus went on His way, and, as He went, He was fol- The terms of disciple-ship.
lowed by great crowds. What was their thought? He
was going up to Jerusalem, and, sure that He was going
thither to declare Himself King of Israel, they designed to
follow Him all the way and share His triumph. Had they
known what was really His destination—not a throne in
Jerusalem but a cross on Calvary, their enthusiasm would
have evaporated and their applause ceased. Suddenly Jesus
wheeled round and, facing the eager throng, told them the
terms of discipleship. " If any one cometh unto Me and
hateth not his father and mother and wife and children and
brothers and sisters, yea, moreover, his own life, he cannot be
My disciple. Whoever doth not carry his cross and come
after Me, cannot be My disciple." Ruthless surrender of all
that is dearest to the human heart when it conflicts with
loyalty to the Master, and resolute endurance for His sake of
the utmost suffering and ignominy that the world can inflict :
such are the terms of discipleship. Were they prepared for
an ordeal like that ? Had they counted the cost ? Let them
do so ere they went further. " Which of you, wishing to
build a tower,[1] doth not first sit down and count the cost ? lest *Cf.* Mt.
haply, when he has laid the foundation and is not able to ^xxi. 33.^
finish it, all that behold should begin to mock at him, saying :
' This man began to build and was not able to finish !' Or
what king, setting out to engage with another king in battle,
will not first sit down and consider whether he is able with
ten thousand to meet one that is coming against him with
twenty thousand ? And, if he be not, while the other is still
at a distance, he sendeth an embassy and asketh terms of
peace. Even so, then, everyone of you who does not bid
farewell to all his possessions, cannot be My disciple." Such
are the terms of discipleship. " If ye would follow Me," says
Jesus, " first count the cost, and do not, in a fit of inconsiderate
enthusiasm, embark upon an enterprise which you will never
have the courage to carry through."

It would seem that this stern declaration cooled the ardour Eating with tax-gatherers and sinners.
of the multitude. They fell back. Jesus, however, was not

[1] Wright, *Palmyra and Zenobia*, pp. 332-4 : " To-day in Syria, every vineyard
and garden has its tower. . . . In the neighbourhood of Damascus men sit in these
mantaras all day, watching a few roods of melon, or a field of maize, or a vineyard,
and they sleep in them during the night."

left alone. The tax-gatherers and sinners of the neighbour-hood who had not dared to mingle with the crowd, saw their opportunity and approached Him. One of them apparently offered Him hospitality ; and Jesus accepted the invitation and took His place at table with a company of outcasts. It was a repetition of the scene in Levi's house at Capernaum ; and now as then the Pharisees were horrified and cried out against the scandal : " This man receiveth sinners and eateth with them ! "

Mt. ix. 9-13
=Mk. ii.
13-7=Lk.
v. 27-32.

In answer to their complaint Jesus spoke three parables—the Lost Sheep, the Lost Drachma, and the Lost Son—which constitute His supreme defence of His attitude toward sinners. He advanced a great claim : Though condemned by the Pharisees, His attitude was approved in Heaven. Even as men sorrow for what they lose and rejoice when they find it, so God sorrows for lost sinners and rejoices at their recovery.

The Lord's defence.

" What man of you, having a hundred sheep and having lost one of them, doth not leave the ninety and nine in the pasture and hie him to the mountains and search for the wanderer until he find it ? And, when he hath found it, he layeth it on his shoulders, rejoicing. And on getting home he calleth together his friends and his neighbours, saying to them : ' Rejoice with me, because I have found my lost sheep.' I tell you that even thus there shall be joy in Heaven over a single repenting sinner rather than over ninety-nine righteous men who have no need of repentance." [2] It was not so much the value of the sheep as the misery of the poor lost creature that excited the shepherd's solicitude ; and Jesus here declares that the sinner's misery moves compassion in the heart of God.

The Lost Sheep.

Mt. xviii. 12.

" Or what woman, having ten *drachmæ*, if she lose one, doth not light a lamp and sweep the house and search diligently until she find it. And, when she hath found it, she calleth together her friends and neighbours, saying : ' Rejoice

The Lost Drachma.

---

[1] The Greek *drachma* was about equivalent to the Roman *denarius*, *i.e.* 8½d. There were four *drachmæ* in a *shekel* or *stater*. *Cf.* Mt. xvii. 24-7, where the δίδραχμον or double *drachma* is the *half-shekel* of the Temple-tax.

[2] Here, as in Mt. ix. 12-3, Jesus ironically takes the Pharisees at their own valuation. They were "perfectly righteous" according to the Rabbinical distinction between *justos tantum* and *justos perfecte*. One of the latter was the young ruler (Mt. xix. 20). *Cf.* Lightfoot.

with me, because I have found the *drachma* which I lost.'
Even thus, I tell you, there ariseth joy in the presence of the
angels of God over a single repenting sinner." It was the
value of her *drachma*, which she could ill afford out of her scanty
store, that moved the peasant woman ; and Jesus here declares
that a sinner is precious in God's sight and his loss is a loss to God.

In the third parable He makes a still more amazing de- The Lost
claration. A sinner is not merely a lost possession, he is a lost Son.
child of God ; and the Father's heart yearns for his recovery,
A man, says Jesus, had two sons. It was common for a father Ecclus.
to distribute his inheritance in his life-time ; and the younger xxxiii. 19-23.
of those two sons requested his portion, which, according to the Deut. xxi.
Law, amounted to half of the first-born's. When he got it, he 17.
went away to a far country and squandered it in prodigality.
He was reduced to want, and, to aggravate his distress, the
country was visited by a severe famine. To save himself
from starvation he hired himself out as a swine-herd, the
most degraded of occupations in Jewish eyes.[1] He was
fain to fill his belly with the swine's bean-pods ; and in
his wretchedness he remembered his father's house where the
very hirelings had bread enough and to spare. " I will arise,"
he said, "and go to my father, and will say to him : ' Father,
I have sinned against Heaven and in thy sight ; no more am
I worthy to be called thy son : make me as one of thy
hirelings.' " It was truly a base speech, revealing the prodigal's
degradation. Had things gone well with him, he would have
felt never a qualm ; and, when he came to himself, it was not
his sin but his misery that troubled him. He did not say :
" I have acted shamefully. I have broken my father's heart.
I am a vile, undeserving wretch." All that he desired was
the bread of his father's house. " How many hirelings of my
father have bread enough and to spare, and I am perishing
here with famine ! I will arise and go to my father." Selfish
in his sin, he was selfish in his repentance. In truth he did
not repent at all until he was in his father's embrace, and then
his heart melted. And is not this the lesson that Jesus here
teaches, that it matters not what brings a sinner to God ? It
is enough that he should perceive his need and lift up his eyes
to Heaven Once he has returned to the Father's House and

[1] *Cf.* Lightfoot on Mt. viii. 30.

discovered the Father's love, he will understand what sin means and will sorrow over it with a godly sorrow.

His welcome home.

Base though his motive may have been, the prodigal arose and went homeward. His father had all the while been mourning in desolation of heart and ever hoping for the wanderer's return. One glad day he descried him afar off. He ran to meet him and clasped him, ragged and filthy, in his arms. "Father," said the penitent, "I have sinned against Heaven and in thy sight ; no more am I worthy to be called thy son——." He got no further. Ere he could make his petition for a hireling's place, his father was shouting to the slaves : "Bring forth a robe, the best in the house,[1] and put it on him, and give him a ring on his hand and shoes on his feet ; and bring the fatted calf, slay it, and let us eat and make merry ; forasmuch as this my son was dead and is alive again, was lost and is found."

The elder son.

The villain of the story is not the prodigal but his elder brother. He was out in the field when the wanderer returned, and, as he approached the house, he heard the din of merry-making and enquired of a servant what it meant. When he was informed, he was indignant and would not enter, though his father came out and besought him. "Behold," cried the churl, "all these years have I been a slave to thee, and I never transgressed a command of thine! And to me thou never gavest a kid that I might make merry with my friends ; but, when this thy son that devoured thy living with harlots came, thou didst slay for him the fatted calf." He was no brother. He disowned the prodigal : "this *thy son*." And he was no son. He had the spirit of a bondsman and regarded his father as a hard taskmaster. Of course he

Gal. v. 1.

represented the Pharisees, who made religion "a yoke of bondage," and would fain have thrust away the tax-gatherers and sinners and made them outcasts from the Father's love. Yet even the Pharisees, Jesus would have it understood, were in God's sight objects rather of pity than of wrath. They were still His sons, though destitute of the filial spirit ; even as the outcasts whom they contemned, were still their brethren. "Child, thou art ever with me, and all that is mine is thine.

[1] στολὴν τὴν πρώτην, perhaps "his former robe," the robe which he had worn in former days. *Cf.* Lightfoot on Lk. xx. 46 ; Aug. *Quæst. Ev.* ii. 33 : "Stola prima est dignitas quam perdidit Adam."

It behoved us to make merry and rejoice, forasmuch as this *thy brother* was dead and is alive, was lost and is found." There was room in the heart of Jesus not only for sinners but for Pharisees. He looked on both with kind and pitiful eyes, and would fain have gathered both into the Father's House.

He followed up His apology for befriending sinners with a parabolic discourse on the use of riches. It was addressed to His disciples—not the Twelve who, being poor men, had no need to be instructed in the use of riches, but all who had received His message and owned Him as their Lord,[1] especially the tax-gatherers whose hospitality, to the indignation of the Pharisees, He had accepted. These were rich men, and it was appropriate that He should discourse to them on this theme. Lesson on the use of riches.

There was, said He, a certain rich man. In true Oriental fashion he allowed his factor absolute control of his estate. It was the story of Potiphar and Joseph over again : " he made him overseer over his house, and all that he had he put into his hand. And he knew not aught that was with him, save the bread which he did eat." The factor abused his trust, and his lord, hearing a report of his malfeasance, took him to task. " What is this that I hear of thee ? Render the account of thy factorship ; for thou canst not any longer be factor." The luckless wight, thus thrown upon the world, debated what he should do. " To dig I have not strength ; to beg I am ashamed." A happy inspiration came to him. " I know what I will do ! " he cried. It is the Oriental fashion for a proprietor to farm out his estate ; and whatever, over and above the proprietor's due, the agent may be able to extort from the tenantry, he appropriates. It is an evil system, inevitably involving oppression unless the agent be a righteous man ; and this factor had been ruthless. Here lay his opportunity. Many of the tenants were overwhelmed with debt, and he summoned them before him. " How much owest thou to my lord ? " he asked the first, keeping up the fiction that the debt was due to the proprietor and not to himself. " A hundred *baths*[2] of oil," was the answer ; and he bade the man enter fifty in his account. " And thou—how much dost thou The parable of the Shrewd Factor. Gen. xxxix. 4, 6. Cf. Lk. xii. 17-8.

---

[1] " The Apostles " in xvii. 5 are contrasted with " the disciples " in xvi. 1.

[2] A *bath* was about 8¼ gallons ; a *cor* about 10 bushels.

owe ? " he asked another. " A hundred *cors* of wheat," was the reply ; and he bade the man put down eighty.

It was a clever trick. The tenants would suppose that the factor had used his influence with the lord and procured them those liberal abatements ; and his hope was that they would remember the good turn which he had done them, and, when they learned that he was thrown out of his office, would come to his assistance and give him shelter under their roofs. He was a shrewd rogue. He knew his men and offered each his price, abating here fifty per cent., there twenty. The transaction came to the lord's knowledge, and it greatly amused him. He could afford to be amused. The manipulation cost him nothing, since the abatements were made not on his rental but on the factor's extortion. He laughed and complimented the rascal on his shrewdness.[1]

Its applica-
tion.
Cf. 2 Cor.
v. 1.

"Learn a lesson," says Jesus, "of this clever knave. Make a wise use of your money. Spend it in charity ;[2] and, when you leave this world and reach the gate of Heaven, you will be greeted there by those whom ye have succoured here. Make yourselves friends with the mammon of un-

Cf. Ps. xv.
1; 2 Cor.
v. 1.

righteousness, that, when it fails, they may welcome you into the Eternal Tents."

"The
mammon
of unright-
eousness."

What is the meaning of that phrase "the mammon of un-righteousness ? " If it meant " money unrighteously acquired," it might be a stinging epithet for the ill-gotten gains of the tax-gatherers ; but there were others than tax-gatherers in the audience, and, moreover, when ill-gotten gains are devoted to charity, it is not meritorious beneficence but simple reparation. Our Lord furnishes the interpretation of the phrase when

xvi. 11.

He presently contrasts " the unrighteous mammon "[3] and " the true." It is a Hebrew phrase. When the Psalmist

Ps. xxiii. 3.

speaks of " the paths of righteousness," he means paths which lead to the desired goal in contrast to " delusive tracks which lead nowhere ; "[4] and even so, when Jesus speaks of " the

---

[1] ὁ κύριος in *v*. 8 is the steward's master ; *cf*. *vv*. 3, 5. According to some (Erasm., Luth.) it is Jesus. But His comment begins at *v*. 9 : καὶ ἐγὼ ὑμῖν λέγω. ὅτι οἱ υἱοί, κ.τ.λ., a parenthetical explanation of φρονίμως ἐποίησεν.

[2] *Cf*. the Rabbinical saying : " Alms is the salt of mammon."

[3] μαμωνᾶ τῆς ἀδικίας and τὸ ἄδικον μαμωνᾶ are identical. τῆς ἀδικίας a descriptive Gen. ; *cf*. Lk. xviii. 6 ; 2 Thess. ii. 3.

[4] Cheyne.

mammon of unrighteousness," He means earthly riches which delude and disappoint. The phrase recalls that other of His, "the deceit of riches," and St Paul's "the uncertainty of riches." It is a prudent speculation to purchase with earth's failing treasure a treasure unfailing in the heavens.

Mt. xiii. 22; 1 Tim. vi. 17.
Lk. xvi. 9; xii. 33.

The Fathers loved to quote a saying of Jesus which is reported by none of the Evangelists : " Show yourselves approved bankers." [1] And does it not find here a very appropriate setting, at once illumining the aphorisms wherewith the parable closes, and borrowing illumination from them ? " Show yourselves approved bankers.   He that is faithful in a very little, in much also is faithful ; and he that in a very little is unrighteous, in much also is unrighteous. If therefore in the unrighteous mammon ye proved not faithful, the true mammon who will entrust to you ? And if in what is another's ye proved not faithful, what is your own who will give you ? " It is indeed thus that God deals with men. There is a beautiful Rabbinical story, that, when Moses was tending Jethro's flocks in Midian, a kid went astray. He sought it and found it drinking at a spring. " Thou art weary," he said, and lifted it on his shoulders and carried it home. And God said to him : " Since thou hast had pity for a man's beast, thou shalt be the shepherd of Israel, My flock." [2]

"Show yourselves approved bankers."

Jesus addressed this discourse to His disciples ; but there were Pharisees listening, and it was very unpalatable to them. Love of money was a characteristic of their order, and they reckoned their prosperity a mark of God's special favour. The Lord's discourse touched them to the quick, and they sneered. [3] He marked the curling of their lips. " Ye are they," He cried, "that make themselves out righteous in the sight of men ; but God readeth your hearts ; forasmuch as what is high among men is an abomination in the sight of God." [4] And then He spoke a parable.   " There was," He says, " a certain rich man " ; and with a few graphic touches He depicts, in St Chrysostom's phrase, " his life baptised with luxury ": his robe of purple and his under-

The parable of the Rich Man and Lazarus. Cf. Mk. xii. 40=Lk. xx. 47.

---

[1] Cf. Introd. § 2.

[2] Wetstein on Lk. xv. 5.

[3] ἐκμυκτηρίζειν, naso suspendere adunco.

[4] Lk. xvi. 16-8 interpolated logia. Cf. Mt. xi. 13 ; v. 18, 32.

clothing of fine linen,[1] his sumptuous and glittering table.[2]
And there was a certain poor man named Lazarus.   The
name, which is a shortened form of Eleazar, meant " God
hath helped," and Jesus chose it to characterise the man.[3]
The godly Lazarus was not only poor but diseased, and he
lay, a mass of loathsome sores, at the rich man's gateway,
longing for scraps from that sumptuous board.   No human
heart had pity on him, yet was he not unbefriended.   God
was his helper; angels hovered round him unseen; and the
dogs, prowling for garbage, would lick with their soft, warm
tongues his festering sores, the only dressing they ever got.[4]
And it came to pass that the poor man died and was carried
away by the angels [5] to Abraham's bosom; and the rich man
also died, and was buried.   " It was a very splendid funeral
in the sight of men that was furnished to that purple-clad
rich man by his crowd of retainers; but a far more splendid
one in God's sight that was afforded to that beggar full of sores
by the ministry of the angels, who did not carry him forth to
a marble tomb but carried him up to Abraham's bosom." [6]

Thus ends the contrast of their earthly lives, and Jesus
lifts the veil and displays their conditions in the hereafter.   The Jews and the Greeks had a like conception of
the unseen world.   The former called it Sheol, the latter
Hades, and both conceived it as the common abode of all
souls, good and bad alike, where they received the due reward
of their deeds.   It was a bitter aggravation of the misery of
the unrighteous that they continually beheld the felicity of

---

[1] Chrysost. *Serm. de Laz. et Div.* βύσσος, linen of a finer sort than λίνον,
chiefly Egyptian. *Cf.* Rev. xix. 8, 14.

[2] εὐφραινόμενος, *cf.* Lk. xii. 19; xv. 23, 29. λαμπρῶς, in allusion perhaps to
the gold and silver plate. '

[3] Since nowhere else does Jesus give a name to a parabolic personage, it has
been supposed that this is not a parable but an actual history (Tert. *De Anim.* § 7;
Iren. *Adv. Hær.* iv. 3. § 2); and a name, Ninevis, has been found for the rich
man. *Cf.* Euth. Zig. Jesus, however, was wont to employ names significantly.
Cf. " Simon, son of *John*," *i.e.* "the Lord's grace" (Mt. xvi. 17; John xxi. 15-7).

[4] Chrysost. : " The dogs nobler than the rich man, kinder than his inhumanity."
Wetstein quotes a proverb: ἔχομεν κύνα τῷ πτωχῷ βοηθοῦντα.   Others regard
their licking as an aggravation of his misery: he was unable to drive away the
unclean creatures.

[5] *Targ. Cant.* iv. 2: " Non possunt ingredi Paradisum nisi justi, quorum animæ
eo feruntur per angelos."

[6] Aug. *De Civit. Dei*, i. 12. § 1.

the righteous, knowing the while that they could never share *Cf.* Enoch
it.[1] Such was the prevailing conception of the state of the xxvii. 3;
departed in our Lord's day, and He makes use of it here, not Rev. xiv.
as being true but as serving to enforce the lesson which He 10.
desired to teach.   It is a startling reversal which meets the
eye when He draws aside the veil and displays the dooms
of those two men.   The rich man died and was buried ; and
in Hades he lifted up his eyes, being in torments.   Afar off
he saw Lazarus, no longer a beggar, hungry and loathsome,
but a guest at the Heavenly Feast, occupying the chief place
and reclining on Abraham's bosom,[2] even as in the Upper John xiii.
Room the beloved disciple reclined on Jesus' breast.   " Father 23.
Abraham ! " he cried ; " have pity on me, and send Lazarus to
dip the tip of his finger in water and cool my tongue ; for I
am in anguish in this flame."   " Child," Abraham replied,
" remember that thou receivedst thy good things in thy life-
time, and Lazarus likewise the evil things ; but now here he
is being comforted, but thou art in anguish.   And in all this
region betwixt us and you a great chasm hath been fixed,
that they that wish to pass over from this side unto you may
not be able, nor those on that side cross over unto us."
According to the Rabbis the abodes of the blessed and the
doomed were nigh one to the other.   According to one there
was only a span betwixt them, according to another the
boundary was a wall.[3]   But Jesus sets a great chasm betwixt
the twain, as though He would say that the sentence is
irrevocable, the separation eternal.

Moreover, He vindicates the justice of the doom.   " I
pray thee, father," pled the rich man when the ministration
of Lazarus had been denied him, " that thou send him to the
house of my father—for I have five brothers—that he may
testify unto them, lest they also come into this place of
torment."   " They have Moses and the Prophets," Abraham
answered ; " let them hearken to them."   " Nay, father
Abraham," urged the wretch, " but if one from the dead go
unto them, they will repent."   " If," came the inexorable and in-

---

[1] Wetstein.

[2] There were three Jewish phrases descriptive of the condition of the souls of the
righteous after death : (1) *In Horto Edenis* or *Paradiso* ; (2) *Sub Throno Gloria*
(*cf.* Rev. vi. 9) ; (3) *In sinu Abrahami*.

[3] *Cf.* Lightfoot.

disputable response, "to Moses and the Prophets they did not
hearken, not even if one rise from the dead, will they be
persuaded." It is not, Jesus here declares, for lack of
opportunity that men perish. Even under the ancient dispensation the way of life was clear to all who would walk
therein. In the Holy Scriptures, which were "read in the
Synagogues every Sabbath," God spake with strong authority
and gracious importunity ; and, if any continued impenitent,
it was not for lack of knowledge but by reason of the
obduracy of their hearts. Not even if one rose from the
dead, would they be persuaded. Had the Lord's adversaries
been persuaded by the raising of Jaïrus' daughter or of the
son of the widow of Nain? Were they persuaded when He
raised Lazarus of Bethany? Nay, were they persuaded when
He Himself rose from the dead on the third day according
to the Scriptures?

Its twofold application: (1) to the disciples; The parable had two audiences and, corresponding to
these, a double purpose. On the one side there were the
disciples, and the parable was for them an enforcement of the
precept wherewith Jesus had concluded His parable of the
Shrewd Factor : "Make yourselves friends with the mammon
of unrighteousness, that, when it fails, they may welcome you
into the Eternal Tents." Well for the rich man had he befriended the beggar at his gate and won his gratitude !
When he passed into the unseen world, Lazarus would have
(2) to the Pharisees. met him and welcomed him to the Heavenly Feast. On the
other side there were the Pharisees, and the parable was for
them an illustration of the aphorism wherewith Jesus had
answered their sneers : "What is high among men is an
abomination in the sight of God."[1] Despite their profession
of sanctity the Pharisees were steeped in worldliness. When
they made feasts, they invited their friends, their brethren,
Lk. xiv. 12-4. their kinsmen, and their rich neighbours, regardless of the
starving poor at their gates ; and in this grim picture they
would recognise their own portraiture and a prophecy of the
doom which awaited them.

---

[1] Wetstein thinks that Jesus had the wealthy and worldly Sadducees in His eye.
Schleiermacher suggests that the rich man was Herod Antipas, *v.* 18 alluding to
his matrimonial relationships and *vv.* 29-31 to his Sadducean scepticism. The
Pharisees, however, were, in their own way, as worldly as the Sadducees.

It is remarkable that the parable imputes no actual wickedness to the rich man. He did not refuse Lazarus the scraps from his table, nor did he drive him from his gate ; neither is there any suggestion that his wealth had been ill acquired. What then was his offence ? Was it simply that he was rich?[1] Nay, in the Lord's eyes there was neither crime in riches nor merit in poverty. Lazarus was not received into Abraham's bosom because he had been poor, but because God had been his help. And the rich man's offence was not that he was rich, but that he lived an easy, selfish, luxurious life, oblivious of the misery around him. He did not use his riches for the glory of God and the good of his fellow-creatures. He did not show himself an approved banker, a shrewd factor of the mammon of unrighteousness.

[1] The parables of the Shrewd Factor and the Rich Man and Lazarus are adduced as instances of Lk.'s alleged Ebionitic tendency (Strauss, Keim, Schmiedel in *E. B.*, art. *Gospels* § 110). It is noteworthy that our Lord's severest saying about riches is recorded also by Mt. and Mk. (Mt. xix. 23-4=Mk. x. 23-5 =Lk. xviii. 24-5).

CHAPTER XXXVI

THE JOURNEY THROUGH SAMARIA

Lk. xvii.
11-21;
xviii. 1-14;
ix. 51-6; x.
17-20; 25-
37.

"Quam despectus, quam dejectus
Rex cœlorum est effectus,
    Ut salvaret seculum?
Esurivit et sitivit,
Pauper et egenus ivit
    Usque ad patibulum."—S. Bonaventura.

The ten lepers. AT length Jesus reached the borders of Samaria,[1] that despised and hostile territory. His coming was expected, since the Seventy had gone two by two before Him, preparing His way; and, as He approached a certain village, He found a company of ten lepers awaiting Him. They knew that He would pass that way, and had stationed themselves there in the hope that He would heal them. "Jesus, Master," they cried when they espied Him, standing in their uncleanness afar off, "have pity on us!" And it was indeed a piteous spectacle. In ordinary circumstances "Jews had no dealings with Samaritans"; but in that company there was at least one Samaritan. Partners in affliction, Jew and Samaritan herded together in a brotherhood of misery. Jesus responded to their appeal, and bade them go and show themselves to their respective priests. Such was their confidence in Him that they obeyed, and, as they went, they were cleansed. They all held on their way save one; and when he felt the blessed change in his flesh, he hastened back, loudly glorifying God the while; and, when he reached Jesus, prostrated himself before Him and poured out the gratitude of his heart. Only one returned to give thanks, and he was a Samaritan. "Were not the ten cleansed?" Jesus exclaimed. "The nine —where are they? Were none found that returned to give glory to God except this alien?"

[1] Lk. xvii. 11: διὰ μέσον Σαμ. καὶ Γαλ., "through the borderland between S. and G."

The incident was painful to Jesus, exemplifying as it did the characteristic ingratitude of the Jewish people. Yet it had its more pleasing aspect. It afforded a fresh evidence that the despised Samaritans were open to His grace ; and it was especially welcome at that crisis. He was just entering Samaria with the design of travelling through it and preaching as He went ; and the behaviour of that poor alien, coupled with the remembrance of what had befallen at Sychar at the commencement of His ministry, seemed a fair augury of success.

Since it had its Pharisees, that border village was plainly Jewish. Chagrined perhaps by His commendation of the grateful Samaritan, they approached Jesus and asked Him : "When cometh the Kingdom of God ? " It was a mocking question. They believed that the Messiah would appear in pomp and triumph ; and, when Jesus came to their village, a wanderer, almost a fugitive, with His little retinue of lowly followers, they laughed at His Messianic claim and asked Him derisively when He purposed setting up His Kingdom.[1] He answered with a terse and scornful epigram : " The Kingdom of God cometh not with observation." *Observation* was a technical term of astrologers and weather-prophets,[2] and Jesus used it perhaps in allusion less to the skill of the Galileans in discerning the signs of the sky than to the rulers' reiterated demand for " a sign from Heaven." " The Kingdom of God," He says, " cometh not with observation. You cannot foretell its approach as in the crimson of the evening sky ye read the promise of a fair morrow. Nor will men say, ' Behold, here ! ' or ' yonder ! ' for, behold, the Kingdom of God is among you."[3] They were asking when the Kingdom would come, all unconscious that it had come already. They were in a like case with those delegates of the Sanhedrin to whom John the Baptist had said : " In the midst of you standeth One whom ye know not."[4]

Mocking Pharisees.

Lk. xii. 54-6=Mt. xvi. 2-3.

John i. 26.

[1] *Cf.* Euth. Zig.

[2] Diod. S. i. 28 : παρατήρησις τῶν ἀστρων. Euth. Zig. understands *outward and visible pomp.*

[3] ἐντὸς ὑμῶν. The rendering "within you," *i.e.* in your hearts (*cf.* Ps. ciii. 1 : πάντα τὰ ἐντός μου) is inadmissible here. The Kingdom of God was not in the hearts of those Pharisees. *Cf.* Euth. Zig.

[4] Lk. xvii. 22-37 is part of the Lord's eschatological discourse to the Twelve (Mt. xxiv = Mk. xiii = Lk. xxi. 1-36).

Parable of the Un-righteous Judge and the Persist-ent Widow. The Pharisees had their answer, but their sneer would rankle in the hearts of the disciples. It chimed in with their own thoughts. They shared the prevailing opinion of the Messianic Kingdom, and their Master's lowly estate was a grievous stumbling-block to their faith. And He knew what searching of heart was in store for them. When they saw Him hanged on the Cross, it would seem to them as though God had declared finally against them and refused to vindi-cate their cause. And therefore Jesus addressed a parable to them with the design of reassuring them in the face of God's apparent neglect and encouraging them to persistent and importunate faith. In a certain city, He said, there was a judge, and a widow who had been wronged appealed to him for redress. It was precisely the sort of case which should have excited a judge's sympathy and enlisted his prompt and energetic assistance;[1] but this was an unrighteous judge. There was no chance of his getting a bribe from a poor widow, and he dismissed the appeal. She would, however, take no denial, but kept coming to him and pressing her suit, until at last, simply to be rid of her, he yielded to her im-portunities. Jesus humorously represents him as soliloquising thus: "Though I fear not God nor regard man,[2] yet, because this widow is a nuisance to me,[3] I will redress her grievance, lest she keep on coming and end by giving me a black eye."[4]

"And God—shall not He," Jesus asks, "give redress to His elect that cry to Him day and night, though He keep them waiting that sinners may have space for repentance?"[5] Who but Jesus durst have spoken thus, comparing God to a wicked and heartless man?[6] The exceeding graciousness of

---

[1] Maim. *Sanhedr.* 1 enumerates seven qualifications of a judge: "prudentia, mansuetudo, pietas, odium mammonæ, amor veritatis, atque ut sint dilecti ab hominibus, et bonæ famæ." Lightfoot.

[2] A proverbial description of an unconscionable and unprincipled man. See Wetstein.

[3] παρέχειν κόπον, "bother." *Cf.* Mt. xxvi. 10 = Mk. xiv. 6; Gal. vi. 17.

[4] ὑπωπιάζειν, *sugillare*, "hit under the eye" like a pugilist. Suid.: ὑπώπια· τὰ ὑπὸ τοὺς ὀφθαλμοὺς πελιδνώματα, ἢ τὰ ἐξ αὐτῶν ἐξιόντα πῦα. *Cf.* 1 Cor. ix. 27.

[5] μακροθυμεῖ ἐπ' αὐτοῖς, "is long-suffering where they are concerned." *Cf.* Rom. ix. 22.

[6] An evidence, according to Keim, of the "late date" of the parable. There are, however, three similar parables in Lk.: (1) the Selfish Neighbour (xi. 5-8); (2) the Shrewd Steward (xvi. 1-9); (3) the Thankless Master (xvii. 7-10).

His doctrine of the Heavenly Father made it possible for Him to speak thus without any risk of being misunderstood. And in truth it is the very villainy of the judge that lends the argument its irresistible force. It is an argument *a fortiori*, like that other : " If ye, being evil, know how to give good gifts unto your children, how much more shall your Heavenly Father give good things to them that ask Him ? " If that unrighteous judge, out of sheer selfishness, yielded to the suppliant's importunities and granted her desire, how much more will God, in the fulness of His love and the tenderness of His sympathy, give ear to His people's prayers and at length, in His own good time, bring them out of their distresses ? Mt. vii. 11 =Lk. xi. 13.

Wherever He went, Jesus proclaimed the good news of His Kingdom, nor would He forbear during His brief sojourn in that border village. It was there apparently that He spoke His memorable parable of the Pharisee and the Tax-gather. It was a Jewish village, and their proximity to Samaria would foster a spirit of Pharisaism in its people. " They had confidence in themselves that they were righteous and set the rest of men at naught " ; and the aim of the Lord's parable was to humble their pride and show them what was their standing in God's sight. The Feast of Tabernacles was nigh, and troops of pilgrims were on their way to Jerusalem ; and Jesus described two men going up to the Temple to pray. A very striking contrast they presented. One was a Pharisee, and it was nothing strange that he should repair to the sacred shrine ; but the other was a tax-gatherer, and it was a great marvel that he should go thither and that he should pray. With elaborate ostentation the holy man took his stand in the posture of devotion. He struck an attitude [1] and prayed : " O God, I thank Thee that I am not as the rest of men, extortioners, unrighteous, adulterers, or even as this tax-gatherer. I fast twice in the week, I tithe all that I get." [2] This would not indeed be the language of his lips. Very seemly and edifying would be the prayer which he uttered in the ears of the Parable of the Pharisee and the Tax-gatherer.

---

[1] σταθείς as distinguished from ἑστώς (*v.* 13) implies *deliberate posture,* " having struck an attitude." *Cf.* Lk. xix. 8. Standing at prayer : p. 103.

[2] *Pir. Ab.* ii. 13 : " Quando oras, noli in precibus bona tua enumerare sed fac preces misericordiarum et pro gratia impetranda coram Deo."

admiring bystanders ; but, whatever his lips may have spoken, that was the thought of his heart. " He prayed thus to himself." Nor were his professions unjustified. It was characteristic of the Pharisees that they strove to outdo the rest of men in "works of righteousness." Fasts were appointed for the Congregation when any occasion arose calling for humiliation before God——war, pestilence, locusts, blight, scarcity, drought, and the like ;[1] but the stricter sort of Pharisees fasted every Monday and Thursday.[2] The Law

Lev. xxvii. required the tithing of the produce of lands and herds ; but the
Num. xviii. Pharisees went beyond the legal requirement and tithed all
30-2 ;
21, 24. their income, with ludicrous scrupulosity bringing even their kitchen herbs under levy.[3] All that this Pharisee professed was true, and the fault of his prayer was that it breathed a spirit of self-righteousness. And therewith went a spirit of cruel contempt for others. He alone was righteous, and all his fellow-mortals were included under one sweeping condemnation. "Descend," apostrophises St Chrysostom,[4] " from thine insolent words. Say even that ' some men ' and not ' the rest of men ' are extortioners, unrighteous, adulterers. Are all extortioners except thee, O Pharisee? Are all unrighteous, and thou alone righteous ? Are all adulterers, and hast thou alone achieved chastity ? "

Meanwhile the tax-gatherer was standing at a distance, the very image of contrition. The Pharisee had observed him and utilised his presence as a background to his own resplendent righteousness, recking nothing of the struggle which was going on within that troubled breast. The sinner " stood," but not like the Pharisee with elaborate and ostentatious pose. His eyes were downcast. So indeed were the Pharisee's, for such was the Jewish manner in prayer ;[5] but it was a sense of guilt that bowed the sinner's head. His iniquities had taken hold upon him, so that he was not able to look up. He durst not lift his eyes to Heaven lest, says St Chrysostom, the very stars should accuse him, and he should see his sentence written across the sky. His prayer was a sob of

---

[1] Lightfoot. [2] *Cf.* p. 104. [3] *Cf.* p. 413.
[4] *Serm. in Publ. et Phar.*
[5] Maim. *in Tephill.* 5: "Orans velet caput suum et spectet deorsum." *Cf.* Lightfoot.

contrition, a cry for mercy : " O God, be merciful to me the sinner ! " Even as the Pharisee deemed that he alone was righteous, so it seemed to the tax-gatherer that there was no sinner on the earth that could be compared with himself.

" I tell you," says Jesus, " this man went down justified to his house rather than the other." Of course it was not his sin but his penitence that commended him to God. It is not said that he left the Temple rejoicing in the mercy which had been vouchsafed to him. Perhaps he would go home with drooping head and continue sorrowing for many a day. Nevertheless in that hour when he confessed his sin and cried for mercy, he was accepted of God, and in due time he would attain to the glad assurance of salvation. Some other day he would go up to the Temple with light step and lighter heart, and declare what God had done for his soul. " Verily God hath heard me ; He hath attended to the voice of my prayer. Blessed be God, which hath not turned away my prayer, nor His mercy from me."

From the border-land Jesus struck into Samaria, and, following the preconcerted route, reached a Samaritan village.[1] It had already been visited by two of His seventy forerunners, and He expected as the result of their ministry to find a welcome for Himself and His message. His expectation, however, was disappointed. The inhabitants, apprised of His approach, were up in arms against Him and refused Him admission, " because," explains the Evangelist, " His face was in the direction of Jerusalem." It is evident that their un-friendliness was more than the habitual antagonism betwixt Jew and Samaritan, and a reasonable explanation lies to hand. When the Galileans went up to the Holy City at the festal seasons, they travelled through Samaria, and their passage was resented by the populace, and frequently occasioned hostile demonstrations.[2] The caravans of pilgrims to the Feast of Tabernacles had lately passed that way ; and it is no

Rejection by the Samaritans.

---

[1] Lk. ix. 53-6 ; x. 17-20; 25-42 should follow xviii. 14. *Cf.* Introd. § 10. ix. 51-2 an anticipation of the departure from Galilee (xiii. 22) and the sending of the Seventy two by two before His face (x. 1). According to Euth. Zig. the " messengers " in ix. 52 were James and John who, as Jesus and His company approached the town, were sent on in advance to procure a lodging (ἐτοιμάσαι) and returned indignant ὡς ἀτιμασθέντος τοῦ διδασκάλου.

[2] Jos. *Ant.* xx. 6 ; *De Bell. Jud.* ii. 12. §§ 3-7.

wonder that, when Jesus and His disciples arrived, they were
ill received. They were Galileans, and their faces were in
the direction of Jerusalem. The disciples were indignant,
especially James and John, the fiery-spirited Sons of Thunder.

2 Kings i.
10-2.
" Lord," they cried, recalling the ancient story of Elijah,[1] " wilt
Thou that we bid fire descend from Heaven and consume
them ? " Jesus turned upon them sharply. " Ye know not,"
He said, " what manner of spirit ye are of. For the Son of
Man came not to destroy men's lives but to save them."[2] And
they went to another village.

Return
of the
Seventy.
The Lord's rejection by the people of that town was only
a foretaste of what awaited Him. A wave of anti-Jewish
sentiment was sweeping over Samaria, and He found no
entrance for His word. He was compelled to abandon His
project of a mission in Samaria and hasten on His way toward
Judæa.[3] Somewhere in the course of His journey He met
the Seventy, who had accomplished their mission and were
returning in a body to tell Him how they had fared. Since
they had preceded the pilgrim travellers through Samaria, they
had encountered no hostility ; and, when they met Jesus, they
were brimming over with wonder and exultation. " Lord,"
they cried, " even the dæmons submit to us at the mention
of Thy name ! " Their speech was little pleasing to Jesus.
Did it not evince a spirit of faithlessness ? He had sent them
forth to do mighty works in His name, and their wonderment
at their achievements proved how ill they had realised what
their commission meant. They were amazed that they had
achieved so much because they had expected so little. And
in truth their achievements were but insignificant. Jesus had

---

[1] ὡς καὶ Ἠλείας ἐποίησεν, an interpretative gloss.

[2] καὶ εἶπεν· οὐκ οἴδατε ποίον (v.l. οἵου) πνεύματός ἐστε ὑμεῖς omitted by best MSS.,
Tisch., W. H., supported by D, Chrysost. (In Matth. xxx, lvii) ; probably genuine
and omitted, as Wetstein suggests, because it was employed as a proof-text of the
Marcionite heresy that the O.T. was the work of the Demiurgus. Cf. Tert. Adv.
Marc. iv. § 23. ὁ γὰρ υἱὸς του ἀνθρ. οὐκ ἦλθ., κ.τ.λ., very weakly attested, but a
genuine logion of Jesus and very suitable here. The Vulg. has both clauses.

[3] On the ground of Mt. xix. 1 and Mk. x. 1 (where read : "cometh into the
borders of Judæa and beyond Jordan ") Keim conceives that Jesus avoided Samaria
and, crossing the Jordan in the north (Lk. xvii. 11), travelled by the alternative route
through Peræa, entering Judæa from the eastern side of Jordan. But between
μετῆρεν ἀπὸ τῆς Γαλιλαίας and ἦλθεν εἰς τὰ ὅρια τῆς Ἰουδαίας πέραν τοῦ Ἰορδάνου (Mt.
xix. 1) come (1) the journey through Samaria (Lk.), (2) the visit to Jerusalem (John
vii. 10—x. 39), (3) the retreat to Bethany beyond Jordan (John x. 40-2).

anticipated greater things. "I had a vision," He says, "of Cf. Is. xiv. 12. Satan fallen as lightning from Heaven.[1] Behold, I have given you authority to trample upon serpents and scorpions and on Cf. Ps. xci. 13. all the power of the Enemy,[2] and nothing shall in any wise hurt you." Though armed with such authority, they had yet expected little and achieved little. Their exultation revealed also a disposition to spiritual pride, and Jesus reminded them that they had a greater reason for rejoicing. "Ye have indeed been Cf. Exod. xxxii. 32-3; endowed with wondrous powers; nevertheless in this rejoice Mal. iii. not that the spirits submit to you, but rejoice that your names 16; Phil. have been enrolled in Heaven." To have his name inscribed iv. 3; Hebr. xii. in God's Book of Life is the proudest dignity whereto a mortal 23; Rev. can attain, and to realise it is the surest safe-guard against iii. 5. pride and the strongest incentive to devoted service.

When He had passed the southern frontier of Samaria A lawyer's and entered Judæa, Jesus arrived at a town, perhaps Jericho.[3] captious question. Apparently He repaired to the Synagogue [4] and preached, and, when He had finished His discourse, one of His hearers, according to the custom of the Synagogue, rose and addressed a question to Him. The man was a Lawyer, one whose business it was to expound and interpret the Sacred Law and determine its meaning. He was versed in subtle dialectic; and he rose, not to seek enlightenment, but to puzzle Jesus, put Him to confusion before the assemblage, and perhaps betray Him into some unorthodox pronouncement which might serve as a ground of accusation.[5] It was a foretaste of the manner of conflict which Jesus must thenceforth maintain against the astute intellects of Judæa, and which reached its height in that memorable series of dialectic encounters during the Passion

---

[1] A bold figure descriptive of the triumph which Jesus had expected to follow the preaching of the Seventy. It is simply an importation of alien ideas to discover special allusions in this saying: (1) Satan's fall when he sinned and was cast down from Heaven: Orig. (*In Matth.* xv. § 27 ; *In Matth. Comm. Ser.* § 49), Theophyl. (2) His overthrow by the Incarnation: Greg. Naz., Euth. Zig. (3) His defeat by Christ at the Temptation: Lange. There was an early opinion that ἐθεώρουν is plur. : "they, *i.e.* the dæmons, beheld." Erasm. : "in quodam Latino codice repperi *videbant*." The idea would then be : "No marvel the dæmons submit to you, since their chief has fallen."

[2] *Cf.* Wetstein.

[3] He is next found at Bethany which lay on the route between Jericho and Jerusalem.

[4] His hearers were seated (*v.* 25).   [5] *Cf.* Euth. Zig.

Week. it would seem that He had been discoursing of Eternal Life, and the Lawyer asked : " Teacher, what shall I *The Lord's* do to inherit .' Eternal Life ' ? " Jesus perceived his crafty *answer.* intent, and, with that amazing resourcefulness which never failed Him in sudden emergencies, He declined to commit Himself and made His assailant answer his own question, thus assuming at the outset the critic's vantage-ground. " What stands written in the Law ? " He asked. " How readest thou ? " The answer came glibly and confidently : " Thou shalt love the Lord thy God from thy whole heart and with thy whole soul and with thy whole strength and with thy whole mind, and thy neighbour as thyself." It was a felicitous combination of two Mosaic precepts,[1] and would seem to have *Cf.* Mk. been the approved summary of religious duty in the Jewish *xii.* 32-3. schools of the period. The Lawyer quoted it with complete assurance and with all the greater alacrity that it promised, as he foresaw, to furnish an opportunity for disputation. It was agreed among the Rabbis that " neighbour " meant a fellow-Jew, but he had a shrewd suspicion that Jesus would give the term a wider comprehension. Jesus approved the answer. " This do," He said, " and thou shalt live." The Lawyer clutched at his opportunity. " And who," he asked, " is my neighbour ? "

Parable of It was a clever ruse, but Jesus proved more than a match *the Good* *Samaritan.* for His wily antagonist. He refused to be entrapped into a barren controversy and answered with a parable. He told how a traveller, going down from Jerusalem to Jericho, was set upon by the brigands who infested that precipitous road of evil name, the Ascent of Blood.[2] They plundered him, maltreated him, and left him half dead. The twenty-four courses of the Jewish priesthood ministered by turns in the Temple, and, since half the officiating course lodged in the City of Palm-trees where food and water were abundant,[3] there were continually priests passing to and fro betwixt Jerusalem

---

[1] Deut. vi. 5 ; Lev. xix. 18. ἐν ὅλῃ τῇ διανοίᾳ σου is an addition to the verse as it stands in the Hebrew text, due perhaps to the LXX rendering of בְּכָל־לְבָבְךָ, ἐξ ὅλης τῆς διανοίας σου.

[2] *Cf.* p. 34. Jer. on Jer. iii. 2 : "Arabas, quæ gens latrociniis dedita usque hodie incursat terminos Palæstinæ et descendentibus de Hierusalem in Hiericho obsidet vias."

[3] Lightfoot.

and Jericho. As the plundered traveller lay weltering in blood, a priest came down the road and spied him, but he passed by on the other side. Next came a Levite, and he also passed by on the other side. Presently there came a Samaritan, jogging on his ass to Jerusalem, a merchant probably and no stranger on that road.[1] He spied the unfortunate man and made haste to succour him. He dressed his wounds, according to the medical prescription of the day, with oil and wine, and bound them up.[2] Then he set the traveller on his beast and conveyed him to an inn and tended him there. He rose betimes in the morning[3] to push forward on his journey, and at the door of the inn gave the host two *denarii* and charged him to tend the invalid. A *denaraius* was a day's wage for a labouring man, and the two would probably Mt. xx. 2. suffice till the traveller was fit for the road again ; but it was possible that more might be needed, and the Samaritan bade the innkeeper spare no expense. " Whatever more thou spendest, I will repay thee on my way back."

" Now," says Jesus, " which of these three seemeth to thee to have proved ' neighbour ' to the man that fell in with the robbers ? " There was but one answer possible. The Lawyer should have answered " The Samaritan," but he could not bring himself to utter the hated word and reluctantly faltered out : " The one that took pity on him." " Go thy way," said Jesus ; " do thou also likewise." His triumph was complete. He had declined to be entangled in a bootless controversy, and with admirable dexterity had compelled His reluctant antagonist to own himself in the wrong.

---

[1] *Cf. v.* 35 : known to the innkeeper, and his credit good.

[2] Colum. vii. 5. § 18 : " Fracta pecudum non aliter quam hominum crura sanantur involuta lanis oleo atque vino insuccatis et mox circumdatis ferulis colligata." See Wetstein.

[3] ἐπὶ τὴν αὔριον, " towards the morrow."

CHAPTER XXXVII

MINISTRY IN JERUSALEM

Lk. x. 38-
42; John
vii. 11-52
(Mt. xi.
28-30);
viii. 12-x.
39; Mt.
xxiii. 37-9
=Lk. xiii.
34-5; Mt.
xi. 25-6=
Lk. x. 21.

*" Then is it nothing to thee? Open, see
Who stands to plead with thee.
Open, lest I should pass thee by, and thou
One day entreat My Face
And howl for grace,
And I be deaf as thou art now.
Open to Me."*—CHRISTINA G. ROSSETTI.

At
Bethany.
WHEN Jesus left Galilee, He had no thought of being present at the Feast of Tabernacles. He meant to travel slowly through the land, preaching as He went, and arrive at Jerusalem in time for the Feast of the Passover. But it had been otherwise ordained in the providence of God, and Jesus, walking ever in the days of His flesh by faith and not by sight and taking each step in obedience to the indication of the Father's will, acquiesced in the dispensation; and, arriving in Judæa while the Feast of Tabernacles was in progress, repaired to the Holy City. Travelling up the Ascent of Blood, He reached Bethany, a village within two miles of Jerusalem just over the brow of Mount Olivet. There dwelt Lazarus and his sisters, Martha and Mary, and Jesus broke His journey in order to visit them. His kindness in rescuing Mary from her life of shame in the northern city of Magdala and restoring her, forgiven and cleansed, to her home, had won Him their gratitude, and He received a glad welcome.

The joy of
the Feast.
The Feast of Tabernacles was the most joyous of all the Jewish festivals. "He who has not seen its joy," said the Rabbis,[1] "knows not what joy is." It commemorated in the first instance the Exodus from Egypt, and in remembrance of the tents wherein their fathers had dwelt during their wanderings in the wilderness, the people built them booths of the branches of thick trees intertwined with boughs of olive and

Lev. xxiii.
33-44;
Neh. viii.
15

---

[1] *Tosaph. Succ.* 4. 2.

myrtle. At the same time it was the feast of harvest, and Deut. xvi. 13-5; Exod. xxiii. 16. celebrated the ingathering of the fruits of field and vineyard. The citizens built their booths on the flat roofs or in the courtyards of their houses, and the strangers built theirs in the streets or round the city walls. And, sitting under those pleasant bowers, they kept holiday for a livelong week. It was a season of feasting and hospitality. They "ate the Neh. viii. 9-18. fat and drank the sweet, and sent portions unto them for whom nothing was prepared, and made great mirth."

It was at this joyous season that Jesus came to Bethany. The good "portion." Martha, the mistress of the house, was busy making ready the festal cheer, and His arrival would increase her anxiety that nothing might be lacking to the entertainment. Mary, on the contrary, oblivious of all else, seated herself at Jesus' feet, Cf. Lk. ii. 46; Acts xxii. 3. the disciple's posture, beholding His dear face and drinking in His discourse. It angered the busy housewife, "distracted about much service," to see her sitting thus. Reverence for the Master restrained her awhile, but at length she could contain herself no longer and broke in :[1] "Lord, dost Thou not care that my sister left me alone to serve? Tell her then that she lend me a helping hand." "Martha, Martha," He replied, "thou art anxious and bustled about many things, but a few are all we need." It was a gentle remonstrance against the sumptuousness of the repast which His hostess was preparing. Far simpler fare would have sufficed. What need of all those viands? "A few things are all we need, or rather," He adds, passing suddenly, after His wont,[2] from the earthly to the heavenly, "one thing;[3] for it is the good 'portion' that Mary chose, one which shall not be taken away from her." At that joyous season they were all feasting and sending "portions," but Mary had no thought for the meat that perisheth. She had chosen a better "portion" and was feasting her soul on heavenly manna.[4]

---

[1] ἐπιστᾶσα of sudden intervention.

[2] Cf. Mt. viii. 22 = Lk. ix. 60 : νεκρούς, dead first spiritually, then physically. Mt. xvi. 25-6 = Mk. viii. 35-7 : ψυχή, first life, then soul.

[3] ὀλίγων δέ ἐστιν χρεία ἢ ἑνός ℵBL, W. H. Simplified to ἑνὸς δέ ἐστιν χρεία AC, T. R., Tisch., R.V., and still further, in several ancient authorities, to Μάρθα, Μάρθα, θορυβάζῃ· Μαριὰμ τὴν ἀγ. μερ. κ.τ.λ.

[4] μερίς, a portion of food ; cf. Gen. xliii. 34. Specially associated with the Feast of Tabernacles ; cf. Neh. viii. 10 (LXX) : ἀποστείλατε μερίδας τοῖς μὴ ἔχουσιν.

Expect-
ancy at
Jerusalem. From Bethany Jesus took His way to Jerusalem. It was a bold thing to do. On the occasion of His last visit to the Holy City He had incensed the rulers by His miracle at the Pool of Bethesda which they deemed a violation of the

John v. 18. Sabbath ; and they had sought to kill Him. Nor had their hostility abated in the interval ; rather had it grown more

John vii. 1. bitter. For eighteen months He had kept away from Jerusalem, shunning, until His time should come, their murderous grasp. It had been a disappointment to rulers and people alike when feast after feast passed by and He never appeared ; and, as the worshippers gathered to the Feast of Tabernacles, the hope of seeing Him revived. It may be that some of the northern pilgrims had observed Him with " His face in the direction of Jerusalem " and brought word that He was on the way. Expectation passed into impatience when the feast began and He did not arrive. "Where is that fellow ? " said the rulers,[1] disdaining to utter His name and concealing their hatred under a mask of contempt.[2] And the people, though they durst not talk freely about one who was in such ill favour with the rulers, were all agog with curiosity and discussed the question of the hour in animated whispers. " He is a good man," said some. " No," said others ; " he leadeth the multitude astray."

His arrival At length, on the fourth day of the Feast [3] when the hope of seeing Him must have well-nigh been abandoned, He appeared and began to teach in the outer court of the Temple. His discourse produced a profound impression. The rulers were astonished. Never had they heard such teaching, and their wonder was how one who had never sat at the feet of the Rabbis in the House of the Midrash,[4] could possess such

His self-
vindica-
tion. wisdom. Jesus replied to their questioning that His teaching was not His own but God's. "And," He said, " if any one willeth to do His will, he will discover in regard to the teaching whether it be of God or whether I speak from

[1] " The Jews ": cf. p. 62.
[2] ἐκεῖνος is contemptuous. Cf. John ix. 12, 28. Chrysost. In Joan. xlviii : ὑπὸ τοι πολλοῦ μίσους καὶ ἀπεχθείας οὐδὲ ὀνομαστὶ αὐτὸν καλεῖν ἐβούλοντο.
[3] John vii. 14. There were properly seven feast-days. According to Wetstein "the middle of the Feast" included all the days between the first and the last.
[4] Cf. p. 21.

Myself." [1]   Here lay the secret of their unbelief. Because they were not faithful to the lesser truth which they already knew, they could not comprehend the greater truth which Jesus revealed.   " Hath not Moses given you the Law ? and none of you keepeth the Law. Why are ye seeking to kill Me ? " The multitude, whereof only a few were citizens of Jerusalem and knew the designs of the rulers, were surprised and cried out after the coarse manner of their kind : " Thou hast a dæmon. Who is seeking to kill thee ? ". Jesus let the interruption pass and elaborated His indictment of the rulers. He accused them of unreasonable inconsistency. They were wroth with Him for healing a man on the Sabbath Day, never considering that they regularly committed a breach of the Sabbath-law quite as flagrant.   The Law directed that a child should be circumcised on the eighth day, and, when the eighth day chanced to be a Sabbath, they had no scruple in circumcising him despite the command that they should do no work on the Sabbath Day.   It was a conflict of ordinances. And surely healing was more important than circumcision. " If a man receiveth circumcision on a Sabbath, that the Law of Moses may not be broken, are ye wroth with Me because I made a man every whit whole on a Sabbath ? " [2]   There was indeed no written ordinance for healing as for circumcising, but there was the unwritten yet imperative requirement of humanity.

Very keen was the discussion which ensued among the multitude.   Here is a group of the citizens of Jerusalem. They know the fell purpose of the rulers, and they marvel that it is not being put into execution.   " Is not this," says one, " he whom they are seeking to kill ? And, see, he is speaking boldly, and they are saying nothing to him. Can it really be that the rulers have recognised that this is the Messiah ? " " Nay," says another, scouting the idea, " we know this man whence he is ; but the Messiah—when He cometh, no one recogniseth whence He is."   Such was the current idea.

Opinions of the multitude.

---

[1] *Cf.* Aug. *In Joan. Ev. Tract.* xlviii. § 1 : " Fides enim meritum est, intellectus præmium." Hamerton, *Intell. Life,* p. 303 : " Hoogstraten, who was a pupil of Rembrandt, asked him many questions, which the great master answered thus :— ' Try to put well in practice what you already know ; in so doing you will, in good time, discover the hidden things which you now inquire about.' "

[2] This very argument was used later by R. Eleasar ben Azariah (*c.* A.D. 100-30). *Cf.* Wetstein on Mt. xii. 10.

Cf. Mt. ii. 4-6. It was indeed allowed that, according to the Scripture, the Messiah would be born at Bethlehem ; but, said the Rabbis, even as the first Redeemer, Moses, was concealed in the wilderness of Midian, so would the second Redeemer be revealed and caught away and then reappear.[1] And His re-appearance would be sudden and unexpected. " Three things," it was said, " come unawares : the Messiah, a treasure-trove, and a scorpion." [2] Apprised of their disputing, Jesus cried : " Ye both know Me and know whence I am ! And on My own errand I have not come, but He that hath sent Me is true, whom ye do not know. I know Him, because from Him I am and He hath sent Me." Thus reasoned those citizens of Jerusalem, versed in the theology of their day ; but they were only a small proportion of the multitude which thronged the Temple-court during the festal season ; and there were many who, unbiassed by theoretical prejudice, considered the Lord's claims with open minds and believed on Him. " The Messiah," they reasoned, " when He cometh, will He do more signs than this man doeth ? "

Embar-rassment of the rulers. It was not indeed because they had been persuaded of His Messiahship that the rulers stayed their hands. They would fain have apprehended Him and wreaked their ven-geance upon Him forthwith ; but they durst not. The multi-tude were on His side. Though they did not all recognise His Messiahship, they were all profoundly impressed. He was Cf. Acts xxi. 27-36. Mt. xxvi. 4-5=Mk. xiv. 1-2 =Lk. xxii. 2. the hero of the hour. The rulers knew the excitability of the mob, and the fear of provoking a tumult restrained them. They perceived that so long as He retained the popular affec-tion, He was impregnable, and from that hour they made it their endeavour to discredit Him in the eyes of the multitude. If only they could effect that, they would have Him at their mercy and might do with Him what they listed.[3] It ex-asperated them when so many confessed their faith in Him in the Temple-court, and they deliberated what they should do. It was unconstitutional for the Sanhedrin to convene during a festal season ; but, on the initiative of the Pharisees, who were ever the dominant party in the national council,[4] they met

---

[1] Lightfoot and Wetstein.   [2] *Bab. Sanhedr.* 97.
[3] John ignores the immediate cause of the Lord's immunity and refers it to the purpose of God (vii. 30).   [4] *Cf.* p. 42.

informally and instructed the officers of the court to arrest
Jesus and bring Him before them as soon as the Feast was
over. Thus far, they reckoned, could they go without excit-
ing the wrath of the populace.

Preaching still in the Temple-court, Jesus appealed to the A call to
waverers. He warned them that the time was short. "For decision.
a little while longer am I with you and I go away to Him
that sent Me. Ye shall seek Me and shall not find Me, and
where I am ye cannot come." It was a call to immediate
decision, but, when it came to the ears of the rulers, it provoked them at once to wonder and to mockery. What could
He mean? Plainly, they thought in their unspiritual fashion,
that He was about to quit the land of Israel and go where they
would never see or hear Him more. But whither would He
go? It did not occur to them that He might betake Himself to the Gentiles: that were too monstrous. But there was "Will He
another course which they conceived possible. All over the go to the
Disper-
world, chiefly in Babylonia, Egypt, Syria, Asia Minor, Greece, sion?"
and Italy, there were colonies of Jews who had settled in
those heathen lands and, with the commercial aptitude of their
race, had usually attained to wealth and influence. They
clung tenaciously to their ancestral faith and came up to
Jerusalem at the great festivals to worship in the Temple;
yet it was impossible for them to remain unaffected by the
atmosphere of the lands where they dwelt. They learned the
language of their neighbours and all unconsciously imbibed
their ideas and acquired their manners. Those Jews of the
Dispersion were regarded with no great kindness by the proud
Judæans; and, when the rulers heard that dark saying of
Jesus, they wondered if He meant to go to the Dispersion Cf. 1 Pet.
among the Gentiles and teach the Gentiles. "What is this i. 1; Ja. i.
word which He spoke: 'Ye shall seek Me and shall not find
Me, and where I am ye cannot come'?"

The Feast of Tabernacles lasted a week, but the eighth The Great
day also had its solemnities, albeit on a lesser scale. On the Day of the
Feast.
first day thirteen bullocks were offered and one fewer each Num. xxix.
succeeding day until the seventh—seventy in all. On the 12-40.
eighth only one bullock was offered. On each of the seven
days two rams and fourteen lambs were offered; on the eighth
one ram and seven lambs. The eighth day was properly

distinct from the Feast,[1] nevertheless it was popularly accounted not only one of the feast-days but the most important of all. It was "the great day of the Feast," and its seeming inferiority was construed by a quaint Rabbinical parable as a proof of its superiority. The seventy bullocks were offered for the seventy nations of the world, the eighth day's bullock was Israel's offering for herself; and it was, said the Rabbis, as though a king made a seven days' feast and bade thereto all the people of the city, and on the eighth day said to his friend: "We have now done our duty by the people of the city; let us now return, thou and I, to whatever may be had, though it be but a single pound of flesh or fish or herbs."[2]

Prayer for dew and rain. The Feast of Tabernacles was the Jewish Harvest Home, and the worshippers gave thanks for the ingathering of the fruits. At sunrise on the sixth day a priest, bearing a golden pitcher and attended by a joyous company, went down to the Pool of Siloam and filled the pitcher, returning just as the sacrifice was conveyed to the altar, and amid a blare of trumpets entering the Temple by the Water Gate, which hence derived its name. On the eastern side of the altar stood a silver basin into which the wine-offering was poured; and on the western side another silver basin, and into it was poured the water from the pitcher. The ceremony was a thankful remembrance of the showers wherewith God had refreshed and fertilised the earth. Nor did the worshippers merely give thanks for the harvest which had been gathered in. They sought also a blessing on the husbandry of the ensuing year. During the seven days of the feast they prayed for dew, on the eighth they prayed for rain.[3]

"Rivers of living water." On the eighth day, while they prayed for that "gift of God" so precious in the arid East, Jesus stood and cried aloud:

Is. lv. 1. Cf. Is. xxxii. 2; xliv. 3; Jer. ii. 13; Ezek. xliv. 3. "If any thirst, let him come unto Me and drink. He that believeth in Me, as the Scripture hath said, rivers out of his heart[4] shall flow, rivers of living water." It was not a quotation but an echo of Scripture, and it was like the word which He had spoken to the Samaritan woman at Jacob's Well:

John iv. 14. "Whosoever drinketh of the water which I shall give him

---

[1] *Succ.* 48. 1 : "Dies octavus est festum per seipsum."

[2] Lightfoot on John vii. 37.   [3] Wetstein on John vii. 37.

[4] ἐκ τῆς κοιλίας, *ex corde.* *Cf.* the N.T. use of σπλάγχνα, *viscera.*

shall never thirst; but the water which I shall give him, will become within him a well of water springing up into life eternal." Nothing else that He said is recorded by the Evangelist; but He must have said much more, or the multitude would hardly have been moved as they were. He would discourse of the thirst of the soul and the living water which alone can assuage it; and perchance it was here that He uttered that gracious invitation which St Matthew has preserved in an alien setting: "Come unto Me, all ye that labour and are heavy laden, and I will refresh you.[1] Take My yoke upon you and learn from Me, because meek am I and lowly in heart; and ye shall find refreshment for your souls. For My yoke is kindly[2] and My burden light." It is the image of a weary beast, thirsty and galled; and the promise is threefold: a refreshing draught of the living water, a kindly yoke, and a light burden. "The yoke of the Law" is a phrase which was much on the lips of the Rabbis,[3] and truly they had made the Law naught else than a galling yoke. Observe the blessing which Jesus bestows. He does not remove a disciple's burden; for a burden is appointed to every man in the wise providence of God. But He gives the disciple a new burden and a new yoke—His own burden and His own yoke. He shares both with His disciple, and it is a burden which does not tire and a yoke which does not chafe. The twain are yoke-fellows. The self-same yoke is on their necks, one end on the neck of Jesus and the other on the disciple's, and they drag the self-same burden side by side, partners in labour and in reward.

Mt. xi. 28-30; cf. Ecclus. li. 23, 26-7.

Cf. Mt. xxiii. 4; Gal. v. 1.

If it was thus indeed that He spoke on that great day of the Feast, it is no marvel that the hearts of His hearers were stirred. Often had such discourse been heard in Galilee, but most of the multitude that thronged the Temple-court on that memorable morning, had come from other parts and had never heard aught like this. They were filled with wonderment. Some surmised that He was the prophet who should arise and prepare the way for the Messiah. Others said that

Diverse opinions of the multitude.

---

[1] ἀναπαύσω, Vulg. *reficiam*. *Cf.* 1 Cor. xvi. 18; 2 Cor. vii. 13; Philem. 7, 20; Mt. xii. 43=Lk. xi. 24.

[2] χρηστός. *Cf.* Lk. vi. 35; Eph. iv. 32; Tit. iii. 4; 1 Cor. xiii. 4.

[3] Lightfoot; Wetstein; Taylor, *Say. of Fath.* iii. 8.

He was the Messiah Himself. " Nay," objected others, "doth the Messiah come out of Galilee? Did not the Scripture say that of the seed of David and from Bethlehem, the village where David was, the Messiah cometh?" They knew the Lord only as Jesus of Nazareth, and, thus ignorantly objecting, they unwittingly bore witness to Him.[1]

A futile meeting of the Sanhedrin.　　It seemed to the Lord's adversaries that this division of opinion offered a favourable opportunity for effecting His arrest. The officers of the Sanhedrin were present, yet they let the opportunity slip, not because they feared a tumult but because they had been impressed by the Lord's discourse. When the Feast was over the Sanhedrin met, and the rulers demanded of the officers why they had not brought Him. " Never," was the reply, " did a man so speak." The Pharisees, ever foremost in the Sanhedrin, retorted with an angry sneer : " Have ye also been led astray? Did any of the rulers believe in Him or any of the Pharisees? But this multitude that doth not understand the Law—accursed are they." It was a bitter sneer, breathing the Pharisaic spirit of contempt for the common folk, " the people of the land," as they were styled.[2] What marvel that Jesus had been moved with compassion when He saw the multitude like shepherdless sheep, nay, worse than shepherdless in that they had such shepherds as these?

Feeble protest of Nicodemus.　　Only a single voice was raised on the Lord's behalf. There was a Pharisee who, all unknown, believed in Him— Nicodemus, who had visited Him under cover of night at the outset of His ministry as the Sanhedrin's delegate. The memory of that interview had haunted him ever since, and he was a disciple at heart ; but he feared to confess his faith, knowing what a storm of wrath and obloquy would burst upon him. He was present at that meeting of the Sanhedrin and ventured upon a feeble protest. He merely raised a point of order, asking whether it were legal to condemn a man unheard. Did his colleagues suspect his secret inclination? They turned upon him with withering scorn. " Art

---

[1] This is the irony of the passage, and it is surprising that critics like Keim should miss it and find here an evidence of the unhistoricity of the birth at Bethlehem.

[2] עַם הָאָרֶץ. Cf. Taylor, Say. of Fath. ii. 6.

thou also of Galilee?" they sneered. "Search, and see that out of Galilee a prophet ariseth not"; overlooking in their blinded prejudice the many names which Galilee had contributed to the prophetic roll.[1] The taunt silenced Nicodemus, and never again was his timorous voice raised in the Sanhedrin on the Lord's behalf.

When the Feast was over, the throng of pilgrims took *The Feast over, Jesus remains at Jerusalem.* their departure, but Jesus remained. The providence of God had brought Him, contrary to His own purpose, to Jerusalem, and He would minister there a while and appeal to His enemies ere they embrued their hands in His blood. The men of Jerusalem were widely different from the Galileans. Their city was the centre of Jewish life and religion, and they prided themselves upon their pre-eminence. And this proved their undoing, They looked askance at Jesus at once because He was a Galilean and because He had never sat· at the feet *John vii. 15.* of the Rabbis. They were versed in Rabbinical lore; and ever and anon, as He taught, they would raise some theological objection and reject His doctrine because it did not square with their theory. Compassed by the goodwill of the populace, the Lord was immune from violence, yet at every turn He was watched and harassed by His malignant adversaries.

The scene of the first encounter was the Temple Treasury. *Controversy in the Treasury.* In the Women's Court, so named not because the women alone might enter it but because they were suffered to proceed no further, stood thirteen boxes, from their shape called Trumpets, whereinto the worshippers cast their offerings.[2] The place was much frequented, and it would seem to have *Cf. Mk. xii. 41 = Lk. xxi. 1.* been a favourite resort of Jesus. As He taught there one day, He said: "I am the Light of the world. He that followeth Me shall not walk in the darkness but will have the light of life." It may be that there is here an allusion to the scene which was enacted on the last day of the Feast of Tabernacles, when at the close of evening the golden candelabra in the Women's Court were lighted and the worshippers danced before them with blazing torches in their hands.

---

[1] *Cf.* p. 17.

[2] שׁוֹפָרוֹת. The narrow end was uppermost to ensure the safety of the contents.

Cf. Lightfoot, ii. pp. 405 *sqq.*

In any case Jesus here advances a great claim. "The Light" was a Jewish title of the Messiah,[1] and, when Jesus said "I am the Light of the world," He asserted His Messiahship. The Pharisees broke in with an objection. It was a principle of Rabbinical law that a man's testimony on his own behalf was incompetent;[2] and they cried: "Thou art testifying regarding thyself: thy testimony is not true." It was a sorry quibble, revealing the petty pedantry of their minds; and Jesus answered it with calm contempt, emitting withal a great declaration. Their legal rule, He told them, was wholly inapplicable. It was necessary that He should testify concerning Himself; for He alone knew whence He had come and whither He was going, and no other could testify truly concerning Him. Nor was His testimony unsupported. "I am not alone, but I and the Father that sent Me. Yea, and in your Law it stands written that the testimony of two men is true. There is I that testify concerning Myself, and the Father that sent Me testifieth concerning Me." "Where is thy father?" they asked, half-sneering, half-bewildered, revealing their utter unspirituality. Had they been at all spiritually minded, they must have recognised the heavenliness of Jesus and known that He was speaking of God.

Deut. xix.
15.

Another
call to
decision. As He taught on another occasion, He said: "I am going away, and ye shall seek Me, and in your sin ye shall die. Where I am going, ye cannot come." It was a reiteration of the warning which He had spoken during the Feast, and which the rulers had taken as an intimation that He would Gross mis-
under-
standing of
the rulers. betake Himself to the Dispersion. They understood the second warning no better than the first and attached a grosser significance to it, led astray by their theology. They leaped John viii.
48, 52; cf.
vii. 20. to the conclusion that Jesus, whom they suspected of insanity, meditated suicide. It was a Jewish belief that such as laid violent hands upon themselves, were not received into the common abode of the departed in the unseen world, but were consigned to a place of deeper darkness;[3] and, when Jesus

---

[1] *Ech. Rabb.* 68. 4: "Lux est nomen Messiæ, sicut dicitur 'Lux cum illo habitat' (Dan. ii. 22)."

[2] *Cf.* Wetstein on John v. 31; Lightfoot on John viii. 13.

[3] Jos. *De Bell. Jud.* iii. 8. § 5. *Cf.* Wetstein.

said : " Where I am going, ye cannot come," they supposed
that He referred to the suicides' hell. It was a coarse and
insulting idea, and it filled Him with disgust and despair.
Those men and He belonged to different worlds, and communion was impossible. " O wherefore," He cried, " do I
speak to you at all ? "[1]   Naught remained but to go forward
to the bitter end ; and, when they had wrought their will
upon Him, they would read, in His Resurrection and the
wonders that would follow, His vindication by God. " When *Cf.* Acts ii
ye have lifted up the Son of Man, then shall ye recognise that 32·3.36.
I am He,[2] and of Myself do nothing, but, as the Father
taught Me, speak these things."

Painful though it had been, the encounter was not unprofit- Rulers that
able. " While He spake these things, many believed in Him." Him." believed
These were true converts, abiding fruits of His ministry in
Jerusalem. And, besides these, there were actually some of *Cf.* John ix.
the rulers who had been impressed. They did not " believe 21, 24.
in Him " but merely " believed Him," that is, according to
the New Testament's succinct distinction, they did not sur- John viii.
render themselves to His grace but hearkened to His teaching 30·1.
and owned its reasonableness.[3]   It was possible that these
men might be brought to discipleship ; and one day Jesus
addressed Himself to them, thinking to win them outright.
His exhortation, however, displeased them, and there was one
sentence which touched them to the quick and transformed
them into angry enemies. " If," He said, " ye abide in My *Cf.* John
Word, ye are truly My disciples, and ye shall discover the vii. 17.
Truth and the Truth shall make you free." That offended
their pride. Their Jewish spirits were fretting under the
Roman yoke ; and, missing His spiritual meaning, they took

---

[1] viii. 25 : a *crux interpretum. Cf.* Meyer, Westcott, Moulton's Winer, pp. 581-2,
Field's *Notes*, Abbott, *Joh. Gram.* pp. 142-4. The choice lies between (1) "even
that which I have also spoken unto you from the beginning" (τὴν ἀρχὴν ὅ, τι καὶ
λαλῶ ὑμῖν). So both Engl. versions. The objection is that this would require λέγω
for λαλῶ. (2) "To think that I am talking to you at all !" *Mene omnino vobiscum
loqui!* The objection is that τὴν ἀρχήν or ἀρχήν had the sense of *omnino* only after
a neg., but this rule was not observed in later Greek. *Cf.* Clem. *Hom.* vi. § 11 : εἰ μὴ
παρακολουθεῖς οἷς λέγω, τί καὶ τὴν ἀρχὴν διαλέγομαι ; It seems decisive that the
sentence was so understood by Chrysost. while Greek was still a living language : ὁ δὲ
λέγει τοιοῦτόν ἐστι· τοῦ ὅλως ἀκούειν τῶν λόγων τῶν παρ' ἐμοῦ ἀνάξιοί ἐστε, μητί γε
καὶ μαθεῖν ὅστίς ἐγώ εἰμι.

[2] ἐγώ εἰμι, sc. the Messiah, the great One who was in the thoughts of every Jew
and did not need to be named. *Cf.* John iv. 26 ; viii. 24 ; xiii. 19 ; Mk. xiv. 62.

[3] *Cf.* Moulton's Winer, p. 267 ; Moulton's *Gram. of N.T. Gk.* i. pp. 67 *sq.*

"We are the Lord's words as an allusion to their national degradation
free." and resented the fancied insult. Ignoring the Egyptian
bondage, the Babylonian captivity, the Greek conquest, and
the Roman domination under which they were even then
groaning, they retorted that they were Abraham's seed and
had never been slaves. Jesus gently explained the spiritual
significance of His words. It was the bondage of sin to which
He had alluded. So long as a man committed sin, he was a
bondsman, and had no standing in the House of God. And
this was the boon which He offered—to give them, in St Paul's
phrase, "the spirit of adoption" and make them, like Himself,
sons of God. "I know," He said, "that ye are Abraham's
seed ; but," He added, marking the menace of their looks, "ye
are seeking to kill Me, because My word hath no place within
you. What I have seen in the Father's presence, I speak.
Do ye also therefore what ye heard from the Father."

"We are   Their indignation was kindled, and they would not listen
Abraham's to reason. "Our father is Abraham," they repeated. "If,"
seed." said Jesus, using some severity, "ye are children of
Abraham, do the works of Abraham. But, as it is, ye are
seeking to kill Me for telling you the truth which I heard from
God. This Abraham did not. Ye are doing the works of
"We are your father." "We are not bastards," they vapoured ; and,
children of thinking to improve upon their claim, they advanced a higher :
God." "One father have we, even God." "If God were your Father,
ye would love Me," Jesus retorted, and told them plainly that
they were children of the Devil and were bent on doing their
father's work—seeking to kill Him and refusing to believe
the truth.

"Thou art   That roused their fury, and they fell to coarse abuse.
a Samari- "Say we not well that thou art a Samaritan and hast a
tan and a
demoniac." dæmon ?" _Samaritan_ was a common term of abuse in
Jerusalem. It was one of the Rabbis' epithets for such as did
not sit at their feet,[1] and, as the Galileans had nicknamed Him
"Friend of Tax-gatherers and Sinners," the Judæans in their
pride of intellect termed him "Samaritan" and "demoniac."
"I have not a dæmon," He answered, "but I honour the

---

[1] _Sot._ **22. 1**: "Qui Scripturam et Mischnam tantum didicit nec magistris
servit, R. Eleazar dicit eum esse plebeium ; R. Samuel filius Nachmani esse rusticum ;
R. Jannai esse Samaritanum ; R. Acha filius Jacobi esse Magum."

Father and seek His glory, heedless of My own. Verily, verily I tell you, if any one keep My word, he shall never behold death." "Now," they cried, "have we found that thou hast a dæmon. Abraham died, and the Prophets; and thou sayest: 'If any one keep My word, he shall never taste of death'! Art thou greater than Abraham and the Prophets? Whom makest thou thyself?" "Abraham your father," *Cf.*Hebr. answered Jesus, "exulted to see My day, and he saw it and xi. 13. rejoiced." "Thou art not yet fifty years old,"[1] they cried, "and hast thou seen Abraham?" "Verily, verily I tell you," He replied, "ere Abraham was born, I am."[2]

They had called Him mad, but this was worse than mad- Attempt to ness. It was rank blasphemy. Stoning was the penalty of stone Him. blasphemy, and they snatched up stones, finding plenty to hand, since the Temple was still a-building and the rough material lay around them.[3] They would have pelted Him to death, but, ere they could execute their purpose, He was gone. He mingled with the multitude which, being friendly, would cover His retreat, and quitted the Temple.

Amid such controversies the days sped by; and one A man Sabbath, when the Feast of Dedication was nigh at hand,[4] born blind. Jesus was passing along in His disciples' company and His eye rested on a spectacle of misery—a young man stone-blind *Cf.* John who sat by the way-side begging alms. Since the Temple- ix. 18. gate was a favourite station for mendicants, it was there be- *Cf.* Acts like that he sat and, as the worshippers passed, published his iii. 2.

---

[1] His burden had aged the Man of Sorrows, and He looked ten years older than He was. Euth. Zig. thinks that they judged His age by "the richness of His experience." Irenæus (*Adv. Hær.* ii. 33), controverting the opinion that the Lord's ministry lasted only a year, asserts that He lived to be upwards of forty (which Keim thinks possible), alleging this passage and the testimony of the Ephesian elders who had been associated with John. Irenæus, however, was not without dogmatic bias. Since Jesus, he argues, came to save all, it was necessary that He should pass through every age: *infans, parvulus, juvenis, senior.* A man was a *senior* from forty to fifty. Chrysost. read τεσσαράκοντα. "Audacter ita correxit," says Matthæi in his note on Euth. Zig.

[2] εἰμι, pregnant pres.: "I was and still am." *Cf.* John xiv. 9; xv. 27.

[3] *Cf.* Lightfoot. Jos. *Ant.* xvii. 9. § 3: during an insurrection in the Temple the worshippers drop their sacrifices and stone the soldiers.

[4] The interpolation in viii. 59: διελθὼν διὰ μέσου αὐτῶν καὶ παρῆγεν οὕτως makes the miracle of the healing of the blind man happen as Jesus quitted the Temple after His controversy with the rulers. This is impossible. His departure on that occasion was a hasty retreat from a murderous assault, and He would not linger by the way.

condition and craved charity, The spectacle arrested Jesus. It awoke compassion in His breast, but in His disciples it merely provoked speculation. According to the current theology suffering was always penal and betokened antecedent sin. Nor did it invalidate the theory that this man had been born blind. It merely threw the sin further back. The Jewish theology recognised the grim fact of heredity, and taught moreover that a child was not only conceived in sin and shapen in iniquity but might actually sin while still in the womb.[1] The disciples, forgetting, if indeed they had heard, the Master's pronouncement regarding the massacre at the altar and the disaster at Siloam, assumed that sin was the cause of this man's blindness and wondered whether it had been ante-natal or hereditary.

Exod. xx. 5; Lam. v. 7; Ezek. xviii. 2.

Lk. xiii. 1-5.

Jesus heals him.

Jesus rejected both alternatives. The man's blindness was no punishment at all. It was a providential visitation, "that the works of God might be manifested in him." And there was no time for idle speculation. "We must work the works of Him that sent Me[2] while it is day. The night cometh when no one can work." The sight of need had ever aroused the Lord's compassion, but, as the end drew near, it was as though He hasted to save. The time was short, and He would fain crowd it with deeds of mercy. Forthwith He addressed Himself to the task of healing the blind man, and He set to work after a curious fashion. He spat on the ground and, making clay of the spittle, smeared therewith the sightless orbs, and bade the man go and wash in the Pool of Siloam. Clay and saliva were accounted efficacious remedies for ocular affections,[3] and Jesus was following the medical prescription of His day when He performed that operation so unpleasing to modern taste. Of course He did not follow it because He believed in its efficacy. It may be that, as in the case of the blind man at Bethsaida Julias whom He treated similarly, He desired to awaken hope in the sufferer's breast ; but He had a further design. It was the manner of the

Mk. viii. 22-6 ; cf. vii. 33.

---

[1] Lightfoot on John ix. 2. *Cf.* Lk. i. 41.

[2] ἡμᾶς δεῖ Tisch., W. H. τοῦ πέμψαντός με W. H. ; τοῦ πέμψαντος ἡμᾶς Tisch. The former is preferable. Jesus always kept His own mission distinct from that of the Twelve : the Father had sent Him ; He sent them.

[3] See classical and Rabbinical quotations in Wetstein ; amusing story of R. Meir in Lightfoot.

prophets of Israel, when deeply moved, to enforce their pro-
clamations by symbolic enactments.   When Ezekiel would
intimate the impending destruction of Jerusalem, he took a
tile and pourtrayed upon it a city and all the enginery of a ^{Ezek. iv.}
vigorous siege—towers, mound, camp and battering-rams. ^{1-3.}
And, when Agabus would warn Paul of the doom which
awaited him at Jerusalem, he took the Apostle's girdle and
bound therewith his own hands and feet, announcing : " Thus ^{Acts xxi. 10}
saith the Holy Spirit : ' The man whose is this girdle, the ^{-1. Cf.}^{Neh. v. 13.}
Jews shall so bind in Jerusalem.' "   Such symbolic actions
are characteristically Oriental.   Grotesque as they seem
now-a-days, they were congenial to the Jewish mind and
served their purpose well.   They startled the spectators and
compelled them to reflect.   And it is remarkable that Jesus
repeatedly adopted this prophetic method during those last
days when He was making His final appeal to Jerusalem.[1]
So did He when He smeared that blind man's eyes with clay
and sent him through the city to the Pool of Siloam.   It
was a parable of the blindness which had happened unto
Israel, and a satire upon her teachers, those blind guides ^{Cf. John}
of the blind.   They professed that they gave light to those ^{ix. 38-41.}
that sat in darkness, but they simply put a veil upon ^{2 Cor. iii.}
men's hearts and seeled their eyes.

The man obeyed the Lord's behest.   He went to the ^{The man}
Pool and, when he had washed the clay from his eyes, he saw. ^{arraigned}^{before the}
When he got home his neighbours were amazed, and wondered ^{Pharisees.}
if it were indeed the blind beggar.   Some said : " It is he."
" No," said others, " he is like him."   " I am he," said the
man, and told them how it had come about : " The man that
is called Jesus made clay and anointed my eyes and said to
me : ' Away to Siloam and wash.'   So I went away and
washed, and I got my sight."   " Where is he ? " they asked.
" I know not," he replied, perchance mistrusting them.   And
thereupon they did a shameful thing.   The rulers had
published an edict that any one who confessed Jesus as
Messiah should be excommunicated.[2]   The terror of the ban

---

[1] *Cf.* the Triumphal Entry, the blasting of the Fig-tree, the feet-washing in the
Upper Room.

[2] There were three degrees of excommunication : (1) נִדּוּי, suspension from religious and social privileges for thirty days.   (2) שַׁמְּתָא, continuance of the sus-

was hanging over the city, and those base caitiffs, eager to evince their loyalty and clear themselves of suspicion, laid hold on their neighbour and brought him before the Pharisees. Of course his offence was that he had suffered himself to be healed of his blindness on the Sabbath. He was the accomplice of Jesus.

His examination.

The Pharisees interrogated him, and then conferred with one another. Opinion was divided. Some of them declared that Jesus could not be from God inasmuch as He did not observe the Sabbath. Others dissented : " How can a sinner do such signs ? " Unable to agree they turned again to the man : " What sayest *thou* regarding him, forasmuch as he opened thine eyes ? " " He is a prophet," was the stout reply. Thereupon the question was raised whether a miracle had really been wrought. Perhaps the man was in collusion with Jesus and had never been blind. Accordingly his parents were summoned in the hope that their evidence might expose the imposture, and three queries were addressed to them : Is this your son ? Was he born blind ? If so, how does he now see ? Dreading the doom of excommunication, they would not commit themselves. The first question and the second they answered in the affirmative, but cautiously disclaimed all knowledge of the last. " Question *him*," they said. " He is of age : he will speak for himself." The baffled rulers, still suspecting collusion, resorted to another stratagem. They consulted together, then summoned the man once more before them, and, as though they had meanwhile ascertained the fact, sternly accosted him : " Make full confession.[1] We know that this fellow is a sinner."

Cf. John iii. 2.

His spirited behaviour.

Very striking is the contrast betwixt the old paralytic at Bethesda who, out of sheer stupidity, betrayed his Benefactor to the rulers, and this quick-witted and courageous youth. He faced his judges undaunted. " Whether he be a sinner I know not. One thing I know, that, whereas I was blind, now I see." Foiled anew, they asked feebly : " What did he unto

---

pension for thirty days more, if the offender remained impenitent. (3) If still impenitent, the curse, חֵרֶם. Cf. Lightfoot on 1 Cor. v. 5.

[1] δὸς δόξαν τῷ Θεῷ, not " Ascribe the miracle to God ὡς παρ' αὐτοῦ ἰαθεὶς καὶ μὴ παρὰ τοῦ Ἰησοῦ " (Euth. Zig.), but " Give glory to God by telling the truth and confessing the imposture." Cf. Josh. vii. 19 ; Ezr. x. 11 (LXX) : δότε αἴνεσιν Κυρίῳ.

thee? How opened he thine eyes?" The answer was a quick flash of mingled contempt and sarcasm : "I told you already, and ye did not hearken. Why do ye again wish to hear it? Can it be that ye also wish to become disciples of his?" It was a galling taunt, and, forgetting their dignity, they broke into reviling : "Thou art a disciple of the fellow ; we are disciples of Moses. We know that to Moses hath God spoken ; but this fellow—we know not whence he is." They gained nothing by thus losing their tempers. They simply demeaned themselves and exposed themselves afresh to their clever adversary's artillery of scorn. Undismayed by their wrath, he plied them with biting sarcasm. Why, here was a marvel! A miracle had been wrought, and they, the wise men of Israel, confessed that they knew not whence the worker of it was. With fine irony he proceeds to enlighten them. "We know that to sinners God doth not hearken ; but, if any one be godly and do His will, to him He hearkeneth. From eternity it was not heard that any one opened the eyes of one born blind. If 'this fellow' had not been from God, he could have done nothing." The audacity of the speech infuriated them. "In sins," they cried, "thou wast born His excom-entirely, and thou teachest us?" And they excommunicated tion. him.[1]

In that hour when the door of the Synagogue was closed Jesus against him, the gate of the Kingdom of Heaven was opened claims him. to him.[2] Jesus sought him and claimed him. "Dost thou believe," He said, "in the Son of Man[3]?" He did not say "the Son of God," since that was a Messianic title much on the lips of the Pharisees and would have repelled one who had been so hardly treated by those proud ecclesiastics. Familiar as that title which Jesus loved, was in Galilee, it was strange in Jerusalem, and the man was puzzled. "And who is he, Lord," he asked, "that I may believe in him?" "Not only hast thou seen Him," Jesus answered, "but it is He that is Cf. John talking with thee." Then the man perceived that it was for iv. 26.

---

[1] ἐξέβαλον αὐτὸν ἔξω, not simply "they cast him out of doors," *ejecerunt eum foras* (Vulg.). Cf. Euth. Zig.

[2] Aug. *In Joan. Ev. Tract* xliv § 10 : "Jam non erat malum fieri extra synagogam. Illi expellebant, sed Christus excipiebat."

[3] אBD, Tisch., W. H. τὸν υἱὸν τοῦ ἀνθρώπου. T. R. τὸν υἱὸν τοῦ Θεοῦ is very ancient, being the reading of Vulg., Tert., Aug., Chrysost. (with variant ἀνθρ.).

Himself that Jesus was claiming his faith, and he gladly
yielded it.   Had not that gracious One proved Himself
worthy of all trust and adoration?   " I believe, Lord," he
cried, and did obeisance to Him.   His darkness was all
dispelled.   His blind eyes had already been opened, and
now " the illumination of the knowledge of the glory of God
in the Face of Christ " poured into his soul.   Was it not
strange that, while one man was thus visited, others should
reject the light?   " For judgment," exclaimed Jesus, " I came
into this world, that they that see not may see, and they that
see may become blind."   Some Pharisees were by, apparently
spying upon Him,[1] and they demanded : " Are we also
blind ? "   " Had ye been blind," Jesus answered, " ye had not
had sin ; but, as it is, ye say ' We see ' : your sin remaineth."
This was their condemnation, that the Light had come into
the world, and they loved the darkness.   Well for them had
they known their blindness !   They would then have sought
the Physician who could give them sight.[2]

2 Cor. iv.
6.

John iii. 19.

Parable of
the True
Shepherd. Grieved at the high-handed procedure of those ecclesiastics
who had driven the man out of the Church and shut the
door against him, Jesus spoke a parable.   He described a
sheep-fold such as His hearers had often seen out in the
wilderness of Judæa, where the flocks pastured which furnished
sacrifices for the Temple and wool for the market.[3]   The fold
was a spacious enclosure whither the shepherds conducted
their flocks at night-fall.   It was in charge of a porter who
would admit none but such as had a right to admission.
Within its shelter the flocks rested together till the morning,
and then they were led out to their several pastures.   The
shepherds had no difficulty in separating their own.   Out on
the lone wilderness a shepherd had no other companions than
his sheep, and a tender relationship was formed betwixt him
and them.   He knew every sheep of his flock and had a name
for it ; and it knew its name and would answer to it.   In the
morning he would call his own, and they would leave the herd
and follow him out to the pasture.   He did not need to drive

---

[1] Chrysost. thinks that they were superficial followers, easily turned aside.

[2] Aug. *In Joan. Ev. Tract.* xliv. § 17 : " Quia dicendo *Videmus* medium non quæritis, in cæcitate vestra remanetis.

[3] Jerusalem had a sheep-market and a wool-market.   *Bab. Kam.* 10. 9.

them. "He goeth before them, and the sheep follow him, because they know his voice ; and a stranger they will in no wise follow, but will flee from him, because they know not the voice of the strangers." The shepherd's office demanded tenderness, courage, and devotion.[1] "He shall gather the lambs with his arm, and carry them in his bosom, and shall gently lead those that are with young." He must oftentimes imperil his life to snatch a lamb from the jaws of a ravening beast and traverse the mountains in weary quest of a lost wanderer. There was no image more attractive to Jewish minds. The saints of old had loved to think of God as the Shepherd of His people ; and the Christian tombs in the Catacombs are adorned with rude sketches of the True Shepherd carrying His lost lamb upon His shoulder.

Is. xl. 11.

1 Sam. xviii. 34-5; Am. iii. 12. Mt. xviii. 12-3=Lk. xv 3-6.

The immediate purpose of the parable was to console that excommunicated man. "I am the Door of the sheep," says Jesus. What did it matter that the man had been thrust out of the Synagogue ? He had found the door into God's Fold. "I am the Door. Through Me if any one go in, he shall be saved, and shall go in and out and find pasture." This, however, was not the sole purpose of the parable, and Jesus gives it another interpretation. "I am the True Shepherd,"[2] He says. Those high-handed rulers were no shepherds. They lacked the essential qualities of love and devotion. They were mere hirelings, and they cared not for the sheep but only for their hire. When the wolf appeared, they would flee and abandon their flock to his devouring jaws. "I am the True Shepherd," says Jesus ; and this was the evidence thereof, that He loved His sheep, yea, and the lost sheep were very dear to His heart. He was the Shepherd not only of Israel but of all mankind. "Other sheep I have which are not of this fold. Them also must I lead, and to My voice they shall hearken ; and there shall come to be one flock, one Shepherd." And He was ready to lay down His life for His sheep, a willing sacrifice. "No man taketh it away from Me,

---

[1] Wetstein quotes Colum. vii. 6: "Magister autem pecoris acer, durus, strenuus, laboris patientissimus, alacer atque audax esse debet; et qui per rupes, per solitudines atque vepres facile vadat : et non, ut alterius generis pastores, sequatur sed plerumque ut antecedat gregem."

[2] ὁ ποιμὴν ὁ καλός, Euth. Zig.: ὁ ἀληθής. καλός, genuine and perfect of its kind ; Suid.: τὸ εὖ πεφυκέναι πρὸς τὸ ἴδιον ἔργον. ·Cf.· Introd. § 2, n. 4.

but I lay it down of Myself. I have authority to lay it down, and I have authority to receive it again. This commandment received I from My Father."

The parable set the rulers once more at variance. "A cleavage again arose among them." The general verdict was that He had a dæmon and was mad, but there were some who dissented from the truculent majority. "These," they said, "are not the words of a demoniac. Can a dæmon open blind men's eyes?" They resolved to approach Him and perchance arrive at an understanding. The days had sped by, and the Feast of Dedication had come round. It was celebrated in the month of Chislev or December, beginning on the twenty-fifth and extending over eight days, and commemorated the purification of the Temple under Judas Maccabæus after its defilement hy Antiochus Epiphanes.[1] It was a joyous festival. While it lasted, mourning and fasting were prohibited, and lamps were lit each night in front of the houses.[2] It differed from the feasts of Passover, Pentecost, and Tabernacles in this, that, since it was celebrated all over the land, it brought no troops of pilgrims to Jerusalem. Along the eastern side of the outer court of the Temple ran a portico which bore the name of Solomon's Cloister, since it was the only part of Solomon's Temple which had escaped the devastating fury of the Babylonian army in B.C. 586.[3] It afforded a pleasant shelter from the cold, and one day in the course of the Feast, as Jesus was walking there, the rulers appeared on the scene and, as though determined that He should not escape until they had satisfaction from Him, ringed Him round and demanded: "How long dost thou keep us in suspense? If thou art the Messiah, tell us plainly." It was no honest question. The majority of them, at all events, had sought Him with malignant hearts, hoping to extort from Him some declaration which might serve as a ground of accusation.[4]

He perceived their intent and would not be ensnared. "I told you," He answered, "and ye do not believe." And had they not the testimony of His works? The explanation

---

[1] I Macc. iv. 52-9; Jos. *Ant.* xii. 11.

[2] Hence the Feast of Dedication (τὰ ἐγκαίνια. חֲנֻכָּה was called also τὰ φῶτα. *Cf.* Lightfoot.

[3] Jos. *Ant.* xx. 9. § 7.   [4] Aug. *In Joan Ev. Tract.* xlviii. § 3.

of their unbelief, He tells them, reverting to the parable which had occasioned their disquietude, was simply that they were not of the number of His sheep. " My sheep hearken to My voice, and I recognise them, and they follow Me ; and I give them eternal life, and they shall never perish, and there is not any that shall snatch [1] them out of My hand." It was an allusion to their sentence of excommunication. The True Shepherd's flock was safe from all alarm. The thief would not carry them off nor the wolf devour them. His flock was very precious in His sight. "What My Father hath given Me is greater than all, and none can snatch it out of the Father's hand." Then, explaining the alternation " My hand," " the Father's hand," He added : " I and the Father are one."

This enraged them. They deemed it rank blasphemy, and, hastening from the Cloister, they got them stones from the builders' litter and bore them back, meaning to pelt Him to death.[2] He confronted them with a dauntless bearing which overawed them and stayed their wild hands. " Many good works," He said with calm irony, " did I show you from the Father. For which of them are ye stoning Me ? " " It is not," they replied, " for a good work that we are stoning thee but for blasphemy and because thou, being a man, makest thyself God." Jesus met this charge with one of those deft turns of dialectic wherewith, in the course of His final conflict at Jerusalem, He was wont to parry the assaults of His captious adversaries. He appealed to the Scripture, quoting the eighty-second Psalm where, in accordance with Hebrew usage,[3] the judges of the people are styled *gods*. " If," He reasoned, " they are called ' gods ' in your Law,[4] why should you count it blasphemy that I call Myself the Son of God ? Those judges were corrupt men, whereas the works which I have wrought, prove that the Father hath sanctified

Another attempt to stone Him.

His defence against the charge of blasphemy.

---

[1] ἁρπάσει. *Cf. v.* 12 : ὁ λύκος ἁρπάζει αὐτά.

[2] ἐβάστασαν, "carried." Contrast viii. 59 : ἦραν, "picked up." The Cloister of Solomon, being an ancient structure, had no rubble lying about it. This delicate distinction betrays the eye-witness.

[3] *Cf.* Exod. xxi. 6 ; xxii. 8, 28 : אֶל־הָאֱלֹהִים, R.V. : "to God," A.V., R.V. marg. : "unto the judges."

[4] In common parlance "the Law" meant simply the Scriptures, the Prophets and the Hagiographa as well as the Books of Moses. *Cf.* 1 Cor. xiv. 21. See Wetstein and p. 420, n. 1.

Me and sent Me into the world." It was a genuine piece of Rabbinical argumentation. Jesus here borrows His assailants' methods and routs them with their own weapons; and His irony is very keen. They regarded the Scripture with a veneration nothing short of idolatrous, and He presents them the embarrassing dilemma of either acquitting Him or condemning it. "If it called them 'gods,' and the Scripture cannot be loosed." Of course it was no serious argument; nevertheless it involved, and He meant it to involve, a high claim. Their grievance was that, being a man, He made Himself God; and He does not repudiate the imputation. On the contrary, He allows it and justifies it. His argument amounts to nothing less than an assertion of His deity.

Departure from Jerusalem. They durst not stone Him. They would have arrested Him, but He eluded their grasp, and the friendly multitude would cover His retreat. He left Jerusalem, to return no more until He returned to die. He took His way westward across the valley of the Kedron and up the climbing ascent of Olivet; and, as He went, solemn emotions struggled in His breast. Ere He crossed the brow of the hill, He looked back on the city, and a cry of poignant and impassioned *Mt. xxiii. 37-9=Lk. xiii. 34-5.* farewell broke from His lips: "Jerusalem, Jerusalem! that killeth the Prophets and stoneth them that have been sent unto her. How often would I have gathered thy children together even as a hen gathereth her brood under her wings, and ye would not! Behold, your house is being left unto you desolate. For I tell you, ye shall never more see Me until ye say: 'Blessed is He that cometh in the name of the *Mt. xxi. 9 =Mk. xi. 9-10=Lk. xix. 38= John xii. 13.* Lord!'" And so it came to pass on that day when He rode into the city amid the plaudits of the attendant throng, avowing Himself her King and making His last appeal. Already He had planned the final *dénouement*.

He left Jerusalem, grieved by her unbelief yet in no wise disappointed. The rulers had rejected Him and sought His *Cf. John vi. 37.* life, yet He had won His own. All that the Father had given Him had come unto Him. They were indeed a little flock, numbering none of the wise or noble or mighty after the flesh; but they sufficed. It was the Father's good *Lk. xii. 32.* pleasure to give them the Kingdom. Perchance it was here that He spoke that great word which St Matthew and St Luke have inserted at random in their narratives : " I thank Thee, Father, Lord of heaven and earth, because Thou didst hide these things from wise and understanding, and didst reveal them to babes. Yea, Father, because thus it seemed good in Thy sight."[1]

Mt. xi. 25-6=Lk. x. 21.

[1] See Introd. § 15.

John x. 40-
2=Mt. xix.
1b-2=Mk.
x. 1 ; Mt.
xix. 3-12=
Mk. x. 2-
12 ; Mt.
xix. 13-5=
Mk. x. 13-
6=Lk.
xviii. 15-7 ;
Mt. xix. 16-
30=Mk. x.
17-31=Lk.
xviii. 18-30
(xvii. 7-10);
Mt. xx. 1-
16.

CHAPTER XXXVIII

RETREAT TO BETHANY BEYOND JORDAN

" I want a sober mind,
A self-renouncing will,
That tramples down and casts behind
The baits of pleasing ill :
A soul inured to pain,
To hardship, grief, and loss ;
Bold to take up, firm to sustain,
The consecrated cross."—CHARLES WESLEY.

At Bethany
beyond
Jordan.
WHEN He left Jerusalem, Jesus went away down to Bethany beyond Jordan. It was natural that He should turn thither. There John had preached ; and there Jesus had been baptised, there He had been manifested unto Israel, there He had met His first disciples. The spot was evermore sacred in His eyes ; and now, when the end is near, He repairs thither to refresh His soul in communion with God and win strength and fortitude for the last, grim ordeal. But His concern was not for Himself alone. He was troubled about His disciples. He knew their weakness, and He would intercede for them that their faith might not fail in the day of trial. And He still yearned over Jerusalem. Though her rulers had rejected Him, He had not forsaken her nor utterly despaired of winning her. He purposed addressing to her yet another appeal, and He would pray that God might incline her to hearken, granting perchance some convincing attestation, some overwhelming vindication of His claims.

Cf. Lk.
xxii. 31-2.

Cf. John
xi. 41-2.

Ministry
there.
Nevertheless He did not go to Bethany merely to commune with God. Learning whither He had gone, a multitude followed Him, and He ministered to them by teaching and miracle. It was a wondrous season. The people recalled the mighty work of grace which they had witnessed there three years before, and confessed that this was a mightier work by far. " John," they said, " did no sign ; but everything that

354

John said regarding this man was true." And it was a
fruitful season. " Many believed in Him there."

The rulers had doubtless flattered themselves that they Question of
were rid of Jesus, and, when they learned that He had left the Phari-
sees about
Jerusalem only to establish Himself at Bethany and there divorce.
continue His labours, they were greatly perturbed. Presently
the Pharisees, ever vigilant, appeared on the scene. They
approached Jesus with a captious question cleverly devised :
" Is it allowable for a husband to divorce his wife for every
cause ? " That was a burning question in those days. The
Mosaic Law permitted divorce when a wife proved faithless ; Deut. xxiv.
but the Rabbinical interpreters after their wont disputed over 1-4.
this enactment. The school of Shammai, adhering to the
letter of the Law, held that a wife should not be divorced
except for unfaithfulness ;[1] whereas the school of Hillel, with
a laxity very agreeable to the general inclination, allowed a
husband to put away his wife " for every cause"—if he dis-
liked her, if he fancied another woman more, if her cookery
were not to his taste.[2] The doctrine of Hillel was the
common practice in our Lord's day, and it operated dis-
astrously. It violated the sanctity of domestic life ; and there
is a hideous passage in the Talmud which shows what havoc
it made of the obligations of morality. It was customary for
a Rabbi of the school of Hillel, when he visited a strange town
to make public advertisement for a woman who would serve as
his wife during his sojourn there.[3] It was an inhuman system
and inflicted cruel wrong upon womankind. It put the wife
at her husband's mercy. She could not divorce him, but for
any whim he might divorce her and cast her upon the world.[4]

Jesus was ever the friend of the oppressed, and His
heart was hot within Him at this foul injustice.[5] The

---

[1] *Gitt.* 9 : "Schola Shammæana : Non dimittenda est uxor nisi ob turpitudinem
solum."

[2] Maim : "Si quis uxorem odio habeat, dimittat." R. Sol.: "Uxorem dimittere
præcipitur si in oculis mariti gratiam non assequatur." *Gitt.* 9 : "Dixit R.
Akibah, Si quis mulierem videat uxore formosiorem, uxorem dimittere licet." *Ibid.*
"Si esculenta mariti nimia salsedine aut nimia tostione male conficiat uxor, est
dimittenda."

[3] Lightfoot on Mt. xix. 3.

[4] Maim. *Gerush.* 1 : "Non dimittebatur uxor nisi libenter volente marito ; re-
luctante enim non erat repudium : at, velit, nolit uxor, repudianda, si vellet
maritus." [5] *Cf.* Introd. § 9, n. 1.

Pharisees expected that He would answer their question with an uncompromising and indignant denial, and thereby offend the general sentiment. Facility of divorce was a cherished privilege. It is amazing how the Jews prized it. They accounted it a singular grace vouchsafed to Israel and withheld from the Gentiles.[1] The Pharisees knew that, if He condemned the system, Jesus would estrange the populace, and perhaps they contemplated the possibility of embroiling Him with Herod Antipas. Might not His condemnation of divorce be represented as a direct and intentional affront to the guilty tetrarch? It was his denunciation of Herod's matrimonial offence that had brought John the Baptist to the dungeon and the block, and might not Jesus be involved in a like doom?

The Lord's answer. Such were their secret designs when they propounded their ensnaring question: "Is it allowable for a husband to divorce his wife for every cause?" With that consummate skill which He ever displayed in encounters of this sort, Jesus avoided entanglement in the Rabbinical controversy and appealed to the Scriptures. "Have ye not read," He asked, ironically charging them with ignorance of those Scriptures whereof they were the official guardians and interpreters, "that the Creator[2] from the beginning made them male and female?[3] Therefore shall a man leave his father and his mother and cleave unto his wife, and the twain shall become one flesh. What therefore God joined together, let man not separate." Such was marriage according to the Creator's design—not the subjection of the woman to the man's caprice, but their union on equal terms as mutual helpers. There was no need for argument. The simple setting forth of the Scriptural ideal was a sufficient condemnation of the prevailing practice.

Cf. Mt. xii. 3=Mk. ii. 25=Lk. vi. 3.

And this the Pharisees perceived. They made no attempt to justify the doctrine of Hillel, but they clutched at a fresh opportunity which the Lord's answer seemed to present. He had said: "What God joined together, let man

---

[1] Lightfoot on Mt. v. 31.

[2] ὁ κτίσας Orig., W. H. ; ὁ ποιήσας Chrysost., Tisch.

[3] Chrysost. *In Matth.* lxiii: "Had He meant that he should put away one and take another in her room, when He made one man, He would have fashioned many women."

not separate "; but did not the Mosaic Law expressly
sanction divorce? Here was indeed a promising snare.
Should Jesus condemn the ordinance of Moses, He would
stand condemned as a heretic, and would forfeit the
popular sympathy and render Himself liable to judicial
procedure. There seemed no way of escape ; nevertheless
Jesus not only extricated Himself triumphantly but turned
His assailants' weapons against their own breasts. Yes,
Moses had permitted divorce ; but that was a departure from
the primal ordinance, necessitated by Israel's inability to rise
to the height thereof. " In view of your hardness of heart [1]
he permitted you to divorce your wives." Solon once said
that his laws were not the best that could have been devised,
but they were the best that the Athenians could receive ; and
even so was Moses constrained to accommodate his legislation
to the capacity of the Israelites.

The Pharisees had their answer. They said no more, Discomfi-
but the disciples pursued the theme. It seemed to them, ture of the
disciples.
being Jews, an intolerable hardship that the fetters of matri-
mony should be thus firmly riveted ; and, when they reached
their lodging, they protested that, if such were the conditions
of marriage, it were better not to marry at all. Ignoring
the petulance of the speech, Jesus assented. It is indeed
better not to marry, but only if the sacrifice be dictated by
devotion to the Kingdom of Heaven. Not all who abstain
are praiseworthy. " There are eunuchs who from their
mother's womb were born thus, and there are eunuchs who
were made eunuchs by men, and there are eunuchs who
made themselves eunuchs for the Kingdom of Heaven's sake."
These last Jesus commends, thinking, however, not of mutilation of the flesh, but of freedom from worldly entanglements,
voluntary surrender, for the Kingdom of Heaven's sake, of
indulgence which a man might enjoy. Such " eunuchs for
the Kingdom of Heaven's sake " are all who, like St Paul,
abstain from marriage that they may care for the things of 1 Cor. viii.
the Lord. This is indeed a noble self-abnegation, but 25-40.

---

[1] σκληροκαρδία, *imperviousness to spiritual truths.* *Cf.* Mk. xvi. 14; Acts vii. 51.
Chrysost. (*In Matth.* xvii) understands σκλ. as *hardheartedness, i.e.* cruelty, and
thinks that the Mosaic permission of divorce was designed to save wives who had
lost favour from being murdered by their husbands : τοιοῦτον γὰρ τῶν Ἰουδαίων τὸ
ἔθνος. So Jerome ; Isidor. Pelus. *Ep.* iii. 76.

in such a cause what sacrifice is too great? Michelangelo never married because, as he used to say, " Art is a sufficiently exacting mistress"; and surely the Kingdom of Heaven may claim an equal devotion from its true-hearted votaries. Jesus was not laying down an absolute law of celibacy. He was thinking of emergencies which would require of His followers that, " by reason of the present necessity," those that had wives should be as those that had not. " It is not every one," He says, " that can receive this saying, but they to whom it hath been given." Incapacity to receive it is apparent alike in those who set self-indulgence above the claims of the Kingdom of Heaven and in those who, with heroic yet mistaken devotion, have mutilated themselves for the Kingdom of Heaven's sake. " He that is able to receive it, let him receive it."

"Suffer the children to come unto Me."   Presently there approached Jesus another company of visitors very different from the last—a troop of parents, fathers and mothers both,[1] bringing their children to the gracious Teacher to receive His benediction. They brought them reverently and adoringly. " They offered[2] them unto Him," say the Evangelists. They presented their little ones like gifts at the altar. It was a solemn act of dedication, and it was well-pleasing to Jesus; but it displeased the disciples. Ruffled, perhaps, by His condemnation of divorce, they were in an irritable mood, and they resented the intrusion. Jesus was vexed at their churlishness. " Suffer the children," He cried, " to come unto Me! Hinder them not! For of such is the Kingdom of Heaven." And then He took them in His arms, laid His hands upon them, and blessed them. It was a wondrous experience for those unconscious babes. Would they not talk of it in after years, and tell it to their children and their children's children?

The young Ruler.   One day during the Lord's sojourn at Bethany a stranger came in quest of Him. He was a young man,[3] and he was

[1] Fathers, because τοῖς προσφέρουσιν (Mk.) is masc.; mothers, because the children were βρέφη (Lk.). The reading αὐτοῖς for τοῖς προσφ. is probably an assimilation to Mt. and Lk.

[2] προσέφερον. Cf. Mt. ii. 11; v. 23-4; viii. 4; Hebr. v. 1, 3, 7; etc.

[3] Mt. xix. 22: νεανίσκος. Cf. Mk. xiv. 51. A vague word; at all events Saul of Tarsus is called νεανίας, though he must have been quite thirty (Acts vii. 58), and Agrippa I, though about forty (Jos. Ant. xviii. 6. § 7).

a personage of importance, being a ruler of the synagogue.[1]
As he approached, he saw Jesus just leaving His abode with Mk. x. 17.
His disciples, and he ran toward Him, knelt down before
Him, and asked : "Good Teacher, what shall I do to inherit
'eternal life'?" It was the very question which the captious
lawyer had addressed to Jesus in a synagogue, probably at Lk. x. 25.
Jericho, where Jesus had preached some three months previously on His way up to Jerusalem ; and it may be that this
man was a ruler of that synagogue and had heard the Lord's
discourse on Eternal Life and His controversy with the lawyer.
The arrow of conviction had pierced his soul, and had been
rankling there ever since ; and, on learning that Jesus was at
Bethany, he had travelled the few miles from Jericho to un-
burden his troubled heart. He was a Pharisee, but a Pharisee
of the nobler sort, one of those who were facetiously styled the
" Let-me-know-what-is-my-duty-and-I-will-do-it Pharisees." [2]
Like Saul of Tarsus in the days of his ignorance, he was a Acts xxii.
zealot for God, as touching the righteousness that is in the [3.]
Law blameless ; yet, for all his diligence in the performance Phil. iii. 6.
of works of righteousness, he had found no rest. His soul
was still unsatisfied. He had done everything, and something
was still lacking. "Good Teacher," he cried, pouring out the
trouble of his soul without preface or explanation, "what shall
I do to inherit 'eternal life'?"

It was precisely the sort of appeal which always "Why
gladdened Jesus and won from Him a ready and gracious dost thou
response. The ruler was a young man and he was an anxious 'good'?"
enquirer, and in either capacity he had a special claim upon
the Lord's sympathy. Nevertheless he met, to all appearance,
with a very chill reception. Jesus answered his impassioned
enquiry with a carping objection. He fastened on the epithet
wherewith, in all sincerity and reverence, the man had
addressed Him. "Why dost thou call Me 'good'?[3] No one

---

[1] Lk. xviii. 18: ἄρχων. *Cf.* Mt. ix. 18: ἄρχων = Mk. v. 22: εἷς τῶν
ἀρχισυναγώγων = Lk. viii. 41 : ἄρχων τῆς συναγωγῆς.

[2] One of the seven kinds of Pharisee enumerated in the Talmud is " Pharisæus
qui dicit: 'Noscam quid sit officium meum, et præstabo.'" *Cf.* Lightfoot and
Wetstein on Mt. iii. 7. Jerome classes the Young Ruler with the Pharisees who
had asked the question about divorce : "Non voto discentis sed tentantis interrogat."
"Mentitur adolescens."

[3] *Cf.* Introd. § 12, 3, (1).

is ' good ' save God alone." Wherefore did He raise so trivial
an objection ? It was in no wise that, conscious of moral
imperfection, He was constrained to disclaim the attribute ;
for many a time He accepted more lavish homage without
demur. Nor was His objection prompted by His characteristic
dislike of pious phrases which meant nothing ; for the man
did not use the word lightly. It was no phrase of conven-
tional courtesy. " Teacher" or " Rabbi " was the common
style, and was employed without addition ;[1] and it evinces
what reverence the man had conceived for Jesus that he
deemed the common style insufficient and addressed Him as
he would never have thought of addressing a Rabbi. In
truth the Lord's objection was a challenge. He read the
enquirer's heart, and, perceiving whereunto he had already
attained, He desired to lead him further. " Consider," He
said, " what your language implies. You have given Me a
title which belongs to God.[2]   Do you mean it ? "

"Keep
the com-
mand-
ments."
When He had flashed this challenge upon the man,
Jesus answered his question. " If," He said, " thou wishest
to enter into life, keep the commandments." It was a vague
prescription. There were many commandments in those
days, not only the commandments of Moses but the
multitudinous requirements of the Rabbinical law. Was it
those commandments that Jesus meant, or did He allude to
new commandments of His own ? " What sort of commandments ? " asked the man ; and Jesus repeated certain familiar
precepts of the Decalogue, all belonging to the second table
which has to do, not with the worship of God, but with the
duty of man to man :[3] " Thou shalt not kill : Thou shalt
not commit adultery : Thou shalt not steal : Thou shalt
not bear false witness : Honour thy father and thy mother."[4]

---

[1] *Rabbi, Mar, Mari* are common, but *Rabbi bone* or *Mar bone* nowhere occurs in
the Talmud. Lightfoot on Lk. xviii. 19.

[2] Not that Jesus denied human goodness. Chrysost. *In Matth.* lxiv : " He says
it, not by way of robbing men of goodness, but in comparison with the goodness
of God." *Cf.* Mt. vii. 11 = Lk. xi. 13.

[3] It is noteworthy that, when the whole Law is mentioned in the N.T., it is
commonly the second table that is meant. *Cf.* Rom. xiii. 8-9 ; Ja. ii. 8, 11.

[4] Mk. adds μὴ ἀποστερήσῃς, an interpolation summarising Exod. xx. 17, the
only commandment of the second table which Jesus omits. Mt.'s "Thou shalt
love thy neighbour as thyself" is also an interpolation (Orig. *In Matth.* xv. § 14).
It was a favourite saying of Jesus. *Cf.* Mt. xxii. 39 = Mk. xii. 31 ; Lk. x. 27.

The answer was a grievous disappointment to the enquirer. Those commandments and many more he had faithfully and laboriously observed, thinking thereby to attain to peace; and, finding no rest for his soul in the way of legal righteousness, he had come to Jesus, hoping to be shown some better way. And, behold, his hope had been disappointed! The teacher of whom he had expected so much, pointed him to the old unprofitable way. Sadly and wearily he replied; "All this I observed from my youth. What lack I yet?"

It was no idle boast; and, when Jesus heard the pathetic protestation, His heart was moved, and He stepped forward and, after the manner of the Rabbis when a disciple pleased them, kissed his brow.[1] His purpose was to reveal to the man the inexorable stringency of God's requirements; and, since he had stood one test, He subjected him to another more severe. He set before him a sacrifice which he had never contemplated, and challenged him to face it. "If," He said, "thou wishest to be perfect, go, sell all that thou hast, and give it to the poor, and thou shalt have treasure in Heaven; and come, follow Me." This staggered the man. He was very wealthy, and he recoiled from the sacrifice. He had believed that eternal life was his supreme desire, but all the while there was something which he prized more, and Jesus revealed it to him. "His face fell, and he went away grieving."

"Sell all that thou hast and give it to the poor."

Jesus made the demand in good earnest, but to suppose that He here makes poverty a universal condition of discipleship were a profound misconception. He dealt with men after the manner of a skilful physician, discovering their diverse plagues and administering to each the appropriate remedy. Had Herod Antipas come to Him, enquiring what he must do to inherit eternal life, He would, like John the Baptist, have laid His hand on the plague-spot and answered: "Put away thy brother's wife." Had Nicodemus come to Him with a like enquiry, He would have said to him: "If thou wishest to be perfect, go, conquer thy craven fear and confess Me before men." And even so, when the young ruler came to Him, He discovered what was the plague of his

---

[1] Mk. x. 21: ἠγάπησεν αὐτόν. Lightfoot on Mk. x. 21 and John xiii. 23. Field, *Notes.* Orig. *In Ev. Matth.* xv. § 14 (vat. interpr.): "dilexit eum, vel, osculatus est eum."

heart, the canker that was eating into his soul. It was his wealth, and Jesus laid His hand upon it and declared that it must go. "If thou wishest to be perfect, go, sell all that thou hast, and give it to the poor, and thou shalt have treasure in Heaven; and come, follow Me." Such is ever the Lord's requirement. Whatever it be that a man prizes most, He lays His hand upon it and claims for the Kingdom of Heaven a prior devotion; and "that man who has anything in the world so dear to him, that he cannot spare it for Christ, if He call for it, is no true Christian."

"How hardly shall a rich man enter into the Kingdom!" As the young ruler withdrew with downcast face and sorrowful heart, making "the great refusal," Jesus spoke one of the sternest words that ever fell on mortal ears. "How hardly," He exclaimed, "shall they that have riches enter into the Kingdom of God!" Then, marking the disciples' amazement, He reiterated the assertion, refusing to qualify it and quoting a common proverb to lend it still greater emphasis: "Children, how hard it is to enter into the Kingdom of God![1] It is easier for a camel to pass through the needle's eye than for a rich man to enter into the Kingdom of God."[2] The declaration fell like a thunder-bolt on the disciples. "They were amazed at His words"; "they were astonished exceedingly." And no wonder; for Jesus had struck a blow at their fondest hope. They clung still to the Jewish ideal of the Messianic Kingdom. What was it that had attached them to Jesus at the outset and nerved them to endure the sacrifices and hardships of discipleship? It was chiefly no doubt the love which they bore Him, yet mingled therewith they had an ignobler motive. They looked for rich amends. When their Master gained His throne, He would, they confidently anticipated, recompense His faithful followers who had continued with Him in His days of humiliation. He would load them with honours and award them the chief places at His royal

Consterna-
tion of the
Twelve.

---

[1] Mk. x. 24 T. R.: τοὺς πεποιθότας ἐπὶ τοῖς χρήμασιν, a frigid gloss.

[2] Attempts have been made to tone down the metaphor (1) by substituting κάμιλος, "cable," for κάμηλος, and (2) by understanding the "needle's eye" as a postern-gate. Cf. Shak. K. Rich. II, V. v:

"It is as hard to come as for a camel
To thread the postern of a needle's eye."

The monstrous exaggeration, however, is thoroughly Oriental. Cf. similar proverbs in Lightfoot, all denoting *impossibilities*. The proverb occurs in *Koran*, vii.

court. They would have lands and houses, and they would
sit, in accordance with that generation's carnal dream of the
Messianic Kingdom, like the council of the Sanhedrin with
Him as their president, judging the nations of the world.[1]
Nor, when they saw the storm gathering, did they relinquish
their hope. They reasoned that it would merely precipitate
the consummation and compel their Master to cast aside His
inexplicable delay and, flashing forth in His rightful glory,
take unto Him His great power and reign.

Hence their consternation at that declaration of Jesus.
They were dreaming of riches in the Kingdom of Heaven,
and He told them that a rich man would hardly enter
into it. The announcement sounded like the death-knell
of their hopes. Were their sacrifices after all to go unre-
quited? Was the recompense whereon they had confidently
reckoned, to be snatched from their grasp? Was the hope
which had lured them to forsake their possessions and cast in
their lot with the homeless Son of Man, to prove all a delusion?
Peter, ever the spokesman of the Twelve, gave voice to their
dismay. "Behold," he said, pointing the contrast betwixt
the Apostles and the young ruler, "*we* have left all and have
followed Thee. What then shall we get?"[2] And how did
Jesus answer? On another occasion, with the design of
beating down in the hearts of His disciples that mercenary
spirit which serves God for the hope of glory and reward, He
had spoken a stern parable.[3] "Who is there of you," He
said, "having a slave ploughing or shepherding, who on the
latter coming in from the field will say to him : 'Come aside
straightway and take thy place at table'; and will not rather
say to him : 'Get my supper ready, and gird thyself and wait
upon me while I eat and drink, and thereafter thou shalt eat
and drink'? Is he grateful to the slave for doing what was
commanded? Even so ye also, when ye have done all that

Peter's question.

Lk. xvii. 7-10.

---

[1] Lightfoot on John iii. 17.

[2] Orig. *In Matth.* xv. § 22 : "Like an athlete after the contest enquiring of the
umpire if he knows not the prizes of the contest."

[3] The occasion of the parable is lost. Lk. introduces it abruptly in an alien
setting. *Cf.* the precept of that ancient Rabbi, Antigonus of Socho : "Be not
as slaves that minister to the lord with a view to receive recompense ; but be
as slaves that minister to the lord without a view to receive recompense ; and let
the fear of Heaven be upon you." Taylor, *Say. of Fath.* i. 3.

was commanded you, say: 'We are unprofitable slaves: only what it was our duty to do have we done.'" It is not thus indeed that God deals with His people. He calls them not slaves but sons; He longs for their love and requites their poor service with a rich recompense. Yet such must ever be their attitude toward Him. They are His bondsmen. He has bought them with a great price, and His love constraineth them. They owe Him a debt which they can never pay, and they gladly acknowledge it, realising that, when they have done their utmost, they are still unprofitable slaves, and, though they had done a thousand-fold more, they would be still His debtors.

The Lord's reply. Jesus might have answered Peter's question: "What then shall we get?" after this fashion; but for very pity He refrained Himself, touched by their distress. Nor did He smile at His apostle's protestation: "Behold, we have left all and have followed Thee." To any one but Jesus it might have seemed a foolish boast. For what had Peter left for the Master's sake? Not lands and gold, but a life of toil and poverty, the reeds by the Lake, his net, his boat, and his fishercraft.[1] In the world's sight it was but little that the disciples had left; but it was all that they had, and Jesus did not make light of their sacrifices for His sake. He made answer in great pity and kindness, and spoke a gracious word of reassurance. He told them that they would in no wise lose their reward. All that they had anticipated, yea, and more than they had anticipated, would come to pass. "Verily I tell you," He says, employing the imagery wherewith they decked their dreams, and surveying them the while with that wondrous face of His,[2] "that ye that have followed Me, in the Regeneration, when the Son of Man shall sit upon His throne of glory, shall yourselves also take your seats upon twelve thrones, judging the twelve tribes of Israel. And everyone who hath left brethren or sisters or father or mother or children or lands or houses for My name's sake, shall receive manifold more and inherit eternal life." And the

[1] Orig. *In Matth.* xv. § 22 ; Chrysost. *In Matth.* lxv.
[2] Mt. xix. 26 ; Mk. x. 27 : ἐμβλέψας. *Cf.* Chrysost. *In Matth.* lxiv : ἡμέρῳ ὄμματι καὶ πράῳ φρίττουσαν αὐτῶν τὴν διάνοιαν παραμυθησάμενος καὶ τὴν ἀγωνίαν καταλύσας.

promise was abundantly fulfilled, though after another fashion
than they expected, when they entered into the large and holy
brotherhood of the Church and inherited, not land and gold,
but the priceless possessions of righteousness, peace, and joy
in the Holy Ghost.

" But," Jesus added, gently insinuating a word of warning, Parable of
" there shall be many first last and last first " ; and in the Labourers in
explanation of this epigrammatic sentence He spoke a parable. the Vine-
He told how a master went out to the market-place one yard.
morning at day-break and hired men to work in his vineyard
at the usual wage of a *denarius* a day. About nine o'clock,
when three hours of the day were gone, he found others
standing idle in the market-place, and sent them also into the
vineyard ; in their case, however, making no stipulation about
wages but simply promising fair payment. Glad to get
employment, they agreed. He did the like about twelve
o'clock, and again about three. About five, when only one
working hour remained, he once more visited the market-place
and found others standing unemployed. They were the poorest
sort of labourers, and they had stood there the livelong day,
seeing others hired and hoping that their turn would come ;
but no one would have them. Their dejected aspect aroused
the compassion of the kindly farmer. " Go ye also into the
vineyard," he said, never mentioning wages ; and they obeyed
with ready alacrity, trusting to his benevolence and glad of the
chance of earning something, however little.

When six o'clock came and the day's work was ended,
the master told his factor to pay the men, bidding him begin
with those who had been hired last. They got a *denarius* a-
piece, a full day's wage, though they had worked only an hour
and shown themselves but sorry workmen. The first hired made
sure that they would get more, but to their disgust they got
only a *denarius*. To be sure, it was what they had bargained
for ; nevertheless they felt aggrieved. They all grumbled,
and one of them, letting his *denarius* lie, protested insolently,
addressing the factor but speaking out so that the master,
who was standing by, might hear : " These last fellows put in
a single hour,[1] and thou hast put them on an equality with us
that have borne the burden of the day and the burning heat."

---

[1] μίαν ὥραν ἐποίησαν, not εἰργάσαντο. *Cf.* Ja. iv. 13 ; Acts **xv.** 33 ; **xx.** 3.

The master interposed. " Mate," he said, " I am doing thee no injustice. Didst thou not bargain with me for a *denarius*? Take up thy pay, and begone ! It is my pleasure to give to 'this last fellow' even as to thee. May I not do what I please with my own ? Or is thine eye grudging because I am generous ? "[1]

" Thus," said Jesus, " shall the last be first and the first last." The parable was designed, in the first instance, to correct the mercenary spirit of the Twelve. If they worked for wages, they would get their wages, but they would be accounted mere hirelings. God would have His workmen serve Him with no thought of recompense, not like those first hired labourers who made their bargain ere they went into the vineyard, but like those that went simply at the master's bidding, leaving it to him to pay them whatever was just ; nay, like " these last " who fell to work with never a thought of requital, thankful that he had regarded them and trusting to his generosity.

The parable was designed, moreover, to beat down the arrogance of the disciples. Did that sentence : " It is my pleasure to give to 'this last fellow' even as to thee," never ring in the ears of " the men who had been with Jesus " when, because he had been hired late, they denied the apostleship of St Paul ? And did the Jewish Christians never think of this parable when they despised the Gentiles whom the Lord had pitied and received into His service, making no difference betwixt them and the Jews who had been hired at the first hour ? It is a lesson which the Church had need to learn in apostolic days and which she still has need to lay to heart, that the Lord will be served for love and not for wages, that He has a special tenderness for the despised and the neglected, and that He looks not at a man's work but at the spirit wherewith he labours.

[1] *Cf.* Introd. § 12, 4.

CHAPTER XXXIX

THE RAISING OF LAZARUS

John xi. 1-53.

"Ille suscitavit hominem, qui fecit hominem. Plus est hominem creare quam resuscitare."—S. AUGUST.

JESUS was thus employed at Bethany beyond Jordan when tidings reached Him from the other Bethany. Lazarus had fallen sick, and his anxious sisters had bethought them of the dear Master and sent Him word. So absolute was their confidence in Him that they made no request. They neither, like the courtier of Capernaum, implored Him to hasten to the rescue, nor, like the centurion, suggested that, abiding where He was, He should send forth His word and heal their brother. They simply informed Him how matters stood, believing that, if only He knew, He would help, and leaving it to Him to do whatever He might deem best.[1] "Lord," their message ran, "he whom Thou lovest is sick." Sickness of Lazarus. John iv. 47. Mt. viii. 8.

The tidings moved Jesus. He recognised the hand of God in the sickness of Lazarus. He had been praying that some occasion might arise which would attest His divine commission and serve at once as a final appeal to Jerusalem and a confirmation of His disciples' faith; and, behold, His desire was fulfilled. "This sickness," He declared when He heard the message, "is not unto death but for the glory of God, that the Son of God," that is, the Messiah, "may be glorified through it." He recognised the Father's purpose, and, that it might come to pass, remained for two days where He was. An answer to Jesus' prayer.

Meanwhile the faith of the sisters was suffering a severe trial. No succour came; Lazarus died;[2] their messenger Death of Lazarus.

---

[1] Aug. *In Joan. Ev. Tract.* xlix. § 5: "Sufficit ut noveris; non enim amas et deseris."

[2] The two Bethanies were some 20 miles apart. If the messenger set out early in the day, he would reach Jesus that night. Jesus tarried two days and started the next. He would arrive that evening. Since Lazarus had then been three full days in his grave (*v.* 39), he must have died soon after the messenger's departure, burial following immediately (*cf. P. E. F. Q.*, Oct. 1905, p. 349).

returned alone, and it would be a cruel aggravation of their distress when they learned what Jesus had said. "This sickness," He had declared, "is not unto death"; nevertheless His promise had been belied. Contrary, as it seemed, to His assurance their brother was dead. They did not know the Lord's purpose nor the love which was hidden beneath His apparent neglect. "Jesus loved Martha and her sister and Lazarus. *Therefore*, when He heard that he was sick, He remained in the place where He was." Yet so absolute was their confidence in Him that they believed in Him still despite His seeming coldness and the seeming falsification of His prediction.

"Let us go into Judæa again."
After two days' tarrying Jesus bade the Twelve accompany Him back to Judæa. All the while Lazarus had never been out of His thoughts, but so little concern had He manifested that they had forgotten the sickness of their friend. Moreover His assurance, as it seemed, that it would not have a fatal issue, had prevented them from feeling any alarm ; and, when He proposed to return to Judæa, they never guessed His errand but naturally supposed that He meant to adventure Himself once more in Jerusalem ; and they were alarmed for

Alarm of the Twelve.
His safety and no less for their own. "Rabbi," they cried, "it is but now that the rulers were seeking to stone Thee, and art Thou again going there?" He calmly replied, apparently quoting a proverb : "Are there not twelve hours in the day? If one walk in the day, he doth not stumble, because he seeth the light of this world ; but, if one walk in the night, he stumbleth, because the light is not in him." "God's children," says old Thomas Fuller, "are immortal while their Father hath anything for them to do on earth" ; and, since the Father called Him thither, Jesus would return to Judæa, confident that, until His time should be fulfilled, His enemies were powerless. Then, thinking to reassure them, He told the Twelve that Bethany and not Jerusalem was His destination. "Lazarus our friend hath fallen asleep, but I am going to awake him." They misunderstood the beautiful metaphor, afterwards so familiar, and clutched at the announcement as an argument against making the perilous journey. Sleep, they represented, betokened returning health ;[1]

[1] *Cf.* Wetstein.

and, if Lazarus had fallen asleep, he would recover, and there
was no need for Jesus to risk His life and theirs by going to
Bethany.[1]   Their reluctance convicted them of stupidity,
cowardice, and selfishness, and Jesus answered sadly and
not without severity : " Lazarus died ; and I rejoice on your
account that I was not there, that ye may believe.   Nay,
let us go unto him."   They were half disposed to let
Him go alone, but for very shame they durst not ; and
Judas the Twin, ever despondent yet a brave man and a
lover of Jesus at heart, determined their vacillation.   " Let
us go too," he cried, "that we may die along with
Him."

The home at Bethany was plunged in woe.   It was the
Jewish fashion that, when a man died, his friends should come
and condole with the survivors for the space of a week.   Not
till three days had elapsed was hope abandoned.   It was
believed that for three days after death the soul hovered
round the sepulchre, fain to re-enter and reanimate its fleshly
tenement ; and stories, very credible in view of the fact that
in that sultry climate immediate interment was necessary,
were told of buried men awaking and coming out of their
graves.   For three days the mourners clung to hope, and
would visit the grave, if haply they might find their dead
alive.   But on the fourth day decomposition set in, and, when
they saw its ghastly disfigurement upon the face, their hope
perished, and, returning home, they abandoned themselves
to unrestrained lamentation.[2]   There was no lack of mourners
in the house of Lazarus.   He was beloved for his goodness
and gentleness by the folk among whom he dwelt, and even
in the adjacent capital he was had in honour.   Despite his
intimacy with Jesus a large deputation of the rulers had come
to condole with his sisters.[3]

On the fourth day Jesus arrived.   He would be descried
afar off climbing with His disciples the Ascent of Blood, and
Martha was informed of His approach.   She hastened out
and met Him ere He entered the village.   " Lord," she cried,

Mourning at Bethany. Ecclus. xxii. 12.

Arrival of Jesus.

Jesus and Martha.

[1] Chrysost. *In Joan.* lxi : ἐγκόψαι βουλόμενοι τὴν ἐκεῖ παρουσίαν.
[2] See Lightfoot on John xi. 39.
[3] When R. Ismael's sons died, four Rabbis came to comfort him.   Lightfoot on
John xi. 19.

" if Thou hadst been here, my brother had not died." Such had been the plaint of the sisters all those heavy days. It seemed as though Jesus had failed them in their sore need, yet had they not utterly abandoned hope. They remembered the daughter of Jaïrus and the son of the widow of Nain, and they deemed it possible that their brother might be restored in like manner. Such was Martha's thought. No sooner had she exclaimed reproachfully : " Lord, if Thou hadst been here, my brother had not died ! " than she added : " Even now I know that all that Thou askest of God, God will give Thee." She hoped that He would recall Lazarus to life, and her heart sank within her when He answered : " Thy brother shall rise again." She would have rejoiced had He said, " Thy brother shall *live* again " ; but when He said " He shall *rise* again," she thought of the Resurrection at the Last Day, and supposed that He was offering her merely one of the trite consolations of religion. She did not indeed disdain that glorious hope ; but the Resurrection seemed far away, and her heart craved present succour. Jesus hastened to uplift her drooping spirit, and vouchsafed to her a great reassurance. " I," He said, " am the Resurrection and the Life. He that believeth in Me, even if he die, shall live , and every one that liveth and believeth in Me shall never die.[1] Believest thou this ? " It was impossible for Martha to comprehend then the full significance of that declaration, yet it was not wholly hidden from her. It was a doctrine of the later Jewish theology that, when the Messiah came, He would summon Israel, at all events the righteous, from their graves to share His glory.[2] Perhaps this doctrine occurred to her, and her confidence in Jesus would reinforce it, emboldening her to believe, on His assurance, more than she could understand. " Yea, Lord," she answered ; " I have believed that Thou art the Messiah, the Son of God, He that cometh into the world."[3]

---

[1] This use of "life" and "death" in a double sense, natural and spiritual, was characteristic of Jesus. *Cf.* Mt. viii. 22 = Lk. ix. 60. Aug. *In Joan. Ev. Tract.* xlix. § 15 : "Unde mors in anima ? Quia non est fides. Unde mors in corpore ? Quia non est ibi anima. Ergo animæ tuæ anima fides est."

[2] *Cf.* Charles on *Enoch* ii. 1.

[3] Simply a strong confession of the Messiahship of Jesus, ὁ υἱὸς τοῦ Θεοῦ and ὁ εἰς τὸν κόσμ. ἐρχ. being variations of ὁ Χριστός.

Therewith she returned to the house where Mary sat [1] Jesus and
mourning, ignorant of the Lord's arrival ; and, knowing the Mary.
enmity of the rulers, whispered to her : " The Teacher hath
come and is calling for thee." Mary started up and sped
away with winged haste. She found Him outside the village
where Martha had left Him ; and, more impassioned than her
sister, she fell at His feet, those blessed feet which she had
bedewed with tears on that great day when He cleansed her Lk. vii. 38.
soul from its defilement in the house of Simon the Pharisee, John xii. 3;
and which were ever after sacred in her eyes. Like Martha xxviii. 9).
she cried : " Lord, if Thou hadst been here, my brother had
not died ! " but she said no more. The dear Lord's presence
sufficed her. She sobbed out the sorrow of her heart at His
feet and left it all with Him.

The company of mourners had marked Mary's hasty Jewish
departure, and, surmising that she was going to weep at the lamenta-
sepulchre, they had followed after her. They found her tion.
weeping at Jesus' feet, and, with the wild abandonment of
Oriental grief, they mingled their lamentations with hers.
Examples of Jewish lamentation are found in the Talmud,
and one marvels at their utter hopelessness, more befitting
heathen than worshippers of the living and true God. When
the sons of R. Ismael died, four Rabbis came to condole
with him. " Should we not," said R. Tarphon, " argue by
the less and the greater ? If it was necessary to bewail
Nadab and Abihu, much more the sons of R. Ismael." Then Lev. x. 6.
Joses of Galilee took up the refrain . " Should we not argue
from the less to the greater ? If all Israel mourned for
Abijah the son of Jeroboam, for the sons of Ismael should we 1 Kings
not weep much more ? " [2] Such lamentation would now xiv. 13.
assail the ears of Jesus, and He was greatly displeased, even
as on that like occasion when he entered the house of Jaïrus
and, finding a company of mourners " weeping and shrieking," Mk. v. 38;
cried : " Withdraw ! Why are ye making a tumult and weep- Mt. ix. 24.
ing ? The child is not dead but sleepeth." A storm of grief
and indignation swept His soul. His brow was knit, His lips
quivered, His breast heaved, His breath came quick and

---

[1] ἐκαθέζετο (v. 20), ἐγείρεται (v. 29). During the days of mourning the beds
were lowered and the mourners sat on them, the comforters sitting on the ground.
Lightfoot on John xi. 19,   [2] Ibid. cf. p. 200.

short.[1] " Where have ye laid him ? " He demanded.   " Lord,"
they answered, " come and see."

"Jesus
wept."   According to the Jewish requirement the burial-place was
situated at least a mile outside the village,[2] and on the way
thither the Lord's emotion found relief in tears.   What made
Him weep ?.   It was not simply His resentment of that outburst of heathenish lamentation.   Neither was it sorrow for
the death of His friend.   It was natural that Martha and
Mary should weep for their bereavement, but wherefore should
Jesus weep, knowing that Lazarus would presently be restored
to life ?   In truth it was naught else than this knowledge
that occasioned His tears.   " He was about," said one long
ago,[3] " to raise him for His own glory ; He wept for him,
almost saying : ' One that has sailed within the haven, I am
calling back to the billows ; one that has already been
crowned, I am bringing again to the contests.' "   If St Paul
Phil. i. 23. had the desire to depart and be with Christ, since it was very
much better, what marvel that Jesus, who knew the felicity
of Heaven, should grieve to summon Lazarus thence and
bring him back to the strife and sorrow of this mortal state ?
Remembering the gladness of the Father's House where He
had dwelt from everlasting and whence He had come on His
errand of redemption, He recognised it as no disaster but an
exceeding gain to fall on sleep and wake in that home of bliss
and inherit the glory which God hath prepared for them that
love Him.

Diverse
comments
of the
rulers.
Cf. John
ix. 16; x.
19.   The rulers in the company were watching Jesus narrowly,
and the spectacle of His emotion set them talking and dis-
puting.   Once more there was a diversity of opinion among
them.   Some exclaimed : " See how he loved him ! " but
others jeered.   This was the man who had passed for a
miracle-worker and only the other week had created such a
stir in Jerusalem by pretending to have opened a blind man's

---

[1] ἐνεβριμήσατο τῷ πνεύματι καὶ ἐτάραξεν ἑαυτόν : an energetic and picturesque
description. For the meaning of ἐνεβριμ. cf. p. 114. Chrysost. understands : " He
checked His emotion," mastering it with a violent effort. But τῷ πνεύματι corresponds to ἐν ἑαυτῷ (v. 38), which discountenances also Wright's rendering (Synops.
p. 139), " sighed deeply in His breath." ἐτάρ. ἑαυτ.: cf. Pss. xlii. 5, 11 ; xliii. 5
(LXX). " He threw Himself into a state of agitation," the indignation of His πνεῦμα
appearing in His bodily movements. There is a touch of docetism in Augustine's
comment : " Quis eum posset, nisi se ipse, turbare ? "

[2] Cf. p. 221, n. 3   [3] Isidor. Pelus. Ep. ii. 173.

eyes; and here he was shedding unavailing and impoten
tears! "Could not this fellow," they sneered, malignant even
in the presence of death, "the opener of the blind man's eyes,
have prevented this man also from dying?"[1] Thus they
exulted in what they deemed the Lord's discomfiture.

Their sneer reached His ears, and, stifling the indigna- The
tion which anew swelled within Him, He approached the miracle.
sepulchre. It was a cave hewn out of the rock, and the
entrance was closed with a great slab of stone. "Take away
the stone," He commanded. Martha remonstrated. It was
the fourth day since the burial, and decomposition had set in.
She was sure of it, since she had that morning visited the
sepulchre and seen on the dear face the loathsome change
which warned the mourners to relinquish their last fond hope;
and, thinking that Jesus meant merely to take a last look at
His friend's remains, she would fain dissuade Him from disclosing the ghastly spectacle. "Said I not unto thee," Jesus *Cf. vv.* 4,
replied, "'If thou believest, thou shalt see the glory of God'?" 25-6.
He knew well the dead man's condition, yet it in no wise
dismayed Him. On the contrary, He rejoiced that things
had gone thus far, since the miracle would carry the greater *Cf. v.* 15.
conviction. Had He arrived a day earlier, the Jews, deeming
it always possible, until decomposition appeared, that the soul
might reanimate its clay, would have pronounced it no miracle
at all. It had been thus ordered by the providence of God
and not by the design of Jesus, who did not discover until
He arrived at Bethany that Lazarus had been four days in *Cf. v.* 17.
his sepulchre. And Jesus recognised all this as no happy
chance but the operation of God and an answer to His prayer.
Standing by the open sepulchre He poured out His gratitude
to the Father whose hand had opened up His way before
Him and led Him to that great hour, vouchsafing the opportunity which He had craved for the manifestation of His

---

[1] *Cf.* Chrysost. *In Joan.* lxii. The adversative δέ, contrasting the second
speech with the first (*cf.* v. 46), and the consequent indignation of Jesus prove de-
cisively that the question was a sneer. According to Strauss their reference to "this
heterogeneous and inadequate example" and their silence about the two earlier re-
suscitations of the dead prove that the latter were unknown to the Fourth Evangelist.
It was, however, natural that they should quote the recent miracle, the immediate
casus belli. Doubtless they had heard the fame of the two miracles in distant
Galilee (*cf.* Lk. vii. 17); but it was an old story, nor was it their policy to revive it.

glory.   Not for Himself had He sought it, since He had the
assurance of His Father's approbation ; but the disciples and
the Jews needed such a manifestation.   " Father," He said, " I
thank Thee that Thou didst hearken unto Me.   Yet I knew
that Thou always hearkenest unto Me, but for the sake of
the multitude that standeth round I spake, that they may
believe that Thou didst commission Me." [1]   Then He cried :
"Lazarus, come forth ! "   He cried, says the Evangelist,
" with a great voice."   It was the shout of Death's Conqueror,
and the dead man heard His voice, and, when he heard it, he
lived and came forth, all wrapped in his grave-clothes.[2]
" Loose him," said Jesus, " and let him go his way."

There was already a division of opinion among those
rulers who had come from Jesusalem to condole with Martha
and Mary ; and the miracle made it more decided.   Many of
them believed in Jesus ; but there were others who " would
not be persuaded though one had risen from the dead," and
they betook themselves to Jerusalem and reported to their
colleagues of the party of the Pharisees, being probably
Pharisees themselves, what had transpired.   The story made
a great sensation among the rulers, and, convening the
Sanhedrin, they debated what course they should pursue.
They foresaw that a miracle so amazing must procure Jesus
a vast access of popularity ; and, knowing the jealous
surveillance which Rome exercised over turbulent Palestine,
they dreaded the consequences, should the multitude rally
round Him and acclaim Him the Messianic King of Israel.
" What are we doing," cried the panic-stricken councillors,
" forasmuch as this fellow is doing many signs ?   If we let
him thus alone, they will all believe in him ; and the
Romans will come and take away our place [3] and our nation
both."   They shuddered at the storm of vengeance which
would sweep over the devoted land, destroying their holy
Temple and obliterating every vestige of Jewish nationality.
The president of the assemblage was the High Priest

Cf. Mt.
xxvii. 50=
Mk. xv. 37
=Lk. xxiii.
46.
Cf. John v.
28.

Resolution
of the
Sanhedrin
to put Jesus
to death.

Lk. xvi.
31.

[1] Origen (*In Joan.* xxviii. § 5) thinks that Jesus gave thanks because He had
observed that the soul of Lazarus had returned into his body.
[2] Augustine (*In Joan. Ev. Tract.* xlix. § 24) thinks it a further miracle that he
should have been able to walk forth thus swathed.   But, if the swathings were
wrapped about each limb separately, they would not interfere with his movements.
[3] The Temple.   *Cf.* Acts vi. 13-4.

Caiaphas, a member of the Sadducean order, and he broke in upon the excited deliberations of his colleagues. The course was clear : Jesus must be got out of the way. It was indeed a violent measure, but what was a single life in comparison with the interests at stake? "Ye know nothing whatever," he blustered with Sadducean insolence [1] and the air of a strong man who sees what the occasion demands and will not palter, "nor do ye reckon that it is in your interest that one man should die for the people and that the whole nation should not perish."

When he thus spoke, the truculent Sanhedrist uttered a deeper truth than he knew. "This he said not of himself," observes the Evangelist, "but, being High Priest that eventful year,[2] he prophesied that Jesus was about to die for the nation, and not for the nation only but to gather together into one all God's dispersed children." It was an unconscious prophecy, and it is the more striking that it was spoken by the High Priest. All unwittingly he proclaimed Jesus the true Paschal Lamb. There was tragic irony in the situation. In his masterful pride Caiaphas was working out God's eternal purpose ; and, when his colleagues acquiesced in his policy, they were defeating the end which they thought to compass, and bringing upon their nation the very disaster which they strove to avert. In that hour when they decreed the death of Jesus, they sealed the doom of Israel.

The prophecy of Caiaphas.

---

[1] *Cf.* p. 43.

[2] The office of High Priest was originally held for life, but in our Lord's day the High Priests were appointed and deposed at the pleasure of Herod and the Romans. Strauss, following Chrysostom and Augustine, imputes to the Evangelist the erroneous notion that it was a yearly office ; but ἀρχιερεὺς ὢν τοῦ ἐνιαυτοῦ ἐκείνου (*vv.* 49, 51 ; *cf.* xviii. 13) does not imply that Caiaphas was High Priest only for that year, but that that memorable year fell during his pontificate.

John xi. 54
7 ; Mt. xx
17-9 = Mk
x. 32-4 =
Lk. xviii.
31-4 ; Mt.
xx. 20-8 =
Mk. x. 35-
45 (Lk.
xxii. 25-6) ;
Mt. xx. 29-
34 = Mk. x.
46-52 = Lk.
xviii. 35-
43 ; Lk.
xix. 1-28 ;
Mt. xxvi.
6-13 = Mk.
xiv. 3-9 =
John xii. 1-
11.

CHAPTER XL

GOING UP TO THE PASSOVER

"All in the April evening,
    April airs were abroad ;
    The sheep with their little lambs
    Passed me by on the road.

"The lambs were weary, and crying
    With a weak, human cry ;
    I thought on the Lamb of God
    Going meekly to die."—KATHERINE TYNAN.

Retreat to Ephraim.

AWARE of the Sanhedrin's resolution Jesus would not adventure Himself in Jerusalem. His time to die had not yet come, and, until it came, He would avoid the rage of His enemies. Had He returned to Bethany beyond Jordan, He would have been within their grasp, and He betook Himself to the town of Ephraim, twenty miles north of Jerusalem and five north-east of Bethel, on the margin of the wilderness of Judæa.[1] Ephraim is unknown to fame.[2] It was situated in a wheat-growing district, and the Jews had a proverb "Carry straw to Ephraim," much like our "Carry coals to Newcastle."[3] What took Jesus thither ? For one reason, Ephraim was close to the Samaritan frontier,[4] and, in the event of any attempt on the part of the rulers to arrest Him, He could have escaped over the border. The Samaritans had indeed shown themselves unfriendly when He was travelling south-ward ; but the self-same animosity against the Jews which had made them His enemies when His face was in the direction of Jerusalem, would have procured Him their good offices had He come amongst them a fugitive from Jewish violence.

Lk. ix. 51-3.

---

[1] Jer. *De Loc. Hebr.* ; Schürer, *H. J. P.* I. i. p. 246.

[2] The very name is uncertain. Some MSS. read 'Εφρέμ. Chrysost.: Εὐφρατά.

[3] *Menach.* 85. 1 : "Dixerunt Jannes et Jambres Mosi : ' Tune stramen affers in Ephraim ?'" *Cf.* Lightfoot, ii. p. 43.

[4] It had been a Samaritan town until B.C. 145, when it was granted by Demetrius II. to the Maccabean High Priest Jonathan and united to Judæa. 1 Macc. xi. 34.

Moreover, Ephraim was nigh to the wilderness where at the outset of His ministry He had been tempted of the Devil ; and it may be that during His sojourn there He would revisit the scene of His early conflict, fortifying Himself by remembrance of His triumph for the last, dread ordeal.

There He tarried till the Passover was at hand, and then *Departure for Jerusalem.* He set out with the Twelve for Jerusalem. They did not strike direct across the wilderness of Judæa but travelled south-eastward for some twelve miles until in the neighbourhood of Jericho they joined the highway from the north. Ephraim sent its contingent of worshippers to the Feast, and these went in company with Jesus and the Twelve. It was customary for the pilgrims to sing glad songs as they journeyed *Ps. xlii. 4.* to the Holy City, but that train marched in silence. Jesus strode on in advance, and His companions followed after Him, the disciples in amazement and the rest in fear.[1] It was His bearing that so impressed them. He knew what was His journey's goal, and, as He travelled amid the sunshine, the shadow of death was upon His soul. Yet He did not bear Himself as one dismayed, else had the disciples gathered about Him and sought to comfort Him. He walked majestic. Never had they seen Him so kingly.

Thus they went their way, and presently Jesus took the *Third announcement of the Passion.* Twelve aside and for the third time forewarned them of His Passion. On the first occasion He had announced simply *Mt. xvi 21. =Mk. viii. 31=Lk. ix. 22.* that He must suffer many things at the hands of the rulers, and be killed, and on the third day be raised. On the second He had added the tragic particular of His betrayal. Here He *Mt. xvii. 22-3=Mk. ix. 31=Lk ix. 44.* unfolds the whole of the grim drama : His betrayal, His condemnation, His surrender to the Romans to be mocked, insulted, spat upon, scourged, and crucified, and His resurrection on the third day. Again He spoke to uncomprehending ears. The thoughts of the Twelve were occupied with the miracle which they had lately witnessed at Bethany. At last, they imagined, the crisis so long postponed had arrived. Their Master could no longer hold back. He must manifest *Cf. Lk.* Himself in His rightful glory and inaugurate His Messianic *xix. 11.* reign. They received the announcement in bewildered silence.

---

[1] Mk. x. 32 : οἱ δὲ ἀκολουθοῦντες, " the others, as they followed." T. R. καὶ ἀκολ. obliterates this significant touch.

Ambition
of Salome
and her
sons. How far it was from dispelling their worldly dream
appears from an incident which presently occurred. They
had, it would seem, reached the highway from the north
and, probably by appointment, joined company with a train
of Galilean pilgrims.[1] Among the latter was Salome, the
mother of James and John. The fame of the miracle at
Bethany had been noised abroad and must have reached
Capernaum. She would eagerly question her sons regarding
it, and betwixt them they arranged a cunning plot.[2] Probably
they had long cherished the design, and now, they thought,
the time had arrived for carrying it into effect. The manifestation of the Kingdom of Heaven was imminent, and thereafter would ensue the distribution of honours among the Lord's
faithful followers. The Twelve had frequently debated who
should be greatest in the Kingdom, and James and John had
been not the least loud in the assertion of their claims. And
Salome, with maternal solicitude for her sons' advancement, had
fanned the flame of their ambition. Since the chief honours
must indubitably fall to the favoured three, Peter seemed
their only rival, and their plot was to oust him by extorting
from Jesus a pledge that they should have the pre-eminence.
It must, they recognised, be now or never ; yet, when the
moment for action came, they held back. They shrank from
approaching Jesus and unfolding their ambition before Him.
Did they remember His severity whenever the Twelve had
betrayed their worldly imaginations ? Did they recall the
" Get thee behind Me, Satan ! " which He had hurled at Peter,
and dread lest they should suffer a like rebuff ? It is indeed
no marvel that, when the moment arrived, they hesitated to
approach Him and prefer their ambitious request. Salome,
however, less acquainted with the Master's spirit, felt no
scruple. She would rally them on their cowardice.

> " Was the hope drunk
> Wherein ye dress'd yourselves ? hath it slept since ?
> And wakes it now, to look so green and pale
> At what it did so freely ? . . . Are ye afeard.
> To be the same in your own act and valour,
> As ye were in desire ? "

---

[1] Unless indeed Salome had been with them at Ephraim.

[2] Mt. (xx. 20 ; cf. Mk. x. 35) mentions Salome's intervention, moved perhaps by the
same solicitude for the Apostles' credit which made Lk. omit the incident altogether.

Her remonstrances proved unavailing, and there was nothing for it but that she should herself undertake the office of approaching Jesus and negotiating with Him on their behalf.

And she discharged it with consummate skill. She *Her* approached Jesus, so soon to be a King, in the fashion of *petition.* a suitor,[1] even as Esther approached Ahasuerus, and prayed *Esth. v.* Him to pledge Himself beforehand, after the large manner of *Cf. Mt. xiv.* Oriental despots, to grant whatever she might request. " What *7=Mk. vi.* dost thou wish ? " He enquired, brushing aside her artful *22-3.* ruse ; and she unfolded her plan. " Say the word that these my two sons may sit one on Thy right and the other on Thy left[2] in Thy Kingdom." It was Salome that spoke, but she was only the mouthpiece of her sons ; and to them Jesus made answer, not in anger but in sorrow that they should still be so worldly-minded. " Ye know not," He said, " what ye *Cf. Ps. xi.* are asking. Can ye drink the cup which I am drinking, *6; Mt.* or with the baptism wherewith I am being baptised, be *Cf. Lk.* baptised ? "[3] With light-hearted assurance they returned : *xii. 50.* " We can." They imagined that Jesus was going up to Jeru-salem to claim His throne, and they allowed that it could not be won without a struggle. When He asked if they could drink His cup and be baptised with His baptism, they con-ceived that He was challenging their courage to bear their parts in the preliminary struggle ; and, believing that, though the ordeal might be severe, the issue was certain, they assured Him of their resolution. Far otherwise had they spoken, had they known whereto they were pledging themselves, had it been revealed to them that a week later He would be lifted up, not on a throne but on a cross, with a cross on His right and a cross on His left. Their love for their Master would surely have kept them faithful ; but they would have spoken with faltering lips, and their answer would have been a trembling prayer for strength to drink that bitter cup and endure that bloody baptism.

Jesus foresaw the stern reality, and He knew that, how- *The Lord's promise.*

[1] προσέρχεσθαι of (1) a worshipper approaching God : cf. Hebr. iv. 16 ; vii. 25, xi. 6 ; (2) an inferior approaching a superior : cf. Mt. xiii. 27 ; Mt. xxvii. 58=Lk. xxiii. 52 ; (3) a candidate approaching an elector : Wetstein on Mk. x. 35.

[2] The places of honour. Cf. Wetstein on Mt. xx. 21.

[3] According to Mk.'s report (for πίνω Mt has μέλλω πίνειν) Jesus speaks as though the Passion had already begun.

ever they might quail at the outset, the Apostles would ultimately emerge victorious from the ordeal. "The cup which I am drinking," He said, "ye shall drink, and with the baptism wherewith I am being baptised, ye shall be baptised , but to sit on My right or left is not Mine to give, but it is for them for whom it hath been prepared."[1] The Apostles pictured the Kingdom of Heaven after the pattern of the corrupt kingdoms of the earth, where the honours were bestowed upon the prince's favourites ; and Jesus tells them that its honours must be won. They are not gifts but rewards. " Let us suppose," says St Chrysostom, "that there is an umpire, and many good athletes enter the lists. Two of the athletes, who are very intimate with the umpire, approach him and say: ' Cause us to be crowned and proclaimed victors,' on the strength of the goodwill and friendship betwixt them. But he says to them : ' This is not mine to give, but it is for them for whom it has been prepared by their efforts and sweat.' " The Lord's words sank into the hearts of the twain, and, though hidden at the moment, their meaning was afterwards revealed. Were they in John's thoughts when he wrote :

Rev. iii. 21; " He that overcometh—I will give to him to sit with Me on
cf. 2 Tim. My throne, as I also overcame and took My seat with My
ii. 12. Father on His Throne " ?

Greatness The incident was abundantly distressing to Jesus. It was
in the so untimeous, following hard after that solemn intimation of
Kingdom
of Heaven. His Passion. And the actors belonged to the inner circle of His chosen. They had enjoyed His especial favour and fellowship, yet they remained unpurged of worldly and selfish ambition. Moreover, their petition kindled resentment in the breasts of their comrades, and this grieved Jesus. He marked the indignation of the ten, and, calling them all about Him, He read them another lesson in self-abnegation, the fundamental law

Mt. xviii. of the Kingdom of Heaven. On a previous occasion He had
1-4=Mk.
ix. 34-7= set a child in their midst and bidden them take him for their
Lk. ix. 46- model ; but now He sets Himself forth as their example. If
8. they would be great in the Kingdom of Heaven, let them be as its King. "Ye know that the princes of the Gentiles lord it over them, and the great men exercise authority over them. Not thus is it among you ; but whosoever desireth among you

---

[1] Mt.'s ὑπὸ τοῦ Πατρός μου is a gloss which spoils the argument.

to become great, must be your servant ; and whosoever desireth
among you to be first, must be your slave ; even as the Son of
Man came not to be served but to serve and to give His life a
ransom for many."

This great saying has a priceless value. Though He "A ransom for many."
continually emphasised the supreme importance and the
absolute necessity of His death, Jesus never taught a doctrine
of the Atonement, leaving it to His Apostles, under the
guidance of the Holy Spirit, to penetrate that sacred
mystery and discover its significance. Nevertheless He let
fall several pregnant suggestions, and the apostolic teaching
is naught else than an explication of these. He spoke in
sacramental language of Himself as "the living bread that John vi. 50-1, 55.
came down from Heaven, that a man might eat thereof and
not die," of His flesh as "true food" and His blood as "true
drink." Again, He called Himself the True Shepherd and
specified it as the characteristic of the True Shepherd that John x. 11.3, 17-8.
He laid down His life for the sheep, to rescue them from
the devouring wolf. And now He speaks of "giving His life
a ransom for many." What image would this conjure up in
the minds of the disciples? It might suggest the half-shekel
which every Jewish adult paid yearly at the Passover-season
into the Temple-treasury, "a ransom for his soul unto the Exod. xxx 12-6.
Lord":[1] but there was another application of the word
which could hardly escape them. Her stormy history had
familiarised the Jewish nation with the usages of war ; and
when, hard after His allusion to the tyrannous princes of the
Gentiles, Jesus spoke of a "ransom," the disciples would
think of the redemption of captives taken in war and held in
bondage by the conqueror.[2] Here is, in germ, the apostolic
doctrine of the Atonement. "As many," says St Paul, "as Gal. iii. 10, 13.
are of the works of the Law, are under a curse. Christ
bought us out from the curse of the Law, having been made
a curse for us." And surely St Peter had this great saying

---

[1] Bruce, *Kingd. of God*, pp. 238 *sqq.* Ritschl makes out a reference to Job
xxxiii. 23-34 ; Ps. xlix. 7.

[2] Suid. : λύτρα· μισθός· ἢ τὰ παρεχόμενα ὑπὲρ ἐλευθερίας ἐπὶ τῷ λυτρώσασθαι βαρ-
βάρων δουλείας. λύτρον occurs nowhere else in N.T. ; but ἀντίλυτρον in 1 Tim.
ii. 6 : λυτροῦσθαι Lk. xxiv. 21 ; Tit. ii. 14 ; 1 Pet. i. 18 : λυτρωτὴς Acts vii. 35 :
λύτρωσις Lk. i. 68 ; ii. 38 ; Hebr. ix. 12 : ἀπολύτρωσις Lk. xxi. 28 ; Rom. iii.
24 ; etc.

1 Pet. i. 18 of the Master in his thoughts when he wrote : " Not with corruptible things, silver or gold, were ye ransomed, but with precious blood, as of a lamb blameless and spotless, even the blood of Christ." It is only a metaphor,[1] but it expresses a truth which is the very heart of the Gospel and without which there is no Gospel at all : that Jesus died for the sin of the world and by His death won eternal life for all believers.[2]

At the gate of Jericho.   Proceeding on their way, Jesus and His retinue reached Jericho which, though it bore the ancient name, stood Deut. about a mile and a half from the ancient City of Palms. xxxiv. 3. It was a fine city, one of the triumphs of Herodian architecture, yet withal a heathenish sort of place with its theatre, its amphitheatre, and its hippodrome. As He approached the gate, He was greeted with importunate cries. They Blind Bar-came from a blind man, named Bartimæus,[3] who sat by timæus. the wayside craving alms of the passers by. It was an excellent station, especially when the troops of pilgrims were arriving at the city on their way to Jerusalem. He heard the tramp of many feet and the acclamation of many voices, and, enquiring what it all meant, learned that Jesus the Nazarene was passing by. The name awoke in his breast the hope of a better boon than alms, and he cried lustily : " Son of David, have pity on me ! " It is significant that he should have given Jesus this Messianic title which the common folk loved. The miracle at Bethany had served its purpose. The fame of it had gone abroad, carrying conviction that Jesus was none other than the Messiah, and Bartimæus was simply echoing the cry which was in every

---

[1] It is simply riding the metaphor to death to raise the question *to whom the ransom was paid*. Origen (*In Matth*. xvi. § 8) answered : *To the Devil*; and Gregory of Nyssa represented the Atonement as a trick practised on the Devil, who accepted Christ as a ransom for mankind but found that he could not retain Him, thus losing both the price and the purchase. Peter Lombard puts the theory in one gruesome sentence : " The Cross was a mouse-trap baited with Christ's blood " (*Sent.* ii. 19). In spite of occasional protests the revolting theory held the field until Anselm (1033-1100) dealt it its death-blow in his *Cur Deus Homo?* the greatest book on the Atonement ever written.

[2] Jerome on Mt. xx. 28 : "*pro multis*, id est, pro his qui credere voluerint."

[3] Mk. x. 46. ὁ υἱὸς Τιμαίου is an interpretation of the patronymic Bartimæus (*cf.* Bartholomew), whether an explanation of the Evangelist for the sake of his Roman readers (*cf.* xiv. 36: ἀββᾶ ὁ πατήρ) or a marginal gloss imported into the text. On the discrepancies of the three narratives *cf.* Introd. § 12, 1.

mouth and which was soon to ring through the streets of Mt. xxi. 9.
Jerusalem.   Resenting the interruption,[1] the bystanders bade
him hold his peace, but he only redoubled his clamour.
Jesus stopped.   He might have healed the man where he
sat   but He would fain have larger dealings with him.
" Call him," He commanded ; and instantly they ceased from
their chiding.   " Courage ! " they said to the blind man ;
" rise ! He is calling thee."   Eagerly Bartimæus obeyed and,
casting off his cloak, made his way through the crowd in the
direction whence that gracious voice had come.   " What wilt
thou," asked Jesus, " that I do to thee ? "   " Rabbûni," he
answered, using the most honourable title that he knew,[2]
" that I may recover sight."   " Go thy way," said Jesus ; " thy
faith hath saved thee."   Forthwith sight came to the blind
eyes, and Bartimæus attached himself to the throng that
followed Jesus, another trophy of His grace, another voice to
swell the chorus of His praise.

Jesus entered the city, and the acclamations of His followers   Progress
attracted an ever-increasing throng.   It was toward evening, through the
and the travellers must halt at Jericho.   Jerusalem was some   city.
fifteen miles distant, and not only was the road perilous after
nightfall, being infested by bandits, but the next day, it would
seem, was the Sabbath.[3]   It was toward evening, and at six
o'clock the Sabbath began.   Jesus took His way through the
streets in quest of a lodging.   It was a priestly city,[4] but the
priests were His bitter enemies, and none of them would receive the Redeemer and minister to His necessities.   Perchance, however, amid that acclaiming throng there might be
one who would think of befriending the weary Son of Man
and bid Him welcome to his house.   He went his homeless
way through the city, making His mute appeal.

Jericho was a prosperous place.   Situated in a fertile   Zacchæus
plain 820 feet below sea-level, it enjoyed a tropical climate   the tax-
and was surrounded by rich groves of palm and balsam trees.   gatherer.

---

[1] Euth. Zig.: εἰς τὴν τιμὴν τοῦ Ἰησοῦ ὡς ἐνοχλοῦντας αὐτόν.   Hilary supposes
that the rebuke came from unbelievers who did not like to hear Jesus styled the
Messiah.   To them He was only "Jesus the Nazarene."   Cf. Chrysost. Serm. de
Cæc. et Zacch.

[2] Rabbi = "my Rab" ; Rabbûni = "my Rabban."   Rabbi was greater than Rab
and Rabban than Rabbi.   Cf. Taylor, Say. of Fath. ii. 1, n. 1.

[3] Cf. Append. VL   [4] Cf. p. 328.

The revenue which accrued therefrom required the presence
of a large staff of tax-gatherers ; and, when Jesus came thither,
one of the chief of that hated fraternity was a man called
Lk. xix. 9. Zacchæus.[1]   He was a Jew.   A Jew and a tax-gatherer, he
was doubly odious in the eyes of his countrymen.   He was
rich, and he might have brazened it out, enjoying his wealth
and scorning public opinion.   But he had a heart for better
things.   His conscience was ill at ease and his soul unsatisfied.
He had heard the fame of Jesus, and what appealed to him
most would not be the miracles of the wondrous prophet but
His kindness to the outcasts.   He was nicknamed " the Friend
of Tax-gatherers and Sinners," and He had actually admitted
a couple of tax-gatherers into the company of His disciples.
Perchance He might do for Zacchæus what He had done for
Levi and James, lifting him also out of the slough of sin and
helping him to a better life.

His deter
mination to
see Jesus. He heard the tramp of many feet and the murmur of
many voices, he saw the crowd, and learned, like Bartimæus,
that Jesus the Nazarene was passing by.   Eagerly he joined
the throng and strove to get near to Jesus and see His face
and haply engage His attention.   But his efforts were unsuccessful.   The multitude knew him.   It was seldom that they
had the tax-gatherer in their midst, and they would welcome
the opportunity of venting their hatred.   When he tried to
push in, they would jostle him and pelt him with insults.   It
was impossible for him to get near Jesus, and he would fall
back breathless and dishevelled to the outskirts of the crowd.
Yet he would not desist.   Jesus was there, and he was resolved to see Him.   He was a little man and could not see
over the heads of his neighbours.   What should he do ?   A
happy thought struck him.   Jesus had passed through the
city and was approaching the southern gate.   Just outside
stood a sycamore tree, overshadowing the road with its spread-
ing boughs.[2]   Zacchæus darted ahead and, climbing the tree,

---

[1] The O.T. Zaccai, *i.e.* " pure."   *Cf.* Ezr. ii. 9.   The father of R. Jochanan,
himself a Rabbi, was called Zaccai, and he lived at Jericho about the time when
Jesus visited it.   See Lightfoot.   Clem. Alex. (*Strom.* iv. 6. § 35) says that some
identified our Zacchæus with Matthias.   This is, of course, impossible, since
Matthias had companied with the disciples from the beginning of the Lord's
ministry (Acts i. 21-2).

[2] See art. *Sycamore* in Hastings' *D. B.*   The sycamore is a large tree, "some-

waited till the procession came up.   From that coign of vantage
he could see Jesus.   And Jesus saw him.   He had witnessed
the behaviour of the crowd and His heart had warmed to the
man.   He comprehended the situation, and, when He came
abreast of the tree, He looked up.   "Zacchæus," He cried, Jesus
"make haste and come down ; for to-day I must stay at thy claims his
house."   It was past six o'clock ; the Sabbath had begun, hospitality.
and Jesus would spend it beneath the tax-gatherer's roof.

It was a double surprise.   It was a surprise to Zacchæus. Surprise
He had desired to see Jesus, hoping that the Friend of Tax- of (1)
gatherers and Sinners might observe him and take pity on him. Zacchæus,
And Jesus far exceeded his hope.   He called him by his
name and, as though He had come to Jericho for no other
purpose, told him that He was going home with him.   This
was indeed good news for Zacchæus.   He hastened to descend and give his guest a joyful welcome.   And it was no
less of a surprise to the bystanders.   When they heard Jesus (2) the
not only greeting the outcast but proposing to go home with crowd.
him and lodge beneath his unholy roof, they were aghast.
They followed in mute amazement till they reached the tax-
gatherer's house.   It would be a stately mansion.   Zacchæus
would dwell as remote as he might from the unfriendly citizens,
and his house would most likely be situated outside the city-
wall on the fair champaign.[1]   Thither he conducted Jesus to
the horror of the multitude.   "He has gone in," they exclaimed, "to lodge with a sinful man!"   Their murmuring
reached the ears of Zacchæus, and he turned and faced them
defiantly, divided betwixt scorn of them and reverence for
Jesus.   "Behold!" he cried, "the half of my property,[2] Lord, Zacchæus
I give to the poor, and whatever I took from any one by vow.
false accusation,[3] I give back fourfold."   It was at once an
answer to the crowd and a vow to the Lord.   And truly it
was a heroic restitution to which Zacchæus pledged himself,
far exceeding the legal requirement and evincing his utter
penitence and his absolute determination to lead thenceforth

times shading an area of 60-80 ft. in diameter," and it is impossible that such a tree
should have grown within the cramped circumference of a walled city.

[1] Strabo xvi. 763 : the *Palmetum* was "full of houses."

[2] *I.e.* what he possessed apart from his ill-gotten gains, perhaps his patrimony.
Cf. Chrysost. *Serm. de Cæc. et Zacch.*

[3] ἐσυκοφάντησα : *cf.* Lk. iii. 14.   On the exactions of the tax-gatherers *cf.* p. 124.

a new life.   The Law claimed only a fifth for the poor,[1] but
he vowed a half.   In cases of fraud the offender was required
to restore the amount and a fifth more ; but he vowed, as in
the case of theft, fourfold restitution.   Already he was a new
creature, and the heart of Jesus rejoiced.   " To-day," He cried,
" salvation came to this house, forasmuch as even he is a son
of Abraham."   His faith had saved him, and they that are
of faith are sons of Abraham.   It is no marvel that Jesus
was glad.   " The Son of Man came to seek and save what is
lost," and in the salvation of Zacchæus He saw of the travail
of His soul and was satisfied.

One would fain know what passed betwixt Jesus and
Zacchæus in the course of that Sabbath which they spent
together—the last Sabbath of the Lord's earthly life ; but, in
the providence of God, it is unrecorded, and the tax-gatherer
appears no more on the page of history.[2]   Jesus would
certainly, as His custom was, go into the Synagogue, and He
would be called upon to address the congregation.   He knew
the thought that was in every mind.   " They were nigh to
Jerusalem, and they opined that the Kingdom of God was
presently about to be manifested."   Their worldly dream was
not hidden from Him, and He essayed to dissipate it.   He
spoke a parable.[3]   Some thirty years before King Herod had
died and bequeathed the Kingdom of Judæa to his son
Archelaus, and the latter had repaired to Rome to have his
title confirmed by Augustus.   Ere the Emperor had given
his decision, an embassy from Judæa appeared and, urging
the misdeeds of Herod, pled that the nation should be
delivered from that odious dynasty and suffered to govern
itself under the suzerainty of Rome.[4]   With evident allusion
to this incident Jesus told how a nobleman went to a far
country to get him a kingdom, and ere his departure entrusted
to ten of his slaves a pound apiece wherewith to trade during
his absence.   But he was hated by his citizens, and they sent
an embassy after him, declaring that they would not have him
for their king ; and on his return he reckoned with his slaves

Lev. vi. 1-
5 ; Num.
v. 6-7.
Exod. xxii.
1.

Gal. iii. 7.

Parable
of the
Pounds.

Lk. iv. 16.

---

[1] *Cf.* Lightfoot.
[2] There is a tradition that he was ordained bishop of Cæsarea by Peter, sore
against his will.   Clem. Rom. *Hom.* iii. §§ 63 *sqq.* ; *Recog.* iii. § 66.
[3] *Cf.* Introd. § 11 ; § 12, 2.   [4] *Cf.* Schürer, *H. J. P.* I. ii. 6.

to whom he had entrusted his money, and took vengeance on
his enemies who had conspired against him.

The nobleman was Jesus, and the parable was designed
to dispel the delusion which His hearers were cherishing.
It was addressed primarily to His disciples. They were
dreaming of reward and glory ere many days should elapse,
and Jesus showed them what really awaited them. He was
going away to a far country. He would indeed one day
return in glory and take unto Him His great power and
reign ; but a long time must elapse ere that consummation,
and He would meanwhile entrust His affairs into their hands
and leave them to trade in His absence. Not glory and
honour but labour and responsibility were their immediate
portion. The parable was also a prophecy. Jesus knew how
His Gospel would fare when He was gone. His claims would
be rejected, and many, even of those who were now acclaiming
Him, would say : " We will not have this man to reign over us."

When the Sabbath was ended, the travellers set forward At
on their journey. Climbing the Ascent of Blood, they Bethany.
reached Bethany, and there Jesus stopped with the Twelve
while the rest went on to Jerusalem. He received a great
welcome. The Sanhedrin had decreed His death and had
published an edict that anyone who knew where He was should
give information in order to His arrest ; but the miracle
which He had wrought there the other week, had filled
Bethany with wonder, and, in defiance of the rulers, He was
received with all reverence. One of the principal men of the
village made a banquet in His honour and invited a large Banquet in
company of guests. His name was Simon. It was a Simon the
very common name among the Jews, and, as one Simon was house.
surnamed Peter, another the Zealot, a third the Man of
Kerioth,[1] and a fourth the Cyrenian, so this Simon was Mk. xv. 21
distinguished as the Leper. He had once been afflicted with
that loathsome disease, and it may be that he was one whom
Jesus had cleansed. It was fitting that he should act as host
on this great occasion ; yet others must participate in the entertainment, and Martha was entrusted with the superintendence
of the banquet. Lazarus, of course, had a place at the table.[2]

---

[1] *Cf.* p. 153.
[2] *Cf.* Introd. § 10; § 12, 3, (2). The idea that the scene of the banquet was

Mary anoints the Lord's feet.

And what of Mary? Being a woman, she was not one of the guests, nor did she, like her sister, bear a hand in setting forth the feast and waiting on the company ; nevertheless she played a conspicuous part in the entertainment. Her heart was full of gratitude and love, and she had resolved to do honour to her dear Lord. She procured an alabaster vase [1] of precious ointment, and, while the feast was in progress, she entered and approached the couch whereon He reclined. It was customary to anoint the head of an honoured guest, and, had Mary done so, she would have occasioned no wonderment. But she did not thus. She poured her ointment on His feet. Nor was that all. She had come into the room with her hair unbound ; and that was a scandal in Jewish eyes, since unbound hair was the token of an harlot.[2] And, after she had poured the ointment on those dear feet, she wiped them with her loose tresses. Though the company must have known the story of Mary's shame, they would not understand her strange behaviour. But Jesus would understand it. It was a reminiscence of the day when He was reclining at table in the house of another Simon, the Pharisee in far northern Magdala, and Mary, a trembling penitent,

Lk. vii. 36-9.

stole in with an alabaster vase of ointment and, standing behind Him, rained tears over His feet, wiped them with her loose tresses, kissed them, and anointed them with the ointment. And now she comes, weeping no longer, since the Lord had wiped away every tear from her eyes, and re-enacts the scene, anointing His feet as she had anointed them then, and wiping them with her hair, though there were no tears to wipe away. She cared not what men might think, for love knows no shame.

Protest of Judas.

The company were surprised and shocked. They whispered one to another and frowned on Mary,[3] and one of them spoke out. It was Judas, the Man of Kerioth. What angered him was not the seeming immodesty of Mary, but

---

the house of Lazarus has given rise to fancies about Simon. Theophyl. mentions the opinion that he was the father, recently deceased (Ewald), of Lazarus.

[1] ἀλάβαστρον· λίθινος μυροθήκη. So called, says Suidas, either because it had no handles (λαβάς) or because it was difficult to grasp (λαβέσθαι) by reason of its smoothness. Cf. Luc. Meretr. Dial. 14. § 2 : ἀλάβαστρον μύρου ἐκ Φοινίκης, δυο καὶ τοῦτο δραχμῶν (a present to a harlot).

[2] Cf. p. 204, n. 1.   [3] Mk. xiv. 5 : ἐνεβριμῶντο αὐτῇ. Cf. p. 114.

what he deemed her wastefulness. He was the treasurer of the disciple-band. "He was a thief," says St John with burning contempt, " and, having the purse, was in the habit of pilfering the contributions." That poor purse not only supplied the necessities of the Master and the Twelve but afforded charity besides. It was chiefly furnished by the generosity of devout women, and, when Mary poured her costly ointment over the Lord's feet, it was a sore vexation to Judas, and he protested against the loss—he the Son of Loss![1] "Wherefore," he demanded, "was not this ointment sold for three hundred *denarii* and given to the poor?" John xiii. 29. *Cf.* Lk. viii. 3.

In the eyes of Judas, nay, of the whole company, Mary's offering seemed mere waste; but it was very welcome to Jesus, and brought gladness to His heart. In His eyes it was "a beautiful work," and He attached to it a greater significance than Mary intended. She had designed it simply as an expression of her grateful love; but Jesus had the Cross in view, and it seemed to Him as though her gentle hands had performed the last office of affection, anointing His body for the tomb, "as the manner of the Jews is to bury." "Suffer her," He cried, "to observe the rite against the day of My burial! For the poor ye have always with you, but Me ye have not always." And then He added a great word of promise: "Verily I tell you, wherever the Gospel is proclaimed in the whole world, the thing also which she did shall be spoken of for a memorial of her." Very grandly was Mary rewarded. The promise of Jesus has been fulfilled. "The memory of what she did," said St Chrysostom long ago,[2] "did not fade, but Persians, Indians, Scythians, Thracians, Sauromatians, the race of the Moors, and the dwellers in the British Isles blaze abroad what was done in Judæa by stealth in a house by a woman that had been an harlot." The Lord's commendation.

---

[1] Mt. xxvi. 8 = Mk xiv. 4 : εἰς τί ἡ ἀπώλεια ; *Cf.* John xvii. 12 : ὁ υἱὸς τῆς ἀπωλείας.

[2] *In Matth.* lxxxi. Chrysostom regarded Mt. xxvi. 6-13 = Mk. xiv. 3-9 and John xii. 1-11 as distinct incidents, accounting the nameless woman of the Synoptics as a penitent harlot.

CHAPTER XLI

THE ENTRY INTO JERUSALEM

"Sis pius ascensor tu, nos quoque simus asellus,
Tecum nos capiat urbs veneranda Dei.
Gloria, laus, et honor tibi sit, rex Christe, redemptor
Cui puerile decus prompsit Hosanna pium."—S. THEODULPH.

THE raising of Lazarus had advanced the fame of Jesus to an unprecedented pitch. The worshippers who gathered to the Passover, could scarce talk of aught else. They hoped that He would come to the Feast and impatiently expected His appearance in their midst, apprehensive lest He should again absent Himself as He had done the previous year. "What think ye?" they would ask each other as they stood in the Temple-court discussing the question of the hour. "That He will not come at all to the Feast?" Presently their doubt was set at rest. Word was brought, not only by the pilgrims who had accompanied Him from Jericho but by some who had gone out to see the wondrous sight of a man raised from the dead, that He had arrived at Bethany and would come to Jerusalem on the morrow. The intelligence fanned the flame of the rulers' wrath, and they determined to put Lazarus also to death;[1] but it increased the enthusiasm of the multitude, and it was resolved that they should go forth to meet Jesus on the morrow and escort Him into the city.

All this lent itself to the Lord's design. He had left Jerusalem with a determination to make a final appeal to the impenitent city, and it had been given Him to work the miracle at Bethany in answer to His earnest prayer for some striking *dénouement* which should excite wonderment and win acceptance for His claims. And He was resolved to improve

[1] Probably Lazarus was compelled to flee; and this may be the reason why he does not appear in the narratives of the Crucifixion and the Resurrection.

390

this advantage. A device presented itself to Him. During His recent sojourn at Jerusalem He had adopted the histrionic method which the prophets had employed and the people loved; and He would pursue it once more. He would do violence to His own instincts and, availing Himself of the enthusiasm of the populace, would invest Himself before their eyes with Messianic dignities. There was a prophecy which was much discussed by the Rabbis and which, at the least suggestion, would leap into men's minds: "Rejoice *Zech. ix. 9.* greatly, O daughter of Zion! Shout, O daughter of Jerusalem! Behold, thy King cometh unto thee: He is righteous and victorious; lowly, and riding upon an ass, even upon a colt, a she-ass's foal."[1] In the East the ass was, as it still is, a fine creature, as large as a small horse, and often very handsome with its rich saddle, its dangling tassels, and its bridle studded with shells and silver. Great men rode upon asses. Jaïr the Gileadite, the judge of Israel, had *Jud. x. 4.* thirty sons who rode on thirty ass-colts. When kings went forth to war, they rode upon horses; when they went on peaceful errands, they rode upon asses; and that ancient oracle made the King of Zion come riding upon an ass *Zech. ix.* because He was the Prince of Peace. The prophecy presented *10.* itself to Jesus, and He determined to enact the Messianic rôle which it pourtrays, and so enter the city.

A little way from Bethany just on the brow of the hill *The ass-* stood the village of Bethphage,[2] and Jesus, it would seem, had *colt.* an understanding with some friend who dwelt there, perhaps a gardener in that district of fig-trees, palms, and olives. When he was setting out for Jerusalem on the morrow, He bade two of His disciples proceed thither. At the entrance to the village, He told them, they would find tethered at a

---

[1] This was recognised as a prophecy of the Messiah's advent, and the question arose how it should be reconciled with Dan. vii. 13. The answer of the Rabbis was that, if Israel were righteous, the Messiah would come with the clouds of Heaven; otherwise, He would come, according to Zechariah's prophecy, riding on an ass. It was argued also from Exod. iv. 20 that He would come on an ass. *Cf.* Lightfoot and Wetstein.

[2] *Cf. P. E. F. Q.*, Apr. 1897, pp. 116 *sqq.* Bethphage, according to Orig. and Jer., was a priestly village: τῶν ἱερέων ἦν χωρίον, *sacerdotum viculus erat.* Since Jerusalem could not accommodate all the worshippers who came up to the Passover and the Paschal bread must be prepared "within the walls," all the district eastward as far as Bethphage was reckoned as "within the walls." Lightfoot, ii. p. 198.

door an ass-colt[1] which had never been ridden and was therefore suitable for sacred use.[2] "Loose it," He said, "and bring it unto Me." As they did so, they would be challenged, and they must reply: "The Lord hath need of it." Such was the watchword which He had. arranged with the owner. The two disciples went their way. They found the colt and, being challenged as Jesus had said, they gave the watchword and were allowed to lead the beast away. The disciples spread their cloaks on its back by way of saddle, and, when Jesus had mounted, they set forward on the way to Jerusalem.

The procession.   The multitude had come out from the city to escort Him thither, and they recognised the part which He was acting. Their exultation was boundless. Here was the Messiah approaching His capital according to that ancient prophecy, and they must accord Him a fitting welcome. After the fashion of royal processions[3] they strewed the road with their garments, and cut boughs from the palm-trees which lined the road, and, waving those emblems of triumph, escorted Him on His way. As they descended the western slope of Olivet, they shouted their acclamations:

Pss. cxviii. 25-6; cxlviii. 1.

> "Hosanna to the Son of David!
> Blessed is He that cometh in the name of the Lord.
> Hosanna in the highest!"

Thus literally was the word fulfilled which Jesus had spoken when He took His departure from Jerusalem: "I tell you, ye shall never more see Me until ye say: 'Blessed is He that cometh in the name of the Lord.'"

Mt. xxiii. 39=Lk. xiii. 35.

Protest of the Pharisees.   It was a royal progress; yet amid the jubilation murmurs were heard, prophetic of the coming storm. The rulers, ever vigilant, had observed the multitude trooping out from the city, and some of the Pharisees had accompanied them to mark what passed. They were bitterly provoked, and they

---

[1] Cf. Introd. § 12, 5; § 13. For Mt.'s ὄνος and John's ὀνάριον Mk. and Lk. substitute πῶλον, "a colt." They knew how the ass was despised by the Greeks and Romans, and, writing for Greeks and Romans, avoided provoking ridicule. Cf. the deliberate elimination of the ass from the O.T. by LXX. See Wetstein's interesting note on Mk. xi. 2.

[2] Cf. Deut. xxi. 3; 1 Sam. vi. 7. For classical quotations see Wetstein.

[3] See Wetstein on Mt. xxi. 8 for illustrations from Jewish and classical literature.

were withal surprised at the complaisance of Jesus who had ever borne Himself so humbly, rejecting the Messianic honours which His followers would fain have thrust upon Him. "Teacher," they cried, "rebuke thy disciples!" "I tell you," answered Jesus, "that, should these men be silent, the stones will cry out." It was a rebuke to the Pharisees whose obdurate hearts had resisted His appeals. Their protest was ominous in His ears. It reminded Him of the implacable enmity which encompassed Him and would never rest until it had shed His blood. And He knew full well what the multitude's enthusiasm was worth. A few days more, and those very mouths which were shouting "Hosanna!" would be clamouring "Crucify him! crucify him!" As the procession wound its way down the mountain-side, the Holy City *The Lord's lament.* lay full in view glittering in the sunshine across the ravine, and the spectacle stirred mournful emotion in the Lord's breast. A lament[1] broke from His lips: "O that thou too hadst recognised during this day the things that make for peace! But, as it is, they have been hidden from thine eyes. For there will come days upon thee when thy foes will embank a trench against thee, and ring thee round, and hem thee in on every side, and dash to the ground thee and thy children within thee, and not leave a stone on a stone within thee; forasmuch as thou didst not recognise the season of thy merciful visitation." All this came to pass some forty years later when the army of Titus blockaded the city. And truly it needed no prophet's eye to foresee what must be the issue, if the Jews persisted in their provocation of imperial Rome. It must happen to *Cf. Is. xxix. 3-6.* Jerusalem even as it happened in the past.

When the multitude surged through the gate, "all the *Astonishment in Jerusalem.* city," says St Matthew, "was shaken as by an earthquake." "Who is this?" they asked, and the multitude answered: "This is the prophet Jesus, the man from Nazareth of Galilee. *Mt. xxi. 11; John xii. 17.* He called Lazarus out of the sepulchre and raised him from the dead." The Pharisees gnashed their teeth in impotent vexation. "Ye behold," they said one to another, each laying the blame on his neighbours, "that ye are doing no good. See! the world hath gone away after him."

---

[1] ἔκλαυσεν, "wailed," as distinguished from ἐδάκρυσεν, "shed tears" (John xi. 35).

The Entry rather a humiliation than a triumph.

That day Jesus did nothing. His heart was heavy within Him, and He would fain rest awhile. That royal progress had been a sore trial to Him. It is commonly called the Triumphal Entry, but in truth it was rather a humiliation than a triumph. It was a piece of acting; and, pleasing as it was to the multitude, it was very distasteful to Jesus. He submitted to it in the hope of winning them and persuading them of His Messiahship, loathing all the while the painful necessity. It is a revelation of His grace that He should thus do violence to Himself and humble Himself to the level of their carnal imagination in order to win men's faith.

The widow's offering.

Mk. xi. 11.

Mk. xii. 41-4 = Lk. xxi. 1-4.

He had no heart that day for aught else, and He betook Himself to the Temple. The court was thronged, and He surveyed the animated scene with wistful eyes. Perchance it was then that an incident occurred which, observed by no other, appealed to His tender sympathy.[1] He had seated Himself in a favourite place over against the Treasury,[2] and was watching the worshippers as they dropped their contributions into the Trumpets. There came a poor widow with her poor offering in her hand—two *lepta* or halves of a *quadrans*, the fourth of an *assarion* which was the sixteenth of a *denarius*. It was a very small sum, and it looked all the smaller in comparison with the contributions which the rich worshippers were casting into the Treasury; but in the eyes of Jesus it was a rich offering. It is evident that the widow was no stranger to Him. The troubled ever found their way to Jesus; and it may be that He had blessed her during His late sojourn at Jerusalem, and this was her thankoffering. It was a poor gift in the world's estimation, but it cost her much: it was all that she possessed. "Verily I tell you," said Jesus to His disciples, observing, perhaps, a look of derision on their faces, " that this poor widow hath contributed more than all they that are contributing to the Treasury. For they all of their superfluity contributed, but she of her penury contributed all that she had, even her whole living."

---

[1] The position of the incident in Mk. and Lk. after the denunciation of the Pharisees is obviously unsuitable and may be due to verbal association with the allusion to widows in Mk. xii. 40 = Lk. xx. 47.

[2] *Cf.* p. 339.

At night-fall Jesus left the city and retraced His steps up His lodging
the slope of Olivet. He did not, however, return to the on Olivet.
village of Bethany. That night and on each succeeding night
until the end He repaired to a garden called Gethsemane on
the side of the mountain, and there He lodged in the open
amid the olive trees with only the blue Syrian sky above His
head.[1] In the morning He betook Himself back to Jerusalem.
As he went, He espied a fig-tree at some distance off, con- The fruit-
spicuous by reason of its luxuriant leafage, and, being hungry, less fig-tree.
He approached in the expectation of finding fruit upon it.
It was a reasonable expectation. It is a peculiarity of the
fig-tree that it forms its fruit ere it puts forth its leaves,[2] and
therefore foliage is a promise of fruit. It was not indeed the
season for figs, but that tree, perhaps because its soil and situation were good, had matured early. Since it was in leaf, it was
reasonable to expect fruit upon its boughs ; but, when Jesus
approached, He found nothing but leaves. In that fig-tree so
advantageously situated, so abundant in promise, yet fruitless,
Jesus saw an emblem of Israel. He had already likened her to
such a tree and warned her of the doom which would overtake Lk. xiii. 6.
her ; and now He reiterates His warning. He pronounces 9.
sentence on the tree. "Nevermore," He says, "let anyone
eat fruit of thee." It was an acted parable after the manner
which He had of late assumed.

He passed on with the Twelve, leaving the fig-tree to its Ministry in
doom ; and, entering the city, He repaired to the Temple. the Temple.
That day was crowded with beneficent activities. He taught
in the Temple-court ; and blind folk and lame, hearing the
testimony of Bartimæus and recalling what the Lord had done
at the Pool of Bethesda, repaired to Him and were healed.
The enthusiasm was boundless. His praises were on every
lip, and the very children joined in the acclamation, repeating
the refrain of yesterday : "Hosanna to the Son of David!"
The rulers were bitterly chagrined. They would fain have
seized Him and executed their murderous resolution ; but
they durst not. They knew well that any attempt upon the

[1] *Cf.* Lk. xxi. 37. αὐλίζεσθαι, "bivouac *sub dio*"; *cf.* Ecclus. xiv. 26. Gethsemane was His habitual resort : Lk. xxii. 39; John xviii. 2. According to Mk:
xi. 11 Jesus "went forth εἰς Βηθανίαν," but the name was given both to the village
and to a tract of the mountain. See Lightfoot, ii. 202. *Cf.* Mt. xxi. 17.
[2] Plin. *H. N.* xvi. 49 : "Ei demum serius folium nascitur quam pomum."

hero of the hour would provoke an outburst of popular fury. Yet they could not refrain themselves, and they found fault where they deemed it safe. They durst not rebuke the enthusiasm of the multitude, but they had naught to fear from the children, and, affecting horror that the stillness of the sacred precincts should be broken by their voices, they approached Jesus and remonstrated: "Hearest thou what these are saying?" "Yea," He replied, retorting upon them with the disdainful formula wherewith He loved to put those teachers of Israel to shame; "did ye never read: 'Out of the mouth of babes and sucklings Thou didst perfect praise'?" Therewith He left them to their discomfiture, and, as evening was closing in, sought His retreat in the garden.

Ps. viii. 2.

John vii. 53-
viii. 2 ; Mk.
xi. 20-5 = Mt.
xxi. 20-2 ;
Mt. xxi. 23-
7 = Mk. xi.
27-33 = Lk.
xx. 1-8 ; Mt.
xxi. 28-32 ;
Mt. xxi. 33-46
= Mk. xii. 1-
12 = Lk. xx.
9-19 ; John
viii. 3-11 ; Mt.
xxii. 15-22 =
Mk. xii. 13-
7 = Lk. xx.
20-6 ; Mt.
xxii. 23-33 =
Mk. xii. 18-
27 = Lk. xx.
27-40 ; Mt.
xxii. 34-40 =
Mk. xii. 28-
34 ; Mt. xxii.
41-6 = Mk.
xii. 35-7 =
Lk. xx. 41-4.

CHAPTER XLII

ENCOUNTERS WITH THE RULERS

"Superbientium
Terat fastigia,
Colla sublimium
Calcet vi propria
Potens in prœlio."
PETR. ABÆLARD.

ON their way to Jerusalem next morning they passed by that The fruitless fig-tree, and the disciples observed with astonishment withered fig-tree. that it was withered from the roots.[1]   "Rabbi," cried Peter, "see !   The fig-tree which Thou cursedst, hath been withered up."   Why should they have been surprised ?   Their Lord's words were not wont to fall to the ground.   "Have faith in God," He answered.   "Verily I tell you, if ye have faith and do not doubt, not only what is done to the fig-tree shall ye do, but even if ye say to this mountain : ' Be lifted up and *Cf.* 1 Cor. be cast into the sea,' it shall come to pass."[2]   xiii. 2.

Passing on to Jerusalem, Jesus repaired to the Temple En- and resumed His teaching in the court.   Presently the rulers counters: 1. The appeared on the scene and interrupted His teaching with rulers challenge a haughty demand : "By what manner of authority art thou His doing these things ? and who gave thee this authority ? " authority. Their design was evidently two-fold.   On the one hand, they thought to impress the multitude by thus asserting their official dignity and jurisdiction ; and, on the other hand, they hoped to elicit from Jesus, not merely an assertion of His Messiahship, but some bolder claim, like that declaration of His oneness with God which had brought His last sojourn at

[1] Mt., after his wont (*cf.* viii. 5-9 = Lk. vii. 2-8 ; ix. 1-8 = Mk. ii. 1-12 = Lk. v. 17-26), condenses the narrative, making the blight and the disciples' comment follow immediately upon the cursing of the tree.

[2] *Cf.* similar proverb in Lk. xvii. 6.   The more distinguished Rabbis were called "uprooters of mountains."   Lightfoot on Mt. xxi. 21.   Mk. xi. 24-5 [6] = Mt. xxi. 22 : alien *logia* about prayer.   *Cf.* John xiv. 13 ; xv. 7, 16, xvi. 23 ; Mt. vi. 14-5.

John x. 30. Jerusalem to an abrupt conclusion. He perceived their malignant design, and, with that amazing resourcefulness which
never failed Him in the most trying emergency, He retorted:
" I also will ask you a single question. Answer Me, and I
will tell you by what manner of authority I am doing these
things. The Baptism of John—was it from Heaven or from
men?" They stood mute in utter embarrassment. What
answer should they make? John had proclaimed Jesus the
Messiah and had administered the rite of baptism in preparation for His advent; and, if they said: " From Heaven,"
Jesus would retort: " Then why did ye not believe him?"
On the other hand, they durst not say: " From men," inasmuch as John was universally accounted a prophet and they
feared to provoke an uproar by offending the popular sentiment. " Answer Me," Jesus insisted as they hesitated, debating what they should say; and they blurted out helplessly:
" We do not know." Quick came the contemptuous and
humiliating rejoinder: " Neither do I tell you by what
authority I am doing these things."

It was a masterpiece of dialectic, but it was very much
more. Jesus did not drag in the Baptism of John at hap-
hazard, grasping at it on the spur of the moment as the first
controversial question which presented itself to His mind. He
adduced it deliberately that He might bring home to His
assailants the reason of their antagonism against Him. They
had at first, like the rest of the nation, been stirred by that
mighty revival which had swept over the land in the days of
John. For awhile they had been seriously impressed. They
John v. 35. had acknowledged the Baptist's power and had been " minded
for a season to rejoice in his light." But in their pride they
had rebelled against his demand for repentance, and had disdained to take their places among the multitude that were
baptised by him in the Jordan, confessing their sins. They
had stifled conviction, closed their eyes to the light, and fought
against the truth. Had they hearkened to the Baptist, they
John i. 35- had hearkened to Jesus and passed, like John and Andrew,
40. by easy and natural transition into the ranks of His disciples.
When He spoke of the Baptism of John, He probed to the
root of their unbelief, and they would wince at the home-
thrust.

"What think ye?" He continued, pursuing His baffled assailants with a parable. "A man had two children. He came to the first and said to him : 'Child, go, work to-day in the vineyard.' 'Yes, sir,' answered the lad, and did not go. He came to the second and said to him likewise. 'I will not,' he answered ; afterwards he repented and went. Which of the two," Jesus asked, "did the will of the father?" The rulers did not perceive the drift of the parable, and indeed only one answer was possible. "The latter," they replied, all unconsciously pronouncing sentence upon themselves, inasmuch as the former of these two lads represented the Jewish people, who, in the prophet's language, "honoured God with their lips while their hearts were far from Him," and the latter the out-casts. "Verily I tell you," said Jesus, "that the tax-gatherers and the harlots are going before you into the Kingdom of God. For John came unto you in the way of righteousness, and ye did not believe him ; but the tax-gatherers and the harlots believed him ; but ye, when ye saw it, did not even repent afterwards that ye should believe him." Jesus seemed an innovator, and their rejection of Him was so far excusable. But they had no excuse for their rejection of John. He had come to them "in the way of righteousness," that is, on the lines of Jewish legalism, proclaiming no novel message but simply reinforcing the moral requirements of the ancient Law and insisting upon faithful observance thereof.

Parable of the two sons.

Cf. Lk. vii. 29-30.

When He had thus discomfited His assailants, Jesus turned to the multitude again and resumed His instruction. The rulers lingered to hear what He might say, and He spoke a parable which, though not addressed to them, concerned them very deeply. He told how a landlord planted a vine-yard, furnishing it with hedge, wine-press, and watch-tower, let it out to husbandmen, and went abroad. At the season of vintage he sent for his share of the fruit, but his messenger was ill received. The husbandmen scourged him and sent him away empty-handed. He sent others, and each in succession was worse treated than the last. Some were scourged, others were killed. He had a well-beloved son, and he resolved to send him, thinking : "They will reverence my son." But, when they spied him, they exclaimed : "Here is the heir! Come, let us kill him, and take his inheritance." And they

Parable of the vine-dressers.

Lk. xx. 9.

seized him, and cast him forth outside the vineyard, and killed him.

"Now," said Jesus, "when the lord of the vineyard cometh, what will he do to those husbandmen?" The multitude had

Mt. xxi. 41. followed the story with keen interest, and they cried: "Miserable men! he will miserably destroy them, and will let out the vineyard to other husbandmen who will render him the fruits at their seasons." They did not perceive the drift of

Mt. v. 12= the parable, but the rulers perceived it. They understood the
Lk. vi. 23; reference to the prophets who had been sent in long succession
Mt. xxiii.
37=Lk. to impenitent and rebellious Israel; and they knew that, when
xiii. 34; Mt.
xxiii. 29-35 Jesus spoke of the heir, He meant Himself. The multitude's
=Lk. xi.
47-51. inconsiderate reply was a confession of Israel's guilt and of

Lk. xiii. 6- the justice of that doom which Jesus had already an-
9. nounced; and they broke in with a protest: "Perish the
Lk. xx. 16. thought!"

"The stone   Jesus turned and, fixing upon them those wondrous
which the eyes which looked men through and through and read the
builders
rejected." secrets of their hearts, asked: "Have ye never read: 'A
Lk. xx. 17. stone which the builders rejected, this hath been made the
Ps. cxviii.
22-3. head of the corner. Of the Lord was it made, and it is
wondrous in our eyes'?" It is a quotation from the hundred and eighteenth Psalm which belongs to the post-exilic period, being a song which was sung by the worshippers as they went up to the restored Temple at one of the great festivals. As they entered, their attention was arrested by a stone over the gateway. Perhaps it was the lintel of the old Temple. All battered and defaced, it had been deemed useless by the builders when they were restoring the ruined House, but the priests had valued it for its sacred associations and retained it in its ancient place. In that pathetic memorial the Psalmist had seen an emblem of Israel despised and persecuted by the nations but chosen and preserved by God; and now Jesus gives it a new application. The Jews are now the persecutors

Cf. Acts iv. and despisers, and He is Himself the stone which the builders
11. have rejected but which God will make the head of the corner. It was a tragic reversal. The words which on the Psalmist's lips had been a parable of God's grace to Israel, were on the lips of Jesus a parable of Israel's rejection. "Therefore I tell you that the Kingdom of God shall be taken away

from you and given to a nation producing the fruits thereof." [1]

The rulers were indignant. They would fain have arrested Jesus, but He was encompassed by the enthusiastic multitude and they durst not harm Him. They left Him and went their way, but they had in no wise abandoned their deadly purpose. They left Him only to consider what they should do. Debarred from violence, they would essay strategy. It happened that they had a culprit on their hands—a woman who had been detected in adultery.[2] Here was their opportunity. They knew the Lord's kindness for sinners, and they perceived the possibility of eliciting from Him a judgment antagonistic to the Law. The affair was entrusted to the Pharisees, the interpreters of the Law and the champions of orthodoxy ; and, with that stinging sentence : " The tax-gatherers and the harlots are going before you in to the Kingdom of God " rankling in their memories, they haled the offender into the Temple-court and set her before Jesus as He sat teaching, the multitude meanwhile looking on with curious eyes and listening with greedy ears. " Teacher," they said, "this woman hath been caught in the very act of adultery ; and in the Law Moses commanded us to stone such. Now what sayest *thou* ? " [3]

It was an ingenious snare. Should Jesus, as they probably anticipated, oppose the execution of the legal sentence, they would raise a cry of blasphemy and arraign Him on that count. Should He, on the contrary, approve the stern enactment, He would alienate the popular sympathy,[4] nor would the rulers have been slow to convict Him of inconsistency and self-condemnation. Was not Mary Magdalene one of His followers ? And had He not, only the other evening, suffered her to

[marginal note: 2. The case of an adulteress]

[marginal note: His verdict.]

---

[1] Lk. xx. 18 (Mt. xxi. 44 is an interpolation) sounds rather like an apostolic comment than a *logion* of Jesus. *Cf*. Rabbinical parallel in Wetstein on Mt. xxi. 42 On Mt. xxii. 1-14 *cf*. Introd. § 12, 2.

[2] On John vii. 53—viii. 11 *cf*. Introd. § 6.

[3] The Law required merely that an unfaithful wife should be put to death (Lev. xx. 10 ; Deut. xxii. 22), *i.e.*, according to the Rabbinical interpretation, strangled. But the punishment was stoning in two cases : (1) if the culprit were a damsel betrothed but yet unwed ; (2) if she were a married woman who was a priest's daughter. If the latter were only betrothed, she was burned. Lightfoot on John viii. 5.

[4] *Cf*. Aug. *In Joan, Ev. Tract*. xxxiii. § 4.

caress His feet without remonstrance, nay, with commendation? Jesus made no reply. He did not, after His wont,
confront them with the calm scrutiny of His great, deep eyes.
Indignant at their heartlessness and hypocrisy, He stooped
and with nervous finger scribbled on the ground.[1] They supposed that He was confounded and knew not what to say;
and, exulting in their triumph, they pressed for an answer,
even as, when they and their colleagues the Sadducees stood
confounded by His question about the Baptism of John, He
had demanded : " Answer Me." They were quickly unde-
ceived. Mastering His emotion, He lifted His glowing face
and hurled His answer at them : " He that is without sin
among you, let him first cast a stone at her." Then He
resumed His attitude. It was like a rapier-thrust. They
hung their heads and, conscience-stricken, took themselves off
one by one. The elder went first and the younger followed,
reversing, in their confusion, the order of voting in the Sanhedrin where, in capital cases, the youngest gave his decision
first.[2] They came as accusers, and He arraigned them before
that stern tribunal which holds its assize in every human
breast. When they were all gone and Jesus was left alone with
the culprit, incarnate Pity with that pitiable one,[3] He lifted
Himself up and asked : " Woman, where are they ? Did none
condemn thee ? " " None, Lord," she answered, expecting reproof. But no word of blame came from those gentle lips.
He would not break the bruised reed. " Neither do I condemn thee," He said. " Go ! Henceforth sin no more."
Her condemnation was all the concern of the Pharisees ; her
salvation was all the concern of Jesus.

---

[1] *Cf.* Euth. Zig. : ὅπερ εἰώθασι πολλάκις ποιεῖν οἱ μὴ θέλοντες ἀποκρίνεσθαι πρὸς
τοὺς ἐρωτῶντας ἄκαιρα καὶ ἀνάξια. Two more specific explanations of our Lord's
action have been suggested : (1) In His writing on the ground Lightfoot finds an
allusion to "the trial of jealousy" (Num. v. 11-31)—the dust which the priest took
from the floor of the Tabernacle and mingled with the water, and the curses which
he wrote in a book. It is vain to inquire what Jesus wrote. He wrote nothing.
He merely scribbled abstractedly on the ground. (2) "He was seized with an
intolerable sense of shame. He could not meet the eye of the crowd, or of the
accusers, and perhaps at that moment least of all of the woman " (*Ecce Homo*, chap.
ix). This, however, is hardly borne out by His dealings either with them or with
her.

[2] *Cf.* p. 472.

[3] Aug. *In Joan. Ev. Tract.* xxxiii. § 5 : " Relicti sunt duo, misera et misericordia."

Resolute to destroy Him, the Lord's adversaries devised another snare, evincing no less skill than villainy. Not daring to resume the attack in person, they sent deputies— several disciples of the Pharisees, young men who, like Saul of Tarsus, were being trained in the Rabbinical schools, and along with them several of that courtly Sadducean order, the Herodians.[1] It was not the first occasion on which their common antagonism to Jesus had united the Pharisees and the Herodians, naturally so wide asunder, in unhallowed alliance. The deputation watched for a fitting opportunity and, approaching Jesus with feigned reverence and unctuous flattery, submitted a question to His decision: "Teacher, we know that thou art true, and teachest the way of God in truth, and carest not for anyone; for thou regardest not the person of men. Tell us, therefore, what thou thinkest: Is it right to give tribute to Cæsar or not?" It was a clever trick. The Jews were groaning under the Roman yoke, and the necessity of paying tribute to the conqueror was very grievous to their proud spirits. It was in truth a burning question of the day, and it came with an appearance of much sincerity from the lips of those enquirers. The Pharisees were the patriotic party, and it might seem natural that these disciples of the Pharisees, in their youthful ardour, should be actuated by a noble solicitude for their nation's honour; while the Herodians, worldly time-servers though they were, had a jealous regard for the dignity of the native dynasty and resented its subjection to the foreign despotism.

3. The question of tribute.

Cf. Mk. iii. 6.

It seemed a reasonable question, but in truth it was a cunning trick. They evidently expected that Jesus would pronounce against payment and thereby expose Himself to the ruthless vengeance which the Romans, steeled by experience of Jewish turbulence, ever wreaked on rebels. Was He not from Galilee? and Galilee was a veritable hot-bed of sedition. And had He not among His intimate adherents a member of the desperate sect of the Zealots? Suppose, on the other hand, that He should pronounce in favour of payment: He would alienate the popular sympathy, and, bereft of that bulwark of defence, He would be at the rulers' mercy. The multitude recognised Him as the Messiah, and

A grave dilemma

---

[1] *Cf.* p. 136.

they followed Him with hosannas because they believed that He was about to ascend the throne and emancipate Israel from the Roman tyranny. Should He counsel submission to the imperial imposition, it would be tantamount in their eyes to a repudiation of the Messiahship, and they would forthwith desert Him.

His escape.   It was a clever plot, excellently disguised, but not for an instant was Jesus deceived. "Why are ye tempting Me?" He cried. "Show Me the tribute-coin." It would seem that the imperial taxes were paid not in Jewish but in Roman coinage, and they handed Him a *denarius* bearing the Emperor's medallion and the superscription: TI. CÆSAR DIVI AUG. F. AUGUSTUS PONTIF. MAXIM. "Whose," He demanded, "are this image and superscription?" "Cæsar's," they replied. "Then pay what is Cæsar's to Cæsar, and what is God's to God." It is not without significance that, whereas they had asked: "Shall we *give*?" Jesus answered: "*Pay*." The tribute-coin was not theirs but Cæsar's, and they had no right to withhold it. Was it not a principle of Jewish jurisprudence that, wherever any king's coinage was current, there that king's sovereignty was recognised?[1] There is an accent of contempt in His language. The debt which they owed to God was other and greater than they conceived.

4. The question of the Resurrection.   The plotters were baffled, and they withdrew without a word, marvelling at the Lord's dexterity. Presently He was approached by another group. They were Sadducees, members of that aristocratic order which stood in direct and bitter antagonism to the order of the Pharisees, separated from the latter alike in politics and in creed. The Sadducees rejected the oral tradition, so sacred and precious in the eyes of the Pharisees, and recognised only the written Law. It is said that they rejected also the Prophets and the Hagiographa and, like the Samaritans, accepted only the books of Moses;[2] and it is at least certain that they acknowledged the Pentateuch as their rule of faith and set less store by the other

---

[1] Euth. Zig.: διὰ τοῦτο γὰρ οὐκ εἶπε "δότε" ἀλλ' "ἀπόδοτε" ὡς ἐκείνου ὄντα. Maim. *Gez.* 5: "Ubicunque numisma regis alicujus obtinet, illic incolæ regem istum pro domino agnoscunt."

[2] Orig. *C. Cels.* i. 49; Jer. on Mt. xxii. 31.

Scriptures.[1]   The latter teach the doctrine of the Resurrection, and this the Sadducees denied, their denial thereof being the chief article of controversy betwixt them and the Pharisees.

Acts xxiii. 6-8. Scoffing Sadducees.

It was a company of Sadducees that now approached Jesus.   They were not in league with the group that had just retired.   On the contrary, they relished the discomfiture of the latter and approached with a pretentious air, confident of their superiority.   Their design was to confound Jesus and the Pharisees both by exposing the absurdity of that ridiculous idea of the Resurrection.   Though they had succeeded, no serious consequence would have ensued.   They would not have embroiled Jesus with the Roman governor, and just a little would they have alienated the multitude from Him.   Rather would they have brought fresh odium upon themselves.   Their scepticism was far from popular.   Indeed it is said that, when a Sadducee held office, he had to pretend agreement with the doctrine of immortality, or he would not have been tolerated by the people.[2]

It seemed to them so easy to refute the doctrine of the Resurrection.   In truth it was a ridiculous notion unworthy of serious argument ; and, thinking to laugh it out of court, they came to Jesus and propounded to Him an imaginary case.[3]   There were seven brothers.   The first died childless and, in accordance with the levirate law, the second took the widow in order to raise up seed for his brother, "that his name might not be blotted out of Israel."   Neither did she conceive by him, and on his death she passed to the third brother.   All the seven in succession had her to wife, and she remained childless to the last.   Then she also died.   The question was : "In the resurrection-life of which of the seven shall she be wife?"

An imaginary case.

Deut. xxv. 5-10.

Jesus might justly have brushed it aside, answering levity with scorn.   It was not only an imaginary but an impossible case, one which had never arisen and never could arise.   St

His answer.

---

[1] Lightfoot on John iv. 25 and Acts xxiii. 8 ; Taylor, *Say. of Fath.*, Exc. iii. 4.

[2] Jos. *Ant.* xviii. i. § 4.

[3] Mt.'s παρ' ἡμῖν makes them state a professedly actual case, but the words are omitted by Mk. and Lk.   In fact the levirate law had fallen into abeyance in our Lord's day. *Cf.* Edersheim, *Life and Times*, ii. p. 400. Chrysost. *In Matth.* lxxi : λόγον δέ τινα πλάττουσι καὶ πρᾶγμα συντίθεασιν, ὡς ἔγωγε οἶμαι, οὐδὲ γεγενημένον

Chrysostom remarks with appropriate jocularity that, when the first two died, the rest of the brothers would have regarded the woman as ill-omened and had nothing to do with her. And the Rabbis held that a woman who was married twice in this world, would in the world to come be restored to her first husband.[1] In fact, according to the levirate law, she remained his wife even when she had been taken by his brother. The latter was not her husband. He merely " performed the duty of an husband's brother unto her." Jesus would have been warranted in treating the question with contempt, but He answered it. It was unlike the question about tribute in that *Cf.* Lk. xii. it did not relate to that secular domain from which throughout 13-4. His ministry He resolutely held aloof, but to that spiritual world which was His home and which He would fain make real and sure to His disciples' faith. It did not excite indignation in His breast. He did not brand those Sadducees as " play-actors," since they did not approach Him veiling a sinister design beneath a mask of courtesy. Neither did their self-assurance provoke Him. It rather moved His compassion. He pitied those vain men who, unconscious of their ignorance, scoffed at the mysteries of that eternal world which He knew so well. " Ye err," He cried, " not knowing the Scriptures nor the power of God."

The   The source of their scepticism was ignorance, and their
mistake ignorance was twofold. They were ignorant of the life to
of the
Sadducees. come ; and this was their supreme mistake, that they imported into it the conditions of the present and reasoned that what is inconceivable here is impossible there, " not knowing the power of God." Had they known the power of God, they would have hesitated to limit the possibilities of the future. *What is* is no measure of *what may be.* " In the resurrection-life," says Jesus, " they neither marry nor are given in marriage, but as God's angels are they in Heaven." Assuredly He did not mean that the life to come will be less rich than the present, or that any relationship which has made the heart glad here, will there disappear. The present relationships will abide, but they will be so transfigured and ennobled that they will need other names. Even as of old, when a man became " a new creature in Christ Jesus," he got a new name, so, when all

[1] *Cf.* Wetstein.

things are made new, they will get new names. In the Rev. ii. 17.
resurrection-life they will not *marry*. It will be no longer
marriage, but something so immeasurably nobler that another
name will be needed. What Jesus here counsels is a prudent
suspense of judgment, an utter confidence in the power of
God, and an assured faith that, whatever the life to come may
be, it will be unspeakably fuller, richer, and more beautiful
than the life that now is : " things which eye saw not, and ear 1 Cor. ii. 9.
heard not, and which entered not into man's heart, even all
the things which God prepared for them that love Him."

In a tone almost of banter Jesus proceeds to convict those Argument
arrogant men of ignorance on another score. They recognised from the Scriptures.
the Pentateuch as their rule of faith, and it contained the
doctrine which they denied. " As regards the Resurrection
of the dead, have ye not read what hath been spoken to you
by God : ' I am the God of Abraham and the God of Isaac
and the God of Jacob ' ? He is not a God of dead men but
of living. Ye greatly err !" How significant this iteration :
" Ye err ; ye greatly err ! " It is the impassioned protestation
of One who knew that unseen world whereof in their ignorance
they reasoned so ill. How foolish their confident talk sounded
to Him whose home was the bosom of the Father ! Of
course there is here no serious argument for immortality. It
was not thus that Jesus handled the Scriptures ; but it was
thus that the Jews handled them,[1] and Jesus with masterly
strategy meets His adversaries on their own ground and routs
them with their own weapons. His triumph was complete.
It exalted Him in the eyes of the multitude : " they were
amazed at His teaching." Some of the Scribes were standing
by, and even they were unable to withhold applause.
" Teacher," they cried, " thou hast spoken well." Exegesis
was their business, and that felicitous stroke compelled their
admiration. It was a veritable masterpiece.

The Lord's adversaries had been worsted in each 5. The chief
encounter, and, had they been wise, they would have acknow- command-
ledged their defeat and troubled Him no more. But the ment.
Pharisees, exulting in the discomfiture of their natural enemies
the Sadducees and hoping to succeed where they had failed,
were minded to make yet another attempt. They deputed

---

[1] *Cf.* Schürer, *H. J. P.* ii. 1, p. 349.

one of their order, a Scribe versed in the Sacred Law, to approach Him and submit a vexed question to His decision. It was reckoned by the Rabbis that the Law contained six hundred and thirteen precepts; and these were distinguished as "heavy" and "light," and very keen was the disputation betwixt the strict school of Shammai and the more liberal school of Hillel which precepts were "heavy" and which

Cf. Gen. xvii. 14; Exod. xii. 15, 19; xxxi. 14; Lev. vii. 20, 25; Num. xix. 20. "light."[1] It was commonly agreed that those were heavy to which the penalty of death was attached; and, since these were in the main laws regarding circumcision, the eating of unleavened bread, Sabbath-observance, sacrifice, and purification, the consequence was that exaltation of ceremonial which was the curse of later Judaism.

His decision. Thinking to entangle Him in this wearisome and unprofitable controversy, the Scribe approached Jesus and asked: "What manner of commandment is first of all?"   "First," Deut. vi. 4-5. answered Jesus, "is: 'Hear, Israel: The Lord your God is one Lord; and thou shalt love the Lord thy God with thy whole heart and with thy whole soul and with thy whole mind Lev. xix. 18. and with thy whole strength.'   Second this: 'Thou shalt love thy neighbour as thyself.'   Greater than these is no other commandment.   On these two commandments the whole Law hangs and the Prophets."   It seems that the combination of these two precepts as summarising religion in both its *Cf.* Lk. x. 27. aspects, the Godward and the manward, was the latest achievement of the Rabbinical theology of that day; and, when Jesus answered thus, He showed that He was acquainted with the doctrine of the schools and, even on that field, was no mean antagonist.   But there was that in His look and tone which went to the heart of His questioner.   The Pharisees, even as when at the outset of His ministry they had sent Nicodemus to interview Jesus, had been unfortunate in their selection of a representative.   They had chosen one versed in Rabbinical theology, but he was an earnest man.   Like Saul of Tarsus he was seeking to be justified before God and had realised the futility of legal observances.   His soul leaped up in response to the Lord's verdict.   "Of a truth, Teacher," He cried, "thou hast spoken well.   For there is one God, and there is none other besides Him; and to love Him with the

---

[1] *Cf.* Wetstein on Mt. xxiii. 23.

whole heart and with the whole understanding and with the whole strength and love one's neighbour as oneself is exceeding more than all the whole burnt offerings and sacrifices." Jesus was touched by the wistfulness of the reply. "Thou art not far," He said kindly, "from the Kingdom of God." It was an invitation to cross the intervening space; and one would fain know what became of the Scribe. Did he obey the gracious invitation and take the decisive step?[1]

The long controversy, so skilfully conducted, so persistently renewed, is ended, and Jesus stands victorious. "No one dared to interrogate Him any more." Hitherto His enemies have been the aggressors and He has sustained assault after assault, repelling each with infinite dexterity; now He changes from defence to attack. He adduces the hundred and tenth Psalm, which is the work of some unknown psalmist and celebrates the invincible prowess of some unknown king, the psalmist's "lord," who owed his triumph to Jehovah's help. It was written during the later period of Israel's history, when the king was, "after the manner of Melchizedek," both king and priest. Such is the plain meaning of the psalm, but it was otherwise interpreted by the Rabbis. Disliking anonymity, they were wont to bring everything under the shadow of some great name, and they ascribed the bulk of the Psalter to David, regardless of probability and sometimes even of possibility. They entitled this *a Psalm of David*, conceiving that he had written it prophetically of his Lord, the Messianic King of Israel. Knowing their interpretation of the psalm, Jesus made use of it to put His adversaries to shame. "What think ye," He asked, addressing the Pharisees and echoing their own phrase, "about the Messiah? Whose son is He?" It seemed an easy question to those learned doctors, and they answered glibly: "David's." "Then," Jesus retorted, "how does David, speaking by inspiration, call Him 'Lord'? 'The Lord said

6. David's Son and David's Lord.

Cf. Mt. xxii. 17.

---

[1] Strauss, followed by Keim and Wright, identifies Mt. xxii. 34-40 = Mk. xii. 28-34 with Lk. x. 25-37, finding here an instance of "the freedom which was used by the early Christian legend in giving various forms to a single fact or idea." The only points of similarity are that in both narratives the interrogator is a lawyer or scribe and the same quotation is made; but the differences are numerous and distinctive. The idea of identification is far older than Strauss: Augustine mentions and rejects it (*De Cons. Ev.* ii. § 75).

unto my Lord : *Sit at My right hand until I put Thine enemies under Thy feet.'* If then David calls Him 'Lord,' how is He his son ? "

It was a genuine piece of Rabbinical casuistry, just such a *theologicalis quæstio* as the Scribes loved to debate in their schools.[1] What was the Lord's purpose in thus adopting the method of His opponents? It was not simply to humble those insolent men and put them to shame before the multitude by meeting them on their own ground and routing them with their own weapons. It was rather to bring home at once to the rulers, to the multitude, and to His disciples the erroneousness of their Messianic ideal. They loved to think of the Messiah as the Son of David, picturing Him as a victorious prince who should deliver Israel from her oppressors and restore her to more than her ancient glory ; and the marvel is not that so many rejected Jesus but that any accepted Him, when He presented Himself before them—a Galilean peasant, meek and lowly in heart. He made many a protest against that worldly dream, but of all His protests there was perhaps none so effective as His *reductio ad absurdum* of the Rabbinical interpretation of the hundred and tenth Psalm. That psalm was His adversaries' grand prooftext for their Messianic ideal, and He demonstrated that their interpretation of it was a preposterous mistake.[2]

---

[1] *Cf.* Lightfoot on Lk. ii. 46.

[2] The notion that Jesus here puts His seal to the Davidic authorship of the psalm, so that to question it is to impugn His authority, is an utter misconception of His argument and involves a startling consequence : If He asserted the Davidic authorship, then He denied the Davidic sonship. The Rabbis acknowledged the force of His argument and—as Jerome says, "ad deludendam interrogationis veritatem"—revised their interpretation of the psalm. They should have abandoned its Davidic authorship, but they preferred to deny its Messianic reference, applying it variously to Abraham, David, and Hezekiah. *C*. Lightfoot on Lk. xx. 42.

CHAPTER XLIII

THE GREAT INDICTMENT

Mt. xxiii. 1-7, 13-36; Mk. xii. 38-40=Lk. xx. 45-7; Lk. xi. 39-54; John xii. 20-50.

"Sinner, here thou dost hear of love, prithee do not provoke it, *by turning it into wantonness.* He that dies for *slighting love,* sinks deepest into hell, and will there be tormented by the remembrance of that evil, more than by the deepest cogitation of all his other sins. Take heed therefore, do not make *love* thy tormentor."—JOHN BUNYAN.

JESUS had put His enemies to silence, and, as they stood con-founded, He addressed them for the last time, exposing and satirising their corruption and perversity. It was a scathing indictment, the most terrible that ever fell on human ears; yet, as it poured from His lips, pity struggled with indignation in His breast. It is justly entitled by an ancient commen-tator a " commiseration of the Scribes and Pharisees."[1] Even while He pronounced their doom, He yearned over them with a great compassion. *"The Commiseration of the Scribes and Pharisees."*

He began with a stroke of biting satire. " On Moses' chair," He said to His disciples and the multitude, " are the Scribes and the Pharisees seated.[2] All therefore that they say unto you do and observe; but according to their works do not ; for they say and do not." [3] This distinction betwixt the men and their office, this requirement of deference to their authority coupled with reprobation of their example, was a heavy indictment of those teachers of Israel. " Their seeming honour," says St Chrysostom, " He makes a condemnation. For what case could be more miserable than a teacher's when it saves his disciples to give no heed to his life ? " It was a damning charge, and Jesus proceeded to establish it. The *improbus astutus* was a byword in those days—the teacher who " enjoined 'light' things upon himself and 'heavy' *Their portraiture.*

---

[1] Euth. Zig. : περὶ τοῦ ταλανισμοῦ τῶν Γραμμ. καὶ Φαρισ. οὐαὶ δὲ ὑμῖν, eight times reiterated, is an exclamation no less of commiseration than of condemnation.

[2] *I.e.* as successors of the legislator of Israel.

[3] *Cf.* Paul's recognition that respect was due to the High Priest in virtue of his office. Acts xxiii. 2-5.

things upon others." [1] And Jesus imputes this offence to the Scribes and Pharisees. Like a merciless camel-driver, they "bound heavy burdens and put them on men's shoulders, and would not themselves move them with their finger." They hungered for praise; they were consumed by petty ambition. They made their phylacteries broad and their fringes long; [2]

Cf. Lk. xiv. they loved the chief places at feasts and the front seats in the
7. synagogues, and, when they walked abroad, it gratified them that the passers by should do obeisance to them and greet them with the reverential salutation: "Hail, Rabbi!" [3]

Their
offences: The rulers were standing by in angry discomfiture, and, when He had thus with a few graphic strokes pourtrayed them for the admonition of His disciples and the multitude, He addressed them with burning indignation and overwhelmed them with a torrent of accusation. It was a terrific indictment, and each count was prefaced with a half indignant, half sorrowful "Woe unto you!"

1. Shutting
the
Kingdom
of Heaven. "Woe unto you, Scribes and Pharisees, play-actors! forasmuch as ye shut the Kingdom of Heaven in men's faces. For ye do not enter, neither them that are entering do ye suffer to enter." Their very teaching blocked the way into the Kingdom of Heaven. They had overlaid the Word of God with their traditions; they had choked the living fountain with the rubbish of their inventions. John had sought to open up the way into the Kingdom of Heaven, and they had hunted him to death; and now they were plotting against Jesus.

2. Proselytism. "Woe unto you, Scribes and Pharisees, play-actors! forasmuch as ye scour sea and land to make a single proselyte; and, when he is gained, you make him twice more a son of Gehenna than yourselves." Scant courtesy was shown to proselytes. The Rabbis declared that they "hindered the advent of the Messiah" and called them "a scurf upon

[1] *Cf.* Lightfoot.
[2] The φυλακτήρια, תְּפִלִּין, "prayers," were strips of parchment inscribed with four passages (Exod. xiii. 3-10; 11-6; Deut. vi. 5-9; xi. 13-21) and fastened to the forehead and left arm in literal obedience to Exod. xiii. 9, 16; Deut. vi. 8; xi. 18. Originally φυλακτήρια meant *observatoria, i.e.* remembrancers, but latterly *conservatoria, i.e.* amulets to put evil spirits to flight. See Lightfoot, iii. p. 31. Jerome and Chrysostom compare the little Gospels and bits of the Cross worn by superstitious women in their day. On the *fringes* see p. 197, n. 4.
[3] On the position of Mt. xxiii. 8-12 *cf.* Introd. § 9.

Israel." [1] Nevertheless the Jews were zealous proselytisers. [2] Not only was it a triumph for the true faith when converts were won from heathenism, but wealthy proselytes, like the cen- turion of Capernaum and Cornelius of Cæsarea, by their munificent liberality augmented the ecclesiastical revenues. And it is remarkable that the proselytes surpassed the Jews in superstition and fanaticism. [3] "Ye make them twice more sons of Gehenna than yourselves." There lay the guilt of the Scribes and Pharisees : they scoured sea and land to make a single proselyte, caring nothing for his soul, eager only for their own aggrandisement and enrichment.

Lk. vii. 5.
Acts x. 1-2.

"Woe unto you, blind guides!" With crushing contempt He exposes their moral obliquity, adducing specimens of the casuistry wherewith, after the manner of the Jesuits, those teachers of Israel played fast and loose with the moral law and corrupted the moral sense. [4] "Swear," they said, "by the Sanctuary : it is naught ; swear by the gold of the Sanctuary : it is binding. Swear by the altar : it is naught ; swear by the gift that is on it : it is binding. Swear by Heaven : it is naught ; swear by the Throne of God : it is binding." As though the greater did not include the less! "Ye fools and blind ! "

3. Casuis-
try.

"Woe unto you, Scribes and Pharisees, play-actors ! for- asmuch as ye tithe your anise and mint and cummin." It was the very climax of scrupulosity when men tithed their kitchen-herbs. [5] There was indeed no harm in the practice ; the sin was that they "neglected the weightier things of the Law—judgment and compassion and faith," compounding for their laxity in matters essential by scrupulosity in matters of no moment. "Blind guides ! " cries Jesus with infinite scorn, hitting them off with a proverb characteristically Oriental in its grotesque exaggeration, "ye that strain out the midge and gulp down the camel."

4. Scrupu-
losity in
trifles,
laxity in
essentials.

"Woe unto you, Scribes and Pharisees, play-actors ! for- asmuch as ye cleanse the outside of the cup and the platter

5. Rapacity
and incon-
tinence.

---

[1] *Babyl. Nidd.* 13. 2 : "Tradunt Rabbini nostri : ' Proselyti et pæderastæ im- pediunt adventum Messiæ. Proselyti sunt scabies Israeli.' "

[2] *Cf.* Taylor, *Say. of Fath.* i. 13, n. 29.

[3] Acts xiii. 43, 50 ; Tac. *Hist.* v. 5 ; Juv. xiv. 96-106.

[4] *Cf.* Lightfoot on Mt. v. 33. Mart. *Ep.* xi. 97. 7-8.

[5] *Cf.* Lightfoot.

while inside they are full of rapacity, and incontinence."
Rapacity and incontinence !   These are strange things to lay
to the charge of grave and reverend men who posed as
paragons of sanctity.   Yet Jesus spoke in all seriousness and
truth.   During the dark ages which preceded the Reformation,
it was the custom in our own land, when a peasant died, for
the priest to visit the stricken dwelling, not to comfort the
widow and orphans, but to claim the "cors-presant"—the
best cow and the coverlet of the bed or the deceased's outer
garment.   There is indeed no evidence that the rapacity of
the Scribes and Pharisees reached such a pitch, yet it was
sufficiently monstrous.   "The stroke of the Pharisees has
touched you," said R. Eleazar to a widow whom R. Sabbatai
had plundered.[1]   The iniquity enkindled the Lord's indignation,
and He branded those faithless shepherds of Israel as hirelings
who cared not for the sheep, nay, thieves who came only to
steal and kill and destroy.   And it was an aggravation of
their iniquity that they practised it in the name of religion
and behind a mask of piety.   "Woe unto you, Scribes and
Pharisees, play-actors ! forasmuch as ye devour widows'
houses, even while by way of pretext ye make long prayers.
Therefore shall ye receive more abundant condemnation."[2]
Thrice daily they prayed for an hour ; and an hour before
and an hour after they spent in meditation, thus devoting
to prayer nine hours daily.   "Long prayer," they said,
"lengthens life."

And it is a deplorable fact that beneath their cloak of
sanctity the Pharisees too often hugged in their bosoms the foul
lusts of the flesh.   Jesus read their secret thoughts, and He
needed no other evidence ; but the pages of the Rabbinical
literature abound in testimonies that His judgment was just.
Their very protestations of an unearthly chastity smack of
lasciviousness.   It is written that R. Simeon delighted to
behold fair women, and the spectacle of their beauty moved
him to praise God.   R. Gidal and R. Jochanan were in the
habit of sitting at the women's bathing-place ; and, when
they were admonished of the danger of lasciviousness, R.

John x. 10, 13.

---

[1] *Cf.* Wetstein.
[2] The best authorities omit Mt. xxiii. 13, but it is certainly part of the discourse.
Cf. Mk. xii. 40=Lk. xx. 47.   [3] See Lightfoot.

Jochanan replied: "I am of the seed of Joseph over whom lust could have no dominion." [1]

"Woe unto you, Scribes and Pharisees, play-actors!" He continues; "forasmuch as ye resemble whitewashed tombs, which outside look beautiful but inside are full of dead men's bones and every sort of filth." Contact with the dead involved ceremonial defilement, and therefore, lest a man should stumble upon them unawares, Jewish tombs were whitewashed. They stood conspicuous, giving warning like the lepers who stood afar off, crying: "Unclean! unclean!" They got weather-stained during the rainy season, and at the close thereof, just before the Passover, they received a fresh coating of whitewash.[2] There they stood around Jerusalem as Jesus spoke, clean and fair to the eye, fit emblems of the Pharisees, so fair without, so foul within. "Even so ye also outside look righteous to men's eyes, but inside ye are stuffed with hypocrisy and lawlessness." *6. Fair without, foul within.*

This allusion to the tombs leads on to the final and most damning count in the indictment. "Woe unto you Scribes and Pharisees, play-actors! forasmuch as ye build the tombs of the Prophets and adorn the sepulchres of the righteous, and say: 'If we had been in the days of our fathers, we would not have been partakers with them in the blood of the Prophets.'" [3] And was not their protestation justified? Yonder on the southern shoulder of Mount Olivet stood the Tombs of the Prophets glistering in the sunshine, monuments which the Jews of later days had reared with penitent hearts and generous hands to the honour of those martyrs whom their fathers had slain. Yet Jesus disallowed their claim. They were like that savage chief who, when he heard the story of the Crucifixion, brandished his weapon and exclaimed: "Ah, had I been there, I would have cut those wicked Jews into a thousand pieces!" Yet he would not give his heart to Jesus or for His sake abandon his wicked ways. What availed it that *7. Guilty of the blood of the Prophets.*

---

[1] *Talm. Hieros. in Ber.* 12. 3; *Babyl. Ber.* 20. 1. *Hieros. Chall.* 58. 3: "Calcaneum mulieris aspiciens est ac si uterum aspiceret; uterum autem aspiciens est ac si cum ea coiret." *Babyl. Ber.* 24. 1: "Intuens vel in minimum digitum fœminæ est ac si intueretur in locum pudendum." See Lightfoot on Mt. v. 28. *Cf.* Susanna and the Elders.   [2] *Cf.* Lightfoot.

[3] *Macc.* 1. 17: "R. Tarphon et R. Akiba dixerunt: 'Si nos fuissemus in Synhedrio, non esset unquam de eo quisquam interfectus.'"

the Jews deplored their fathers' deeds when their fathers' spirit
was in their hearts and they were doing to the new prophets even
as their fathers had done to the old, proving themselves their
fathers' sons and filling up the measure of their fathers' guilt?
Jesus knew what awaited Himself, and He knew also how it
would fare with His Apostles. "Some of them ye will kill and
crucify, and some of them ye will scourge in your synagogues
and chase from city to city, that upon you may come every
drop of innocent blood shed upon the earth, from the blood
of Abel the righteous even to the blood of Zechariah [1] whom
ye murdered betwixt the Sanctuary and the Altar."

The murder of Zechariah. The words would send a thrill of horror through the
listening multitude. They knew well the awful story—how,
nigh nine hundred years ago in the days of King Joash after
the death of the good priest Jehoiada, Judah and Jerusalem
fell into idolatry, and, when Zechariah the son of Jehoiada,
2. Chron. xxiv. 20-2. raised his protest, they "stoned him with stones in the court
of the House of the Lord." It was a horrid crime, and, eager
to expiate it, the Jews had reared a shrine in honour of
Zechariah just across the Kedron; but still the memory of it
haunted them. It was, they said, a seven-fold crime: the
victim was at once a priest, a prophet, and a judge; innocent
blood had been shed; the sacred court had been defiled; the
day on which it was perpetrated, had been the Sabbath and
the Day of Atonement. "The Lord look upon it and require
it!" had been the martyr's dying words, and generation after
generation they had kept ringing in the nation's ears. Tradition told how, long after, on the desecrated spot blood had
bubbled up from the pavement and would not cease.[2] The
very name of Zechariah was fateful in Jewish ears, and the
Lord's allusion would fill His hearers with shuddering dread.
It was indeed an ancient crime, and much innocent blood
had since been shed in Jerusalem; but the story is told in
the second Book of Chronicles, and in the Hebrew Bible that
book stands last. It was as though the Lord had said: "All
the crimes that your history records from the first page of the
Scriptures to the last will be visited on you. Ye are the
heirs of all the guilt of all the centuries, and on you the ac-
cumulated vengeance will fall. Verily I tell you, all this will
come upon this generation."

[1] *Cf.* Append. VII.   [2] *Cf.* Lightfoot.

It was a dreadful prophecy; yet it merely exasperated the rulers, and they went away and consulted how they might compass the death of Jesus. The day was declining, and Jesus, it would seem, rested in the Temple while His disciples were busy here and there ere they should quit the city and repair to their lodging on Mount Olivet. As Philip went his errand, perhaps to the market-place, he was accosted by a company of strangers. They were Greeks,[1] and they requested him to procure them an interview with the Master. "Sir," they said, "we are wishing to see Jesus." Who were they? A curious story is told by the ecclesiastical chronicler Eusebius. Abgarus, King of Edessa in Mesopotamia, was sick with a painful and incurable disease, and, when he heard the fame of Jesus, he sent to Him and entreated Him to come and heal him. Eusebius found a record of the incident in the archives at Edessa, and he gives both the letter of Abgarus and the reply of Jesus, literally translated from the original Syriac. The former runs thus:

"*Abgarus, prince of Edessa, to Jesus the good Saviour who hath appeared in the district of Jerusalem, greeting. The story hath reached my ears of Thee and Thy healings as wrought by Thee without drugs and simples. For, it is said, Thou makest blind men to see, lame to walk, Thou cleansest lepers, and castest out unclean spirits and dæmons, and them that are tormented with long sickness Thou curest, and Thou raisest dead men. And when I heard all this about Thee, I inferred one or other of the twain: either that Thou art God and, having come down from Heaven, art doing these things, or Thou art a Son of God in that Thou doest these things. For this reason then I have written and prayed Thee to travel unto me and cure the sickness which I have. For I have heard that the Jews also are murmuring against Thee and wishing to do Thee damage. My city, however, though but small, is a goodly one, and it is sufficient for us both.*"

Jesus replied that He must remain at Jerusalem and accomplish

Margin notes:
A deputation of Greeks.
Mt. xxvi. 3, 5=Mk. xiv. 1-2= Lk. xxii. 2.

[1] The fact that they had "come up to worship at the Feast" does not imply that they were either proselytes or Hellenistic Jews. It was a singular provision of the Jewish Law that a Gentile might bring an offering to Jerusalem, and men of cosmopolitan spirit frequently availed themselves thereof. At the Passover of A.D 37 the Syrian governor interrupted his march to go up to Jerusalem and offer sacrifice. Jos. *Ant.* xviii. 5. § 3. *Cf.* Lightfoot on John xii. 19; Schürer, *H J. P.* ii. 1, pp. 299-305.

His mission, but He promised that after He had been received up He would send one of His disciples to heal Abgarus and give life to him and his people. And in fulfilment of this promise Thaddæus was sent to Edessa.[1]

Emotion of Jesus :

It is a curious story. Though the authenticity of the correspondence is very questionable, there is no reason to doubt the fact of the embassy ; and there is much probability in the suggestion that those Greeks who came in quest of Jesus, may have been the messengers of Abgarus. Uncertain

John vi. 7-8; Mk. xiii. 3.

what he should do, Philip consulted with Andrew, always the man of his counsel and a favourite with the Master, and the two went and told Jesus. Their story excited a storm of

(1) exulta- tion ;

emotion in the Lord's breast. It inspired Him with exultant gladness. He recognised those Greeks as harbingers of that innumerable multitude out of every nation and all tribes and peoples and tongues that should believe in His name and call Him Lord. Already those other sheep which were not of Israel's fold, were hearkening to their Shepherd's voice and gathering unto Him. It was an earnest of greater things to come, a pledge that His sacrifice would not prove unavailing. " The hour hath come," He cried, " that the Son of Man should be glorified. Verily, verily I tell you, if the grain of wheat do not fall into the earth and die, by itself alone it remaineth ; but, if it die, much fruit it beareth." Not in vain had He trodden His weary path ; and it was the path which His disciples must tread, winning the world by sacrifice. " He that loveth his life loseth it, and he that hateth his life in this world unto life eternal shall guard it. If any one serve Me, let him follow Me, and where I am, there My servant also shall be. If any one serve Me, the Father will honour him."

(2) per- plexity.

Presently His exultation was checked. There rushed upon Him that old temptation which had assailed Him in the wilderness at the outset of His ministry and pursued Him throughout the course thereof. Was it necessary that He should die ? Had not a door of escape been opened before Him in the providence of God ? Should He not obey the call which had been addressed to Him, and, quitting impeni-tent Jerusalem and His bloodthirsty foes, go away with those

---

[1] Eus. *H. E.* i. 13.

kindly Greeks and establish the Kingdom of Heaven in their midst? Such was the counsel of His frail humanity, trembling and shrinking in the near prospect of the Cross. "Now," He cried, "hath My soul been troubled; and what am I to say? Father," He prayed, "save Me from this hour." And His prayer was answered. It was the eternal purpose of God that He should die, a sacrifice for the sin of the world. That was His mission, and He would not flinch from it. "Nay," He exclaimed, rallying Himself from His momentary irresolution, "it was for this that I came unto this hour. Father, glorify Thy name."

It was a momentous crisis. On the issue of the conflict which was being waged in the Redeemer's breast, hung the hope of the world's salvation, and all Heaven watched the event. It is no marvel that again, as on the bank of the Jordan and on the Mount of Transfiguration, the silence was broken by a voice from Heaven. God answered the prayer of His beloved Son: "I both have glorified it and will glorify it again." Jesus needed no audible assurance of the Father's approval of His past ministry and sympathy with Him in the ensuing ordeal; but the multitude needed it, and the voice should have told them what was passing in their midst. But they did not understand it. Some thought that it was thunder, others that an angel had spoken to Jesus. "Not for My sake," said He, "hath this voice come, but for yours. Now is this world on its trial; now shall the Prince of this world be cast out. And I," He added, exulting afresh in anticipation of the day when there should be no longer Jew and Greek but a universal brotherhood of redeemed men, "if I be lifted up from the earth, will draw all men unto Myself." [1]

A voice from Heaven.

Mt. iii. 17 = Mk. i. 11 = Lk. iii. 22; Mt. xvii. 5 = Mk. ix. 7 = Lk. ix. 35.

"This He said," explains the Evangelist, "signifying by what manner of death He was about to die." Their acquaintance with Rabbinical theology was always a stumbling-block to the men of Jerusalem, a hindrance to their comprehension and acceptance of the Lord's claims. Their minds were prepossessed, and, whatever He said, they raised some scholastic quibble. So it happened now. "We have heard out of the

Bewilderment of the multitude.

Cf. John vii. 41-2; viii. 13.

---

[1] According to Strauss John xii. 20-32 is a blending together of "the two Synoptical anecdotes of the Transfiguration and the Agony in the Garden."

Cf. Pss.
xxxix. 36 ;
cx. 4. Law," [1] they objected, " that the Messiah remaineth for ever,
and how dost thou say that the Son of Man must be lifted up ?
Who is this ' Son of Man ' ? " Jesus had said " I " : wherefore
did they substitute " the Son of Man " ? Was it that He had
often repeated in their hearing His declaration to Nicodemus :
John iii. 14. " The Son of Man must be lifted up " ? They had understood
that, when He spoke of the Son of Man, He meant Himself.
They knew that He claimed to be the Messiah, and they believed it ; and, sure that the Messiah would " remain for ever,"
they thought that they must have erred in thinking that by
the Son of Man Jesus meant Himself. " Who," they asked in
bewilderment, " is this ' Son of Man ' ? " He did not stay to
resolve their perplexity. A greater business claimed Him.
Those Greeks awaited Him, and He must hasten to them.
" A little time longer," He said, " is the Light among you.
Walk as ye have the Light, lest darkness overtake you ; and
he that walketh in the darkness knoweth not where he goeth.
As ye have the Light, believe in the Light, that sons of Light
ye may become." It was His last word to the men of
Jerusalem. " This spoke Jesus, and went away and was
hidden from them."

**Discourse
to the
Greeks.** In that retreat where Jesus hid from the multitude, He
accorded to the Greeks the interview which they desired.
They would have much to ask of Him, and He would vouch-
safe to them an abundant disclosure of His mind and heart.
Yet only the barest outline of His discourse has been preserved, and the reason is doubtless that the Evangelist was
not present and did not hear it. Probably Philip and Andrew
were the only representatives of the Twelve that heard it, and
St John has reported only so much as he learned from them.
It is a mere summary, yet it reveals much. Jesus spoke with
Cf. John
vii. 28, 37. deep emotion : " He *cried* and said." He set forth the Gospel
in all its fulness, omitting none of the great truths which He
had proclaimed in the course of His ministry : His oneness
with the Father, His errand of redemption, the guilt of rejecting His revelation, His gift of Eternal Life. And, speaking
not to Jews but to Gentiles, He proclaimed the universality of

---

[1] The Law is the Scripture generally in opposition to the teaching of the Scribes.
Lightfoot : " Frequentissime occurrit *Hoc est ex Lege* : cui appositum *Hoc est ex
Rabbinis.*" Cf. p. 351, n. 4.

His salvation : " I have come a light into *the world* " ; " I came not to judge *the world* but to save *the world.*" [1]

[1] It was John's manner to introduce discourses of Jesus abruptly (*cf.* the insertion of chaps. xv-xvii between the exit from the Upper Room and the departure from Jerusalem with no indication where they were spoken) ; and the recognition of xii. 44-50 as the Lord's address to the Greeks removes a *crux interpretum.* This additional address ("quite isolated and introduced without locality, without one new idea") after Jesus "went away and was hidden from them" is pronounced by Keim "an impossibility, in truth only the reflection of the Evangelist continued in a pretended utterance of Jesus." Several explanations have been suggested : (1) After his departure Jesus returned and again addressed the Jews (Chrysostom, followed by the older expositors). (2) Over against the unbelief of the Jews (*vv.* 37-43) John gives (*vv.* 44-50) "an energetic summing up, a condensed summary of that which Jesus has hitherto clearly and openly preached " (Meyer). (3) The section has got misplaced and should stand between 36a and 36b (Wendt).

CHAPTER XLIV

DISCOURSE ABOUT THINGS TO COME

" Judex ergo cum sedebit,
    Quidquid latet apparebit,
    Nil inultum remanebit.

" Rex tremendæ majestatis
Qui salvandos salvas gratis,
Salva me, fons pietatis.

" Inter oves locum præsta
Et ab hædis me sequestra,
Statuens in parte dextra."—THOM. DE CEL.

Retiral to Olivet. EVENING came on, and Jesus and the Twelve retired from the city and betook themselves to the Mount of Olives. As they quitted the Temple, the disciples remarked upon the grandeur of the sacred edifice. It was indeed an imposing spectacle for those northern peasants. When King Herod embellished his capital, the old Temple of Zerubbabel accorded ill with its surroundings, and the astute Idumæan, thinking thereby to ingratiate himself with his subjects, rebuilt it in Magnificence of the Temple. magnificent style. It was an imposing pile, a triumph of architecture, justifying the Rabbinical eulogy that one who had never seen Herod's Temple, had never seen a beautiful edifice.[1] It was built of marble, some of the blocks measuring five and forty cubits in length, five in height, and six in breadth, and all set with gold. Crowning a steep hill, it looked from afar like a mountain of snow; and, when it caught the first beams of morning, it shone with a splendour which dazzled the eyes.[2] "Teacher," exclaimed one of the disciples, "see what manner of stones and what manner of Prediction of its over-throw. buildings!" "Thou art looking," returned Jesus, "on these great buildings? There shall not be left one stone upon another which shall not be pulled down."

Things to come. It was a startling announcement; and, when they reached their retreat, four of the disciples, Peter, James, John, and

---

[1] Wetstein on Mt. xxiv. 1.

[2] Jos. *De Bell. Jud.* v. 5; *Ant.* xv. 11. Nonn. *Paraphr. S. Ev. Joan.* v. 1-2:

δόμος αἰθέρι γείτων

χιονέην ἀμάρυσσε λίθων ἑτερόχροον αἴγλην.

Andrew, ventured to approach Jesus, as He sat apart, and ask Him for an explanation. " Tell us, when will this be ? And what is the sign when all this is about to be consummated ? " He acceded to their request, and there in the still evening on the mountain-side, with City and Temple full in view across the valley, He discoursed to the Twelve of things to come, foretelling two tremendous crises—the destruction of Jerusalem which befell in A.D. 70, and His Second Advent which after the lapse of nearly nineteen centuries is still future.[1]   His purpose was not to gratify the curiosity of His disciples, but to prepare them for the ordeal which awaited them, lest their faith should fail in the day of trial.   The doom of Jerusalem *Destruc-* was plain to every eye which could read the signs of the *tion of Jeru-* *salem.* times, and it was ever a cause of wonderment to Jesus that His contemporaries should be so blind to the impending catastrophe.   They could read the tokens of the sky, but not *Lk. xii. 56.* the signs of the times.   The moral order of Providence was the key that opened the future to Jesus.   Jerusalem must fall because she was ripe for judgment.   The cup of her iniquity was full.   She was as a dead carcase, and the law stands written on the page of history that " wheresoever the carcase *Mt. xxiv. 28* is, there shall the eagles be gathered together." [2]   And there *= Lk. xvii.* *37.* could be only one issue of the smouldering disaffection, ever and anon bursting into flame as the gusts of Messianic fanaticism swept over the land.   Jesus understood the temper of His countrymen, and He knew that Rome would ere long lose patience and with her iron heel crush the rebellion of the turbulent province.   All this He foresaw, and it was very grievous to Him.   He loved Jerusalem.   She was to Him the City of the Great King.   Her Temple was His Father's House.   She was the centre of Israel's faith, the stage whereon the mighty drama of redeeming love had been enacted.   Hers were the saints who all down the long centuries of Israel's history had prayed and toiled and poured out their martyr blood.   She was dear and sacred in His eyes. Her unbelief was the bitterest ingredient in His cup of sorrow, and the thought of her doom lay like a heavy burden on His

[1] *Cf* Introd. § 12, 6 and 7.

[2] *Cf.* Wright, *Palmyra and Zenobia*, p. 383.   The scavenger-bird is properly the vulture (γύψ).   Jesus probably says ἀετοί in reference to the Roman *aquilæ.*

heart. It is no marvel that, when He spoke thereof to the Twelve, there swelled within Him a great flood of emotion.

In the spirit of the ancient prophets He depicts the Jewish state going down amid storm and thunder and eclipse. It is no precise picture of the things which actually came to pass. Wars and rumours of wars, nation rising against nation and kingdom against kingdom, earthquakes, famines, and pestilences : these are not historical events announced in literal detail ere they came to pass, but lurid strokes of prophetic imagery designed to bring home to His hearers the horror of the approaching desolation.[1] It was a terrible prospect, and, lest it should surprise and overwhelm them, Jesus set it before the imaginations of His disciples in all its grim terror. He warned them that not only would they share those national calamities but they would suffer peculiar distresses as Apostles of the Kingdom of Heaven. They would encounter persecution and martyrdom ; they would be hated of all men for His name's sake ; nor would they be spared the pain of witnessing wide-spread defection in the hour of trial : "the love of most would wax cold." And deceivers would arise—false prophets and false Messiahs,[2] and deceive, if it were possible, even the elect. "Be not dismayed," says Jesus. "Behold, I have foretold you."

The Second Advent. With the signs of the times before His eyes Jesus clearly perceived that the issue of the protracted conflict betwixt the Jews and their conquerors could not be long delayed. The nation was hastening to its doom, and, ere that generation had passed away, Jerusalem must fall. But regarding the date of the supreme crisis of His Second Advent He was less explicit. He expressly declared that it was hidden from Him. In the John v. 20, days of His flesh the Lord walked by faith and not by sight, 30. knowing only what was revealed to Him by the Father ; and Mt. xxiv. "of that day and hour none knew, neither the angels in 36=Mk. xiii. 32; cf. Heaven nor the Son, but the Father alone."[3] Of this, how-Acts i. 7.

[1] Cf. Is. xiii. 9 sqq. ; xxiv. 18 sqq. ; Jer. iv. 23 sq. ; Ezek. xxxii. 7 sqq. ; Joel iii. 9 sqq. ; Am. viii. 9.

[2] It was the outbreak of Messianic fanaticism that precipitated the disaster. Cf. Jos. De Bell. Jud. vi. 5. § 4.

[3] On dogmatic grounds T. R. of Mt. om. οὐδὲ ὁ υἱός. "These words," says Origen (In Matth. Comm. Ser. § 55), "seem to convict those who profess that they have knowledge of the end and the destruction of the world, and make announcements as though the Day of the Lord were at hand."

ever, He assured the Twelve, that the great consummation
might lie in the remote future, and the Church must lay her
account for long waiting. "When ye hear of wars and
rumours of wars, be not dismayed. It must so come to pass,
but not yet the end." "These things are the beginning of
the birth-pangs." "And this Gospel of the Kingdom shall be
preached in the whole world for a testimony unto all the
nations, and then shall come the end."

And, as though to lay this lesson home to the hearts of Two
His disciples, He spoke two parables—the Ten Virgins and parables:
the Talents—which sum up His teaching about the Second
Advent.[1] Watch! Work! are the precepts thereof, and the
Church, weary of waiting and full of heaviness, has need in
every generation to have them sounded in her ears. The
former depicts a scene very familiar to the disciples—a 1. The Ten
wedding. Eastern weddings are celebrated after night-fall, Virgins.
and their principal features are the procession and the
banquet. Jesus tells how a company of virgins, the friends of
the bride, fared forth with lighted lamps to meet the bridegroom and escort him to the house of the bride's father, the
scene of the wedding.[2] Something, however, detained him,
and they sat waiting for him by the way. The slow hours
passed, and still he tarried; and the weary virgins all grew
drowsy and fell asleep. At midnight the cry was raised:
"Behold, the bridegroom! Come forth to meet him." They
started up. Their lamps had burned low, and they must
needs replenish them with oil. Then it appeared that five of
them were prudent and five foolish. The former, apprehensive
of emergencies, had carried oil-flasks with them; but the
latter, never dreaming that the bridegroom's advent would be
delayed, had merely filled the cups of their lamps. All had
gone well had the bridegroom come betimes; but he had
tarried, and during the weary hours of waiting the thirsty

[1] Mt. alone records these parables, but they both appear in Lk. in a confused
form, blended with other parabolic sayings (xii. 35-8 ; xix. 11-28). Mk. xiii. 34-7
is a mutilated version of the parable of the Talents.

[2] Sometimes the wedding ceremony was in the bride's home, the bridegroom
providing the feast (Jud. xiv. 10). Sometimes it was in the bridegroom's house, and
he escorted the bride thither from her home (1 Macc. ix. 37-42). The latter
arrangement is implied by the reading of some MSS. in v. 1 : εἰς ὑπάντησιν του
νυμφίου καὶ τῆς νύμφης.

flame had been drinking up the scanty supply ; and now the cups were empty. The prudent virgins replenished their exhausted lamps from their flasks, but their improvident companions had no such resource. "Give us of your oil," they cried, "because our lamps are going out." "Perhaps," was the reply, "there will not be enough for us and you. Go rather to the sellers and buy for yourselves." Whatever the oil may signify, the fact remains that on that great Day each will have need of all the grace that he has, and "none will be able by any means to redeem his brother." It evinces the folly of the foolish virgins that they followed their companions' advice and hurried away to buy oil at midnight, never bethinking themselves that the merchants would have gone to rest and that, ere they could return, the bridegroom would have passed by. Improvident at the first, they were improvident to the last. "As they were going away to buy, the bridegroom came ; and they that were ready went in with him to the wedding-feast ; and the door was shut." By and by the foolish virgins came knocking at the door. "Sir, sir," they cried, "open to us." "Verily I tell you," came the answer from within, "I do not know you."

"Keep awake!"

"Keep awake therefore," says Jesus, pointing the lesson of the parable, "because ye know not the day nor the hour." He would fain at His coming find His disciples standing with Lk. xii. 35- their loins girt and their lamps burning like men that are 6. waiting for their lord ; but He foresaw how it would fare with them when He was gone. As the generations passed Cf. 2 Pet. and the promise of His coming remained still unfulfilled, iii. expectancy would flag and ardour burn low. The Church will be asleep when the Lord returns ; but well for such as carry in their souls a deep spring of faith and love, and, when the cry is raised at midnight, awaken with glad surprise to greet Him. It will be too late then to think of making ready. "In whatsoever condition I find you," Jesus is reported to have said, "therein will I judge you."[1] We may be asleep when the Lord comes, yet, if our hearts be true to Him and leap up in gladness to bid Him welcome, all will be well

---

[1] Just. M. *Dial. cum Tryph.*, Sylburg. ed. p. 267 A : διὸ καὶ ὁ ἡμέτερος κύριος Ἰησοῦς Χριστὸς εἶπεν· ἐν οἷς ἂν ὑμᾶς καταλάβω, ἐν τούτοις καὶ κρινῶ. Clem. Alex. *De Div. Serv.* § 40 : ἐφ' οἷς γὰρ ἂν εὕρω ὑμᾶς, φησίν, ἐπὶ τούτοις καὶ κρινῶ.

with us; we are ready and we shall go in with Him to the feast.

Jesus spoke another parable. He told how a man went abroad and, ere he left home, summoned three of his slaves, the most trustworthy of his household, and put them in charge of his property. To the first he entrusted five talents,[1] to the next two, and to the third one, according to his knowledge of their abilities; and charged them to trade therewith during his absence. He was a long time away, and on his return he called them to account. The first and the second had acquitted themselves well. No sooner had their master gone than they set to work: and their enterprises had prospered greatly. Each had doubled the sum entrusted to him. "Well done, good and faithful slave!" cried the delighted master, as he heard the account of each. "Thou hast been faithful over a few things: over many things will I set thee. Enter into the joy of thy lord."[2] The third had a very different story to tell. A man of less ability than his fellows, he had been entrusted with a proportionately smaller sum, and he had taken offence thereat and conceived hard thoughts of his master. There was no pleasing such an unconscionable tyrant, he had said petulantly to himself. Whatever he might gain would be deemed insufficient, and, should his speculations miscarry, he would suffer for it. The safest course was to run no risks. So he had deposited his talent in the ground, that primitive repository of treasure;[3] and now he produces it intact, and, conscious how ill a part he has acted, tries to brazen it out. "Sir, I recognised that thou art a hard man, 'reaping where thou didst not sow and gathering where thou didst not thresh';[4] and I was afraid, and went away and hid thy talent in the ground. See! thou hast thine own." "Ungenerous slave and slothful!" cried the master, convicting him on his own admission. "Thou knewest that I 'reap where I did not sow and gather where I did not thresh'? Thou shouldst therefore have deposited my money with the bankers, and on my coming I would have received my own

---

[1] A talent was about £213.
[2] *I.e.* "Be no longer my slave but my friend." *Cf.* John xv. 11, 15.
[3] *Cf.* Wetstein on Mt. xiii. 44.
[4] A proverbial description of a grasping man.

with interest. Therefore take away from him the talent and give it to him that hath the ten talents; and cast forth the useless slave into the outer darkness."

"Do busi-
ness till I
come."

Lk. xix. 13.

2 Thess. iii.
11-2.

Mt. xxiv.
14=Mk.
xiii. 10.

Reckoning
and
reward.

" *Do business till I come* " is the Lord's behest in view of the uncertainty of His Second Advent. How needful it was appears from what befell at Thessalonica ere many years had elapsed. The idea that the Day of the Lord was at hand took possession of the believers there and wrought grievous mischief. The excitement was intense ; the Church was in confusion ; the business of life was at a standstill. So serious was the situation that St Paul wrote to them and sought to recall them to sobriety. "We hear," he says, " of some that walk among you disorderly, that work not at all but are busybodies Now them that are such we command and exhort in the Lord Jesus Christ, that with quietness they work and eat their own bread." And precisely similar is the Lord's exhortation in this parable. He would have His disciples watch for His appearing, but meanwhile there was much work to be done : " This Gospel of the Kingdom shall be preached in the whole world for a testimony unto all the nations, and then shall come the end " ; and they would best prepare to meet Him and most effectually hasten His advent, not by scanning the sky for the sign of His appearing, but by addressing themselves strenuously to their mission and carrying His Gospel to the nations of the earth. Since the work is great, the very uncertainty of the Second Advent should serve as an incentive to activity. There is much to be done, and the time may be very short. " The Last Day," says St Augustine,[1] " is hidden that all days may be observed."

The parable is fraught with far-reaching and profitable truth. It shows how the Lord will reckon with His servants at His appearing. He will consider their capacities and reward them not so much according to their achievements as according to their zeal and faithfulness. Since the first slave had larger ability than the second, he received a larger trust ; yet, since they displayed equal diligence, each doubling his deposit, they got the self-same commendation and the self-same reward. And, had the third done business with his single talent and made it two, he would have had a like

[1] *Serm.* xxxix. § 1.

recompense; yea, had he earned three talents, tripling his trust, he would have been greeted with the loftiest eulogy of all.   His condemnation was not that he earned less than his fellows but that he earned nothing.   And what is meant by the Master's remonstrance: "Thou shouldest have deposited my money with the bankers, and on my coming I would have received my own with interest"?   It is surely an admonition to such as hold positions of trust, that, if they have not the heart to be faithful, they should stand aside and resign their places to others who will diligently improve the sacred opportunities.   The man who hid his talent in the earth, was doubly guilty, forasmuch as he neither traded with it himself nor suffered another to trade with it.   And, finally, the parable teaches that the reward which the Lord will bestow upon His faithful servants, is not discharge from labour but a call to further and larger service.   "Take away from him the talent, and give it to him that hath the ten talents.   For to every one that hath shall be given, and he shall have more abundantly."[1]   And this is the prayer of every true-hearted disciple:

> " Dismiss me not Thy service, Lord,
>   But train me for Thy will;
> For even I, in fields so broad,
>   Some duties may fulfil:
> And I will ask for no reward
>   Except to serve Thee still."

The secret of devotion to the Lord's service is recognition of His goodness.   His service may be heavy, demanding unwearied labour and boundless sacrifice, yet it is a blessed service.   Jesus is no hard master.   If the way which His disciples must take be difficult, it is the way which He trod before them; and, if they must share His suffering, they shall enter into His joy.

The discourse closes with a picture of the Last Judgment. The Last Since He was speaking to Jews, Jesus employed Jewish Judgment. language, and, borrowing a familiar image from the Book of Dan. vii. Daniel, told how "the Son of Man would come in His glory, 13.

---

[1] A favourite saying of Jesus.   R. Hillel said: " He who increases not decreases," meaning that knowledge unimproved perishes.   *Cf.* Taylor, *Say. of Fath.* i. 14 The Lord's maxim is similarly applied in Mt. xiii. 12; Mk. iv. 25=Lk. viii. 18.

and all the angels with Him."[1] Perhaps He was thinking of
the repeated demand of the Pharisees and Sadducees for a
sign from heaven. When last they made it, He had refused
it with indignant contempt, but now He declares that on
that great Day they will have their desire : " Then shall
appear the sign of the Son of Man in heaven, and all the
tribes of the earth shall mourn, and they shall see the Son of
Man coming on the clouds of heaven with power and much
glory." Still employing prophetic imagery, He proceeds to
depict the solemn Assize : " He shall sit on His throne of
glory, and there shall be gathered before Him all the nations."
Who are they that shall be thus arraigned before the
Judgment-seat of the Son of Man? From ancient times it
has been generally supposed that they are all mankind.[2] So
early, however, as the third century this assumption was
challenged ;[3] and in truth it is more than doubtful. It is
distinctly said that " all the nations " shall be gathered before
that dread tribunal, and in the Scriptures " the nations " are
ever *the heathen*. Indeed the imagery of the parable is
borrowed from Joel's prophecy of the judgment of the nations
in the Valley of Jehoshaphat, and the nations are there distinguished from Israel, Jehovah's people and heritage. Nor is
it without significance that the Judge is styled *the King*. He
is the Messiah of Israel, but He is the King of the nations.
It might be concluded that what is here depicted is the judgment of the Gentile world, were it not for the wondering
question wherewith the Judge's sentences are greeted : " Lord,
when saw we Thee an-hungered ? " This is the language of
utter strangers to Jesus, and it seems indubitable that what is
here depicted is the judgment of those who have never heard
His name. No Christian will be there, and no Jew, since
neither Christian nor Jew is a stranger to Jesus. No heathen
who has known the Gospel will be there ; none but heathen
who have never heard the name of Jesus and never had the

Marginal notes:
Mt. xvi. 1
=Mk. viii.
11.

Mt. xxiv.
30 ; *cf.*
Zech. xii.
12.

Cf. Joel iii.
2, 11, 12,
14.

Only for
such as
have never
heard the
Gospel.

---

[1] In a curious passage (*De Bell. Jua.* v. 6. § 3) Josephus says that during the
siege of Jerusalem at every discharge of the Roman catapults the watchers on the
ramparts shouted by way of warning : ὁ υἱὸς ἔρχεται, "The Son is coming !" *lós,
missile*, is a suggested emendation of υἱός.

[2] Chrysost. : πᾶσα ἡ των ἀνθρώπων φύσις.

[3] *Cf.* Orig. *In Matth. Comm. Ser.* § 70. Lactantius held that what is here depicted is the judgment of Christians. So Euth. Zig., Neand., Mey.

offer of His salvation.   In truth such is our Lord's constant
representation.   According to His teaching the judgment of
such as know the Gospel is not reserved to the Last Day.   It
is not future but present.   "God sent not His Son into the John iii. 17
world that He might judge the world, but that the world 9.
might be saved through Him.   He that believeth in Him is
not being judged ; he that believeth not hath already been
judged, because he hath not believed in the name of the only
begotten Son of God.   And this is the judgment, that the
light hath come into the world, and the men loved the darkness rather than the light."   Judgment implies the possibility
of acquittal, and such as have rejected the Saviour will be
arraigned before Him at the last not for trial but for sentence,
not for judgment but for condemnation.

What then shall be the judgment of such as have never The separa-
heard the Gospel?   "He shall separate them from one tion of the
righteous
another, as the shepherd separateth the sheep from the goats, from the
un-
and shall set the sheep on His right and the goats on His righteous.
left."   The significance of the similitude does not lie in some
fancied superiority of sheep over goats,[1] but in the separation
of the promiscuous multitude into two well-defined and plainly
recognisable companies.   Like sheep and goats in one pasture,
like tares and wheat in one field, like good fish and bad Mt. xiii. 24-
in one net, men are mingled during this life ; but on the 30, 36-43,
47-50.
Day of Judgment, in presence of that Face which discerns the
secrets of the soul, they will be parted according to their
moral affinities.

The test is character evinced by deeds of kindness, but The test.
Jesus attaches thereto a profound and wonderful significance.
Sitting on His throne the King addresses first the multitude
on His right, hailing them as His Father's blessed ones and
bidding them inherit the Kingdom which, all unknown to
them, has been prepared for them since the world's foundation.   And this felicity they have earned by kindness to
Himself.   He was hungry, and they gave Him food ; thirsty,
and they gave Him drink ; a stranger, and they showed Him
hospitality ; naked, and they clothed Him ; sick, and they

---

[1] Chrysost. : Sheep more *profitable* than goats, yielding wool, milk, lambs.   Jer. :
" Hædos, lascivum animal et petulcum, et fervens semper ad coitum."   Euth. Zig. :
Goats malodorous like sin   The distinction is not of *quality* but of *kind*.

visited Him ; in prison, and they came to Him. It is an
amazing announcement. Never till this hour have they seen
Him, and how have they done Him all these kindnesses?
The King explains. There are poor folk in the throng who
have suffered such ills, and they have crept near His throne
attracted by the grace which ever shone in His blessed face
and drew the wretched to Him.[1] With such the Son of the
Fallen always claimed kinship ; and, pointing to them, He replies : " Verily I tell you, inasmuch as ye did it unto one of
these My brethren, even the least, unto Me ye did it." Then,
turning to those on His left and charging them with neglect
of all those deeds of charity, He calls them " accursed " and
bids them depart from Him. They have steeled their hearts
against the miseries of their fellow-mortals, and in neglecting
them they have neglected Him.

Un-
conscious
disciple-
ship.

It is a wonderful claim that Jesus here advances ; no less
than this, that He is everywhere present, even where He is
unknown, observing whatever befalls ; and so tender is His
sympathy, so deep His entrance into human ill and so utter
His appropriation thereof, that it is as though He were incarnate in every sufferer, presenting Himself to the world and
claiming its succour and service.[2] There is no spot on earth
without His presence. " Raise the stone," He is reported to
have said, " and there thou shalt find Me ; cleave the wood,
and I am there."[3] There is no human soul that is not encompassed by His love.

> " Nor bounds, nor clime, nor creed thou know'st,
>   Wide as our need thy favours fall ;
>   The white wings of the Holy Ghost
> Stoop, seen or unseen, o'er the heads of all."

Each striving against evil, each yearning after good, each
generous emotion that stirs in the human breast, is an inspiration of that Saviour who is near even to such as do not know
Him, compassing their path and their lying down, besetting
them behind and before, and laying His hand upon them.

[1] Keim conceives the " brethren " to be the Christians, who surround the throne,
spectators of the scene, the heathen being judged according to their treatment of the
Church. Cf. Acts ix. 1, 4-5.

[2] Cf. Lowell's Vision of Sir Launfal and Tolstoï's Where Love is, God is also.
Saying of R. Abin : " Remember, when a poor man stands at your door, the Holy
One stands at his right hand."

[3] One of the 1897 Oxyrhynchus logia : ἔγειρον τὸν λίθον κἀκεῖ εὑρήσεις με, σχίσον
τὸ ξύλον κἀγὼ ἐκεῖ εἰμί.

How gracious are the Lord's thoughts towards the dark world of heathendom! How righteous His judgments! Unlike the Rabbis, who comprehended the Gentiles in one indiscriminate condemnation and reckoned them mere "fuel for Gehenna," He claims as His disciples all who, though they have never heard His name, are actuated by a Christ-like spirit and do Christ-like deeds.[1] Some of the early Greek Fathers shared His humane and large-hearted attitude. In marked contrast to the Rabbis, who banned the *Chokmath Javanith*, Justin Martyr recognised how much of truth and goodness there is in the writings of the Greek philosophers, poets, and historians, and claimed for them a share in the inspiration of Christ, speaking of a "seminal divine Word," which was His, implanted in their minds.[2] And Clement of Alexandria regarded Philosophy as a preparation for Christianity. It was the pædagogue that led the Greeks to Christ even as the Law led the Jews.[3] Plato, though he never knew Gal. iii. 24 Jesus, was His disciple, and all the truth that he knew was revealed to him by the Holy Spirit. It is indeed plain from many declarations of Jesus that the test for such as know Him is their attitude toward Himself, their acceptance or rejection of His claims ; but none will be condemned for not believing in a Saviour whom they never knew or not accepting an invitation which they never heard.[4] It is required of every man that he be faithful to the trust committed to him and obedient to the truth revealed to him—that and no more, that and no less.

The kindness of Jesus to the heathen world appears not Mercy merely in His recognition of its righteous sons as His un- tempering conscious disciples, but in His attitude towards the un- doom. righteous. It is true that the latter have not followed the light which they had ; yet, had they seen "the light of the knowledge of the glory of God in the face of Jesus Christ," they might have welcomed it ; and therefore it is just that their judgment should be more lenient and their doom less awful. And it is even so. They are indeed sent away into the Eternal Fire prepared—not for them, since God would *Cf.* Enoch liv. 5.

---

[1] They pronounced the same malediction on one who reared swine and one who taught his son Greek. See Ottho, *Hist. Doct. Misn.* pp. 68-70; Wetstein on Acts vi. 1.

[2] *Apol.* i, Sylburg. ed. p. 51 C.   [3] *Strom.* i. 5. § 28.

have all be saved, and, if any perish, it is contrary to His purpose; but—for the Devil and his angels; yet even this awful doom has its alleviations. "That slave," said Jesus, in another connection, "that knew his lord's will and did not make ready or do according to his will shall be beaten with many stripes; whereas he that knew it not and did things worthy of stripes shall be beaten with few. And every one to whom was given much, much shall be required from him; and with whom they deposited much, exceeding more shall they ask of him." [1] Such is the Lord's judgment, and the heart rises up and confesses at once its righteousness and its mercy.

Lk. xii. 47-8.

[1] Mt. xxv. 46 (*cf.* Dan. xii. 2-3) is a gloss, probably catechetical. *Cf.* Introd. § 12, 7.

John xiii. 1 ; Mt.
xxvi. 1-5=Mk.
xiv. 1-2=Lk.
xxii. 1-2; Mt.
xxvi. 14-20=Mk.
xiv. 10-7=Lk.
xxii. 3-14; Lk.
xxii. 24-30; 15
8; John xiii. 2
20 (Mt. xxiii. 8
12); Mt. xxvi.
21-5=Mk. xiv.
18-21=Lk. xxit.
21-3=John xiii.
21-35; Mt. xxvi
31-5=Mk. xiv.
27-31=Lk. xxii.
31-8=John xiii.
36-8; Mt. xxvi.
26-9=Mk. xiv.
22-5=Lk. xxii.
19-20 (1 Cor. xi
23-5); John xiv

CHAPTER XLV

THE UPPER ROOM

" I will remember all Thy Love divine ;
Oh meet Thou with me where Thy saints are met,
Revive me with the holy bread and wine,
And may my love, O God, lay hold on Thine,
And ne'er forget."—WALTER C. SMITH.

As the Lord sat thus on Olivet and discoursed to the Twelve
of things to come, the end was nigh. That evening, according
to Jewish reckoning, had ushered in the fourteenth day of
Nisan, and the morrow would be the Day of Preparation when
all must be got ready for the Paschal Supper, that sacred
feast which commemorated the deliverance of Israel from her
bondage in Egypt, and which was celebrated in the Holy City
after nightfall at the commencement of the fifteenth day. On
the ensuing evening Jesus would eat the Passover with the
Twelve, and immediately thereafter the tragedy of the Passion
would be enacted, beginning with the Betrayal in the Garden
of Gethsemane and culminating in the Crucifixion on the Hill
of Calvary.[1]

The eve of the Preparation.

Exod. xii.

So nigh was the end. The following night Jesus would
be in the grasp of His malignant foes ; and He knew it.
How was He affected by the prospect? St John, remembering
well his dear Lord's every act and word and look, has added
to the picture some significant touches which show how He
bore Himself at that dread crisis. He did not blench or
falter. Where the world saw only defeat, He saw triumph ;
and, when He spoke, there was exultation in His tone. " Now
hath the Son of Man been glorified, and God hath been glorified
in Him." And, as the end drew near, the disciples observed in
His bearing toward them an access of unwonted tenderness.
" Before the Feast of the Passover Jesus, knowing that His

The Lord's bearing.

John xiii. 31.

[1] *Cf.* Append. VI.

hour had come to pass out of this world unto the Father,[1] having loved His own that were in the world, loved them to the utmost."[2]   It was the tenderness of imminent farewell ; nor was there wanting a generous recognition of the steadfast loyalty of the men who, amid much weakness, had stood by Him in all His conflicts and privations.

Lk. xxii. 28.

Consultation of the rulers. The storm was fast gathering.   The succession of defeats which they had sustained in their encounters with Jesus and the heavy indictment which He had brought against them in the hearing of the multitude, had enraged the rulers beyond endurance, and they had met in the High Priest's palace and consulted how they might put Him to death.   They were still confronted by the difficulty that He was the hero of the populace and His arrest would have excited a dangerous tumult.   The issue of their deliberation was a two-fold resolution : they must arrest Him by stealth, and they must wait until the Feast was over and the throng of worshippers, especially those turbulent Galileans, had departed from the city.

Their agreement with Judas. It was with extreme reluctance that they recognised the expediency of delay, and great was their exultation when an unexpected turn of events brought an opportunity for immediate action.   A man presented himself at the High Priest's palace and craved audience.   It was Judas the Man of Kerioth, and he came on an infamous errand.   He was a disappointed man.   He had attached himself to Jesus because he deemed Him the Messiah and expected reward and honour in the Messianic Kingdom.   Gradually the truth had come home to him, and he had discovered the vanity of his expectation.   His disillusionment was complete when he realised that what awaited Jesus was not a crown but a cross. He perceived that he had embarked on a ruinous enterprise, and to his worldly judgment it appeared the wisest policy to come out of it on the best possible terms.   It may be also

---

[1] Cf. Augustine's beautiful fancy (In Joan. Ev. Tract. lv. § 1) : " Pascha, quod latine transitus nuncupatur, velut interpretans nobis beatus Evangelista, ' Ante diem,' inquit, ' festum Paschæ, sciens Jesus quia venit hora ejus ut transeat ex hoc mundo ad Patrem.'   Ecce Pascha, ecce transitus."

[2] εἰς τέλος not to the end but to the utmost, as He had never loved them before. Cf. Chrysost. In Joan. lxix ; Euth. Zig. ἠγάπησεν implies demonstrations of affection, Cf. p. 361.

that he was actuated by a desire to be avenged on the Master who, as he deemed, had fooled him ; and a plan had presented itself which promised at once profit and revenge. While Jesus was engaged with the Greeks, Judas betook himself to the High Priests and offered, if they would adequately remunerate him, to betray their troubler into their hands. They joyfully welcomed the proposal and offered him thirty shekels of silver. It was the price of a slave,[1] and, when they named it, the insult was aimed less at Jesus than at Judas. It was the traitor that they purchased at a slave's price, and, conscious of the degradation of trafficking with the wretch, they salved their consciences by treating him with undisguised contumely. Lost to self-respect and impervious to contempt, he accepted their offer, and they paid over the money on the spot as though in haste to be done with him.[2]

Exod. xxi. 32.

The next day was the Preparation ; and, never doubting that Jesus according to His wont would eat the Paschal Supper in the evening, the disciples asked Him where He would have them make ready. He had arranged the matter with a friend in the city ; and in view of subsequent developments it is a tempting conjecture that the friend was John Mark afterwards the Evangelist. He was cousin to Barnabas, a wealthy believer, and resided in Jerusalem with his widowed mother, Mary, who threw her hospitable door open to the Apostles in after days.[3] He had a large upper room in his house, and he had granted the use of it to Jesus that He might eat the Supper there with His disciples, promising to furnish it with table and couches. Jesus might have named the house to His disciples, but, cognisant of the traitor's purpose, He would not have Judas know the place, lest he should reveal it to the rulers and bring them in upon Him in

The Lord's direction regarding preparation.

Col. iv. 10, R.V.

Acts xii. 12

---

[1] *Cf.* Wetstein.

[2] Mt. xxvi. 15 : ἔστησαν, "weighed." *Cf. P. E. F. Q.* Apr. 1896, p. 152 : "To this day it is usual in Jerusalem to examine and test carefully all coins received. Thus a Medjidie (silver) is not only examined by the eye, but also by noticing its ring on the stone pavement, and English sterling gold is carefully weighed, and returned when defaced." Mk. and Lk. represent the money as merely promised, but Mt. xxvii. 3-10 proves that it was paid. There is no good reason for regarding Mt.'s graphic details ἔστησαν, τριάκοντα ἀργύρια, and the Potter's Field as borrowed from Zech. xi. 12-3 (Mt. xxvii. 9-10).

[3] So Ewald. Theophylact. (on Mt. xxvi. 6) quotes the opinion that the friend was Simon the Leper. Keim suggests Joseph of Arimathæa.

Lk. xxii.
15. the midst of the Supper. He would fain eat that Passover with His disciples ere He suffered and commune with them undisturbed ; and therefore He had laid a plan with His host. He chose Peter and John for the errand. " Go into the city," He said, " and there shall meet you a man carrying a pitcher of water. Follow him ; and, wheresoever he entereth, say to the master of the house : ' The Teacher saith : *Where is My room where I am to eat the Passover with My disciples ?*' " Since drawing water was a woman's office, a man carrying a pitcher would be sufficiently noticeable ; and, since he was evidently one of their host's slaves, he would be known to the disciples. The direction afforded Judas no clue, and he durst not track the messengers.[1]

Dispute in
the Upper
Room. Their task included the conveyance of the lamb to the Temple,[2] its offering at the altar, and the roasting of its flesh, besides the procuring of the wine, the unleavened cakes, and the bitter herbs and the preparation of the *charosheth*, a paste of crushed fruits moistened with vinegar symbolising the clay wherewith the Israelites had made bricks in Egypt. When all was ready, they returned to Jesus, and toward evening the whole company repaired to Jersualem and took possession of the apartment. Their host had furnished it bravely. It was seldom that Jesus and the Twelve had enjoyed such state, and even at that solemn crisis the unaccustomed grandeur provoked contention among the disciples, and, each anxious to vindicate his superiority in view of the impending distribution of rewards and honours, they fell Cf. Lk. xiv.
7-11. a-disputing about the places which they should occupy at table.[3]

The first
cup. Jesus paid no heed at the moment. They took their places, and the Supper began. By the aid of the Talmud it is possible to follow with comparative certainty the course of

---

[1] *Cf.* Euth. Zig. on Mt. xxvi. 18.

[2] It had already been procured on 10th Nisan. *Cf.* Exod. xii. 3.

[3] The primitive fashion had been to eat the Supper *standing* (Exod. xii. 11) ; but this had fallen into abeyance, and they reclined at table in token that they were no longer slaves but the Lord's freemen. *Cf. Hieros. Pesach.* 37. 2. The contention is implied by John, but it is expressly mentioned only by Lk., who erroneously inserts it after the announcement of the betrayal (xxii. 24-30), evidently suggesting that the matter of dispute was which was least capable of treachery. At that moment, however, they were unfit for contention. They were stricken dumb. Lk.'s account is further defective in that it is obviously assimilated to Mt. xx. 25-6 = Mk. x. 42-3.

that memorable feast.[1] It began, according to the paschal
rubric, with the mixing of a cup of wine[2] and the giving of Lk. xxii.
thanks. Anxious to awaken His disciples to the solemnity [17.]
of the occasion, Jesus preluded this with the announcement
that never again would He eat the Passover with them on
earth, and, as the cup went round, He added: "I tell you,
I shall not hereafter drink of this fruit of the vine until that
day when I shall drink it with you new in the Kingdom of
My Father."[3] Then the various viands were brought forward
—the bitter herbs, which symbolised the bitterness of the
Egyptian bondage, the unleavened bread, the *charosheth*, and
the lamb already carved. After a blessing had been asked
the herbs were dipped in the paste and eaten, and then a
second cup was prepared.

At this point it was customary for the head of the house- Lesson in
hold to explain the origin and significance of the Passover ; humility.
and probably it was here that Jesus found occasion to refer to
that unseemly contention, administering to His disciples an
effective rebuke and teaching them a memorable lesson in
humility. He did it in a very remarkable manner. "He An acted
riseth from the Supper and layeth aside His robes, and took parable.
a towel and girded it about Him. Then He putteth water
into the basin and began to wash the feet of the disciples and
wipe them with the towel wherewith He was girded."[4] What
did He mean? Among Jews, Greeks, and Romans alike it
was the fashion that, when guests arrived at the house of their
entertainer, slaves should receive them and, taking off their
sandals, wash their feet heated with travel and soiled with the
dust of the way.[5] And this custom is commonly deemed a
sufficient explanation of the scene in the Upper Room. Our
Lord's purpose was to rebuke the selfish ambition of His
disciples, and it was assuredly a very striking enforcement of
humility when He, their Lord and Teacher, went round the

---

[1] *Cf.* Lightfoot on Mt. xxvi. 26, 27.

[2] The paschal cups were mixed with water *ad salubritatem atque ad fugam ebrietatis.*
It was required, however, that they should retain the taste and colour of wine.

[3] The earthly feast was a shadow of the heavenly. *Cf.* Hebr. viii. 5 ; ix. 23-4.

[4] *Cf.* Augustine's fine comment (*In Joan. Ev. Tract.* lv. § 7); "Crucifigendus
sane suis exspoliatus est vestimentis, et mortuus involutus est linteis : et tota illa
ejus passio, nostra purgatio est."

[5] *Cf.* Lk. vii. 44. See Becker, *Charicles,* sc. vi, exc. 1 ; Wetstein on John xiii. 5.

astonished circle and wrought on each that menial office. Yet, obvious and sufficient as this explanation may at the first glance appear, a difficulty emerges on a more attentive scrutiny. The customary feet-washing was performed at the entrance of the guests; but here it is not until the company have taken their places at table that Jesus rises and addresses Himself to the servile task.[1]

"With unwashed feet." The truth is that, when Jesus rose from the Supper and washed the feet of the Twelve, it was not the ordinary usage at all. It was another acted parable, nor would its significance be obscure to the disciples. The Greeks had a proverb, which was apparently derived from the ritual of the Mysteries and which, forasmuch as the Mysteries were of Oriental origin, must have been no less intelligible in the East than in the West. They spoke of entering upon an undertaking "with unwashed feet" or, in precisely the same sense, "with unwashed hands."[2] According to the ancient lexicographer the proverb meant "without any preparation"; and it is aptly exemplified by a passage in Lucian's sketch of his ideal wise man, Demonax the eclectic philosopher. Demonax, says his biographer, was no novice when he entered on his profession. "He did not rush at it, as the saying goes, 'with unwashed feet,' but he had been nurtured with poets and remembered most of them, and had been trained to speak, and had a thorough acquaintance with the philosophic schools." Is not this proverb the key to our Lord's symbolic action, His acted parable, in the Upper Room? Even in that solemn hour the disciples were disputing "which of them should be accounted the greatest"; and, when He arose and washed their feet, it was as though He had said: "If ye be not clothed with

---

[1] The true reading in *v.* 2 is δείπνου γινομένου, "during Supper," not δείπ. γενομένου, "Supper being ended." Augustine with the latter reading before him insisted nevertheless, in view of the situation, that it could not mean "after Supper." *In Joan. Ev. Tract.* lv. § 3.

[2] ἀνίπτοις ποσίν, ἀνίπτοις χερσίν. Suidas: χωρὶς τινος παρασκευῆς. ἐπὶ τῶν ἀμαθῶς ἐπί τινα ἔργα καὶ πράξεις ἀφικνουμένων. Erasmus in his *Adagia* applies the proverb to the quarrel between the scholars of the Renaissance and the obscurantist monks, "who, equipped with some frigid syllogisms and childish sophistries—eternal God!—dare anything, enjoin anything, determine anything. . . . One who is ignorant of the three tongues [Greek, Latin, and Hebrew], is no theologian but a violator of sacred Theology. Truly, with hands and feet alike unwashed, he does not treat of the most sacred of all subjects, but profanes, defiles, and violates it."

humility, ye are none of Mine. Your worldly and selfish ambition proves you still uninitiated into the mysteries of the Kingdom of Heaven, whose law is love and whose glory is service. Think not to enter it 'with unwashed feet.' If I wash you not, ye have no part with Me." *Cf.* Mt. xiii.
11 = Mk. iv.
11 = Lk.
viii. 10.

He began with Peter.[1] "Lord," cried the horrified disciple, "*Thou* wash *my* feet!" "What I am doing," Jesus answered, "thou knowest not just now, but thou shalt recognise presently." Still Peter persisted, deeming it an impiety that his feet should be washed by those blessed hands : "Never shalt thou wash *my* feet." "If I wash thee not," Jesus returned, "thou hast no part with Me";[2] and at that the disciple gave way and, with characteristic impetuosity, bounded to the opposite extreme. "Lord," he cried, "not my feet only but also my hands and my head." It was ever thus with Peter, and there would be a kindly smile on the face of Jesus when He made reply : "He that hath been bathed hath no need save to wash his feet,[3] but is clean all over." It was only their feet that the guests needed to wash ere taking their places at table ; and the disciples, bathed once for all in "the laver of regeneration," needed only to be cleansed from the soiling of the way. "Daily," says St Augustine, "He washes our feet who intercedes for us ; and that we have daily need to wash our feet, that is, to direct the ways of our spiritual steps, we confess when we pray : 'Forgive us our debts as we forgive our debtors.'" It was a playful answer, but the smile would fade from the Lord's face as, thinking of the traitor, He added : "And ye are clean, but not all." He went round the circle, encountering no further resistance, and He would come to Judas in his turn. He knew the errand on which those feet had gone yesterday, yet He laved them and wiped them with His gentle hands.[4] Peter's
protest.

Tit. iii. 5

---

[1] Aug. *In Joan. Ev. Tract.* lvi. § 1. Chrysostom thinks Judas was first, then Peter. The chief seat belonged to Peter, ἀλλ' εἰκὸς τὸν προδότην ἰταμὸν ὄντα καὶ πρὸ τοῦ κορυφαίου κατακλιθῆναι.

[2] Aug. *ibid.* § 2 : "Salvator ægrum reluctantem de ipsius salutis periculo exterrens."

[3] ἢ (*al.* εἰ μή) τοὺς πόδας omitted by ℵ, but well attested.

[4] Aug. *In Joan. Ev. Tract.* lvi. § 6 : "Etiam illi non dedignatus est pedes lavare cujus manus jam prævidebat in scelere."

The Lord's
explana-
tion.
John xiii.
12-20; Lk.
xxii. 24-
30; Mt.
xxiii. 8-12.
As soon as He had resumed His garments and His place at
table, He fulfilled His promise to Peter and explained what He
had done.   He discoursed to the company of the humility
which makes men great in the Kingdom of Heaven, setting
Himself forth as their Exemplar and bidding them observe how
He had borne Himself among them, not only in that singular
act of self-abasement, but in His whole ministry of redeeming
love : " I have washed your feet ; I am in your midst as he
that serveth.   An example have I given you, that, even as I
have done to you, ye also should do."   It is told of Godfrey
de Bouillon, the hero of the first Crusade, that, though he
undertook the government of Jerusalem, a trust as full of
danger as of glory, he would not wear the name and ensigns of
royalty in a city where his Saviour had been crowned with
thorns ; and even so should the disciples, remembering their
Lord's infinite sacrifice, make themselves of no reputation.
Dignity was dear to the hearts of the Pharisees.   They loved
to be styled *Rabbi, Father, Leader*.[1] " Be not ye called
' Rabbi,'" says Jesus ;[1] " for One is your Teacher, and all ye
are brethren.   And call none your ' Father' on the earth ;
for One is your Father, even the Heavenly One.   Neither be
called ' Leaders'; for your Leader is One, the Messiah."[2]
Here at the close of His ministry the Lord reiterates the
lesson which throughout its course He had inculcated by word
and deed : " The greater of you shall be your servant.   Learn
of Me ; for I am meek and lowly in heart."   It is one of the
achievements of Jesus that He introduced into the world a
new ideal of greatness, such an ideal as men had never
dreamed of.   He lived the divine life before their eyes, and,
behold, it was a life of utter self-abasement and boundless
self-sacrifice.   " Proud man," says St Augustine, " would have
perished for ever, had not a lowly God found him."

Announce-
ment of the
Betrayal.
Pss. cxiii-
cxiv.
According to the rubric, when the master of the house had
discoursed on the significance of the Passover, the company
sang the first part of the Hallel, and the cup was passed
round.   Thereafter followed a rite of peculiar solemnity preliminary to the eating of the lamb which was the feast proper.

---

[1] *Father = Abba.* *Cf.* Wetstein.
[2] Mt. xxiii. 8-12, incorporated inaptly wiih the indictment of the Pharisees,
find its true place here. So Keim. *Cf.* Introd. § 9.

The master washed his hands, took two loaves and, breaking one, laid the fragments on the other; then, after a blessing, he enfolded the fragments in the bitter herbs, dipped them in the *charosheth*, and, saying : " Blessed be Thou, O Lord God, our Eternal King, who hast sanctified us by Thy commandments and commanded us to eat," ate of the bread and the herbs. It was probably at this stage that Jesus startled the disciples by an appalling announcement. The bitter herbs were in His hands, and bitterness was in His soul. " He was troubled in spirit and testified and said : " Verily, verily I tell you that one of you shall betray Me." Twice already He had told them that He should be betrayed, but now He brings the crime home into their midst. He had a design in so doing. He had gathered the Twelve in the Upper Room, not merely that He might eat the Passover with them, but that He might institute a sacred rite which should perpetuate the remembrance of His immortal love ; and ere its institution, since it was fitting that only His true disciples should particpate therein, the traitor must depart.[1]

Mt. xvii. 22 = Mk. ix. 31 = Lk. ix. 44 ; Mt. xx. 18 = Mk. x. 33 = Lk. xviii. 32.

The announcement fell upon them like a thunder-bolt, and " they looked at one another, wondering of whom He spoke." Peter would naturally have questioned Him, but two things prevented. What had happened at the feet-washing a little before had put an awe upon him and bridled his impetuosity, and his position rendered it difficult for him to address Jesus. The couches were set aslant round a low table, each of the company resting on his left elbow with his right arm free. The middle place was the most honourable, and it would be occupied by Jesus. The couch behind Him, adjoining His neck, was occupied by Peter. That in front of Him, adjoining His breast, was occupied by John.[2] Peter might have questioned Jesus, but, reclining thus behind Him, he could not. Catching John's eye, as the latter turned round in

Consternation of the disciples.

---

[1] John alone mentions the departure of Judas, and, since he does not record the institution of the Supper, it is a question whether the traitor took his departure before or after it. The old opinion, relying on Lk. xxii. 17-21, is that he was present at it. *Cf.* Lightfoot on Lk. xxii. 21. But Lk.'s arrangement differs from that of Mt. and Mk. who put the institution after the announcement. From John's narrative it appears that Judas departed immediately after the announcement, and the institution probably follows John xiii. 38, chap. xiv being the Communion Address.

[2] *Cf.* Lightfoot on Mt. xxvi. 20 and John xiii. 23.

amazement, he made a sign to him, unseen by Jesus, that he should put the question; and John, with the familiarity of the best beloved disciple, laid back his head on Jesus' breast and asked: "Lord, who is it?" An open declaration would have created a painful scene, and Jesus whispered His reply: "It is the man for whom I shall dip the sop and give it to him."[1] Thereupon He took a scrap of bread and, dipping it in the *charosheth*, handed it to Judas. The latter durst not decline it, albeit, observing the whispered colloquy, he must have surmised the purport of the Lord's action. His crime was known, and it was impossible for him now to draw back. "After the sop then Satan entered into the wretch."[2]

The with-
drawal of
Judas.

As he lay confounded and irresolute, Jesus said to him curtly and significantly: "What thou art doing do promptly"[3]; and instantly he rose, hurried from the room, and went out into the night on his errand of darkness. His withdrawal was tantamount to a confession of guilt; but only John knew that he was the traitor, and no one suspected the reason of his going, else would they have sprung up and arrested him. He went at the Lord's bidding, and they supposed that he was going on some errand connected with his office as treasurer—to purchase something for the paschal season or to give something to the poor. Ere they recovered from their confusion, Jesus spoke. The traitor's departure removed a load from the Lord's heart. That malign presence had been a restraint upon Him, and now He might commune freely with the faithful Eleven. "Now," He exclaimed exultantly, "hath the Son of Man been glorified, and God hath been glorified in Him. My children, a little longer am I with you;

John viii.
21; *cf.* vii.
33-4.

ye will seek Me, and, as I said to the Jews: 'Where I am going away, ye cannot come,' I now tell you also. A new commandment I give you, that ye love one another—that, as I have loved you, ye also love one another. By this shall all recognise that ye are My disciples, if ye have love one for another."

---

[1] Chrysost. *In Joan.* lxxi: λάθρα εἴρηκεν ὥστε μηδένα ἀκοῦσαι· καὶ γὰρ ὁ Ἰωάννης διὰ τοῦτο παρὰ τὸ στῆθος ἀναπεσὼν ἐρωτᾷ μονονουχὶ πρὸς τὸ οὖς· ὥστε μὴ γενέσθαι φανερὸν τὸν προδότην. *Cf.* Introd. § 13.

[2] Keim's trivial gibe that, "if Jesus so prostituted him, as John represents, he was to a certain extent irresponsible," is very old. *Cf.* Aug. *In Joan. Ev. Tract.* lxii. § 13.   [3] Moulton's *Gram. of N.T. Gk.* i. pp. 78, 236.

Then [1] He made a second announcement well-nigh as *Announcement of the Desertion.* horrifying as that of the Betrayal : " All of you shall stumble at Me in the course of this night ; for it hath been written : *Zech. xiii. 7.* ' I will smite the Shepherd, and the sheep shall be scattered abroad.' " It was a terrible announcement, yet Jesus never spoke more graciously. He did not dwell upon the cowardice of the disciples or His own utter desolation. To the last He was the True Shepherd, and all His care was for His sheep. He saw them shepherdless at the mercy of the spoiler ; and His heart was sore for their piteous plight. And, lest dismay should overwhelm them, He had no sooner announced the desertion than He added a great promise of hope, and told them that He would meet them again in that dear northern land where He and they had laboured and held sweet fellowship. " After I have risen, I will go before you into Galilee."

The intimation of their infidelity amazed the disciples. *Incredulity of the disciples.* They deemed it incredible, and Peter, after his impulsive and self-confident manner, protested : " Though all shall stumble at Thee, I will never stumble." " Simon, Simon," Jesus answered, recurring to the old name, as He was wont when He would reprove the rash disciple, reminding him what he had been ere grace found him, " behold, Satan hath requested *Cf. Job i. 11-2, ii. 5-6.* you all, that he may sift you like the wheat ; but," He adds, singling out Peter with the design at once of shaking his self-confidence and of delivering him from despair in the hour of his apostasy, " I have prayed for thee, that thy faith may not fail. And do thou, when anon thou hast rallied, strengthen thy brethren." " Lord," asseverated the disciple, " I am ready to accompany Thee both to prison and to death. Lord, where is it that Thou art going away ? " " Where I am going away," Jesus replied, " thou canst not now follow Me, but thou *Cf. John xxi. 18-9.* shalt follow Me afterwards." " Lord," he persisted, supposing merely that Jesus contemplated some perilous enterprise, " why cannot I follow Thee just now ? I will lay down my life for Thy sake." " Thou wilt lay down thy life for My sake ? Verily, verily I tell thee, the cock shall not crow until thou shalt deny Me repeatedly." [2] " If I must die with Thee," protested Peter, " I will in no wise deny Thee." And the others echoed the protestation.

[1] *Cf.* Introd. § 13.   [2] *Cf.* Introd. § 12, 3, (2).

Warning of
the gravity
of the
situation.

Mt. x. 9-10
=Mk. vi.
8-9=Lk.
ix. 3.
Jesus let them have their way and endeavoured to awaken them to the seriousness of the impending crisis. "When I sent you forth," He asked, "without purse and wallet and shoes, lacked ye anything?" "Nothing," they replied, and He warns them that a very different experience now awaits them. A storm of murderous passions will presently break upon them, and they will hardly escape. They will need every resource. "Now he that hath a purse, let him take it up, and likewise a wallet; and he that hath no purse, let him sell his cloak and buy a sword. For I tell you that this that hath been written must be fulfilled in Me: 'And with transgressors He was reckoned'; for what concerneth Me is having its fulfilment." What this meant they would under-stand when they saw their Master in the grasp of an armed band and fled for their lives; but at the moment they did not understand it. They took it literally. So threatening had the situation of late become that, despite the law which prohibited the bearing of arms on the Passover Day,[1] Peter

and another, perhaps his comrade John, had swords concealed beneath their cloaks.[2] "Lord," they said, producing their weapons, "see, here are two swords." "It is sufficient," said Jesus wearily. It was not a sneer at so ample an equip-

ment, but a dismissal of the subject. Their stupidity was desperate. He felt the pathos of the situation. Poor souls, so dull yet withal so faithful! they little realised what awaited them.

The Feast was well nigh ended. There remained only the eating of the lamb. This was the actual Passover, and Jesus invested it with a new significance. As they were eating, He took a loaf, and after giving thanks broke it and handed it to the disciples. "This," He said, "is My body that is for you. This do in remembrance of Me." The Paschal supper ended with the eating of the lamb, and thereafter no food was tasted. But, ere the company dispersed, they drank a third cup, the Cup of Blessing,[3] and sang the

---

[1] *Mish. Shabb.* 6. 4: "Non exibit vir cum gladio neque cum arcu neque cum scuto neque cum funda neque cum lancea. Quodsi exierit, peccati reus erit."

[2] Chrysostom thinks that the μάχαιραι were the knives which Peter and John had used in slaying and dressing the paschal lamb: εἰκὸς οὖν καὶ μαχαίρας εἶναι διὰ τὸ ἀρνίον. *Cf.* Euth. Zig. μάχαιρα meant both *sword* and *knife*. *Cf.* Field, *Notes*.

[3] I Cor. x. 16: τὸ ποτήριον τῆς εὐλογίας, כּוֹס הַבְּרָכָה So called because thanks were given over it.

second part of the Hallel. This also Jesus invested with a Pss. cxv-cxviii.
new significance. He took the cup after the Supper and
said : "This cup is the New Covenant in My blood. This
do in remembrance of Me."

Thus did Jesus institute the Sacrament of the Supper. A memorial of the Lord's Death.
It was no new rite. It was simply the ancient Feast of the
Passover, but Jesus gave it a new significance. He said :
"When ye keep this feast which your fathers have observed
all those centuries, think no longer of the deliverance from
Egypt's house of bondage, but of the greater deliverance
which I have wrought." The Christian Passover no less
than the Jewish is a memorial feast. Jesus ordained it in His
Church that He might never be forgotten, and it is very
remarkable what He chose to be remembered by. He was
famous for His teaching, and still more for His miracles, yet He
chose neither. He chose His death. "When ye would remember Me," He said to the Eleven and to all who should
afterwards believe in Him, "turn your eyes to Calvary." He
had come into the world to give His life a ransom for many.
His death was no disaster but His supreme act of redeeming
sacrifice.

The Lord's Supper is, in the first instance, a commemora- An inter-pretation thereof : (1) fellow-ship of food ;
tion of His death ; but it is more. It is an interpretation
thereof. It embodies two ancient ideas which are full of
significance. It is a common meal, and all over the East to
this day eating in company constitutes a sacred and indis-
soluble bond. "So far was this principle carried by the old
Arabs, that Zaid al-Khail, a famous warrior in the days of
Mohammed, refused to slay a vagabond who carried off his
camels, because the thief had surreptitiously drunk from his
father's milk-bowl before committing the theft."[1] It was a
heavy aggravation of Judas' treachery that he had eaten and
drunk with Jesus, sharing His "table and salt." "Verily I Mk. xiv. 18; cf. John xiii. 18.
tell you that one of you shall betray Me, a man that eateth
with Me." To be the Lord's guest, eating of the provision of
His house, was the Hebrew ideal of union and fellowship with
God. "Thou preparest a table before me," says the Psalmist, Ps. xxiii. 5.
"in the presence of mine enemies : Thou hast anointed my
head with oil ; my cup runneth over." And thus it is with

---

[1] Robertson Smith, *Rel. of the Sem.* p. 252. *Cf.* Josh. ix. 14-5.

those who are bidden to the Lord's Supper.   He is their
Host, and He receives them into loving fellowship, and binds
them to Himself and to one another by sacred ties of friendship and loyalty.

(2) cove-
nant re-
lationship.
Jer. xxxi.
31-4; *cf.*
Hebr. viii.
8-12.

It embodies also the ancient idea of federal relationship.
"This cup is the New Covenant in My blood," says Jesus,
alluding to the prophecy of Jeremiah: "Behold, days are
coming, saith the Lord, when I will make with the house of
Israel and the house of Judah a new covenant ; not according
to the covenant which I made with their fathers in the day
when I took them by the hand to bring them forth from the
land of Egypt.   For this is My covenant which I will make
with the house of Israel : I will put My laws into their mind
and on their hearts will I write them ; and I will be to them
a God, and they shall be to Me a people.   For I will be
merciful to their unrighteousnesses, and their sins will I remember no more."[1]   Even as the Jewish Passover commemorated the Exodus from Egypt, so the Christian Passover
commemorates the grander redemption whereof the Exodus
was a symbol.[2]   It is the Messiah's new and better covenant ;

Exod. xxiv.
4-8.

and, as of old a covenant was always ratified with the blood
of sacrifice, so it is ratified with the blood of Jesus.   "This
cup is the New Covenant in My blood."[3]

Com-
munion
address.

After the institution of the memorial rite Jesus poured
out His heart in words of consolation and reassurance.   It
had been necessary for Him in the course of that evening to
speak terrible things to His disciples, and now He would fain
compose their disquietude.   He was about to leave them, and
He spoke to them like a dying father to his sorrowful children.   His discourse throbs with emotion and breathes an
unutterable tenderness, and all down the ages it has been a
stay and a strength to troubled souls in every sore strait
of life and in the awful hour of death.

"Room in
theFather's
House."

"Let not your heart be troubled," He began.   "Believe

[1] Hence doubtless Mt.'s addition εἰς ἄφεσιν ἁμαρτιῶν (xxvi. 28), proving that he,
like the author of the *Ep. to the Hebr.*, had the prophecy in his mind.
[2] *Cf.* p. 274.
[3] Weizsäcker (*Apost. Zeit.* v. 1. §2), following the Pauline account, regards the
wine alone as referring to Christ's death.   τὸ σῶμα τὸ ὑπὲρ ὑμῶν applies to "the
living personal presence promised in Mt. xviii. 20."   But, though κλώμενον in
1 Cor. xi. 24 be an interpolation, Jesus symbolised His body by *broken* bread.

in God; in Me also believe." It was the prospect of His departure that troubled them, and He explained to them what His departure really meant, making use of homely yet exquisite imagery. At intervals along the highways of the land stood the *caravanserais* where travellers lodged.[1] It happened sometimes, especially at the festal seasons when the ways were thronged, that a traveller would arrive at the gate only to find that the place was crowded and he must fare shelterless on his way. More than thirty years before a traveller had arrived at the *caravanserai* near Bethlehem, accompanied by his espoused wife who was great with child. Her pangs had taken hold upon her and, since every lodging-place was occupied, she had to lie down in the court-yard among the beasts, oxen, asses, and camels. And there she brought forth her first-born Son and laid Him in a manger, "because there was no room for them in the inn." Hence Jesus derives His illustration. The disciples were like travellers, and His companionship had hitherto cheered them on their journey. And now He must leave them. But He was not forsaking them. He was only hastening on in advance to make ready for them. And, when they arrived, He would be waiting for them and would bid them welcome. " In My Father's House there are many lodging-places.[2] If there were not, I would have told you, because I am going to prepare room for you. And, if I go and prepare room for you, I am coming again, and will receive you unto Myself, that, where I am, ye also may be. And where I am going away, ye know the way."

"Lord," interrupted Judas the Twin, ever despondent, Objection of Judas the Twin. "we do not know where Thou art going, and how do we know the way?" Had he not learned the Master's all-sufficiency? Could he not go forward, following in His steps, rejoicing in His revelation of the Father, and trusting His guidance to the end? " I," answered Jesus, "am the Way and the Truth and the Life.[3] None cometh unto the Father

---

[1] *Cf.* p. 3.

[2] μονή, *mansio*, "station," "resting-place for the night." *Cf.* Paus. x. 31. § 7 ; Jerome's Ep. *De xlii. Mansionibus* of the Israelites in the wilderness. μονή only here and *v.* 23 in N.T., but μένειν, "lodge," frequently : Lk. i. 56 ; xix. 5 ; xxiv. 29 ; John i. 39, 40; Acts xvi. 15 ; xviii. 3. τόπον : *cf.* Lk. ii. 7 ; xiv. 22.

[3] *Cf.* Bern. *Serm. ii. de Ascens. Dom.* : " Via in exemplo, veritas in promisso, vita in præmio."

but through Me. If ye had recognised Me, the Father also ye would have known. Henceforth ye recognise Him and have seen Him." Philip, ever slow in spiritual understanding,

Request of Philip. was puzzled. "Lord," he said, "show us the Father, and it is enough for us." Jesus was vexed and disappointed. Was it in vain that He had lived His wondrous life before His disciples? Had they not perceived the Father's hand and the Father's heart in all that He had done and spoken and

John viii. 19. been? It was no marvel that the rulers, not knowing Him, had not known the Father; but did not His disciples know Him? Had they not recognised who He was and whence He had come? "So long time am I with you," He cried, " and hast thou not recognised Me, Philip? He that hath seen Me hath seen the Father. How sayest thou: 'Show us the Father'? Dost thou not believe that I am in the Father and the Father in Me?"

Promise of the Advocate. Since it was amid the toils and perils of the way that they needed their Lord's succour and inspiration, the assurance that He would meet them at their journey's end, might seem a poor consolation; and therefore He proceeded to assure them further that, though He was about to leave them, He would be always with them. He had

Mt. xviii. 20. already promised His spiritual presence wherever His people should assemble in His name; and now He reiterates and enlarges the promise: "I will ask the Father, and another Advocate[1] will He give you to be with you for ever. I will not leave you orphans; I am coming unto you." During His sojourn on the earth Jesus had been God's Advocate with men, representing Him and pleading with them on His behalf. Henceforth He would appear in the presence of God on their

1 John ii. 1. behalf, their Advocate with the Father; but God would not leave Himself without a representative on the earth. He would send another Advocate, the Holy Spirit, who would

---

[1] παράκλητος only in John's Gospel (xiv. 16, 26 ; xv. 26 ; xvi. 7) and First Epistle (ii. 1). In the latter it must mean Advocate, and it is inconceivable that John should have used it in a different sense in his Gospel. In fact, being pass. not act., the word cannot mean "Comforter," as both our versions render it, though the Revisers put "Advocate" in the margin. This interpretation, accepted, singularly enough, by the Greek Fathers, may be due to the fact that a Jewish name for the Messiah was *Menahem, Consolator*, and His days were called "the days of consolation." *Cf. Targ. in Hierem.* 31. 6 : "Qui desiderant annos consolationis venturos." Lk. ii. 25. See Cremer ; J. B. Lightfoot's *Fresh Revision*, pp. 50-6 ; Field, *Notes.*

take the place of Jesus and carry forward His work, " teaching His disciples all things and reminding them of all things which He had told them." If they loved Him, they would keep His commandments ; and, if they kept His commandments, they would enjoy His spiritual fellowship. " He that hath My commandments and keepeth them, he it is that loveth Me ; and he that loveth Me shall be loved by My Father, and I will love him and manifest Myself unto him."

This puzzled the disciples. Even in that hour they clung to their Jewish expectation. Their Master, they believed, would extricate Himself from His embarrassments and display His power and glory to an astonished world. What did He mean by that promise to manifest Himself to His disciples? Had something happened to delay still further the Messianic *dénouement* which they had so long anticipated? " Lord," exclaimed Judas Lebbæus, " what hath come to pass that to us Thou art about to manifest Thyself and not to the world?" Jesus made no attempt to disabuse their minds. The course of events would soon dispel that worldly dream, and the Holy Spirit would in due time reveal to them the true glory of the Messiah. " If," He said, reiterating His declaration, " a man love Me, he will keep My Word, and My Father will love him, and we will come unto him and lodge with him. Peace I am leaving to you, My peace I am giving to you. Not as the world giveth, am I giving it to you." Such was the dying Lord's bequest to His children : peace, not such peace as the Stoic philosophy gave to its votaries, but His own peace, the peace which had attended Him at every step of His weary and painful way, and which was with Him at that dread hour, a peace which the world could neither give nor take away.

Question of Judas Lebbæus.

Cf. John vii. 4.

It was waxing late, and the hour was nigh. " Arise!" said Jesus, " let us go hence " ; and, when they had sung the Hallel,[1] they fared forth from the Upper Room into the silent street.

Departure from the Upper Room.

[1] Mt. xxvi. 30=Mk. xiv. 26: ὑμνήσαντες. Lightfoot: "Ipsissima vox הימנן occurrit in *Midras Till.* fol. 4. 2 et 42. 1."

CHAPTER XLVI

THE ARREST IN GETHSEMANE

John xv-
xvii ; Mt.
xxvi. 30=
Mk. xiv. 26
=Lk. xxii.
39=John
xviii. 1 ;
Mt. xxvi.
36-46=
Mk. xiv.
32-42=Lk.
xxii. 40-6 ;
Mt. xxvi.
47-56=
Mk. xiv.
43-52=Lk.
xxii. 47-53
=John
xviii. 2-11.

> " Heu ! Dei Filius quot pœnis premitur ;
> Latrone vilius huic vita demitur.
> Ah flete, flete lumina,
> Dent lacrymarum flumina.
> Jesu, Jesu, amor dulcissime !
> Quo raperis, quæ pateris
> Pro mundi scelere?"—*Med. Hymn.*

Further commun-ing. JESUS had still much to say to His disciples after He had led them forth from the Upper Room, nor did He quit Jerusalem until He had spoken all. Wherefore did He leave that quiet retreat ere He had done communing with them? It is likely that He apprehended an invasion of His sanctuary by the traitor and the Sanhedrin's emissaries, and therefore, that He might speak all that was in His heart, He sought another retreat. The Evangelist does not tell whither He betook Himself, but there is reason to believe that, when He left the Upper Room, He repaired to the court of the Temple and there continued communing with the Eleven. At midnight the Paschal Supper ended and the gates of the Temple were thrown open.[1] At so untimeous an hour the sacred court would be deserted and would afford a quiet haven. And, though the Temple was the very stronghold of His adversaries, there was no place in the city where He ran less risk of arrest: it was the last place where they would look for Him.[2]

---

[1] Jos. *Ant.* xviii. 2. § 2. On account of Exod. xi. 4 ; xii. 29 the Paschal Supper must end by midnight. *Pesach.* 10: "Pascha post mediam noctem polluit manus."

[2] John xv-xvii between the exit from the Upper Room (xiv. 31) and the departure from the city (xviii. 1). Where did Jesus go with the Eleven? Chrysostom thinks that, since the disciples were apprehensive lest Judas should break in upon them, Jesus led them away " to another place" where they might listen without distraction to what He still had to say. The parable of the Vine suggests the Temple. Other opinions : (1) The parable was spoken on the way to Gethsemane, being suggested by the vines on the slope of Olivet (Wetstein). But Jesus did

Over the gateway of the Temple was wrought a sacred The Real Vine. emblem which caught the eyes of all who entered—a wreath of golden vines with clusters a man's stature in length.[1] This exquisite ` adornment was one of the marvels of Herod's magnificent Temple ; and, when the Romans invaded the Holy Land, it attracted their observation, and some concluded that, since it bore his emblem, the Temple must be sacred to the god Bacchus.[2] In truth it was a characteristically Jewish device. In ancient days the vine had been employed by Prophets and Psalmists as a symbol of Israel, but in later days it was a symbol of the Messiah.[3] "O God of Hosts," Ps. lxxx. 15-6. runs the Psalmist's prayer according to the Targum's Aramaic paraphrase, "turn now again, look from Heaven and see, and remember in mercy this vine. And the vine-shoot which Thy right hand hath planted, and the King Messiah, whom Thou hast established for Thyself." Being thus a Messianic emblem, that device over the Temple-gate lent itself to the Lord's use and furnished Him with an impressive parable. "I am the real Vine," He said, "and My Father is the Husbandman." His disciples were the branches, and their business was to bear fruit : "Herein is My Father glorified." And in order to this end, even as a branch can bear fruit only as it is united to the parent stem, so must they abide in vital union with Him : "Apart from Me ye can do nothing."

With this preface Jesus resumed the discourse which He Encouragements had begun in the Upper Room. He told them that they would encounter persecution, but in the midst thereof they would have two great consolations. First, whatever they might suffer, they would know that their Lord had suffered it all and still worse before them. "If the world hate you, recognise that Me before you it hath hated. Remember the

---

not cross the Kedron till His discourse and prayer were ended (John xviii. 1). (2) They lingered in the Upper Room after ἐγείρεσθε, ἄγωμεν ἐντεῦθεν, and a vine trailing over the window (*cf.* Ps. cxxviii. 3) suggested the parable (Tholuck). (3) Chaps. xv-xvii have got displaced : they should stand in chap. xiii—between *vv.* 35 and 36 (Wendt), between 31a and 31b (Spitta). The theory of displacement is the resource of exegetical despair.

[1] Jos. *Ant.* xv. 11. § 3 ; *De Bell. Jud.* v. 5. § 4.
[2] Tac. *Hist.* iv. § 5.
[3] See Delitzsch in *Expositor*, Jan. 1886, pp. 68-9. Sacramental prayer in *Didache*, ix : εὐχαριστοῦμέν σοι, πάτερ ἡμῶν, ὑπὲρ τῆς ἁγίας ἀμπέλου Δαβὶδ τοι παιδός σου, κ.τ.λ.

Mt. x. 24; John xiii. 16. word which I spoke to you : ' A slave is not greater than his lord.' " Moreover, they would have the succour of the Holy Spirit. And it should reconcile them to their Lord's departure that the promise of His spiritual presence could not otherwise be fulfilled. His departure was really a gain not only for Him but for them. " I tell you the truth : it is expedient for you that I should depart. For, if I do not depart, the Advocate shall not come unto you. But, if I go, I will send Him unto you." While they retained Jesus among them in bodily presence, it was impossible for them to realise the spirituality of the Kingdom of Heaven. They could conceive no other way of holding communion with Him than approaching Him, accosting Him, and hearing His gracious voice. In after days, when He had departed from them and, scattered over the wide earth and sundered one from another by leagues of land and sea, they still had access to their glorified Lord through His Spirit shed abroad in their souls, they discovered what His promise meant : " Where there are two or three assembled in My name, there I am in their midst."

The Redeemer's Prayer. " These things have I spoken unto you that in Me ye may have peace. In the world ye have tribulation ; but courage ! I have conquered the world." With this ringing sentence Jesus concluded His discourse to the Eleven, and then He lifted up His eyes to Heaven and addressed Himself to the Father in prayer. It was a prayer of self-consecration, thanksgiving, and intercession. He did not intercede for the world which He had come to redeem and which was very dear to His heart, but for His disciples : first for the Eleven who were with Him while He prayed, the men whom the Father had given Him out of the world, whom He had kept in the Father's name, and whom He was leaving as His representatives, charged with the self-same mission whereon He had Himself been sent ; and then for all who should be won by their preaching, and all who from generation to generation should share their faith and carry on their work even to the end. There is nothing more remarkable about this prayer than the note of exultant triumph which rings through it. As Jesus spoke, the end was nigh ; and in the world's judgment it seemed as though His life-work were closing in dire and tragic failure. Where was His throne? Where His crown? He should, if He were the Messiah, have been the nation's hero, encompassed by acclaiming thousands; but there He stood, despised and rejected, with only that little band of Galilean peasants by His side; and, ere many hours had passed, His insulting enemies would be dragging Him to the cross of shame. Yet He bore Himself as a conqueror, and, lifting up His eyes to Heaven, He declared: "I have glorified Thee upon the earth, having accomplished the work which Thou hast given Me to do." One thinks of the dying scholar's piteous cry: "My book, my book! I shall never finish my book!" And it is thus that mortals ever face death—with a sad consciousness of the imperfection and incompleteness of their life-work. But Jesus faced death without regret and without disappointment. His life seemed to the world to be closing in darkness and defeat; but He saw the final issue, and He knew that what seemed darkness was glory and what seemed defeat was triumph.

When He had done communing with His disciples and with God, Jesus left the city. He led the Eleven along the silent street and, passing through the gate, crossed the Kedron and sought His accustomed retreat on the slope of Olivet. It is not without a mystic significance that St John alludes to the crossing of the Kedron. It was no pleasant stream. The sacrificial blood wherewith the Temple's altars were sprinkled, drained into it,[1] and it was running red with the blood of the paschal lambs as the Lamb of God passed over it. Nothing was said by the way;[2] for Jesus had spoken His last words of warning and encouragement, and an awe had fallen upon the disciples. There was no spare ground within the circle of its walls, and there was, moreover, a ceremonial objection to the use of manure in the Holy City;[3] and therefore the wealthier citizens had their gardens and pleasure grounds outside the gates, especially on the western slope of Olivet.[4] One of these, the property of some friend of Jesus, perhaps Mary, the mother of John Mark, had been

Departure to Gethsemane.

---

[1] Lightfoot on John xviii. 1.
[2] On the position of Mt. xxvi. 31-5 = Mk. xiv. 27-31 *cf.* Introd. § 13.
[3] Lightfoot on Mt. xxvi. 36.
[4] *Cf.* Jos. *De Bell. Jud.* v. 3. § 2; vi. 1. § 1, Lightfoot on John xviii. 1.

His nightly retreat during the Passion-week. It was an olive-grove, thence called the Close or Garden of Gethsemane, that is, the Oil-press.[1] Thither Jesus betook Himself with the Eleven.

The Lord's distress.
It was late, and the weary disciples would fain have wrapped themselves in their cloaks and laid them down to sleep. But Jesus had other thoughts. "Sit down here," He said, "while I go away and pray yonder"; and, taking Peter, James, and John, He went aside with them. As soon as they were beyond hearing of the rest, He opened His heart to His companions, and they perceived that their Master, a little ago so calm and triumphant, had been stricken by a storm of distress. What was it that ailed Him? It was not the fear of death. He had conquered that; and it is inconceivable that the prospect which in the Upper Room He had faced with exultation, should so quickly have been overcast and clothed itself with terror in His eyes. It was something more awful that shook the Redeemer's soul.[2] The anguish of His vicarious passion had begun. Already He was entering into that black cloud which enfolded Him as He hung on the Cross. It is impossible for us to understand the experience of the Eternal Son of God at that supreme crisis when He was "carrying up our sins in His body to the Tree"; and, where under-standing fails, it becomes us to refrain our lips and be silent.

1 Pet. ii. 24.

> " Deep waters have come in, O Lord !
> All darkly on Thy Human Soul ;
> And clouds of supernatural gloom
> Around Thee are allowed to roll.
>
> " And Thou hast shuddered at each act
> And shrunk with an astonished fear,
> As if Thou couldst not bear to see
> The loathsomeness of sin so near."

---

[1] χωρίον (Mt. xxvi. 36 = Mk. xiv. 32), not simply *a place*, but *an enclosed piece of ground* (*cf.* Acts i. 18), corresponding to κῆπος (John xviii. 1. Jer. : *in villam* (Mt.), *in prædium* (Mk.). Tradition fixes as the site of Gethsemane a plot of ground some 50 yards beyond the Kedron, and claims that eight olive trees which grow upon it, were there in our Lord's day and witnessed His Agony and Arrest. This is impossible. Not only are two thousand years too great an age for olive trees, but Josephus (*l.c.*) says that during the siege all the trees around Jerusalem were cut down by the Romans. The actual site is probably higher up.

[2] If Hebr. v. 7 refers to the scene in Gethsemane, the author of the Epistle con-ceived the perturbation of Jesus as due to the fear of death. But the phrase ἐν ταῖς

There, in the Garden of Gethsemane, the first gust of that awful storm swept over His soul. "He began," says St Matthew, "to be grieved and bewildered." "He began," says St Mark, "to be amazed and bewildered."[1]

In that dread hour Jesus craved for sympathy. "My soul," He said to the faithful three, "is sore grieved even unto death. Stay here," He pleaded, "and watch with Me." He withdrew from them a stone's cast, and fell on His face and prayed, crying aloud in the anguish of His soul. His voice reached their ears through the still night-air : " Father, if it be possible, let this cup pass away from Me. Nevertheless," He added, "not as I will, but as Thou wilt." For nigh an hour He lay prostrate thus, and the three disciples, overcome by weariness and sorrow, fell asleep. By and by He came to them and, waking them, reproachfully addressed Peter who had so lately boasted that he would lay down his life for His sake : " Thus ![2] Had ye not strength for a single hour to watch with Me? Watch and pray lest ye enter into temptation. The spirit," He added, making generous excuse for their frailty, " is eager, but the flesh is weak." He withdrew again and prayed, no longer asking release but making submission to the Father's will[3] : " My Father, if this cannot pass away unless I drink it, Thy will be done." Again He returned and found them asleep, for their eyes were heavy. They were ashamed, and He did not upbraid them but withdrew once more and repeated that prayer of resignation to the Father's will. Thereupon He heard the tramp of many feet and saw through the trees the gleam of torches and burnished armour. He hastened to the disciples and addressed them with sad irony : "Sleep on and rest you. Enough! the hour is come. Behold! the Son of Man is being betrayed into the hands of

His struggle. Pss. xlii. 5-11; xliii. 5 (LXX).

Mt. xxvi. 40=Mk. xiv. 37.

ἡμέραις τῆς σαρκὸς αὐτοῦ, "quamdiu habitavit in corpore mortali," proves that the passage has a wider reference. Strauss, insisting that it was the fear of death that troubled Jesus, presents "the dilemma, that either the farewell discourses in John, or else the events in Gethsemane, cannot be historical."

[1] ἀδημονεῖν, a word of uncertain derivation, used by Plato of *bewilderment of soul amid unaccustomed surroundings*. *Phædr.* 251 D : ἡ ψυχὴ . . . ἀδημονεῖ τε τῇ ἀτοπίᾳ τοῦ πάθους καὶ ἀποροῦσα λυττᾷ. *Theæt.* 175 D : ὑπ' ἀηθείας ἀδημονῶν τε καὶ ἀπορῶν. The suggested derivation from ἄδημος = ἀπόδημος hits the idea. *Cf.* Aug. *Enarr. in Ps.* xl. § 6

[2] *Cf.* Euth. Zig.

[3] W. H. bracket τὸν αὐτὸν λόγον εἰπών in Mk. xiv. 39.

sinners. Arise! let us be going. Behold! My betrayer is at hand."[1]

Judas and his band. As He spoke, the company whose approach He had perceived, emerged into view. On his withdrawal from the Upper Room Judas has betaken himself to the rulers and told them that he would that night implement his bargain, and they had mustered a band for the Lord's arrest. It consisted, in the first place, of some of the officers of the Temple. These might have sufficed, but they were reinforced by a detachment of Roman soldiers. It was contrary to the Law for a Jew to bear arms on the Passover day, and, though Jesus was defenceless, the rulers would be apprehensive lest an alarm should be raised and the multitude flock to their hero's rescue. Moreover, the governor, ever jealous for the maintenance of public order, especially at festal seasons when the city was crowded and a spark might set it ablaze, would have resented such an enterprise on the part of the Jewish rulers ; and, since his countenance and co-operation were of the utmost consequence to the success of their scheme, they had, fretting the while at the delay, appealed to him and had been granted a detachment of soldiers, under the command of a tribune, from Fort Antonia.[2] The soldiers wore their armour and would march in order, but the undisciplined **Mt. xxvi.** Temple-servants, armed only with cudgels and carrying lamps **47=Mk.** and torches, gave the company a disorderly appearance. It **xiv. 43=** **Lk. xxii.** looked a mere rabble. Judas led the way, for he knew that **47.** **John xviii.** retreat whither he had repaired each evening with his Master **2.** and his fellow-disciples. The motley band followed after him, and with the rest, their dignity forgotten in their eagerness, came some of the High Priests, the Temple-captains,[3] and the Elders.

The Betrayal. It lay with the soldiers to make the arrest ; but they did not know Jesus, and, as they approached and in the light of the torches and lanterns saw not one man but twelve, they were

[1] On Lk. xxii. 43-4, *cf.* Introd. § 13, 7.

[2] John xviii. 3, 12. The regular garrison at Jerusalem was a single cohort (σπεῖρα), *i.e.* 500 men. *Cf.* Schürer, *H. J. P.* I. ii. p. 55. John's λαβὼν τὴν σπεῖραν does not mean that the whole cohort was sent, but only a detachment. *Cf.* our phrases "call out the military," "summon the police."

[3] Lk. xxii. 4, 52 : στρατηγοὶ τοῦ ἱεροῦ, the סְגָנִים, officials next in dignity to the priests. Their business was to preserve order in the Temple. See Schürer, *H.J. P.*, ii. 1. pp. 257 *sqq.*

puzzled which they should apprehend. Judas came to the rescue. " The one whom I shall kiss," he said, " is he. Take him ;" and, advancing, he greeted Jesus with a show of reverence : " Hail, Rabbi !" and kissed Him effusively.[1] It was a piece of shameless and heartless effrontery, and Jesus answered with a stinging sentence quivering with scorn and indignation. " Comrade," He said, in that single word expressing all the traitor's baseness, " to thine errand !" Waving Judas aside, He stepped forward and addressed the soldiers : " Whom are ye seeking ? " There was that in His tone and bearing which overawed them, and they faltered : " Jesus the Nazarene." " I am He," He replied. They were standing irresolute beside the guilty traitor, and, when Jesus said calmly : " I am He," perhaps making to advance towards them and surrender Himself into their hands, they gave back in consternation and fell on the ground. There is no miracle here. It is told of John Bunyan that once, when a body of constables entered the house where he was preaching and one of them was ordered to arrest him, he fixed his eyes steadfastly on the man, holding the while an open Bible in his hand. The constable turned pale and fell back. " See," cried Bunyan, looking round upon the company, " how this man trembleth at the Word of God !" And it is told of John Wesley that once, in the days of his persecution, he was beset on the street by a gang of ruffians. " Which is he ? which is he ? " they cried, uncertain of their victim amid the throng. " I am he," said the man of God, stepping forward and facing them undaunted ; and they retreated in amazement.[2] And what marvel is it that His assailants bowed before the majesty of the Son of Man ? It had overawed the lawless Nazarenes, Lk. iv. 29-30. and stayed their wild hands when they would have hurled Him over the precipice ; and what marvel is it that now in Gethsemane, amid the weird shadows of the night, this band should quail in His presence ?

Jesus repeated His question : " Whom are ye seeking ? " The Arrest. and again they made answer : " Jesus the Nazarene." " I told you," He said, " that I am He. If then," He added, solicitous for His disciples even in that dread hour, " ye are

---

[1] φιλεῖν, kiss ; καταφιλεῖν, kiss effusively.   Cf. Lk. vii. 38, 45.
[2] Cf. Plut. C. Mar. § 39 : οὐ δύναμαι Γαἱον Μάριον ἀποκτεῖναι:

seeking *Me*, let these men go their way." Recovering from
their panic, the soldiers laid hold upon Him and they would
handle Him the more roughly that they were ashamed of the
weakness which they had displayed. The Eleven were terror-
stricken ; but, when he saw those rude hands binding his
Peter's attack on Malchus. dear Master, Peter could not restrain himself. With the
courage of desperation, he plucked out the sword which he
carried under his cloak and, falling upon the man who stood
nearest, struck off his right ear. The unfortunate man was
Malchus, the High Priest's slave. He had stood in the background during the altercation between Jesus and the soldiers,
and, when the latter had arrested Him and were binding
Him, Malchus, like his fellows, had closed in and was watching the operation from the outskirts of the throng, when
Peter assailed him from behind. It seemed as though the
wild act had sealed the rash disciple's fate. A moment more,
and he would have been stricken to the earth ; but, ere a
blade could flash from its sheath, Jesus interposed. "Put the
sword into its sheath," He commanded Peter, and, working
His hands free from the yet unfastened cords and saying to
the soldiers : "Let Me go ; just thus far," He stepped forward to Malchus and, touching the dissevered ear, healed his
wound. The miracle saved Peter's life. But for it he would
have been cut in pieces by a score of vengeful blades.

The Lord's reproof of Peter. While Malchus' comrades crowded round him, examining
and congratulating him, Jesus remonstrated with Peter. "All
that take sword," He said in language that has the ring of
a proverb, "by sword shall perish. Dost thou suppose that
I cannot appeal to My Father and He will even now send
to My support more than twelve legions of angels ? How
then are the Scriptures to be fulfilled that even thus it must
come to pass ? " Did He refer, as St Chrysostom fancies,
2 Kings xix. 35. to the Old Testament story of the destruction of Sennacherib's
army ? There were six thousand in a legion ; and, if a single
angel smote that great host of an hundred fourscore and five
thousand, what could this rabble avail against seventy-two
thousand angels ?

His satire on the Priests and Pharisees. The Lord's calm self-possession at that dread crisis is
revealed by His remonstrance with Peter and still more by
what He said thereafter. He turned to the Priests and

Pharisees who accompanied the band, and scornfully addressed
them. "As though against a brigand, ye have come out
with swords and cudgels to capture Me!" What had they
ever seen so terrible about Him that they should beset Him
like a fierce desperado with armed men? "Daily in the
Temple I was wont to sit teaching, and," He adds with cutting
satire, "ye did not take Me." They would feel the sting of
His taunt. They had not taken Him in the Temple because
they were afraid of the multitude. Cowards then, they were
cowards still, coming against Him, solitary and defenceless,
with that armed band. Did His speech provoke them? The
Did they break out into clamorous menace? Something Desertion.
happened at this juncture which struck terror into the hearts
of the disciples. "They all forsook Him and fled."

Here St Mark introduces a singular incident. A solitary The young
figure [1] strangely attired had all the while been hovering near man with
the linen
—a young man with a linen sheet wrapped about him "over sheet
his undress." He was not one of the Lord's company, yet
he was plainly a friend and a sympathiser; and, when the
scared disciples took to flight, the angry rulers [2] laid hold
upon him; but he dropped his garment and, leaving it in
their hands, fled undressed.[3] One marvels that such an
incident should have been rescued from oblivion. It seems
merely to render the young man ridiculous besides introducing
an incongruous touch of comedy into the tragic narrative.
There must have been some reason for recounting it, and
it is an attractive conjecture that the young man was none
other than St Mark himself, who has here, according to the Probably
custom of the sacred writers, affixed his signature to his book John Mark.
in cryptic fashion.[4] Long ago it was suggested that the
young man had come from the house where Jesus had eaten
the Passover with His disciples; [5] and, if it was indeed the
house of Mary, the likelihood is that he was her son. The

---

[1] Mk. xiv. 51 : εἶς τις.

[2] T. R. "the young men"; Tisch., W. H. om.

[3] γυμνός, not absolutely *nude*. *Cf.* John xxi. 7. Wetstein on Mk. xiv. 51.

[4] Olshausen, Godet. Gregory (*Moral.* xiv. 23) guesses John who returned from
his flight and followed Jesus to the High Priest's palace. Epiphanius and Theophylact think of James, the Lord's brother, who always after his conversion wore
linen garments (Eus. *H. E.* ii. 23). *Cf.* Petavel's interesting art. in *Expositor*,
March, 1891.

[5] See Euth. Zig., Theophyl.

linen sheet which he wore, was a bed-cloth ; [1] and Mark, it may be gathered, had gone to rest after the Paschal Supper, but, with an uneasy foreboding of trouble, he had lain awake, and, when he heard Jesus and the Eleven descend from the Upper Room and quit the house, he had risen and, hastily wrapping his sheet about him, had followed after them to observe what might befall.

Mark the Stump-fingered. The incident was trivial enough, yet it would be engraved on Mark's memory ; and it has a peculiar value, attesting as it does that the Evangelist was an eye-witness of the scene. And perhaps it was less trivial than his modesty makes it appear. In the early Church Mark was distinguished by a curious epithet. He was styled Mark the Stump-fingered,[2] and, in the absence of any trustworthy explanation, it may be surmised that in the scuffle on that memorable night his fingers were shorn off by the slash of a sword-blade. If it be so, he would wear the epithet proudly, and would feel no shame for the mutilation which told of his devotion to the Master in the hour of His desertion.

[1] *Cf.* Dionysius' account of his arrest in Eus. *H. E.* vi. 40 : μένων ἐπὶ τῆς εὐνῆς, ἧς ἤμην γυμνὸς, ἐν τῷ λινῷ ἐσθήματι, where Heinichen comments : "ἐν τῷ λινῷ ἐσθήματι idem est quod alias vocatur σινδών," comparing our passage.

[2] Hippol. *Philosoph.* vii. 30 : οὔτε Παῦλος ὁ ἀπόστολος οὔτε Μάρκος ὁ κολοβοδάκτυλος.

CHAPTER XLVII

BEFORE THE HIGH PRIESTS

" Nox insomnis itaque tota ducebatur,
Nulla prorsus requies Jesu parabatur :
Magistrorum impia plebs injuriatur,
Alapis et colaphis innocens mactatur."—*Med. Hymn.*

John xviii.
12-27=Mt.
xxvi. 57-75
=Mk. xiv.
53-72=Lk.
xxii. 54-71;
Mt. xxvii.
3-10.

FROM Gethsemane they led Jesus away to His trial. The Sanhedrin situation was complicated by the political condition of the and Pro- curator. Jewish nation. Had the nation been independent, it would have sufficed that the Sanhedrin should condemn Him ; but, since the Roman conquest, the power of the Sanhedrin had been abridged, and, ere sentence of death could be executed, it was necessary that the Roman governor's sanction should be obtained.[1] Thus it came to pass that Jesus had to under- go two trials. He was in the first instance arraigned before the Sanhedrin, and then He was brought for sentence before the Roman governor.

The High Priest was, in virtue of his office, President of The house the Sanhedrin, and at that crisis the High Priest was Joseph of Annas. Caiaphas, a remarkable man and allied with a remarkable family. He was son-in-law to old Annas, who not only had held the high priesthood from A.D. 6 to 15 but enjoyed this unique distinction, that after his deposition by the Roman governor Quirinius his four sons and his son-in-law held the sacred office. Such good fortune, remarks the historian,[2] " has fallen to the lot of no other of our High Priests." Yet it was in no wise to the credit of Annas and his family. In those days the high-priesthood was at the disposal of the Roman governors and the Herodian princes, and went commonly to the highest bidder ;[3] and the prolonged ascendancy of the house of Annas is an evidence no less of their corruption than of their astuteness. It was great good fortune to themselves,

---

[1] Jos. *De Bell. Jud.* ii. 8. § 1 ; *Ant.* xx. 9. § 1 ; Lightfoot on John xviii. 31.
[2] Jos. *Ant.* xx. 9. § 1.   [3] *Cf.* Lightfoot on John xviii. 13.

but to the Jewish people it was a heavy calamity. It is written in the Talmud: "Woe to the house of Annas! Woe to their serpent's hiss! They are High Priests; their sons are keepers of the Treasury; their sons-in-law are guardians of the Temple; and their servants beat the people with staves."[1] They were a mercenary as well as a tyrannical race. It was they that had made the Temple "a house of merchandize" and "a robbers' den." They had a country-seat, probably on the Mount of Olives, where they drove a lucrative traffic in doves and all the materials for the offerings of purification; and the place was known, apparently in derision, as the Booths of the Sons of Annas.[2]

Cf. Mt. iii. 7; xii. 34; xxiii. 33.

John ii. 16; Mt. xxi. 13 =Mk. xi. 17=Lk. xix. 46.

Influence of Annas.

Annas was merely High Priest *emeritus* at the time of our Lord's arrest, but as well in fact as in sentiment the High Priest retained his prestige after his demission of office. He was still called the High Priest[3] and retained all his obligations and many of his prerogatives.[4] Nor was Annas the man to be lightly set aside; whether in office or out of it he must exert a predominant influence. It is therefore in no wise surprising that, when they had arrested Jesus, they "led Him to Annas first."[5] It was still the dead of night; and, since the Sanhedrin could not meet till day-break,[6] how better could the intervening hours be spent than in an examination of the prisoner by that astute veteran for the guidance of the Sanhedrin in its conduct of the trial?

John xviii. 13.

Peter and John follow Jesus.

It is probable that he resided at the Booths on the slope of Olivet hard by the Garden of Gethsemane, and thither Jesus was conducted. Two of the disciples, Peter and John, had rallied from the panic which seized them when they saw

---

[1] *Pesach.* 57. i.

[2] *Tabernæ filiorum Chanan. Cf.* Lightfoot, ii. pp. 409-10. The residence of Annas where Jesus was arraigned, was probably the *Tabernæ*, and it must have been outside the city, since (1) doves were bred there for the sacrifices, and a *columbarium* might not be built within 50 cubits of Jerusalem: Lightfoot, ii. p. 239; (2) for ceremonial reasons cocks (*cf.* Mt. xxvi. 74=Mk. xiv. 72=Lk. xxii. 60 =John xviii. 27) were not allowed to be kept in the city. *Cf.* Lightfoot on Mt. xxvi. 34.

[3] John xviii. 15, 16, 19, 22; Jos. *Vit.* § 38; *De Bell. Jud.* ii. 12. § 6; iv. 3. § 7; 4. § 3.

[4] Schürer, *H. J. P.* II. i. p. 203.   [5] *Cf.* Introd. § 13.

[6] The Sanhedrin might meet between the morning and afternoon sacrifices. *Cf.* Lightfoot on Mk. xv. 1. The morning sacrifice was offered whenever the flush of dawn was seen on Hebron. *Cf.* Lightfoot, ii. p. 207.

their Master in the grasp of His enemies ; and they followed at a safe distance. When the troop reached the gateway of the Booths, Peter remained outside, but John passed in ; not because he was bolder than his comrade, but because he had some sort of acquaintance with the High Priest. What acquaintanceship could there be betwixt a Galilean fisherman and that exalted dignitary, as proud an aristocrat as ever sat on a chair of state and spurned the populace like the dust beneath his feet ? It has been supposed, on the strength of an ancient description of St John as "a priest wearing the mitre,"[1] that, though a Galilean fisherman, he was of priestly lineage.[2] But Annas would hardly have acknowledged such a claim ; and in fact the description is nothing more than a figurative expression of the veneration which was felt in early days for St John, that true priest of the Lord. There is much attractiveness in an ancient tradition which has it that he was known to the High Priest "from his fisher craft."[3] Since he had plied the fishing industry on the Lake of Galilee on a somewhat large scale in company with his father Zebedee and his brother James, it may well be that he had a business connection with the capital and supplied that wealthy mansion. Thus it came to pass that he got admission to the court-yard on that memorable night. It was by no means his first visit to the Booths. He had often been there in the way of business. The portress would admit him without demur, and all the servants would greet him.

John's acquaintance with the High Priest.

Mk. i. 20.

Peter had no such pass-port ; and, moreover, after his attack on Malchus he had reason to fear reprisal. He lingered outside the gate until John, mindful of his comrade, interceded with the portress and procured him admittance. As he passed in, the girl looked hard at him and said : "Thou too art one of this fellow's disciples, art thou not ?" It was an innocent question prompted by mere curiosity, and, had Peter assented or held his peace, the affair would have gone no further ; but he was at his wits' end with fright and, blurting out : "No, I am not !"[4] he hurried in confusion into

Peter denies Jesus at the gate.

[1] Ep. of Polycrates in Eus. *H. E.* iii. 31 ; v. 24.   [2] So Ewald.
[3] Noun. *Paraphr.* xviii. 71 : ἰχθυβόλου παρὰ τέχνης. Caspari thinks that Zebedee and his sons were citizens of Jerusalem and resided at Bethsaida during the fishing season.
[4] Aug. *In Joan. Ev. Tract.* cxiii. § 2 : "Debemus advertere non solum ab eo

the court-yard. It was unusually cold that night, and the servants had lit a fire and clustered round it ; and Peter, anxious to seem at his ease, joined the group and stood warming himself with an ill-assumed air of nonchalance.

Precognition by Annas.
Mk. xiv. 66.
Lk. xxii. 59. Meanwhile Jesus had been conducted upstairs to the audience-chamber of Annas and was there undergoing an examination which lasted about an hour. No disciple, no friend was present, yet a report of the memorable scene reached the ears of St John. Jesus comported Himself with fearless dignity and displayed His accustomed resourcefulness, proving Himself more than a match for that wily diplomatist. Annas questioned Him regarding His disciples and His teaching, and He answered proudly : " I have spoken openly to the world. I always taught in Synagogue and in the Temple where all the rulers assemble, and in secret spoke I nothing. Why question Me ? Question them that have heard Me what I spoke unto them. See," He exclaimed, pointing to the spectators, " these men know what I said." It was a crushing rejoinder. Legal procedure required that witnesses should first of all be summoned for the defence,[1] and in departing from this rule and seeking to extort from Jesus some damning admission Annas was guilty of flagrant illegality. It was a stinging rebuke, all the more effective that it was spoken so calmly, and Annas would wince and flush crimson. Observing his discomfiture and anxious, after the fashion of his sort, to curry favour, one of the officers gave Jesus a buffet, crying with an affectation of horror : " Is it thus that thou answerest the High Priest ? " Perpetrated in a hall of judgment such a deed of violence was an outrage upon justice itself, and Jesus answered with quiet dignity not without sarcasm : " If I spoke ill, bear witness regarding the ill ; but, if well, why smite Me ? " Another scene rises up in Acts xxiii. 1-6. striking contrast to the Lord's bearing at this juncture. When St Paul was making his defence before the Sanhedrin, by command of the High Priest, Ananias, he was smitten on the mouth. His indignation blazed up, and he cried : " God shall smite thee, thou white-washed wall ! " The bystanders

negari Christum qui dicit eum non esse Christum ; sed ab illo etiam qui cum est, negat se esse Christianum."

[1] *Cf.* Lightfoot on John xviii. 15, 21.

protested : " Revilest thou God's High Priest ? " and immediately he made an apology : " I knew not, brethren, that he was the High Priest." St Paul recognised that he had blundered ; but from the beginning of His long and vexatious trial to the end not a single wrong move did Jesus make, not a single false step did He take ; He never blundered, never spoke a word which He needed to retract. He bore Himself throughout the ordeal with calm self-possession, with fearless dignity, conscious that He was not alone, that the Father was with Him.

Baffled and angry Annas ended the interview, and ordered Jesus to be led away bound to Caiaphas to stand His trial before the Sanhedrin. Meanwhile rough play had been going on in the court-yard.[1] When Peter disowned his discipleship at the gateway, thinking thus to escape molestation, he delivered himself into the hands of the tormentors. The portress was a mischievous maid. She noticed his perturbation at her question, and by and by, when she could leave her post, she approached the group about the fire and, pointing to the shrinking figure, informed them : " This fellow is one of them." Every eye turned in Peter's direction. He denied it, but it was useless. His very denial, spoken with the broad northern accent, convicted him. " Certainly thou art one of them," cried a chorus of voices ; " for thy speech bewrayeth thee." Of course it did not necessarily follow that, because he was a Galilean, he was a disciple of Jesus, but they perceived his alarm and, having nothing else to do, they thought it good sport to bait him. " I am not," he vociferated wildly ; " I do not know what ye are talking about." As ill-luck would have it, there was in the company a slave of the High Priest who was a kinsman of Malchus and had been in Gethsemane and witnessed Peter's frantic assault. He chimed in : " Did not I see thee in the Garden with him ? " Poor Peter was hard put to it. He was fairly run to earth. He had recourse to the desperate man's resort. The habit of his

Peter denies Jesus in the court-yard.

---

[1] On the differences between the accounts of the Denial *cf.* Introd. § 12, 3, (2). Whatever their differences, all the Evangelists report the Denial. *Cf.* Chrysost. *In Psalm* l. (li.): "The philanthropy of God, in consideration for the weakness of the human race, not only caused the successes of the saints to be written but turned their sins into medicines, that their wounds might prove medicines to their fellows, and the righteous man's shipwreck constitute a haven for the sinner."

old fisher days, dormant these three years, revived, and he began to curse and swear: "I do not know the fellow!"

His re- pentance. Just then a cock crew. The sound checked Peter. It reminded him of the Lord's prediction in the Upper Room: "Ere cock-crow thou shalt repeatedly deny Me." To complete his humiliation it chanced that Jesus was at that moment being conducted, with His hands pinioned behind His back, through the court-yard on His way to the judgment-hall of Caiaphas. He had heard those wild imprecations, that brutal abjuration; and, when Peter paused conscience-stricken and looked guiltily about him, he espied his Lord. Jesus had turned His head and was gazing back at His faithless disciple. "He looked on Peter," and that look broke Peter's heart. He muffled up his face in his cloak,[1] hurried from the court-yard, and wept bitterly.

Before the Sanhedrin. Mt. xxvi. 57, 59; Mk. xiv. 55. They led Jesus into the city ere yet it was astir. The eager Sanhedrin met betimes. There was a full house that morning, and the President would have no need to ascertain whether the minimum of twenty-three were present.[2] Caiaphas, the acting High Priest, presided, and he was supported by his Mt. xxvi. 59=Mk. xiv. 55. predecessors, who still retained the title of High Priest— his father-in-law Annas and at least three others, Ismael the son of Phabi, Eleasar the son of Annas, and Simon the son of Kamithos, who had each held office for a brief term under the procurator Valerius Gratus.[3] The meeting-place was the Hall of Hewn Stone within the Temple area; and the President sat at the western end of the chamber with his colleagues on either hand forming a semi-circle. In the midst, fronting the President, stood the prisoner, and officers were in attendance to guard him, summon witnesses, and execute the sentence.[4]

Illegal pro- cedure. The procedure of the Sanhedrin on that memorable

---

[1] Mk. xiv. 72 : ἐπιβαλὼν ἔκλαιεν has been rendered (1) "He began to weep," cœpit flere (Vulg.). Euth. Zig. : ἐπιβαλὼν ἀντὶ τοῦ ἀρξάμενος. (2) "When he thought thereon, he wept" (A.V., R.V.). See Wetstein. (3) "Muffling up his face he wept," ἐπικαλυψάμενος τὴν κεφαλήν (Theophyl.). The choice lies between (2) and (3), the latter being preferable. The phrase was proverbial. Cf. Erasm. Adag. under Nudo capite : "Qui rem pudendam faciebant, üs mos erat centonibus caput operire." See Field, Notes.

[2] Lightfoot on John xviii. 15.   [3] Jos. Ant. xviii. 2. § 2.

[4] Lightfoot, ii. pp. 194, 773.

morning was a succession of flagrant illegalities.[1]   Justice
was straightway thrown to the winds without excuse or
shame.   With a humane sense of the value of human life
the Jewish law had laid down a very complete code of
regulations for the conduct of capital trials.   It was required
that the witnesses for the defence should be summoned first
and that, ere those for the prosecution gave evidence, they
should be reminded of the solemnity of their position and
enjoined to speak only from certain knowledge and affirm
nothing on hearsay.[2]   It was required also that adverse
evidence should be subjected to a searching scrutiny and
admitted only when corroborated by a second witness.[3]   Those
just and merciful regulations Caiaphas and his colleagues un-
blushingly disregarded.   Their troubler had been delivered
into their hands, and they were bent on making short work
of Him.   One consideration alone, restrained them.   It lay
with the Roman governor to pronounce and execute sentence
of death, and, when they handed their prisoner over to him,
they must specify His offence.   It was therefore necessary
that they should go through the form of a trial and condemn
Him on some plausible ground.   They met not to try but to
condemn Him.   They summoned no witnesses for the defence,
but they hunted up witnesses against Him with an undisguised
determination to effect His condemnation and with no attempt
to preserve even the appearance of judicial impartiality.   Of Useless
adverse witnesses they had no lack.   Many were ready at evidence.
their call to come forward with stories against Jesus, but so
foolish and contradictory were their allegations that they
afforded no ground for condemnation.   It was out of the
question to go to the governor with such charges.   Had there
been no governor to reckon with, they could easily have condemned Jesus.   Was there not the crime of Sabbath-breaking
to be laid to His charge?   He had frequently committed it,
and nothing that He had done in the course of His ministry
had given them more grievous offence.   And according to the
Jewish law it was a capital offence.   But then, had they gone
to the governor with a complaint about Sabbath-observance,

[1] It should not have met at all on a feast-day.   See Lightfoot on Mt. xxvii. 1 ;
Schürer, H. J. P. II. i. p. 190.

[2] Lightfoot on John xviii. 15 ; Schürer, H. J. P. II. i. p. 194.

[3] Lightfoot on Mk. xiv. 56.

they would have fared like the Jews at Corinth in after days,

Acts xviii. 12-6. when they impeached St Paul before Gallio for "persuading men to worship God contrary to the Law," and the proconsul told them that he would be no judge of such matters, and drove them contumeliously from his presence.

A promising charge. At length a charge was preferred which looked promising, inasmuch as it was supported by two witnesses and smacked of anarchy. "We heard him," they alleged, "saying: 'I can pull down the Sanctuary of God and in the course of three days build it.'" It was a distorted version of that mystic John ii. 19-22. saying which He had spoken after the cleansing of the Temple at the outset of His ministry. The two witnesses were probably honest men. They had heard that saying of Jesus, and, if it was misunderstood by the rulers, if its meaning was hidden even from the disciples until "He was raised from the dead," what marvel is it that two plain citizens should have misinterpreted it? Here was promising evidence. It seemed to warrant not only a charge of blasphemy against the Jews' Holy Place but a charge of revolutionary intentions such as the governor durst not ignore. It promised well, but, when the witnesses were further questioned, they got confused and invalidated their evidence by mutual contradiction.

Silence of Jesus. All the while Jesus had stood silent, uttering no protest, deigning no explanation. "His whole life and His deeds among the Jews," says an ancient apologist,[1] "were better than a voice refuting the false testimony or words making defence against the accusations." His life and deeds were His defence, and He stood silent in "proud disdain." His judges were troubled. They were impressed by the majesty of His bearing and angry withal at their ill success. It seemed as though it were impossible to bring home to Jesus any charge which would pass with the governor. Was their prey after all to escape from their clutches? If only He would speak, He might perhaps say something which could be employed to His Adjuration of Caiaphas. disadvantage. Starting from his chair Caiaphas advanced into the centre of the circle and, confronting the prisoner, demanded: "Answerest thou nothing? What is it that these men are witnessing against thee?" Jesus held His peace. "I put thee on oath," said the High Priest, half

[1] Orig. *C. Cels.* i. 2.

awed, half enraged, "to say to us whether thou art the Messiah, the Son of God." Then Jesus spoke. The adjuration was a challenge. Had He kept silence, His silence would have been interpreted as a denial of His Messiahship, a dereliction of all His claims. At such a crisis silence would have been disloyalty to His mission and a betrayal of the souls that had believed in Him and owned Him as their Lord. "Thou hast said,"[1] He replied ; "and,"[2] He continued, surveying the assembly, "ye shall see the Son of Man seated at the Right Hand of Power and coming upon the clouds of Heaven."

Caiaphas had gained his end. He had compelled Jesus to speak and, with consummate dexterity, had extorted from Him precisely such a declaration as the Sanhedrin's malign purpose required. Disguising his exultation by an affectation of horror, he rent his garments, as the law directed a judge to do when blasphemy was uttered or reported in his hearing.[3] It was no involuntary manifestation of horror but a histrionic conventionality. His emotion was a mere pretence. There was no blasphemy in the Lord's declaration. It was nothing uncommon in those restless days for an enthusiast to arise and give out that he was the Messiah, and the worst that could be laid to his charge was that he was either a fanatic or an impostor. It was no blasphemy on the part of Jesus to declare that He was the Messiah, though the piteousness of His condition might well render His claim ridiculous in His judges' eyes. Nevertheless it served their turn to raise the cry of blasphemy. It not only gave them a pretext for condemning Jesus according to their Law but furnished them with a specious complaint to urge against Him before the governor. They knew how jealously the Romans regarded that Messianic enthusiasm which in those dark days was continually stirring the hearts of the enslaved Jews and inciting them to desperate insurrection. Jesus had declared Himself the Messiah, and they could forthwith delate Him to the governor as a seditious plot- monger, an aspirant to the Jewish throne, an enemy of Cæsar.

---

[1] A formula of assent. Mk. gives "I am."

[2] Mt.'s ἀπάρτι, "henceforth," is probably an interpolation due to the primitive expectation of an immediate παρουσία.

Cf. Lightfoot, Wetstein.

Con-
demnation
of Jesus. "Blasphemy!" cried Caiaphas. "What further need
have we of witnesses? Behold, just now ye heard the
blasphemy. What is your verdict?" Instantly came the
unanimous response: "He is liable to death"; and Jesus
stood condemned. Was there no one in the assembly who
sympathised with Him? What of Nicodemus, that ruler of
the Jews, and Joseph of Arimathæa, that honourable councillor,
who were both "disciples but secret ones for fear of the Jews"?
Did their fear seal their lips? Or did they, with hardly less
cowardice, absent themselves from the Sanhedrin on that fateful morning?[1]

Violence
of the
Sanhedrin. Consider the shameless illegality of the procedure.
Lesser cases might be concluded on a single day; but in
capital cases, while sentence of absolution was pronounced on
the same day, it was required that sentence of condemnation
should be delayed until the day following. It was required,
moreover, that the votes of the judges should be taken down
in writing, each standing up in turn, the youngest first, and
intimating his verdict.[2] Not thus was Jesus condemned.
They did not wait until the morrow but sentenced Him
forthwith; nor did they vote in deliberate succession, but
declared Him guilty by tumultuous acclamation. It was
further required that after condemning a criminal to death
the Sanhedrin should mourn and fast all that day; but no
sooner was Jesus condemned than those grave councillors,
the custodians of Israel's law and faith, arose from their seats
and compassed Him with contumely.[3] They spat on His
face, they buffeted Him, they blindfolded Him and, striking
Him, challenged Him, as He was a prophet, to divine who
smote Him. And the officers of the court abetted their
superiors in the brutal sport. The conduct of the Sanhedrin
on that woeful morning imprinted on the reputation of the
august court an indelible stain which by and by the Jews
would fain have obliterated. Vainly seeking to rewrite
history, they told how for forty days Jesus was led through

[1] According to the apocryphal *Ev. Nicod.* v Nicodemus pled for Jesus both in
the Sanhedrin and before Pilate.

[2] Lightfoot on Mt. xxvii. 1; Schürer, *H. J. P.* II. i. p. 194.

[3] Mt. and Mk. make it plain that the mockery was done by the Sanhedrists.
Lk., perhaps deeming this incredible, has put the incident before the meeting of
Sanhedrin and attributed the brutality to "the men that held Jesus."

the city, and a herald went before Him, proclaiming that He had been sentenced to stoning as a deceiver of the people, and inviting any who could attest His innocence, to come forward and do so.[1]

The Sanhedrin had found Jesus guilty of blasphemy, and, according to the Law, He should have been forthwith stoned to death. But it was necessary in those days that the Roman governor's consent should be obtained. He resided at Cæsarea Stratonis, the Roman capital of Palestine, but he had, according to custom, come to Jerusalem to maintain order during the Feast, and thus the case could be immediately submitted to his adjudication. As they left the Hall of Hewn Stone and passed out into the Temple-court, the Sanhedrists encountered a weird figure. It was the traitor Judas, haggard and wild. Truly " man knows the beginning of sin, but who knows the issues thereof? " Without a qualm Judas had carried his crime through; and then, like the matricide Nero,[2] when it was accomplished, he perceived its enormity and recoiled affrighted by what he had done and stricken with remorse. Horror had taken hold of him in Gethsemane, when before the face of his betrayed Lord he fell to the earth; and, in an agony of guilt and remorse, he had followed to the house of Annas and thence to the Hall of Hewn Stone, and had waited without until he should know the issue, hoping that even yet Jesus might be acquitted. When the sentence was pronounced, his last hope was swept away. A desperate device occurred to him : might he not even now cancel the bargain? Clutching the accursed shekels in his wild hands, he confronted the retiring Sanhedrists, and, addressing the High Priests who had paid him his price, cried: " I have sinned in betraying innocent blood! " " What is that to us? " they sneered. " *Thou* must see to that "; and, spurning the wretch, they passed on. That the Sanhedrin might " sit near the Divine Majesty," the Hall of Hewn Stone adjoined the Sanctuary[3] with its two chambers—the inner chamber, the Holy of Holies, and, separated therefrom by a veil, the outer, the Holy Place.[4] Thither the High Priests betook themselves less to per-

Remorse of Judas.

---

[1] Lightfoot on Mt. xxvii. 31 and Acts i. 3.
[2] Tac. *Ann.* xiv. 10.
[3] Lightfoot on John xviii. 31.
[4] *Cf.* p. 63.

form their priestly duties than to be rid of Judas. Even in
his frenzy he durst not intrude into that sacred shrine where
none but priestly feet might tread ; but he followed them to
the threshold and, ere they could close the entrance, hurled the
the ringing coins into the Sanctuary. Before the priests had
recovered from their astonishment, he was gone. " He went
away and hanged himself."

<p style="margin-left:2em">Later legends. Such is St Matthew's story, and it bears the stamp of
truth. The traitor's crime was awful in the eyes of the
primitive Church, and it is in no wise surprising that his doom
was early invested with lurid circumstances. In the Acts of
the Apostles St Luke reports the story which was current
in his day.[1] It tells how Judas, unvisited by remorse,
purchased a field with the price of his iniquity and was
stricken by a manifest judgment of Heaven : "falling headlong, he burst asunder in the midst, and his bowels all gushed
out." And hence that field was known ever after as
Akeldama, the Field of Blood. In process of time the
legend developed apace. It was told how the traitor was
horribly afflicted. His body swelled till he could not pass
where a wagon had room ; it flowed with loathsome dis-
charges ; and, when he died, he was buried in his field, and
no one could pass by the place for the stench, " even if he
stopped his nostrils with his hands." [2] It is no marvel that
such legends should have arisen. In like manner did the
Scottish Covenanters invest their arch-persecutor, the bloody
Claverhouse, with supernatural terrors. His coal-black steed,
they said, was a creature of no earthly sire. It was a gift
which he had received from his master, the Devil. He was
furthermore, by the same master's grace, proof against lead,
and, when he fell on the field of Killiecrankie, he was shot,
they believed, by a silver button wherewith his waiting-
servant, "taking a resolution to rid the world of this truculent
bloody monster," had loaded his musket.

Pathos of the traitor's end. St Matthew's story, so grave, so restrained, so impressive
in its very simplicity, must be historical ; else had it resembled
those wild legends. It is impossible to repress a throb of pity

---

[1] Acts i. 18-9 is no part of Peter's speech but an explanatory parenthesis from
Lk.'s hand.

[2] Papiæ Fragm. iii in Patr. Apost. Op.; Routh, Reliq. Sacr. ii. pp. 9, 25-6.

for the wretch who so terribly sinned and so terribly repented.
It is a quaint fancy of one of the Fathers that, knowing that
His Master must die, he hastened to die before Him, thinking
to meet Him in the other world with naked soul, that, confessing his sin and imploring forgiveness, he might obtain mercy.[1]
Would that, like Peter, he had sorrowed with a godly sorrow
and sought mercy at the Cross from that gracious Saviour
who died with pardon on His lips! There was grace enough
in the heart of Jesus even for "such an ugly man as Judas."

The priests were not a little embarrassed when they found
their money thus thrown back upon their hands. What
should they do with it? It was blood-money, and therefore
they might not put it into the sacred Treasury. With characteristic moral obliquity, "straining out the midge and gulp-
ing down the camel," they shuddered at the blood-stained
shekels and never thought of the deeper stain wherewith their
souls were dyed. What should they do with the money?
After deliberation they hit upon an appropiate use. Outside
the city [2] there lay a worked-out clay-bed, at once useless and
unsightly. The potter was glad to be rid of it, and for the
poor pittance of thirty shekels they purchased it from him
and converted it into a burial-ground for strangers, that is,
Gentiles who chanced to die in the Holy City.[3] How could
the money be more contumeliously employed than in the
purchase of a burial-place for the carcases of Gentile dogs?

Thus they salved their consciences and evinced their
loathing of the blood-stained shekels, blind to the grim irony
of the transaction. When they bestowed upon the heathen
the purchase of the Redeemer's blood, they were all unconsciously prophets of His world-wide grace.[4] And, moreover,
they put themselves to an abiding shame. The place was
called the Field of Blood, and it remained for centuries [5]

The Potter's Field.

Cf. Deut. xxiii. 18.

Unconscious self-condemnation.

[1] Orig. *In Matth. Comm. Ser.* § 117.

[2] On account of the smoke a pottery had to be at a distance from dwellings, "in
some out-of-the-way place, among plants and hedges"; *cf.* 1 Chron. iv. 23.
P. E. F. Q., Jan. 1904, pp. 51-2.

[3] Not foreign Jews sojourning in Jerusalem: they would not have been buried
in that unclean place.

[4] Calv.: "Non improbo quod veteres quidam scripserunt, hoc symbolo datam
fuisse spem salutis Gentibus, quia in pretio mortis Christi inclusæ essent."

[5] Jer. *De Loc. Hebr.*: "Hodieque monstratur in Ælia ad australem plagam
montis Sion."

a monument of their crime, the ghastly name proclaiming
it trumpet-tongued and keeping its memory alive. The
Evangelist recognised in the episode a fulfilment of that
ancient Scripture where the prophet tells how an ungrateful
people requited his shepherd-care with a slave's price.[1] " They
weighed for my price thirty pieces of silver."   And in scorn
of this " goodly price wherewith he had been priced of them,"
he " cast it to the potter "—a proverb for contemptuous rejection, a potter's handiworks being frail and little worth [2]—" in
the House of the Lord."   The coincidence is more than
accidental.   The words of the Prophets have ever a deeper
meaning than they knew.   The Spirit of Messiah was in
them, testifying aforehand the sufferings that should befall
Messiah and the glories that should follow these.

1 Pet. i. 11.

[1] Zech. xi. 12-3. Mt.'s "Jeremiah" is perhaps a mere *lapsus memoriæ*, due to
Jer. xviii. 1-6; xxxii. 6-10. Calv. : "How the name of Jeremiah has crept in, I
confess I know not ; nor does it greatly trouble me.   That the name of Jeremiah
has certainly been put by an error for ' Zechariah ' the fact shows, since nothing of
the sort is read in Jeremiah, nor anything approaching it."   Origen suspects that it
is either a scribe's error (*errorem esse scripturæ*) or a quotation from some secret
scripture of Jeremiah.   And Jerome, while regarding it as a quotation from
Zechariah, says : "I read lately in a Hebrew book, which a Hebrew of the
Nazarene sect presented to me, an apocryphal writing of Jeremiah in which I found
this passage written word for word."   *Cf.* Aug. *De Cons. Ev.* iii. §§ 28-31.   It is
recognised that the latter half of Zechariah (ix-xv) is a collection of prophecies
belonging to different periods, ix-xi being thought by many to have been written
before the Exile.   What if xi. 12-3 were a prophecy of Jeremiah after all?

[2] *Cf.* Lam. iv. 2 ; Eccl. xii. 6 ; Arabic proverb: "The turning pitcher (of the
water-wheel) must one day receive a knock."

CHAPTER XLVIII

BEFORE PONTIUS PILATE

Mt. xxvii.
1-2, 11-4=
Mk. xv. 1-5
=Lk. xxiii.
1-5=John
xviii. 28-
38 ; Lk.
xxiii. 6-16;
Mt. xxvii.
15-30=
Mk. xv. 6-
19=Lk.
xxiii. 17-25
=John
xviii. 39-
xix. 16.

"Ejus corona splendicat,
    Sed est contexta rubo ;
Et gemmæ, quot intermicant,
    Nascuntur mari rubro,
Scintillant sicut faculæ,
Nam sunt cruoris maculæ."—*Med. Hymn.*

THUS "by impious show of law condemned," Jesus was led To the pro-curator. John xviii. 28. without delay to the governor. It was early in the morning, somewhere betwixt daybreak and six o'clock [1]—an unusual hour even in the East where, since it is impossible to transact business during the sultry hours of broad day, it is necessary to begin betimes.[2] So eager were the rulers for the ratification and execution of their sentence.

The man who at that juncture held the office of governor of Pontius Pilate, Judaea was Pontius Pilate, and for the part which he bore in the crime of the Lord's death, he has stood ever since on the pillory of the world's scorn and execration. Nevertheless, when his position is understood, it appears that he was to a large extent the victim of circumstances, and may even claim a measure of pity.[3] He was a typical Roman, stern and practical, with all the Roman contempt for superstition, which at that period was synonymous with religion of every variety,[4]

---

[1] At the close of the trial before Pilate ὥρα ἦν ὡς ἕκτη (John xix. 14), *i.e.*, according to John's reckoning, about 6 A.M. The Crucifixion was at 9 A.M. (Mk. xv. 25). Mt. xxvii. 19 implies that the trial was at an early hour : Pilate had gone to the Prætorium ere his wife was astir.

[2] At Rome the clients paid their visits from 6 to 8 A.M. ; the law-courts sat from 8 to 9 A.M. *Cf.* Mart. iv. 8.

[3] Though prompted by a desire to throw the guilt on the Jews, the tendency of some early writers to exculpate Pilate is not unjustifiable. *Cf. Ev. Nicod.* xii ; *Ev. Petr.*, ed. Robinson and James, pp. 16-7.

[4] Gibbon defines the Roman attitude toward religion in a pithy epigram : " The various modes of worship which prevailed in the Roman world, were all considered by the people as equally true ; by the philosopher as equally false ; and by the magistrate as equally useful."

2 K   477

and all the Roman hatred of the Jews, "that horde of circumcised." Had he been set over another province, he might have proved a successful ruler, but he was ill adapted for the government of a race so tenacious of its faith and so quick to resent whatever seemed a slight upon its cherished traditions. The Jews required very tactful management, and Pilate was a man of imperious temper, disposed to carry things with a high hand and compel obedience.

The offence of the standards. Trouble was inevitable, and no sooner had he set foot on his province than it began. His predecessors, prudently respecting the Jewish prejudice against images, had always taken care that, when their troops entered Jerusalem, they should not carry their ensigns emblazoned with the Emperor's effigy; but Pilate, disdaining what he deemed weak deference to a contemptible prejudice, bade the cohort which garrisoned the Holy City, march in with their standards and plant them on the citadel. Since the entry was made by night, the outrage was unobserved at the moment; but, when morning broke and they saw the standards floating over the citadel, the indignant citizens thronged out to Cæsarea and requested that the offensive insignia be removed. Pilate scorned their request, and for five days and as many nights they lay prostrate on the ground in sorrowful entreaty. On the sixth day he convened them in the race-course, and on their renewing their appeal he gave a signal, and a company of soldiers whom he had set in ambush, sprang forward and, surrounding the defenceless suppliants, threatened them with instant death unless they desisted from their clamour and returned peaceably home. He thought to intimidate them, but to his amazement they flung themselves on their faces and, baring their necks, declared themselves ready to die rather than endure the violation of their laws. Thereupon he gave way and ordered the removal of the ensigns.[1]

Sacrilegious use of Temple-treasure. It is always a grievous blunder to resile from an ultimatum, and Pilate's compliance was fatal to his authority ever after. His subjects took his measure. They perceived that he could be concussed by clamour. Ere long another issue emerged. Jerusalem had great need of an adequate supply of water, and Pilate determined to build an aqueduct.

[1] Jos. *Ant.* xviii. 3. § 1; *De Bell. Jud.* ii. 9. §§ 2-3.

It was a laudable project, but he conceived the unlucky idea
of defraying the cost out of the Temple-treasury. The Jews
were indignant at the sacrilege, and, when the governor visited
Jerusalem, he found himself beset by a clamorous and abusive
mob. Aware of the popular sentiment and apprehensive of
trouble, he had bidden his soldiers mingle in plain clothes
with the multitude and, should it prove necessary, fall upon
them with cudgels and beat them into subjection. Finding
remonstrance of no avail, he gave the signal, and the soldiers
assailed the unarmed mob with a severity greater than Pilate
had intended. Many were beaten to death, and many more
were trampled under foot. The tumult was suppressed, but
the populace was the more exasperated.[1]

The misguided governor had plunged ever deeper into Growing
barbarity. Quite recently he had fallen upon a company of disaffec-
Galileans in the Temple-court and had mingled their blood tion.
with the blood of their sacrifices—an atrocity which had sent Lk. xiii. 1.
a shudder through the land. The province was seething
with disaffection, which came to a head when, " less for the
honour of Tiberius than for the annoyance of the Jewish
people," Pilate hung votive shields richly gilded and engraved with the Emperor's name, in the Palace of Herod in
Jerusalem. It was perhaps a lesser outrage than the introduction of the standards, but it roused the exasperated people.
Headed by a company of their nobles, including the four sons
of Herod, they approached the governor and requested that
the shields be removed. He obdurately refused, and they
addressed a complaint to the Emperor. So long as the two Imperial
great imperial interests, revenue and order, were conserved, reprimand.
Tiberius cared little what went on in the provinces, least of all
in despised Judæa ; but woe to the luckless governor if the
taxes fell into arrears or an insurrection arose requiring
military operations for its suppression. The complaint from
Judæa provoked the Emperor's displeasure. He administered
a rebuke to Pilate and peremptorily ordered the removal of
the offending shields.[2]

---

[1] Jos. *Ant.* xviii. 3. § 1 ; *De Bell. Jud.* ii. 9. § 4.

[2] Phil. *De Leg. ad Cai.* § 38. This is probably the quarrel alluded to in Lk.
xxiii. 12. On the somewhat precarious ground that Sejanus was the arch-enemy of
the Jews and, while he lived, his baleful influence would have prevented Tiberius
from siding with the appellants, Schürer (*H. J. P.* I. ii. p. 86) regards the incident

Pilate's difficult position. Thus sorely strained were the relations betwixt Pilate and his subjects. He hated them and would have crushed them had he dared ; but he had the dread of deposition and disgrace before his eyes, and was obliged to walk warily and shun offence. He hated his subjects, but he also feared them. He was at their mercy, and they knew it.

At the Prætorium. The governor's residence at Jerusalem, called the Prætorium, was the palace which King Herod had built for himself in the days when Judæa retained the semblance of freedom. It stood on the western side of the city, and its magnificence, Josephus declares,[1] baffled description. Thither the Sanhedrists brought Jesus bound. Eager though they were, they would not enter. By entering a heathen dwelling they would have incurred ceremonial pollution and been debarred from further participation in the solemnities of the festal season.[2] Therefore they remained outside, and Pilate was obliged, with no good grace, to come forth and hear their complaint. There they stood face to face, the antagonists in the most momentous combat ever fought on earth : on the one side, Pilate full of scorn which he must repress yet could not conceal, and, on the other, the Jewish rulers aware of their opponent's weakness and bent on forcing him to do their will. " What accusation," he demanded, " are ye bringing against this man ? " and, meeting hauteur with hauteur, they answered : " Had he not been an evil-doer we would not have delivered him unto thee." It was an intimation that they would not be trifled with, and it stung Pilate to the quick. " Take ye him," he cried impatiently, " and judge him according to your law " ; and they answered : " We may not put anyone to death." It was a significant sentence. With insolent brevity it informed the governor how far the case had proceeded. They had already tried the prisoner and brought in a capital verdict ; and they had come to have their sentence confirmed and a death-warrant granted. Pilate would fain have bidden them begone, but they had the law on their side. They had tried the case in due form and were now bringing it under his review, and he must take it up.

as subsequent to the death of Sejanus in A.D. 31 and therefore subsequent to the trial of our Lord. It was not, however, sympathy with the Jews that moved the Emperor but solicitude for the peace of the province.

[1] De. Bell. Jud. v. 4. § 4.   [2] Cf. p. 538.

Thus ended the first bout, and Pilate had been worsted. Pilate compelled to take up the case.
He was obliged reluctantly to take up the case, and ere
returning to the judgment-hall he ascertained the precise
nature of the charge.   Here the villainy of the Lord's
accusers appeared.   They reported truly enough that He had
been condemned for claiming to be the Messiah, but they put
a new construction on the offence.   In the Hall of Hewn
Stone, that they might sentence Him to death under the
Jewish law, they had interpreted the claim as blasphemy.
They knew, however, that the governor would not listen for a
moment to a cry of blasphemy, and therefore, that they might
secure His condemnation under the Roman law, they gave
His claim a political significance and charged Him with
plotting sedition.   "We found this fellow," they said, "per- Lk. xxiii.
verting our nation, and preventing the payment of taxes to 2.
the Emperor, and alleging himself to be Messiah, a King."
It was bad enough that they should juggle with the indictment, attaching one meaning to it in the Hall of Hewn Stone
and another at the Prætorium ; it was worse that they should
set down a deliberate falsehood, accusing Him of opposing
the payment of tribute despite His pronouncement only a few Mt. xxii.
days previously in the court of the Temple ; but it was worst 15-22=
Mk. xii. 13-
of all that they should trample upon the instincts of patriotism 7=Lk. xx.
20-6.
and the ideals of religion.   When they delivered Jesus to
Pilate, did they not remember that their Law forbade the
delivery of an Israelite into the hands of the Gentiles on pain
of forfeiture of any place in the world to come ?[1]   And, when
they represented His claim to Messiahship as disloyalty to
the Emperor, did they not bethink themselves that the
Emperor was Israel's tyrant and that the advent of the
Messiah had been the hope and dream of her sons all down
the generations of her sacred history ?

When he had thus ascertained the charge the governor Examina-
retired into the Prætorium and, summoning the prisoner, tion of
Jesus.
proceeded to examine Him.   It needed no shrewdness to
perceive the absurdity of the accusation.   Pilate looked at
Jesus.   "Thou !" he exclaimed.   "Art thou the King of the
Jews ? "   It was no sneer.   It happened with Pilate as with
all who had to do with Jesus in the days of His flesh and

[1] Lightfoot on Mt. x. 4.

encountered the gaze of His wondrous Face, "always with that high look of godlike calm": he involuntarily bowed before Him and marvelled what manner of man He might be. "Sayest thou this," Jesus replied, "of thyself, or did others tell thee about Me?" The question recalled the governor from his unaccustomed mood, and, as though ashamed of his momentary weakness, he retorted brusquely: "Am I a Jew? Thy nation and the High Priests handed thee over to me. What didst thou do?" Jesus knew well that the governor's soul was beset by strange questionings and that his rudeness were merely an attempt to daff these aside. "My Kingdom," He said, "is not of this world. Had My Kingdom been of this world, My servants had been striving that I might not be handed over to the rulers. But, as it is, My Kingdom is not from hence." It was at once a denial of the charge which had been laid against Him and a gracious self-manifestation to Pilate's wondering soul. "Then," exclaimed the latter, "thou *art* a king?" "Thou sayest it," was the reply; "because a king I am. It is for this end that I have been born and for this end that I have come into the world, that I may testify to the Truth. Everyone that is of the Truth hearkeneth to My voice." Ah, now Pilate perceived the situation. He had heard that sort of talk before. Rome was infested by Greek sophists, "men fonder of contention than of truth," eternally wrangling about "the truth" to the weariness of sensible folk.[1] "I cannot away with a Greek Rome!" cried the satirist of a later generation; and Pilate would have echoed the sentiment. "The Truth!" he sneered. "What is 'Truth'?" It was clear to him how matters stood. Jesus was certainly no dangerous revolutionary. He was nothing but a sophist, a harmless visionary. He was a king as the Wise Man of the Stoics was a king.

Pilate pronounces Him innocent. Thus resolved, Pilate conducted the prisoner forth and said to the expectant rulers: "I find no fault in him." It was in no wise the verdict which they desired, and they raised a clamour, pouring forth a torrent of accusations. Jesus held His peace, disdaining to reply; and Pilate wondered at His silence so unlike His frankness with himself a little agone.

---

[1] Cic. *De Orat.* i. § 47: "Verbi enim controversia jam diu torquet Græculos, homines contentionis cupidiores quam veritatis."

Wherefore did He not repeat His repudiation of sedition and explain in what sense He claimed to be a king? "Answerest thou nothing?" he said. "See how many things they are accusing thee of." Still He held His peace. Pilate was astonished and withal greatly embarrassed. Justice required him to dismiss the case and set the prisoner at liberty; but he durst not, in his unfortunate situation, thwart the Jewish rulers. Amid the babel he caught the word "Galilee," and learned that Jesus was a Galilean. This discovery opened a door of escape to the perplexed governor. Being a Galilean, Jesus was under the jurisdiction of Herod Antipas, the tetrarch of Galilee. It chanced opportunely that Antipas had come up to keep the Feast and was at that moment at Jerusalem in the old Palace of the Asmonæans; and Pilate, anxious to extricate himself from a difficult position, remitted the case to him. *Pilate's first evasion: the case referred to Herod Antipas.*

Antipas was delighted when the prisoner was brought before him. He had heard the fame of Jesus in the north, and with a sceptic's superstition had conceived the notion that He was the murdered Baptist come back to life. The idea had haunted him. He had wished to see Jesus, and had latterly, at the instigation probably of the Jewish rulers, been minded to kill Him; but, partly from the indolence which characterised him, partly from that singular reluctance which cowards feel to know the worst, he had never procured an interview, preferring rather to remain in harassing uncertainty than have his doubt resolved. At length all unexpectedly he found himself face to face with the mysterious personage, and discovered to his relief that He was not the Baptist. In truth Jesus was utterly unlike the stern prophet who had lashed his guilty conscience with the stinging scourge of imperious and indignant rebuke. Curiosity had mingled with alarm in the breast of the frivolous tetrarch, and he had been in hopes of witnessing one of those miracles whereof he heard so much. But Jesus would not gratify him. He maintained a contemptuous silence, deigning no reply either to the questions of the tetrarch or to the shrill accusations of the attendant rulers. Antipas could make nothing of Him. He was not in the mood to treat the affair seriously, and by way of venting his spleen for all the uneasiness which he had suffered, he made a mock of Jesus, his bodyguards lending their aid, and, *Before Antipas.* *Mt. xiv. 1-2=Mk. vi. 14-6=Lk. ix. 7-9.* *Lk. xiii. 31.*

attiring Him in a splendid garment from his own sumptuous wardrobe in derision of His regal claim, sent Him back to Pilate.

Pilate's second evasion: a compromise. The stratagem had failed, and Pilate, to his chagrin, was obliged to resume the awkward case. He knew that the Jewish rulers were set upon the death of Jesus; but his Roman reverence for justice revolted from the idea of condemning an innocent man, and he made a feeble attempt at compromise, consenting to a lesser wrong in the hope of averting a greater. "Ye brought this man unto me," he said, "as a perverter of the people; and, behold, on examination I found in this man none of the faults whereof ye accuse him. Nay, neither did Herod; for he sent him back to us, and, behold, nothing worthy of death hath been committed by him." [1] It was a complete and absolute declaration of the prisoner's innocence, and Pilate would fain have concluded, perhaps he meant to conclude: "I will therefore release him." But he quailed before those ruthless faces and concluded with faltering inconsequence: "I will therefore chastise him and release him."

The annual release. It was a poor compromise, and it would have been greeted with a clamour of disapproval but for the sudden appearance of a fresh company of actors on the scene. It was customary for the Roman governors, with politic deference to Jewish sentiment, to signalise the Passover by granting pardon to a prisoner, allowing the people to name the fortunate recipient of the imperial clemency. Just at that moment a crowd came thronging to the gate [2] and craved the annual boon.

Pilate's third evasion: Jesus or Bar Abba? Pilate welcomed the interruption. It opened to him another door of escape from the odious necessity of condemning Jesus. There was lying in prison at that crisis a notorious criminal, one of those brigands who infested the mountains of Judæa and rendered the Ascent of Blood so perilous to travellers betwixt Jerusalem and Jericho. He had been concerned in a recent insurrection, one of those tumults which were so frequent during Pilate's term of office, and had been taken red-handed and was awaiting execution.

---

[1] Lk. xxiii. 14: ἐνώπιον ὑμῶν is inconsistent with John xviii. 28, 33. See Introd. § 13.

[2] Mk. xv. 8: ἀναβὰς ὁ ὄχλος Tisch., W. H. ἀναβοήσας T. R.

By a singular coincidence the desperado's name was Jesus.[1]
He was the son of one of the Rabbis, and he was known
generally, perhaps in wonderment at his fall, as *Bar Abba*,
the Son of the Father, that is, the Rabbi.[2] Pilate perceived
his opportunity and, with dexterous alacrity, presented his
petitioners with the alternative : "Which will ye that I release
unto you—Jesus the Son of the Rabbi or Jesus that is called
Messiah ? "

It seemed as though the ruse would succeed. Jesus was
the popular hero, and, though that throng would be the
rabble of the city, they would have no ill-will to Jesus. It
seemed inconceivable that they should "deny the Holy and
Righteous One, and ask that a murderer should be granted
unto them." Just then, however, a message was brought to
Pilate. It was a communication from his wife. Tradition
says that she was named Claudia Procula and was a proselyte
to the Jewish religion.[3] It is plain that she had some acquaintance with Jesus. If she was indeed a proselyte, she
must have heard Him teaching in the Temple-court during
the busy days of the Passion-week. And her soul had been
stirred. When the High Priests visited Pilate on the previous
night, requesting a detachment of soldiers for the Lord's
arrest, she would learn their errand and would retire to rest
full of uneasy forebodings. Since dreams are but reflections
of waking thoughts, it is no marvel that, while she slept, she
dreamed of that wondrous Man.[4] When she woke, her dream
haunted her. Her husband was already abroad, and she
learned that he had gone to the judgment-hall and that the

A message from Claudia.

---

[1] According to several min., vers. Arm. Syr. Schol. 41 : παλαιοῖς δὲ πάνυ
ἀντιγράφοις ἐντυχὼν εὗρον καὶ αὐτὸν τὸν Βαραββᾶν Ἰησοῦν λεγόμενον· οὕτως γοῦν εἶχεν
ἡ τοῦ Πιλάτου πεῦσις ἐκεῖ· "τίνα θέλετε τῶν δύο ἀπολύσω ὑμῖν, Ἰησοῦν τὸν Βαραββᾶν
ἢ Ἰησοῦν τὸν λεγόμενον Χριστόν;" Origen's text had this reading, but he did not
approve it, thinking it unfit that a robber should bear the sacred name (*In Matth.
Comm. Ser.* § 121; *cf.* § 33.

[2] *Cf.* p. 442. Βαραββᾶς = בַּר אַבָּא. Wetstein : "Nomen apud Thalmudicos
usitatissimum. R. Samuel *bar Abba*, R. Nathan *bar Abba*, Abba *bar Abba*."
Jerome says that in the *Gosp. of the Hebr.* the name was interpreted "Filius
Magistri eorum."

[3] Niceph. *H. E.* i. 30; *Act. Pil.* §§ 2, 4. Origen (*In Matth. Comm. Ser.* § 122)
says that she was converted to Christianity, and sees in her *mysterium ecclesiæ
ex gentibus.*

[4] *Cf.* Lucr. iv. 962 *sqq.* The dreams of Calpurnia : Plut. *C. Cæs.* § 63; Shak.
Jul. Cæs. II. ii. Plin. *Ep.* iii. 5.

business on hand was the trial of Jesus. In keen apprehension she sent him a warning message: "Have thou nothing to do with that righteous man; for I suffered much to-day[1] in consequence of a dream on his account."

Bar Abba chosen. Little did Claudia think, when she thus intervened on behalf of Jesus, that she was sealing His doom. Her message diverted Pilate's attention, and the astute priests and elders clutched at their opportunity and incited the crowd to demand the release of Bar Abba and the death of Jesus. "Well," said Pilate, resuming the business, "which of the twain will ye that I release unto you?" "Bar Abba" they shouted. "Then what," asked the disconcerted governor, "shall I do to Jesus that is called Messiah?" and they shouted back: "Let him be crucified!" "Why," he remonstrated, "what ill hath he done?" His opposition only irritated them and provoked them to the assertion of their right of choice. "Let him be crucified!" they shouted loud and long.

Jesus condemned. Grievously reluctant Pilate gave way. "He released him that for insurrection and murder had been thrown into prison, whom they claimed, and Jesus he handed over to their will." He felt himself the while nothing else than a murderer. Among the ancients, Romans, Greeks, and Jews, it was customary for a man, after he had shed blood, to wash his hands, thus symbolically cleansing away the stain;[2] and the conscience-stricken governor had water fetched to him and in sight of the assemblage washed his hands exclaiming: "I am innocent of this blood. Ye shall see to it." The thoughtless rabble had no misgivings. "His blood," they cried, "be upon us and upon our children!" It was indeed, says St Jerome, a goodly inheritance that they left to their sons. Were those stout words recalled a generation later when Jerusalem fell, and her wretched citizens were crucified around her walls till, in the historian's grim language,[3] "space was wanting for the crosses and crosses for the bodies"?

Scourging and mockery. The Romans were wont to scourge a criminal ere they crucified him.[4] The scourge was a frightful instrument—a

[1] The Jewish day began at 6 P.M.
[2] Schol. on Soph. *Aj.* 663: ἔθος ἦν παλαιοῖς ὅτε ἡ φόνον ἀνθρώπου ἡ ἄλλας σφαγὰς ἐποίουν, ὕδατι ἀπονίπτειν τὰς χεῖρας εἰς κάθαρσιν τοῦ μιάσματος. Deut. xxi. 6; Ps. xxvi. 6.   [3] Jos. *De Bell. Jud.* v. 11. § 11.
[4] Cf. Lips. *De Cruc.* I. ii-iv; Wetstein on Mt. xxvii. 6.

whip with several thongs, each loaded with acorn-shaped
balls of lead or sharp pieces of bone.   Six lictors took the
victim, stripped him, bound him to a post, and plied the cruel
lash.   Each stroke cut into the quivering flesh ; the veins
and sometimes the very entrails were laid bare,[1] and often the
teeth and eyes were knocked out.   It is no wonder that not
unfrequently the sufferer expired under the torture.   The
soldiers led Jesus away and scourged Him ; and then they
took Him, faint and bleeding, and compassed Him with
ribald mockery.   Over His lacerated back they put Herod's
purple[2] robe ; they plaited a crown of thorns and put it on
His head ; and in His right hand, by way of sceptre, they put
a reed ; then in mock homage they knelt before Him and
saluted Him : " Hail ! King of the Jews."   And they spat
upon His face, buffeted Him, and, snatching the reed from
His hand, smote Him on the head, at each stroke driving the
thorns into His tortured brow.

When the soldiers thus added mockery to the scourging, *Pilate's*
they overstepped the limits of Roman usage.[3]   It was a *fourth evasion :*
superfluous barbarity.   Yet Pilate did not restrain them. *an appeal*
Perhaps he encouraged them ; for he had an end in view. *ad miseri-*
He hoped, says St Augustine,[4] that the Jews would be satis- *cordiam.*
fied with scourging and mockery, and refrain for very pity
from putting Jesus to death.   When the brutal sport was
ended, he strode forth and said to the multitude : " See ! I am
bringing him forth to you, that ye may recognise that no
fault do I find ———." [5]   He was about to say " in him " ; but
he stopped short.   His eye had lighted on Jesus painfully
making His way from the Prætorium, pale and bleeding,
tricked out in the piteous bravery of His thorny crown and
purple robe ; and, pointing to Him, he cried : " Behold, the
Man ! "   It was an appeal to their compassion.   Surely the
spectacle must soften them.

---

[1] Jos. *De Bell. Jud.* ii. 21. § 5.

[2] Mk. xv. 17 : πορφύραν, John xix. 2 : ἱμάτιον πορφυροῦν, Mt. xxvii. 28 :
χλαμύδα κοκκίνην.   Wetstein : "Coccinæ et purpuræ vicinus est color, unde sæpe
confunduntur."

[3] Orig. *In Matth. Comm. Ser.* § 125.   Field quotes from Plut. *Pomp.* xxiv. a
similar exhibition of mockery on the part of the Mediterranean pirates.

[4] *In Joan Ev. Tract.* cxvi. § 1.

[5] John xix. 4 : ὅτι αἰτίαν οὐχ εὑρίσκω ℵ* Tisch.

" O quanta vis doloris est
  In Jesu patiente !
  Plorare, nisi tigris es,
  Debes ac redamare."

The crowd apparently were not unmoved. At all events
they were silent ; but the priests, very wild beasts in their
ferocity, shouted : " Crucify him ! crucify him ! " their officers,
after the fashion of servile minions, joining in the clamour.

His agita-   Sick at heart Pilate retorted : " Take ye him and crucify
tion. him ; for *I* find no fault in him." It was the speech of one
who had lost all patience and would have nothing further to
do with the odious business. Of course it was impossible for
him to maintain that attitude. Sentence had been passed,
and he was bound to see it executed. And he was promptly
recalled to the dire necessity. " We have a law," said those
relentless rulers, " and according to the law he ought to die,
because he made himself God's Son." The statement was
scarcely accurate. It was no blasphemy that Jesus had called
Himself the Son of God, which was merely a Messianic title.
Cf. John v. His blasphemy in their eyes lay in His calling Himself the
18. Son of God in a manner which amounted to an assertion of
His equality with God. Such a refinement, however, would
have been meaningless to Pilate ; and in truth their answer
was not so much a statement of the prisoner's offence as an
intimation that there must be no trifling. It threw the
governor into sudden agitation. Here was a new aspect of
the case. He had been impressed by the mystery which
encompassed that wondrous Man ; and, when he heard that
He had made Himself God's Son, his soul, unemancipated
from the superstition which he despised, was shaken with
Interview vague dread. He conducted Jesus within and asked Him
with Jesus. earnestly : " Whence art Thou ? " Jesus made no reply. He
had witnessed Pilate's pusillanimity, his repeated surrenders,
his base betrayals of justice ; and He despised the man. He
surveyed him in contemptuous silence. Pilate winced and
tried to brazen it out. " Speakest thou not to me ? Knowest
thou not that I have authority to release thee and I have
authority to crucify thee ? " Half in scorn, half in pity Jesus
answered : " Thou hadst no authority against Me, unless it
had been given thee from above. Therefore," He added

making generous allowance for Pilate's ignorance and casting the guilt upon the Jews, and particularly Caiaphas, " he that handed Me over to thee hath greater sin."

At their first interview, when Jesus spoke of His unearthly Kingdom and His mission to testify to the Truth, Pilate had sneered ; but in the interval he had perceived the majesty of Jesus, and his soul bowed before the thorn-crowned Man. The terrors of the unseen had taken hold of him, and at all hazards he must get the prisoner off. He went out and told the Jews that he would release Him. The announcement raised a wild storm. "They fell a-howling," says the Evangelist. " If thou release this fellow," they cried, "thou art no friend of the Emperor. Every one that maketh himself a king, opposeth the Emperor." It was a clever stroke. In those dark days, when a gloomy and suspicious tyrant sat upon the imperial throne, *læsa majestas* was the crime of crimes, and men were hurried to death on the most trivial evidence.[1] It would be an ugly story to reach the ears of Tiberius that his procurator in the turbulent province of Judæa had sided with a ringleader of sedition. Pilate was in an awkward predicament, yet he persisted in his resolution to save Jesus. He was standing at the entrance to the Prætorium on the broad landing richly tessellated and known as the Gabbatha,[2] and there, in full view of the assemblage, setting Jesus down, thorn-crowned and purple-clad, upon a seat,[3] like a king upon his throne, he pointed to Him and said : " See ! your King ! " It was as though he had said : " Can you seriously maintain that this poor broken man is a dangerous person, a rival of the Emperor?" At the same time he appealed to their Jewish sentiment. " It was," says St John, " the Passover Friday " ; and could they at that season, sacred to the memory of the great deliverance which had made Israel a nation, doom a fellow-countryman to an ignominious death for

Marginal notes: Determination to release Him.

Marginal notes: Pilate's fifth evasion : an appeal to reason and patriotism.

---

[1] Tac. *Ann.* iii. 38 : "Majestatis crimine, quod tum omnium accusationum complementum erat." Philostratus (*Vit. Apoll.* iv. 39) tells of a drunken fellow who went about the streets of Rome singing Nero's songs and arresting every one who gave him nothing ὡς ἀσεβοῦντα. *Cf.* Senec. *De Benef.* iii. § 26.

[2] Perhaps connected with גַּב, "back," and so *a broad, elevated platform*. See Hastings' *D. B.*

[3] Taking ἐκάθισεν as act. *Cf. Ev. Petr.* § 3 : καὶ ἐκάθισεν αὐτὸν ἐπὶ καθέδραν κρίσεως.

seeking to make Israel once more free and rid her of the foreign yoke?

Clamour of the crowd. It was Pilate's final attempt to save Jesus, and it failed. Impervious to ridicule, deaf to the voices of patriotism and religion, they howled like wolves athirst for blood : "Away with him! away with him! Crucify him!" "Shall I crucify your King?" asked the governor in scorn and disgust ; and the reply came : "We have no King but the Emperor." It was the High Priests, worldly and sceptical Sadducees, that uttered the ominous sentence. The Pharisees and the multitude were silent. They had not sunk so low as to abjure thus their country's liberties and swear fealty to the heathen tyrant. Nevertheless they were silent. They made no protest. Surely the sceptre had departed from Judah.

Sentence of crucifixion. The contest was ended. Pilate had struggled hard, but all in vain. Since he had not the courage to do justice and set the consequences at defiance, there was no more that he could do. "Then, therefore, he handed Him over to them to be crucified." *Ibis ad crucem. I, miles, expedi crucem.*

CHAPTER XLIX

THE CRUCIFIXION

" Found guilty of excess of love,
It was Thine own sweet will that tied
Thee tighter far than helpless nails ;
Jesus, our Love, is crucified ! "—FABER.

Mt. xxvii.
31-66=
Mk. xv. 20
47=Lk.
xxiii. 26-56
=John xix.
17-42.

No sooner had the sentence been pronounced than the Prepara-
soldiers proceeded to carry it out. First of all, they stripped tions.
Jesus of the purple robe and reclothed Him with His own
attire. Then from the pile which lay always ready to hand
in the Prætorium,[1] they selected a cross. It was a grim
custom that a criminal should carry his cross to the place of
execution ;[2] and they laid the ghastly gibbet on the shoulders
of Jesus. It was also the custom that, as the criminal was
led to the place of execution, he should be preceded by a
herald carrying a board whereon his name and his offence
were written, that all might know who he was and wherefore
he had been condemned.[3] Here Pilate saw an opportunity
for venting his spleen against those odious Jews. He put on
the board : JESUS THE NAZARENE, THE KING OF THE JEWS,
writing it, that all might be able to read it, in Hebrew, Latin,
and Greek. It was a piece of petty malice, and it was keenly
resented. " Do not," remonstrated the High Priests, " write :
The King of the Jews, but : *He said: ' I am King of the
Jews.'* " " What I have written, I have written," was the
scornful answer.[4]

[1] Lightfoot, ii. p. 56.
[2] Lips. *De Cruc.* II. v ; Wetstein on Mt. x. 38. In Isaac carrying the wood for
his own sacrifice (Gen. xxii. 6) Tertullian sees a prefiguration of Jesus carrying
His cross (*Adv. Jud.* § 10).
[3] Eus. *H. E.* v. 1 : καὶ περιαχθεὶς κύκλῳ τοῦ ἀμφιθεάτρου, πίνακος αὐτὸν προ-
άγοντος ἐν ᾧ ἐπεγέγραπτο Ῥωμαϊστί · οὗτός ἐστιν Ἄτταλος ὁ Χριστιανός. *Cf.* Lips.
De Cruc. II. xi.
[4] *Cf.* Shak. *Two Gentl. of Ver.* I. iii : "For what I will, I will, and there an
end."

The pro-
cession.

Jesus did not go alone to execution. Two brigands, like
Bar Abba, were lying under sentence, and Pilate, regardless of
the Jewish law which forbade more than one execution on
the same day,[1] sent them with Him to their doom. Setting
forth from the Prætorium, the procession passed along the
most frequented streets of the city, that the populace might
be duly impressed by so signal an exhibition of the terrors of
justice.[2] The prisoners were escorted by a detachment of
soldiers under the command of a centurion ; and, staggering
under their crosses, they were driven forward by lash and
goad.[3] Forgetful of their dignity in their eagerness to witness
the destruction of their victim, the High Priests joined the
train ; and the rascal multitude swarmed in the rear, a jostling,
curious, thoughtless rabble. Yet Jesus was not wholly unbefriended as He went His sorrowful way. John, the best
beloved of His disciples, was there when the procession started,
and saw his dear Lord set forth with His cross on His
shoulders. It would seem, however, that he did not follow the
procession. He hastened away to inform Mary of the issue
of the trial and support her beneath the weight of her sorrow ;
and by and by, in company with her and the rest of the
Galilean women, he went forth and stood beside the Cross.[4]
No disciple attended Jesus on His way to death ; but there

Lk. xxiii.
27.

were women in the crowd, and they were moved by the
spectacle of His woe and poured forth lamentations. No other
tokens of kindness did He receive as He went His way to die.

The im-
pressment
of Simon of
Cyrene.

Enfeebled by fasting, excitement, and brutal handling,
Jesus staggered along beneath His burden as far as the city
gate,[5] and there His strength utterly failed. Tradition says
that He fell. There was nothing for it but to relieve Him of
the cross and transfer it to stouter shoulders. Looking round
for one whom they might impress,[6] the soldiers spied a man

[1] Lightfoot on Mt. xxvii. 31.

[2] Jos. *Ant.* xx. 6. § 3 ; *De Bell. Jud.* iv. 6. § 1 ; Quinct. *Decl.* 274.

[3] Lips. *De Cruc.* II. vi.

[4] Such is the account of the apocryphal *Act. Pil.* (x. 2), and it explains
why John omits certain things which the Synoptists mention : (1) The impressment
of Simon. He saw Jesus set out "carrying the cross for Himself " ; he did not see
it transferred to Simon's shoulders. (2) The offering of the myrrhed wine to Jesus
before the crucifixion.

[5] Mt. xxvii. 32 : ἐξερχόμενοι, "as they were going forth," *i.e.* from the city.

[6] *Cf.* p. 160.

who had been about to enter the city as the procession came pouring through the gateway. He was a Hellenistic Jew named Simon from Cyrene, a North African city where a large Jewish colony resided ;[1] and he had come up to Jerusalem to celebrate the Feast. He had his lodging in the country outside the walls of the city, and he was on his way to the Temple to join in the morning prayer. All unexpectedly and sorely against his will he was called to a holier service. The soldiers arrested him in the Emperor's name, and, laying that ghastly burden on his shoulders, compelled him to turn his back upon the city and accompany them on their grim errand. Nothing further is recorded of Simon save that he had two sons, Alexander and Rufus, who were evidently believers in connection with the Church at Rome.[2] Surely Simon also believed. It were indeed a strange irony had the man who carried the Cross, missed the salvation whereof it is the instrument and the symbol.

Mk. xv. 21.

While the soldiers were busy about Simon, the women lamented Jesus, beating their breasts and chanting a dirge, regardless of the law which forbade open lamentation for one sentenced to death.[3] Their sympathy would be sweet and comforting to His heart. Yet even in that hour of utter weakness He bore Himself right royally. He knew what would come to pass, and He turned and said to them : " Daughters of Jerusalem, weep not for Me ; but for yourselves weep and for your children. For, behold, there are coming days wherein they shall say : ' Blessed are the barren and the wombs which did not bear and breasts which did not give suck.' "

"Daughters of Jerusalem."
Cf. Mt. xi. 17 = Lk. vii. 32.

The procession resumed its march, but so shaken was Jesus that, though no longer burdened with His cross, He was unable to walk unsupported and had to be borne along,[4] until the place of execution was reached. Where was that place, at once the most tragic and the most sacred on the earth ?[5] Tradition, resting upon the alleged discovery of the Holy

Cf. Lk. xi. 27-8 ; xxi. 23.
Calvary.

---

[1] Jos. *Ant.* xiv. 7. § 2 ; Acts ii. 10.

[2] Mk., writing at Rome, mentions them as well-known persons. The Rufus of Rom. xvi. 13 is commonly identified with the son of Simon. His mother had shown Paul kindness.   [3] Lightfoot on Mt. xxvii. 31.

[4] Mk. xv. 22 : φέρουσιν αὐτόν, probably " they carry Him." *Cf.* Mk. ii. 3 = Lk. v. 18 ; Mt. xiv. 11 = Mk. vi. 28 ; Lk. xxiii. 26.

[5] According to *Ev. Nicod.* ix, " in the garden where He had been arrested."

Sepulchre by the Emperor Constantine,[1] fixes the site on the western side of Jerusalem ; but the discovery is a mere fable, and the probability is that the place lay to the north of the city. It was called Golgotha, which signifies in Latin Calvaria and in English a Skull ; and the name is variously explained. A legend of great antiquity says that it was the place where Adam died and was buried ; and "Jesus, in the place where death reigned, set up His trophy."[2] St Jerome, rejecting the ancient fable, puts forward the opinion that Golgotha was a place of execution and got its name from the skulls which bestrewed it. The prevailing opinion in modern times is that the name was derived from the configuration of the ground :

Mt. xxvii. Golgotha was a skull-shaped knoll. It appears from the
32; cf. Gospel narratives that it lay outside the city ; that it was near
Hebr. xiii.
12-3; John the city ; that it was an eminence, since it could be seen from
xix. 20;
Mt. xxvii. afar ; and that a highway ran hard by it. And just outside
55=Mk.
xv. 40; Mt. the Damascus Gate there is a knoll, known as Jeremiah's
xxvii. 39= Grotto, which answers to all these requirements.[3]
Mk. xv. 29.

Cruci- It was nine o'clock when they reached the place and
fixion. addressed themselves to their brutal work. Crucifixion was a
Mk. xv. 25.
horrible punishment. Originally Oriental, the Romans had borrowed it from their enemies the Carthaginians, and they reserved it for slaves and provincials, accounting it a sacrilege that a Roman citizen should endure either the scourge or the cross.[4] Though the ignominy of the *crudelissimum tæterrimumque supplicium* was its chief terror, at all events in Jewish eyes, the torture was appalling, insomuch that, when the Romans would express the extremity of anguish, they fashioned a word from *crux* and called it *cruciatus*, whence also the English *excruciating* is derived. The cross was a ghastly instrument. It was either *crux simplex*, a single stake whereon the victim was impaled,[5] or *crux compacta*, which had three forms : the *Crux Decussata*, shaped like the letter X and

---

[1] Gibbon, *Decl. and Fall*, chap. xxiii.

[2] Orig. *In Matth. Comm. Ser.* § 126 ; Chrysost. *In Joan.* lxxxiv ; Jer. ; Euth. Zig.

[3] *Cf.* arts. Golgotha in Hastings' *D. B.* and *E. B.* ; Henderson's *Palestine*, § 117 ; *P. E. F. Q.*, Oct. 1898, p. 248 ; Sanday, *Sacr. Sit.*, plates xliv. and xlv.

[4] Cic. *In Verr.* v. 66 : "Facinus est vinciri civem Romanum ; scelus verberari ; prope parricidium necari : quid dicam in crucem tollere? Verbo satis digno tam nefaria res appellari nullo modo potest."

[5] Sen. *Consol. ad Marc.* § 20.

known as St Andrew's Cross, since on such a cross he is
reported to have died at Patræ; the *Crux Commissa* or St
Anthony's Cross, shaped like the letter T;[1] and the *Crux
Immissa*, whereof the upright (*stipes, staticulum*) projected
above the transom (*antenna, patibulum*), ✝.[2] The last was
apparently the commonest. The victim, called *cruciarius*,
was first of all stripped naked,[3] his garments falling to the
executioners as their recognised perquisites;[4] then he was
laid across the transom with outstretched arms, and his hands
were made fast to either end, usually by nails hammered
through the palms or the wrists but sometimes, to prolong
the suffering, merely by cords.[5] Thereafter the transom with
its quivering load was hoisted on the upright; and, to support
its weight which must else have torn the hands, the body
rested, as on a saddle, on a projecting peg (*sedile, cornu*).[6]
Sometimes the feet, like the hands, were merely tied, but
usually they were nailed to the upright either through the
instep by two nails or through the Achilles tendon by a single
nail transfixing both.[7] And thus the victim hung in agony,
lingering on, unless the end were hastened, as long as two
days.[8]

Jesus suffered, it seems, on a *crux immissa*.[9] It was a
humane custom among the Jews that, ere a criminal was
executed, a potion of medicated wine should be administered
to him in order to dull his sensibility, in accordance with the
scriptural precept: "Give strong drink unto him that is ready
to perish, and wine unto the bitter in soul." And there was
a society of charitable ladies in Jerusalem who charged themselves with the preparation of the merciful potion.[10] Ere the

The narcotic draught.

Prov. xxxi. 6.

---

[1] *Cf.* Barn. *Ep.* § 9; Luc. *Jud. Vocal.* § 12.

[2] Lips. *De Cruc.* I. vi-ix.

[3] According to *Ev. Nicod.* x, Jesus had a loin-cloth.

[4] Wetstein on Mt. xxvii. 35.   [5] Lips. *De Cruc.* II. viii.

[6] Just. M. *Dial. cum Tryph.*, ed. Sylburg., p. 318 C: καὶ τὸ ἐν τῷ μέσῳ πηγνύ-
μενον ὡς κέρας καὶ αὐτὸ ἐξέχον, ἐστιν, ἐφ' ᾧ ἐποχοῦνται οἱ σταυρούμενοι. *Cf.* Iren.
Adv. Hær. ii. 36. § 2.   [7] Lips. *De Cruc.* II. ix.

[8] Orig. *In Matth. Comm. Ser.* § 140; Lips. *De Cruc.* II. xii.

[9] So Iren. *l.c. Cf.* Lips. *De Cruc.* I. x. The title was probably fixed to the
projection of the upright.

[10] *Bab. Sanhedr.* 43. 1: "Prodeunti ad supplicium capitis potum dederunt,
granum thuris in poculo vini, ut turbaretur intellectus ejus; sicut dicitur Prov.
xxxi. 6. Traditio est fæminas generosas Hierosolymitanas hoc e spontaneo sumptu
suo exhibuisse." Various drugs were used: frankincense, laudanum, myrrh, resin,

nails were driven through His hands, it was presented to Jesus. Parched with thirst He put it to His lips, but, as soon as He tasted it, He recognised what it was and refused to drink it. It was not that He disdained relief, as though there were virtue in mere suffering ; neither was it simply that He would fain meet death with open eyes, like him who prayed that he might " render up his soul to God unclouded." Was it not rather that He still had work to do? With his parting breath He would speak pardon to sinners and glorify the Father.

"Father,
forgive
them."
Cf. John
xix. 23.

Four soldiers were told off to do the brutal work of crucifixion. It was usual for the victims of that dreadful doom, frenzied with pain, to shriek, entreat, curse, and spit at the spectators ;[1] but neither moan nor malediction escaped the lips of Jesus. As He lay in agony, He spoke, and His words were a prayer—not an entreaty to His executioners to spare Him but a supplication to God that they might be forgiven the wrong which they were doing. " Father," He cried, " forgive them ; for they know not what they are doing." [2] Those rude soldiers had no acquaintance with Jesus. In their eyes He was merely a rebel Jew who had earned his doom. When they stripped Him and nailed Him to the cross, they were simply obeying orders. It was bloody work ; but they were accustomed to it, and they would do it without a qualm. It was indeed the foulest crime ever perpetrated on the earth, but they knew not what they were doing.

The divi-
sion of
Jesus'
garments.

Hoisting the transom on the upright, they fastened His feet, not nailing them but only tying them with cords.[3] They fixed above His head the board with Pilate's mocking

---

saffron, mastich. *Cf.* Wetstein on Mk. xv. 23. Mk.'s ἐσμυρνισμένον οἶνον is in entire agreement with Mt.'s οἶνον (ὄξος is a copyist's assimilation to Ps. lxix. 21) μετὰ χολῆς μεμιγμένον, since χολή, " wormwood " (*cf.* Prov. v. 4 ; Lam. iii. 15) was used of any bitter draught.

[1] Cic. *In Verr.* i. 3 ; v. 46 ; *Pro Cluent.* 66 ; Jos. *De Bell. Jud.* iv. 6. § 1 ; Sen. *De Vit. Beat.* § 19.

[2] *Cf.* Introd. § 6.

[3] D. Smith is mistaken here. The fact that Jesus' feet were also nailed to the cross is suggested strongly in Lk. xxiv. 39, *cf.* Jn. xx. 25. Archaeological proof that also the feet of crucified victims were nailed to the cross is supplied in Paul L. Maier, *First Easter* (Harper & Row, 1973), pp. 78 ff., where a spike is photographed in first-century heel bones. —ED.

THE CRUCIFIXION

497

inscription, that all who passed along the highway might read it and learn who He was and wherefore He was hanging there. Then, their task being ended, they took His raiment and divided the spoil. There were four of them, and one got His cloak, another His girdle, the third His sandals, and the fourth His turban. There remained still His under-garment, the tunic. They would naturally have torn it into four pieces, but there was a peculiarity about it which caught their eyes and arrested their hands. It was seamless, woven all in one piece. It was thus that the tunics of the Galilean peasantry were fashioned, and it is said by ancient tradition that this tunic of Jesus had been woven by Mary for the Son of her love.[1] It was a poor man's tunic, and no Jew would have regarded it; but it was a novelty to the soldiers. They had never seen the like, and, loath to rend it, they agreed to cast lots for it, all unconsciously fulfilling the Scripture: "They parted My garments among themselves, and for My vesture they cast lots." Ps. xxii. 18.

Meanwhile Jesus was hanging in agony. The brigands Mockery. also had been crucified, and were hanging on either hand, but it was the central cross that drew every eye. The High Priests had gathered round it, exulting in the success of their machinations, and they wagged their heads at Him, and taunted Him, abetted by the unthinking rabble. Gibe after gibe was flung at the meek Sufferer. "Ah, thou that pullest down the Sanctuary and buildest it in three days! Save thyself by coming down from the cross." "Others he saved; himself he cannot save." "He is King of Israel! Let him come down now from the cross, and we will believe on him." "He hath set his trust on God: let Him rescue him now, if He desireth him; for he said: 'I am God's Son.'" The soldiers were seated hard by, guarding the crosses in case a rescue should be attempted.[2] They had with them a beaker of their *posca* or vinegar-water, the drink Cf. 2 Kings xix. 21; Pss. xxii. 8, cix. 25; Lam. ii. 15. Mt. xxvii 36. John xix. 29

---

[1] Isidor. Pelus. *Ep.* i. 74; Chrysost. *In Joan.* lxxxiv. Euth. Zig. Thus baseless is the idea that the "seamless tunic" is a Johannine fiction investing Jesus with symbolic dignity by assigning Him a garment like the High Priest's (*cf.* Jos. *Ant.* iii. 7. § 4) or like that of Philo's Divine Word (*De Profug.*, ed. Pfeiffer, iv. pp. 270 *sq.*).

[2] Petron. *Sat.*: "Cruciarii unius parentes ut viderunt noctu laxatam custodiam, detraxere pendentem." *Cf.* Lips. *De Cruc.* II. xvi.

of slaves and of soldiers on duty,[1] and, heated by their toil, they had filled their cups. As they drank, they heard the priests and the rabble deriding " the King," and, approaching the cross, they held up their cups and drank jestingly to His Majesty.

Lk. xxiii. 36-7.

The penitent brigand.

Nor were these the only voices that assailed the ears of Jesus. In the frenzy of their agony the two brigands, thinking perhaps to propitiate their executioners and win them to mercy, joined in the chorus and reviled their fellow-sufferer. Presently, however, one of them relented. It may be that he had never seen Jesus before that dreadful day, but rumours of the wondrous Prophet must have reached the outlaw in his mountain-fastness; and he had heard the prayer: " Father, forgive them," and marked the majesty of that meek face. His soul bowed in awe, and he ceased from his reviling.[2] His callous comrade continued his blasphemies. " Art thou not the Messiah?" he cried. " Save thyself and us." The taunt moved the penitent to remonstrance. " Dost thou not even fear God," he said, " forasmuch as thou art in the same condemnation? And we justly, for we are receiving what our deeds deserve; but this man did nothing amiss." Then he prayed: " Jesus, remember me when Thou comest into Thy Kingdom." It was a strangely mingled prayer, combining ignorance and faith. He knew only that Jesus claimed to be the Messiah, the King of the Jews: it was written on the board above His head. But he recognised in that gracious and kingly Sufferer One who was worthy of all trust and reverence; and his dark and groping faith won an instant and generous response. " Verily I tell thee," said Jesus, employing with compassionate condescension Jewish language such as that poor dark soul could understand, and granting him a boon beyond his expectation, " to-day thou shalt be with Me in Paradise."[3] There is a legend that these

[1] Æl. Spart. Hadr. 10: " Jussit vinum in expeditione neminem bibere sed aceto universos esse contentos." Lightfoot and Wetstein on Mt. xxvii. 34. Gibbon, Decl. and Fall, chap. xxiv: " The vigilant humanity of Julian had embarked a very large magazine of vinegar and biscuit for the use of the soldiers, but he prohibited the indulgence of wine."

[2] Thus, not unreasonably, is the apparent discrepancy between Mt. xxvii. 44 =Mk. xv. 32 and Lk. xxiii. 39-43 explained by Orig., Jer., Chrysost. (Serm. lxii in Paralyt. Demiss. per Tect.).

[3] Cf. Lightfoot and Wetstein.

two brigands were named Titus and Dumachus[1] and met the Holy Family fleeing from King Herod into Egypt. Dumachus would have plundered them, but Titus interposed. He saw the wondrous Infant in His mother's arms and, taking Him lovingly in his own, he said : " O blessed Child ! if ever a day shall come for having mercy on me, then remember me and do not forget this day."

By this time John had arrived on the scene, conducting Mary and three others with her,[2] her sister Salome, Mary the wife of Clopas, and Mary Magdalene. Reckless in their grief, they had pressed close to the Cross. Solicitude for His widowed mother was the one earthly care of Jesus in the hour of death. She had indeed other sons who might have tended her ; but they were unbelievers as yet and would have proved sorry comforters. He would not leave her to them. John was His cousin after the flesh and the best beloved of His disciples. He was worthy of the sacred charge, and Jesus bequeathed it to him as a precious legacy.[3] " Woman," He said to Mary, " see ! thy son. See !" He said to John, " thy mother." And right loyally did the disciple guard his trust. For the rest of her life Mary dwelt in his house compassed with affection and honour ; and it would be a source of constant wonder and gratitude to him that he was privileged to stand thus in his Lord's room, like Simon of Cyrene, though in a far more sacred way, the *vicarius Christi*. He accepted the trust in reverent silence. As for Mary, it would seem that she was overcome by emotion.

Jesus' bequest to John. [marginal note]

> " O quam tristis et afflicta
> Fuit illa benedicta
> Mater Unigeniti !
> Quæ mœrebat et dolebat
> Et tremebat, cum videbat
> Nati pœnas inclyti."

John tenderly conveyed her from the scene of horror. " From that hour the disciple took her to his own home." [4]

It was now mid-day, and Jesus had hung for three hours *Darkness at noon.* [marginal note]

---

[1] Otherwise Dysmas and Gestas. *Ev. Nicod.* ix-x ; *Ev. Infant. Arab.* xxiii; "Aug." *De Vit. Erem.* § 48.   [2] *Cf.* p. 147, n. 2.

[3] *Cf.* Luc. *Toxar.* § 22 : the bequest of Eudamidas.

[4] His departure explains his silence regarding the darkness and the Lord's cry of desolation.

John xviii. on the Cross.   The unusual cold during the previous night
18 had betokened a disturbance of the atmospheric conditions,
and the storm now broke.   It was high noon, yet darkness
overspread the earth.[1]   It frequently happens thus in Syria
when the sirocco comes up from the desert; and, though the
phenomenon generally passes quietly, it is sometimes the
harbinger of an earthquake.   A traveller has thus described
the scene which preluded an earthquake at Beirut on 1st
Jan. 1837.   It was "a quiet Sabbath evening.   A pale,
smoky haze obscured the sun, and threw an air of sadness
over the closing day, and a lifeless and oppressive calm had
settled down over the face of nature."[2]   It was such a
darkness that overspread the earth on that dread noon-day.
Though incommoded by the attendant heat,[3] the spectators
would feel no apprehension.   It was, they would suppose,
an entirely natural phenomenon, and it would presently disappear.   It was indeed a natural phenomenon, yet the hand
of God was in it.   It was as though creation were mourning
for her Lord and the sun, loathing the impious spectacle, had
veiled his face.   In after days men recognised a portentous
significance in those signs of earth and sky, and added other
marvels, telling, for instance, that, when Jesus died, every
green leaf in the world withered.   It is no slight evidence of
the sobriety and veracity of the Evangelists that they simply
and briefly recount what befell, neither calling it a miracle
nor investing it with a judicial significance.

The dere-   The darkness had continued some three hours when
liction.
Ps. xxii. 1. suddenly a cry was heard from the Cross: "My God, My
God, why hast Thou forsaken Me?"   It was a sentence from
that wondrous Psalm which, as an ancient Father[4] said, "contains the whole Passion of Christ."   It is not given to blind
and feeble man to know what passed in the Redeemer's soul
at that dread season and wrung from His holy lips that exceeding bitter cry.   The Evangelists make no attempt to draw

---

[1] It was not an eclipse, since it was the season of full moon. Lk.'s τοῦ ἡλίου
ἐκλείποντος need mean nothing more than "the sun's light failing." T. R. has
καὶ ἐσκοτίσθη ὁ ἥλιος, which Orig. (*In Matth. Comm. Ser.* § 134) accepts, suggesting
that enemies of the Church had changed it to τοῦ ἡλ. ἐκλ. in order to discredit the
Gospel by introducing an impossible phenomenon.

[2] Thomson, *Land and Book*, chap. xix.

[3] *Ibid.* chap. xxxv.   [4] Tert. *Adv. Marc.* iii. § 19.

the veil aside, and it may well become us to refrain from curious enquiry and rather bow our heads in awe. And, if Jesus was indeed the Eternal Son of God, "putting away sin by the sacrifice of Himself," then the confession that here we are face to face with an inscrutable mystery is no weak evasion but a most reasonable recognition of our human limitations. Yet may we, without irreverence, seek to enter some little way into the mystery, if only that we may realise its greatness and be delivered from narrow thoughts regarding it.

There are two opinions which should be dismissed at the outset. One is that the desolation of our Blessed Lord was due to naught else than human weakness. His soul was clouded by the sore anguish of His flesh and spirit. It seemed, in view of all that had come upon Him, as though God had abandoned Him and given Him over to the will of His enemies ; and His faith, hitherto victorious, gave way. This sort of explanation is utterly insufficient. Is it credible that, after enduring with steadfast fortitude the sharpest pangs, He should have faltered when the bitterness of death was well-nigh past ? In truth it was nothing that man inflicted or that man may fully understand that so terribly shook His soul and wrung that cry of desolation from His lips. It was a visitation of God. And equally false is the opposite opinion that in that awful hour Jesus was enduring the wrath of God in the room of sinners. God was not angry with His Beloved Son as He hung upon the Cross, obedient even unto death, consummating by that supreme act of self-devotion the work which had been given Him to do. On the contrary, He was never so dear to God, never so manifestly the Beloved Son in whom the Father was well pleased.[1]

Nevertheless His desolation was a visitation of God, and He suffered it as the bearer of sin. At the outset of His ministry He had accepted as His vocation the Baptist's announcement : "Behold, the Lamb of God that taketh away the sin of the world," and throughout its course the burden of the world's sin had been lying on Him, but He knew that on the Cross He would feel the uttermost stress of that awful load and drain the last dregs of the bitter cup which He had accepted from the Father's hand. And, as the hour approached,

Two erroneous opinions.

The dereliction a visitation of God.

---

[1] *Cf.* Calv. *Instit.* ii. 16. § 11.

the darkness had gathered about His soul. "The cords of death had compassed Him, and the pains of the grave had gat hold upon Him: He had found trouble and sorrow." And now the dread hour had come.

A withholding of the Father's ministration.

Gal. iii. 13. Hebr. ii. 18.

A gleam of light is cast upon the dark mystery by the apostolic doctrine that it was needful for Jesus, in order that He might redeem us, to identify Himself with us in our misery and make it all His own. "Christ redeemed us from the curse of the Law, having become a curse for us." "In that He hath Himself suffered being tempted, He is able to succour them that are tempted." Had He, in going down into the Dark Valley, been cheered by the presence of God and sustained by His good hand, He had then been exempted from the most awful of human experiences, and His sympathy would have failed us just where it is most needed. And therefore, that He might be identified with us at all points and know the worst that can befall us, He was forsaken by God at that supreme crisis. It was not that God was angry with Him and poured upon His innocent head the wrath which is our due. On the contrary, He never pleased the Father so well as in that hour when He hung, a willing Victim, on the Cross. It needed not the Father's displeasure that He might lose the sense of the Father's presence. All the days of His flesh He depended on the Father. His wisdom was not His own, but the Father's gift; His knowledge of the Father's will was the Father's revelation; His works were wrought by the Father's co-operation. "He went about doing good and healing all that were under the tyranny of the Devil, *because God was with Him.*" Had the Father at any moment refrained from His ministration and left Him alone, Jesus had been weak and blind as any of the children of men. And thus it may be dimly perceived how it came to pass that He was forsaken on the Cross. That He might be one with us in our sorest strait, the Father ceased for a space to visit the soul of His Beloved Son with His communion. It had been the comfort of Jesus when the Eleven forsook Him and fled, that He was not alone, because the Father was with Him; but now He was bereft of that support. "My God, My God," He cried astonied, "why hast Thou forsaken Me?"

John vii. 16; v. 20; v. 30; vi. 37; xiv. 10.

Acts x. 38.

John xvi. 32.

Jesus spoke the words in Hebrew as they were written by "I thirst."
the Psalmist: *Eli, Eli lama azabhtani?*[1] The cry would
be understood by the Jews, but it fell strangely on the ears of
the soldiers.[2] They caught the word *Eli* and took it for
Elias. They knew nothing about the ancient prophet; but
Elias was an ordinary Jewish name, and they supposed that
Jesus was calling for some friend. The sirocco's sultry breath
aggravated the anguish of the fevered Sufferer, and, as they
were debating what His cry might mean, He moaned : " I
thirst." One of them took pity on Him, and, running to the
beaker of *posca*, dipped a sponge-stopper in the liquor and,
putting it on the end of a reed, held it up to His parched
lips.[3] " Hold ! "[4] cried his comrades. " Let us see if Elias
is coming to take Him down."[5] But the man persevered in
his ministry of mercy, and Jesus accepted it.

The end had come, and He hailed it exultantly. As His **The death**
eyes closed upon the scene of His mortal anguish, the dark- **of Jesus.**
ness which had enwrapped His soul, melted away and He beheld God's face. " Father," He cried, employing the language
of another psalm but prefixing thereto that dear name which
no psalmist had ever used, " into Thy hands I commit My **Ps. xxxi. 5.**
Spirit." " He cried," says the Evangelist, " with a great
voice." It was a shout of triumph. His warfare was
accomplished. He had " finished transgression, and made an
end of sins, and made reconciliation for iniquity, and brought
in everlasting righteousness." He had perfected Love's
sacrifice and sealed with His heart's blood the new covenant
betwixt God and man. All the days of His flesh " the Son **Mt. viii. 20**
of Man had not where to lay down His head "; but at length **=Lk. ix.**
His work was done, and He entered into His rest. " He **58.**
said : ' It is finished,' and He laid down His head and handed **John xix.**
over His spirit." **30.**

His cry was still ringing in the ears of the astonished **The rend-**
ing of the
Veil.

---

[1] *Cf.* Dalman, *Words of Jesus*, p. 53.

[2] The actors in this scene are not Jews, else they would have understood the cry
of Jesus. *Cf.* Jerome, Euth. Zig.

[3] *Cf.* Aristoph. *Ach.* 439 : χυτρίδιον σπογγίῳ βεβυσμένον.

[4] ἄφες may be simply the sign of the imperative, like ἄς in Mod. Grk. ; *cf.* Mt.
vii. 4 = Lk. vi. 42. See Moulton's Winer, p. 356, n. 3 ; Moulton's *Gram. of N. T. Gk.*
i. p. 175. But to take it as an independent imperative is equally permissible on the
score of grammar and preferable in point of sense. *Cf.* Epict. IV. i. 79.

[5] So Mt. According to Mk. the offering of the *posca* was a piece of ribaldry.
But Jesus did not so regard it (John xix. 30).

spectators when, as though a shuddering had seized it, the earth trembled and shook. Syria is a volcanic region, and all down the course of history Palestine has experienced seismic disturbances. It was nothing strange or unprecedented that happened when an earthquake shook the Hill of Calvary. The last shock was well remembered. It had occurred in B.C. 31, when King Herod was engaged in military operations against the Arabians. About ten thousand of the people of Judæa had been buried beneath the ruins of their houses, and the army had escaped disaster only because it was encamped in the open.[1] It was a like convulsion that shook the land on this solemn day,[2] and, though less calamitous, it was nevertheless sufficiently severe. The close-built city suffered most, and there was one disaster which created a profound impression. The curiously wrought veil which separated the Holy Place from the Holy of Holies,[3] was rent in twain from top to bottom, laying open that sacred shrine which the High Priest alone might enter and only once every year on the Day of Atonement.[4] In the eyes of the disciples it was no accident. It was the stroke of God's hand, symbolically declaring what had been achieved by the Sacrifice on Calvary. "Having therefore, brethren, boldness to enter into the Holy Place by the blood of Jesus, by the way which He dedicated for us, a new and living way through the Veil, that is, His flesh, let us draw near with a true heart in full assurance of faith."

Hebr. ix. 7.

Hebr. x. 19-22.

The centurion's testimony. The death of Jesus and the attendant circumstances inspired the spectators with wonderment and awe, especially

---

[1] Jos. *Ant.* xv. 5. § 2.

[2] Mt. xxvii. 51b-3, where alone the earthquake is expressly mentioned, is an addition to the Evangelic Tradition, explanatory of Mt. xxvii. 51a=Mk. xv. 38 = Lk. xxiii. 45b. *Ev. Petr.* § 6 has ἡ γῆ πᾶσα ἐσείσθη, but omits the ensuing marvels which unquestionably belong to the Synoptic cycle of unhistorical tradition. *Cf.* Introd. § 20.

[3] Jos. *De Bell. Jud.* v. 5. § 4.

[4] There is a singular story in the Talmud that forty years before the destruction of Jerusalem, *i.e.* about the time of the Crucifixion, the doors of the Temple opened of their own accord, a premonition of the approaching catastrophe. See Lightfoot, ii. p. 641. According to the *Gospel of the Hebrews* it was the lintel of the Temple that was shattered by the earthquake. *Cf.* Jer. on Mt. xxvii. 51. Nestle regards this as the true account, the Synoptic καταπέτασμα being due to a confusion of כַּפְתּוֹר, *lintel*, with פָּרֹכֶת, *curtain*. But see Dalman, *Words of Jesus*, p. 56.

the centurion who had command of the soldiers. It would seem that he had been present at the trial in the Prætorium. He had heard Pilate's repeated assertion of the prisoner's innocence, and had witnessed his perturbation on learning that He claimed to be "God's Son." It all came back to him at that dread crisis. "Indeed," he exclaimed, "this man *was* 'righteous'; truly he *was* 'God's Son.'" The multitude also, who had thronged forth to Calvary with no animosity against Jesus but from mere curiosity to witness the spectacle of a crucifixion, were deeply affected. Scared by the earthquake and stricken with awe, they took themselves off and wended their way to the city, beating their breasts.

Lk. xxiii.
47 ; Mt.
xxvii. 54=
Mk. xv. 39.

It was three o'clock when Jesus died, and the day was fast declining toward Sabbath-eve. According to Roman custom it was usual for the crucified, unless mercifully despatched, to hang until they perished slowly of loss of blood and famine or were torn in pieces by beasts and birds of prey ;[1] but it was contrary to the Jewish law that they should be left hanging overnight,[2] and the offence would in this instance have been the greater inasmuch as the next day was the paschal Sabbath. Pilate therefore, at the request of the rulers, had ordered that the three victims should be despatched and taken down from their crosses at the close of day. The soldiers administered the *coup de grace* in the customary way by shattering blows with a heavy mallet.[3] They performed the brutal operation on the two brigands, but, when they came to Jesus and found that He was already dead, they held their hands. One of them, however, whom tradition names Longinus,[4] to make sure that He was really dead, drove his spear into His side. And thereupon a strange thing happened. As the spear was withdrawn, it was followed by a gush of blood and water.

The *cruri-
fragium.*

Deut. xxi.
23.

St John alone recounts the incident, and it was evidently wholly inexplicable to him. He could only asseverate solemnly that he had beheld it with his own eyes. Yet it is

The blood
and the
water.

---

[1] Lips. *De Cruc.* II. xii-xiii.

[2] *Cf.* Lightfoot on Mt. xxvii. 58.

[3] On the *crurifragium*, σκελοκοπία see Lips. *De Cruc.* II. xiv ; Wetstein on John xix. 21.

[4] *Ev. Nicod.* xvi. *Cf.* "Aug." *Man.* xxiii : "Longinus aperuit mihi latus lancea, et ego intravi, et ibi requiesco securus." Longinus is perhaps derived from λόγχη, *spear.*

in no wise incredible ; and medical science has confirmed the
Evangelist's testimony, and has so explained the phenomenon
that it sheds light upon the death of our Blessed Lord and
reveals somewhat of the anguish of His Passion.[1]   Jesus
died literally of a broken heart—of "agony of mind, producing rupture of the heart."   In that awful hour when He
was forsaken by the Father, His heart swelled with grief
until it burst, and then the blood was "effused into the
distended sac of the pericardium, and afterwards separated, as
is usual with *extravasated* blood, into these two parts, viz.,
(1) crassamentum or red clot, and (2) watery serum."   When
the distended sac was pierced from beneath, it discharged
"its sanguineous contents in the form of red clots of blood
and a stream of watery serum, exactly corresponding to the
description given in the sacred narrative, 'and forthwith came
there out blood and water.'"[2]

Joseph's petition to Pilate. Lk. xxiii. 49.

Among the acquaintance of Jesus who watched the crucifixion from afar in company with the faithful women, was
a Sanhedrist named Joseph, belonging to Arimathæa, the
ancient Ramathaim-Zophim.[3]   He was a devout Israelite, one
"who was expecting the Kingdom of God"; and, like his
colleague Nicodemus, he was at heart a disciple, but "a secret
one for fear of the Jews."   He had not supported the Sanhedrin's sentence of condemnation that morning, but neither
had he opposed it.   Probably he had adopted the prudent
course of absenting himself from the meeting.   At length,
when it was too late, he had realised how ill a part he had
played ;   and   there he stood, with grief and shame in his
heart, surveying the tragedy which he had done nothing to
avert.   It was impossible to undo the past, but he resolved
forthwith to declare himself on the side of Jesus and make
such amends as he could.   He knew what would be done with
the bodies of the victims.   They would be taken down and flung
out as refuse to be devoured by pariah dogs and carrion birds;[4]
and he determined that at least the poor boon of an honour-

[1] *Cf. Treatise on the Physical Cause of the Death of Christ,* by William Stroud, M.D.

[2] Prof. J. Y. Simpson in Append. to Hanna's *Last Day of our Lord's Passion. Cf.* Calv. on John xix. 34.   Orig. (*C. Cels.* ii. 36), Euth. Zig. regard it as a miracle.

[3] Eus. and Jer.   [4] *Cf.* Lightfoot on Mt. xxvii. 58.

able burial should be accorded to Jesus. It was common for the friends of the crucified to purchase their bodies and inter them decently,[1] and Joseph was rich and could easily pay the price. " He plucked up courage and went in unto Pilate and asked for the body of Jesus." The awe wherewith Jesus had inspired him, still oppressed the soul of the governor. It surprised him that Jesus had died so soon, and on communicating with the centurion and learning from him all that had occurred, he was the more troubled, and evinced his agitation in a striking manner. The unhappy procurator had earned himself an evil reputation for greed of gold, and, when he was impeached before the Emperor, the taking of bribes was one of the chief counts in the indictment[2]; yet such was his agitation that he refused the price which Joseph offered, and made him a free gift of the body of Jesus.[3]

Joseph hastened back to Calvary, and there joined his colleague Nicodemus, his partner in remorse as he had been his partner in cowardice. Each bore his part in the mournful ministration. Together they took the mangled corpse down from the Cross and swathed it in linen cloths. Joseph had provided these, and he provided also a tomb. He had a garden hard by where he had hewn a tomb out of the rock for his own last resting-place ; and he gave it up to Jesus. It was the custom of the Jews to embalm their dead with fragrant spices, and this office Nicodemus took upon him. With lavish profuseness he had brought a hundred pounds' weight of myrrh and aloes, atoning for his stinted loyalty by giving Jesus a kingly burial.

The burial of Jesus.

Cf. 2 Chron. xvi. 14.

Thus they laid the Lord to rest. And the women watched them as they wrought their sad office, observing where they laid Him.

Mt. xxvii. 61=Mk. xv. 47= Lk. xxiii 55-6.

---

[1] *Cf.* Wetstein on Mk. xv. 45.

[2] Schurer, H. J. P. I. ii. p. 83. (By way of exception, D. Smith has misused his source here, as Schurer reports only *legends* of Pilate with such claims. No early source states that Pilate had any trial before the Roman emperor, or that he was accused of taking bribes as part of the indictment. —ED.)

[3] Mk. xv. 45; *cf.* Wetstein.

John xx. 1-
18 (Mt.
xxviii. 1-10
=Mk. xvi.
1-8=Lk.
xxiv. 1-11
[12]) ; Lk.
xxiv. 13-35;
John xx.
19-25 (Lk.
xxiv. 36-
43) ; John
xx. 26-31 ;
John xxi.
(Mt. xxviii.
16-20);Acts
i. 3-12 (Lk.
xxiv. 44-
53); 1 Cor.
xv. 4-8 ;
Acts ix. 1-9
=xxii. 6-11
=xxvi. 12-
20.

CHAPTER L

THE RESURRECTION

" But now Thou art in the Shadowless Land,
  Behind the light of the setting Sun ;
And the worst is forgotten which Evil planned,
  And the best which Love's glory could win is won."
                              SIR EDWIN ARNOLD.

Despair of the disciples.

THE death of Jesus seemed to His disciples a heavy and irretrievable disaster. They had deemed Him the Messiah, and, despite His repeated and emphatic protests, they had clung with pathetic tenacity to their Jewish ideal and expected confidently that He would manifest Himself to the world in regal splendour, claim the throne of His father David, and reign in Jerusalem over an emancipated and regenerate Israel. The Crucifixion had dispelled their dream. It was not only a heavy bereavement but a cruel disenchantment. It had put them to shame. They stood convicted in the eyes of the nation and in their own as the foolish dupes of a preposterous delusion ; and it seemed that nothing remained for them but to creep back to their old homes and, amid the derision of their acquaintance, resume the occupations which they had abandoned in quest of a Kingdom. They had fled panic-stricken when their Master was arrested, and their first impulse was doubtless to get them back to Galilee and put the length of the land betwixt themselves and the truculent rulers ; but presently they changed their purpose. They repented of their cowardice and, returning to the neighbourhood of Jerusalem, lurked there in concealment. The Sabbath-eve was closing in when the Lord was laid to rest in Joseph's garden, and that Sabbath was a great day, being the paschal Sabbath ; but they kept close and took no part in its solemnities.

The empty Sepulchre.

For three days after the burial of the dead the Jews were wont to visit the sepulchre to see if haply the soul had returned to its tenement of clay.[1]   None of the Eleven thought of visiting the Sepulchre of Jesus.   They durst not.   It had been madness to expose themselves to the fury of the triumphant rulers.   But there was one heart in which love had conquered fear.   In her home at Bethany Mary Magdalene remained inactive, according to the commandment, until the Sabbath was past ; and then, too eager to wait for day-light and glad perhaps of the covert of the darkness, she repaired to the garden on the slope of Olivet, accompanied by others of the women.[2]   To their surprise they found that the heavy slab of stone which closed the cavern's entrance, had been removed. It must have been done by strong hands from without, and they concluded that the body had been carried off and deposited elsewhere.   Knowing the retreat of Peter and John, Mary ran thither and told them her discovery and her surmise.   They hurried wondering to the Sepulchre ; and John, being the younger and the nimbler, outstripped his comrade and was the first to arrive.   Passing through the open entrance, he found himself on a floor skirted on either hand by an excavation four cubits deep where the bodies were laid in niches ;[3] and, peering down at the place where the Lord's body should have been, he saw the cerements lying loose.   He refrained from descending and making a closer inspection, whether because he dreaded pollution or because he saw plainly enough that the body was gone.[4]   As he stooped and gazed, Peter broke into the Sepulchre after him, and with characteristic impetuosity leaped down and examined the grave.   It was indeed empty, but its condition was puzzling.   If the body had been stolen, the marauders would have taken it away in its cerements ; but these were lying flat as though the body had evaporated, and the napkin which had been bound about His head, covering His face, was lying *Cf.* John xi apart from the linen cloths where His head had rested, still [44.] retaining its fold.   It had not collapsed when His head was withdrawn.[5]   Prompted perhaps by an astonished exclamation from his companion, John descended and saw how matters

[1] *Cf.* p. 369.   [2] *Cf.* Introd. § 19, 1.
[3] Lightfoot, ii. p. 240.   Latham (*Risen Master*, pp. 33-5, Note A) gives a different representation.
[4] Wetstein: "Ne pollueretur.   Num. xix. 16."   Euth. Zig. : φρίξας ἢ ἀρκεσθείς.
[5] *Cf.* Latham, *Risen Master.*

stood. The wondrous truth dawned upon him : Jesus had risen. It should have been no surprise ; the evidence of the vacant grave and the empty cerements should have been unnecessary ; but "not yet," he confesses with an accent of shame, "did they know the Scripture, that He must rise from the dead."

Appearance to Mary. The two disciples quitted the Sepulchre and returned home, leaving Mary weeping by the entrance. Presently she entered and peered down at the grave. To her amazement it was no longer untenanted. Two angels were there, one at the head and the other at the feet where the Lord's body had lain. "Woman," they said, "why art thou weeping ? " "They have taken away my Lord," she sobbed, "and I know not where they have put Him." Did some look or gesture of the angels apprise her that one had entered behind her ?[1] She looked round and beheld one standing there. It was Jesus, but she did not recognise Him. "Woman," He asked, "why art thou weeping ? Whom art thou seeking ? " She supposed that it was the gardener charging her with trespass, and the idea occurred to her that perhaps it was he that had removed the body, lest his plots should be trampled by visitors to the Sepulchre.[2] "Sir," she cried, "if thou didst carry Him off, tell me where thou didst put Him, and I will take Him away." "Mary!" He said, and that was enough. "Rabbûni!"[3] she cried, and turned herself about. "Love," says St Bernard, "knows no reverence," and, flinging herself at His feet, she would have embraced them and covered them with kisses. She thought that He had been restored to her as of old and that their former intercourse would straightway be resumed. Cf. Lk. vii. 39. "Cling not to Me," He said, gently repulsing her ; "for I have not yet ascended unto the Father ; but go unto My brethren and tell them : 'I ascend unto My Father and your Father, and My God and your God.'"[4]

---

[1] Chrysost. *In Joan.* lxxxv : ἐμοὶ δοκεῖ ταῦτα λεγούσης αὐτῆς ἄφνω φανεὶς ὁ Χριστὸς ὄπισθεν αὐτῆς ἐκπλῆξαι τοὺς ἀγγέλους.

[2] It is curious that this is one of the theories whereby the Jews sought to explain away the Resurrection. *Cf.* Tert. *De Spect.* § 30. Rénan approves the theory.

[3] *Cf.* p. 383.

[4] Aug. *In Joan. Ev. Tract.* cxxi. § 3 : "Non ait, Patrem nostrum : aliter ergo meum, aliter vestrum ; natura meum, gratia vestrum."

That afternoon two disciples were journeying to Emmaus, Appear-
a village some seven or eight miles from Jerusalem.[1] One of ance at
them was called Cleopas, and the name of his companion is Emmaus.
unrecorded.[2] They were not apostles. They belonged to the
rank and file of the Lord's followers, and they were departing
from Jerusalem in deep dejection, believing that all was over.
They had heard of the strange events of the morning : how
Peter and John had found the Sepulchre empty, and how
some of the women had seen a vision of angels who said that
Jesus lived. Of His appearance to Mary, however, they
had heard nothing, else they would hardly have left
Jerusalem.

It was all very bewildering, and, as they journeyed, they On the
were debating what it might mean. They were men of diverse road.
temperaments, Cleopas being, like Judas the Twin, prone to
despond, whereas his companion was of a sanguine turn ; and
a somewhat heated controversy arose betwixt them. In the
midst thereof a stranger joined them. It was Jesus, but they
did not know Him. " Their eyes were holden that they should
not recognise Him." He accosted them : " What are these
arguments which ye are bandying one with another as ye
walk ? " Ashamed that their quarrel had been overheard,
they stood with downcast faces.[3] The gloomy Cleopas
answered, not without petulance, perhaps resenting the intrusion : " Art thou sojourning all alone at Jerusalem that
thou knowest not the things that have been done therein
during these days ? " " What manner of things ? " asked the
stranger. " The things about Jesus the Nazarene," they
replied together, " who proved a prophet mighty in work
and word before God and all the people, and how the High

[1] Probably *El-Khamasa*, S.W. of Jerusalem. *Cf.* Henderson, *Palestine*, § 118.
Jerome identifies the village with Emmaus (*Amwas*), 160 stadia W.N.W. of
Jerusalem, known later as Nicopolis ; and for ἑξήκοντα some MSS., including א,
read ἑκατὸν ἑξήκοντα. But this Emmaus was more than a "village," nor could the two
disciples have travelled back to Jerusalem 22 miles that same night. Lk.'s Emmaus
is mentioned by Josephus : *De Bell. Jud.* vii. 6. § 6. Emmaus = *Hammath*, "hot
springs." There was a third town of this name near Tiberias, famed for its baths.
Some Old Lat. MSS. mistake Emmaus for the name of the companion of Cleopas.
Cf. Expos. Times, June, 1902, pp. 429-30.
[2] Various conjectures : (1) Simon (Orig.). Hence the *v.l.* λέγοντες in *v.* 34.
(2) Luke (Theophyl.). *Cf.* Carr in *Expos.*, Feb. 1904. Lk., however, on his own
showing, had never seen Jesus (i. 2). (3) Nathanael (Epiphan.).
[3] Reading in *v.* 17 καὶ ἐστάθησαν σκυθρωποί.

Priests and our rulers handed Him over for sentence of death and crucified Him." "And," sighed Cleopas, "we were hoping that it was He that should redeem Israel ; but, to crown all, this is the third day since these things were done."[1] "Yes," broke in the other, who thought there might still be hope, "but some women of our number amazed us. They went early to the Sepulchre, and they did not find His body and came saying that they had actually seen a vision of angels. who said that He lived. And some of our company went away to the Sepulchre and found it even as the women said." "But Him," added the incredulous Cleopas, "they did not see." "Ye foolish men," exclaimed Jesus, 'and slow of heart to put your trust on all that the Prophets spoke ! Was it not necessary that the Messiah should suffer these things and enter into His glory ? " Then He quoted to them passage after passage of the Scriptures from Moses onward through the Prophets, showing how they had all been fulfilled by His Passion.

In the house. The two men listened with kindling hearts. At length they reached Emmaus, and Jesus made as though He would go further. "Lodge with us," they pled, loath to part with the wondrous stranger and fain to hear more ; "forasmuch as it is toward evening, and the day is now far spent." "Methinks," says St Bernard, "they perhaps accosted Him with plaints like these : 'Depart not, thou sweet one, O depart not from us ; but still of Jesus the Nazarene let thy voice sound in our ears. Speak, we entreat, of the joy of the Resurrection ; lodge with us, forasmuch as it is toward evening and the day is far spent, but we will keep night-vigils. For the day is not sufficient that our ears may be sated with hearing of sweet Jesus.'" He acceded to their importunities, and presently the table was spread. He was the guest, yet He assumed the part of host and gave thanks ere they should eat. Such was the devout custom in every Jewish home,[2] but Jesus observed it after a peculiar fashion. "He took the loaf, and blessed it, and brake it, and handed it to them." Mt. xiv. 39 Thus had He done twice before : when He fed the five

---

[1] There was no longer any hope, he thought, not knowing the Lord's promise to the Twelve that He would rise " on the third day."

[2] Wetstein on Mt. xiv. 19. *Cf.* Rom. xiv. 6 ; 1 Cor. x. 30 ; 1 Tim. iv. 3.

thousand in the wilderness, and when He instituted the
Sacrament of the Supper in the Upper Room. Cleopas and his
companion ·had not been present at the Supper, but they may
have witnessed the miracle. Perhaps, however, there was no
particular reminiscence. None ever prayed like Jesus, and
His prayer revealed Him : " He was recognised by them in
the breaking of the loaf." [1] Ere they could accost Him, He
was gone : " He vanished out of their sight." They understood all now. " Was not our heart burning [2] within us," they
cried, " as He was talking to us on the road, as He was
opening to us the Scriptures ? "

=Mk. vi.
41=Lk. ix.
16=John
vi. 11 ; Mt
xxvi. 26
=Mk. xiv.
22=Lk.
xxii. 19.

Forthwith they arose and returned to Jerusalem. On
their arrival they found that much had happened since their
departure. The Apostles were no longer dispersed here and
there, dismayed and despairing. With certain of their
associates they had assembled in a lodging in the city ; and,
late as it was, they were engaged in animated and excited
converse. It was perilous for them to meet thus at the very
gates of the vengeful rulers, and for safety's sake they had
the doors fast shut. All the Apostles were there save Judas
the Twin, who had probably fled farthest in the panic of the
Arrest and had not yet returned. Cleopas and his comrade
found the meeting-place and gained admittance, but, ere they
could tell their story, they were greeted by a chorus of eager
voices : " The Lord hath indeed risen, and He hath appeared
to Simon ! " This appearance to Peter is mentioned also by
St Paul, but no account is anywhere given of it ; the reason
being, perhaps, that his interview with the dear Master whom
he had so basely denied, was too sacred to divulge, and the
Apostle hid it away in his own heart.

At Jeru-
salem.

Appear-
ance to
Simon
Peter.
1 Cor. xv.
5.

When at length they got their turn, the new-comers told
their story, enkindling fresh wonderment. Suddenly a hush
fell upon the company. *Jesus was present.* None had heard
Him knock, none had unbarred the door, none had seen Him
enter ; yet there He stood. He advanced into the midst of
the company with the accustomed greeting : " Peace to you ! "
They were fluttered and affrighted. They doubted whether

Appear-
ance to ten
of the
Apostles
and others.

---

[1] Euth. Zig. : ἰδόντων τὴν συνήθη καὶ γνώριμον εὐλογίαν τοῦ ἄρτου.

[2] There is an interesting Western reading, due probably to 2 Cor. iii. 14-6 : οὐχὶ
ἡ καρδ. ἦν ἡμῶν κεκαλυμμένη ; " was not our heart veiled ? "

it were indeed He, and were disposed to think that they beheld a spirit, until He gave them a token. He showed them His wounded hands and side ; and, when they saw those marks of His sore Passion, their doubt vanished, and they rejoiced. Did the Apostles, amid their rejoicing, recall His promise in the Upper Room : "I will see you again, and your heart shall rejoice, and your joy none shall take away from you"? Then He greeted them anew, and gave them another token. "As the Father hath commissioned Me," He said, "I also send you"; and, after the symbolic manner so congenial to the Jewish mind, He breathed upon them and said : "Receive the Holy Spirit. Whosesoever sins ye remit, they have been remitted unto them ; whosesoever ye retain, they have been retained." It was a renewal of their apostolic commission, and it would assure them that His purpose and their calling stood fast.

Judas the Twin was the only apostle who was absent on that memorable night ; and, when by and by he rejoined his brethren and was informed that they had seen the Lord, true to his character, he refused to believe it. They assured him that it was even so : they had seen the Lord, and He had showed them His wounds. But he would not be persuaded. "Unless," he asseverated, "I see in His hands the print of the nails, and put my finger into the print of the nails, and put my hand into His side, I will in no wise believe it." The following Sunday the disciples met again in their room with closed doors, and this time the Twin was with them. Once more Jesus appeared in their midst and greeted them. It was for the doubter's sake that He had come, like the shepherd seeking his one lost sheep. "Reach thy finger here," He said, "and see My hands ; and reach thy hand, and put it into My side ; and prove not unbelieving but believing." "My Lord and my God!" cried the Twin, leaping from the depth of despair to the very summit of faith. And Jesus answered gently : "Because thou hast seen Me, thou hast believed? Blessed are they that saw not and believed." Though addressed to one, it was a reproach to all the Apostles, since they had all been slow of heart to believe the Scripture's testimony and the Lord's reiterated declaration that He would rise from the dead on the

Marginal notes:
John xvi. 22.

Mt. xviii. 18.

Appearance to the Eleven.

third day. And it has a meaning for all time. "When," observes St Chrysostom, "one says now : ' Would that I had been in those days and seen Christ working wonders !' let him consider that ' blessed are they that saw not and believed.'"

The Risen Lord had much to say to His Apostles ere He should bid them farewell and go home to the Father ; and the hostile capital was no fitting scene for His manifesta- tions. Already in the Upper Room He had promised to meet them in Galilee ; and thither at His behest they repaired, betaking themselves apparently to their old abodes at Capernaum. There they waited for His appearing. It was necessary meanwhile that they should procure a livelihood ; and one evening, when seven of them were ˋgathered, perhaps in Peter's house,[1] Peter, always the leader and always impulsive, said suddenly : "I am off to fish." His companions were Judas the Twin, Nathanael the son of Talmai, James and John, and two others ; and they said : "We also are going with thee." Forthwith they went down to the beach and pushed off. All night they fished, but they caught nothing ; and, as morning broke, they spied one standing on the shore. It was Jesus, but they did not recognise Him. They were only about a hundred yards from the land, and He hailed them like a merchant who would do business with them :[2] "Lads, have ye caught any fish ?"[3] "No," they answered, and He called back : "Cast the net on the right side of the boat, and ye will have a take." Suppos- ing naturally that the stranger had skill in fisher-craft and had perhaps observed indications of a shoal,[4] they obeyed, and their net was so filled that they could not draw it. The token flashed home to John's quick mind, recalling the kindred wonder which he had witnessed in that very neighbourhood three years earlier, and which had determined himself and his brother and their partners, Peter and Andrew, to cast in their lot with Jesus. "It is the Lord!" he exclaimed to Peter ; and the latter, slower of understanding

Marginal notes:
Appear- ance by the Lake of Galilee.
Mt. xxvi. 32=Mk. xiv. 28.
Mt. xxviii. 16.
Lk. v. 1-11.

---

[1] *Cf.* John xxi. 3 : ἐξῆλθαν, "they went out of the house."

[2] Chrysost. *In Joan.* lxxxvi : τέως ἀνθρωπινώτερον διαλέγεται ὡς μέλλων τι ὠνεῖσθαι παρ' αὐτῶν.

[3] παιδία· *cf.* Euth. Zig. : ἔθος γὰρ τοὺς ἐργατικοὺς οὕτως ὀνομάζειν. προσφάγιον, like ὄψον, *something taken along with bread, especially fish. Cf.* Wetstein ; Moulton's *Gram. of N.T. Gk.* i. p. 170.   [4] *Cf.* Euth. Zig.

but prompter in action, girt about him his fisher's cloak [1] whereof he had disencumbered himself while at work, and, even as on that night when Jesus came walking over the

Mt. xiv. 28- waves, flung himself overboard in his haste and swam to the
31. land.[2] His comrades got into the small-boat [3] and rowed ashore, dragging the full net.

On landing they found that preparations had been made for a meal.   There was a loaf of bread, and a fire had been kindled and fish laid thereon to broil.   Jesus bade them fetch also some of the fish which they had caught, and Peter got into the small boat and drew the net ashore.   It was found to contain a hundred and fifty three large fish.[4]   It was a huge haul, and the wonder was that the net had stood the strain.   "Come and breakfast," said Jesus when all was ready ; and He blessed and distributed the bread and the fish in the old manner which they knew so well.[5]

Colloquy Jesus vouchsafed this manifestation of Himself to those
with Peter. seven disciples, who were probably all apostles, in order that, ere His departure, He might commune with them and counsel them concerning their mission.   As soon as the meal was ended, He addressed Himself to the task.   He accosted Peter, and He did what seems a very cruel thing.   He deliberately recalled the vain boast which the disciple had made in the Upper Room, and which he had so terribly belied in the courtyard of Annas a few hours later : "Though all shall stumble at Thee, I will never stumble."   Peter had bitterly repented of his unfaithfulness, and surely he had confessed it

Lk. xxiv. and been forgiven at that meeting with Jesus on the day of
34; 1 Cor. the Resurrection.   Yet here Jesus brings it up again and
xv. 5.

---

[1] ἐπενδύτης an upper-garment, ὑποδύτης an under-garment (Suid.). According to Euth. Zig. ἐπενδύτης was a sort of tunic without sleeves, reaching to the knees, worn by seamen.

[2] John xxi. 7 *Sin. Palimps.* : "He took his coat and girt it about his loins, and cast himself into the lake and was swimming, and came, for they were not far from the land."

[3] τῷ πλοιαρίῳ ἦλθον.

[4] The Fathers exercised their ingenuity to discover mystic meanings in the number. *Cf.* Aug. *In Joan. Ev. Tract.* cxxii. § 8.   Calv. sensibly remarks : "As regards the number of the fish, there is not any sublime mystery to be sought therein."

[5] John xxi. 13. *Sin. Palimps.* : "Jesus took the bread and the fish, and blessed them (literally, *blessed upon them*), and gave to them."

casts it in his face in presence of his comrades. "Simon, son of John,"[1] He said, "dost thou regard[2] Me more than these?" *Regard* was no name for the tenderness wherewith the heart of Peter was overflowing. "Yea, Lord," he answered humbly, "Thou knowest that I *love* Thee." "Feed My lambs," said Jesus. Then He repeated His question: "Simon, son of John, dost thou regard Me?" and Peter repeated his assurance: "Yea, Lord, Thou knowest that I *love* Thee." "Tend My sheep," said Jesus. A third time He put the question: "Simon, son of John, dost thou love Me?" He had accepted the correction, but this only grieved Peter the more. It seemed as though the Lord were now challenging not merely his regard but his love. Surely "those eyes of far perception" could see the overflowing passion of his heart. "Lord," he cried, "Thou knowest all things; Thou perceivest that I love Thee." "Feed My sheep," said Jesus.

Was it not very ungenerous, was it not very unlike Jesus, thus to cast up his sin to Peter, especially in the presence of the others? Nay, it would hardly seem to the latter that their comrade was singled out for reproach. Had they acquitted themselves better than he? He had indeed denied the Lord, but they had all alike proved faithless. They had all protested in the Upper Room that they would die with Jesus, and in Gethsemane they had all forsaken Him and fled. And in truth Peter had done better than any save John, inasmuch as he had presently rallied and followed the soldiers and their prisoner to the house of Annas. The reproach was addressed to him, but they would all take it home to themselves. And the purpose of Jesus was in no wise merely to upbraid them with their unfaithfulness but to show them how they might make amends for it. Did they protest with Peter that they loved Him? Then His answer was: "Feed My lambs; tend My sheep." As they had forsaken the Shepherd, let them lay down their lives for His

The purpose thereof.

[1] *Cf.* p. 262.

[2] For the distinction between ἀγαπᾶν, *diligere*, and φιλεῖν, *amare*, see Wetstein on John xi. 4; Trench, *N.T. Synon.* Following Erasm. and Grot. some allege that the terms are used here without distinction; *cf.* Cross in *Expos.*, Apr. 1893; Dods in *Expos. Gk. Test.* Certainly they are used interchangeably in John xiii. 23 and xx. 2, but the case is different when they stand in close collocation.

flock and thus attest at once their penitence and their love.[1]

1 Pet. v. 2-3. Nor was the charge forgotten. " Tend the flock of God that is among you," wrote St Peter by and by to his fellow-elders, " not of constraint but willingly, neither for filthy lucre but of a ready mind, neither as lording it over your charges but proving ensamples to the flock. And, when the Chief Shepherd is manifested, ye shall win the unwithering crown of glory."

Prophecy of Peter's crucifixion. How far it was from the Lord's purpose to put Peter to shame before his fellows appears in the sequel. " Verily, verily I tell thee," He continued, " when thou wast younger, thou wast wont to gird thyself and walk where thou wouldest ; but, when thou growest old, thou shalt stretch forth thine hands, and another will gird thee and drive [2] thee where thou wilt not." It was a dark saying at the moment, but afterwards when Peter suffered martyrdom by crucifixion,[3] it was remembered and understood. " This He said, signifying by what manner of death he would glorify God." " This end," says St Augustine, " that denier and lover found : by presumption uplifted, by denial crushed, by weeping purged, by confession proved, by suffering crowned. This end he found—to die with perfect love for His name's sake with whom in perverse haste he had promised to die." Albeit dark at the moment, the saying was clearly a prediction of suffering for the Lord's sake after long and faithful service. It was a glorious future that Jesus foretold for Peter. His comrades would envy him. If he had been humbled in their sight, he had also been greatly exalted.

Cf. John xiii. 36.

Fancy that John would never die. Peter and John were the chiefs of the apostolic company, and Jesus desired, ere His departure, to commune with them alone. " Follow Me," He said to the former ; and, as they withdrew, Peter observed that John also was following. " Lord," he asked, " and what of this man ? " It was a foolish question, characteristic of the impulsive disciple ; and Jesus retorted : " If I will that he remain until I come, what is it to thee ? Follow thou Me." He named His coming again as

---

[1] Aug. *In Joan. Ev. Tract.* cxxiii. § 4 : " Sit amoris officium pascere dominicum gregem, si fuit timoris indicium negare pastorem."

[2] So *Sin. Palimps.* The cross-laden victim was driven with scourge and goad to execution. *Cf.* p. 492. Perhaps, however, οἴσει recalls Mk. xv. 22 : φέρουσιν αὐτόν. See p. 493.   [3] *Cf.* pp. 146-7.

the supreme consummation, the goal of His Church's toil and desire. The slow-hearted disciples misconstrued His words, taking them to mean that John would not die but would live on until the Lord returned in His glory. The idea seemed reasonable enough in early days when it was believed that the Second Advent was imminent; and it was confidently believed notwithstanding the protest of the Apostle, when he wrote his Gospel in extreme old age, that Jesus had said merely : "If I will that he remain until I come." Nay, even after he had actually died, it still persisted. His grave was shown at Ephesus for centuries, and as late as St Augustine's day it was alleged that he was not really dead but only lying asleep, and that the earth which covered him heaved gently to his breathing.[1] And in the eighteenth century the saintly Lavater clung to the idea. He believed that John was alive upon the earth, and it was his heart's desire and prayer that it might be given him to meet the Apostle whom Jesus loved ; and he would wistfully scan the face of every stranger, if haply it might be he.

Neither Peter nor John has divulged what passed betwixt Jesus and them when they followed Him apart. It was a secret interview, and it was fitting that what the rest of the Apostles might not hear should be concealed from the world. Whither did He conduct them ? It would seem that He led the way to the uplands behind Capernaum,[2] to the retreat whither in former days, when weary with labour and controversy, He had been wont to betake Himself for repose and prayer ; and in that spot fragrant with holy memories the disciple whom Jesus loved and the disciple who loved Jesus, received His latest behests. *Secret interview with Peter and John. Mt. xxviii. 16.*

During the space of forty days the Risen Lord manifested Himself to His disciples. These, which the Evangelists have thus recorded, were not His only manifestations. St Paul mentions, besides that to himself on the road to Damascus, five manifestations, whereof two—that to the company of five hundred brethren and that to James, the Lord's brother [3]— *Other appearances, Acts i. 3. 1 Cor. xv. 4-8. Cf. Acts xiii. 31.*

[1] Aug. *In Joan. Ev. Tract.* cxxiv. § 2.

[2] Mt. xxviii. 16-20 is probably a vague tradition of the journey to Galilee and what befell there.

[3] The account of the appearance to James in the *Gospel of the Hebrews* (Jer. *Script. Eccl.*) is plainly unhistorical.

are recorded by no Evangelist. None of the sacred writers would know all the manifestations which the Lord vouchsafed in the course of those forty days ; and none would record all *Cf.* John that he knew, but only such as sufficed for the establishment xx. 30-1. of the great fact of the Resurrection[1]. At length the wondrous Final ap season drew to a close. He had appointed a last meeting pearance in with the Eleven at Jerusalem ; and there, perhaps in that room Jerusalem. where He had visited them on the night after the Resurrection, He appeared to them and communed with them of His Passion and Resurrection, showing how these had been foretold in the Law and the Prophets and the Psalms, and opening their mind to understand the Scriptures. They still clung to their Jewish ideal of a worldly Kingdom. The Crucifixion had dealt it a heavy blow, but the Resurrection had revived it, and it was only when they were enlightened by the Holy Spirit that they perceived the spirituality of the Kingdom of Acts i. 6-8. Heaven. "Lord," they said, "is it at this time that Thou restorest the Kingdom unto Israel?" "It is not yours," He answered, "to learn times or crises which the Father set in His own authority ; but ye shall receive power when the Holy Spirit hath come upon you, and ye shall be witnesses for Me both in Jerusalem and in all Judæa and Samaria and unto the end of the earth." He had promised in the Upper Room to send the Holy Spirit to them after His departure, and He bade them remain at Jerusalem until the promise should be "Begin at fulfilled, and there begin their preaching. "Begin at Jerusa- Jerusalem," He said. It was a great word of grace. lem." Lk. xxiv. 47. Jerusalem had been the scene of His shame, His suffering, and His death ; and He desired that His mercy should be offered first to the men who had wrought these things upon Him—to the men who had falsely accused Him, to the men who had chosen Bar Abba and sent Him to the Cross, to the men who had spat on His face, buffeted Him, and crowned Him with the crown of thorns, to the men who had hammered

---

[1] There is no reason to suppose with Keim that Paul professed to give either "the complete list or the definite sequence of the appearances." He omits the appearance to Mary, probably not only because he would have women "keep silence in the Church" (1 Cor. xiv. 34) but because he would adduce only apostolic testimony. For the same reason, though he records the appearance to Mary, John omits it from his enumeration (xxi. 14), counting only appearances τοῖς μαθηταῖς, not ταῖς μαθητρίαις (Euth. Zig.).

the nails through His hands, to the man who had driven the spear into His side, yea, to Pilate and the High Priests. "Oh the greatness of the grace of Christ! that he should be thus in love with the souls of Jerusalem-sinners! that he should not only will that his gospel should be offered them, but that it should be offered unto them first, and before other sinners were admitted to a hearing of it! *Begin at Jerusalem.*"

When He had done communing with them, He led them Farewell. forth to Olivet, and there in the neighbourhood of Bethany "He lifted up His hands and blessed them. And it came to pass, while He was blessing them, He parted from them."

Jesus had risen from the dead, as He had predicted. It Veritable was a veritable resurrection. The Evangelists are very care- resurrec- ful to make it plain that what the disciples saw was no the Lord's ghostly apparition of their Master's disembodied spirit but body. Himself in the body which He had worn while He companied with them, which had been nailed to the Cross and laid in Joseph's Sepulchre, and which had been reanimated by the power of God. When He appeared to the ten Apostles and their companions in Jerusalem on the night after His Resurrection, they were disposed to think that they beheld Lk. xxiv. a spirit, until He assured them of His corporeality by showing 37. them His wounds. And in the empty Sepulchre they had an evidence no less convincing.[1] Had it been merely His spirit that appeared to them, His body would have remained where it had been laid; but Peter and John and Mary had seen the vacant grave and the cast-off cerements. This is indeed a strong evidence of the reality of the Resurrection, yet it involves a serious difficulty. There was no difficulty in it to the Anthropomorphites of early days, who believed in a material Heaven and a corporeal God;[2] but, if it be true that, in the language of St Paul, "flesh and blood cannot 1 Cor. xv. 50.

---

[1] From the very first unbelievers have recognised the force of this evidence and sought to explain it away. The Jews alleged that the disciples had stolen their Master's body and given out that He had risen. *Cf.* Mt. xxvii. 62-6; xxviii. 11-5; Just. M. *Dial. cum Tryph.*, ed. Sylburg., p. 335 C; Tert. *Apol.* § 21 ; *De Spect.* § 30. So Reimarus, Rénan. Origen (*C. Cels.* ii. 56) argues convincingly against the allegation.

[2] *Cf.* Jer. on Ps. xciv (xciii). 9.

inherit the Kingdom of God, neither doth corruption inherit incorruption," is it conceivable that Jesus carried thither the body which He had worn while He tabernacled among men, and wears it there at this hour?

St Paul comes to our aid in this perplexity with his wondrous conception of the resurrection-body—a conception whereto assuredly he attained not by his own wisdom but by the revelation of the Holy Spirit. "Some one will say: 'How are the dead raised, and with what manner of body do they come?' Thou foolish one! What thou sowest is not quickened except it die. And what thou sowest, it is not the body that will come into being that thou sowest, but a bare grain, perchance of wheat or of some of the other sorts; and God giveth it a body even as He willed, and to each of the seeds a body of its own. Thus also the resurrection of the dead. It is sown in corruption, it is raised in incorruption; it is sown in dishonour, it is raised in glory; it is sown in weakness, it is raised in power; it is sown a natural body, it is raised a spiritual body. If there is a natural body, there is also a spiritual body." It happened to the body of Jesus even as it will happen to the bodies of believers, whether alive or dead, at the Resurrection. It was laid in the Sepulchre a corruptible body, a body of humiliation; it was raised a spiritual body, a body of glory.

It is not given us in our present ignorance to know the change which was wrought on our Lord's body when it was raised by the power of God; yet something of the mystery is revealed by the sacred narrative and claims reverent consideration. It is evident from the Evangelists' accounts of the Risen Lord's appearances, in the first place, that, while it retained its identity, His glorified body had been wonderfully changed. He appeared to the disciples even as He had appeared to Peter and James and John on the Mount of Transfiguration. So utter was the transformation that Mary failed to recognise Him when He stood beside her in the Sepulchre, and took Him for the gardener. It might

The resur-
rection-
body.

1 Cor. xv.
35-8, 42-4.

Phil. iii. 21.

(1) Trans-
figured.

be thought that her failure was due merely to the gloom and the dimness of her weeping eyes, were it not that it happened so in every instance. When He joined the two disciples on the road to Emmaus, they never dreamed that it was He. They took Him for a stranger and told Him their mournful story. And, when He appeared to the seven by the Lake of Galilee, they took Him for a stranger until He revealed Himself; and even then they wavered betwixt certainty and doubt, knowing that it was the Lord, yet half disposed to ask: "Who art Thou?"[1] In every instance it was necessary that He should make Himself known by some token which revealed Him and assured them that it was He. He gave Mary a token when He called her by her name with the old accent of tenderness; He gave the two at Emmaus a token when He blessed the bread and broke it; He gave the ten in Jerusalem a token when He showed them His wounds; He gave the seven a token when He filled their net with fish, repeating the miracle which He had wrought at the outset of His ministry.

Again, the Lord's resurrection-body was not subject to the laws which govern ordinary matter. It was able, like the ethereal bodies whereof Science dreams, to "move freely amongst and through ordinary matter without let or hindrance." The doors of that room in Jerusalem where the disciples had gathered on the night of the Resurrection Day, were closed when He appeared in the midst of the company. Doors and walls had been no barrier to His entrance.[2] Space too were naught to the ethereal bodies. "With the swiftness of light or gravitation they could speed from where old Boötes leads his leash to where Sagittarius draws his bow in the south." And within the space of a single evening the Risen Lord appeared to Peter at Jerusalem, to Cleopas

(2) Not subject to the laws of ordinary matter.

---

[1] Chrysost. *In Joan.* lxxxvi: τὴν δὲ μορφὴν ἀλλοιοτέραν ὁρῶντες καὶ πολλῆς ἐκπλήξεως γέμουσαν σφόδρα ἦσαν καταπεπληγμένοι.

[2] *Cf.* Aug. *In Joan. Ev. Tract.* cxxi. § 4: "Moli autem corporis ubi divinitas erat, ostia clausa non obstiterunt. Ille quippe non eis apertis intrare potuit, quo nascente virginitas matris inviolata permausit." Calvin, while holding that He entered miraculously, denies that His body "penetrated through the closed doors." His judgment, however, was in this instance biassed by antagonism to the contention of Popish sacramentarianism that the Lord's body was infinite and ubiquitous.

and his companion at Emmaus, and again to the disciples at Jerusalem.

(3) Invisible to the eye of sense.

And He was invisible to the eye of sense. It was very early urged against belief in the Resurrection that Jesus appeared only to disciples, and never to enemies, who stood more in need of conviction and could not have been suspected of partiality ; and the objection has been urged also in modern times.[1] It is probably in answer hereto that the apocryphal *Gospel of the Hebrews* makes Jesus appear to the High Priest's servant,[2] and the *Gospel of Peter* represents Him as coming forth from the Sepulchre betwixt the two angels in sight of the centurion Petronius and his soldiers and the Jewish elders.[3] In truth, however, such apologetic embellishments of the evangelic narrative are no less ill-advised than unhistorical. The Lord's resurrection-body was a spiritual body, and it was invisible to the natural eye. When He visited His disciples, it was needful that they should be endowed with spiritual vision ; and, until this miracle had been wrought upon them, they were unaware of His presence ; though He were by their side, they never perceived Him.[4] Evidently His appearance to the two on the road to Emmaus took them by surprise. They did not observe His approach nor did they hear the sound of footsteps behind them. Their spiritual vision was suddenly unveiled, and, behold, He was by their side ! So changed was He that, like Mary, they never recognised Him until He gave them a token ; and then straightway " He vanished out of their sight." The veil had been lifted from their hearts ; and no sooner had they recognised Him than it fell, and they saw naught but what was visible to their natural eyes. Since only to such as are subject to the operation of the Holy Spirit is the gift of spiritual vision vouchsafed, to such alone was it possible for the Risen Lord to appear. " Him," says St Peter

x. 41. in the *Acts of the Apostles*, " God raised on the third day and gave to become visible, not to all the people, but to witnesses that had been before chosen by God." Only such as had the

---

[1] Orig. *C. Cels.* ii. 63 ; Tert. *Apol.* § 21. Strauss, Keim.

[2] Jer. *Script. Eccles.* under *Jacobus qui appellatur frater Domini.*

[3] *Ev. Petr.* §§ 9-10.

[4] *Cf.* Chrysost. *In Joan.* lxxxvi: τί δέ ἐστι τὸ " ἐφανέρωσεν " (John xxi. 1); ἐκ τούτου δῆλον ὅτι οὐχ ἑωρᾶτο εἰ μὴ συγκατέβη διὰ τὸ λοιπὸν ἄφθαρτον εἶναι τὸ σῶμα καὶ ἀκήρατον. Probably this applies also to the visions of angels.

veil taken from their hearts could see Him ; and therefore it
is that on the day of His departure, as He passed through the
city on His way to Olivet, none marvelled or lifted a hand
against Him. To the Eleven He was visible, but the people
who thronged the streets, though they saw the Eleven, saw
not the wondrous form that walked in their midst.[1] Lk. xxiv.
50.

In the light of this conception a profound significance is
discovered in the Lord's promise to be with His people in
every generation. "Where there are two or three assembled
in My name, there am I in the midst of them." "Behold, I
am with you all the days until the consummation of the age."
These words are literally true. When He parted from the
Eleven on Olivet, He did not forsake the earth and migrate
to a distant Heaven. He ceased to manifest Himself ; but
He continued His presence, and He has never withdrawn it
all down the centuries. He is here at this hour no otherwise
than during those forty days after His Resurrection ; and at
any moment He might lift the veil from our hearts and
manifest Himself unto us, even as He did to Mary and
Peter and John. He actually wrought this miracle on that
great day when He met Saul of Tarsus on the road to
Damascus. St Paul never doubted that in that wondrous
hour he saw Jesus our Lord. It was no vision, but an actual
appearance, in no wise different from those which had been
vouchsafed to the earlier disciples during the forty days.
Saul beheld Him, but he did not recognise Him until he
received a token ; and, since he had never known Jesus in the
days of His flesh, the token was no reminiscence but an express declaration : "I am Jesus whom thou art persecuting."
Saul saw Him because the veil had been lifted from his heart,
but his companions beheld no one.[2]

Perpetual presence of the Risen Lord. Mt. xviii. 20. Mt. xxviii. 20. Acts ix. 1-9. 1 Cor. ix. 1.

[1] As the Lord's spiritual body was invisible, so probably it was impalpable, to the
ordinary sense. It is, however, in no wise incredible that the grace which had endowed Thomas with spiritual vision, should have wrought a like miracle on another
of his faculties—if indeed he did actually touch the wounds (John xx. 27). *Cf.*
Chrysost. *In Joan.* lxxxvi. Curious tradition in Clem. Alex. *Adumbr. in Ep. Joan.* i
(Dindorf's ed., iii. p. 485) of the intangibility of the Risen Lord's body.

[2] The appearance to Paul was thus precisely similar to the earlier appearances,
and not a mere "internal influence of Christ on his mind," as the advocates of the
Vision theory of the Resurrection maintain, arguing hence that, since he classes his
own vision with the others, they also were merely subjective. *Cf.* Weizsäcker : "There
is absolutely no proof that Paul presupposed a physical Christophany in the case of

And Jesus is with His people now. " Where there are two or three assembled in His name, there is He in the midst of them," no otherwise than He was in the midst of that company assembled in Jerusalem on that memorable first day of the week, " the doors being shut where they were for fear **1 Kings vi.** of the rulers." " Lord," prayed the ancient prophet, " open **17.** his eyes that he may see." And the Lord opened the eyes of the young man ; and, behold, the mountain was full of horses and chariots of fire round about Elisha. And, if only the veil were lifted from our hearts when we gather believingly in His blessed name, we would see a far more wondrous sight : we would see Jesus.

Lord Jesus, Who in the greatness of Thy compassion dídst leave Thy Glory, didst take our nature and dwell here, a man of sorrows and acquainted with grief, and didst suffer for us on the cruel Cross, that Thou mightest reveal the Father's Heart and open for us the way to the Father's House ; as Thou art the same yesterday and to-day, yea and for ever, may we endure as seeing Thee Who art invisible ; may we know Thee and the power of Thy Resurrection and the fellowship of Thy sufferings ; believing utterly and steadfastly the Gospel of Thy salvation, may we possess the peace and gladness thereof and walk through the world like a people that carry the broad seal of Heaven upon them. And thus witnessing for Thee and faithfully following in Thy steps, may we be received at last into Thy Glory and behold Thy blessed Face. Amen.

the older Apostles. Had he done so, he could not have put his own experience on a level with theirs." So Strauss, Keim.

APPENDIXES

I

OBJECTIONS TO THE MIRACULOUS CONCEPTION   P ∘

1. The story is of one sort with the heathen fables of commerce betwixt gods and mortals. So Celsus,[1] who cites the myths of Danae, Melanippe, Auge, and Antiope, and above all the story about Plato that Periktione bore him to Apollo ere she had connection with her husband Ariston.[2] *Cf.* the stories of Romulus and Alexander.[3]

Such stories, though congenial to the Greeks who conceived of their gods as simply "magnified men," would have seemed nothing less than blasphemies to Jewish minds. It is true that Philo had an idea that uncommon men, while begotten by human fathers, were born of divine seed, as it were by the special co-operation of God. "I will mention the holy Moses," he says,[4] "as a credible witness to what I say. For he introduces Sarah as conceiving when God visits her in her barrenness, yet bearing not to Him but to Abraham. And more plainly does he teach it in the case of Leah, saying that God opened her womb. To open a womb is a man's office, and, she, when she conceived, bare not to God, but to Jacob." This, however, is obviously very different from a birth wherein a human father has no part. And it is really a Greek idea. Philo was an Alexandrian Jew, and his mind was so steeped in Greek pantheism that a saying was current: "Either Plato philonises or Philo platonises."[5] The idea of a virgin conceiving by the operation of the Holy Spirit is utterly un-Jewish; and the mere fact that it arose on Jewish soil is a singular attestation of the evangelic story.

2. According to Strauss Jesus was really the offspring of an ordinary marriage between Joseph and Mary, but in conformity with Is. vii. 14 the belief prevailed that the Messiah would be born of a virgin by divine operation, and the history was squared with the prophecy. As a matter of fact, however, no such belief prevailed among the Jews.[6] They expected that the Messiah would be born "a man of man."[7]

---

[1] Orig. *C. Cels.* i. 37.
[3] Plut. *Rom.* § 2 ; *Alex.* § 3. *Cf. Lys.* § 26.
[5] Suidas under *Philo.*
[7] *Cf.* p. 142.

[2] *Cf.* Diog. Laert. iii. 2.
[4] *De Cherub.*, ed. Pfeiffer, ii. p. 26.
[6] *Cf.* Gore, *Dissert.*, pp. 289-91.

And that prophecy of Isaiah does not really contain the idea. The word
עַלְמָה which Matthew (i. 23), following the LXX, renders παρθένος,
means merely a *young woman*, and it is rightly rendered νεᾶνις by
Aquila, Theodotion, and Symmachus.[1] The prophecy had a contemporary reference. In face of confederate Syria and Ephraim Isaiah
assures King Ahaz of deliverance and gives him a sign : ere a young
woman, perhaps the prophet's betrothed (*cf.* viii. 3), bring forth a son,
Assyria shall intervene. No Jew ever understood the prophecy of the
Messiah,[2] and the Evangelist's far-fetched application of it proves that
the virgin-birth of Jesus was a fact. The history was not adapted to the
prophecy; on the contrary, the prophecy was adapted to the history.

3. It discredits the story of the virgin-birth that it is never alluded
to, at least expressly, by John or Paul. It is hardly likely that there
is an allusion to it in Gal. iv. 4 : γενόμενον ἐκ γυναικός, and it is a
precarious contention that Mary's anticipation of help from Jesus at
the wedding at Cana was founded on her knowledge of His wondrous
Birth.[3]

But may it not be that they knew and believed the story and
yet had reason for keeping silence regarding it ? Aware how it was
perverted by the malignant Jews, who mentioned even the name of
Mary's paramour,[4] they would judge it unmeet to give occasion for
blasphemy and would "keep the Lord's mystery for the sons of His
house." It was indeed necessary that a biographer of Jesus should
tell the story, but, when John wrote, it had already been sufficiently
told by Matthew and Luke. Besides, he was not concerned about
the human birth. His task was to tell of the Eternal Word made
flesh, and so he begins with that sublime Prologue. And as for Paul :
(1) He says practically nothing about the earthly life of our Lord
(*cf.* 2 Cor. v. 16). If all that he does not allude to be unhistorical,
how little is left ! (2) The "argument from silence" is specially
precarious in the case of one who wrote much that has perished. One
thing is certain : whatever be the explanation of their silence about
the virgin-birth, each of those great apostles recognised Jesus as the
Lord from Heaven : "the Word made flesh," "in God's form primally
existing."

4. The virgin-birth served no end. It did not secure our Lord's
sinlessness ; for, though He had no inherited sin on the father's side,
He must have shared the evil heritage on the mother's side.

But observe the Scriptural representation. Jesus never called Mary

[1] Irenæus (*Adv. Hær.* iii. 23) pronounces this rendering an attempt to "frustrate
the testimony of the prophets."
[2] *Cf.* Wetstein on Mt. i. 23.   [3] Chrysost. *In Joan.* xx.
[4] Orig. *C. Cels.* i. 28, 32.

"mother." *Cf.* His emphatic repudiation (Mt. xii. 46-50) and a striking passage in the *Gospel of the Hebrews* which makes Him say "My Mother the Holy Spirit." He styled her "woman" at Cana (John ii. 4) and on the Cross (John xix. 26). The mystery of His Birth is best viewed in the light of the Pauline thought of Christ as the Second Adam, the Head of a new Humanity (1 Cor. xv. 22, 45-7). Humanity had in Him a fresh beginning. He stood where Adam stood when he came from the hand of God. His Birth was a creation. He was not generated; He was created by the operation of the Creator Spirit in the womb of the Virgin. He derived nothing from her. She was, as it were, His cradle, and the Law of Heredity had nothing to do with Him. Thus the Second Adam began where the first Adam had begun, and conquered where the first Adam had failed. *Cf.* Newman :—

> "O loving wisdom of our God !
> When all was sin and shame,
> A second Adam to the fight
> And to the rescue came.

> "O wisest love ! that flesh and blood
> Which did in Adam fail,
> Should strive afresh against their foe,
> Should strive and should prevail."

Observe : (1) This is not opposed to the true humanity of our Lord. The Second Adam was as truly man as the first. (2) It does not imply that He was exempt from temptation and moral conflict. He fought Adam's battle over again, and conquered on the field of his defeat.

It is noteworthy, as proving how early the virgin-birth was accepted in the Church, that it was denied by Cerinthus, John's adversary at Ephesus, and that Irenæus includes in the apostolic *Prædicatio Veritatis* τὴν ἐκ Παρθίνου γέννησιν.[1]

II

ST JOHN'S METHOD OF RECKONING THE HOURS OF THE DAY

Pp. 45, 74, 477.

The Jewish day began at 6 P.M., and the hours were reckoned from 6 P.M. to 6 A.M. and again from 6 A.M. to 6 P.M. The modern method, however, was not unknown in the ancient world. The Romans

---

[1] *Adv. Hær.* i. 2, 21.

reckoned their sacerdotal and their civil day from midnight to noon and again from noon to midnight. So also the Egyptians counted their hours.[1] Nor is evidence lacking that a like system obtained in Asia Minor. Polycarp was martyred in the Stadium at Smyrna ὥρᾳ ὀγδόῃ,[2] and this must mean 8 A.M. since public spectacles began at an early hour.[3] The Synoptists follow the ordinary Jewish method, but it were natural that John, writing at Ephesus, should follow the method in vogue in Asia Minor, and so he appears actually to have done.

1. i. 39. If "the tenth hour" be here 4 P.M., it could hardly be said that "they lodged with Him that day." Since the Jewish day began at 6 P.M., only two hours remained.

2. iv. 6. The weariness of Jesus indicates that He had done a long day's journey, and it was in the evening that the women came to draw water (Gen. xxiv. 11). *Cf. P. E. F. Q.*, July 1897, p. 196.

3. According to John xix. 14 it was "about the sixth hour" when Jesus was condemned by Pilate. If this means noon, it is irreconcilable with the Synoptic representation that He was crucified at 9 A.M. (Mk. xv. 25) and died at 3 P.M. (Mt. xxvii. 46 = Mk. xv. 34 = Lk. xxiii. 44); but, if it means 6 A.M., the narratives agree.

The other side of the question is argued by Ramsay in *Expositor*, March, 1893, pp. 216-23 ; June, 1896, pp. 457-9.

III

Pp. 49-52.

THE SON OF MAN

There is no question in the whole range of N.T. study which has been more largely discussed or regarding which there is less agreement than the meaning of this title. According to one opinion it means the Ideal Man, and constitutes a claim on the part of Jesus to a unique character and mission; according to another it means the Mere Man, and identifies Him with the other members of the human race, "the sons of men" (*cf.* Mk. iii. 28: τοῖς υἱοῖς τῶν ἀνθρώπων = Mt. xii. 31: τοῖς ἀνθρώποις). Some regard it as a Messianic title; others maintain that it has nothing to do with Messiahship. And recently, on the ground that in Aramaic "the son of man" would mean simply "the man," the startling opinion has been propounded that the title is unauthentic and never was used by Jesus at all.

In face of such wide divergence of opinion there is reason to

---

[1] Plin. *H. N.* ii. 79.   [2] *Martyr. Polyc.* xxi.
[3] Becker, *Charicles*, p. 409.

suspect that the investigation has been prosecuted along false paths, and a fresh starting-point and a new clue are necessary in order to a satisfactory solution of the problem. Nor is the initial fallacy far to seek. It has been generally assumed that Jesus derived the title from the apocalyptic literature, in the first instance from the Book of Daniel and then from the Book of Enoch. This, however, is very questionable. It is even doubtful whether the Enoch-passages be pre-Christian (cf. Schürer, H. J. P. II. iii. pp. 54 sqq.); and in neither book is "son of man" an appellation. In Dan. vii. 13 "one like unto a son of man" means merely *a figure with a human form*, and the Book of Enoch simply quotes the phrase when it speaks of the Messiah as "that son of man." As Jesus used it, the title has no connection with the apocalyptic literature.

And it is certain that it is not a Messianic title. Indeed it is surprising that it should ever have been taken as such in view of the use which Jesus made of it. "Who," He asked at Cæsarea Philippi, "do men say that the Son of Man is?" And Simon Peter answered: "Thou art the Messiah." The point here is that the title, so far from being Messianic, concealed the Messiahship of Jesus and made the recognition thereof difficult, nay, impossible without divine illumination. "Flesh and blood did not reveal it unto thee, but My Father in Heaven" (Mt. xvi. 13, 16-7).

See Bruce, *Hum. of Chr.*, pp. 225 sqq.; *Kingd. of God*, pp. 166 sqq.; Westcott, *St John*, pp. 33-5; Charles, *Book of Enoch*, App. B.; Dalman, *Words of Jesus*, pp. 234 sqq.; Driver's art. *Son of Man* in Hastings' *D. B.*

IV

"SECOND-FIRST SABBATH"   P. 133.

ἐν σαββάτῳ δευτεροπρώτῳ

(Lk. vi. 1)

This cumbrous compound occurs nowhere else. It was a sore puzzle to the Fathers, and it is significant that they knew of no traditional explanation. They had nothing but conjecture to guide them, and their explanations are, for the most part, a chaos of contradictions and impossibilities. It is possible that a technical term of the Jewish calendar should have passed into disuse in the course of two or three centuries, but its meaning could hardly have been utterly forgotten.

It were weary and unprofitable work to exhume the multitude of discredited and forgotten theories. "I have," says Erasmus, "found

nothing satisfactory on the subject in authors hitherto"; and his
verdict may be reiterated now after other four centuries of discussion
and conjecture. "It were simpler," remarks the caustic humanist,
"to say 'I do not know.'" As early as the fourth century Jerome
recognised the hopelessness of a reasonable solution. "I once," he
says (*Ep.* ii, *ad Nepotianum*), "asked my teacher, Gregory of
Nazianzus, to explain what is meant by 'a second-first Sabbath' in
Luke; and he answered with a pretty jest. 'I will teach you on the
subject,' quoth he, 'in Church where, amid the applause of the
congregation, you will be compelled in spite of yourself to know what
you don't know, or, depend upon it, if you be the only one silent, you
will be condemned as the only fool in the congregation.'"

Erasmus tells another anecdote. Once at a banquet—was it that
immortal symposium at the house of Richard Charnock, Prior of St
Mary's College, Oxford (*Ep.* v. 1, *Joanni Sixtino*; ed. Lond. 1642)?
—a certain monk, who was likewise a professor of Theology, was asked
by a learned man of another profession, probably Erasmus himself,
what Luke's "second-first Sabbath" meant. He replied that there
was nothing of the sort anywhere in the Gospels. The other insisted
that it was in Luke, and the professor laid a wager that it was not.
"I will doff my cowl," he declared, "if Luke wrote anything of the
sort." Did he mean that the word was an interpolation? If he did,
he was probably in the right. Om. אBL. It is most likely that the
bewildering word is a confused marginal note which has found its
way into the text. Some copyist, with his eye on *v.* 6: "on another
Sabbath," wrote "first" over against *v.* 1; then some other, in view of
iv. 31, prefixed "second" by way of correction. It is remarkable that
several MSS. have actually δευτέρῳ πρώτῳ. *Cf.* Vulg. *secundo primo.*

See Field, *Notes*; W. H., *Notes.*

V

THE UNNAMED FEAST

(John v. 1)

The Evangelist says merely: "There was a feast" (ABD, Orig.,
Chrysost., W. H., A.V., R.V.) or: "the feast (אCL, Tisch.) of the
Jews"; and it has been much disputed which feast it was. The
opinion that it was the Passover seems most reasonable. (1) It is
supported by the earliest tradition. *Cf.* Iren. *Adv. Hær.* ii. 32. § 1.
Nor is it without significance that an 8th c. MS. reads "the Feast
of Unleavened Bread" (A τῶν ἀζύμων). (2) The very vagueness of

the Evangelist's reference indicates the Passover (*cf.* Mk. xv. 6). It was the only feast which all Israelites were required to attend. It was the custom of Jesus to go up yearly to its celebration ; and, had this been another feast, it must have been specially designated. *Cf.* John vii. 2 ; x. 22. (3) The open and murderous enmity of the rulers when Jesus went up to Jerusalem (*v.* 18), proves that John v. must be placed not near the outset of His ministry but after the declaration of hostility. Their knowledge that " He was in the habit of breaking the Sabbath " (*v.* 18) implies a date subsequent to the Sabbatarian controversies at Capernaum (Mt. xii. 1-14 = Mk. ii. 23—iii. 6 = Lk. vi. 1-11). Between John iv. and v. comes the Synoptic record of the Lord's varied activity during the first year of His ministry.

VI

CHRONOLOGY OF THE PASSION-WEEK P. 383.

John xii. 1 is the basis of calculation. τὸ πάσχα, not identical with ἡ πρώτη ἡμέρα τῶν ἀζύμων, ὅτε τὸ πάσχα ἔθυον (Mk. xiv. 12 = Mt. xxvi. 17 = Lk. xxii. 7), is the Paschal Supper on the evening which ushered in Friday, 15th Nisan. Six days before the 15th, according to the ancient reckoning which included the *terminus a quo* and the *terminus ad quem*, would be Sunday, 10th Nisan. The following arrangement seems justified by the narratives :—

Sabbath, 9th Nisan.—At Jericho with Zacchæus.

Sunday, 10th Nisan.—Journey continued ; arrival at Bethany ; supper in the house of Simon the Leper.

Monday, 11th Nisan.—Entry into Jerusalem ; retiral to Olivet.

Tuesday, 12th Nisan.—Cursing of the Fig-tree ; teaching in the Temple-court (Mk. xi. 17 ; Lk. xix. 47) and miracles (Mt. xxi. 15); children's acclamations and remonstrance of rulers ; retiral to Olivet.

Wednesday, 13th Nisan.—Disciples remark on the withering of the Fig-tree ; captious questions ; the Great Indictment ; visit of the Greeks ; consultation of rulers in the High Priest's palace and compact with Judas ; retiral to Olivet.

Thursday, 14th Nisan.—Discourse on Olivet about things to come ; the Preparation.

Friday, 15th Nisan.—The Supper in the Upper Room ; Gethsemane ; the Betrayal and Arrest ; the Crucifixion.

Sabbath, 16th Nisan.—" Sabbatizat in sepulchro."

Sunday, 17th Nisan.—The Resurrection.

VII

P. 416.

THE MURDER OF ZECHARIAH

(Mt. xxiii. 35 = Lk. xi. 51)

Matthew's reading "Zechariah son of Barachiah" has occasioned much perplexity. It seems indubitable that υἱοῦ Βαραχίου is merely a gloss on our Lord's words, whether by the Evangelist or by some early copyist, due to Zech. i. 1. It is omitted by ℵ* and several cursives. Accepting it, Origen takes Zechariah the son of Barachiah as Zechariah, the father of John the Baptist,[1] who, according to the apocryphal *Protevangelium*, was murdered in the Temple by the servants of Herod. This was the prevailing opinion in early days. Jerome and Chrysostom mention three opinions. The martyr in question was (1) Zechariah son of Barachiah, the Minor Prophet, (2) the father of John, (3) Zechariah son of Jehoiada. According to Chrysostom, Jehoiada had two names. Jerome mentions that in the *Gospel of the Hebrews* the reading was "son of Jehoiada"—manifestly a correction.

These ancient fancies are far surpassed in wild improbability by the modern identification of Zechariah son of Barachiah with that Zechariah son of Baruch who was slain in the Temple in A.D. 68.[2] Strauss rejects the suggestion, but Keim welcomes it as proving the passage a late interpolation and disposing of the prediction in *v.* 34. The idea is utterly unreasonable. It is true that both the martyrs were named Zechariah and both perished in the Temple; but Barachiah and Baruch are different names, and the Zechariah of Josephus fell by the hands of the Essenes in league with the Idumæans.

VIII

Pp. 491-507.

THE DAY OF THE CRUCIFIXION

All the Evangelists agree that our Lord was crucified on a Friday and rose on the ensuing Sunday; and, were the Synoptics the sole records, it would be no less certain that the Friday was Passover-day, 15th Nisan, and the supper which He had eaten with His disciples in the Upper Room on the previous evening the regular Paschal meal (Mt.

---

[1] *In Matth. Comm. Ser.* § 25. Elsewhere he suggests that our Lord was referring to some extra-canonical history (*In Ev. Matth.* x. § 18).

[2] Jos. *De Bell. Jud.* iv. 5. § 4.

xxvi. 17 = Mk. xiv. 12 = Lk. xxii. 7). But, turning to the Fourth
Gospel, one finds what looks like a different representation. (1) John
xiii. 1 seems to put the Last Supper "before the Feast of the Passover."
(2) Next morning, when they brought Jesus before Pilate, the rulers
would not enter the Prætorium, "that they might not be defiled, but
might eat the Passover" (xviii. 28)—a clear evidence, apparently,
that they had not eaten the Paschal meal the previous evening but
had it still in prospect. (3) Thrice over (xix. 14, 31, 42) it is said that
the day of the Crucifixion was παρασκευή, meaning, it is supposed, 14th
Nisan, the day of preparation for the Passover.

Hence it would appear that, according to John, the Friday on
which Jesus was crucified, was not, as the Synoptists represent, Passover day, 15th Nisan, but Preparation-day, the 14th ; and the supper
which He had eaten with His disciples the previous evening, if it
was indeed the Paschal meal, had been eaten a day too soon, on the
evening which closed the 13th day of Nisan, and which, according
to the Jewish reckoning, ushered in the 14th.

Here is no mere question of curious scholarship but one which
involves great issues. Not only is such a discrepancy regarding that
supremely sacred event painful to religious sentiment, but it touches
the historicity of the evangelic narratives ; and therefore it is no
wonder that students of the N.T. have laboured, often with amazing
ingenuity, to effect a reconciliation. Perhaps the boldest device is
that of Lightfoot, who identifies the Johannine supper, not with the
Synoptists' Passover supper in the Upper Room, but with the supper
in Simon the Leper's house (Mk. xiv. 3-9 = Mt. xxvi. 6-13), which,
misled by Mk. xiv. 1 = Mt. xxvi. 2, he supposes to have been held
at Bethany two days before the Passover.[1] It is true that St John
says nothing about the Passover, and does not report the institution
of the Lord's Supper; but a comparison of John xiii. 38 with Mt.
xxvi. 34 = Mk. xiv. 30 = Lk. xxii. 34 suffices to establish the identity
of the Johannine supper with that of the Synoptists in the Upper
Room.

Reconciliation has been attempted along two main lines :

1. *John's account has been accepted and that of the Synoptists brought
into harmony therewith.*

(1) *The supper in the Upper Room was not a Passover at all.* So
Clem. Alex. : In previous years Jesus had kept the Passover and
eaten the lamb, but on the day before He suffered as the true
Paschal Lamb He taught His disciples the mystery of the type.[2]

---

[1] The supper in Simon the Leper's house is unquestionably identical with the
Johannine supper at Bethany six days before the Passover. *Cf.* Introd. § 10.

[2] Fragm. in *Chron. Pasch.* See Dindorf's *Clem. Alex. Op.* iii. p. 498.

So also, according to the *Chronicon Paschale*, Apolinarius of Hierapolis, Hippolytus, and Peter of Alexandria.

(2) *Since the Passover-day, falling that year on Friday, was reckoned as a Sabbath* (Lev. xxiii. 6, 7, 11, 15), *the Jews, to avoid the inconvenience of two successive Sabbaths, postponed the Passover by a day: Jesus adhered to the day fixed by the Law.* So Calvin.[1] The Synoptists are therefore right in calling the Lord's Supper a Passover, and John also is right in saying that, when the Jews crucified Jesus, they had their Passover still in prospect. The objection to this is that, while in certain circumstances the Passover might be postponed to a later *month*, it had always to be celebrated on the 15th day; nor, moreover, would the priests have suffered any, least of all Jesus and His disciples, to sacrifice their lamb in the Temple on another day than that appointed by the Sanhedrin.[2]

(3) *Jesus anticipated the Passover,* knowing that at the proper time He would be lying in His grave. This is put forward by Chrysostom [3] as an alternative explanation of John xviii. 28; and it is the theory of Grotius, who holds that there was no lamb at the Lord's Supper; it was a πάσχα μνημονευτικόν, not a πάσχα θύσιμον. Fatal, however, alike to this theory and to Calvin's is Luke's express statement (xxii. 7) that Jesus ate the Passover on the general Passover-day, ἐν ᾗ ἔδει θύεσθαι τὸ πάσχα.

The supposed Johannine account is not without a certain attractiveness, since there are facts which seem at the first glance to tell against the Synoptic representation and to prove that the Lord's Supper must have taken place on the evening before the Passover-day. The Synoptists all record that after the Supper Jesus and the Eleven left the city and went out to Olivet (Mt. xxiv. 30 = Mk. xiv. 26 = Lk. xxii. 39), whereas the Law required that no one should "go out at the door of his house until the morning" (Exod. xii. 22). This requirement, however, had been set aside in the time of our Lord;[4] and even had it been still in force, it would hardly have restrained Jesus. "Permit," says Lightfoot, "the Lion of the tribe of Judah not to be bound by those spider-webs." Again, since the

---

[1] On Mt. xxvi. 17. *Cf.* Chrysost. *In Matth.* lxxxv: The rulers spent the night waiting for the return of the arrest-party with Jesus, and therefore they did not eat the Passover. Next day they ate it and broke the Law διὰ τὴν ἐπιθυμίαν τὴν περὶ τὴν σφαγὴν ταύτην.

[2] *Cf.* Lightfoot on Mk. xiv. 12.

[3] *In Joan.* lxxxii: ἤτοι οὖν τὸ πάσχα τὴν ἑορτὴν πᾶσαν λέγει, ἢ ὅτι τότε ἐποίουν τὸ πάσχα, αὐτὸς δὲ πρὸ μιᾶς αὐτὸ παρέδωκε τηρῶν τὴν ἑαυτοῦ σφαγὴν τῇ παρασκευῇ ὅτε καὶ τὸ παλαιὸν ἐγίνετο τὸ πάσχα. This sentence, it has been remarked, writes the programme for subsequent discussion down to the present day.

[4] Wetstein on Mk. xiv. 26.

Passover-day was reckoned as a Sabbath, it has been deemed inconceivable not merely that Judas, Joseph of Arimathæa, and the women should have gone to the market (John xiii. 29; Mk. xv. 46; Mk. xvi. 1), but, above all, that Jesus should have been crucified on that day. In fact, however, the Passover-day, though called a Sabbath, was less strictly observed than the ordinary Sabbath. Servile work was prohibited, but trade went on.[1] And, while the Athenian law forbade the execution of criminals during religious festivals,[2] Jewish sentiment, singularly enough, was less fastidious. Executions during the Passover season were in no wise uncommon, instances occurring from King David's time (2 Sam. xxi. 9) down to apostolic days: James the Apostle was executed during the days of Unleavened Bread (Acts xii. 1-4), and James the Lord's brother on the Passover-day.[3] The strict R. Akiba ordained that a certain criminal should be conveyed to Jerusalem and kept till the Passover, and then executed in the sight of the people, in accordance with Deut. xvii. 13.[4] The Talmud indeed asserts that Jesus was executed on the day before the Passover,[5] but this is nothing else than an attempt on the part of the later Jews to eliminate an ugly fact by rewriting history and thus silence the taunts of Christian writers. Once more, when Simon of Cyrene was impressed, he was coming ἀπ' ἀγροῦ, from his work, it is supposed; and he would not have been working in his field had it been the Passover-day. But Simon was not a resident in Jerusalem. He was one of the multitude of strangers who had come up to celebrate the Feast, and, lodging, as so many, including Jesus and the Twelve, were obliged or preferred to do, outside the gates, he was coming "from the country" (ἀπ' ἀγροῦ, *rure*) to worship in the Temple at the hour of morning prayer.

2. *The Synoptists' account has been accepted and that of John brought into harmony therewith.*

Recent criticism[6] rejects the latter as unhistorical, and explains it as originating in the idea, suggested by St Paul (1 Cor. v. 7) and expressly asserted by Clement of Alexandria, Apolinarius, Hippolytus, and Peter of Alexandria, that, since Jesus was Himself the Paschal Lamb, He must have been slain on 14th Nisan. In support of this theory it is pointed out that John, by way of proving Him the true Paschal Lamb, cites the legal requirement that the lamb's bones

---

[1] Edersheim, *Life and Times*, ii. p. 508; Lightfoot, ii. p. 759.
[2] *Cf.* Plat. *Phæd.* 58 A; Plut. *Phoc.* § 37.
[3] Hegesippus apud Eus. *H. E.* ii. 23.
[4] Wetstein on Mt. xxvi. 5.   [5] Lightfoot on Mt. xxvii. 31.
[6] After Strauss Keim, Schmiedel (in *E. B.*, art. *John, son of Zebedee*).

should not be broken (Exod. xii. 46; Num. ix. 12) as fulfilled in the case of Jesus (xix. 36);[1] that he throws the anointing at Bethany back to the 10th Nisan (xii. 1), the day on which the Paschal lamb was chosen (Exod. xii. 3); and that, in opposition to the Synoptists (Mk. xv. 25; Mt. xxvii. 45 = Mk. xv. 33 = Lk. xxiii. 44), he represents Jesus as still before Pilate at the sixth hour, *i.e.* noon (xix. 14), with the design, it is alleged, of making the Crucifixion coincide with the sacrifice of the Paschal lambs, which were slain in the Temple from 3 to 5 P.M.[2] The theory is more ingenious than convincing. It takes no account of the probability that John reckoned the hours, not, like the Synoptists, from 6 o'clock, but, according to the alternative method from midnight and from noon;[3] and since by the "sixth hour" he means 6 A.M., he is in full agreement with the Synoptists (*cf.* Mt. xxvii. 1-2 = Mk. xv. 1). Moreover, Jesus was none the less the true Paschal Lamb though He was not crucified between 3 and 5 P.M. on 14th Nisan but at 9 A.M. on the 15th. Although he spoke of Christ as "our Paschal Lamb" (1 Cor. v. 7), Paul regarded the Last Supper as the regular Paschal meal, calling the communion cup in the same Epistle (x. 16) "the Cup of Blessing."[4]

While recent critics are right in accepting the Synoptic account, it may be questioned whether their rejection of the Johannine account as irreconcilable therewith be not a hasty verdict, due partly to a foregone conviction of the unhistoricity of the Fourth Gospel and partly to misunderstanding of the passages at issue. Let us consider these afresh:—

John xiii. 1 is the crucial passage, and the difficulty connected with it is due to misapprehension of its significance. It is in truth an independent paragraph, and has no bearing whatever on the date of the Supper. What the Evangelist says is that, as the end drew near, the disciples observed a singular access of tenderness in their Master's bearing toward them. He had always loved them, but then He showed them His heart and demonstrated His affection as He had never done before.[5] It was the tenderness of imminent farewell. Then, beginning a new paragraph, the Evangelist goes on to recount the story of the Supper (*vv.* 2 *sqq.*), assuming, according to his wont, an acquaintance on the part of his readers with the details of time and arrangement given by the Synoptists (Mt. xxvi. 17-9 = Mk. xiv. 12-6 = Lk. xxii. 7-13). Had he been dating the Supper, he would not have used so vague a phrase as "before the Feast." Had he differed from the Synoptists, he would, as in other

---

[1] Probably John refers rather to Ps. xxxiv. 20.   [2] Jos. *De Bell. Jud.* vi. 9. § 3.
[3] *Cf.* Append. II.   [4] *Cf.* p. 446.   [5] *Cf.* pp. 435-6.

APPENDIXES
539

instances, have corrected their error with a precise definition of
the day.

Again, it is a mistaken inference from John xviii. 28 that on the
day of the Crucifixion the Jews had the Paschal meal still in prospect,
and that it was therefore the Preparation-day, 14th Nisan. They
would indeed have been defiled had they entered a heathen house,
but the defilement would have lasted only until evening, and then,
after due ablution, they could have eaten the Paschal meal. The
reply of Strauss, that they would nevertheless have been disqualified
for the business of preparing the Passover on the afternoon of the
14th, overlooks the fact that it was not necessary for them to make
the preparations themselves; according to the Law they could have
deputed the business to their servants, even as Jesus deputed it to
Peter and John.[1] It was not the Paschal supper that they would have
been debarred from eating had they entered Pilate's prætorium, but
the *Chagigah* or thankoffering, which consisted usually of a bullock.
And not only was 15th Nisan the day on which the *Chagigah* should
be offered,[2] but every worshipper had to present it in the Temple *in
propriâ personâ*.[3] To our minds the phrase " eat the Passover "
naturally suggests the Paschal supper, but on Jewish lips it had also
a larger significance.   Alike in the Scriptures and in the Talmud it is
used of the celebration of the entire feast, including the *Chagigah*.[4]
Nor should it be overlooked that elsewhere in the Fourth Gospel τὸ
πάσχα is invariably employed in its larger sense, denoting not the
Paschal supper as in Mt. xxvi. 17 = Mk. xiv. 12 = Lk. xxii. 7-8, but
the whole feast, τὴν ἑορτὴν πᾶσαν.[5] It is inconceivable that in this
solitary instance John should have departed from his *usus loquendi*.
It is noteworthy in this connection that after the Crucifixion, ὀψίας
γενομένης, Joseph of Arimathæa visited Pilate and requested the Lord's
body (Mt. xxvii. 57-8 = Mk. xv. 42-3 = Lk. xxiii 50-2 = John xix. 38).
He had no less reason than his fellow-Sanhedrists to dread pollution,
and he went without scruple to Pilate's house because, unlike them in
the morning, he had already that afternoon celebrated the solemnity
of the *Chagigah*.

Finally, with regard to St John's reiterated statement that the day
of the Crucifixion was Preparation, it is a hasty assumption that
παρασκευή here means the day of preparation for the Passover, *i.e.*
14th Nisan.   It is true that the word was used of the preparation for

[1] *Cf.* Lightfoot on Mk. xiv. 26.
[2] *Cf.* Lightfoot on John xviii. 28.   [3] *Id.* on Mk. xv. 25.
[4] Deut. xvi. 2 ; 2 Chron. xxx. 1, 23, 24 ; xxxv. 1, 8-19 ; Ezek. xlv. 21-4.
Menach. 3. 1 : " Vitulus et juvencus quem mactant nomine Paschatis." *Nota illud*,
says Lightfoot, *vitulus est Pascha uti et agnus.*
[5] *Cf.* John ii. 13, 23 ; vi. 4 ; xi. 55 ; xii. 1 ; xiii. 1.

the Passover or any other feast, but it was also used by the Jews, alternatively with προσάββατον,[1] as the regular name for Friday, the day of preparation for the weekly Sabbath.[2] The term was taken over by the Christians,[3] and to this day it remains the regular name for Friday on the Greek calendar. It means Friday in Mk. xv. 42, Mt. xxvii. 62, Lk. xxiii. 54; and a false presupposition is the sole reason for attaching to it a different significance on the lips of John. When he says ἦν παρασκευὴ τοῦ πάσχα (xix. 14), he means, not "it was the Preparation for the Passover," but "it was Friday of the Passover-season." And if by παρασκευή he means Friday in xix. 31, the reason of his statement is obvious. "That Sabbath-day was a great one," not because, being at once the weekly Sabbath and Passover-day, it was Sabbath in a double sense, but, as Lightfoot puts it, because (1) it was a Sabbath, (2) it was the day on which the people appeared before the Lord in the Temple (Exod. xxiii. 17), and (3) it was the day on which the sheaf of the first-fruits was reaped (Lev. xxiii. 11).

In his account of the Quartodeciman controversy Eusebius[4] quotes from Irenæus a remarkable story. The Christians of Asia Minor "observed the 14th day of the moon in connection with the Feast of the Saviour's Passover," and, when Polycarp, John's disciple and friend, visited Anicetus at Rome, he defended the usage on the ground that it had been the usage of John and the rest of the Apostles in the days when he companied with them. That is to say, Polycarp had it from John that the Lord had celebrated the Passover and instituted the Supper, agreeably to the Synoptic representation, on the 14th day of the moon or, according to the Jewish reckoning, on 15th Nisan; and it follows either that, as Baur argues, the Fourth Gospel is not John's or that, in accordance with our reasoning, the Johannine and the Synoptic accounts agree.

---

[1] Mk. xv. 42; Epiphan. *Hæres.* 72. § 2.
[2] Jos. *Ant.* xvi. 6. § 2.   Wetstein on Mt. xxvii. 62.
[3] *Didache*, viii; Clem. Alex. *Strom.* vii. § 75 ; Tert. *De Jejun.* § 14.
[4] *H. E.* v. 23-4.

INDEXES

I

NAMES AND SUBJECTS

II

GREEK WORDS AND PHRASES

III
THE GOSPEL TEXT